Professional
Linux® Programming

Professional
Linux® Programming

Jon Masters
Richard Blum

BICENTENNIAL
1807
WILEY
2007
BICENTENNIAL

Wiley Publishing, Inc.

Professional Linux® Programming

Published by
Wiley Publishing, Inc.
10475 Crosspoint Boulevard
Indianapolis, IN 46256
www.wiley.com

Copyright © 2007 by Wiley Publishing, Inc., Indianapolis, Indiana

Published simultaneously in Canada

Manufactured in the United States of America

10 9 8 7 6 5 4 3 2 1

Library of Congress Cataloging-in-Publication Data:
Masters, Jon, 1981-
  Professional Linux programming / Jon Masters, Richard Blum.
    p. cm.
  Includes index.
  ISBN: 978-0-471-77613-0 (paper/website)
  1. Linux. 2. Operating systems (Computers) I. Blum, Richard, 1962- II. Title.
  QA76.76.O63M37153 2007
  005.4'32—dc22
                              2006102202

For Karin, whom I love very much.—**Jon Masters**

To my wife Barbara.—**Richard Blum**

About the Authors

Jon Masters is a 25-year-old British-born Linux kernel engineer, embedded systems specialist, and author who lives and works in the United States for Red Hat. Jon made UK history by becoming one of the youngest University students the country had ever seen, at the tender age of just 13. Having been through college twice by the time his peers were completing their first time around, and having been published over 100 times in a wide range of technical magazines, journals and books, Jon went on to work for a variety of multinational technology companies. He has worked extensively in the field of Embedded Systems, Enterprise Linux and Scientific instrumentation and has helped design anything and everything from Set Top Boxes to future NMR (MRI) imaging platforms.

When not working on Enterprise Linux software for Red Hat, Jon likes to drink tea on Boston Common and read the collective works of Thomas Paine and other great American Revolutionaries of a bygone age. He dreams of a time when the world was driven not by electrons, but by wooden sailing ships and a universal struggle for the birth of modern nations. He plays the violin, and occasionally sings in choral ensembles, for which he has won several awards. For relaxation, Jon enjoys engaging in a little rock climbing. He lives in Cambridge, Massachusetts, just across the river Charles from historic Boston, and enjoys every minute of it.

Jon has extensive experience in speaking about and training people to use a wide variety of Linux technologies and enjoys actively participating in many Linux User Groups the world over.

Richard Blum has worked for over 18 years for a large U.S. government organization as a network and systems administrator. During this time he has had plenty of opportunities to work with Microsoft, Novell, and of course, UNIX and Linux servers. He has written applications and utilities using C, C++, Java, C#, Visual Basic, and shell script.

Rich has a Bachelors of Science degree in Electrical Engineering, and a Masters of Science degree in Management, specializing in Management Information Systems, from Purdue University. He is the author of several books, including *"sendmail for Linux"* (2000, Sams publishing), *"Running qmail"* (2000, Sams publishing), *"Postfix"* (2001, Sams Publishing), *"Open Source E-mail Security"* (2001, Sams Publishing), *"C# Network Programming"* (2002, Sybex), *"Network Performance Open Source Toolkit"* (2003, John Wiley & Sons), and *"Professional Assembly Language Programming"* (2005, Wrox).

When he is not being a computer nerd, Rich plays electric bass for the church worship and praise band, and enjoys spending time with his wife Barbara, and daughters Katie Jane and Jessica.

Credits

Contributing Writers
Christopher Aillon
Katherine and David Goodwin
Matthew Walton

Acquisitions Editor
Kit Kemper

Development Editor
Howard A. Jones

Production Editor
Eric Charbonneau

Copy Editor
Foxxe Editorial

Editorial Manager
Mary Beth Wakefield

Production Manager
Tim Tate

Vice President and Executive Group Publisher
Richard Swadley

Vice President and Executive Publisher
Joseph B. Wikert

Graphics and Production Specialists
Carrie A. Foster
Jennifer Mayberry
Barbara Moore
Alicia B. South

Quality Control Technicians
Cynthia Fields
John Greenough

Project Coordinator
Adrienne Martinez

Proofreading and Indexing
Techbooks

Anniversary Logo Design
Richard Pacifico

Acknowledgments

I sit here writing these acknowledgements on my 25th birthday, having spent many long evenings over the last year pouring over schedules, planning and even occasionally actually getting some writing done. When I first undertook to write this book, I could never have fully appreciated the amount of work it takes to put such a thing together nor the difficulties that would need to be overcome along the way. I started writing this book living just outside London and finished it less than a year later from my new home in Cambridge, Massachusetts, having decided to leave the country in the interim. Over the last year, a lot has changed for me both personally and professionally, but I am supported by a great network of friends and family who have helped make it possible.

First and foremost I would like to thank the team I have worked with at Wiley — Debra, Adaobi, Kit, Howard and Carol as well as numerous others whose job it is to turn this manuscript into a finished book. Kit Kemper deserves special thanks for enduring my writing schedule and somehow making that just about work out in the end, as does Debra Williams-Cauley for believing that this project was a good idea in the first place. Howard Jones helped to keep me honest by doing an excellent job as my editor. This book would not exist without the inspiration I received from my good friends (and former bosses) Malcolm Buckingham and Jamie McKendry at Resonance Instruments (later Oxford Instruments), who used to moan about the lack of Linux-specific programming books. This book would also not exist without the kind contributions from several good friends of mine — Kat and David Goodwin, Matthew Walton, and Chris Aillon, thank you. Thanks also to Richard Blum for stepping up and joining the team once it became apparent to me that I couldn't hope to finish this in time. You've all done a great job and I really do thank you very much.

I have been helped along the way by my fantastic family — my parents Paula and Charles, my sisters Hannah Wrigley and Holly, my brother-in-law Joe, and occasional inspiration too from my grandmothers. I have also benefited from some of the best friends anyone could ask for — there are too many to list everyone individually, but I would like to specifically mention Hussein Jodiyawalla, Johannes Kling, Ben Swan, Paul Sladen, Markus Kobler, Tom Hawley, Sidarshan Guru Ratnavellu, Chris and Mad Ball (and Zoe, the cat), Emma Maule, John and Jan Buckman, Toby Jaffey and Sara, Sven Thorsten-Dietrich, Bill Weinberg, Daniel James, Joe Casad and Andrew Hutton and Emilie. Special thanks also to all of my friends at Red Hat, my boss and all the other hard-working people who help to make our company truly the greatest place to work anywhere in the world. Red Hat really understands what it means to work on Linux, and I am extremely grateful for having such a cool work environment, which really does encourage involvement in projects such as this one, in the true spirit of the Linux community — thanks, guys, you rock.

Finally, I would like to thank Karin Worley for her friendship, which provided me with ample opportunity for procrastination during the final stages of this project. Karin, I'm not sure I would have completed it without the new-found sense of happiness that recently entered into my life.

Jon Masters
Cambridge, Massachusetts

Acknowledgments

Many thanks go to the great team of people at Wiley for their outstanding work on this project. Thanks to Kit Kemper, the Acquisitions Editor, for offering me the opportunity to work on this book. Also thanks to Howard Jones, the Developmental Editor, for keeping things on track and helping make this book presentable. I would also like to thank Carole McClendon at Waterside Productions, Inc. for arranging this opportunity for me, and for helping out in my writing career.

Finally, I would like to thank my parents, Mike and Joyce Blum, for their dedication and support while raising me, and to my wife Barbara and daughters Katie Jane and Jessica for their love, patience, and understanding, especially while I'm writing.

Richard Blum

Contents

Contents

Contents

Contents

Contents

Introduction

Linux has come a long way in the last few years. From relatively humble beginnings, Linux now powers a growing number of Fortune 500 companies. Everything from your cell phone right on up to the largest supercomputing clusters are now built using the Linux kernel and the software distributions built around it. But what really is Linux? What makes it different from any other UNIX-like Operating System on the market today? Most importantly, how can you harness the full power of Linux and the wider Free, Libre, and Open Source Software (FLOSS) revolution in your own software projects?

This book aims to address these and other questions. The *raison d'etre* for this book really stems from a need to impart to you, the reader, those things that make Linux unique, while going beyond the basic Beginner's guides that are already available on the market. As a professional Linux programmer, the author has, over the years, found himself working with highly skilled software engineers who have little or no Linux experience. Some were searching for a book like this one – only to be later disappointed. Born out of their frustration, this book should help you to understand the powerful sense of community, the established software development model and the way things are done in the Linux world.

There are many other books that claim to be dedicated to Linux programming. Many of those books are truly excellent, but they often concentrate too much on the ways in which Linux simply follows what came before. You won't find that in this book; it's not merely about those things Linux has in common with the UNIX systems of old. It's about the modern Linux Operating System. This is not just another UNIX programming book; it's an attempt to explain to why Linux has been so successful and to show you some of those parts of the system that other books on the subject brush over or completely ignore.

In this book, you will learn about what drives the Linux development process. You will discover the wide variety of tools commonly used by Linux developers – compilers, debuggers, Software Configuration Management – and how those tools are used to build application software, tools, utilities and even the Linux kernel itself. You will learn about the unique components of a Linux system that really set it apart from other UNIX-like systems, and you will delve into the inner workings of the system in order to better understand your role as one of a budding new generation of Linux developers.

You will learn about novel development methods, including the use of virtualization technology, cross-compilation as a means to build software for different compatible platforms. You will also learn about the importance of internationalization to a community that has no borders – Linux is truly international and so are its users. Finally, you will learn about wider uses of Linux with the modern Internet by writing software for the oft-touted LAMP (Linux, Apache, MySQL, Perl/Python) stack. Linux is about so much more than just the Linux kernel itself – and it's important to realize that as a Linux developer.

Most importantly, this book is about learning. It's about presenting you, the reader, with informed discussion of the key topics that drive Linux development so that you will be better equipped to discover the world of Free and Open Source software projects out there. After reading this book, you should better understand what it is that you need to know; you won't get all the answers in this book, but you'll be able to go out and learn for yourself. Whether you're writing Free Software or working on a large commercial software project using Linux, you will gain from reading this book.

Who This Book Is For

This book is written for two different kinds of reader. First and foremost, this book is targeted at existing programmers looking to make the switch to Linux. Such readers will already have some familiarity with the C programming language and understand fundamental concepts – compilers, linkers, debuggers, and so on. They will have likely read an introductory text on the subject – for example, Wrox's *Beginning Linux Programming* (Wiley 2004), but will have little practical experience.

For those who are new to professionally developing software for Linux, the content of the book is ordered for your benefit. You should be able to begin reading at the beginning and read right through in the order presented. Optionally, you might decide to skip over the kernel material (Chapters 7-9) and concentrate more on the higher level applications and tools used in everyday projects outside of the Linux kernel. You will find the background on Toolchains, Portability, and SCMs of particular use.

This book also includes material targeted at Linux enthusiasts, managers and other interested parties, who already use Linux in their day-to-day lives but want to understand the internals of a typical Linux system to a great extent – without necessarily developing software in the process. How does a moodern Linux system handle hardware detection? Why does the Linux kernel not provide a Device Driver Model? How does Linux support internationalization? There are many questions covered herein.

For those who are not new to Linux, you won't need to read all of this book, though you should find something new and interesting in each chapter nonetheless. Often, footnotes and commentary include examples and advice that you may not have encountered previously. These include anecdotes and lessons learned from the experience of others. Nonetheless, you will likely choose to focus more substantively on the latter chapters in this book – covering the Linux kernel, desktop and LAMP.

The bottom line is that whether you are a Microsoft Windows developer with some basic Linux and UNIX knowledge who's looking to broaden your horizons or a die-hard UNIX programmer from the days of yore who wants to understand what makes Linux tick, you should this book helpful to you.

What This Book Covers

This book covers a wide variety of technologies used both in Linux software development and in that same software itself. These include a background on the history of modern UNIX, UNIX-like, and Linux systems, software portability from one platform to another, and the tools that facilitate achieving this on modern Linux software distributions. You will learn about interacting with Linux systems through network interfaces, graphical user environments, complex modern web-based LAMP stacks, and even address extending the Linux kernel itself. You will learn about modern Linux development.

This book tracks the state of the art at the time of writing, but versions of software do change over time. For this reason, most topics don't require a specific version of a utility, source code or distribution package. Where a specific release is covered, it will be noted; otherwise, you should assume that examples will work with any recent Linux distribution that you may have at your disposal.

How This Book Is Structured

This book is loosely grouped into four parts. In the first few chapters, you will learn about fundamental tools and technologies that are designed to make your life as a professional Linux programmer easier. You will learn about the GNU Toolchain, the importance of software portability, and the need for Internationalization, as well as many other topics designed to get you up to speed and working on software projects of your own. You will want to read this material first and refer to it often.

The second part of this book covers the lower-level parts of a typical Linux system – traditional systems programming topics – including networking, database concepts, and the Linux kernel. You can use this material in order to gain a better understanding of those topics that will be of interest to you, but you will not learn all there is to know in the space of these pages. That's especially true of the kernel material – this book isn't a Linux kernel programming book, but it should whet your appetite.

In the third part of this book, you'll look at higher level concepts, including the GNOME Desktop environment and its many software libraries. You will learn about the Free Desktop Project and have an opportunity to write a simple CD player application by harnessing the power of the Gstreamer library, as used by modern GNOME Desktop multimedia applications. You will discover how much can be achieved through software re-use and gain some insight into writing your own GNOME software.

Finally, the last chapter of this book is devoted to LAMP. Based upon a commodity software stack, and built using Linux, Apache, MySQL, and Perl or Python, LAMP allows you to write very powerful web applications using only Free and Open Source software. The chapter will introduce you to each of these components and provide a few examples of their use.

Conventions

To help you get the most from the text and keep track of what's happening, we've used a number of conventions throughout the book.

> **Boxes like this one hold important, not-to-be forgotten information that is directly relevant to the surrounding text.**

Tips, hints, tricks, and asides to the current discussion are offset and placed in italics like this.

As for styles in the text:

❑ We *highlight* new terms and important words when we introduce them.

❑ We show keyboard strokes like this: Ctrl+A.

❑ We show file names, URLs, and code within the text like so: `persistence.properties`.

❑ We present code in two different ways:

```
In code examples we highlight new and important code with a gray background.
```

```
The gray highlighting is not used for code that's less important in the present
context, or has been shown before.
```

Source Code

As you work through the examples in this book, you may choose either to type in all the code manually or to use the source code files that accompany the book. All of the source code used in this book is available for download at http://www.wrox.com. Once at the site, simply locate the book's title (either by using the Search box or by using one of the title lists) and click the Download Code link on the book's detail page to obtain all the source code for the book.

> *Because many books have similar titles, you may find it easiest to search by ISBN; this book's ISBN is 978-0-471-77613-0.*

Once you download the code, just decompress it with your favorite compression tool. Alternately, you can go to the main Wrox code download page at http://www.wrox.com/dynamic/books/download.aspx to see the code available for this book and all other Wrox books.

Errata

We make every effort to ensure that there are no errors in the text or in the code. However, no one is perfect, and mistakes do occur. If you find an error in one of our books, like a spelling mistake or faulty piece of code, we would be very grateful for your feedback. By sending in errata you may save another reader hours of frustration and at the same time you will be helping us provide even higher quality information.

To find the errata page for this book, go to http://www.wrox.com and locate the title using the Search box or one of the title lists. Then, on the book details page, click the Book Errata link. On this page you can view all errata that has been submitted for this book and posted by Wrox editors. A complete book list including links to each book's errata is also available at www.wrox.com/misc-pages/booklist.shtml.

If you don't spot "your" error on the Book Errata page, go to www.wrox.com/contact/techsupport.shtml and complete the form there to send us the error you have found. We'll check the information and, if appropriate, post a message to the book's errata page and fix the problem in subsequent editions of the book.

p2p.wrox.com

For author and peer discussion, join the P2P forums at p2p.wrox.com. The forums are a Web-based system for you to post messages relating to Wrox books and related technologies and interact with other readers and technology users. The forums offer a subscription feature to e-mail you topics of interest of your choosing when new posts are made to the forums. Wrox authors, editors, other industry experts, and your fellow readers are present on these forums.

At http://p2p.wrox.com you will find a number of different forums that will help you not only as you read this book, but also as you develop your own applications. To join the forums, just follow these steps:

1. Go to p2p.wrox.com and click the Register link.
2. Read the terms of use and click Agree.

3. Complete the required information to join as well as any optional information you wish to provide and click Submit.

4. You will receive an e-mail with information describing how to verify your account and complete the joining process.

You can read messages in the forums without joining P2P but in order to post your own messages, you must join.

Once you join, you can post new messages and respond to messages other users post. You can read messages at any time on the Web. If you would like to have new messages from a particular forum e-mailed to you, click the Subscribe to this Forum icon by the forum name in the forum listing.

For more information about how to use the Wrox P2P, be sure to read the P2P FAQs for answers to questions about how the forum software works as well as many common questions specific to P2P and Wrox books. To read the FAQs, click the FAQ link on any P2P page.

1

Working with Linux

One of the biggest stumbling blocks when writing software for Linux is understanding what Linux is and is not. Linux means different things to different people. Technically, Linux itself is an operating system kernel written by the Finnish born Linus Torvalds, though most people today casually refer to an entire Linux-based system by the same name. In just a few years, Linux has risen from obscurity and become widely accepted by some of the largest and most powerful computing users on the planet.

Linux is now a big-money, enterprise-quality operating system. It's used in some of the largest supercomputers and also many of the smallest gadgets, which you would never expect to have Linux underneath. Yet for all its prevalence — for such a big name in modern computing — Linux isn't owned by any one corporation that pulls the strings. Linux is so successful because of the many thousands of developers around the world who constantly strive to make it better. They, like you, are interested in writing high-quality software that draws upon the experience of others within the Linux community.

Whatever Linux means to you, you're reading this book because you're interested in learning more about becoming a professional Linux programmer. As you embark on this journey, you will find it helpful to tool yourself up with an understanding of the different flavors of Linux, how to get going in developing for them, and how working with Linux differs from working with many other popular platforms on the market today. If you're already a Linux expert, you need only skim this chapter. If you're working toward becoming the next expert, this chapter should provide some useful pointers.

In this chapter, you will learn what Linux is and how the individual components of a Linux distribution fit together, from a professional programmer's point of view. You will learn about the development process behind much of the Free, Libre, and Open Source Software (FLOSS) that is used on Linux systems and discover the wealth of online communities that power the open source revolution. Finally, you'll also discover a few of the ways in which Linux differs from other operating systems you've encountered in the past — more on that throughout the rest of the book, too.

A Brief History of Linux

Linux has a very diverse and interesting history, which dates back much further than you may at first think. In fact, Linux has heritage spanning more than 30 years, since the earliest UNIX systems of the 1970s. This fact isn't just relevant to die-hard enthusiasts. It's important for you to have at least a general understanding of the unique history that has lead to the modern Linux systems that you will encounter today. Doing so will better equip you to understand the little idiosyncrasies that differentiate Linux from alternatives on the market — and help to make Linux development more interesting, too.

The earliest work on Linux itself began back in the summer of 1991, but long before there was Linux, there was the GNU project. That project had already spent well over a decade working on producing much of the necessary Free Software components in order to be able to create a fully Free operating system, such as Linux. Without the GNU project, Linux could never have happened — and without Linux, you might not be reading about the GNU project right now. Both projects have benefited enormously from one another, as you'll discover in the topics throughout this book.

The GNU Project

Back in 1983, Richard Stallman (aka RMS) was working in the artificial intelligence (AI) lab at MIT. Up until that time, many software applications had been supplied in source code form, or otherwise had source code available that users could modify for their own systems, if it was necessary. But at this time, it was a growing trend for software vendors to ship only binary versions of their software applications. Software source code had quickly become the "trade secret" of corporations, who would later become highly protective of their — what open source developers now often term — "secret sauce."

The initial goal of the GNU project was to produce a Free UNIX-like operating system, complete with all of the necessary tools and utilities necessary in order to build such a system from source. It took well over a decade to produce most of the tools and utilities needed, including the GCC compiler, the GNU emacs text editor, and dozens of other utilities and documentation. Many of these tools have become renowned for their high quality and rich features — for example, GCC and the GNU debugger.

GNU enjoyed many early successes, but it had one crucial missing component throughout the 1980s. It had no kernel of its own — the core of the operating system — and instead relied upon users installing the GNU tools within existing commercial operating systems, such as proprietary UNIX. Though this didn't bother many of the people who used the GNU tools and utilities on their proprietary systems, the project as a whole could never be complete without a kernel of its own. There was intensive debate for years over alternatives (such as the developmental GNU HURD), before Linux came along.

Linux has never truly formed part of the GNU operating system that Richard Stallman had envisioned. In fact, for many years the GNU project has continued to advocate the GNU HURD microkernel over the Linux kernel in its conceptual GNU system, despite the fact that Linux has become the poster child for a new generation of users and developers and is by far more popular. Nevertheless, you will still occasionally see the term "GNU/Linux" used to refer to a complete Linux system in recognition of the large part played by the many GNU tools in both building and running any modern Linux system.

The Linux Kernel

The Linux kernel came along much later than the GNU project itself, over a decade after Richard Stallman made his initial announcement. In that time, other alternate systems had been developed. These included the HURD microkernel (which has since garnered limited general interest outside of the enthusiastic core developer community), as well as the educational Minix microkernel that had been written by Andrew Tanenbaum. For various reasons, neither of these alternative systems was widely considered ready for prime time by general computer users when Linux first hit the scene.

Meanwhile, a young Finnish student, working at the University of Helsinki had become frustrated about many of the things that he considered broken in the Minix operating system.[1] Thus, he began work on his own system, designed specifically for his (at the time cutting-edge) AT-386 microcomputer. That person was Linus Torvalds, and he would go on to lead the project that has created a whole industry of Linux companies and spurred on a new generation.

Linus sent out the following announcement to the comp.os.minic Usenet newsgroup upon the initial release of Linux in the summer of 1991:

> Date: 25Aug 91 20:57:08 GMT
>
> Organization: University of Helsinki
>
> Hello everybody out three using minix – I'm doing a (free) Operating system (just a hobby, won't be big and professional like gnu) for 386(486) AT clones. This has been brewing since April, and is starting to get ready. I'd like any feedback on Things people like/dislike in minix, as my OS resembles it somewhat (same physical layout of the file-system (due to practical reasons) among other things).
>
> I've currently ported bash (1.08) and gcc(1.40), and things seem to work. This implies that I'll get something practical within a few months, and I'd like to know what features most people would want. Any Suggestions are welcome, but I won't promise I'll implement them.

Despite Linus's initial modesty, interest in the Linux kernel grew quickly around the world. It wasn't long before several release cycles had passed and a growing community of users — all of whom were necessarily developers; simply installing Linux required a great deal of expertise — were working to solve technical challenges and implement new ideas as they were first conceived. Many of the now infamous Linux developers became involved early on. They enjoyed being able to work on a modern entirely Free UNIX-like system that didn't suffer from design complexities of alternative systems.

Linux developers relied upon the many existing GNU tools to build the Linux kernel and to develop new features for it. Indeed, it wasn't long before interest grew beyond the early developers, and Minix users began to work on Linux instead — something that ultimately led to a series of well-known "flame wars" between the creator of Minix (Andrew Tanenbaum) and Linus Torvalds. Tanenbaum maintains to this day that the design of Linux is fundamentally inferior to that of Minix. Philosophically, this may be true, but the same can be said of other modern operating systems.

You can learn more about the historical heritage of Linux and other UNIX-like operating systems in the book *A Quarter Century of UNIX* by Peter H. Salus (Addison-Wesley, 1994).

---

[1]Many of these issues remained for a number of years and would prove the topic of a large amount of conversation on the early Minix and Linux newsgroups. In latter years, the rivalry has largely subsided as Linux has asserted its dominance in the marketplace and Minix (and its various successors) has continued to be of academic interest to those contemplating future Operating System design.

Linux Distributions

With the growing popularity of the Linux kernel came an interest in making Linux more accessible to those who didn't already happen to have advanced knowledge of its internal programming. To create a usable Linux system, you need more than just the Linux kernel alone. In fact, the average Linux desktop system available today makes use of many thousands of individual software programs in order to go from system power on to a feature-rich graphical desktop environment such as GNOME.

When Linux was first released, there wasn't such a rich multitude of software available. In fact, Linus started out with just one application — the GNU Borne Again SHell (bash). Those who have ever had to boot a Linux or UNIX system into a limited "single-user" mode (where only a bash shell is run) will know what this experience feels like. Linus did much of his early testing of Linux from within a solitary bash command shell, but even that didn't just magically run on Linux; it first had to be `ported`, or modified to run on a Linux system instead of an existing system, such as Minix.

As more and more people began to use and develop software for Linux, a wide range of software became available to those with the patience to build and install it. Over time, it became apparent that building every single Linux system from scratch was an unsupportable, nonupgradeable nightmare that prevented all but the most enthusiastic from experiencing what Linux had to offer. The solution came in the form of Linux distributions, or precreated collections of applications and a Linux kernel that could be supplied on floppy disk (and later on CD) to a wide range of potential users.

Early Linux distributions were simply a convenience for those who wanted to avoid building the entire system from scratch for themselves, and did little to track what software had been installed or handle the safe removal and addition of new software. It wasn't until package managers like Red Hat's RPM and Debian's dpkg had been invented that it was possible for regular users to install a Linux system from scratch without very detailed expert knowledge. You'll discover more about package management in later in the book, when you look at building your own prepackaged Linux software for distribution.

Modern Linux distributions come in many shapes and sizes and are targeted at a variety of different markets. There are those written for regular desktop Linux users; those written for enterprise users with demands of scalable, robust performance; and even distributions designed for embedded devices such as PDAs, cellular telephones and set-top boxes. Despite the different packaging, Linux distributions usually have commonalities that you can exploit. For example, most distributions strive to be compatible on some level with the Linux Standard Base (LSB) de facto set of standards for compatible Linux environments.

Free Software vs. Open Source

Richard Stallman started the GNU project and founded the Free Software Foundation as a nonprofit organization to oversee it. He also worked on the first version of the General Public License — the GPL — under which a large proportion of software written for systems that run Linux is licensed. The GPL is an interesting document in its own right because its goal is not to restrict your use of GPL licensed software, but to protect the right of users and developers to have access to the source code.[2]

---

[2]The GPL is currently undergoing its third major rewrite at the time that this book is being written. The new version is likely to be one of the most controversial Free Software licenses yet. It includes stipulations about the licensing of patents and other technology, attempts to outlaw Digital Rights Management (termed "Digital Restrictions Management" by Richard Stallman) and a great deal of other requirements besides.

The GPL allows you to make changes to the Linux kernel and other GPL-licensed Free Software, in return for you publishing those changes so that other people may use them (or incorporate them back into the next official release of a given piece of software). For example, the GPL allows you to fix a bug in a major application such as Open Office, or to add custom audio file support to the totem multimedia player on a GNOME desktop system. The GPL affords you, as a developer, a great deal of flexibility to use Linux for whatever purpose you choose, just as long as you make your modifications available for others to do likewise. That's the key point — the GPL tries to keep the development process open.

Unfortunately for Richard Stallman, the English language isn't well equipped with an equivalent of the French word libre (free as in liberty), so many people confuse the concept of Free Software with software that is monetarily free. In fact, much Free Software is entirely free of charge, but there are also companies who make money from selling GPL-licensed software (including its freely redistributable source code). They are able to make money not through the software itself, but by offering a variety of support options and additional professional services for when things go wrong.

To reduce the confusion associated with the term "Free Software," the term "Open Source" was coined and became popular during the 1990s. Unlike Free Software, open source does not specifically refer to GPL-licensed software. Instead, it refers to the general desire for software to come with source code included (so that it can be tuned, debugged, and improved by others), even if that source code is actually under a more restrictive license than the GPL itself. For this reason, there is a lot more software available technically meeting the definition of open source, while simultaneously not being Free.

It is very important that you have an understanding of the requirements that the GPL places on the work that you may do in modifying existing GPL-licensed software. Although you are not required to use the GPL in your own programs, you must respect the rights of others who have done so. There are numerous examples of potential GPL infringement on the Internet — usually from companies who didn't know that they needed to make their modifications to software such as the Linux kernel available for others to take a look at. You don't want to become the next example case, so always ensure that both you and your colleagues are aware of the GPL, and decide early on how you want to work with it.

Beginning Development

The first step you take as a Linux developer is to tool yourself up for the tasks that lie ahead. This means that you'll need to have a suitable development system available to you on which you can compile and test your own Linux programs. Almost any reasonable workstation will be sufficient, at least at first — though if you end up building a lot of software, you might elect for a higher-performance machine to reduce build times. There's little else more demotivating than constantly waiting for large software builds to complete. Still, it's always good to walk before you try to run.

It should be stressed at this point that the authors of this book are not going to suggest to you that you install or use a particular Linux distribution. There are plenty of good alternatives out there, and it's the job of corporate marketing and community interest to convince you of the merits of working with and supporting a particular set of Linux distributions over any others. Nonetheless, it does make sense to look at well-known distributions (at least at first) so that you'll have better access to a highly active community of developers who can help you as and when you make your first mistakes.

You can track the current trends in modern Linux distributions through impartial websites, such as www.distrowatch.com. Distrowatch also provide useful informational resources about each one.

Choosing a Linux Distribution

At the time that this book is being written, there are well over 300 Linux distributions in use around the world, and that number is growing almost daily. Since most (if not all) of the software shipped in the average Linux distribution is covered by the GNU General Public License (GPL), literally anyone can take that software and package it for themselves into their own distribution. This encourages initiative and experimentation, but it would also quickly lead to an unmanageable support nightmare for those who decided to package software for use by those with the 300 different distributions in use.

Fortunately for you as a software developer, most of the Linux users you will need to support are using a mere handful of popular Linux distributions. Those who are not apparently using one of these well-known distributions may well have a distribution that is based upon one. It's very common for newer distributions to be built upon the niche requirements of a subset of existing users. Obviously, it stands to reason that the 100 people using a particular specialist Linux distribution may not necessarily receive the same level of support as the many hundreds of thousands of people who use another.

Here are 10 of the more popular Linux distributions available today:

❑ Debian GNU/Linux

❑ Fedora (previously known as Fedora Core)

❑ Gentoo Linux

❑ Mandriva Linux

❑ Red Hat Enterprise Linux (RHEL)

❑ Slackware Linux

❑ OpenSuSE

❑ SuSE Linux Enterprise Server (SLES)

❑ Ubuntu

Linux Distributions from Red Hat

Red Hat once produced a version of Linux known as Red Hat Linux (RHL). This was available up until release 9.0, at which point the commercial product became known as Red Hat Enterprise Linux. Around the same time, the Fedora community Linux distribution became available for those who would prefer an entirely open source version without commercial support. Fedora is very popular with desktop users and enthusiasts and is widely used by Free Software developers, as well as commercial vendors — who will later need to test and certify their software against the Enterprise release as a separate endeavor.

For more information about Red Hat, see www.redhat.com. The Fedora project has a separate website, www.fedoraproject.org.

Linux Distributions from Novell

Novell bought SuSE in 2004 and gained full control over SuSE Linux. At around the same time, a variety of marketing and branding decisions affected the future naming of Linux products from Novell. Like Red Hat, Novell provide a community release of their operating system — known as OpenSUSE. It is maintained by a growing community of users, who help to cultivate new technologies that may ultimately feed back into the next release of the commercial SuSE Linux Enterprise Server. Red Hat and Novell are usually considered to be the two big commercial Linux vendors in the marketplace.

For more information about Novell and SuSE, see `www.novell.com`. The OpenSUSE project has a separate website, `www.opensuse.org`.

Debian and Ubuntu GNU/Linux

Debian has been around for as long as Red Hat and SuSE and has a large group of core supporters. As an entirely community-maintained distribution, it is not motivated by the goals of any one particular corporation but strives simply to advance the state of the art. This is a laudable goal indeed, though Debian has suffered in the past from extremely large development cycles — often many years between major releases. A variety of "Debian derivatives" have been produced in the past, including Progeny Linux, which was one of the first attempts at producing a commercial version of Debian.

Mark Shuttleworth, one-time founder of Thwate made a fortune developing a business that had some reliance on Debian systems. Thus, he was heavily involved in the Debian community, and in 2004 founded the Ubuntu project. Ubuntu is based upon Debian, but it doesn't aim to replace it. Rather, the goal of the Ubuntu project is to provide stable release cycles and productize Debian into a distribution for the masses. Canonical, the company backing Ubuntu development has developed various tools as part of this process, including the Launchpad and Rosetta tools mentioned later in this book.

For more information about Debian GNU/Linux, see `www.debian.org`. The Ubuntu project has a separate website, `www.ubuntulinux.org`.

Classes of Linux Distribution

Distributions can be broadly broken down into three different classes, depending upon their goals, whether they are a derivative of another popular distribution, and whether they are designed for ease of use or for those with more advanced requirements. For example, the average desktop user is unlikely to rebuild his or her entire Linux distribution on a whim, whereas some server administrators actively enjoy the power and flexibility of squeezing every last possible drop of performance out of their machines.

It's important to remember that Linux delivers great flexibility — if someone can think of a way to use Linux and create a new distribution, somebody else is probably already working on implementing it.

RPM based Distributions

RPM-based distributions are so called because they use Red Hat's RPM package management tools in order to package and distribute the individual components of the distribution. In early fall 1995, RPM was one of the first package management tools available for Linux. It was quickly adopted by other distributions, such as SuSE Linux. RPM has since been renamed from Red Hat Package Manager to RPM Package Manager — reflecting the independent development of the RPM tools happening today — but a number of distributions using RPM continue to share commonalities with Red Hat distributions.

RPM-based distributions such as Red Hat's Enterprise Linux (RHEL) and Novell's SuSE Linux Enterprise Server (SLES) make up a bulk of commercial Linux offerings used throughout the world today. If you're writing software for use in the enterprise, you'll want to ensure that you have support for RPM-based distributions such as these. You needn't buy a copy of the Enterprise version of these distributions simply for everyday software development. Instead, you can use one of the community-maintained releases of the Fedora (Red Hat Linux derived) or OpenSuSE Linux distributions.

Debian Derivatives

As you will discover later in this book, Debian-derived distributions are based on the Debian Linux distribution and package management tools such as apt. Debian's dpkg package management tool was written around the same time that the original work was done on RPM, although different design decisions and philosophy have seen the two tools continue along separate paths ever since. Debian has a reputation for forming the basis of a variety of community and commercial Linux distributions.

Debian is a community-maintained Linux distribution, coordinated by a nonprofit organization known as Software in the Public Interest (SPI). Since the earliest releases, there has been an interest in customizing Debian and in distributing variants aimed at addressing a particular need. One of the most high-profile Debian derivatives is the Ubuntu Linux distribution, which aims to encourage widespread adoption through regulated release cycles and by steering overall development to meet certain goals.

Source Distributions

Linux distributions don't need to be based upon one of the common package management systems. There are many alternatives out there that use little or no package management beyond keeping software components in separate file archives. In addition, there are distributions that are actually intended for you to build when they are installed. This can be the case for any number of practical (or ideological) reasons but such distributions are usually confined to very niche Linux markets.

Build-from-source distributions such as Gentoo are designed to be easy to use but at the same time deliver high performance through locally customized software for each installed system. Gentoo uses a system known as portage to automate the process of downloading and building each individual software application whenever you require. Just bear in mind that it can take many hours for Open Office to build the first time you decide you need to use it and instruct portage to build it up for you.

You won't usually concern yourself with source-based distributions if you're producing an application for the mass market. Most customers prefer to use popular commercial or community distributions with standardized packaging processes. It reduces support headaches and often seems to make life easier. If you're interested in Gentoo Linux, don't forget to visit the project website at www.gentoo.org.

Roll Your Own

As you'll discover later in this book, it's possible to build your own Linux distribution from component parts. There are any number of reasons that you might want to do this — curiosity, the need for greater flexibility than is otherwise available, customizability, and so on. The fact is that many of the Embedded Linux devices on the market today are built entirely from scratch by the vendor producing the device. Needless to say, we do not encourage you to try building your own Linux distribution before you have become familiar with the internal packages, software, and utilities required by distributions in general.

The Linux From Scratch project is an example of one self-help guide you can use in building your own Linux distributions from scratch. Their website is www.linuxfromscratch.org. You can also check out automated distribution build tools such as PTXdist at http://ptxdist.sf.net.

Installing a Linux Distribution

Once you have decided upon which Linux distributions you will be working with, you'll need to set up at least one development machine. It's important to realize that you won't need to install every single distribution you might want to later support when you start your development. Instead, choose one that you feel comfortable spending a lot of time working with as you try to get your software up and running. Later, you can port your software over to any other distributions that may be required. Don't forget that virtualization products – such as Xen and VMware – can greatly ease testing, as you can install any modern Linux distribution in its own virtualized sandbox away from your existing setup.

Later in this chapter, you'll find links to online groups and resources where you can discuss your choice of Linux distribution and ask any questions you may have while getting yourself set up.

Getting Hold of Linux

Most modern Linux distributions are supplied on CD or DVD media or are available to download in the form of CD or DVD images (ISOs) over the Internet. Distributions generally will use mirror sites to spread the load of the enormous numbers of people who wish to download CD or DVD images over their high-speed links. You can do your bit to help them out by always downloading from a mirror site that is geographically located near you. That way, you won't clog up international links unnecessarily with your large downloads — remember that Linux is international by its very nature.

> *Don't forget to check out BitTorrent as a means to harness peer-to-peer technology to speed up your download. Linux distributions covered under the terms of the GPL are freely redistributable, so many people have set up BitTorrent trackers to allow them to get faster downloads, while actually helping others speed up their downloads at the same time – look for explanations from vendor websites.*

Be forewarned that downloading a particular distribution can take many hours, even on modern high-speed Internet connections. If you don't want to wait so long to download multiple CD or DVD images, you can often perform an online install instead. This process will take longer, but you will only install those packages that you select — so the installer won't need to retrieve as much data overall. To perform an online install, look for smaller network install CD images on vendor websites. These are often under 100MB in size and will download very quickly, while still allowing you to do a full install.

Of course, you might also elect to buy an off-the-shelf boxed product and save some of the time and hassle in downloading and burning media for yourself. If you choose to buy a copy of a commercial Linux distribution, look for a local Linux supplier that might be able to help you directly. They can come in handy later when you need to pick up any additional software — so use the opportunity to establish a relationship if you have the chance. You might also find that your local Linux user group additionally has a preferential deal with certain Linux vendors and suppliers for products for use by enthusiasts.

Determining Install-Time Package Selection

Installation of most modern Linux distributions is a smooth and painless process requiring that you answer just a few questions. Tell the installer the name you'd like to give to your Linux machine, what its network settings will be, and a few other details, and in no time at all, it'll be installing a lot of shiny software onto your machine. This is the ease with which a regular installation goes these days — certainly far removed from the days of having to build up the system from scratch yourself.

Most installers won't automatically include development tools when setting up a regular Linux desktop or server system. In particular, it is unusual to find the GNU toolchain and related build tools available out of the box with popular distributions — such as those from Red Hat, SuSE, or Ubuntu. You'll need to modify the package selection at install time to include what is usually labeled as "development tools" or similar. To do this, you might need to choose a custom install option, depending upon the specific version of the distribution that you are using. Check the documentation for advice.

Figure 1-1 shows the development packages being installed on a Fedora Core 5 system.

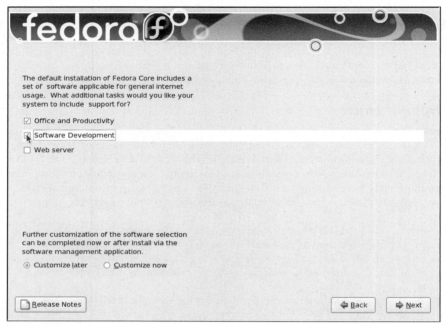

Figure 1-1

If you missed the opportunity to add development tools during system installation, you can go back and add in development tools at a later stage. This is usually best accomplished by using a graphical package management tool included with you distribution. Graphical package management tools such as yumex (Fedora), YaST (SuSE) and synaptic (Ubuntu) offer groups of related packages and ease the process of identifying what components you will need to install. If all else fails, you'll experience some strange errors when you try out some of the example code from this book — look out for missing tools.

Setting Up Your Development Environment

A newly installed Linux system will usually automatically load up a graphical desktop environment. Most Linux systems available today choose either of the GNOME or KDE graphical desktops (or in some cases both, allowing you to choose which you would like to use). Although this book attempts to be unbiased as possible, it is nevertheless not possible to cover all technologies to the same degree within a single volume. As a result, the authors have chosen to focus upon the GNOME desktop environment whenever it is necessary to talk specifically about desktop-related issues.

GNOME is the default graphical desktop environment used by both the Fedora and Ubuntu projects, but whatever your personal or organizational preference is, you should find the interfaces appear similar. You will quickly discover the administration and management tools located in the system menus, as well as those development tools that have been preinstalled by your distribution. Several distributions now ship with the Eclipse IDE development environment installed by default — a good place to start if you're familiar with other graphical development tools such as Microsoft Visual Studio on Windows.

Finding a Terminal

Linux systems, like other UNIX systems, are built upon many different tools and utilities that work together to get the job done. Although graphical desktop environments have become very popular over the last few years, it's still commonplace to perform everyday software source file editing and to drive software build processes entirely from within a system terminal. You can use a graphical development environment such as Eclipse, but it's a good idea to know how to work at the command line.

As you work through this book, most of the example code will include simple commands that you can use at the command line in order to build the software. You will usually find that a terminal is available to you via the system menus, or in some cases by right-clicking on your desktop and selecting Open Terminal from the menu. On Fedora systems, you'll need to install an extra system package (use the Software Updater tool in the System Tools menu, under the Applications menu) to have the terminal option readily available in your desktop menu — it's there by default on OpenSUSE and Ubuntu.

Editing Source Files

Throughout this book, you will find example source code that you can try out and modify for your own purposes. You'll find out more about how to build software on Linux systems in subsequent chapters. You'll also find many examples that are available from the website accompanying this book, which you can download in order to avoid typing them in each time. Despite this, you will clearly want to produce your own programs early on. It is, therefore, recommended that you find a text editor that you feel comfortable working with as you develop your Linux software.

Most Linux developers choose to use popular editors such as vim (derived from the ancient UNIX vi editor) or GNU emacs (Richard Stallman's original GNU project editor). These work both from the command line and as graphical applications, depending upon the precise version you have installed. Each comes with a rich set of features that will enhance your productivity, as well as a set of documentation and tutorials to help you get up to speed quickly. For those who prefer a graphical editor, the GNOME and KDE desktops are supplied with several powerful alternatives.

It's worth noting the tradition of vi and emacs rivalry. Historically, vi and emacs users were mutually exclusive. Those who use one typically dislike the other with a passion (and other users of the other). There are few sources of contention more pointless than the editor flame wars started from time to time by people on mailing lists, but the sheer range of vi vs. emacs T-shirts and other merchandise available on the Internet should demonstrate the seriousness with which some people take these editor wars. It's never a good idea to try to understand precisely why people care so much about this — just live with it.

> *Whatever text editor you choose, don't try using a word processor such as Open Office writer or abiword to edit program source code. While it is technically possible to do so, these tools usually mangle source and even when editing text files will attempt to embed various rich text formatting that will confuse the build tools you later use to build the software.*

Figures 1-2 and 1-3 show examples of source files being edited with the vim and emacs text editors.

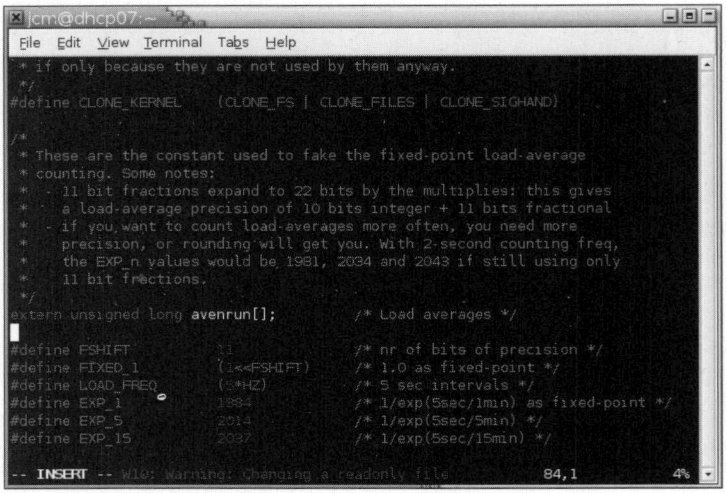

Figure 1-2

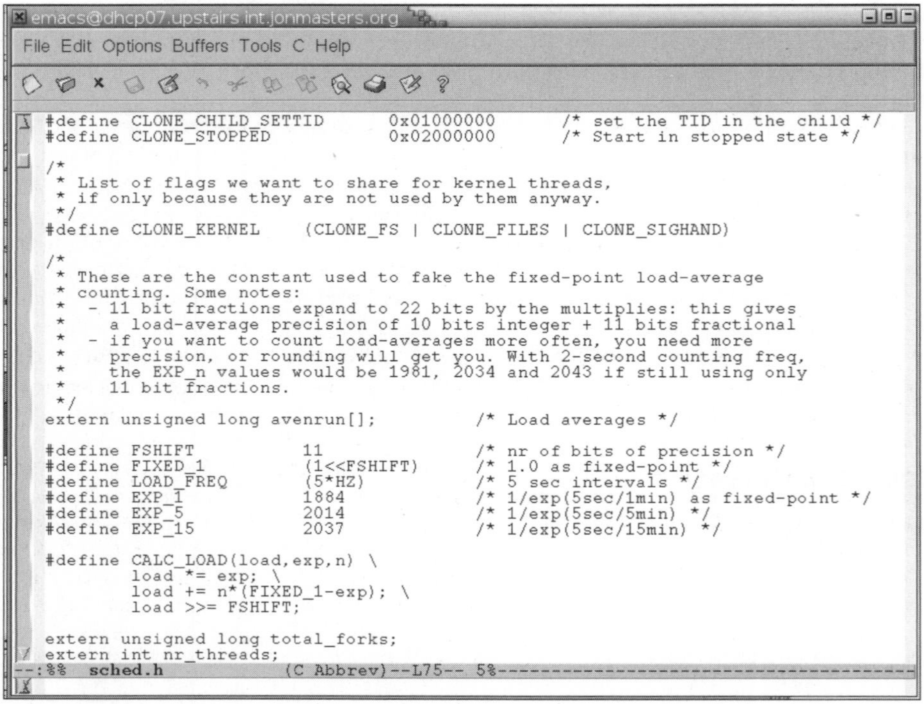

Figure 1-3

Using the Root Account

To avoid occasional accidental system damage — the removal of core system files, accidentally wiping out system utilities with your own, and so on — it's usual to do your everyday work as a regular user on your machine. A regular user has full access to his or her home directory (under /home) and can easily build and test out most regular application software. This is sufficient for most development tasks, but there are times when you will need to gain access to the administrative (root) account in order to modify global system settings, install test software, and generally to get the job done.

Rather than using your system entirely as the root user, or logging out and logging in as root whenever you need access to the root account, it's recommended that you use the sudo utility. Sudo enables you to run a single command as the root user, without running the risk of having to be logged in with such powers all of the time. It's amazing how easily you can accidentally trash a system with a single mistaken command as the root user. Hence, most developers generally use their own accounts.

To use sudo, you'll need to ensure that your regular user account is listed in /etc/sudoers. For example, the user account "jcm" can be granted sudo permission with the following entry:

```
jcm     ALL=(ALL) ALL
```

This grants jcm permission to run any command as the root user (on any machine – there's only the local machine to worry about in most cases, but if you're on a network, check with your IS/IT folks). To actually run a command with root permissions, you can use the sudo command:

```
$ sudo whoami
root
```

You will be asked for a password, if you have not entered one recently.

The first time you use it, sudo warns you about the dangerous things you can do as a root user and then asks for a password, which may not be the same as your login password. On some distributions, sudo is configured to ask for the root account password by default, others will use your own login password in order to gain access to the sudo tool. You'll want to check your distribution's documentation or use the UNIX man command to find out more information about the local installation.

> *If you're working within a corporate environment, don't forget to notify your IT or IS department that you will require administrative access to your development machine. It'll save a lot of hassle later on, unless they specifically want to support you every time you need to use the root account.*

Development Releases

Linux distributions usually have a development version that closely tracks ongoing development of the distribution itself. Such versions are updated far more often that their stable release counterparts. Stable distribution releases usually vary between 6 months and 18 months apart, while a development version might change on even a daily basis. The big three distributions — those from Red Hat, SuSE, and Ubuntu — all have unstable development releases available on a daily basis. You won't normally need to look at these, but it helps to know they're out there, so here's a quick overview of the alternatives.

> *Development releases of modern distributions are explained here for your interest and education. They may aid in some of your development decisions, but you should not directly build or develop production software on them. Changes occur frequently, making it extremely difficult to achieve reproducible results. Complete system breakage is also not that uncommon.*

Red Hat calls their unstable Fedora release rawhide. It's available via the Fedora website, but you'll usually perform a "yum update" (after uncommenting the development YUM repository entries in `/etc/yum.repos.d`) from the most recent stable release in order to switch over, rather than trying to perform an install of rawhide directly. Rawhide is a hive of activity from which you can often garner some insight into what might make it into the next Fedora release — ultimately, that may even affect what goes into the Red Hat Enterprise product at some point in the future.

Novell calls its unstable OpenSuSE release Factory. It's available from the OpenSuSE website and can be installed using network bootable images that are available for download. You will need to follow the installation instructions carefully if you perform a network install as to do so necessitates changing various options early on in the boot process — before the YaST installer has even started. You can also upgrade using YUM (documented online), but that process is much newer as of this writing. Factory is updated on a semi-regular basis, ultimately feeding technology into SuSE Linux Enterprise Server.

Ubuntu, like Debian, is available in an unstable release. This release is updated frequently, whenever the packages within it are modified. Thus, it's sometimes the case that a given system is unable to perform an update to the latest unstable release at a particular moment in time. Unlike the other distributions mentioned here, Ubuntu and Debian provide an interim testing version of their distribution, which always contains packages that have been known to be usable after being released into unstable release of the distribution. You will usually "apt-get upgrade" your system to unstable after modifying `/etc/apt/sources.list`).

Scratch Boxes and Virtualization Technologies

As you become happier with Linux development and become more adventurous, you'll want to have a scratch box that you can just test out ideas on (or completely trash) without risking breaking anything it had installed. This is especially true if you later decide to write your own Linux kernel device drivers or otherwise modify critical system components — you don't want to be doing that on a machine you need to remain stable during that process. Many hackers resort to using old PCs for this purpose.

Virtualization technologies, such as VWware, qemu and Xen, can be useful ways to gain access to a large number of test virtual machines that you can happily trash all day long, all without actually having to buy any additional hardware. Not only is virtualization is good cost-saving idea, but it's also very practical when it comes to setting up standard test environments and sharing ideas with your colleagues. Most virtualization technologies will allow you to set up snapshots of systems configured in a particular way that you can then store or send to your coworkers via a network storage area of some kind.

VWware

VWware allows you to manage large collections of virtual machines using their proprietary graphical software. It's trivial to configure a new virtual machine and to then install a Linux distribution within it. Using VWware, you can easily install a range of different PC-based Linux distributions, all without actually changing the software on your machine. Great when you want to store preconfigured test machines or try out some experimental features that don't rely on having some specific custom hardware device, not so great for testing out your custom Linux kernel device drivers!

You can find out more information about VWware at www.vmware.com.

Qemu

Qemu is an open source virtualization technology that can be used to run Linux. It's entirely free, but somewhat more limited than proprietary offerings like VWware. Using the qemu command line utilities, you can create a virtual machine environment and then install a Linux distribution within it. Since qemu is covered by the GNU General Public License, it's possible to modify the software itself and add in interesting new capabilities. As you'll discover later in the book, possible modifications include custom virtualized hardware devices for which you can write your own device drivers—all without having to risk the stability of your regular development environment.

For more information about qemu, see the project website at `www.qemu.org`.

Xen

Over the past few years, there has been a growing interest in a virtualization technology known as Xen. At the time that this book is being written, Xen is making headlines most every other week. Like VWware, Xen is capable of running any operating system within a virtualized environment. Unlike VWware, Xen is also Free Software, and there are a variety of graphical configuration tools available for those who want to use them. Most recent Linux distributions include some level of specific support for building and configuring Xen virtualized environments that you can use to test out your software.

For more information about Xen, see the project website at `www.cl.cam.ac.uk/Research/SRG/netos/xen`.

Linux Community

One of the most important things to realize when developing software for Linux is that you are very much not alone. A large community of fellow developers exists all over the world. Many of these people are interested in trading stories or helping you out when you get yourself into a jam. There are numerous different ways in which you can contact fellow Linux users and developers—and you'll want to look into joining the wider community well before you run up against your first roadblock.

In addition to getting involved with the wider Linux community, you'll probably want to start reading one of the regular magazines. The oldest of these is the *Linux Journal* (`www.linuxjournal.com`), but at the time this book is being written, there are literally dozens of magazines from around the world.

Linux User Groups

Wherever you are in the world, you're probably located nearer to other Linux users than you may think. Most major towns or cities have their own Linux user group (LUG) that is made up of local Linux enthusiasts working in a wide range of different areas. Some members, like you, may be less familiar with Linux and be seeking advice from those who have been involved in the community for perhaps a decade or longer. In fact, some LUGs are well over 10 years old by this point.

You can find out more information about your local Linux user group via the Internet. Just type your local town or city name into Google's special Linux search engine at `www.google.com/linux`.

Mailing lists

Most of the Linux developers around the world today communicate new ideas, exchange software patches, and participate in general discussion via electronic mailing lists. There are so many different mailing lists on so many different topics that it would be impossible to cover them all in this book. Everything from the smallest subsystem of the Linux kernel to entire Linux distributions and even the most remote regions of the planet will have a mailing list of some kind. You are encouraged to join the mailing list from your local Linux user group and user lists provided by your distribution vendor as a starting point.

Throughout this book, you will find references to mailing lists and other similar resources that might help you to get more involved or better understand a particular topic.

IRC

Developers frequently wish to participate in more interactive discussion than a mailing list is designed to allow. IRC (Internet Relay Chat) facilitates the process of joining various channels on IRC networks around the world, and many groups that have a mailing list will also have an IRC channel of some kind to complement mailing list discussion. You can discover a wealth of online resources within IRC networks such as Freenode, OFTC, and others. Each of these is preconfigured into graphical IRC clients such as the xchat client that comes with most modern Linux distributions.

Private Communities

The Linux developer community isn't always quite as open as you may think it is. A number of closed groups do exist around the world in the name of facilitating discussion between bona fide core developers of a particular technology. These groups occasionally hold special events, but more often than not will simply communicate using nonpublic mailing lists and IRC networks. It's important to realize that Linux does have an open development process, despite the occasional private club.

An example of a private group is the many security groups around the world that look to quickly fix problems that are discovered in Linux software. They necessarily do not publish the precise details of what they're working on until they have found the security bug and made a coordinated release with any vendors and other third parties involved. This helps to reduce the number of security incidents. If you ever discover a security bug in Linux software, always use the appropriate channels to report it.

There is no Linux Cabal.

Key Differences

Linux isn't like other operating systems you may have encountered in the past. Most operating systems have been designed over a period of many years by a small team of highly skilled people. Those designers then handed over a specification document to software engineers for them to implement the design. Linux isn't about closed teams of any kind. Sure, there are many vendors working on Linux technology behind semi-closed doors, but the core of the development process happens out in the open for all to see — warts and all.

Having an open development process means that the whole world gets to dissect the implementation of various features within the Linux distributions and propose their own changes. Thus, Linux benefits from the "many eyeballs" scalability of allowing anyone to make a contribution — greatly exceeding the resources of even the largest proprietary software companies. Having an open development process means that it's very hard to have bad ideas accepted into the core of your Linux system. Everyone makes mistakes, but the Linux community is usually very picky about what changes it will accept.

Linux Is Modular

A typical Linux system is built from many smaller components that work together to form the larger whole. Unlike Microsoft Windows, Linux explicitly breaks out even the smallest functionality into a separate dedicated utility. There are several different utilities designed solely to set the system clock, others to control the sound volume mixers on your sound card, still other dedicated tools for individual networking operations, and so on. Take a look in the standard /bin and /usr/bin directories on any Linux system, and you'll see a few of these individual utilities for yourself.

Like many older UNIX systems, Linux is built upon a principal of KISS ("keep it simple, stupid"). This follows the principal that it's better to do one thing and do it well, than try to overload functionality into giant monolithic programs. Unlike Microsoft Windows, Linux systems have been designed so that they are easily user modifiable. You are encouraged to customize your system in whatever manner you choose; such is the point of Free and Open Source software.

Throughout this book, you'll see references to many tools that you may not have encountered previously. Don't panic. As you'll quickly discover, knowing the right people to turn to — the right resources and community groups — and using the documentation that is provided with every Linux system is often enough to get you out of a jam. Many so-called experts are in fact highly skilled Googlers who know how to get at the information that will help them to do whatever they need to.

Linux Is Portable

As you'll discover in Chapter 3, Linux itself is one of the most portable operating systems available today. Linux distributions have been released for the smallest embedded devices like your cell phone, PDA, and digital video recorder (DVR) set-top box, while at the same time others support mainframe systems or supercomputers being used to process the human genome. Software written for Linux is often designed with portability in mind, and since it may automatically be built for a range of different target systems as part of being in a Linux distribution, it's common to find portability issues early on.

When you write software for Linux, always consider whether your decisions will affect how portable your software will be in the future. Will you ever need to run it on 64-bit systems? Will you always have a full-featured graphical desktop environment based on GNOME, or might someone want to use your software on a resource-constrained embedded device? These are questions you should keep in mind so that you won't have unnecessary surprises later on.

Linux Is Generic

The Linux kernel itself strives to be as generic as possible. That means that the same source code can be built to run on the smallest gadget or the largest mainframe with scalability built right in. There should not be any need to make fundamental adjustments in order to support this wide range of target systems, because the software was built with this kind of flexibility in mind. Of course, certain features can and will be tuned for specific systems, but the core algorithms will remain the same. The same should be true of the majority of software released within modern Linux distributions.

Keeping things as generic as possible and allowing the users to decide how they will use a Linux system is one of the reasons that Linux has been so successful. You should always try to think about the ways that people might want to use your software and avoid incorporating unnecessary design constraints. You don't have to support people who want to use your software in nonrecommended ways, but don't artificially impose limits unless it's absolutely necessary.

Summary

In this chapter, you learned about working with Linux. You learned that the term Linux has different meanings in different contexts. Technically, Linux refers to the core operating system kernel written by Linus Torvalds and maintained by many thousands of skilled developers around the world. But Linux can also be used to refer to distributions of software that are built on top of Linus's original kernel. This software includes many thousands of tools and utilities, modern graphical desktop environments, and many other components that users expect to find in a complete modern OS.

The success of Linux over the past decade has a lot to do with the communities, which have helped to make it so popular as an alternative to big proprietary UNIX and other operating systems on the market today. You now know how to get involved in your local Linux User Group and how to make contact with a larger world of Linux developers, who are keen to help you on your way to becoming an expert. You also have gained an understanding of the many differences between Linux and other operating systems.

2

Toolchains

Toolchains are the silent workhorses behind every major Open Source engineering project, including the Linux kernel itself. They are a collection of the necessary tools and utilities to build and debug anything from the simplest utility to the most complex Linux kernel feature imaginable. If you've done any Linux programming at all, then you have likely already encountered the GNU Compiler Collection (GCC), but there's a lot more to producing a finished application than simply compiling source code. To produce a finished application, you need the aid of a complete set of tools, commonly referred to as a *toolchain*.

A toolchain includes a compiler, a linker, and assembler as well as a debugger to aid in tracking down the inevitable bugs present in all but the most trivial of programs. In addition, a variety of miscellaneous utilities allow for manipulation of the resulting application binaries as may be necessary — for example, the processing of Linux kernel binaries into machine bootable images. The overwhelming majority of Linux applications are built using the GNU Toolchain, formed from tools released by the GNU project.

This chapter introduces you to the myriad tools that make up the GNU Toolchain, as well as a few other related tools that are also used by Linux developers to build and debug applications. These tools include many nonstandard features that are commonly used by Linux applications as well as the kernel. You will learn how to use the GNU Toolchain and become familiar with some of its more advanced features. After reading this chapter, you will be able to build and debug applications, and you will begin to feel comfortable with concepts such as inline assembly and the powerful capabilities of the GNU binutils.

The Linux Development Process

To understand the individual tools used to build software on Linux, you must first have a high-level understanding of the overall software development process and just what the individual tools within a toolchain are designed to achieve. You will then find it much easier to apply these concepts to more advanced uses for individual tools as you come to experiment with them later in the chapter.

Modern Linux software is formed from a relatively large number of individual components that are combined at build time into a small number of executable and nonexecutable files. These include the application binaries themselves, as well as many supporting resources, documentation, and extraneous data used in source code management (SCM) and revision control. Together, these individual parts may be packaged into a single distribution-specific installable software package, shipped to users.

Of course, certain applications may also not be designed to be end-user installable. This is often the case with embedded devices or other OEM solutions where a full system running Linux is supplied as part of a larger product. In these cases, you will write and build the software in the standard fashion, but replace the packaging steps with an automated process for installing the software onto a target.

In this section, you will learn how to work with source code, how to obtain it, and how to configure a set of program sources into a working development tree. You will also begin to examine the common build processes that are shared among most of the applications on your Linux system and with which you will need to be familiar as you come to write your own applications.

Working with Sources

Developers rarely work directly with the end- user-installable software packages. Instead, they work with a source package or archive that contains an application's sources as well as any additional scripts and configuration data that are necessary in order to rebuild the application from source. These external supporting scripts and configuration data are used to automatically determine software prerequisites as well as those features that will be necessary to use the software in a given Linux target environment.

Linux software is usually distributed to developers in one of two forms. The first and most basic is a source archive, commonly referred to as a *tarball* (because the standard compressed archive file has a .tar.gz or a .tar.bz2 extension). This source archive must first be unpacked using an appropriate tool, such as the command line tar command or a graphical archive management tool (supplied by your graphical desktop environment) before it can be built using a standard procedure.

The second way to distribute source to developers is via an SCM tool. These tools automate the process of obtaining source code, tracking local changes, and submitting patches or modified versions of the source *upstream* to the central repository or higher-level developers. A selection of these tools will be examined later in the book. If you do use an SCM, then it is important to follow the procedures and practices agreed on between the individual members of the development team.

You will find that the example code for most of this book is stored within a regular Linux tar archive, although you may find it easier to import examples into your own SCM and keep track of the changes that you make as you work with the code (see Chapter 4, "Software Configuration Management). To unpack the archive containing the example code used in this chapter, you can use the following Linux tar command:

```
tar xvfj toolchains.tar.bz2
```

The xvfj option flags instruct the standard tar command that it is to extract and verify the filename given, which is stored in a bzip2-compressed tar archive. If it were stored in the older and still widely used gzip-compressed tar archive format (usually using the .tar.gz filename extension), then you would have instructed tar to uncompress a gzip tarball with the xvfz option flags instead.

Configuring to the Local Environment

The example project archive contains a single top-level directory and several other subdirectories. At the top level are the README and INSTALL files that describe the standard process used to (re)build the software. This process involves first configuring the local build environment before actually running the additional commands that will build an executable application.

Configuring the local build environment is a necessary step in developing software on Linux because of the wide variety of different target platforms on which Linux is available. Each different hardware environment may have specific limitations — for example, ordering its memory as big or little endian or having specific requirements of executables that are compiled to run on a given target processor — and each different Linux distribution will come with a variety of possible software environments — different versions of utilities and system libraries — which will vary from one release to the next.

Since very few Linux (or indeed other UNIX) environments are identical, it is necessary to introduce a range of tools that can handle these differences in a portable and abstract way. Thus, the first tool of interest is GNU Autoconf, and its presence is characterized by the existence of a configure script. When executed, the configure script will automatically determine whether the necessary build tools are installed on your system and which versions are available, in case there are any specific requirements.

Try asking the example configure script for some usage instructions:

```
$ ./configure --help
`configure' configures hello_world 1.0 to adapt to many kinds of systems.

Usage: ./configure [OPTION]... [VAR=VALUE]...
```

The output has been abridged for brevity.

The output from the configure program lists a variety of possible options and values according to how it has itself been configured. Most of these options are not necessary in this case, since the configure script in the example has been instructed only to determine whether you have the necessary GNU Toolchain components installed correctly for use with the code from this chapter. Later examples, such as those in the next chapter, will exploit more powerful functionality of Autoconf and discuss its internals in detail.

Configure the example code by running the included configure script:

```
./configure
checking for gcc... gcc
checking for C compiler default output file name... a.out
checking whether the C compiler works... yes
checking whether we are cross compiling... no
checking for suffix of executables...
checking for suffix of object files... o
checking whether we are using the GNU C compiler... yes
checking whether gcc accepts -g... yes
checking for gcc option to accept ANSI C... none needed
checking how to run the C preprocessor... gcc -E
```

```
checking for egrep... grep -E
checking for ANSI C header files... yes
configure: creating ./config.status
```

The configure script will automatically determine whether the necessary GNU tools are installed and verify that they work by actually attempting to compile an extremely simple test program. You will learn more about writing `configure` scripts of your own later in the book.

Your output may vary according to the specific environment on your workstation. If there are any errors at this stage, there's a good chance that you don't have the appropriate tools installed on your system. Many Linux distributions no longer install the full GNU Toolchain as part of their installation process, so it will be necessary for you to install whatever development tools are missing. Usually, a vendor provides a "Development" option during installation, which results in the correct tools being installed (but see the Introduction for more details on getting an appropriately configured base Linux system).

Building the Sources

The `README` file supplied with the example source code gives you an overview of the purpose of the example code. It then refers to the more detailed `INSTALL` file, which describes how to actually build and install the example sources on your workstation. As with all Linux software, the documentation also explains how to remove the software, should it not be required any longer.

You can build and test the example code using the following commands:

```
$ cd src
$ make
$ ./hello
Hello, World!
```

As with most UNIX-like systems, the majority of software on Linux is built under the control of GNU make. This handy utility reads in a `Makefile` and uses it to determine which sequence of commands must be called and in what order to produce a working program from the given source code (stored within the `src` subdirectory of the example sources). GNU make understands how to build the majority of simple executables with very few specific instructions, although it is not infallible.

The exact sequence of commands to be called by make is determined by dependency information, which is specified in the `Makefile`. In the example, a single source file named `hello.c` is automatically compiled into a single executable called hello, which you can then execute. Make allows various make targets to be specified, depending upon the desired action. For example, you can use the command `make clean` or `make distclean` to clean up the source code that is ready for distribution to developers.

The example Makefile contains dependency rules such as these:

```
all: hello

hello: hello.c
```

There is no need to tell GNU make how to compile the `hello.c` source into an executable because it already understands that a C source file dependency indicates a requirement that the appropriate invocation of the GNU C compiler and other tools are necessary. In fact, GNU make supports a variety of default file extensions, which it uses to determine default rules for various types of source code.

Makefiles may, in some cases, have been generated by another automated tool. This is often done as part of the process used to generate `configure` scripts, in order to produce software that is widely portable to a variety of different types of target Linux machines. The Makefile will then automatically use the specific GNU tools detected by the configure script and behave according to any additional options given during the configuration process, for example using a specific cross-compiler to build software for a target running on a different processor architecture than that of your workstation.

The Free Software Foundation recommends that you always use such automatic configuration tools, because they abstract away the complexities of building everyday Linux software applications. As a result, you don't need to know anything about the sources to build and use many Linux applications. More important, the same should be true of those who want to build your application from source.

Components of the GNU Toolchain

The previous section introduced the almost universal "`configure, make`" sequence for building most Linux software. As you can see, by using GNU Autoconf and GNU make in the appropriate combination it is possible to build an application from source by using just a couple of commands. You will discover later in the chapter how you can streamline the entire process by using a graphical development environment such as Eclipse to reduce the entire build cycle to a single button click.

Automation is an important part of software development because it both streamlines repetitive build cycles and improves reproducibility by removing potential to make mistakes. Many developers (the authors included) have learned the hard way how important it is to always make building Linux software as simple as possible, after wasting whole days debugging nonexistent "bugs," which turned out actually to be side effects from having too complex a build process to contend with.

While you should always endeavor to use the automation tools at hand, it is not good programming practice to rely solely on them. It is important to have at least an overview of the individual parts of the GNU Toolchain so that you can correctly handle situations in which the tools are unable to help you. Therefore, the remainder of this chapter will focus on the individual tools behind the build process, taking you through what each tool does and how it fits into the overall GNU Toolchain.

The GNU Compiler Collection

The GNU Compiler Collection (formerly the GNU C Compiler) began life back in 1987. Richard Stallman, the founder of the GNU Project, wanted to create a compiler that satisfied his recently defined notion of Free Software and could be used to build other software released the GNU project. The GNU C compiler quickly became popular among the free software community and has become famous over the years for its robustness and portability. It serves as the basis of a number of integrated development tools that have been released by vendors around the world for both Linux and other operating systems.

GCC is no longer a small C compiler used primarily by the GNU project for its own software. Today, it includes support for many different languages — including C and C++ but also Ada, Fortran, Objective C, and even Java. Indeed, modern Linux systems can proudly boast support for a multitude of languages other than those supported directly by the GNU tools. The growing popularity of Perl, Python, and Ruby as scripting languages, as well as the ongoing development of the mono portable C# implementation, has really served to dilute what it can mean to "program" for Linux, but that's another issue entirely.

This chapter concentrates on the uses of GCC as a C compiler. The Linux kernel and many other Free Software and Open Source applications are written in C and compiled using GCC. Therefore, it is essential to have a level of understanding of the concepts covered by this chapter, even if you do not intend to use GCC directly in your projects or if you are using GCC for a purpose other than compiling C source. You should be able to take the general concepts covered in this chapter and apply them to other similar language tools with a little help from their own documentation and third-party online resources.

In addition to its wide range of language support, GCC is a favorite for many developers because it has been ported to such a wide range of available hardware targets (machines based upon differing processor architectures). The standard GCC release includes support for over 20 families of microprocessor, including the Intel IA32 ("x86") and AMD64 processors used in many workstations and servers. GCC also supports high-end SPARC and POWER/PowerPC processors, as well as an increasingly large number of specialized embedded microprocessors, used in Linux-enabled gadgets and other devices. If it's commercially available, GCC can probably compile code for it.

Compiling a Single Source File

As you have already discovered, the process of building software on Linux involves many different tools that work together. GCC is a very flexible and powerful modern C compiler, but it is, at the end of the day, just a C compiler. It is very good at parsing C source and churning out assembly language code for a given processor family, but it is unable to actually produce working executable programs on its own due to its lack of a built-in assembler or linker capable of targeting a given machine.

This design is quite intentional. Following the UNIX philosophy, GCC does one thing and does it well. GCC supports a wide variety of different target processors, but it relies upon external tools to perform the assembly and linking stages, which will result in compiled source code first being turned into object code by an assembler and then being linked by a linker into a suitable container file that can actually be loaded and executed by a particular family of Linux target machines.

GCC may not be able to produce a working executable program on its own, but it does understand which additional GNU tools are usually necessary in order to actually achieve that. The gcc driver program, which forms the front end to GCC, understands that a C source file must be assembled and linked by the GNU assembler and linker tools and will by default perform these additional steps when you give it a C source file to compile.

To test this out, you can create the infamous "Hello World" example:

```
/*
 * Professional Linux Programming - Hello World
 */

#include <stdio.h>
```

```
#include <stdlib.h>

int main(int argc, char **argv)
{
printf("Hello, World!\n");
exit(0);
}
```

You can compile and test this code, using the following commands:

```
$ gcc -o hello hello.c
$ ./hello
Hello, World!
```

By default, the `gcc` driver performs all of the steps necessary in order to compile the `hello.c` source code into an executable program binary. This includes calling the actual C compiler (cc1), which forms an internal part of GCC, as well as the external GNU assembler and linker tools that will actually produce executable code from the output of the GNU C compiler. For historical reasons, resulting executables are called `a.out` by default, but you will usually specify your own with the `-o` option to `gcc`, as shown in the preceding code.

Compiling Multiple Source Files

Most applications are based upon many individual files of source code that are individually compiled and then linked together to form the final executable program. This both simplifies development and allows different teams to work on different parts of a project, while encouraging suitable code reuse. Later in this book you will learn how the Linux kernel is formed from many hundreds of individual source files and also how graphical GNOME desktop applications are built from many separate components, but for the moment, begin by compiling two source files into a single program.

The `gcc` driver application not only understands how to compile individual source files into an executable program but also can link together several different object files by appropriately invoking the GNU linker on its behalf. GCC will do this automatically when given several object (`.o`) files as its input arguments, resulting in a single executable output file. To test this, you can create a program formed from two separate source files, which will be linked together into a single executable.

Start with a single file that contains a simple message-printing function, `message.c`:

```
#include <stdio.h>

void goodbye_world(void)
{
        printf("Goodbye, World!\n");
}
```

The `goodbye_world` function in this example forms a simple software library that can be used by other source code. The function relies upon the standard `printf` C library routine to actually perform the necessary low-level IO to print a message onto a terminal. The C library will later be made available at linking time. Since this code does not form a complete program (there is no main function), GCC will complain if you attempt to compile and link it as you did in the previous example:

```
$ gcc -o goodbye message.c
/usr/lib/gcc/i486-linux-gnu/4.0.3/../../../../lib/crt1.o: In function
`_start':../sysdeps/i386/elf/start.S:115: undefined reference to `main'
collect2: ld returned 1 exit status
```

It is, instead, necessary to instruct GCC not to perform any additional linking stages and to finish after it has assembled the source file into object code with the aid of the GNU assembler. Since the linker is not being executed in this case, the output object file will not contain the necessary information for a Linux machine to load and execute this code as a program, but it will, instead, be linked into a program later on.

Compile the supporting library code using the -c flag to gcc:

```
gcc -c message.c
```

This will instruct the gcc driver program to call its internal C compiler and pass the output on to the external GNU assembler. The resulting output from this process is a file named message.o that contains compiled object code suitable for linking into a larger program.

To use the messaging function goodbye_world in a larger program, you can create a simple example wrapper program, which contains a main function that calls goodbye_world:

```
#include <stdlib.h>

void goodbye_world(void);

int main(int argc, char **argv)
{
        goodbye_world();
        exit(0);
}
```

This file includes a declaration of the external message-printing function as a void function that takes no parameters. As you know, such a declaration is necessary, since GCC would otherwise assume that any undeclared external functions were of integer type and implicitly declare them as such. This might result in unnecessary warnings during compilation. You will generally follow best practices and place these definitions into your own header file, as you have likely have done previously.

You can compile this wrapper program using GCC:

```
gcc -c main.c
```

Now you have two object files, named message.o and main.o that contain object code capable of being executed by your Linux workstation. To create a Linux executable program from this object code, you will need to invoke GCC one more time to perform the linking stages for you:

```
gcc -o goodbye message.o main.o
```

GCC recognizes the .o extension on object code and understands how to call the external GNU linker on your behalf. Remember that GCC will name all executables a.out by default, so it is necessary to specify the desired name of the executable on the command line. Having successfully compiled and linked multiple source files into a single executable, you can execute the program in the normal way:

```
./goodbye
Goodbye, World!
```

The previous individual steps can also be reduced into a single command, since GCC has built-in knowledge for compiling multiple source files into a single executable:

```
gcc -o goodbye message.c main.c
./goodbye
Goodbye, World!
```

Using External Libraries

GCC is frequently used with external software libraries containing standard routines, which provide much needed functionality for C programs running on Linux. This is a side effect of the design of the C programming language as a feature-light language that relies on certain standardized external library routines to perform even basic activities, such as I/O to and from a file or a terminal display window.

Almost every single Linux application relies on routines provided by the GNU C library, GLIBC. This is the library that supplies basic I/O routines such as printf as well as the exit function used in the previous example, which is used to request that the Linux kernel terminate the program under normal conditions (in fact, functions like exit will be called whether you explicitly request them to be run or not—but there is more on that later in the book when looking at the Linux kernel).

As you will learn in later chapters, the GNU C library forms a thin layer on top of the Linux kernel and provides many useful routines, which would be more expensive (in terms of code efficiency and added complexity) if they were provided by the Linux kernel itself. In fact, GCC will assume that GLIBC is to be included in your programs by default in any compilation you ask it to perform. This inclusion happens at the linking stage, so it is still necessary for you to add any library header files to your application sources that may provide prototype definitions for library functions themselves.

The special treatment given to the GNU C library comes as a result of its almost universal usefulness and the fact that few applications would function without it. Although it is unusual to compile source code without GLIBC, it is indeed possible to do so. In fact, the Linux kernel doesn't use GLIBC at all, since GLIBC relies on the Linux kernel to perform various services on its behalf! The kernel instead contains its own simplified implementations of many standard C library functions.

You can create your own software libraries for use with Linux applications by following some simple guidelines, which are explained here. Begin by creating a simple program, trig.c, which will compute various trigonometric values from an angle specified in radians:

```
/*
 * Professional Linux Programming - Trig Functions
 */

#include <stdio.h>
#include <stdlib.h>
```

```
#include <math.h>

#define MAX_INPUT 25

int main(int argc, char **argv)
{
        char input[MAX_INPUT];
        double angle;

        printf("Give me an angle (in radians) ==> ");
        if (!fgets(input, MAX_INPUT, stdin)) {
                perror("an error occurred.\n");
        }
        angle = strtod(input, NULL);

        printf("sin(%e) = %e\n", angle, sin(angle));
        printf("cos(%e) = %e\n", angle, cos(angle));
        printf("tan(%e) = %e\n", angle, tan(angle));

        return 0;
}
```

This program relies upon external math functions provided by the system math library (which is shipped as part of the GLIBC package on Linux systems — but that's incidental to the point that it isn't included automatically in every regular application you compile using GCC). Thus, it is necessary to instruct GCC to include the external library in its search for library functions at link time:

```
gcc -o trig -lm trig.c
```

Note the -lm option given to GCC, which tells it to look in the system-supplied math library (libm). System libraries on Linux and UNIX systems usually begin with the "lib" prefix, so its presence is assumed. The actual library location will vary from system to system, but it typically lives in /lib or /usr/lib, along with many hundreds of other necessary system libraries you may use later.

Shared vs. Static

Libraries on Linux systems come in two different varieties, shared and static. The latter are a holdover from the olden days of UNIX, when all software libraries were statically linked against code that used routines from those libraries. Every time an application is compiled against a statically linked library, the code for any referenced library routine is included directly in the resulting program binary. This results in very large application executables because each one contains a duplicate of standard routines.

Modern Linux (and UNIX) systems use a shared library approach in most cases. Shared libraries contain the same routines as their static counterparts, but those routines are not directly inserted into every program that is linked against them. Instead, shared libraries contain a single, global version of each library routine, which is shared between all applications. The mechanics behind the process are quite complex but rely upon the virtual memory capabilities of modern computers, allowing physical memory containing library routines to be shared safely between multiple independent user programs.

Shared libraries not only reduce the file size and in-memory footprint of Linux applications, but they also actually increase system security. In today's world, new security vulnerabilities in software are discovered daily and fixes come out just as quickly. When security problems exist in system libraries, large numbers of applications can suddenly become a security nightmare. By using shared library resources as much as possible, you can help to ensure that your software is up to date by removing the need for your application to be rebuilt—a global library update automatically corrects your application, too.

As a further benefit of using shared libraries, a single shared library being used by many different programs simultaneously is more likely to remain loaded in memory and available immediately when it is needed rather than sitting in a swap partition on a disk. This can help to further reduce the load time for some of the larger Linux applications available today.

An Example Shared Library

Creating a shared library is a relatively straightforward process. In fact, you can recompile the previous multiple source file example to use a shared library instead of statically linking the different source files into a single executable. Since shared libraries are used by many different applications at the same time, it is necessary to build shared library code in such a way that it can be used in a "position-independent" way (that is, it can be loaded at any memory location and it will still execute).

Recompile the `message.c` source using the `-fPIC` option to GCC:

```
gcc -fPIC -c message.c
```

The `PIC` command line flag tells GCC to produce code that does not contain references to specific memory locations for functions and variables, since it is not yet possible to know where the message code will be linked into the memory address space of any application that uses it. The `message.o` output file is thus capable of being used in a shared library, which GCC is able to create by specifying the convenient `-shared` flag to the `gcc` driver command:

```
gcc -shared -o libmessage.so message.o
```

You can use the shared library with the wrapper `main.c` program from the previous message example. Rather than linking the message-printing routine into the resulting goodbye executable, you can instruct the GCC to inform the linker that it is to use the `libmessage.so` shared library resource instead:

```
gcc -o goodbye -lmessage -L. main.o
```

Notice the `-lmessage` flag is used to inform the GCC driver program that a shared library called `libmessage.so` is to be referenced during linking. The `-L.` flag informs GCC that libraries may be located within the current directory (the directory containing the program sources), as the GNU linker will otherwise look in the standard system library directories and (in this case) find no usable library.

Any shared library you build could be used just like any other library installed on your Linux system, although it must be installed in the correct place to make any such use fully automatic. The runtime dynamic linker/loader provided on modern Linux systems - `ld-linux`—which is automatically invoked whenever an application using shared libraries is loaded—expects to find libraries in the standard system locations under `/lib` and `/usr/lib` (although this could also be overridden using the

/etc/ld.so.conf configuration file on many systems). When you ship your application, you will install any necessary libraries within a location automatically searched by the runtime as part of software installation. Depending upon the system, it may be necessary to then re-run ldconfig.

To discover which libraries are required by a particular application, you can use the ldd command. ldd searches the standard system library paths and shows which library versions would be used by a particular program. Trying this with the above example yields:

```
$ ldd goodbye
        linux-gate.so.1 =>  (0xffffe000)
        libmessage.so => not found
        libc.so.6 => /lib/tls/libc.so.6 (0xb7e03000)
        /lib/ld-linux.so.2 (0xb7f59000)
```

The libmessage.so library file cannot be found in any of the standard search locations and the system provided configuration file /etc/ld.so.conf does not contain an additional override entry for the directory containing the libmessage.so library. Therefore, running the program will yield the following output:

```
$ ./goodbye_shared
./goodbye_shared: error while loading shared libraries: libmessage.so: cannot open
shared object file: No such file or directory
```

Rather than modify your standard Linux system settings or install the libmessage.so library into one of the system library directories just for testing an example, it is possible to instead set an environment variable, LD_LIBRARY_PATH, which will contain additional library search locations. The runtime linker will then search the additional path for libraries that are not in the standard location.

You can run the example code by first setting a suitable LD_LIBRARY_PATH:

```
$ export LD_LIBRARY_PATH=`pwd`
$ ldd goodbye_shared
        linux-gate.so.1 =>  (0xffffe000)
        libmessage.so => /home/jcm/PLP/src/toolchains/libmessage.so (0xb7f5b000)
        libc.so.6 => /lib/tls/libc.so.6 (0xb7e06000)
        /lib/ld-linux.so.2 (0xb7f5e000)
$ ./goodbye
Goodbye, World!
```

GCC options

GCC has a myriad of command line option flags that can be used to control almost every aspect of the compilation process, as well as the operation of any external tools that may be relied upon. You won't normally specify more than a handful of these options when compiling your applications. You will, however, quickly become accustomed to the various debugging and warning options GCC makes available to you as you use it in your own projects.

GCC options are grouped into various categories:

- ❏ General options
- ❏ Language options
- ❏ Warning levels
- ❏ Debugging
- ❏ Optimization
- ❏ Hardware options

General Options

General options include the output name of any executable file produced by GCC as well as whether GCC will complete the build process or terminate after it has performed the basic compilation. You have already seen how you can instruct GCC to perform only compilation and assembly (without linking) by specifying the -c flag on the command line. It is also possible to specify an -S flag, which will cause GCC to stop after the compilation proper and emit assembly language code as output.

Language Options

Language-specific options allow you to control GCC's interpretation of the relevant language standards for the current source language in use. In the case of C, GCC by default uses its own variant of ANSI C (GNU89 or GNU99), which supports some relaxed conventions that are popular among programmers but which may not strictly conform to the official C89 or C99 language specifications. You can override the language behavior through these language-specific options. Several of the more common options are:

-ansi	This disables certain GCC features that are incompatible with the C90 specification, such as the asm and typeof keywords (more about those later in the chapter).
-std	Specifying -std=c89 will instruct GCC to work to the C89 ANSI C specification. The default of gnu89 includes various GNU extensions to the C89 standard. More recent releases of GCC support c99 and gnu99 as language variants here.
-fno-builtin	GCC by default includes built-in versions of common functions like memcpy and even printf, which are more efficient than those present in external libraries. You can disable these built-in versions from being used by specifying this option.

You will usually not need to alter language options except in extreme cases (for example, if you are writing your own C library) or where you are running language verification testing of your own.

Warning Levels

GCC provides a variety of warning levels that can help to track down certain types of bad programming practices or help warn you if you are potentially misusing language features that you instructed GCC not to make available to your program. Several of the more common warning options are:

`-pedantic`	This instructs GCC to strictly interpret the relevant C standards and provide a warning about programs that do not conform to the standard in use. A related option, `--pedantic-errors` will force these warnings to result in an error during compilation.
`-Wformat`	This is one of many related options that will instruct GCC to look at individual function calls to determine whether they are likely to result in runtime problems. `-Wformat` will look for incorrect uses of the `printf` family of functions, while `-Wformat-security` will issue a warning about some potential security vulnerabilities.
`-Wall`	This enables a wide variety of warning options and can result in verbose output.

You will generally benefit from getting into a habit of using the `-Wall` option when compiling your own programs. Additionally, the authors recommend that you also consider using `-pedantic-errors` wherever possible, as this will help to isolate many common problems before they occur, while at the same time helping to ensure that your code is as close to standard compliant as possible.

An example compilation, with extra options is:

```
gcc -o hello -Wall -pedantic-errors hello.c
```

Debugging

GCC provides a variety of options that are necessary to facilitate the debugging of your application, as you will discover later in the chapter. Chief among these is the `-g` option, which will include debugging information within a suitable debugging data section of the application executable. This information can be used by GDB in order to perform source-level debugging and to facilitate other more advanced forms of debugging mentioned later in the book.

To build the previous application with useful debugging information as well as suitable warnings enabled during the compilation, you can use the following command:

```
gcc -g -o hello -Wall -pedantic-errors hello.c
```

Optimization

GCC is capable of performing various optimizations on the code that it compiles. The options available include numeric optimization levels -O0 through -O3, which vary from no optimization through to instructing GCC to perform the most aggressive optimizations possible. Each of these numeric levels results in a variety of additional options being enabled or disabled, depending upon the level specified.

Optimization doesn't come at zero cost. It often greatly increases compilation time and the memory resources required by the compiler during the compilation process. It also doesn't guarantee not to actually increase the size of the resulting executable, since often unrolling loops and functions so that they are repeated inline, rather than making function calls, results in a significant performance gain. Should you wish to do so, size optimization can be requested by using the additional -Os option flag.

Note that some optimization can be necessary. GCC will not by default inline functions[1] (more on this later in the chapter) unless it is called with an appropriate set of optimization flags. This can cause problems when building Linux kernels if you choose to reduce the optimization level in use. One reason to actually reduce the optimization level is to avoid having GCC reorder instructions for more efficient execution on modern processors. While, otherwise beneficial, instruction reordering can make some debugging much harder, especially with very large and complex programs like the Linux kernel.

Hardware Options

GCC is an extremely portable C compiler, which supports a wide variety of different hardware targets. A hardware target is a type of machine and is characterized by the particular family of microprocessor installed within it. Your workstation may well be based upon an Intel-compatible processor, which comes in a variety of different models, each with different capabilities. When you compile code, your version of GCC will, by default, target the processor model that was configured by your distribution vendor.

In the case that you are compiling code solely for use on your own computer (or machines which are of a similar persuasion), there is no need to override any hardware options in order to build code that will execute quite successfully. The situation changes when you use cross-compilers or otherwise wish to build code that will execute on a machine that substantially differs from your own.

Depending upon the hardware in use, some or all of the following options may be available:

-march	Instructs GCC to target a specific model of CPU and emit generated code, which includes instructions specific to that model.
-msoft-float	Instructs GCC not to use hardware floating point instructions and instead to rely upon library calls for floating point arithmetic. This is most commonly used when building software for embedded devices without hardware floating point support.
-mbig-endian -mlittle-endian	Specify whether the hardware target operates in big or little endian mode. This only applies to specific types of target processor (such as the PowerPC), which can either function in or is available in both configurations. Most Intel CPUs are little endian.
-mabi	Some processors can support a variety of different Application Binary Interfaces (ABIs), which may require you to specify a nondefault ABI version. A similar situation arises (with differing options) when a processor family supports both 32- and 64-bit variants and there is a need to specify this at build time.

---

[1]Inlining a function means to literally insert the executable code of a called function inline in place of a function call. Since a function call is not made, there is no need to undergo the overhead of making a function call, especially when calling very small functions."

As a side note, some developers (and a growing number of enthusiasts with aspirations to squeeze every last bit of performance out of their machines) will use GCC hardware option flags to override the default processor target or set other options specific to their local CPU model. In such cases, they are seeking to get maximum performance from their locally compiled applications, but portability to other machines is reduced. This is not a problem if you never intend to distribute your application or if you are an Embedded Linux developer who is seeking to take advantage of every last possible hardware performance optimization.

Further Documentation

Full documentation covering the range of available GCC options can be found in the online help in your local GCC installation. To view the GCC documentation, you can use the Linux man command or the GNU info utilities from within any terminal window. The older-style man pages contain an overview of possible command options, which you can view by typing:

```
man gcc
```

The Free Software Foundation generally discourages all new use of man pages in its own projects and instead recommends the GNU info system, which it considers to be more flexible. You can view the extended documentation available via GNU info by using the following command:

```
info gcc
```

The GNU binutils

The GNU GCC is a visible and fairly obvious part of any Linux development environment, but it is heavily reliant on a number of external tools to actually carry out any useful work on the behalf of a Linux developer. Many of those external tools are provided by the GNU binutils, a collection of utilities for producing and manipulating binary application code in Linux.

Each of the binutils has a specific purpose and performs one task very well, following the standard UNIX philosophy. Some have more obvious uses than others, but each is necessary in order to build large and complex software projects such as the Linux kernel, and all are relied upon every day by thousands of developers, many of whom may not even realize it. Even if you won't actually use these tools directly, it is important that you are aware of them and their general function.

The GNU Assembler

The GNU assembler — as — is perhaps the most natural counterpart to the GNU Compiler Collection. It is responsible for turning compiled C code (which is expressed in assembly language form) into object code that is capable of execution on a specific target processor. GNU as supports many different families of microprocessors, including the Intel IA32 (most people refer to this as "x86") family commonly used on Linux workstations.

The version of GNU as installed on your workstation by your Linux vendor will come preconfigured to target the specific family of processor on which your system is based, although it is also possible to have other configurations installed (see the later section on cross-compilation for more information). Whatever the configuration of the installed assembler, it should behave similarly on all platforms.

You can experiment with the assembler by instructing GCC to emit assembly code for the previous Hello World example and then assembling that into executable object code. To produce some example assembly code, specify the -S option flag when compiling the hello.c source:

```
gcc -S hello.c
```

GCC will emit an assembly language version of your program in the hello.s file. Here is the output generated by GCC 4.0 running on an Intel workstation:

```
        .file   "hello.c"
        .section        .rodata
.LC0:
        .string "Hello, World!"
        .text
.globl main
        .type   main, @function
main:
        pushl   %ebp
        movl    %esp, %ebp
        subl    $8, %esp
        andl    $-16, %esp
        movl    $0, %eax
        addl    $15, %eax
        addl    $15, %eax
        shrl    $4, %eax
        sall    $4, %eax
        subl    %eax, %esp
        movl    $.LC0, (%esp)
        call    puts
        movl    $0, %eax
        leave
        ret
        .size   main, .-main
        .ident  "GCC: (GNU) 4.0.3 20060115 (prerelease) (Debian 4.0.2-7)"
        .section        .note.GNU-stack,"",@progbits
```

You don't need to understand every line of this assembly language listing in order to learn a few interesting things about using GNU as on Linux. There are plenty of good references for Intel assembly language programming on Linux, including Professional Assembly Language (also Wrox), as well as the many other architectures for which one can write assembly language code using Linux.

In the assembly listing, notice how the source is divided into multiple sections using the .section command. Each of these sections will later form a separate part of the executable code used by the program, determined by the GNU linker and its associated linker script. Global symbols are marked in the assembly language, and it includes calls to external library functions, such as puts:

```
call    puts
```

The `puts` function is provided by the GNU C library. This function is not a part of the program, but it will be made available to the program if it is later linked against the standard system libraries, for example when the GNU linker is called in order to produce a runnable executable program file.

You can compile the `hello.s` source code using the GNU assembler as follows:

```
as -o hello.o hello.s
```

This produces a file, `hello.o`, which contains executable object code for the assembly source file specified. Note that you cannot actually run this file on your own Linux workstation because it has not been processed by the GNU linker and so does not contain additional information that is required by any Linux system when it attempts to load and begin executing your application on your behalf.

The GNU Linker

Linking is an important stage in the production of working executable programs on Linux. To build an executable, source code must first be compiled, assembled, and then linked into a standard container format that is understood by the target Linux system. On Linux and modern UNIX/UNIX-like systems, this container format is the ELF or Executable and Linking Format, and it is the file format of choice for both compiled object code and applications. It is also the format of choice for GNU ld.

Linux applications are stored in ELF files composed of many sections. These include code and data sections for the program itself and also various metadata concerning the application itself. Without the appropriate linking stages, an executable does not contain sufficient additional data needed by the Linux runtime loader to successfully load and begin execution. Although the program code may physically be present within a particular file of object code, this is not sufficient for it to be in any way useful.

In addition to churning out executable programs that can be run on Linux systems, the linker is also responsible for ensuring that any necessary environmental setup code is located at the correct location within every executable that must be loaded and run on a Linux target machine. In the case of code compiled with GNU C, this startup code is contained within a file known as `crtbegin.o` (contained within your installation of GCC) that is automatically linked into an application when it is built. A similar file, `crtend.o`, provides code that handles a clean exit when your application terminates.

Operation of the Linker

The GNU Linker follows a series of prewritten commands known as a linker script as it processes various files of object code and produces whatever output has been requested of it. Your workstation already has several of these installed in a directory such as `/usr/lib/ldscripts`, each of which is used by ld when it needs to create a particular type of Linux executable file. Take a look at the scripts installed on your own system for an example of the hidden complexity behind every Linux program.

You will not normally need to invoke the GNU linker — ld — directly when producing regular applications with GCC. Its operation is complex and ultimately determined by the specific version of GCC installed as well as the location and version of various external software libraries. You *will* need to understand how the linker uses linker scripts if you wish to modify the in-memory layout of a Linux kernel, which you might do if you were creating your own version of Linux for your own hardware.

You will learn more about the uses of the linker by the Linux kernel later in this book.

GNU objcopy and objdump

GNU binutils includes several tools that are specifically designed to manipulate and transform binary object code from one format into another. These tools are known as objcopy and objdump and are heavily relied upon during the build phases of much of the low-level software used on your Linux machine and even during some regular application debugging.

The objcopy tool can be used to copy object code from one file into another, performing a variety of transformations in the process. Using objcopy, it is possible to automatically convert between different object code formats as well as to manipulate the contents in the process. objdump and objcopy are both built on the extraordinary flexible bfd binary manipulation library. This library is used by a whole host of handy utilities designed to manipulate binary object files in any which way imaginable.

The objdump tool is designed to make it easy to visualize the contents of an executable and perform a variety of tasks to make that visualization process easier. Using objdump, you can examine the contents of the Hello World example code used earlier in this chapter:

```
$ objdump -x -d -S hello
```

The accompanying command switches instruct objdump to display all headers within the hello binary, to attempt to disassemble the contents of any executable sections, and to intermix the program's source code with its disassembly. The last option will only yield readable output under certain circumstances. It is generally necessary to have built the source with full debugging information (using the -g GCC command switch) and without any GCC instruction scheduling optimizations (for added readability).

The output produced by objdump may be similar to the following. Here, you can see an objdump of the headers of the Hello World example on a PowerPC platform running Linux:

```
hello:     file format elf32-powerpc
hello
architecture: powerpc:common, flags 0x00000112:
EXEC_P, HAS_SYMS, D_PAGED
start address 0x100002a0

Program Header:
    PHDR off    0x00000034 vaddr 0x10000034 paddr 0x10000034 align 2**2
         filesz 0x00000100 memsz 0x00000100 flags r-x
  INTERP off    0x00000134 vaddr 0x10000134 paddr 0x10000134 align 2**0
   STACK off    0x00000000 vaddr 0x00000000 paddr 0x00000000 align 2**2
         filesz 0x00000000 memsz 0x00000000 flags rwx

Dynamic Section:
  NEEDED      libc.so.6
  INIT        0x10000278
  FINI        0x100007ac
  HASH        0x10000164
  PLTGOT      0x100108fc

Version References:
```

```
required from libc.so.6:
  0x0d696910 0x00 02 GLIBC_2.0

Sections:
Idx Name          Size      VMA       LMA       File off  Algn
  0 .interp       0000000d  10000134  10000134  00000134  2**0
                  CONTENTS, ALLOC, LOAD, READONLY, DATA
  5 .gnu.version  0000000a  10000228  10000228  00000228  2**1
                  CONTENTS, ALLOC, LOAD, READONLY, DATA
  9 .init         00000028  10000278  10000278  00000278  2**2
                  CONTENTS, ALLOC, LOAD, READONLY, CODE
 10 .text         0000050c  100002a0  100002a0  000002a0  2**2
                  CONTENTS, ALLOC, LOAD, READONLY, CODE
 11 .fini         00000020  100007ac  100007ac  000007ac  2**2
                  CONTENTS, ALLOC, LOAD, READONLY, CODE
```

The ELF header indicates that this is a 32-bit PowerPC object file. Since Linux is a portable operating system, examples in this book are written and tested on various different Linux platforms, such as PowerPC. ELF too is a cross-platform binary standard, so there's no mention of Linux in the objdump output. In theory, you could attempt to run this code on any PowerPC operating system conforming to the same ABI and capable of loading an ELF file and its libraries.

Output from objdump can also include a full disassembly of the application source code, if the code was compiled using the -g debugging flag on the gcc command line. Here's part of the objdump output from an IA32 (x86) Linux workstation, showing the disassembly and source code for the main function:

```
int main(int argc, char **argv)
{
 8048384:        55                      push   %ebp
 8048385:        89 e5                   mov    %esp,%ebp
 8048387:        83 ec 08                sub    $0x8,%esp
 804838a:        83 e4 f0                and    $0xfffffff0,%esp
 804838d:        b8 00 00 00 00          mov    $0x0,%eax
 8048392:        83 c0 0f                add    $0xf,%eax
 8048395:        83 c0 0f                add    $0xf,%eax
 8048398:        c1 e8 04                shr    $0x4,%eax
 804839b:        c1 e0 04                shl    $0x4,%eax
 804839e:        29 c4                   sub    %eax,%esp

        printf("Hello, World!\n");
 80483a0:        c7 04 24 e8 84 04 08    movl   $0x80484e8,(%esp)
 80483a7:        e8 fc fe ff ff          call   80482a8 <puts@plt>

        return 0;
 80483ac:        b8 00 00 00 00          mov    $0x0,%eax
}
 80483b1:        c9                      leave
 80483b2:        c3                      ret
```

The mechanics of ELF files are beyond the scope of this book, but you should at least be familiar with the `objdump` tool if you really want to understand the layout of a Linux application binary. There are many more usage examples in the `objdump` documentation as well as online. The output from `objdump` can be used to aid in certain debugging processes or viewed out of curiosity. You will learn later that GDB can provide similar information, but sometimes (albeit rarely) GDB isn't there to save the day.

GNU Make

As has been previously noted, the majority of software that is built on Linux machines is built using the GNU Make software. GNU Make is essentially a simple dependency tracker tool, which is able to follow a series of rules that determine the individual actions that must be performed on individual source files within a larger project. You saw a couple of simple `Makefile` rules earlier in this chapter when you learned about the various other build tools that make up the GNU Toolchain.

Here is a more complex `Makefile`, which can be used to build the examples given so far:

```
# Makefile to build Toolchains examples

CFLAGS := -Wall -pedantic-errors

all: hello goodbye trig

clean:
        -rm -rf *.o *.so hello goodbye trig

hello:

goodbye: main.o message.o

trig:
        $(CC) $(CFLAGS) -lm -o trig trig.c
```

The `Makefile` defines a series of rules for possible targets. These include rules for actually building the three individual examples (Hello, Goodbye and Trig), as well as a rule that defines how the sources can be cleaned prior to their distribution to other developers. A rule is defined using a named tag followed by a colon and then a separated list of dependencies, which must first be satisfied in order to consider the result a success. A rule may be followed by detailed commands in the case that make can't automatically determine how to do what is being asked of it through the rule alone.

GNU Make rules vary from trivial source file dependencies to complex hierarchies of other dependencies, but they can always be broken down into simple sequences of commands. In addition to individual rules, make supports defined variables, conditionals, and many other features one might expect from a regular programming language. GNU Make also understands many standard variables, such as $CFLAGS, the flags that will be passed to the C compiler, $CC (set to gcc by default).

Within the example `Makefile`, the default action (all) is to attempt to build each of the three examples — Hello, Goodbye, and Trig — by using the specific rules given for each one. In the case of hello, there are no dependencies given, so make will automatically assume that it has to compile the hello.c source into an executable of the name `hello`. In the case of goodbye, make will automatically compile the two dependencies before linking them together into a single resultant executable program.

The build process for the Trig example is a little different. In this case, no dependencies are specified following the trig rule, but a compiler command is given on the line following the empty rule. GNU Make will instead execute this as a shell command, substituting the variable expansions given in brackets. Thus `$(CC)` becomes `gcc`, and `$(CFLAGS)` is expanded into the flags specified at the start of the `Makefile`. Note that it is necessary to include both `CFLAGS` and `CC` when such an explicit command is given.

You can find more information about Make rules and how to use GNU Make by reading the online documentation installed on your local workstation or on the Free Software Foundation website. Better yet, download a large Free Software project and take a look at the Makefiles it uses — you'll quickly come to understand the complex rulesets that can be built using GNU make.

You can find out more about the design and implementation of the ELF file format and the operation of standard tools, such as the GNU linker in the humor-packed book *Linkers and Loaders* by John R. Levine (Morgan Kaufman, 2000).

The GNU Debugger

The GNU debugger (GDB) is one of the most powerful tools in a Linux developer's toolbox. Not only is GDB a flexible tool used by thousands of people every day, but it is also one of the most ubiquitous debuggers around. This is, in part, due to the number of vendors who choose to reuse GDB in their products rather than reinvent its capabilities from scratch. No matter where you buy your tools from, it's very likely there's some form of GDB inside.

GDB comes as a standalone software package and is usually installed as part of any development tools included in modern Linux distributions. Starting out with GDB is pretty simple — take the trigonometry program as a simple example. You can debug the application by running it under gdb, using the following command (be sure the program was built using the -g debugging symbol's gcc flag):

```
$ gdb trig
GNU gdb 6.3
Copyright 2004 Free Software Foundation, Inc.
GDB is free software, covered by the GNU General Public License, and you are
welcome to change it and/or distribute copies of it under certain conditions.
Type "show copying" to see the conditions.
There is absolutely no warranty for GDB.  Type "show warranty" for details.
This GDB was configured as "i386-linux"...Using host libthread_db library
"/lib/tls/libthread_db.so.1".

(gdb)
```

GDB presents its default prompt and waits for your commands. Begin by using the `list` command to view some source code context for this debugging session:

```
(gdb) list
8        #include <math.h>
9
10       #define MAX_INPUT 25
11
12       int main(int argc, char **argv)
13       {
14               char input[MAX_INPUT];
gle;
16
17               printf("Give me an angle (in radians) ==> ");
```

The program is not running at this point, but you can change that by using the run command. Before running a program under gdb, however, it is a good idea to insert at least one breakpoint into the code. This way, GDB will stop the program when it reaches a particular line in the source and allow you to perform any interrogation that may be necessary to aid your debugging. It is customary to insert the first program breakpoint at entry to the main function and then at other points of interest in the program.

Insert a breakpoint into the example code and run it as follows:

```
(gdb) break main
Breakpoint 1 at 0x8048520: file trig.c, line 17.
(gdb) run
Starting program: /home/jcm/PLP/src/toolchains/src/trig

Breakpoint 1, main (argc=1, argv=0xbfd87184) at trig.c:17
                printf("Give me an angle (in radians) ==> ");
```

GDB will breakpoint on the first instruction of the main function within the trig program, in this case located on line 17 of the source file trig.c. At this point, the list command can be used to show the surrounding lines within the main function, in addition to the single call to printf already automatically displayed by GDB when the breakpoint is hit. Each line of code may be executed in single steps by using the step and next commands — the former stopping after each machine instruction; the latter performing similarly, but skipping over calls to external subroutines.

Test this by skipping over the calls to printf and stopping after the user has entered an angle on the command line:

```
(gdb) next
18               if (!fgets(input, MAX_INPUT, stdin)) {
(gdb)
Give me an angle (in radians) ==> 3.14
angle = strtod(input, NULL);
```

GDB stops the program before it can call the library function strtod() to convert a string into a double floating point number. You can visualize the value of the angle variable both before and after this function is called by using the GDB print command:

```
(gdb) print angle
$1 = -4.8190317876499021e-39
(gdb) next
23                      printf("sin(%e) = %e\n", angle, sin(angle));
(gdb) print angle
$2 = 3.1400000000000001
```

*By default, program input and output is performed to the same terminal through which you enter com-
mands to GDB. You can change this by using the* tty *command within GDB to redirect IO to a specific
Linux terminal. For example, within a graphical desktop environment, you may debug an application in
one X terminal window and have its input and output passed to another. Find the terminal number of
an appropriate X terminal by using the identically named* tty *command.*

Finally, you can allow the program to continue until it terminates (or hits another breakpoint) by using
the continue command, also shortened to just c:

```
(gdb) c
Continuing.
sin(3.140000e+00) = 1.592653e-03
cos(3.140000e+00) = -9.999987e-01
tan(3.140000e+00) = -1.592655e-03

Program exited normally.
```

If at any time while you're using GDB need some help, just type "help" and you'll be presented with a
choice of help, split into various sections, depending upon the class of command:

```
(gdb) help
List of classes of commands:

aliases -- Aliases of other commands
breakpoints -- Making program stop at certain points
data -- Examining data
files -- Specifying and examining files
internals -- Maintenance commands
obscure -- Obscure features
running -- Running the program
stack -- Examining the stack
status -- Status inquiries
support -- Support facilities
tracepoints -- Tracing of program execution without stopping the program
user-defined -- User-defined commands

Type "help" followed by a class name for a list of commands in that class.
Type "help" followed by command name for full documentation.
Command name abbreviations are allowed if unambiguous.
```

Another frequent use of GDB is in debugging program core dumps — crash files containing the state of an application when it crashed, which can be used to ascertain the circumstances of the crash — in much the same way that airplane black box recorders are used following an incident. These core files are automatically generated by Linux whenever an application does something untoward that forces Linux to cause the program to terminate — typically, in the case of an illegal access to memory or in a deference of a null pointer somewhere within the program.

> *Your chosen Linux distribution may not create core (crash dump) files by default. In this case, it may be necessary to instruct your system to do so – consult your vendor's documentation for details.*

The Linux kernel itself presents a constantly updated view of its internal state via a read-only file in /proc known as /proc/kcore. It is possible to use gdb with this fake core dump in order to obtain some limited information about the current state of your Linux workstation. For example, you can view the current time as seen by the Linux kernel, in terms of system timer ticks, since the system booted, as follows:

```
# sudo gdb /lib/modules/`uname -r`/build/vmlinux /proc/kcore
GNU gdb 6.3-debian
Copyright 2004 Free Software Foundation, Inc.
GDB is free software, covered by the GNU General Public License, and you are
welcome to change it and/or distribute copies of it under certain conditions.
Type "show copying" to see the conditions.
There is absolutely no warranty for GDB.  Type "show warranty" for details.
This GDB was configured as "i386-linux"...Using host libthread_db library
"/lib/tls/libthread_db.so.1".

Core was generated by `BOOT_IMAGE=linux ro root=303'.
#0  0x00000000 in ?? ()
(gdb) print jiffies
$1 = 72266006
```

Since the value of jiffies is cached at the time you invoke GDB, attempting to redisplay the value will yield the same result – try restarting GDB again in order to verify that the value has changed.

> *This GDB hack relies on a symbolic link within /lib/modules from the current kernel version to the directory that was used to build it, and instructs GDB to use the fake core file image exported through /proc/kcore. If you didn't build the kernel running on your workstation, you won't be able to run this command because you will have no vmlinux file at hand. There is more on building and debugging the Linux kernel later in this book.*

GDB is capable of many more commands than have been briefly introduced in this chapter. Indeed, to fully cover the functionality contained within GDB would require a great deal more space than is available in a book such as this. You are encouraged to experiment with GDB yourself, though it will be used throughout the rest of this book whenever the need arises.

The Linux Kernel and the GNU Toolchain

The GNU Toolchain is used by countless software projects around the world, but few of these singularly exercise as much functionality within the tools as does the Linux kernel. As you will discover later in the book, the Linux kernel heavily relies upon many language extensions present in GCC as well as GNU extensions available within numerous other common system tools. It is theoretically possible to build the Linux kernel without relying upon the GNU Toolchain, but this is seldom done in practice.

Inline Assembly

Low-level Linux kernel code makes frequent use of an extension present in the GNU C compiler to support inline assembly code. Literally, this is assembly language code, which is inserted inline within the regular C functions that make up the bulk of the kernel. Although the kernel aims to be as portable as is possible — and thus is written mostly in platform-independent C code — some operations can only be performed using machine-specific instructions. Inline assembly helps to make this a clean process.

Here is a simple example C function, which contains some inline assembly language code:

```
void write_reg32(unsigned long address, unsigned long data) {

    __asm__ __volatile ("stw %0,0(%1); eieio"
                        : // no output registers here
                        : "r" (data), "r" (address));

}
```

This function takes two parameters — an address and some data. The PowerPC assembly language following the __asm__ attribute tag stores the data passed to the function at the address in memory that has been specified and finishes up with a special machine-specific instruction (eieio) that forces the hardware to commit whatever value has been written out to some hardware device. The __volatile__ tag tells GCC not to attempt to optimize the example code because it must execute exactly as it is written.

The example code requires a few machine-specific processor registers to contain the data and address variables before the assembly language code can be executed. Note how the r flag indicates in the example that the data and address variables will only be read and not updated by the inline assembly language code fragment. In the case that the inline assembly language command were to changes its input registers, these could be marked with a w so GCC knows those registers will be clobbered.

You don't need to worry about the specifics of the assembly language in this example, but be aware of the format used for inline assembly in general:

```
__asm__ ( Machine specific assembly instructions
                    : Machine specific registers affected by the instruction
                    : Machine specific registers required as inputs
```

You will find more examples of inline assembly in use within the sources of the Linux kernel.

Attribute Tags

The Linux kernel heavily relies upon GCC attributes. These are special tags used within the source to supply additional in-band information to the GNU C compiler about the way in which it must specially process the kernel sources. Attributes include nonnull and noreturn, which inform the compiler that a function may not take NULL parameters or that it is specifically okay for a function not to return.

Here is an example attribute definition used by the Linux kernel:

```
#define module_init(initfn)                                 \
        static inline initcall_t __inittest(void)           \
        { return initfn; }                                  \
        int init_module(void) __attribute__((alias(#initfn)));
```

This defines the module_init function, used by every Linux kernel module (LKM) to declare the function that will run when a module is first loaded. In the example, among many other things, the alias attribute is used to set up an alias, #initfn, for the module initialization function. Whenever a header file later needs to refer to the function, it can use the #initfn macro in place of the full function name.

Linux kernel functions frequently make use of the section attribute, used to specify that certain functions must be placed within a specific section of the Linux kernel binary. The kernel also uses alignment, which forces a particular in-memory alignment on variable declarations. Due to the necessity for high performance, memory alignment of variables within the Linux kernel is often very strict indeed. This helps to ensure efficient transfer of certain data to and from main memory.

Attributes can help various code analysis tools — such as Linus Torvalds' sparse source code checker — to infer additional information about specific functions and variables used within the Linux kernel. For example, function parameters marked with the nonnull attribute tag might be checked to see whether they could ever be passed NULL values.

Custom Linker Scripts

The Linux kernel and other low-level software rely heavily upon linker scripts in order to create executables with a specific binary image layout. This is important for a number of reasons, including a desire to group certain related kernel features into logical sections within the kernel binary image. For example, certain functions within the Linux kernel are marked with the tags __init__ or __initdata__. These are defined as GCC attributes that cause such functions to be grouped into a special section within the kernel.

Once a Linux kernel has successfully booted, it no longer requires code and data marked with such init tags and so the memory that was used to store them should be freed. This is achievable because such code and data are stored within a special section of the kernel that can be released as one large chunk of reclaimable memory. The physical position of these special sections within the final kernel binary image is determined by a special kernel linker script, which includes such considerations.

Sometimes, precise binary image layout is mandated by the hardware of the target machine upon which the kernel will run. Many modern microprocessors expect to find certain low-level operating system functions at precise offsets within the kernel image. This includes hardware exception handlers — code that will run in response to certain synchronous or asynchronous processor events, as well as a multitude of other uses. Since the Linux kernel image is loaded at a precise offset within the physical memory of the machine, this physical requirement can be satisfied with the aid of a little linker magic.

The Linux kernel uses a specific set of linker scripts for each of the architectures on which it runs. Check out the contents of the `arch/i386/kernel/vmlinux.lds` linker script within your local Linux kernel sources. You'll see entries like the following fragment:

```
  .text : AT(ADDR(.text) - (0xC0000000)) {
*(.text)
. = ALIGN(8); __sched_text_start = .; *(.sched.text) __sched_text_end = .;
. = ALIGN(8); __lock_text_start = .; *(.spinlock.text) __lock_text_end = .;
. = ALIGN(8); __kprobes_text_start = .; *(.kprobes.text) __kprobes_text_end = .
```

These entries perform a variety of different tasks, as detailed in the GNU linker documentation. In this case, specifying that all kernel code begins at the virtual address 0xC000_0000 within memory and that several specific symbols must be aligned on 8-byte boundaries. The full linker script is extremely complicated, since the requirements of the Linux kernel are extremely complex on many platforms.

Cross-Compilation

Most software development that happens on Linux takes place on the same type of machine as that which will eventually run the finished application. A developer working on an Intel IA32 (x86) workstation will write applications that are shipped and run by customers (or Free Software users) who also own Intel-based workstations of a similar class.

Things aren't always as easy for Embedded Linux developers. They must work with a variety of different machines, each of which may be running Linux on a completely different processor architecture. Often, individual target devices — such as PDAs and cell phones — do not have nearly enough processing power or storage space available to make it feasible to do software development directly on the target. Instead, cross-compilation is used from more powerful Linux host.

Cross-compilation (or cross-building) is the process of building software on one machine architecture that will execute on another completely different architecture. A common example would be building applications on an Intel-based workstation, which must execute on an ARM-, PowerPC-, or MIPS-based target device. Fortunately, the GNU tools make this process much less painful than it sounds.

Regular tools within the GNU Toolchain are usually executed by invoking a command name such as `gcc` from the command line. In the case of cross-compilation, these tools are named according to the target for which they have been built. For example, to compile a simple Hello World program using a cross toolchain targeted at a PowerPC, you might run a command such as the following:

```
$ powerpc-eabi-gcc -o hello hello.c
```

Notice how the cross target, `powerpc-eabi`, is prefixed to the name of the particular tool. A similar naming convention applies to the remainder of the tools within a cross toolchain, although the precise name very much depends upon the specific target device for which the tools have been built. Many Embedded Linux vendors sell a variety of device-specific toolchains that you can use, but you can also build your own by following the examples given in the next section.

In addition to using cross toolchains directly, you may frequently find yourself needing to build large existing projects which are based upon automated build tools, such as GNU Autoconf. In the case that you need to educate an existing `configure` script about your desire to cross-compile some software for an specific target, you may find the following option flags come in handy:

`--build`	Configure to build on the given build host type.
`--host`	Cross-compile programs to run on the given host type.

Building the GNU Toolchain

As you have no doubt already realized, the GNU Toolchain is formed from many individual components, which are independently developed but which must work together to achieve particular goals. At some point, these individual GNU tools must themselves be built from the sources available on the Internet. This is a *very* time-consuming process, which your Linux vendor has already addressed for your local Linux workstation. They have spent many hours figuring this out so that you don't have to.

There are, however, times when available tools are not up to the task at hand. This can happen for a number of different reasons, including:

❑ Needing a more recent version than is available from your vendor

❑ Cross-compiling applications for a specific or unusual target

❑ Modifying specific build-time options for individual tools

In such cases, it will be necessary for you to obtain and build the GNU Toolchain from scratch for yourself or to pay for one to be made available for you. Building a toolchain from scratch is an extremely difficult and time-consuming process because of the number of patches that need to be applied for different target processors, as well as the sheer interdependencies between the tools themselves. In order to build a toolchain, you'll need to piece together at the following individual components:

❑ GCC

❑ binutils

❑ GLIBC

❑ GDB

It gets worse. In order to build a GCC capable of compiling regular user programs, you'll need a prebuilt GNU C library, but in order to get a working GNU C library, you first need a compiler. For this reason, the build process is actually divided into multiple phases, with a minimal GCC being built in order to first compile GLIBC (which itself requires a copy of the Linux kernel headers) and then a later rebuild for a full toolchain able to build useful programs.

Incidentally, building a toolchain that will only be used to compile Linux kernels or other low-level embedded applications doesn't require GLIBC, so the build process could be simplified somewhat at the cost of a toolchain that's only good for compiling custom kernels or writing some specific low-level firmware for a specific embedded board. If that's what you need, life is a little easier for you.

Fortunately, the toolchain build process has gotten a lot easier in recent years, thanks to a number of automated scripts, which are designed to help you to automate the building of a custom toolchain for your specific application. By far the most popular of these scripts is Dan Kegel's crosstool. It has been used by many enthusiasts and vendors alike as the basis for building their custom toolchains and is freely available online. You'll save yourself many headaches if you use it, too.

You can obtain crosstool from Kegel's website at `http://kegel.com/crosstool`. It comes in the form of a tarball, which must first be unpacked, and a bunch of demo scripts written for each CPU type supported by the GNU Toolchain. You can modify the demo scripts to create a suitable configuration for the toolchain that you require. For example, you might create a cross toolchain for your Intel IA32 (x86) based workstation that is able to build applications for a PowerPC target. Or you might also use crosstool to build a regular toolchain for the same architecture as the host Linux workstation.

crosstool automates the process of downloading individual toolchain sources from their respective project websites and will apply whatever patches are known to be necessary for the desired target combination. crosstool will then build the individual parts of the toolchain in the correct sequence. It'll finish by optionally running standard regression tests, which ship as part of the GNU Toolchain sources.

Summary

The individual tools within the GNU Toolchain are heavily relied upon by thousands of users, developers, and vendors worldwide. They use the GNU tools every day to build many different types of application for many different operating systems. On Linux, GCC and related tools are used to build everything from the Linux kernel itself right up to the most elaborate graphical desktop environments.

In this chapter, you were introduced to the individual elements of the GNU Toolchain — GCC, binutils, gdb, and so on. You also discovered some of the more advanced capabilities of these tools as well as their practical uses in larger Linux software development projects. A special focus was placed upon the requirements of more unusual projects, such as the Linux kernel, which relies upon unique features specific to the GNU Toolchain.

Flexibility is a key part of the job performed using the GNU tools, but all too often their function remains a mystery to all but the most advanced developers. While it is possible to rely upon graphical development tools that perform many of the operations covered in this chapter on your behalf, it is nonetheless essential to retain an overall understanding for those times when the graphical tools let you down or otherwise are unable to live up to the task at hand.

3

Portability

Software and hardware portability is of key importance when working with modern Linux systems. But what exactly does *portability* mean? How can you achieve the desired flexibility from your application so that users with a wide range of target hardware and software platforms can use your software with little or no source modification? These are questions that often plague developers. This chapter aims to address the variety of hardware and software portability issues commonly faced when using Linux.

The chapter is loosely divided into two parts. The first covers pure software portability. It this case, software portability refers to a need for software to run on a wide range of Linux distributions from different vendors or even different releases from the same vendor). Ideally, all software should build automatically, with as little human interaction as possible, especially if it is to be included in a larger project or become part of a Linux distribution. Using the tools and techniques introduced, you will be able to write software that is more portable to the wide array of Linux distributions around today.

The latter part of this chapter focuses on writing software for differing hardware platforms. Modern hardware is complex and machine architectures are quite daunting. Although this chapter won't endeavor to explain how modern computers are constructed, it will attempt to address several fundamental issues that will affect you if you intend to write software for differing hardware platforms running Linux. You'll learn about big and little endian computers, writing code that is 32/64-bit clean and briefly touch upon the need for the Linux kernel as a form of portable hardware abstraction layer in Linux systems.

After reading this chapter, you will feel more confident in writing software for end users. Although you won't learn all you need to know in the space of these pages, you'll be well equipped to consider and learn about many other practical portability issues that you may face in the field as you develop your own software. Remember one golden rule: there are few hard limits when working with software, but you should always remember to consider how your decisions affect application portability later on.

The Need for Portability

Portability is not a new concept. Since the very first computers, there has been a desire to write software that can be used as widely as possible, across a broad range of different machines, with little or no modification being required in the process. To define what is meant by portability, consider the average amount of time spent in developing a complex piece of modern software. If that software is originally written in one particular software or hardware environment, then it may be desirable to be able to *port* that software to other *similar* environments without incurring a massive redevelopment.

> *More formally, software is said to be portable if the effort required to transport and adapt it to a new environment is less than the effort of redeveloping that same software from scratch.*

Portable software dates back almost as far as digital computers themselves. In the early days, computers were built from plug boards and switches that were literally *programmed* by hand. A "program" consisted of a particular configuration of wires that had been crafted to a specific machine. In those days — before even the first assembly language programs — there were no model numbers, families of related microprocessors, or many of the other concepts with which we are so familiar today.

As time moved on, hardware became more complex but users wanted flexibility to buy machines for which existing software was available. So, in 1964, IBM released the System/360. This was the first series of *compatible* computers. These mainframe machines could execute the same code and run the same programs as one another, but otherwise they varied in their construction. This was the first time that software from one machine could be used on another from the same *family* without modification.

With computers becoming more powerful and complex, programming software for them became more abstract in nature. Programs that had once been written in assembly language (or handcrafted machine code) would instead be written using higher-level languages, such as C, Pascal, or FORTRAN. While these languages were arguably easier for developers to learn and use, they also allowed developers to write code that was *portable* from one machine to another. Porting an application between machines required only that it be recompiled and that modifications be made to handle differences between hardware available in differing machines. This was time-consuming but a step in the right direction.

The growth in high-level programming languages allowed for complex operating systems such as UNIX to be developed. UNIX was later considered to be a portable operating system because it had been rewritten in the C programming language (which its authors had also invented). Since a C compiler could be written for many different computers, it was possible to *port* the UNIX operating system from one machine to another. The process was cumbersome and complex, but it was far easier than rewriting the entire system from scratch and shielded individual applications from changes to their environment to a greater extent than had ever been possible previously.

UNIX was a powerful operating system that provided a solid software platform for complex user applications. It introduced a number of fundamental concepts and abstractions that are heavily relied upon to this day and greatly improved the process of writing portable user application software. By abstracting the physical hardware within a machine, a programmer could write code targeted at UNIX rather than at a specific machine from a specific manufacturer. Of course, the result was that different manufacturers attempted to outdo one another in their UNIX offering — leading to the "UNIX Wars."

During the later 1980s and the 1990s, the UNIX marketplace gradually (and at times, somewhat more turbulently) settled down and different manufacturers, faced with growing competition from non-UNIX vendors, began to work together to provide a common UNIX standard. By standardizing what it meant to be UNIX, application developers could more easily write portable software and make that software available to many different UNIX systems. The standardization effort directly resulted in the Portable Operating System Interface (POSIX) standard. POSIX was later complemented by the (freely available) Single UNIX Specification (SUS).

Software portability has taken another leap over the past decade. In the 1990s, Sun's Green project (later leading to Java) sought the creation of an entire virtual machine as an aid to address the wide range of different embedded software platforms available at the time. With a Java Virtual Machine, software would only have to be compiled once and would then run on any platform to which it was possible to *port* the virtual machine. The Java Virtual Machine (JVM) and the Java programming language have since become well known to a new generation of programmers.

As time has moved on, the concept of portability has changed. While software may once have been portable if it could be used on a variety of machines from the same manufacturer, modern Linux (and UNIX) software is expected to be *portable* across a wide range of different machines, distributions, configurations, and the like. Today, it is almost taken for granted that software written on a basic 32-bit Intel-based computer can be rebuilt for an Itanium, PowerPC, or SPARC machine without modification. The remainder of this chapter will introduce you to concepts that help make this a reality on Linux.

The Portability of Linux

Portability means different things to different users and developers of Linux software. Some people are more concerned with platform portability between Linux and other UNIX and UNIX-like systems such as Sun Solaris or Apple Mac OS X. Other people care more about distribution portability—having a Linux application that will run on the multitude of Linux distributions available. Then there are those who want both of these things and also want the freedom to have their software used on 32- and 64-bit systems from a multitude of vendors shipping a wide variety of different types of hardware platform.

Well-designed Linux software, that relies upon portable libraries and that is written to take full advantage of the variety of automated configuration tools available will stand up to each of these requirements. Even if it is not your initial goal to make your software widely available beyond a specific distribution on a specific hardware platform, it is always a good idea to think ahead. One inevitable truth of software is that it will sometimes outlive its original purpose or lifespan. You probably want to make life a little easier for those who need to maintain it into the future.

Layers of Abstraction

The core of any Linux system is the Linux kernel. It supports more than 24 different architectures of hardware platform in the standard "stock" release alone. When you think that a regular PC workstation is just one variant of the i386 architecture, you start to see the scale involved. In addition to amazing levels of hardware portability, Linux also provides numerous device drivers that allow a wide range of peripheral devices to be attached to a system running Linux. In a way, the Linux kernel's main purpose is to provide a portable software abstraction above the raw hardware of these different machines.

When you write software for Linux, you will use standardized system libraries that rely upon specific features of the Linux kernel. The libraries will take care of providing commonly used software routines, while the kernel handles the pesky hardware details. In this way, you don't need to concern yourself with the underlying hardware of the machine for many regular applications. Of course, if you are building customized devices or need to get every ounce of performance out of the machine, then you might choose to voluntarily break this abstraction in your application, to further some greater goal. Take a look at Figure 3-1 to see how an application fits into a typical system running Linux.

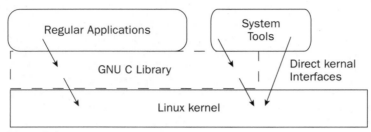

Figure 3-1

Life is a series of trade-offs, and so it is with Linux development. Greater levels of abstraction can lead to lower performance compared with assuming a particular hardware and software environment. However, modern computers are cheap and the average user has a desktop well beyond their minimal requirements. If you work with more resource-constrained systems, then you may need to bend these rules a little. For example, on an embedded device that you have created, you may (obviously) assume a particular hardware platform and use whatever cunning hacks are necessary to create a finished product within the bounds of maintaining a level of design flexibility.[1]

You may not need to worry about the hardware within a machine, but you do need to concern yourself with the software environment provided for you on top of the Linux kernel. This is where distributions — perhaps even different releases of the same distribution — as well as the versions of individual system software and libraries can become a major headache. This second point is important — library versions can pose problems that will be discussed later in the chapter when you learn more about the GNU Autotools.

Linux Distributions

While Linux may be highly portable in and of itself, most users and developers are far more concerned about *distribution portability* than they are about which hardware platforms the software will run on. They are, after all, more than likely to be using a regular Linux PC workstation than a dedicated cluster (and if they are, you'd probably be targeting that cluster as a specific platform requirement and may not be so concerned about distribution portability in general — yes, even in today's world). There are many distributions in use today, each with its own unique nuances that differentiate it from the rest.

You learned about Linux distributions back in Chapter 1. You learned that there are a wide variety of different distributions or *flavors* of Linux on the market. These are both commercial (for example, Red Hat and SuSE) and non-commercial (for example Gentoo and Debian derivatives such as Ubuntu and Knoppix) and are in use by users all over the world. Despite their many differences, distributions are, fundamentally, merely collections of vendor supplied (and possibly supported) prepackaged software.

---

[1]One common hack used on embedded devices known to be based on standard flat 32-bit memory maps (where hardware is just another address in memory) is to mmap() peripheral memory from userspace via the /dev/mem device. Regular application code (albeit with root privileges) can then talk to hardware without a kernel driver. It's ugly, but efficient, and thus widely employed.

Packages

A package represents the fundamental unit of atomicity as far as most distributions are concerned. This is usually a single software application or a group of a (small number of) related utilities that are usually supplied together. Packages are usually based upon an "upstream" Linux community project and share a similar name. For example, most modern Linux distributions provide a package named "module-init-tools" (replacing the older "modutils" package) that contains a collection of utilities supplied in the upstream Linux kernel project of the same name.

Each different application and utility (or a simple collection of obviously related utilities) that will be made available to the user is likely to be supplied in its own package, complete with descriptive meta-data that includes documentation and — most important — dependency information. Dependency information allows the Linux distribution's package manager to automatically resolve package dependencies against a vendor-supplied database summarizing the state of known packages.

Dependency resolution means having the distribution's package manager (a system-supplied utility for the purpose of installing, removing, and managing packages) determine which other packages must first be installed prior to installation of a particular package. Often, complex hierarchies of dependent packages are built up into a logical tree so that installing one package may require 10 or more others to be installed — especially on a newly installed system that has been built with a minimal configuration.

Look at the dependency tree in Figure 3-2.

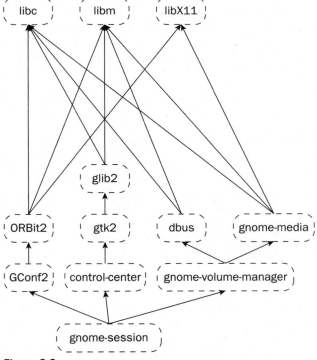

Figure 3-2

Modern package management software is able to automatically handle obtaining and installing any necessary dependency packages without resorting to the user doing this by hand (this is a fundamental advantage of having a distribution over a collection of miscellaneous files). Still, the process is not always as clean as you may desire it to be. Different distributions have slightly different package-naming conventions, and subtle differences in the ways that dependencies and conflicting packages are handled exist. So, there's no substitute for actually testing your software on various distributions.

Different Linux distributions can ship with a wide variety of vendor supplied pre-packaged software dependent upon various system library versions and with a similar level of variance in the resulting configuration of the software. Indeed, differences occur even between one release of a distribution and the next. With all of these references to difference between distributions, you could be forgiven in thinking that Linux is a nightmare for third-party software developers. While this may be true on occasion, developers on other OS platforms are well aware of the limitations of the alternatives — in short, nothing in life is perfect, so you'll just have to deal with distribution issues when they arise.

You will learn more about packages later in this chapter when you build example packages using the RPM and Debian package managers. These two popular package management systems cover the vast majority of Linux distributions available today. If you can get your software to play nicely with both of these, then there's a good chance you'll be able to cope with anything else that becomes popular later.

The Linux Standard Base

Although there is no such thing as a truly *standard* Linux system (yet), there are de facto standards (and a few more official standards besides) that determine, among other issues, the normal filesystem location and availability of libraries, configuration files, and applications. These Linux standards include the popular Linux Standard Base (LSB). The LSB is actually based upon the POSIX and Single UNIX specifications, but it also adds additional considerations for computer graphics, the desktop, and many other areas besides. LSB favors the adoption of existing standards as a base rather than reinventing the wheel. You can obtain the latest version of the LSB (with examples) from: `www.freestandards.org`.

The Linux Standard Base aims to offer true binary compatibility between different vendor distributions — and between vendor releases — on a given host architecture conforming to a particular version of the LSB. The LSB is not Linux-specific, since it is possible (in theory) for any modern operating system to implement a particular level of the LSB (though in practice none do). Since the LSB is a binary ABI (Application Binary Interface) standard, your LSB-compliant packages should (in theory) be wildly portable between many systems and everything should just work — reality is somewhat different.

LSB uses RPM packages as the basis for its notion of a portable packaging format and provides various stipulations upon the naming and internal content of LSB-compliant packages. This chapter aims to be broadly in conformance with the standard (you'll find a section later on testing LSB compliance in your application), but for a full understanding of the dos and don'ts of LSB-compliant packaging, you'll want to check out one of the books specifically devoted to the current standard — check out the LSB website.

LSB as a Panacea

Alas, life is never as simple as one may desire it to be, and there are a number of stumbling blocks along the road to achieving universal portability through the LSB. Not least of these is the fact that the LSB is an evolving specification that is supported to varying extents by the existing Linux distributions. Each vendor supports particular levels of the LSB and may have been certified as meeting the various LSB requirements in particular configurations of a distribution. Thus, the LSB is not a panacea that will cure all of your inter-distribution ailments and make your life as a developer forever a life free from pain. What the LSB does offer in the long term, however, is the chance to make portability simpler.

The fact that some level of standardization exists doesn't mean that you won't have to deal with petty differences when they do arise. As a goal, aim to keep your assumptions as simple as you can. Avoid relying upon distribution-specific system capabilities that you don't provide and that aren't available on other Linux systems. If you must support a specific Linux distribution, you can usually detect which flavor of Linux is installed through a vendor-supplied release or version file and act accordingly.

The LSB is covered in a little more detail later in this chapter when building example packages with the RPM package management tool. An effort has been made to discuss certain criteria for LSB compliance and to explain these criteria as the examples progress. However, this book does not aim to replace the up-to-date documentation and examples available from the LSB website.

The Role of the Linux vendor

Linux vendors play a tough game of continual catch-up with upstream community software releases and must consider trends and changing interests as they decide what software to package with a given distribution. It's not any easy game to be in, and it's not possible to be all things to all people. This is one reason why there are so many different distributions in the first place — audio fanatics need real-time-capable audio support on a level that many regular desktop users simply couldn't care less about.

The job of the vendor is one of continual compromise. It is necessary to pre-package a set of software and to deliver it according to the requirements of the majority of users. Those with a specific need may find optional software packages available at system installation time, or they may not. In which case, they'd need to look elsewhere or to community support efforts. To continue the audio example, many high-end Linux audio users now use an audio system known as JACK. It provides system libraries that are very useful for high-end audio development but that won't be installed by many distributions.

When you write your Linux application, you will need to factor into your design considerations which external software and libraries you will rely upon, which software you will ship yourself (if necessary) and how (if) you will support distributions that don't meet your application's requirements. There are some absolute constraints. For example, if your application requires the latest Linux Real Time (RT) support, then your users must have a distribution that ships with a kernel supporting this feature. This is because it is normally unreasonable to upgrade such fundamental system software on behalf of a user.

Some of the typical issues facing developers and vendors include:

❑ Availability of packages and libraries

❑ Versions of pre-installed software

❑ Distribution-specific configuration

Each of these poses different problems for you as a software developer. There are various ways of dealing with these problems, but it usually comes back to supporting the lowest common denominator. If you rely only upon well-established features, which have been present in major Linux distributions for some time, then you're likely to have fewer problems with the varying manner in which newer features are initially adopted in different ways by distribution vendors.

A Word on Quality

While anyone can release a custom-created Linux distribution, quality remains an important issue. The major Linux vendors and community projects exert considerable effort on the stabilization and testing of their Linux offerings in order to make various guarantees as to their performance. Many other projects may also be of high quality, but they cannot necessarily guarantee the same level of testing has taken place — it's simply a question of resource. It is up to you as a developer to decide which commercial and community-maintained Linux distributions, and which versions thereof, that you will support.

Whatever you decide to support, don't discriminate against noncommercial Linux distributions such as Debian solely because they're not backed up by the support of a major Linux vendor. Several extremely popular Linux distributions are almost entirely community supported. These are especially popular with hobbyists and home users, in addition to a large number of commercial users. Make a reasoned decision based upon the target audience for which your software has been created and your resources. Software that is well written will be portable to other Linux environments with little redevelopment.

RPM-Based Distributions

Several popular Linux distributions are built from packages that are stored in the RPM package format. RPM originally stood for Red Hat Package Manager, but is today used by many more distributions than those created by Red Hat alone and so it has been retrospectively renamed the RPM Package Manager (creating a recursive acronym — one of a Free Software developer's favorite pastimes). RPM is the standard packaging format used by the LSB, is widely adopted by anyone working with Linux systems and as a result is supported on some level by various distributions that don't use it for regular system package management. Debian and Ubuntu are good examples of this.

> *RPM isn't necessarily the best packaging format around, but it is one of the oldest and most widely used. You'll definitely want to package your own applications using the RPM package format (in addition to any others – such as those used by Debian GNU/Linux and Ubuntu) because of its near universal acceptance. As you'll learn later, powerful tools such as* alien *do exist on other types of Linux distribution and can allow those other systems to work with RPM (on various levels).*

Few users will invoke RPM directly from the command line. Many will choose to use a graphical installer of some kind, clicking on your package and expecting the package manager to take care of the rest. To this end, various higher-level tools are layered above RPM. One of the most widely used tools on Fedora is yum. Like apt on Debian, yum isn't a packaging system per se, but is rather an automated front-end that is capable of resolving other RPM dependencies that may arise during installation. Other RPM-based distributions have their own package managers — please do refer to their documentation.

Debian Derivatives

Those distributions that are based upon Debian (including Ubuntu and all of its variants) don't use RPM natively. Debian has never decided to make any switchover to RPM, largely because they prefer some of the advanced capabilities of their own package management system, dpkg. Debian derivatives rely upon dpkg, the higher-level package resolution tool apt and graphical package managers like synaptic. There is a brief description of the build process for Debian packages included in this chapter but for more information (including detailed HOWTO guides), check out www.debian.org.

It is worth noting that much of the Debian project documentation is truly of excellent quality. Even though RPM may be a prevalent "de facto standard," Debian makes it easy to use dpkg, too.

Source Distributions

Source-level distributions don't tend to have very extensive package management systems, although there are always exceptions. Gentoo is an example of a powerful source-based distribution that has layered a concept of packages upon the basic notion of working directly with source code. Older distributions such as Slackware prefer working purely with binary tarballs and other archives.

This chapter doesn't address source-level distributions directly, since it's unlikely you'd be so concerned about portability when working directly with unpackaged software. If you'd like to find out more about layering software package versioning onto a pure source-based distribution, check out the GNU project website for examples of several groups working to make your life easier — www.gnu.org.

Rolling Your Own

Sometimes it may be necessary to create your own Linux distribution. This is actively discouraged, since users are unlikely to install a Linux distribution merely to obtain a single piece of software. Having said this, there are some software vendors who provide dedicated standalone systems that ship with a custom Linux distribution, pre-integrated with all necessary software. If you do decide to take this extraordinary step, be sure to base your Linux environment on one of the popular distributions. Some provide explicit instructions for creating your own derived distribution, if it is necessary.

A far more common reason for rolling your own Linux environment occurs in dedicated Linux devices. Very resource-constrained embedded systems typically require specially cut-down versions of common Linux software, utilities, and libraries. There are Embedded Linux vendors who sell products aimed at solving just this problem, but many people still choose the flexibility (and much greater effort) of creating their own environment and having precise control over everything that goes into it.

It's not just embedded devices that use their own Linux distribution. Large financial institutions occasionally create their own cut-down Linux in order to facilitate auditing or for mass deployment on a very large scale, where storage space becomes a very legitimate concern. Customized distributions are sometimes created for high performance or scientific computing. In that case, optimization becomes a very real concern. Most of these custom Linux environments are based upon popular distributions.

If you do decide to create your own Linux distribution, check out the Linux From Scratch project — www.linuxfromscratch.org. You'll find a complete guide to the necessary system libraries and tools, where they live in the filesystem, and how to put it all together for yourself. This is certainly a very educational (if not very time-consuming) process and is not encouraged in most cases.

> *Don't take discouragement to mean that you shouldn't pursue your intellectual curiosity — just bear in mind that many users are less inclined to install "Larry's Unfrangible Linux 9000" over a well-known distribution that has had many years of testing and is widely adopted.*

Building Packages

Most distribution packages are automatically built from upstream sources (community software source code releases) using detailed build descriptions contained within source package files. It is quite common for vendors to supply their own patches that modify the functionality of the software within a package (at build time) to bring it in line with the standards for a particular distribution — the location of system configuration files and defaults are taken account of here — or simply to fix known bugs and provide stabilization. If you're not working with a large community project, and instead are working alone or with a third party, company then it's less likely you'll need to apply many custom patches.

When you package your software, you will likely use one of the two major packaging formats discussed above — RPM or Debian packages. You're not limited to these two packaging mechanisms, however. You may decide that your software is sufficiently self-contained that a simple tarball is all that is needed in order to ship a package to your users. You would have to handle updates and conflicts yourself, but there are several high-visibility precedents for doing this among popular Linux software today. Tarball distribution is especially popular amongst those who bundle with a graphical installer – that doesn't make it a good idea over having properly tracked packages, but it is fairly popular.

> *Several of the "universal installer" utilities that are designed to supply software for multiple platforms choose to package up Linux software as a single executable containing both the installer and a section filled with a tarball of the software itself — the installer then handles detecting preinstalled versions, often ignoring the system package database. This is not something to be actively encouraged because it actively works against the system's package management.*

Building RPM Packages

RPM is one of the most widely used Linux packaging formats, and it is extremely likely that you will encounter (or have already encountered) RPMs as part of your use of a Linux workstation (even if you're not using a variant of Red Hat or SuSE). Indeed, RPM packages are universally useful, right after plain old tarballs, as a way of packaging your own source, binary, library, documentation, and other application files into a single logical unit for distribution to users and fellow developers.

Writing Spec Files

All RPM packages are built by following a series of instructions contained within a *spec* (specification) file. The spec file describes, in turn, how the RPM build process must first obtain program sources, then patch them up to the appropriate version for distribution, build against a particular build environment, and finally produce a single package file that is able to install (and uninstall) itself from a (possibly LSB-compliant) target system. Some of the sections within a spec file include:

❑ **General header information:** This includes the name of the package, a summary of its purpose in life, version, license(s), and original source location. The name of a package is significant because the LSB places constraints upon valid names that you may use for general distribution. LSB-compliant non-vendor supplied packages must begin with the lsb- prefix followed by a name that has been assigned by the LANANA.[2] You'll find more about this in the specification itself but you will want to bear this in mind if you choose to follow the LSB standard yourself.

❑ **Prep:** The section marked with %prep specifies those actions that must be taken in order to prepare the sources for building. RPM already understands how to actually unpack the sources and apply patches in order (source and patches are numbered from zero upward — or without a number if there is only one), but here you can manage and take ownership over this process.

---

[2]Linux Assigned Names And Numbers Authority. The name is loosely modeled on others such as IANA (the Internet Assigned Numbers Authority) and is hosted by the folks at kernel.org as a public service to the Linux community. LANANA maintains not only assigned package LSB names but also various other master number lists used by the Linux kernel and other Linux community projects.

❑ **Build:** The section marked with `%build` tells RPM how it must go about building the sources. This might be as simple as a call to GNU Make (possibly with a call to GNU configure and other GNU Autotools also), but it could be more complex, especially in the case of a project as large as the official Linux kernel, where various additional steps must precede the build proper.

❑ **Clean:** The section marked with `%clean` tells RPM how to clean up after it has finished doing its build. This is typically a simple call to `rm` in order to remove the temporary build directory, but you can implement more complex handling, if necessary.

❑ **Post:** The section marked with `%post` contains a series of commands that will be executed after the package has been installed. This could include calls to start newly added system services, perform post-installation updates or to remind the user that additional configuration may be required. One well-known virtualization product builds its kernel modules at this point.

❑ **Files:** The `%files` section tells RPM about which directories and files will be installed. There is no need to list every file individually. If your application installs files in the standard system locations, then you can use macros such as `%{_bindir}/*` to refer to "every file in the `bin` directory within my application." Don't forget to set a `%defattr` default set of file attributes and ownerships so that the RPM knows what permissions to assign to files it will later install.

❑ **Changelog:** The `%changelog` section is quite self-explanatory. It contains a free-form text area where brief descriptions of fixes made to an RPM can be listed. Developers tend to vary between integrating full application changelogs here or merely those changes made to accommodate the RPM-packaged version of an application on a given Linux distribution.

❑ **Extras:** There are many other optional sections that you may include in your own RPM spec file (as always, check the documentation for more details). For example, you may need to implement some special case handling when a package is uninstalled from the system, stopping appropriate system services as may be necessary for a full uninstall.

It is perhaps simplest to look at an example of RPM in action. Here is a typical RPM spec file for a simple application (a trivially simple "Hello World" program — a classic and still the best):

```
Name: hello
Summary: A simple hello world program
Version: 1.0
Release: 1
License: GPL
Group: Applications/Productivity
URL: http://p2p.wrox.com/
Source0: %{name}-%{version}.tar.gz
Patch0: hello-1.0-hack.patch
Buildroot: %{_tmppath}/%{name}-buildroot

%description
  This is a simple hello world program which prints
  the words "Hello, World!" except we've modified it
  to print the words "Goodbye, World!" via a patch.
%prep
%setup -q
%patch0 -p1

%build
```

```
make

%install
rm -rf %{buildroot}

%makeinstall

%clean
rm -rf %{buildroot}

%post
echo "The files are now installed, here we do anything else we need to."
echo "You should never actually print output in normal use since users"
echo "with regular graphical package management software won't see it."

%preun
if [ "$1" = 0 ];
then
    echo "The package is being removed, here we cleanup, stop services before"
    echo "we pull the files from underneath, etc."
fi

%postun
if [ "$1" -ge "1"];
then
    echo "The package is still on the system, so restart dependent services"
fi

%files
%defattr(-,root,root)
%{_bindir}/*

%changelog

* Mon Feb 21 2006 Jon Masters <jcm@jonmasters.org>
- initial release of hello with added goodbye
```

The example spec file contains a few sections of interest. Notice how it is divided into logical sections describing the different phases of a typical build sequence. First come the general headers that describe the package, its license, and where to find the sources. Then follows a description (for the benefit of the user who may decide whether to install the package) and finally a sequence of instructions for unpacking the source and building it into executable binary code for a particular target architecture.

Building an Example RPM

The source code accompanying this chapter includes an RPM example. You will find the following files within the rpm subdirectory of the portability chapter directory:

❑   hello-1.0-1.spec

❑   hello-1.0-hack.patch

❑   hello-1.0.tar.gz

These three files are all that is required in order to build an installable RPM package for yourself. The RPM contents and build directives are specified within the `hello-1.0-1.spec` file previously described. This spec file directs the RPM build process that it must unpack the source code contained within `hello-1.0.tar.gz` and apply a patch (`hello-1.0-hack.patch`) that is required specifically for the RPM package. You can use such patches to add any modifications necessary in order to package your software for the given target software environment in which it will be used — for example, "upstream" software is frequently patched by distributions to use their own (and differing) configuration file locations. It's about making life easier for those who follow.

Patching Your Sources

The patch in the example code is extremely simple because it merely replaces the greeting string in the original `hello-1.0.tar.gz` sources with an alternate message. The patch file was generated by copying the original sources into a new directory and modifying the `hello.c` source:

```
$ cd portability/rpm
```

```
$tar xvfz hello-1.0.tar.gz
```

```
$cp -ax hello-1.0 hello-1.0_patched
```

The modified code in the example looks like this:

```
int main(int argc, char **argv)
{

        printf("Goodbye, World!\n");

        return 0;
}
```

Finally, you can generate a suitable patch by using the GNU diff utility from the top-level directory of the example sources:

```
$ diff -urN hello-1.0 hello-1.0_patched
diff -urN hello-1.0/hello.c hello-1.0_patched/hello.c
--- hello-1.0/hello.c    2006-02-21 01:06:31.000000000 +0000
+++ hello-1.0_patched/hello.c    2006-03-18 21:59:46.000000000 +0000
@@ -8,7 +8,7 @@
 int main(int argc, char **argv)
 {

-        printf("Hello, World!\n");
+        printf("Goodbye, World!\n");

        return 0;
 }
```

Configuring the Build Environment

RPM will, by default, look for any files it needs in /usr/src/rpm. This is the standard location as used on existing Red Hat– and SuSE derived-distributions, but it is not necessarily appropriate as a location for individual users to build their own packages. For one thing, the aforementioned directory is a system-level directory normally owned by the root user (or with similarly restrictive permissions), so you'll do better (usually) using your own home directory or a development area for staging your own builds. To use your own home directory, you will need to make a small change to your environment.

Configure your RPM build environment by editing the rpmmacros file in your home directory:

```
$ vi ~/.rpmmacros
```

At a minimum, you'll need to tell RPM where to look for necessary source files and where to place any packages that are produced. The rpmmacros file allows for many flexible extensions to the entire build process and more information is available in the online (manual pages and the Internet) documentation.

Here is a minimal example file:

```
%home %(echo $HOME)
%_topdir %{home}/rpm
```

You'll also need to create the directories that RPM will later look for during any build. Do this by using the following command from your terminal:

```
$ mkdir -p $HOME/rpm/{SPECS,SOURCES,BUILD,SRPMS,RPMS}
```

The -p option to mkdir will create all path components if they do not already exist.

Then, copy the example files into the appropriate locations within your local RPM environment:

```
$ cp hello-1.0-1.spec $HOME/rpm/SPECS
$cp hello-1.0.tar.gz $HOME/rpm/SOURCES
$ cp hello-1.0-hack.patch $HOME/rpm/SOURCES
```

Kicking Off the Build

To begin the build proper, you simply need to invoke the rpmbuild command on the appropriate spec file. In the case of Debian derivatives and other non-RPM distributions, this command may be subtly different — for example, on one of the author's machines it is rpm and not rpmbuild that must be used. Here is the correct invocation and output for a standard RPM-based distribution:

```
$ rpmbuild -ba /home/jcm/rpm/SPECS/hello-1.0-1.spec
Executing(%prep): /bin/sh -e /var/tmp/rpm-tmp.15663
+ umask 022
+ cd /home/jcm/rpm/BUILD
+ cd /home/jcm/rpm/BUILD
+ rm -rf hello-1.0
+ /bin/gzip -dc /home/jcm/rpm/SOURCES/hello-1.0.tar.gz
+ tar -xf -
+ STATUS=0
```

```
+ '[' 0 -ne 0 ']'
+ cd hello-1.0
+ echo 'Patch #0 (hello-1.0-hack.patch):'
Patch #0 (hello-1.0-hack.patch):
+ patch -p1 -s
+ exit 0
Executing(%build): /bin/sh -e /var/tmp/rpm-tmp.15663
+ umask 022
+ cd /home/jcm/rpm/BUILD
+ cd hello-1.0
+ make
cc      hello.c   -o hello
+ exit 0
Executing(%install): /bin/sh -e /var/tmp/rpm-tmp.86515
+ umask 022
+ cd /home/jcm/rpm/BUILD
+ cd hello-1.0
+ rm -rf /var/tmp/hello-buildroot
+ make prefix=/var/tmp/hello-buildroot/usr exec_prefix=/var/tmp/hello-buildroot/usr
bindir=/var/tmp/hello-buildroot/usr/bin sbindir=/var/tmp/hello-buildroot/usr/sbin
sysconfdir=/var/tmp/hello-buildroot/usr/etc datadir=/var/tmp/hello-
buildroot/usr/share includedir=/var/tmp/hello-buildroot/usr/include
libdir=/var/tmp/hello-buildroot/usr/lib libexecdir=/var/tmp/hello-
buildroot/usr/libexec localstatedir=/var/tmp/hello-buildroot/usr/var
sharedstatedir=/var/tmp/hello-buildroot/usr/com mandir=/var/tmp/hello-
buildroot/usr/share/man infodir=/var/tmp/hello-buildroot/usr/info install
mkdir -p /var/tmp/hello-buildroot/usr/bin
cp hello /var/tmp/hello-buildroot/usr/bin
+ /usr/lib/rpm/brp-compress
+ /usr/lib/rpm/brp-strip
+ /usr/lib/rpm/brp-strip-comment-note
Processing files: hello-1.0-1
Finding  Provides: (using /usr/lib/rpm/find-provides)...
Finding  Requires: (using /usr/lib/rpm/find-requires)...
PreReq: /bin/sh /bin/sh /bin/sh rpmlib(PayloadFilesHavePrefix) <= 4.0-1
rpmlib(CompressedFileNames) <= 3.0.4-1
Requires(interp): /bin/sh /bin/sh /bin/sh
Requires(rpmlib): rpmlib(PayloadFilesHavePrefix) <= 4.0-1
rpmlib(CompressedFileNames) <= 3.0.4-1
Requires(post): /bin/sh
Requires(preun): /bin/sh
Requires(postun): /bin/sh
Requires: libc.so.6 linux-gate.so.1 libc.so.6(GLIBC_2.0)
Wrote: /home/jcm/rpm/SRPMS/hello-1.0-1.src.rpm
Wrote: /home/jcm/rpm/RPMS/i386/hello-1.0-1.i386.rpm
Executing(%clean): /bin/sh -e /var/tmp/rpm-tmp.17511
+ umask 022
+ cd /home/jcm/rpm/BUILD
+ cd hello-1.0
+ rm -rf /var/tmp/hello-buildroot
exit 0
```

The end result of this process is a correctly built output binary RPM package in `$HOME/rpm/RPMS/i386/hello-1.0-1.i386.rpm`. If your system uses RPM as its package manager, then you may also install this package (replacing, as necessary, the use of i386 with the architecture used on your development machine – for example ia64, s390x or ppc64):

```
$ sudo rpm -ivh $HOME/rpm/RPMS/i386/hello-1.0-1.i386.rpm
$ hello
Goodbye, World!
```

Please refer to your distribution's manual (and the RPM documentation) for additional instructions on installing, removing, and configuring packages for your Linux environment.

Installing RPMs on Non-RPM-Based Systems

Some systems (notably Debian) that are not RPM-based may not actually allow you to install this package cleanly. In the Debian example, an attempt to use RPM for a package installation will result in a message similar to the following:

```
$ sudo rpm -ivh /home/jcm/rpm/RPMS/i386/hello-1.0-1.i386.rpm
rpm: To install rpm packages on Debian systems, use alien. See README.Debian.
error: cannot open Packages index using db3 - No such file or directory (2)
error: cannot open Packages database in /var/lib/rpm
```

Notice the reference to alien. This is a Debian-provided tool for automatically converting between various packaging formats. alien is able to convert RPM packages into Debian packages and perform a number of other operations that are documented in the online manual. Although it is not perfect (and thus only a partial substitute for a proper Debian package), alien is often able to get Debian and Ubuntu users[3] out of a jam when there is no native distribution available package to them.

To convert the `hello-1.0-1.i386.rpm` package into an equivalent Debian package, use the `alien` command. Here is an example you can use to test alien for yourself:

```
$ fakeroot alien /home/jcm/rpm/RPMS/i386/hello-1.0-1.i386.rpm
```

The `alien` command will, by default, assume that it is being asked to convert the specified RPM into a Debian package and perform the conversion exercise. By default, alien also requires root privileges (in order to create some of the files used during the package build), but you can overcome this by wrapping the call to `alien` with one to `fakeroot`. `fakeroot` temporarily overrides the standard C library functions and presents the `alien` process (and all of its children) with the view that they really are the root user.

Note that no actual root permission is conferred when using `fakeroot`, but `alien` will think it is able to create files and directories owned by root. This is fine because any created files are immediately placed into an archive within a package and never need to exist on the disk owned by the system root user. Thus `fakeroot` is appropriate in a limited number of situations such as this where a mere illusion of power is all that is required. If you need to give a process real root privileges, then you should use the sudo command instead. Your Linux distribution should have documented this.

---

[3]And those using one of the many many Debian/Ubuntu derivatives out there.

Debian Packages

Debian packages are produced by the dpkg package management utility. Like RPM, dpkg follows a series of instructions that are given to it via a single text file. In Debian, this file is known as a control file (the parallel with RPM being the SPEC file), and it contains much the same kind of information as that you have already seen in the previous RPM example. There's a control file included in the example Debian package, which you will learn how to build in this section.

Creating a single Debian package can be fairly straightforward, thanks to the automated Debian helper scripts. In this case, dh_make can be used from the command line in order to create a new package, given an existing source code project to work with. For example, you can copy the existing hello-1.0.tar.gz into a new directory and use it as the basis for a brand-new Debian package.

Copy the hello-1.0.tar.gz code into a working directory and unpack it:

```
$ tar xvfz hello-1.0.tar.gz
```

Inside the newly extracted directory, you'll find the familiar example source code. To create a Debian package, you can call the dh_make script from within this directory:

```
$ dh_make -e jcm@jonmasters.org -f ../hello-1.0.tar.gz
```

Although there are many option flags available for dh_make (see the man page for a lengthy description), you need only two to get started. In the above command, -e informs dh_make that the email address of the package author is jcm@jonmasters.org, while the -f option specifies the location of the original unmodified sources for the current source tree.

When you run dh_make, you will be asked what type of package you would like to create:

```
Type of package: single binary, multiple binary, library, kernel module or cdbs?
[s/m/l/k/b]
```

Since you are creating a single binary package, you want the s option (the others are more complex and documented elsewhere). Here is the output from a typical invocation of dh_make:

```
$ dh_make -e jcm@jonmasters.org -f ../hello-1.0.tar.gz

Type of package: single binary, multiple binary, library, kernel module or cdbs?
[s/m/l/k/b] s

Maintainer name : Jon Masters
Email-Address   : jcm@jonmasters.org
Date            : Mon, 01 Jan 2007 14:54:00 +0000
Package Name    : hello
Version         : 1.0
License         : blank
Type of Package : Single
Hit <enter> to confirm:
Done. Please edit the files in the debian/ subdirectory now. You should also
check that the hello Makefiles install into $DESTDIR and not in / .
```

If all goes according to plan, you'll soon have a new `debian` subdirectory within the existing project sources. Here is what you should see when using the `ls` command from within that subdirectory:

```
$ ls
Makefile   debian   hello   hello.c
```

The `debian` directory is where all of the Debian magic happens. In this directory, you will find that `dh_make` has created many standard files on your behalf:

```
README.Debian   dirs                  init.d.ex         preinst.ex
changelog       docs                  manpage.1.ex      prerm.ex
compat          emacsen-install.ex    manpage.sgml.ex   rules
conffiles.ex    emacsen-remove.ex     manpage.xml.ex    watch.ex
control         emacsen-startup.ex    menu.ex
copyright       hello-default.ex      postinst.ex
cron.d.ex       hello.doc-base.EX     postrm.ex
```

Fortunately, you don't need to modify many of these to create a standard package. You will need to change the control file however, in order to provide information about your particular package. The control file created by `dh_make` is quite basic:

```
Source: hello
Section: unknown
Priority: optional
Maintainer: Jon Masters <jcm@jonmasters.org>
Build-Depends: debhelper (>= 4.0.0)
Standards-Version: 3.6.2

Package: hello
Architecture: any
Depends: ${shlibs:Depends}, ${misc:Depends}
Description: <insert up to 60 chars description>
 <insert long description, indented with spaces>
```

Your first task will be to modify this information in order to provide similar meta-data to that which you provided in the previous RPM SPEC file. Note that you don't need to specify the sources for this package because you're already in the source tree (the `debian` subdirectory lives within your own application's sources – it's a Debian thing).

Here is a modified control file for the example:

```
Source: hello
Section: devel
Priority: optional
Maintainer: Jon Masters <jcm@jonmasters.org>
Build-Depends: debhelper (>= 4.0.0)
Standards-Version: 3.6.2

Package: hello
Architecture: any
Depends: ${shlibs:Depends}, ${misc:Depends}
Description: A simple Hello World example program.
```

```
This program changes the world in many ways. Firstly, it uses the Debian
package management system to demonstrate how you can create your very own
Debian packages. But there's so much more. Call now! Operators are standing
by for /your/ call. And if you call right now, your order will be doubled!
```

The `Source` and `Package` lines refer to the name of the package/application itself. The `Source` line refers to the name of the newly created Debian source package and not to the location of the program sources that are currently being used. The `Section` name is similar to the RPM package `Group`. Various standard groups are defined by the Debian project—you'll need to check out their documentation for further examples of valid group names (as is the case with RPM, don't just make up random Group names – it'll work out badly in the end when your users come back to you complaining about it). The control file ends with a summary description followed by a more wordy verbose description of exactly how this package will serve to change the world (for better, or worse).

Debian Dependencies

So far, you might be wondering what advantage Debian packages offer over merely using RPMs (aside from requiring you to spin your own copy of the program sources with Debian files and directory added in for the benefit of their tools). The real power of Debian comes in the form of its lightweight `apt` (Advanced Package Tool) package management tool[4]. Apt enables Debian to automatically resolve any dependencies that may exist by installing prerequisite packages and ensuring that package conflicts are avoided. apt can't do all of this without a little help from the packager, however.

Debian package control files can include many different types of dependency. Here are some examples taken from the official documentation:

❑ **Depends:** Lines beginning with "Depends:" specify packages that must be installed in order for the successful installation of a given package. These are pure dependencies used to avoid severe system breakage. You don't want to get this bit wrong, for the sake of your sanity.

❑ **Suggests:** Lines beginning with "Suggests:" detail packages that are not required for the successful operation of a particular package, but their presence would enhance functionality in some way. For example, you might like to have (but not require) a graphics utility to assist in formatting the words "Hello World" into a neon-style sign, if the user were to request this.

❑ **Conflicts:** Lines beginning with "Conflicts:" detail packages that must not be installed concurrently with a particular package. For example, if you are providing a mail server, you may decide that the Debian default "exim" mail server (and its notorious configuration scripts) software being installed conflicts with your own mail server application software.

❑ **Provides:** Debian sometimes defines virtual packages, or packages that do not exist but provide a nice friendly way to refer to a particular type of software for which many alternatives may be available. This aids users in finding where an existing package, or a well-known package, has moved to in the latest Debian release without needing to understand the policy behind that.

There are many more examples provided in the online documentation, details of which are provided at the end of the next section. In the worst case, it's a good bedside reader.

---

[4]It has super cow powers. Don't ask. It's a Debian thing.

Building Debian Packages

The build process used by Debian packages differs somewhat from that used by RPM. But just as with RPM, in order to successfully build a Debian package, you'll need to modify the program `Makefile`(s) so that software is installed under a temporary directory hierarchy and not on the root of your filesystem. If you look at the `Makefile` used in this example, you can see how all files are installed relative to `${DESTDIR}`, which is defined by `dpkg` when the package is built.

Here is an example `dpkg` `Makefile`, taken from the example package:

```
all: hello

install:
        mkdir -p ${DESTDIR}
        cp hello ${DESTDIR}
```

Once you have successfully prepared your program sources, you can go ahead and build your Debian package. From within the top level (i.e., outside of the `debian` subdirectory), run the following command:

```
$ dpkg-buildpackage -rfakeroot
```

Just like `rpmbuild`, `dpkg-buildpackage` will first clean your program sources, then build your application and produce a Debian package from it. As before, note the use of `fakeroot` in order to trick the package building software into thinking it is running with full root permissions. This works because the software doesn't actually need to write into standard system file locations in order to build the package, but might need to create files apparently owned by the root user during the self-contained package build process. Remember, `fakeroot` isn't really giving any root privileges away.

A successful run of `dpkg-buildpackage` will produce the following output:

```
$ dpkg-buildpackage -rfakeroot
dpkg-buildpackage: source package is hello
dpkg-buildpackage: source version is 1.0-1
dpkg-buildpackage: source changed by Jon Masters <jcm@jonmasters.org>
dpkg-buildpackage: host architecture i386
 fakeroot debian/rules clean
dh_testdir
dh_testroot
rm -f build-stamp configure-stamp
/usr/bin/make clean
make[1]: Entering directory `/home/jcm/PLP/src/portability/dpkg/hello-1.0'
make[1]: *** No rule to make target `clean'.  Stop.
make[1]: Leaving directory `/home/jcm/PLP/src/portability/dpkg/hello-1.0'
make: [clean] Error 2 (ignored)
dh_clean
 dpkg-source -b hello-1.0
dpkg-source: building hello using existing hello_1.0.orig.tar.gz
dpkg-source: building hello in hello_1.0-1.diff.gz
dpkg-source: building hello in hello_1.0-1.dsc
 debian/rules build
dh_testdir
```

```
touch configure-stamp
dh_testdir
/usr/bin/make
make[1]: Entering directory `/home/jcm/PLP/src/portability/dpkg/hello-1.0'
make[1]: Nothing to be done for `all'.
make[1]: Leaving directory `/home/jcm/PLP/src/portability/dpkg/hello-1.0'
#docbook-to-man debian/hello.sgml > hello.1
touch build-stamp
 fakeroot debian/rules binary
dh_testdir
dh_testroot
dh_clean -k
dh_installdirs
/usr/bin/make install DESTDIR=/home/jcm/PLP/src/portability/dpkg/hello-
1.0/debian/hello
make[1]: Entering directory `/home/jcm/PLP/src/portability/dpkg/hello-1.0'
mkdir -p /home/jcm/PLP/src/portability/dpkg/hello-1.0/debian/hello
cp hello /home/jcm/PLP/src/portability/dpkg/hello-1.0/debian/hello
make[1]: Leaving directory `/home/jcm/PLP/src/portability/dpkg/hello-1.0'
dh_testdir
dh_testroot
dh_installchangelogs
dh_installdocs
dh_installexamples
dh_installman
dh_link
dh_strip
dh_compress
dh_fixperms
dh_installdeb
dh_shlibdeps
dh_gencontrol
dpkg-gencontrol: warning: unknown substitution variable ${misc:Depends}
dh_md5sums
dh_builddeb
dpkg-deb: building package `hello' in `../hello_1.0-1_i386.deb'.
 signfile hello_1.0-1.dsc
gpg: skipped "Jon Masters <jcm@jonmasters.org>": secret key not available
gpg: [stdin]: clearsign failed: secret key not available
```

Note that the output from this build will appear in the directory immediately above the package sources. So, if you unpacked hello-1.0.tar.gz into your home directory, look in the root of your home directory for the output package file hello_1.0-1_i386.deb. In addition to the binary package file, you'll also see that several other files have been created:

```
hello_1.0-1.diff.gz   hello_1.0-1.dsc   hello_1.0-1.dsc.asc
```

These are files that can be used by another developer to recreate the binary package.

You will notice that several warnings were generated during the previous example build. First, GNU Make complained that it was unable to clean the source. That's a problem simply cured by ensuring a clean target is added to every Makefile in order to ensure your project can be cleaned if needed. The second problem observed in the build was that the user did not have GPG installed (or available) at the time the package was build. Properly distributed Debian packages should be GPG (PGP) signed whenever possible and this is electronic signing will be performed for you, if you choose to allow it.

Debian Developers (DDs)

A person who regularly works on the Debian Linux distribution and/or who is responsible for packages in the official Debian distribution is known as a Debian Developer, affectionately abbreviated as "DD". Debian is unlike many of the other distributions, not only in terms of its mission statement, but also in terms of its developer community. It is relatively difficult to become a Debian Developer, usually requiring various mentoring steps and formal processes are undergone.

The good news is, you don't need to be a Debian Developer in order to ship packages for the Debian distribution (and you don't need to be an official Ubuntu developer either). But since it's unlikely that you are or will be an officially sanctioned developer, you'll have to make do with providing your packages via your own website. If you make any `apt` repositories available, packages you produce will not automatically show up in user's `apt` search package lists — they'll need to tell their `apt` explicitly.[5]

Further Information

The Debian package management tools are complex and evolving constantly, so you'll want to refer to the Debian New Maintainer's Guide (available at the Debian website — `www.debian.org`) for more information. Debian maintains its own sets of distribution standards and rules for what constitute valid packages. Once again, the website is the best location for up-to-date reference material.

Portable Source Code

Software that is written for Linux should not only be as binary compatible between distributions running on the same hardware platform as is possible, but should also build correctly on most systems for which the correct libraries and other prerequisites are available. The build process must take care of determining differences that exist between one software environment and the next. This applies both between Linux distributions and also between Linux and other commercial UNIX environments.

To aid in source- level portability between build environments, the GNU Autotools were created. Autoconf, Autoheader, Libtool, Automake, and many other scripts and utilities work together and collectively form the GNU Build System. Each tool will automatically run through a series of tests in order to obtain an understanding of the hardware and software environment available to the user, then determine whether it is possible to build an application in that particular software environment.

With an appropriately prepped set of sources, building your software will become the familiar "configure, make, make install" sequence with which you may already have some familiarity. The following section serves as an introduction to the GNU Autotools. For further information, check out the *Autotools* book, which is freely available online at `http://sources.redhat.com/autobook`.

---

[5] By modifying the `/etc/apt/sources` file to add in your repository, if you provide one.

GNU Autotools

It is perhaps easier to understand how the GNU Autotools work by using an example. In this case, a simple program (`hello.c`) displays a message. It has been modified to use a library (`libhello`) routine called `print_message` to perform the actual message printing operation. Additionally, the program attempts to determine whether the machine upon which it is built is big or little endian in nature and prints out an optional greeting if the machine is big endian (endianness is covered later in this chapter – read on to find out more about how Jonathan Swift influenced Computer Science).

You can create the `hello.c` example program:

```
#include "hello.h"

int main(int argc, char **argv)
{

        print_message("Hello World!\n");

#ifdef WORDS_BIGENDIAN
        printf("This system is Big Endian.\n");
#endif

        return 0;
}
```

The program uses a library called `libhello` that contains a single message-printing function:

```
void print_message(char *msg)
{
        printf("The message was %s\n", msg);

}
```

Building Autotools Projects

Building the example program and library will take several steps. Each individual step relies upon a different piece of the GNU Autotools family of utilities, as explained in the following sections. You have already seen similar example code in the last chapter when you learned how to use the GNU Toolchain to build such code and libraries for yourself. Now, you'll learn how to rely upon the powerful GNU build tools to perform these operations for you — if you'll let them. Remember that the GNU Autotools are complex in themselves and that not all of that complexity is covered here. Please see the GNU Autotools documentation for further detail or consult the online copy of the GNU *Autotools* book.

Within the `portability` example directory, you'll need to prepare an `aclocal.m4` macro file that contains lots of definitions used by automake, depending upon the content of your `configure.in`. Fortunately, this is done for you when you run the aclocal utility:

```
$ aclocal
```

Use `autoconf` to process the `configure.in` and generate an configure script:

```
$ autoconf
```

Use `autoheader` to prepare a `config.h.in` file that will be used to generate a useful `config.h` include file when the configure script is later run on a target system:

```
$ autoheader
```

Prepare for the library to be built automatically with `libtool`:

```
$ libtoolize
```

Finally, have `automake` generate `Makefile.in` files so that a later invocation of the `configure` utility script is able to generate `Makefiles` for the project:

```
$ automake --add-missing
automake: configure.in: installing `./install-sh'
automake: configure.in: installing `./mkinstalldirs'
automake: configure.in: installing `./missing'
automake: configure.in: installing `./config.guess'
automake: configure.in: installing `./config.sub'
automake: Makefile.am: installing `./INSTALL'
automake: Makefile.am: installing `./COPYING'
```

These individual stages seem complex and unwieldy right now, but that's okay because each stage will be explained soon enough. You'll finish reading this chapter with many more questions about GNU Autotools than can be addressed in these pages, but at least you'll know these tools exist and where to look for further information as you build your own projects. That's half the battle won.

You can kick off a configure cycle by calling the newly created `configure` script:

```
$ ./configure
checking build system type... i686-pc-linux-gnu
checking host system type... i686-pc-linux-gnu
checking target system type... i686-pc-linux-gnu
checking for a BSD-compatible install... /usr/bin/ginstall -c
checking whether build environment is sane... yes
checking whether make sets $(MAKE)... yes
checking for working aclocal-1.4... found
checking for working autoconf... found
checking for working automake-1.4... found
checking for working autoheader... found
checking for working makeinfo... found
checking for gcc... gcc
checking for C compiler default output file name... a.out
checking whether the C compiler works... yes
checking whether we are cross compiling... no
checking for suffix of executables...
checking for suffix of object files... o
checking whether we are using the GNU C compiler... yes
checking whether gcc accepts -g... yes
checking for gcc option to accept ANSI C... none needed
checking for a sed that does not truncate output... /bin/sed
checking for egrep... grep -E
checking for ld used by gcc... /usr/bin/ld
```

```
checking if the linker (/usr/bin/ld) is GNU ld... yes
checking for /usr/bin/ld option to reload object files... -r
checking for BSD-compatible nm... /usr/bin/nm -B
checking whether ln -s works... yes
checking how to recognise dependent libraries... pass_all
checking how to run the C preprocessor... gcc -E
checking for ANSI C header files... yes
checking for sys/types.h... yes
checking for sys/stat.h... yes
checking for stdlib.h... yes
checking for string.h... yes
checking for memory.h... yes
checking for strings.h... yes
checking for inttypes.h... yes
checking for stdint.h... yes
checking for unistd.h... yes
checking dlfcn.h usability... yes
checking dlfcn.h presence... yes
checking for dlfcn.h... yes
checking for g++... g++
checking whether we are using the GNU C++ compiler... yes
checking whether g++ accepts -g... yes
checking how to run the C++ preprocessor... g++ -E
checking for g77... g77
checking whether we are using the GNU Fortran 77 compiler... yes
checking whether g77 accepts -g... yes
checking the maximum length of command line arguments... 32768
checking command to parse /usr/bin/nm -B output from gcc object... ok
checking for objdir... .libs
checking for ar... ar
checking for ranlib... ranlib
checking for strip... strip
checking if gcc static flag  works... yes
checking if gcc supports -fno-rtti -fno-exceptions... no
checking for gcc option to produce PIC... -fPIC
checking if gcc PIC flag -fPIC works... yes
checking if gcc supports -c -o file.o... yes
checking whether the gcc linker (/usr/bin/ld) supports shared libraries... yes
checking whether -lc should be explicitly linked in... no
checking dynamic linker characteristics... GNU/Linux ld.so
checking how to hardcode library paths into programs... immediate
checking whether stripping libraries is possible... yes
checking if libtool supports shared libraries... yes
checking whether to build shared libraries... yes
checking whether to build static libraries... yes
configure: creating libtool
appending configuration tag "CXX" to libtool
checking for ld used by g++... /usr/bin/ld
checking if the linker (/usr/bin/ld) is GNU ld... yes
checking whether the g++ linker (/usr/bin/ld) supports shared libraries... yes
checking for g++ option to produce PIC... -fPIC
checking if g++ PIC flag -fPIC works... yes
checking if g++ supports -c -o file.o... yes
checking whether the g++ linker (/usr/bin/ld) supports shared libraries... yes
```

```
checking dynamic linker characteristics... GNU/Linux ld.so
checking how to hardcode library paths into programs... immediate
checking whether stripping libraries is possible... yes
appending configuration tag "F77" to libtool
checking if libtool supports shared libraries... yes
checking whether to build shared libraries... yes
checking whether to build static libraries... yes
checking for g77 option to produce PIC... -fPIC
checking if g77 PIC flag -fPIC works... yes
checking if g77 supports -c -o file.o... yes
checking whether the g77 linker (/usr/bin/ld) supports shared libraries... yes
checking dynamic linker characteristics... GNU/Linux ld.so
checking how to hardcode library paths into programs... immediate
checking whether stripping libraries is possible... yes
checking for gcc... (cached) gcc
checking whether we are using the GNU C compiler... (cached) yes
checking whether gcc accepts -g... (cached) yes
checking for gcc option to accept ANSI C... (cached) none needed
checking for ANSI C header files... (cached) yes
checking whether byte ordering is bigendian... no
checking for unistd.h... (cached) yes
checking for stdlib.h... (cached) yes
checking stdio.h usability... yes
checking stdio.h presence... yes
checking for stdio.h... yes
configure: creating ./config.status
config.status: creating Makefile
config.status: creating src/Makefile
config.status: creating include/config.h
config.status: executing default-1 commands


=============================================================================
Thanks for testing this example. You could add some output here
and refer to any AC environment variables if needed.


=============================================================================
```

Notice how `configure` reports on the status of individual tests it is performing. You can see a lot of output similar to `checking for stdio.h usability` that indicates configure is performing many tests on your behalf. After running configure, you'll notice that a `config.h` file has been created in the include directory within the project sources:

```
/* include/config.h.  Generated by configure.  */
/* include/config.h.in.  Generated from configure.in by autoheader.  */

/* Define to 1 if you have the <dlfcn.h> header file. */
#define HAVE_DLFCN_H 1

/* Define to 1 if you have the <inttypes.h> header file. */
#define HAVE_INTTYPES_H 1

/* Define to 1 if you have the <memory.h> header file. */
#define HAVE_MEMORY_H 1
```

```
/* Define to 1 if you have the <stdint.h> header file. */
#define HAVE_STDINT_H 1

/* Define to 1 if you have the <stdio.h> header file. */
#define HAVE_STDIO_H 1

/* Define to 1 if you have the <stdlib.h> header file. */
#define HAVE_STDLIB_H 1

/* Define to 1 if you have the <strings.h> header file. */
#define HAVE_STRINGS_H 1

/* Define to 1 if you have the <string.h> header file. */
#define HAVE_STRING_H 1

/* Define to 1 if you have the <sys/stat.h> header file. */
#define HAVE_SYS_STAT_H 1

/* Define to 1 if you have the <sys/types.h> header file. */
#define HAVE_SYS_TYPES_H 1

/* Define to 1 if you have the <unistd.h> header file. */
#define HAVE_UNISTD_H 1

/* Name of package */
#define PACKAGE "1.9"

/* Define to the address where bug reports for this package should be sent. */
#define PACKAGE_BUGREPORT "jcm@jonmasters.org"

/* Define to the full name of this package. */
#define PACKAGE_NAME "hello"

/* Define to the full name and version of this package. */
#define PACKAGE_STRING "hello 1.0"

/* Define to the one symbol short name of this package. */
#define PACKAGE_TARNAME "hello"

/* Define to the version of this package. */
#define PACKAGE_VERSION "1.0"

/* Define to 1 if you have the ANSI C header files. */
#define STDC_HEADERS 1

/* Version number of package */
#define VERSION ""

/* Define to 1 if your processor stores words with the most significant byte
   first (like Motorola and SPARC, unlike Intel and VAX). */
/* #undef WORDS_BIGENDIAN */
```

Each of the `#define` statements came about because of a test that was successfully passed during the configure process. Your `hello.c` source code can use these definitions and indeed does so when determining whether to print an additional greeting message. The `hello.h` include header also uses these defines in order to pedantically determine what header files to include:

```
#ifndef HELLO_H
#define HELLO_H 1

#if HAVE_CONFIG_H
#   include <config.h>
#endif

#if HAVE_STDIO_H
#   include <stdio.h>
#endif

#if STDC_HEADERS
#   include <stdlib.h>
#endif

#if HAVE_UNISTD_H
#   include <unistd.h>
#endif

#endif /* HELLO_H */
```

You won't necessarily bother with such a level of pedantry, but you will use the `config.h` output file as a means to have your source code adjust to the local build environment as far as is possible. For example, when porting to other UNIX-like systems, you might find some memory allocation routines are missing or don't behave as you expect — you can use the configure script to pick up on the presence or lack of many standard library features and provide your own alternative implementation, if necessary. Check out the GNU Autoconf documentation for a full list of tests and features that it supports.

Once the software is configured, you can build it in the normal way, using GNU `make`:

```
$ make
Making all in src
make[1]: Entering directory `/home/jcm/PLP/src/portability/autotools/src'
/bin/sh ../libtool --mode=compile gcc -DHAVE_CONFIG_H -I. -I. -I../include     -g -
O2 -c hello_msg.c
mkdir .libs
 gcc -DHAVE_CONFIG_H -I. -I. -I../include -g -O2 -Wp,-MD,.deps/hello_msg.pp -c
hello_msg.c  -fPIC -DPIC -o .libs/hello_msg.o
hello_msg.c: In function 'print_message':
hello_msg.c:7: warning: incompatible implicit declaration of built-in function
'printf'
 gcc -DHAVE_CONFIG_H -I. -I. -I../include -g -O2 -Wp,-MD,.deps/hello_msg.pp -c
hello_msg.c -o hello_msg.o >/dev/null 2>&1
/bin/sh ../libtool --mode=link gcc  -g -O2  -o libhello.la -rpath /usr/local/lib
hello_msg.lo
gcc -shared  .libs/hello_msg.o   -Wl,-soname -Wl,libhello.so.0 -o
.libs/libhello.so.0.0.0
(cd .libs && rm -f libhello.so.0 && ln -s libhello.so.0.0.0 libhello.so.0)
```

```
(cd .libs && rm -f libhello.so && ln -s libhello.so.0.0.0 libhello.so)
ar cru .libs/libhello.a  hello_msg.o
ranlib .libs/libhello.a
creating libhello.la
(cd .libs && rm -f libhello.la && ln -s ../libhello.la libhello.la)
gcc -DHAVE_CONFIG_H -I. -I. -I../include     -g -O2 -c hello.c
/bin/sh ../libtool --mode=link gcc  -g -O2  -o hello  hello.o libhello.la
gcc -g -O2 -o .libs/hello hello.o  ./.libs/libhello.so
creating hello
make[1]: Leaving directory `/home/jcm/PLP/src/portability/autotools/src'
make[1]: Entering directory `/home/jcm/PLP/src/portability/autotools'
make[1]: Nothing to be done for `all-am'.
make[1]: Leaving directory `/home/jcm/PLP/src/portability/autotools'
```

A quick call to make install (with the appropriate root permissions) will install the hello binary and the necessary library into /usr/local/bin/hello (a default location, customizable in configure.in or through --prefix arguments to the configure script, especially if you don't want to install this to the main filesystem of your development machine – you could choose, e.g. $HOME/bin, instead):

```
$ sudo make install
Making install in src
make[1]: Entering directory `/home/jcm/PLP/src/portability/autotools/src'
make[2]: Entering directory `/home/jcm/PLP/src/portability/autotools/src'
/bin/sh ../mkinstalldirs /usr/local/lib
/bin/sh ../libtool  --mode=install /usr/bin/ginstall -c libhello.la
/usr/local/lib/libhello.la
/usr/bin/ginstall -c .libs/libhello.so.0.0.0 /usr/local/lib/libhello.so.0.0.0
(cd /usr/local/lib && { ln -s -f libhello.so.0.0.0 libhello.so.0 || { rm -f
libhello.so.0 && ln -s libhello.so.0.0.0 libhello.so.0; }; })
(cd /usr/local/lib && { ln -s -f libhello.so.0.0.0 libhello.so || { rm -f
libhello.so && ln -s libhello.so.0.0.0 libhello.so; }; })
/usr/bin/ginstall -c .libs/libhello.lai /usr/local/lib/libhello.la
/usr/bin/ginstall -c .libs/libhello.a /usr/local/lib/libhello.a
ranlib /usr/local/lib/libhello.a
chmod 644 /usr/local/lib/libhello.a
PATH="$PATH:/sbin" ldconfig -n /usr/local/lib
----------------------------------------------------------------------
Libraries have been installed in:
   /usr/local/lib

If you ever happen to want to link against installed libraries
in a given directory, LIBDIR, you must either use libtool, and
specify the full pathname of the library, or use the `-LLIBDIR'
flag during linking and do at least one of the following:
    - add LIBDIR to the `LD_LIBRARY_PATH' environment variable
      during execution
    - add LIBDIR to the `LD_RUN_PATH' environment variable
      during linking
    - use the `-Wl,--rpath -Wl,LIBDIR' linker flag
    - have your system administrator add LIBDIR to `/etc/ld.so.conf'

See any operating system documentation about shared libraries for
more information, such as the ld(1) and ld.so(8) manual pages.
----------------------------------------------------------------------
```

```
/bin/sh ../mkinstalldirs /usr/local/bin
 /bin/sh ../libtool  --mode=install /usr/bin/ginstall -c  hello
/usr/local/bin/hello
/usr/bin/ginstall -c .libs/hello /usr/local/bin/hello
make[2]: Nothing to be done for `install-data-am'.
make[2]: Leaving directory `/home/jcm/PLP/src/portability/autotools/src'
make[1]: Leaving directory `/home/jcm/PLP/src/portability/autotools/src'
make[1]: Entering directory `/home/jcm/PLP/src/portability/autotools'
make[2]: Entering directory `/home/jcm/PLP/src/portability/autotools'
make[2]: Nothing to be done for `install-exec-am'.
make[2]: Nothing to be done for `install-data-am'.
make[2]: Leaving directory `/home/jcm/PLP/src/portability/autotools'
make[1]: Leaving directory `/home/jcm/PLP/src/portability/autotools'
```

At this point, you might try running the program for yourself:

```
$ hello
```

```
hello: error while loading shared libraries: libhello.so.0: cannot open shared
object file: No such file or directory
```

The system can't find `libhello.so.0`, which was just installed. Why? Because the dynamic linker needs to refresh its cache of known libraries. The linker knows about directories that are listed in `/etc/ld.so.conf` and will include certain standard directories (such as `/usr/local/lib` used in this example) when rebuilding its cache. You can cause this to happen by running `ldconfig`:

```
$ sudo ldconfig
```

Once this is done, the `hello` program should behave normally:

```
$ hello
The message was Hello World!
```

Congratulations on your first GNU Autotools project. Now that you've started down this path and after you have read the explanatory information in the following sections, you'll want to experiment for yourself. Use the documentation available with the GNU Autotools themselves to guide you..

> *If you're building a project that will later be part of GNU (that becomes an official project of the Free Software Foundation), you'll want to ensure that the example project contains a few more important files. Every GNU project must contain an AUTHORS file with information about each of the authors involved in its creation, a NEWS file tracking project news, a README file with basic information about the project and a ChangeLog file tracking individual project code releases.*

GNU Autoconf

GNU Autoconf is used to produce a `configure` script that is run prior to an application being built. The `configure` script is able to run a series of tests that the developer has asked for in order to ascertain whether the software can be built in a particular environment. This might, for example, determine the version of the (GNU or non-GNU) C compiler installed on your machine and ensure that certain standard C header files are in place. Or, it might do something more complex—there's a lot of flexibility in GNU `autoconf`.

GNU configure can be used to build header files containing dynamic information about a particular system for use in source tests. So, for example, it's typical that a build cycle result in the creation of a config.h header file that contains #define statements for many of the features that have been tested for. If GNU configure determines that the local software environment is suitable for building the software, then these defines aid flexibility by allowing conditional code compilation as is necessary.

You will quickly realize that you want to use GNU configure, because it will simplify your development on Linux, greatly.

Here is an example configure.in from which a configure script is generated:

```
# This is a sample configure.in that you can process with autoconf in order
# to produce a configure script.

# Require Autoconf 2.59 (version installed on author's workstation)
AC_PREREQ([2.59])

AC_INIT([hello], [1.0], [jcm@jonmasters.org])

# Check the system
AC_CANONICAL_SYSTEM

AM_CONFIG_HEADER(include/config.h)
AC_CONFIG_SRCDIR(src/hello.c)
AM_INIT_AUTOMAKE([1.9])
AM_PROG_LIBTOOL

AC_PROG_CC
AC_HEADER_STDC
AC_C_BIGENDIAN
AC_CHECK_HEADERS([unistd.h stdlib.h stdio.h])
AC_OUTPUT(Makefile src/Makefile)

# Pretty print some output
AC_MSG_RESULT([])
AC_MSG_RESULT([[====================================================================
============]])
AC_MSG_RESULT([])
AC_MSG_RESULT([Thanks for testing this example. You could add some output
here])AC_MSG_RESULT([and refer to any AC environment variables if needed.])
AC_MSG_RESULT([])
AC_MSG_RESULT([[====================================================================
============]])
```

You can see that this file is relatively short and contains just a few commands (actually macros, many of these tools are built using the M4 macro processor, but that's immaterial to this discussion). The configure.in file begins with the command AC_PREREQ in order to require that the minimum version of Autoconf used be 2.59. Thus, the system used to generate the configure script must have GNU Autoconf 2.59 installed. AC_INIT is then used to tell Autoconf about the package name, the version, and the email address of the author. What follows after that is a series of commands beginning with AC, directly determining what features and tests will be in the configure script.

You'll learn more about the other lines in configure.in soon.

The main Autoconf commands in this example file are:

- ❏ **AC_CANONICAL_SYSTEM:** Cause Autoconf to determine whether to build for the host or for a target and to handle cross-compilation[6] if necessary.

- ❏ **AC_CONFIG_SRCDIR:** Test for the presence of `src/hello.c` and complain loudly if it is missing. This is used to ensure that the user is running the correct scripts in the correct directory location, and so forth.

- ❏ **AC_PROG_CC:** Test for the existence of a C compiler (for example, this will detect GCC, if installed).

- ❏ **AC_HEADER_STDC:** Test for the availability of the standard C headers (in `/usr/include`).

- ❏ **AC_C_BIGENDIAN:** Determine the endianess of the machine — an example of one of the many custom tests you can add, if needed (see the next section on hardware portability).

- ❏ **AC_CHECK_HEADERS:** Specify additional system header files to test for.

- ❏ **AC_OUPUT:** Specifies a list of files that will be output after GNU Autoconf is run. In this case, GNU Autoconf will lead to the generation of `Makefiles` at the top level and under the `src` subdirectories.

The `configure` script is automatically generated from `configure.in` and is based on portable shell code. This is very important because it is difficult (impossible) to know which shells will be installed on any given Linux or UNIX system. While it's true to say there are few Linux systems without bash, it pays to be flexible when the option exists. You won't need to worry about writing your own portable shell code unless you decide to write your own configure tests (really, do see the Autoconf documentation).

GNU Automake

Automake is used to build the project `Makefiles`, so that the software can easily be built by using regular calls to GNU `make`, as you saw in the build example. GNU Automake takes as its input `makefile.am` input files, and there are two such files used in the example project. The first, at the top level simply informs GNU Automake to descend into the `src` subdirectory:

```
# A simple GNU Automake example

SUBDIRS        = src
```

Within the `src` subdirectory is another `Makefile.am`, this time with more useful content:

```
# A simple GNU Automake example

bin_PROGRAMS          = hello

hello_SOURCES         = hello.c
hello_LDADD           = libhello.la

lib_LTLIBRARIES       = libhello.la
libhello_la_SOURCES   = hello_msg.c
```

---

[6]GNU Autoconf will automatically handle detection of cross-compilation environments, where a special version of the GNU Compiler Collection (GCC) and related parts of the GNU Toolchain may be needed in order to support building on one system to run on another different kind of computer platform.

Notice the simple format of this file. You don't need to tell GNU Automake about the C compiler or regular C compiler compile flags normally required to build program source, or in fact anything other than what source is to be compiled and what dependencies it has — the GNU Autotools will take care of the rest. The program produced in the example will be called hello, so there is a bin_PROGRAMS line in the Makefile.am file telling Automake about this. Then, a hello_SOURCES line informs Automake of the sources needed to build hello.

The final three lines of the example Makefile.am file are used by GNU Libtool and are explained in the next section.

GNU Libtool

Libtool is designed to take much of the hassle out of building static and shared libraries on many of the different Linux and UNIX-like systems that your project source may be built on. There is a heavy tie-in between the other GNU Autotools and GNU Libtool, so you don't need to work with GNU Libtool directly. It is instead sufficient for you to add a single line to your configure.in, as seen in the previous listing (repeated here for your convenience):

```
AM_PROG_LIBTOOL
```

This will cause the resulting GNU configure script to know about GNU Libtool. In addition to that, you need to tell GNU Automake about your libraries, as the previous Makefile.am listing also showed:

```
hello_LDADD              = libhello.la

lib_LTLIBRARIES          = libhello.la
libhello_la_SOURCES      = hello_msg.c
```

These three lines tell GNU Automake that hello requires an additional linking stage against the library file libhello, and then provide the build dependencies for the library itself.

GNU Libtool is able to perform many more operations than those it is indirectly being asked to perform in this example. You are encouraged to explore the GNU Libtool documentation for further examples of the power of this portable library generation utility for yourself.

Internationalization

As you develop on your particular workstation, remember that Linux is in use all over the world. Distribution popularity varies greatly from one geographical location to the next. Sometimes, this is a factor of the origin of a particular distribution. For example, SuSE Linux remains extremely popular in Germany and in mainland Europe because of its German roots (despite now being part of Novell), while Red Hat is traditionally very popular in the United States. The lines have blurred somewhat with time but the point remains — different distributions are popular in different locales around the world.

Sometimes, whole countries standardize on local distributions because they have greater levels of localization and support for a multitude of different languages. These days, Linux does have reasonably good support for internationalization, thanks in part to efforts such as the Open Internationalisation Initiative (OpenI18N) from the Free Standards Group (the same group that publish the LSB standard of which the Open Insternationalisation Initiative forms a part). You'll find more about the specification on the OpenI18N website at www.openI18N.org.

While good support for internationalization may exist, it is important to make good use of this capability whenever possible. To serve this end, Canonical — the makers of the Ubuntu Linux distribution — have recently pioneered a project known as Rosetta (`www.launchpad.net`) that, among other things, allows those of all abilities (both programmers and nonprogrammers alike) to quickly contribute language translations for popular Linux software applications, via a web interface.

Languages and Locales

Linux was first released more than a decade ago, and early distributions were composed of little more than just the kernel and a few simple utilities, originally written for a mostly Western (English speaking) audience. That was great at the time, but today's systems are almost a world apart in terms of user interaction with the system. As you'll learn later in this book, graphical desktop environments such as GNOME allow for a very powerful and easy to use end-user experience on a modern Linux desktop.

But what good is an easy-to-use interface if it doesn't speak your (or, more important, your users') language? This is where locales come into play. Extensive work has gone into providing great support for a wide range of languages, countries, and other preferences that a user might reasonably expect to be tailored to their location.[7] Much of this work was originally inspired by large corporate efforts in the United States (and elsewhere) by those who were shipping software around the world. These days, thanks to powerful translation tools like that provided by Rosetta, anyone anywhere can contribute.

Linux handles different regions of the world through the concept of a locale. You can determine the current available locales on your Linux system by running the following command from any terminal:

```
$ locale -a
```

The list of supported locales could be quite substantial on a modern Linux distribution or it might be very minimal indeed. For example, unless you chose to install many optional locales, your system might feature little more than just the locale needed for your current location. You can consult your vendor-supplied documentation for further information about the locales that they support.

Here is a selection of available locales on one of the author's machines:

```
$ locale -a

en_GB

en_GB.iso88591

en_GB.iso885915

en_GB.utf8

en_US

en_US.iso88591
```

---

[7] For example, you might reasonably expect that your monetary and date display format would vary based on your location. These issues are not discussed specifically in the text — but they're part of the wider issue of making Linux distributions more portable to different locales around the world.

```
en_US.iso885915
```

```
en_US.utf8
```

Formally, a locale identifier consists of a string of the form:

```
[language[_territory][.codeset][@modifier]]
```

In the above listing, you can see that the test system has support for the English language in the United Kingdom (for various reasons internationally referred to as Great Britain with a GB abbreviation) and the United States. Each of these available locales includes support for a different character encoding, including the UTF-8 Unicode character set, which is covered in more detail in the next section.

You may have noticed locales during the installation of your Linux distribution, although any explicit references to setting an appropriate locale may have been massaged into straightforward questions of your geographical location and chosen language. You probably want to offer your users the same level of abstraction from having to understand exactly what any of this means.

Working with Character Sets

For the last 20 years, work has gone into a set of international standards for character encoding and representation. Software vendors, tired of implementing their own character encoding systems for handling multilingual releases of their products worked together to produce a common solution that could be adapted and used universally to handle the growing need for language localization of software well into the future. One of the major outcomes of this work has been the Unicode standard.

Unless you've been living with the monks in Tibet for the past decade, you've probably encountered (and used) Unicode in your own software. Writing software for Linux that uses Unicode characters is relatively straightforward, but you'll need to bear in mind that Linux (like other UNIX-like systems) was originally based around 8-bit (single-byte) US ASCII[8] character encoding (and even older stuff!). As a result, there are many system utilities that don't (yet) handle Unicode correctly. This isn't a major problem, since it is also usual to use the UTF-8 encoding to store such characters on Linux systems.

UTF-8 solves many of the problems that would otherwise arise in using Unicode on Linux. Since the alternative multi-byte Unicode encodings allow for single byte \0 (NULL) or / characters their use in text files or file paths could cause severe problems. For example, the NULL character has special meaning to the C library on Linux and UNIX-like systems as an end of string marker, so its use could cause problems using the standard C library functions on potential Unicode strings. UTF-8 is stored using multiple single bytes in a backward-compatible fashion (ASCII is a valid subset of UTF-8).

UTF-8 varies the width of individual character (in terms of its memory footprint) according to the character itself. Those that fit within the existing 7-bit base ASCII character set can continue to be represented as a single byte, while other characters require an escape byte to indicate the presence of a multi-byte-encoded UTF-8 character. UTF-8 characters can vary from 1 to 6 bytes in length, but you'll probably not have to worry about the exact way in which UTF-8 is constructed — you'll use a library routine to handle conversion to and from an internal representation that's easier to work with.

---

[8]American Standard Code for Information Interchange. Strictly speaking, ASCII is a 7-bit character encoding standard, which was originally based upon telegraphic codes. Although the standard hasn't been updated in two decades, it is still widely used, especially in the UNIX world.

You will discover later in this book that writing software for graphical desktop environments involves using libraries that already have good internal support for Unicode. This should not detract from your interest in this material because much of it will remain relevant, both within and outside the desktop. Besides, it's good to have an idea about what's going on underneath.

Wide Characters

Unicode is an encoding system used to represent character sets such that different applications can work with strings of various shapes and sizes. Internally, a program can use whatever data types it likes for storage. It is usually the case that programmers wish to make their lives easier by using a little more memory than may technically be required, with the benefit of making string and character handling a lot easier. Therefore, it is acceptable to use several bytes per character stored in memory even if a variable width encoding such as UTF-8 would result in lower overall memory usage.

Modern Linux systems (and the ISO C90 standard in particular) support the notion of *wide characters*. A wide character (wchar_t) is a multi-byte data type used to internally represent each individual character of (for example) a Unicode string. On most systems, a wchar_t is 4 bytes wide, or one memory word in width on most 32-bit workstations. Using wide characters requires that the wchar.h system header file be included, which may not be available on more ancient Linux distributions.

Here is an example of wide characters in action. In the example, you can see how printing a wide character string using wchar_t compares with printing a plain old char string with printf:

```
/* Test program for wide characters
 * Note than use of strlen is merely for demonstrative purposes. You should
 * never use strlen with untrusted strings!
 */

#include <stdio.h>
#include <stdlib.h>
#include <string.h>
#include <wchar.h>

int main(int argc, char **argv)
{

        char *sc = "short characters";
        wchar_t *wc = L"wider characters";

        printf("%ls are more universally useful than %s, ",
                wc, sc);

        printf("but they do use more space (%d as opposed to %d bytes).\n",
                wcslen(wc)*sizeof(wchar_t), strlen(sc));

        exit(0);

}
```

You can see that the wchar_t data type is used to represent a wide character string and that wide character versions of standard C library functions exist. In the example, wcslen — the wide character version of the standard C library strlen function is used to calculate the number of characters in a wide string (as opposed to the number of bytes, which would be returned by the strlen alternative), and this is then multiplied by the internal size of the wchar_t opaque[9] data type.

Here is the output from the previous example on a test workstation:

```
$ ./wide_characters
```

```
wider characters are more universally useful than short characters, but they do use
more space (64 as opposed to 16 bytes).
```

The example code uses the plain old printf C library routine, but it instructs printf to use wide characters with the aid of the l modifier prefixed into the usual %s format string. The declaration of a wide character is performed using the L modifier on a standard string declaration, as you can see when the wc wide character string is declared. Note that there is a "wide characters" version of printf — wprintf — that you can use if you want to have flexibility over the on screen width of displayed characters. The plain old printf routine treats its width modifiers as byte widths, which can cause badly aligned output.

For more information about wide characters, check out the full text of the Single UNIX Specification, which includes a full listing of API functions that support wide character display and transformation. You should be aware, however, that not all parts of the Single UNIX Specification are supported on non-Linux systems — for truly portable Unicode, you may need to confine yourself still further, for example by using only those functions and representations defined in the ISO C90 standard. This is somewhat of a grey area — true Unicode portability across UNIX/UNIX-like and non-UNIX.

You may also refer to the manual pages that come with your Linux system. Type "man -k wide characters" for a starting point. Finally, you may like to check out Ulrich Drepper's iconv utility and library routines as a means for easy conversion from one character encoding to another. Your distribution should provide documentation and a copy of this utility, in a standard location.

Speaking Your User's Language

One of the biggest speed bumps on the road to making your software globally usable comes from the need to be able to provide useful output to the users in their own native language. Until natural language processing really takes off (by which time computers will probably write software themselves), you'll need to provide translations for every major output dialog that your application has with the outside world (via the user). Fortunately, the gettext library can help you to make this less painful than it sounds, and you can get the added bonus of farming out translations to those with a flair for languages.

---

[9]Opaque means that the internal representation is intentionally hidden from view. It doesn't matter too much how much memory wide characters take, except when such calculations are being performed.

The gettext library routines can simply take a regular ASCII text string (conventionally written in English) and use that as an index into a table of translations for a given piece of software. Each translation is stored in a .po (portable object) file that can be shipped with your software. Some applications may have dozens of available translations (and certainly the Rosetta project is working to improve upon even that) stored in subdirectories under /usr/share/locale/<language>_<region>. For example, the following example will target users with a en_US and en_GB locale.[10]

Here is a simple program that can output a different greeting to different users, depending upon where they live in the world (what they have set their default locale to via the LANG environment variable):

```c
/* A sample gettext program
 */

#include <stdio.h>

#include <locale.h>      /* LC_ environment variables */
#include <libintl.h>     /* Internationalized library */
#include <stdlib.h>

#define _(String) gettext (String)
#define gettext_noop(String) String
#define N_(String) gettext_noop (String)

int main(int argc, char **argv)
{

        setlocale(LC_ALL, "");

        bindtextdomain("gettext_example", ".");
        textdomain("gettext_example");

        printf("%s\n", gettext("Hello, World!"));

        return 0;
}
```

The code begins by including various standard headers (including the libintl.h header file) and then defines some macros as advised by the gettext documentation on the Free Software Foundation website. A call to setlocale forces any later calls to gettext to base their choices for translation upon various environment variables that the user may or may not have set. Somewhat more important, their distribution may have set these variables on their behalf — typically to the install time selected locale. Nonetheless, in this case, you will be declaring a specific locale via the LANG environment variable in order to temporarily override the locale and test out different application behaviors.

In order to use gettext, some initialization is required. You need to inform the gettext library functions of the location of the translation files that will be used. Typically, these live in /usr/share/locale under various application subdirectories (you'll find hundreds on your system), but to make the example code reasonably straightforward, the example will look for translations in subdirectories of the program binary itself. A call to bindtextdomain informs gettext of the location of the translation files, while textdomain is called as a means to force the current application to use these translations.

---

[10]A somewhat contrived example, but as a British author living in the United States, sometimes it can feel as if you need to translate from one language to another. The point is nonetheless made, if contrived.

Whenever the example program makes a call to gettext, a suitable translation string will be returned, if one is available for the specific translation. Failing a suitable result, the default text will be used instead. In the case of the example, it prints the words "Hello, World" by default, unless a translation exists. You can create a translation (po) file using the xgettext utility:

```
$ xgettext -ao gettext_example.po gettext_example.c
```

This will create a file gettext_example.po that contains each potentially translatable string in the example program. In this case, you only need to supply a translation for the "Hello, World" string, so the content can be trimmed down significantly. For the sake of an example, the first two translations that will be supported by the program will be provided for US and UK users. To that end, two copies of the po file should be made — one for the US and one for the UK.

Here is the gettext_example.po file for hard-core code-hacking US coffee drinkers:

```
# gettext_example
# US Translations

#: gettext_example.c:18
msgid "Hello, World!"
msgstr "cup of coffee?"
```

British users get a slightly different greeting, more for the tea-drinking inclined:

```
# gettext_example
# UK Translations

#: gettext_example.c:18
msgid "Hello, World!"
msgstr "cup of tea?"
```

These files won't be picked up by default because they're not in the correct location (according to the initialization calls made to gettext). To test the example, create the correct directory structure:

```
$ mkdir -p en_GB/LC_MESSAGES en_US/LC_MESSAGES
```

You'll need to convert the po text files into machine readable binary translation files, by using msgfmt utility. For example, to produce a usable en_US binary translation file:

```
$ msgfmt -o en_US/LC_MESSAGES/gettext_example.mo gettext_example_en_US.po
```

In reality, the gettext_example.mo files for each language supported by your application would live under /usr/share/locale, along with the many existing translations supplied by other software programs. In the case of US English, this would normally be in /usr/share/locale/en_US/LC_MESSAGES. Check out your existing system to get a feel for the number of translations that are already provided, just in case you need to use one. You'll be surprised by how many everyday applications have translations.

To test the program, try exporting a LANG environment variable equal to en_US or en_GB (or whichever locale you want to test against). You'll see input/output similar to the following.

Setting a US locale:

```
$ export LANG=en_US
$ ./gettext_example
cup of coffee?
```

Setting a UK locale:

```
$ export LANG=en_GB
$ ./gettext_example
cup of tea?
```

There are many supported locales on the average system (and some less supported — a Klingon[11] language locale does exist, but may very well not be available on your system). It would make little sense to provide multiple English language translations along the lines of those used in this section, but the examples merely serve as an indicator of what is possible when you use non-English translations for your own local country or region. For further information about using `gettext`, check out the online manual pages as well as the Free Software Foundation website.

Languages Other Than C/C++

You should note that higher-level languages such as Perl and Python implement their own internal Unicode handling that is distinct from that used at the Linux system level. You can continue to write your Perl and Python programs in the same way that you do on other operating system platforms. You'll also want to look at the graphical desktop issue separately — see the GNOME chapter later is this book for more consideration of internationalization within modern graphical desktop environments.

Hardware Portability

Portable Linux software can mean different things to different people. Linux is a highly versatile operating system, which has itself been ported to a wide variety of different hardware, though many still consider Linux to mean Linux for Intel IA32 (x86) processors running on a standard PC. Indeed, most (if not all) third-party software vendors continue to ship software "for Linux" without adequately making this distinction. That's marketing for you. But you understand that there is a distinction. Whether you choose to support more than the most popular platforms is a commercial decision.[12]

The Linux kernel has many different internal APIs, header files, and other supporting code that serves to abstract and manage the many differences between hardware platforms in as portable a fashion as is possible. You will learn more about this capability when you begin to explore the internals of the Linux kernel later in this book. Hardware portability isn't merely an issue that affects the Linux kernel, however. Regular user applications routinely need to concern themselves with endian differences — between one machine and another and also between one Linux machine and the outside world.

---

[11]This being said, the Klingon language has no official word for "hello," so the literal translation of this example would have become roughly along the lines of "What do you want?" Typically blunt.

[12]Or possibly limited by availability of hardware. Linux community projects typically face huge problems testing their software on more esoteric platforms — though vendors are increasingly helping out whenever a large tool of interest to their users needs a little help to get ported over.

64-Bit Cleanliness

If there's one thing that this chapter should have impressed upon you up to this point, that would be that Linux is as broad as it gets. There is support for literally any and all kinds of systems in many different kinds of software configurations. As time passes, Linux is increasingly becoming popular on so called "Big Iron" machines (very large "room-sized" machines from companies like IBM and SGI), which are usually at least 64-bit systems. These days, you don't need big iron to find Linux on a 64-bit computer though. Many of the current and next generation hardware platforms are based upon 64-bit technology.

But what does 64-bit really mean? In the context of modern computer systems, it often means computers based upon an LP64 data model. This is a computer scientist's way of saying that such machines use 64-bit representation for long and pointer data types but that other data types might be stored using 32-bit representation (or indeed, some other representation — for example for use in 128-bit floating point or vector calculations).

The main issue you'll face in ensuring your code is "64-bit clean" is that of unsafe typecasts. A pointer on 32-bit machines is usually the same length as an integer, so it has become relatively common to perform horrible things that amount to the following:

```
int i = (int)some_pointer;
```

This is never a clean idea, but especially isn't a good idea on 64-bit machines where you're about to wind up with a pointer of a truncated value that'll potentially result in subtle corruption of your program's data structures at some later time. For reasons such as this, the void * type was retroactively introduced into the C standards and is supported by GCC:

```
void *p = some_pointer;
```

This ensures a safe way to store a pointer to some generic type, without casting to an int. There are many other similar examples of breakage that can happen when you move to a 64-bit machine and have gotten used to making certain assumptions (there is no real good alternative to just trying this and testing for yourself). The bottom line is that testing and ensuring that your code runs on 64-bit platforms is an excellent way of spotting and correcting bad practice that may have crept into an existing code base. You can save a lot of hassle by simply testing on a 64-bit development machine.

Endian Neutrality

"He had good Reasons to think you were a *Big-Endian* in your heart; and as Treason begins in the Heart, before it appears in Overt-Acts, so he accused you as a Traytor on that Account."

—Guilliver's Travels by Jonathan Swift.

The concept of endianess is interesting, especially if you've never encountered it before. Essentially, it boils down (pun intended — read on!) to deciding which way is up, or in the case of modern computers, which way around in memory multi-byte data structures should be stored. In a modern 32-bit or 64-bit computer system using 4-byte integer words, one can physically store numbers in memory with the most significant byte coming first or last, followed by the three remaining bytes of the number.

As Figure 3-3 shows, the number 1234 may physically be stored in the computer's memory at ascending memory locations as 1234 (big endian) or as 4321 (little endian).

Figure 3-3

It doesn't matter which storage convention is used so long as the memory is accessed consistently. The processor is internally designed to handle data stored in one format or the other so does not produce incorrect results. The bottom line is that nether storage format should affect the outcome of any calculations that are performed.

So, why is endianess an important issue? Check out the following code for an example:

```c
/*
 * Test the endianess of this machine
 */

#include <stdio.h>
#include <stdlib.h>

static inline int little_endian() {
        int endian = 1;
        return (0 == (*(char *)&endian));
}

void broken_endian_example() {

        union {
                int i;
                char j[sizeof(int)];
            } test = {0xdeadbeef};
        int i = 0;

        for (i=0;i<sizeof(int);i++) {
                printf("test.j[%d] = 0x%x\n",
                        i, test.j[i]);
        }
}

int main(int argc, char **argv)
{

        printf("This machine is ");
        little_endian() ? printf("little") : printf("big");
        printf(" endian\n");

        printf("This program was build on a machine that is: ");
#if BYTE_ORDER == BIG_ENDIAN
        printf("big endian\n");
#else
#if BYTE_ORDER == LITTLE_ENDIAN
        printf("little endian\n");
#else
        printf("something weird\n");
```

```
#endif
#endif

        printf("and here's a silly example...\n");
        broken_endian_example();

        exit(0);
}
```

You can compile this code in the standard way:

```
$ gcc -o endian endian.c
```

When this code is run on an IBM POWER5 big-endian system, the following output is obtained:

```
$ ./endian
This machine is little endian
This program was build on a machine that is: big endian
and here's a silly example...
test.j[0] = 0xde
test.j[1] = 0xad
test.j[2] = 0xbe
test.j[3] = 0xef
```

However, when it is run on a x86 (IA32) little-endian PC workstation, the following output is obtained:

```
$ ./endian
This machine is big endian
This program was build on a machine that is: little endian
and here's a silly example...
test.j[0] = 0xffffffef
test.j[1] = 0xffffffbe
test.j[2] = 0xffffffad
test.j[3] = 0xffffffde
```

Clearly, some quite different output is observed on the two different types of hardware platform. This happens because so-called system-level languages such as C allow you to have very low-level access to data structures stored within memory. By treating a 32-bit integer within a union as individual 8-bit characters, it's possible to access memory elements in such a way that you can expose the endian differences between two machines. Note, too, that accessing memory in this fashion is inefficient.

Modern computers, often being internally based on some variant of the RISC processor concept, have natural memory ordering and memory access granularity for which they have been optimized. 32-bit PowerPC microprocessors in older Apple notebooks are optimized to read/write 32-bit (or larger) data into memory in any given operation—attempting to read and write a single byte might actually require the processor to perform a full 32-bit operation and truncate to get you the byte you wanted. Things get even worse when you ask for data that doesn't fall on a natural 32-bit alignment.

The bottom line is, be careful. Always think about how your pointer arithmetic and typecasts might affect your application if it is to be used on a machine with a different endianness from that on which you have developed it. Test your code on machines of different endianness to ensure that there are no accidental bugs, and wrap your code with endian-specifc functions to work around differences. You can use GNU Autotool tests to automatically substitute in replacement functions for transparent portability.

Endian "Holy Wars"

The term endianess comes from the story *Guilliver's Travels*[13] by Jonathan Swift. In the story, Guilliver happens upon an island whose inhabitants literally do battle over the correct way to open a soft-boiled egg — using the little or the big end. The little endians and big end endians are each totally convinced that their method is the only correct method for opening an egg and cannot understand why the others won't see reality their way. While this story is amusing in and of itself, it should help you to understand how the endian question is seen among computer scientists — it's just another pointless argument.

Endianess often turns into "holy wars" because developers have their own personal views on the correct way in which computers should store numbers and refuse to accept that any other method should be used. In fact, many modern RISC computers allow data to be stored in either format — just as long as it knows which. The PowerPC is an example of an modern machine architecture where this support is mandated. Internally, most PowerPC processors are big endian (they have IBM heritage[14]) but will automatically perform conversions between big and little endian if placed into little endian mode.

This author often prefers big endian when debugging hardware, because physical memory locations contain data in a natural order that is easily readable. But in almost all other situations, there is no real practical difference between big and little endian — just as long as you know which you are (and which you are supposed to be) using in a given situation. Watch out for those network operations where you need to convert to/from network endian ordering — check out the networking chapter for further examples.

Summary

This chapter introduced you to a wide variety of topics related to writing portable software. Strictly speaking, this author views portability as it refers to "writing software such that the effort required to transport and adapt it to a new environment is less than the effort of redeveloping that same software from scratch." This definition allows for a wide interpretation of just what it means to write portable software. As you have discovered, there's more to it than carefully written source code.

Modern Linux systems are built into a wide range of distributions, each with varying capabilities. Several efforts exist that aim to allow you to produce prepackaged software that will run across the spectrum of available distributions. Standardization efforts such as the LSB — Linux Standard Base — serve to help you, but there will be times when you will have to address issues between distributions for yourself. It's not all about distribution portability either. Modern Linux software should build and run on a wide range of target machine architectures and platforms — you discovered a few tools to help.

Having read this chapter, you should feel empowered to write software for a wide range of distributions, hardware and software platforms and in many different languages for different regions of the world. You won't have learned everything you need here, but you should now have a good base on which to build your knowledge as you experiment for yourself. Take a look at some of the online guides to internationalization, help out with the Rosetta project — get involved and learn as you code!

---

[13]One of those books commonly referenced in texts such as this but seldom actually read by the authors.

[14]Traditionally, IBM is known for being "big endian" and Intel is known for inventing "little endian."

4

Software Configuration Management

Writing modern software is a complex, time-consuming process, filled with many long, repeated build cycles, bug concerns, and quality assurance issues. Developers need to keep apace of the status of an entire software project in order to ensure the reproducibility of results obtained during build and testing, and also to maintain overall productivity. As a result, software configuration management (SCM) forms a big part of the overall software development process. Choosing the right SCM solution is thus an important, potentially expensive process — especially if you were to need to switch to new tools mid-project.

Linux developers use two common and yet diametrically opposed forms of SCM. The first is based on the more traditional, centralized development model in which developers modify individual source files and pass their changes through a central system in order to preserve consistency and manage who is allowed to work on which sources at a given time. The second is truly distributed, does not rely upon any centralization, and is more suited for large, geographically distributed projects.

In this chapter, you will learn about the different types of SCM available for Linux and will experiment with a variety of implementations. You won't learn all there is to know about the tools, but you'll gain enough knowledge to find out what you don't already know by the end of the chapter. Additionally, you will learn about how integrated tools, such as the Eclipse, can be augmented with SCM capability. After reading this chapter, you'll have an understanding of a variety of different SCM tools you may encounter using Linux and the broader understanding necessary to work with various other commercial SCM tools too.

The Need for SCM

Software configuration management may be a term you have rarely encountered in the past, as is often the case when more modern terms are applied to processes that have been happening quite happily for many years. SCM can mean different things to different people, but in the context of this book, it refers to tracking and control of software development and its associated activities.

Some of the broad activities associated with SCM include:

❑   Checking sources into and out of a shared repository

❑   Synchronizing with other developers

❑   Maintaining versions (and branches)

❑   Managing builds

❑   Integrating software development processes

Most SCM solutions involve some form of source repository. In the traditional sense, a repository forms a central store for the entire project from which developers can check in and check out their individual modifications as they happen. Developers must begin by setting up a workspace for their local changes and check out whatever files they need to modify. Those changes are tested and then checked back into the repository once the particular modifications are deemed to be satisfactory.

A developer working with an SCM solution is usually involved with one or more other developers who are working on other parts of the same project (or even on the same file, in some situations). One of the primary functions of an SCM tool is, thus, to manage these individual changes and present a coherent view of the repository to developers at all times. As changes (sometimes referred to as *changesets*) come and go, the repository is updated to reflect these changes, and developers are able to ascertain whether they must update their own local view of the project to pull down recent modifications.

Once a development cycle has been completed, a typical SCM tool allows you to tag a particular state of the repository as being "good for release." This is in addition to the regular versioning, which is performed each time a source file is modified and checked back into the repository. Many tools also support a notion of branching, allowing for several different simultaneous variants of the same project. This might happen, for example, when a project must support several different platforms, and work to support these different hardware or software platforms is being performed by different teams.

As you can see, SCM is all about maintaining control over a software project. It is important to be able to visualize the entire development process as it happens, both for individual developers and for project managers and others involved in the software project. A good SCM solution is as unobtrusive and easy to use as possible as this encourages individual developers to make good use of the available tools. There is nothing more frustrating than slow and cumbersome tools that must be used on a repetitive, daily basis. The git SCM used by the Linux kernel community is one such good tool, which will be discussed later in this chapter — it is both fast and very lightweight for its level of functionality.

Centralized vs. Decentralized Development

One of the first decisions you'll face when working with SCM tools on Linux systems is not what tool to use but which *type* of tool. In the traditional, centralized situation, you would work with a central repository and use a tool such as a CVS — *concurrent versioning system* — to track changes into and out of the central repository as your work calls you to deal with specific source files within a project. In this situation, you would typically take ownership of specific parts of the project in order to avoid many conflicting modifications being made to the project sources at the same time.

In recent years, there has been a focus on decentralized SCM. This has lead to the creation of powerful tools, such as Linus Torvalds' Linux kernel SCM tool, git ("the stupid content tracker"). In decentralized SCM environments, there is no single central repository from which developers must manage all changes made to a project. Instead, each developer maintains their own project tree in which they are free to make whatever changes they like. These changes are then merged back into an upstream maintainer's tree, while conflict resolution processes help to take care of conflicting changes.

There are benefits and disadvantages offered by both approaches. A centralized system works well in a very heavily structured environment where servers are available at all times and developers are expected to follow rigorous procedures in order to submit their modifications. Decentralized SCM solutions are inherently less organized but offer the benefits of having no one single point of failure in the system, an ability to work whenever and wherever you like, and the ability to intelligently handle merging many different developer's simultaneous contributions back into a project over time.

Which tool you should use really depends upon your local development environment. If you are working as a single developer or in a small team within a single company, then it may make more sense to install and use a centralized SCM solution. There are few inherent limitations in such environments, and it is less likely for two developers to be working on exactly the same issue at the same time (most companies don't have the capacity to duplicate work on that level!), so a single developer can easily "take ownership" of a particular source file for the period of time he or she is working on it.

If you become involved in a much larger software project, either commercial or in the wider Linux community, then you may well need to consider a distributed SCM solution in order for individual developers to be as productive and independent as possible. The Linux kernel is one such project that is managed using a distributed SCM approach, but there are a growing number of other projects choosing the decentralized approach — making the code more free and open for others to work on simultaneously.

Centralized Tools

There exist a variety of centralized SCM tools that are commonly used on Linux. In fact, there are too many tools to focus on each one individually. Fortunately, most centralized tools have similar behavior and share a common set of core capabilities — though they, of course, vary in certain details. You can try out these tools for yourself and decide which one works best for you in a centralized environment.

There's no "right" or "wrong" choice here (though there are many opinions on the matter), as on some level it's a question of individual taste (and company policy) which tool you use and personally feel comfortable with. With that in mind, this section introduces you to CVS and Subversion as examples of widely used centralized SCM tools, which are used by thousands of Linux developers. These two tools between them manage some extremely large projects around the world.

The Concurrent Version System

Project website: www.nongnu.org/cvs

The Concurrent Version System (CVS) is one of the most popular (if not the most popular) SCM tools used by Linux developers today. It is also one of the oldest tools available, being loosely related to several much older revision control systems, such as the original RCS (Revision Control System) that was developed during the 1980s. It is based around a central repository that contains individual source projects under CVS control. You use the cvs driver command to interact with the repository and to the manage sources within a project.

> *Almost all Linux distributions come with CVS preinstalled as part of their development packages. If you find that CVS is not available from your workstation, try checking whether you installed the necessary development tools during installation or use another workstation for experimentation.*

Unlike many of the other tools that came before it, CVS supports *concurrent* development (the "C" in CVS). This means that developers who check out a specific source file and begin working on it do not block any other developers from doing the same. Previous version control systems required that developers explicitly flag their intention to edit a particular source file, locking it from modification by anyone else. It was, to say the least, incredibly frustrating when someone went on vacation with locked files sitting in the repository. Thus, when CVS first came on the scene, it was truly revolutionary.

Of course, CVS isn't magical. To support concurrent development there are some trade-offs. It is possible for two people to both edit the same file at the same time and for both people to wish to check in changes to the same file at around the same time. Since it isn't possible to equip CVS with black magic, it instead has a conflict resolution capability that allows the developer to compare their changes with those of another and decide how to successfully perform the integration of the combination.

To get up to speed with CVS quickly, the following sections contain some useful information about how to create and manage CVS repositories. You don't need to create your own CVS repository in order to experiment, but you'll have a greater degree of freedom if you do and you'll be able to try out ideas safe in the knowledge that nothing you do can cause any problems for someone else. As an alternative to setting up your own repository, many large open source projects are managed using CVS, so you could use the CVS server provided by your favorite open source project instead.

The popular Source Forge website (www.sourceforge.net), used by many open source projects, provides CVS server facilities to each of the projects hosted by the website and hosts a guide that explains how you can use those facilitates as an anonymous remote user. You won't be able to check changes back into a CVS repository as an anonymous user, but you can experiment nonetheless.

Creating a CVS Repository

To create your own CVS repository, you can use the following command:

```
$ cvs -d /usr/local/cvsroot init
```

This instructs CVS to create a new repository under /usr/local/cvsroot. Note that the /usr/local directory is usually protected so that only the superuser may write to it. Since you will not usually be logged into your workstation as the root user, you can either create the repository as the root user (using the sudo command in place of logging in as the root user directly) and correct the file permissions on the cvsroot directory (using the chown command – or setup a shared user group for CVS access to the central repository) or choose a different location for the repository.

> *It doesn't matter where you store the CVS repository—if you wish to have your own private CVS repository for experimentation, you could use a subdirectory of your home directory.*

The cvsroot name is significant. It is the root of the CVS managed repository, which will contain each project held under CVS control. All CVS operations will take place relative to this directory, so it's a good idea to export the CVSROOT environment variable in order to avoid having to tell CVS about the repository root each time you invoke a command:

```
$ export CVSROOT=/usr/local/cvsroot
```

Creating a New CVS project

Once a CVS repository has been created and a CVSROOT setup, you can create new CVS managed projects or import existing projects into the repository, to place them under CVS control. Typically, you will have already created a project and wish to enter it into an existing CVS repository, as in the case described here. You can use any existing project as an example, such as the example code from Chapter 2. Check the toolchains directory into your new CVS repository using the following command:

```
$ cd toolchains
$ cvs import -m "toolchains example" plp/toolchains plp start
```

You'll see output from CVS that is similar to the following (shortened for brevity):

```
cvs import: Importing /usr/local/cvsroot/plp/toolchains/src
N plp/toolchains/src/Makefile
N plp/toolchains/src/hello.c
N plp/toolchains/src/hello
I plp/toolchains/src/main.o
N plp/toolchains/src/message.c
N plp/toolchains/src/hello.s
N plp/toolchains/src/main.c
I plp/toolchains/src/message.o
N plp/toolchains/src/trig
I plp/toolchains/src/libmessage.so
N plp/toolchains/src/trig.c
N plp/toolchains/src/goodbye_shared

No conflicts created by this import
```

> *Notice how CVS displays "N" or "I" to the left of each filename that is imported. This is a code indicating the status of that file within the repository. "N" indicates that a file has been newly created on this import, while the "I", which appears next to object files such as* main.o, message.o, *and* libmessage.so, *indicates that CVS is aware these are object code files and that it is to ignore them. You can control which files are ignored by CVS via a special* .cvsignore *file, which you can later create within specific project directories. See the CVS documentation for further details.*

The preceding CVS commands import the toolchains project into the CVS repository pointed to by the $CVSROOT environment variable. The project code itself is stored within the CVS repository under the directory $CVSROOT/plp/toolchains, allowing other related projects to be grouped together under the same plp directory at a later stage. The additional use of plp in the above command occurs as a vendor tag for this project, while start specifies an initial release tag. You won't need to use these two additional tags immediately, but CVS requires them to be present when creating a new repository, so they are included in the above.

By default, when checking in any sources into a repository, CVS will launch an editor (usually determined by your $EDITOR environment variable) and give you the opportunity to enter some descriptive text for a particular check-in. By specifying the -m command line flag in the previous command, you inform CVS to use the text "toolchains example" as the message for this particular checkin and to avoid launching any external text editor. Graphical CVS tools (including extensions to the open source Eclipse IDE) will usually present whatever editor they have built-in at check-in time.

Checking Sources out of CVS

Once a project has been imported into a CVS repository, you'll need to check out the sources before you can work with it. To do this, create a new working directory and ensure that your CVSROOT environment variable is properly set (to the location of the repository previously created), then run the following command from within the working directory where the checked out sources are to be stored:

```
$ cvs co plp/toolchains
```

You can also specify the –d flag to the cvs driver command in order to override the CVSROOT variable — refer to the CVS manual page for some examples of this, including overriding the access method. It is possible, for example to inform CVS that it must authenticate using Kerberos security tickets to your secure company CVS server, or to inform CVS that it must use SSH to talk to a remote CVS server located on the other side of the planet. CVS is powerful, if you choose to make use of it.

After requesting that CVS check some sources out of the central project repository, you'll see output similar to the following as directories are created and files are checked out:

```
cvs checkout: Updating plp/toolchains/src
U plp/toolchains/src/Makefile
U plp/toolchains/src/goodbye_shared
U plp/toolchains/src/hello
U plp/toolchains/src/hello.c
U plp/toolchains/src/hello.s
U plp/toolchains/src/main.c
U plp/toolchains/src/message.c
U plp/toolchains/src/trig
U plp/toolchains/src/trig.c
```

The CVS check-out process creates a directory called plp, under which the toolchains directory contains the sources for the example project. Note how the "U" alongside the filenames indicates that the version that has been checked out from the repository has updated the local file, in this by creating it.

To check out future versions of the project, for example those that include changes made by other developers independently of yourself, you can run the following command:

```
$ cvs update
```

Any files that have changed in the central repository will be downloaded. Changes you may have made locally will be flagged at this point in order for you to resolve any conflicts. It is usually good practice to ask CVS for it to check the project out of CVS before attempting a check-in. This ensures that your changes are known to work against as recent a version of the CVS repository tree as possible. You'll learn more about actually checking in your project modifications into CVS in the next section.

Checking in Modifications

Modifying individual source files and checking them back into the central repository is easy with CVS. As an example of this, make a modification to the trivial `hello.c` C program source file (as highlighted):

```
/*
 * Professional Linux Programming - Hello World
 */

#include <stdio.h>
#include <stdlib.h>

int main(int argc, char **argv)
{

        printf("CVS is a Software Configuration Management tool!\n");

        return 0;
}
```

Build and test the program using the make command as you normally would; then check the modified file back into the CVS repository using the following command:

```
$ cvs commit
```

On this occasion, by not specifying a -m flag on the CVS command line, an editor is loaded into which you can type a short descriptive summary of the changes made (for example, "silly message added to hello world example at the request of the Bob in support"). Enter a description and save the file using whichever editor you have installed on your system.

CVS will produce output similar to the following as it finishes the commit action:

```
cvs commit: Examining .
/usr/local/cvsroot/plp/toolchains/src/hello,v   <--   hello
new revision: 1.2; previous revision: 1.1
/usr/local/cvsroot/plp/toolchains/src/hello.c,v   <--   hello.c
new revision: 1.2; previous revision: 1.1
```

Adding and Removing Files and Directories

By default, CVS will track only those files that it knows about. It won't automatically add and remove files from the repository just because they may have changed in your local version of the project. Therefore, you'll need to use the CVS `add` and `rm` commands to add and remove files and directories to and from a CVS project. Here's an example, creating a new directory and removing some older cruft:

```
$ mkdir rev2
$ cvs add rev2
Directory /usr/local/cvsroot/plp/toolchains/src/rev2 added to the repository
$ cd ..
$ rm README
$ cvs rm README
cvs remove: scheduling `README' for removal
cvs remove: use `cvs commit' to remove this file permanently
```

The removal of files or directories from a repository won't actually take place until the next CVS commit activity is performed:

```
$ cvs commit
cvs commit: Examining .
cvs commit: Examining src
/usr/local/cvsroot/plp/toolchains/README,v  <--  README
new revision: delete; previous revision: 1.1.1.1
```

Browsing CVS History

CVS maintains extensive logs of its activities as well as a complete diff between each version of a file that is checked into a repository. To view the history of a given repository, you can use the CVS `history` command. For example, to view all changes made to the file `hello.c`:

```
$ cvs history -c hello.c
M 2006-02-12 01:52 +0000 jcm 1.2 hello.c plp/toolchains/src ==
~/cvs/plp/toolchains/src
M 2006-02-12 02:19 +0000 jcm 1.3 hello.c plp/toolchains/src ==
~/cvs/plp/toolchains/src/cvs1/plp/toolchains/src
M 2006-02-12 02:29 +0000 jcm 1.4 hello.c plp/toolchains/src ==
~/cvs/plp/toolchains/src/cvs2/plp/toolchains/src
M 2006-02-12 02:30 +0000 jcm 1.5 hello.c plp/toolchains/src ==
~/cvs/plp/toolchains/src/cvs1/plp/toolchains/src
```

The option flags available with the CVS history command are documented in the CVS manual, as well as the online man and GNU info documentation.

Conflict Resolution

The true power of CVS as a concurrent development tool is in its ability to handle conflicts. A conflict arises when two developers attempt to make changes to the same file and then both developers attempt to commit their changes back into the central repository, one after the other (there is always an ordering, even if two developers commit changes together, because the repository is locked during the actual check-in operation). This situation is a conflict that cannot easily be resolved through automated action alone.

Because changes to the same source file may involve subtle semantic changes (ABI breakage, changes to locking hierarchies, and more annoying problems besides) that cannot be automatically resolved, CVS enters into a conflict resolution mode and invites you to help it to figure out how to proceed.

To test the CVS conflict resolution feature, you can create two test directories and check out two separate copies of the example project using the commands already described. Then, modify both hello.c files to print different text strings. Without updating either repository, check in one copy and then the other. Although the first check-in succeeds, the second produces the following message:

```
$ cvs commit
cvs commit: Examining .
cvs commit: Up-to-date check failed for `hello.c'
cvs [commit aborted]: correct above errors first!
```

CVS knows that the central repository has changed since you last checked out your copy of the project, and you are now attempting to commit changes back into the repository. To correct this situation, you must first run an update to synchronize your local project with the repository:

```
$ cvs update
cvs update: Updating .
RCS file: /usr/local/cvsroot/plp/toolchains/src/hello.c,v
retrieving revision 1.2
retrieving revision 1.3
Merging differences between 1.2 and 1.3 into hello.c
rcsmerge: warning: conflicts during merge
cvs update: conflicts found in hello.c
C hello.c
```

The update process notices that you have made modifications to the file hello.c and attempts to help to resolve those conflicts by modifying your copy of the file, so that you can take corrective action:

```
/*
 * Professional Linux Programming - Hello World
 */

#include <stdio.h>
#include <stdlib.h>

int main(int argc, char **argv)
{

<<<<<<< hello.c
        printf("goodbye!\n");
=======
        printf("hello!\n");
>>>>>>> 1.3

        return 0;
}
```

You can now correct the conflicting modifications and attempt another check-in, as before.

> If you find that you are experiencing an excessive number of conflicts — and consider it justified — then you can lock files against changes using CVS. While it is not recommended that you do this for every check-out, you may find that it is easier to have the option of guaranteeing you are the only person modifying a particular file on a certain occasion. Read about the CVS admin command in the CVS documentation for further information and examples on locking files with CVS.

Tagging and Branching

CVS provides a mechanism that allows you to name a particular revision of your project at a certain point in time. This is useful during project development when you need to refer to a particular development version of your application but have not released it or for other similar purposes. To create a tag, use the `tag` CVS command:

```
$ cvs tag dev_rev123
```

CVS will produce output similar to the following as it tags every file in the working directory:

```
cvs tag: Tagging src
T src/Makefile
T src/goodbye_shared
T src/hello
T src/hello.c
T src/hello.s
T src/main.c
T src/message.c
T src/trig
T src/trig.c
```

Nothing has changed in the project except that each file has been tagged as being part of a specifically named version of the project — in this case `dev_rev123`.

In addition to tagging, CVS supports a stronger mechanism for identifying obvious branch points in your project. Branches are a convenient mechanism for freezing a particular version of your project and pursuing a parallel line of development. This might occur, for example, after a new release of your application. Although you want to continue development of your project, you also wish to preserve the state of the software as it was at release time by branching away from that point.

To create a CVS branch, you can specify the remote repository location using the `rtag` command:

```
$ cvs rtag -b release_1 plp/toolchains
```

This immediately creates the branch `release_1` and does not require a CVS commit to complete.

Branches allow you to keep an older release of your software tracked in CVS, since you will need to support that release for some time into the future. Although active development may no longer take place in an older branch of the software project, a separate team can provide legacy support and provide occasional updates — for example, to correct an urgent security vulnerability in a released product.

You might be wondering what the practical difference is between branching and tagging. In many project development environments (especially corporate), branches are used on major product releases, while tags are used whenever a test build of a project is made. There may be many thousands of tagged versions of a CVS repository, but only a handful of branches — that is, essentially, how it goes.

For more information about branching and tagging, check out the CVS documentation.

Distributed Development

The examples given thus far in this section have dealt with a local CVS repository, which exists on the same machine as the developer who is working with the repository. This mode of operation is very suitable when using a shared Linux server environment, but is not so practical when large distances[1] separate developers who must connect to the central server from a remote location.

There are two easy ways to work with CVS servers remotely:

❑   CVS using an SSH connection

❑   CVS using a remote pserver

Which of these two solutions you will choose very much depends upon your local development environment and the policies of the project with which you are working. In an untrusted environment, such as is introduced when working over the Internet, the pserver approach is to be discouraged over using an SSH server. The SSH server introduces stronger accountability and has the added benefit of providing an encrypted, secured connection between the developer and the remote repository server.

CVS over an SSH Connection

You have probably encountered SSH previously since it is the preferred mechanism for remotely connecting to Linux servers that are located across a network connection. Using SSH with CVS is actually an extremely simple process, you just need to have an account on the remote SSH server hosting the CVS repository, and then you can export a single environment variable to enable SSH:

```
$ export CVS_RSH=ssh
```

This instructs CVS to connect to the repository server using the SSH protocol.

Your CVSROOT environment variable will, of course, need updating to reflect the new remote repository location. This will take the form:

```
$ export CVSROOT=username@hostname:/path/to/cvsroot
```

CVS with a Remote pserver

For those not using the SSH protocol, the less secure CVS pserver is available. This is often used by open source projects that have publicly available repositories because it is not possible to give every possible developer an account on a central repository server. This is mostly for security reasons, since it is extremely undesirable to give login credentials to untrusted, unknown third parties over the Internet.

You'll use a CVSROOT of the form: :pserver:cvs@pserver:/path/to/cvsroot to connect to a remote pserver. You'll then need to use the cvs login command to connect and authenticate:

```
$ cvs login
```

The regular CVS commands will then be available as before; there is no concept of "logging out."

---

[1]Think beyond time zones here. All kinds of issues affect community Linux project development — conferences, vacations, time zones, different work practices. On a large project, developers are checking in source changes at all times of the day and irrespective of your favorite national holiday.

As an example of the use of a pserver, you can check out the source code for the popular Samba project from any Linux workstation with CVS installed by using the following commands:

```
$ export CVSROOT=:pserver:cvs@pserver.samba.org:/cvsroot
$ cvs login
$ cvs co samba
```

Limitations

CVS has a number of limitations that have caught up with it in recent years. First and foremost, project changes are tracked on a per-file basis, rather than on a per-change basis. Often, developers change more than a single file to fix a bug or implement a new software feature, and so it is desirable to be able to visualize all of these changes together as a single changeset. With CVS, figuring out which files were modified by a set of changes is cumbersome and difficult. There are ways to work around this (by using excessive amounts of tagging, for example) but that's not entirely elegant either.

Perhaps the most severe design flaw with CVS is that it doesn't handle commits as an atomic operation. You might reasonably expect that if one developer runs a CVS commit while another simultaneously performs a CVS update or checks source out that the user performing, the update will see *all* of the repository changes or *none* of them. Unfortunately, this is not the case with CVS. It is possible for two developers to overlap their activities, at which point it can be annoying attempting to figure out what went wrong. While this isn't a situation that will arise often, you will want to watch out for it.

A final problem with CVS is that it doesn't handle file renames very well. Since changes are tied to a particular file, CVS will get very unhappy if you go changing filenames from underneath it. Varying solutions to this problem include manually hacking the repository structure, checking in the renamed file as a new file and removing the old one, and so on. As a final nail in the coffin for the longevity of CVS, its main developers now consider its various issues too ingrained to fix and have developed Subversion as a replacement. Even so, CVS is likely to be around for *many* years yet.

Subversion

Project website: `http://subversion.tigris.org`

As you learned in the previous section, Subversion is a replacement for CVS. It is designed to fix many of the issues that plagued the original design of CVS, while introducing a level of additional flexibility. Like CVS, Subversion is designed to support a centralized, shared, developer repository although it is worth drawing attention to the entirely separate `svk` project, which has created an extension on top of Subversion to support decentralized development. Thus, Subversion offers a nice bridging solution if you're not entirely sure about what form of development to use and want to hedge your bets.

Unlike CVS, Subversion stores not only version information for file contents but also metadata associated with directories, copies, and renames. It thus handles the tricky file rename problem that has plagued CVS users for many years. In addition, commits performed with Subversion are guaranteed to be atomic. It is guaranteed that no part of a commit action will take effect until the entire commit has succeeded — so there's no more developer-driven race conditions when two people try to commit and update from the same repository at precisely (well, more or less precisely) the same time.

Because CVS and Subversion can be so similar,[2] this section does not delve into the same level of detail that was the case with CVS. If you would like to know more about day-to-day usage of Subversion, you are encouraged to refer to the excellent online documentation, which is inevitably going to be more up to date than this book. Subversion is a moving target, and it really is better to find out about the latest and greatest developments directly from the project website itself.

Note that, unlike CVS, Subversion may well not be installed by default on your Linux workstation. If you find that you do not have the tools described here available on your system, check your distribution's website for any updates that may have been made available. Alternatively, consult the Subversion website directly — they provide packages for many different Linux distributions.

Creating a Subversion Repository

To create a new subversion repository, you can use the `svnadmin` command:

```
$ svnadmin create /usr/local/subrepos
```

This new repository is extremely similar to its CVS counterpart, except that the repository metadata is now stored inside BerkleyDB files rather than the older style RCS files, which are employed by CVS. You generally won't need to worry about the internal file types and structure of the repository.

Creating a New Subversion Project

Importing an existing project into a Subversion repository is easier than when working CVS. Although Subversion also can work with tags and branches, it is no longer necessary to specify any at project creation time. Instead, you simply need to tell Subversion about the directory containing the project that you wish to place under Subversion control:

```
$ svn import toolchains file:///usr/local/subrepos/trunk
```

The `/usr/local/subrepos` location has been chosen arbitrarily — you can locate your Subversion repository wherever is appropriate for your system.

Subversion will produce output similar to the following as it performs the initial import:

```
Adding          toolchains/src
Adding  (bin)   toolchains/src/hello
Adding          toolchains/src/hello.c
Adding          toolchains/src/hello.s
Adding          toolchains/src/message.c
Adding          toolchains/src/main.c
Adding  (bin)   toolchains/src/trig
Adding          toolchains/src/trig.c
Adding  (bin)   toolchains/src/libmessage.so
Adding          toolchains/src/Makefile
Adding  (bin)   toolchains/src/goodbye_shared
```

Note that this is extremely similar to the behavior with CVS, except now you can clearly see which files are binary (the "bin" in parenthesis) and which files are regular program sources (or at least not binary).

---

[2]As has been said, CVS and Subversion share many of the same developers, so this is not surprising.

Checking Sources out of Subversion

Checking sources out of a Subversion repository may seem familiar also:

```
$ svn checkout file:///usr/local/subrepos/trunk toolchains
```

The output from this process is similar to the following:

```
A    toolchains/src
A    toolchains/src/hello
A    toolchains/src/hello.c
A    toolchains/src/hello.s
A    toolchains/src/main.c
A    toolchains/src/message.c
A    toolchains/src/trig
A    toolchains/src/trig.c
A    toolchains/src/libmessage.so
A    toolchains/src/Makefile
A    toolchains/src/goodbye_shared
A    toolchains/README
Checked out revision 1.
```

Checking in Modifications

In order to test out the check-in process for Subversion, make another simple change to the previous hello.c example code:

```
/*
 * Professional Linux Programming - Hello World
 */

#include <stdio.h>
#include <stdlib.h>

int main(int argc, char **argv)
{

        printf("Subversion rocks!\n");

        return 0;
}
```

Additionally, modify the source file message.c, changing the printed message to something more appropriate to this example:

```
#include <stdio.h>

void goodbye_world(void)
{

        printf("Look! Subversion uses proper changesets!\n");
}
```

You can find out about the files that you have edited through the Subversion `status` command:

```
$ svn status
M      hello.c
M      message.c
```

Subversion knows that you have modified these two files as part of one transaction and it is ready to bunch them together as an entire changeset when it comes to committing those changes back.

Changesets

Recall from the earlier discussion of the failings present in the design of CVS that CVS works on a file-by-file basis and does not group changes into a combined entity representing all of the changes made in a single development cycle. With CVS, it is not easy to visualize all of the changes made to fix a single bug or add a new feature, but this is not a problem that plagues its successor (Subversion). To prove the point, merge your changes back into the Subversion repository using the `commit` command:

```
$ svn commit
Sending        src/hello.c
Sending        src/message.c
Transmitting file data ..
Committed revision 1.
```

The Subversion log command can be used to see all changes committed to the repository, for example, to view the files changed in revision 1:

```
$ svn log -r 1 -v
------------------------------------------------------------------------
r1 | jcm | 2006-02-12 05:19:46 +0000 (Sun, 12 Feb 2006) | 2 lines
Changed paths:
   M /trunk/src/hello.c
   M /trunk/src/message.c

checked in a bunch of files
```

You can clearly see that the related changes have been grouped together into a single entity referred to as revision 1 of the `toolchains` example project.

Distributed Development

Subversion does not use the traditional CVS pserver approach for sharing projects with a wider audience. Instead, Subversion uses the more up-to-date HTTP-based WebDAB/DeltaV protocol for network communication while the Apache web server takes can of serving out the repository itself. By relying upon Apache as its server, Subversion uses any of the authentication and compression options available to regular web pages served via Apache and does not need its own implementation.

From a regular developer's point of view, working with remote Subversion repositories is very similar to working with their CVS counterparts. For example, to check out the source for the Samba project using Subversion, you can use the following command:

```
$ svn co svn://svnanon.samba.org/samba/trunk samba-trunk
```

There is no need to log in or specify any additional options, as Subversion will take care of the rest.

Decentralized tools

Decentralized SCM tools have become very popular over the past few years, especially with Linux community projects. Developers are often spread all around the world and are working on many different issues simultaneously — often far more than can easily be tracked by a single person or by forcing every activity to go via a central server. Besides, centralized SCM solutions don't tend to work very well when you're sitting at a conference on a laptop and get a burning desire to hack some code.

There are too many different decentralized SCM projects to consider all of the candidates in a book such as this (there are, after all, whole books on the topic). By the time you read this, there may well be a completely new and revolutionary tool that has yet to be invented — take the phenomenal development of git as an example of this. The good news is that the behavior and usage of individual tools tends to be similar enough that the concepts you learn when using any one single tool can be quickly applied to others.

Most decentralized tools continue to operate on repositories — though they may not use the term — and day-to-day developer activities are very similar to what they would be when using a centralized SCM tool. While it is usual with a centralized SCM solution to have only one local copy of a remote repository, in decentralized SCM environments it is common to have many different copies of the same repository — one for each different line of development (or branch) that you are getting involved with.

The biggest difference between the two SCM approaches comes in handling the equivalent of an upstream repository commit action. In the case of a decentralized SCM, this commit process actually happens between one developer and another. Either one developer pushes changes to another, or (more likely) asks the second developer to pull down a copy of the modified repository to merge. The real power of a particular decentralized SCM is in intelligently handling merging source trees that may share a common ancestor but that have been developed heavily since they were last one tree.

It should be obvious that decentralization in the tool does not detract from some kind of centralized project management. After all, without some kind of steering, there would be no official version of a particular project. Decentralized SCMs don't try to resolve the issues of managing a large and complex project — they just make it easier for the day-to-day developer to get on with writing code. The task of actually integrating developer changes into an official release as part of a series of "pull" actions requires a little patience and a few hours of spare time once in a while to keep things in sync.

Two common tools being developed that offer the decentralized approach are Bazaar-NG (based on GNU Arch) and Linus Torvalds' "git" Linux kernel SCM tool. The former has been developed as a general solution and is being heavily used by the Canonical (Ubuntu) developers as they use Bazaar to manage a variety of other projects. The latter tool has been developed specifically for the Linux kernel. Its design initially trades features for sheer speed — git is one of the fastest SCM tools in existence. You will learn more about git later in this chapter, but first, the next section looks briefly at Bazaar.

Bazaar-NG

Bazaar-NG (bzr) is the successor to Bazaar 1.x, which was itself an attempt to build a user-friendly layer above an SCM called GNU Arch. GNU Arch is a powerful SCM tool, but it was not designed for ease of use by end users and developers.[3] Instead, GNU Arch focuses on solving interesting computer science problems concerning decentralized SCM technology. As a result, Bazaar has become quite popular, since it *is* designed with the consideration that developers must use it time and time again. Bazaar and Arch are not identical, as fragmentation has occurred, but remain broadly compatible.

Differences between GNU Arch and Bazaar-NG center on usability, for example:

❑   Bazaar can accept URLs for most commands. It is possible to directly specify a remote location as part of a `baz get` command, rather than passing additional option flags.

❑   Bazaar doesn't need to be told which repository to work with, if none is specified, it'll work with the current local source tree, whenever possible.

❑   When conflicts occur during merging, the entire project tree is marked as having a conflict. Commands like commit won't work until such conflicts are fully resolved.

Configuring Bazaar

Many decentralized SCM tools necessarily require some form of unique user identifier in order to track changes made by an individual developer and to tie those changes to a unique token when they are passed from one developer to another. There are other approaches, but Bazaar requires an email address as an identifier that will be used in all of the work you will do under the control of Bazaar.

User information is stored in a configuration file named bazzar.conf, which itself lives within the `.bazzar` subdirectory of your home directory (`$HOME/.bazaar/bazaar.conf`). You can configure a suitable email address for bazaar, as in the following example:

```
[DEFAULT]
email=jcm@jonmasters.org
```

Bazaar will now use the default identifier of jcm@jonmasters.org whenever it manipulates repositories and branches on behalf of the user account for which it has been configured.

Creating a New Bazaar Branch

You can begin working with Bazaar by copying the existing `toolchains` example code into a newly created working directory on your workstation. With the directory setup, use the `bzr init` command to place the directory under Bazaar control:

```
$ bzr init
```

---

[3]Like many other GNU projects, the idea was good but developed more for theoretical interest initially.

This will create the `.bzr` directory within your project sources that is used by Bazaar as it tracks changes made to your project.

To actually track a file, or files within Bazaar, you need to add them using the `bzr add` command:

```
$ bzr add .
```

You'll see output from Bazaar as it adds each file within your project, viz.:

```
added src/Makefile
added src/hello.c
added src/hello
added src/message.c
added src/hello.s
added src/main.c
added src/trig
added src/trig.c
added src/goodbye_shared
ignored 4 file(s) matching "*.o"
ignored 2 file(s) matching "*.so"
If you wish to add some of these files, please add them by name.
```

As an alternative to creating your own repository, you can specify the URL of an existing Bazaar repository and Bazaar will attempt to download it.

Note that Bazaar automatically ignored several object files and library files during the add operation. Like CVS, Bazaar knows about several standard file extensions that it should generally ignore when performing such sweeping operations—most people don't track versions of binary prebuilt libraries in their SCM system, though it might be prudent to do so in some cases (for example, when tracking ABI changes between different library versions using some form of automated tool based around the SCM).

Checking in Modifications

Although Bazaar is a decentralized SCM solution, it nonetheless supports the concept of committing changes into your local project branch. When you edit files within a project that is under Bazaar control, these changes won't automatically persist as part of the Bazaar branch you have created. In order to maintain a record of modifications within Bazaar, it is necessary to perform a commit. You can try this for yourself by making another trivial modification to the `hello.c` example source and checking that change back into the Bazaar repository:

```
$ bzr commit -m "modified hello.c"
Committed revision 1.
```

Like Subversion and other recent SCM tools, Bazaar works in units of changesets, so you'll see just one revision for every set of source files that you modify in one go. You can use the `bzr log` command to review your repository history, much as you could with the tools discussed previously:

```
$ bzr log -v
------------------------------------------------------------
revno: 2
committer: Jon Masters <jcm@jonmasters.org>
```

```
branch nick: toolbaz
timestamp: Sun 2006-02-12 09:55:34 +0000
message:
  changeset
modified:
  src/hello.c
  src/trig.c
```

Merging Bazaar Branches

When working with projects managed using Bazaar, where you have made your own modifications to your local branch and wish to integrate those changes alongside an outside Bazaar branch, you can use the bzr merge command. This command takes the location of another Bazaar repository as an argument and attempts to merge your local changes with any included in the other repository. For an example, you can create a second create a copy of your existing Bazaar branch, modify both copies, and then attempt to merge the trees together — it's a little contrived, but suffices to simulate real-life merges.

To copy your existing Bazaar branch, you can use the branch command:

```
$ bzr branch toolchains toolchains1
```

Next, to test out conflict resolution in action, modify both projects and commit those changes with bzr commit. Now you can try to use the merge command to attempt to rejoin these separated trees:

```
$ bzr merge ../toolbaz1
bzr: WARNING: Diff3 conflict encountered in
     /home/jcm/toolchains/./src/hello.c
1 conflicts encountered.
```

In this case, Bazaar has determined that incompatible changes were made to the same file (hello.c) in both repositories. To resolve this, Bazaar creates two additional files, hello.c.BASE (the original hello.c) and hello.c.OTHER (the merge candidate) in addition to modifying the original hello.c source, annotating it with the incompatible modification:

```
/*
 * Professional Linux Programming - Hello World
 */

#include <stdio.h>
#include <stdlib.h>

int main(int argc, char **argv)
{

<<<<<<< TREE
        printf("Bazaar1!\n");
=======
        printf("Bazaar2!\n");
>>>>>>> MERGE-SOURCE


        return 0;
}
```

Your job is to decide which change is kept, clean up `hello.c`, and remove (or rename) both `hello.c.BASE` and `hello.c.OTHER` before Bazaar will allow you to perform the merge, as well as many other management commands that are temporarily unavailable while a "conflict" is in place.

Linux kernel SCM (git)

Project website: `www.kernel.org/pub/software/scm/git`

For the past few years, the Linux kernel has been developed using a proprietary SCM tool known as BitKeeper. This tool has been made available to the kernel developer community on a zero-cost basis and was regarded as singularly responsible for many of the gains in developer productivity achieved in recent times. Using BitKeeper, a decentralized SCM tool, it was possible for developers to quickly and efficiently work with extremely large numbers of changesets — and many individual changesets include dozens of files at a time — without the performance issues other SCM solutions would have faced.

The Linux kernel is an extremely large and active software project, which has hundreds of contributors and many more testers and third parties working on it besides that. As of this writing, the size of the total changesets on any given month for the Linux kernel can be around 30MB. This is larger than the entire kernel was for many years during its early development and now represents only a month's worth of development. As you can no doubt imagine, a lot of work goes into those kernel development cycles.

For various complicated reasons, use of the proprietary BitKeeper solution was abruptly terminated in April 2005, leaving the kernel developers urgently seeking a replacement. When none could be found that any of the developers (chiefly Linus Torvalds, the creator of the Linux kernel) could agree on, Linus Torvalds decided to disappear for a few days and write his own. Less than a week later, git was born. Git is an extremely fast object-based SCM that can be used to manage large projects, such as the Linux kernel, very efficiently indeed. It is now used by a growing number of nonkernel projects too.

The pace of development of git has been nothing short of phenomenal. At the beginning of April 2005, nobody had ever heard of git, yet within a few months it was in widespread use and had become the "official" tool used to manage kernel releases. Within a matter of weeks after the initial release of git, a wide variety of other tools had been created. First came the "easy to use" front ends, then the graphical repository browsers, and finally the whole suite of tools and utilities that are available today.

Git is primarily designed for use by kernel hackers, so you'll probably use it for that purpose if you use it at all. This section includes a brief description of the processes involved in creating a repository from scratch, but most of the time when working with the Linux kernel you will clone an existing publicly available git source tree in order to make modifications to an existing set of public kernel sources.

> *Git doesn't ship as a standard installation package on most distributions as of this writing, but it is likely to quickly become a standard feature that will be present in future. In the meantime, you can obtain the current release of git from the website, both in source and in various prepackaged forms.*

Everything Is an Object

When it comes to git, everything's an object. This is because git is really an extremely fast object-based filesystem that just so happens to also offer a level of software configuration management. When Linus initially created git, he was interested in solving the problem of rapidly cloning a kernel tree from one place to another or pulling out all of the changes in a particular changeset without having to wait an entire afternoon for the process to complete. This was one major reason why existing SCMs weren't deemed to be up to managing the Linux kernel — they were too slow for kernel developers to use.

When a file is checked into a git repository, it is stored as the SHA1 hash of its current contents. Git employs an extremely efficient sorted directory hierarchy under the `.git` directory within your project with each of these objects living in `.git/objects`. Each time a file modification is checked into the repository, a new copy of the file is stored as an entirely new object — the old object is simply discarded. This is an intentional design decision made in the interest of boosting speed for developers, while at the same time consuming (small) additional amounts of disk space for each changeset being checked into the repository over and above that used by other common SCM solutions.

Git vs. Cogito

Git comes in various different forms. The standard git distribution consists of over 100 simple utilities that collectively offer the necessary functionality to developers. You may find yourself quite comfortable using git from the outset. For those who don't, there are various front-end utilities that wrap around git and aim to offer a more pleasant developer experience. By far the most popular of these tools, as of this writing, is called Cogito. In the examples that follow, you can easily substitute the appropriate Cogito commands by reading the excellent online documentation that accompanies it.

Creating a New git Repository

You can begin working with git by creating your own repository from an existing code base. To try out the git SCM for yourself, copy the example source code from Chapter 2 once again. This time, place the directory into a new location and then create a new git repository from those sources:

```
$ cd toolchains
$ git-init-db
defaulting to local storage area
$ git-add .
$ git commit
```

You'll be asked to type a few words for posterity after asking for the commit. In the newly opened editor window, you can see a list of files that will be altered by this commit action. In this case, git informs you that every file in the repository will be affected because the repository has just been created. After you enter a commit message when prompted, git will confirm the commit:

```
Committing initial tree 370eeb1d55789681888d29c4bb85c21ef6cd6317H
```

Git has created a new object, 370eeb1d55789681888d29c4bb85c21ef6cd6317H, which represents the initial state of the source tree when it is created. Additionally, these actions will have resulted in git creating the `.git` directory and populating it as well as its internal object database.

Cloning an Existing git Repository

Most of the time that you spend working with git (if indeed you work with git at all) will be spent working on git repository trees being supplied by someone else. This might be a specific developer's tree, but you are more likely to be working with a local copy of, for example. the official Linux kernel sources, which are managed using git. You will make some changes and then send those (or request that they be pulled from you) back to the upstream project community, who will then deal with releasing the kernel.

To obtain your own copy of the latest Linux kernel for the purpose of git experimentation, create a new directory and pull down the official Linux kernel git tree via the aptly named `git pull` command:

```
$ mkdir linux-2.6
$ cd linux-2.6
$ git pull rsync://rsync.kernel.org/pub/scm/linux/kernel/git/torvalds/linux-2.6.git
```

You will now have a full copy of the 2.6 Linux kernel in a directory called linux-2.6.

It is also possible to clone your local git tree and create another copy using the `git clone` command:

```
$ git clone toolchains toolchains1
defaulting to local storage area
Packing 38 objects
```

This might be especially useful in the case that you were pursuing many different lines of experimentation with a set of sources and wanted to keep your modifications separate.

Managing Sources with git

If you modify a file within your local git repository and wish to have this change checked back in to git (so that it can manage your local git repository tree), you can use the `git-update-index` and `git-commit` commands to do this:

```
$ git-update-index src/hello.c
$ git-commit
```

To see a list of all the commits made to a particular repository, you can use the `git-whatchanged` command:

```
diff-tree 78edf00... (from c2d4eb6...)
Author: Jon Masters <jcm@perihelion.(none)>
Date:   Sun Feb 12 11:18:43 2006 +0000

    modified hello

:100644 100644 b45f4f6... d1378a6... M  src/hello.c

diff-tree c2d4eb6... (from f77bb2b...)
Author: Jon Masters <jcm@perihelion.(none)>
Date:   Sun Feb 12 11:10:14 2006 +0000

    foo

:100644 100644 3c13431... b45f4f6... M  src/hello.c
```

Git as a Debugging Aid

SCM tools have uses beyond those that might at first be apparent. This is especially true when it comes to debugging a project as large as the Linux kernel. Often, a bug report will come into the LKML (Linux Kernel Mailing List) describing how some version of the Linux kernel failed in some fashion when run on a particular machine under certain circumstances (actually many bug reports are far less detailed that that — but kernel developers are ever optimistic of receiving well-written bug reports).

When a particular release of the Linux kernel is known to be "bad," it is normally necessary to begin the debugging process by looking at the last kernel version that *did* work normally for the person reporting the bug. Often, there will be some number of releases between the last known-good kernel and one that does not work correctly. The debugging process thus starts out with a binary search algorithm — trying various kernels until the exact one that introduced a broken changeset is discovered.

Since this binary search debugging approach is so common, git actually includes special functionality to make the process less time-consuming and painful for kernel developers. The `git bisect` command allows you to educate git about specific known-good and known-bad versions. Begin with:

```
$ git bisect start
```

Then educate git about the bad and good kernel versions as follows:

```
$ git bisect bad v2.6.16

$ git bisect good v2.6.15
```

Git will find whatever commit took place exactly halfway between 2.6.15 and 2.6.16 and populate the local directory with this version of the kernel sources, which you can then build, test boot, and mark as good or bad via the "git bisect good" or "git bisect bad" commands. The process continues ad nauseum until eventually git will identify the precise patch that introduced the behavior being experienced.

Integrated SCM Tools

A variety of tools are available that attempt to integrate the various SCM functionality you have learned about in this chapter. Integrated tools are often ideal, because they remove the chore of explicitly calling an SCM tool for yourself while you are developing your software and free up your time to concentrate instead on the issues that really matter — developing code, that kind of thing.

Eclipse

Graphical tools such as those based on the powerful and open source Eclipse framework provide a great opportunity to integrate all of the SCM functionality described in this chapter with a visual IDE tool. You have already learned how powerful Eclipse can be, thanks to the wide array of modules that have been written for it and will know that if there's a feature you want as a developer, then there's a good chance someone has at least attempted to create an eclipse plugin for it. This is true of SCM tools as much as language support, or anything else.

Eclipse provides out-of-the-box support for CVS repositories, while third-party support plugins exist for Subversion (called Subclipse) and various other commercial SCM tools besides. As of this writing, work is in progress on a plugin for GNU Arch and a plugin for the git Linux kernel SCM tool. Whatever SCM you decide to standardize on, there's a good chance there's an Eclipse plugin.

The CVS Repository Perspective

The Eclipse CVS repository perspective can be located via the perspectives menu. Once loaded, eclipse displays a list of known CVS repositories in the left-hand Repositories pane, which is initially empty. To add a new CVS repository, right-click on the CVS Repositories pane and select New and then Repository Location.

A dialog similar to that shown in Figure 4-1 will appear.

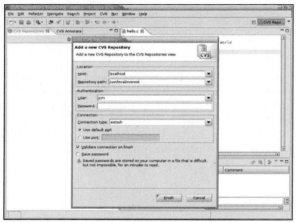

Figure 4-1

You should enter the appropriate details for your CVS server into the box and click on Finish to add this as a new CVS repository, which will then show up in the CVS Repositories pane in Eclipse.

Placing a Project under CVS Control

A typical use for the CVS repository is to place an existing Eclipse project under CVS control. You can do this by switching back to the C/C++ perspective (or whichever language perspective you had selected previously) and right-clicking on the project name in the left-hand pane. Click on the Team menu item and then Share Project. A wizard automatically loads and lists the CVS repository previously configured. You should choose the correct CVS repository from the list presented and complete the wizard.

A dialog similar to that shown in Figure 4-2 will appear.

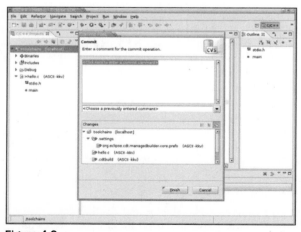

Figure 4-2

Commit the project into the CVS repository and allow the process to complete. Once the main Eclipse window is visible once more, you'll see the project exactly as it was before, but it will now be shared via CVS. You'll see the current CVS version number and other metadata is displayed right alongside the filename, so it's easy to track the current state of your project without having to dig around.

Controlling a CVS Repository

You'll see that a new set of items has appeared in the context menu that appears when you right-click on a source file within your Eclipse project. From this menu, you can now commit file changes to the CVS repository, pull down updates, and handle tagging and branching conveniently. In fact, you can perform all of the available CVS commands from within the CVS perspective. For more information, check out the online Eclipse documentation and the manuals which came with your particular version of Eclipse.

Summary

This chapter introduced you to a several software configuration management (SCM) tools that are available on Linux systems and that can be used in your own software projects. You learned about the processes involved in managing source code and handling revisions, branches, and other version information, while at the same time discovering the flexibility available from some of these tools.

SCM tools can be broken down into those that are specifically targeted at decentralized software development and those that aren't. You learned how different tools benefit different projects in accordance with their specific requirements. The Linux kernel hackers were one group that was so unable to agree on an existing SCM tool that they wound up writing their own!

Writing your own SCM is very much an extreme step, but the point remains — each person has their own personal preference and differing tastes in software and tools used in the development process. Some people prefer simpler tools; some prefer having a graphical front end through an Eclipse plugin. The question of which SCM tool you should use in your own projects remains very much up to you.

5

Network Programming

In today's world, it is not uncommon to have your Linux workstation or server connected to a network. It has become almost a necessity for applications to be network-capable. Knowing how to pass data between network devices is a crucial skill for the professional Linux programmer.

This chapter shows how to add network capabilities to your Linux programs using two different methods. The first method demonstrates how to perform raw socket programming, directly interfacing with the Linux network subsystem. Using this method, you can program any communications protocol required to communicate with any network device.

The second method demonstrates how to utilize prepackaged network programming libraries within your applications. Prepackaged network libraries provide the network programming functions already for you. All you need to do is interface with the library to interact with network devices using common network protocols.

Linux Socket Programming

The UNIX operating system provided many features that revolutionized many things in the programming world. One of these features was file descriptors. A file descriptor provides a programming interface to a file object. Since nearly every object contained in a UNIX system is defined as a file, a file descriptor can be used to send and receive data with lots of different objects on the UNIX system. This makes life much simpler for UNIX (and now Linux) programmers. The same type of programming model works no matter what type of device you are trying to access.

Starting in the 4.2BSD UNIX release, network access has also been defined using file descriptors. Sending data to a remote device across a network is as easy as sending data to a local file. Linux utilizes network file descriptors to allow programs to access the networking subsystem. This section describes how to utilize the different features of Linux network programming.

Sockets

In Linux network programming, you do not need to directly access the network interface device to send and receive packets. Instead, an intermediary file descriptor is created to handle the programming interface to the network. The Linux operating system handles the details of which network interface device the data should be sent out, and how it should be sent.

The special file descriptors used to reference network connections are called *sockets*. The socket defines a specific communication domain (such as a network connection or a Linux Interprocess Communication (IPC) pipe), a specific communication type (such as stream or datagram), and a specific protocol (such as TCP or UDP). Once the socket is created, you must bind the socket either to a specific network address and port on the system (for a server application) or to a remote network address and port (for a client application). After the socket is bound, it can be used to send and receive data from the network. Figure 5-1 shows an example of what this looks like.

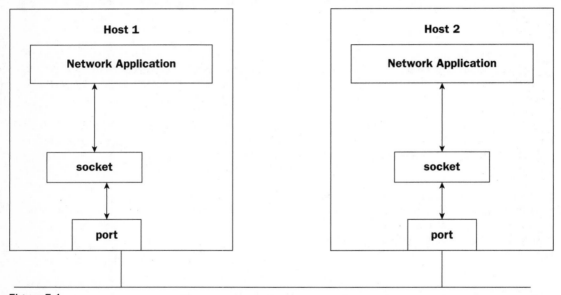

Figure 5-1

The socket becomes the middleman between the application and the network interface on the system. All network data passes through the socket. Linux provides the `socket` C function to create new sockets:

```
int socket(int domain, int type, int protocol)
```

The `socket()` function returns a socket descriptor, which can then be used to send and receive data from the network (but more on that later). The three parameters that are used to create the socket define the communications *domain*, *type*, and *protocol* used. The possible *domain* values that can be use are listed in the following table.

VALUE	DESCRIPTION
PF_UNIX	UNIX IPC communication
PF_INET	IPv4 Internet protocol
PF_INET6	IPv6 Internet protocol
PF_IPX	Novell protocol
PF_NETLINK	Kernel user interface driver
PF_X25	ITU-T X.25 /ISO-8208 protocol
PF_AX25	Amateur radio AX.25 protocol
PF_ATMPVC	Access to raw ATM PVC's
PF_APPLETALK	Appletalk protocol
PF_PACKET	Low-level packet interface

For IP communications, the PF_INET value should be used. The *type* value defines the type of network communication used for transmitting the data packets on the domain. The valid *type* values that can be used are shown in the following table.

VALUE	DESCRIPTION
SOCK_STREAM	Use connection-oriented communication packets.
SOCK_DGRAM	Use connectionless communication packets.
SOCK_SEQPACKET	Use connection-oriented packets with a fixed maximum length.
SOCK_RAW	Use raw IP packets.
SOCK_RDM	Use a reliable datagram layer that does not guarantee ordering.

The two most popular *type* values used for IP communications are SOCK_STREAM, for connection-oriented communication, and SOCK_DGRAM, for connectionless communication.

The specific *protocol* value used to create the socket depends on which type value you choose. Most types (such as SOCK_STREAM and SOCK_DGRAM) can only be safely used with their default protocols (TCP for SOCK_STREAM, and UDP for SOCK_DGRAM). To specify the default protocol, you can place a zero value in the *protocol* parameter instead of a normal protocol value.

Using these guidelines, creating a socket in Linux for network communication is fairly straightforward:

```
int newsocket;
newsocket = socket(PF_INET, SOCK_STREAM, 0);
```

This example creates a standard TCP socket for transferring data to a remote host using connection-oriented streams. Creating the socket itself does not define where the socket will connect. That will come later.

Once the socket is created, you can reference it using the returned file descriptor value; in the preceding example it is the `newsocket` variable.

Network Addresses

After the socket is created it must be bound to a network address/port pair. The way that the Linux socket system uses IP addresses and TCP or UDP ports is one of the more confusing parts of network programming. A special C structure is used to designate the address information.

The `sockaddr` structure contains two elements:

❑   `sa_family`: An address family (defined as a short type)

❑   `sa_data`: An address for a device (defined as 14 bytes)

The `sa_data` element is designed to allow the `sockaddr` structure reference many different types of network addresses. Because of this, the 14-byte address element is difficult to use directly. Instead, Linux provides an IP-specific address structure, `sockaddr_in`, which uses the following elements:

❑   `sin_family`: An address family (defined as a short type)

❑   `sin_port`: A port number (defined as a short type)

❑   `sin_addr`: An address (defined as a long type [4-byte] IP address)

❑   `sin_data`: 8 bytes of padding

For IP communications, the `sin_family` element should be set to the `AF_INET` value, to indicate the Internetwork family of addresses. The `sin_port` and `sin_addr` values are also a little different from what you might expect.

One of the big problems with referencing addresses and ports in Linux is the byte order. Since different systems represent bytes in different orders (high bit versus low bit first), Linux includes function calls to ensure the address and port values are in a consistent format. The `htons()` function converts a value represented on the host to a generic network order for short values. Since the port value is represented as a short, this function works for converting port values for the `sin_port` element.

There are several different methods to use to convert an IP address to network byte order. The simplest is the `inet_addr()` function. This function converts a string representation of a dotted decimal IP address to a long type in network order. If the IP address is represented by a host name, you must use the `gethostbyname()` function to retrieve the associated IP address for the host name.

Using these functions, the code to obtain an IP address/port pair for a host would be:

```
sruct sockaddr_in myconnection;
memset(&myconnection, 0, sizeof(myconnection));
myconnection.sin_family = AF_INET;
myconnection.sin_port = htons(8000);
myconnection.sin_addr.s_addr = inet_addr("192.168.1.1");
```

After creating the `sockaddr_in` variable `myconnection`, it is a good idea to make sure that all of the elements are zeroed out, thus the call to `memset()`. After that, the individual elements are defined. Note that the `sin_addr` element also uses elements to define the address. The `s_addr` element is used to represent the IP address. The `inet_addr()` function is used to convert a text IP numeric address into the IP address structure used by `s_addr`.

Now that you know how to define IP address/port pairs, you can match the sockets to an IP address and start moving data. The socket interface uses different function calls depending on whether the socket is connection-oriented or connectionless. The following sections describe how to use these two methods.

Using Connection-Oriented Sockets

In a connection-oriented socket (one that uses the `SOCK_STREAM` Type) the TCP protocol is used to establish a session (connection) between two IP address endpoints. The TCP protocol guarantees delivery (barring a network failure) of data between the two endpoints. There is a fair amount of overhead involved with establishing the connection, but once it is established data can be reliably transferred between the devices.

To create a connection-oriented socket, a separate sequence of functions must be used for server programs and client programs. Figure 5-2 shows the sequence of functions for each type of program.

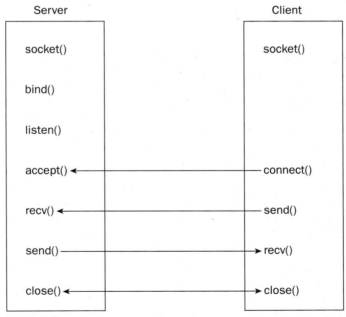

Figure 5-2

The following sections detail the events that distinguish a server program from a client program.

The Server Functions

For the server program, the created socket must be bound to a local IP address and port number that will be used for the TCP communication. The Linux bind() function is used to accomplish this:

```
int bind(int socket, sockaddr *addr, int length);
```

The *socket* parameter references the return value from the socket() function. The *addr* parameter references a sockaddr address/port pair to define the local network connection. Since the server usually accepts connections on its own IP address, this is the IP address of the local device, along with the assigned TCP port for the application. If you do not know the IP address of the local system, you can use the INADDR_ANY value to allow the socket to bind to any local address on the system. The *length* parameter defines the length of the sockaddr structure. An example of this is:

```
struct sockaddr_in myaddr;
bind(s, (struct sockaddr *)&my_addr, sizeof(struct sockaddr));
```

The bind() function returns an integer value of -1 if it fails, or 0 if it succeeds. This can be checked using a standard if statement.

After binding the socket to an address and port, the server program must be ready to accept connections from remote clients. This is a two-step process.

The program must first use the listen() to begin listening for client connection attempts, then the accept() function to actually accept a connection attempt from a client. The format of the listen() function is:

```
int listen(int socket, int backlog);
```

As expected, the *socket* parameter refers to the socket descriptor created with the socket() function. The *backlog* parameter refers to the number of pending connections the system can accept waiting to be processed. If this value is set to 2, two separate client attempts to connect to the port will be accepted. One will be immediately processed, and one will be placed on hold, waiting for the first to finish. If a third connection attempt arrives, the system refuses it, since the backlog value has already been met.

After the listen() function, the accept() function must be called to wait for incoming connections. The accept() function is a blocking function. Program execution will halt at the accept() function until a connection attempt is made from a client device. The format of the accept() function is:

```
int accept(int socket, sockaddr *from, int *fromlen);
```

By now you should recognize the *socket* parameter. The *from* and *fromlen* parameters point to a sockaddr address structure and its length, respectively. The remote address information from the client is stored in this structure, so you can access it if necessary.

When a connection is accepted, the accept() function returns a new socket file descriptor. This new socket is then used to communicate with the remote client. The original socket created by the socket() function can still be used to listen for additional client connections.

Once the connection has been accepted, the server can send or receive data from the client using the new socket file descriptor, and the send() or recv() function calls:

```
int send(int socket, const void *message, int length, int flags)
int recv(int socket, void *message, int length, int flags)
```

The *socket* parameters again reference the newly opened socket from the accept() function for the connection. The *message* parameter references either the buffer of data to send or an empty buffer to receive data into. The *length* parameter indicates the size of the buffer, and the *flags* parameter indicates if any special flags are necessary (such as if you want to tag the data as urgent in the TCP packet). For normal TCP communication, the *flags* parameter should be set to 0.

The send() function does not block program execution. The buffer data is sent to the underlying TCP transport on the system, and the function finishes. It is possible that the entire buffer of data defined in the send() function may not all be sent. The send() function returns an integer value indicating how many bytes of data were sent to the transport buffer. It is important to check to make sure that this value matches the buffer size to ensure that all of the data has been sent.

The recv() function is a blocking function. Program execution will halt until either the recv() function receives data from the remote client, or the remote client cleanly disconnects the TCP session. If the client disconnects the session, the recv() function will return with a 0 value. If the client sends a data packet, the recv() function places the data into the defined buffer, and returns the number of bytes received.

When designing a client and server application, it is important to synchronize the sending and receiving functions. If both the server and client are waiting on recv() functions, they will deadlock and no communication will occur.

Here is an example of a typical server. The tcpserver.c program shown in Listing 5-1 demonstrates a simple server that accepts a connection on TCP port 8000 and echoes back any data it receives.

Listing 5-1: A simple TCP server

```c
/*
 * Professional Linux Programming - Simple TCP server
 *
 */
#include <stdio.h>
#include <sys/types.h>
#include <sys/socket.h>
#include <netinet/in.h>
#include <arpa/inet.h>

int main(argc, argv)
{
        int s, fd, len;
        struct sockaddr_in my_addr;
        struct sockaddr_in remote_addr;
        int sin_size;
```

(continued)

Listing 5-1: *(continued)*

```
        char buf[BUFSIZ];

        memset(&my_addr, 0, sizeof(my_addr));
        my_addr.sin_family = AF_INET;
        my_addr.sin_addr.s_addr = INADDR_ANY;
        my_addr.sin_port = htons(8000);

        if ((s = socket(AF_INET, SOCK_STREAM, 0)) < 0)
        {
                perror("socket");
                return 1;
        }

        if (bind(s,(struct sockaddr *)&my_addr,sizeof(struct sockaddr))<0)
        {
                perror("bind");
                return 1;
        }

        listen(s, 5);
        sin_size = sizeof(struct sockaddr_in);
        if ((fd =accept(s,(struct sockaddr *)&remote_addr,&sin_size)) < 0)
        {
                perror("accept");
                return 1;
        }
        printf("accepted client %s\n", inet_ntoa(remote_addr.sin_addr));
        len = send(fd, "Welcome to my server\n", 21, 0);
        while ((len = recv(fd, buf, BUFSIZ, 0)) > 0)
        {
                buf[len] = '\0';
                printf("%s\n", buf);
                if (send(fd, buf, len, 0) < 0)
                {
                        perror("write");
                        return 1;
                }
        }
        close(fd);
        close(s);
        return 0;
}
```

Notice that the `tcpserver.c` program uses several header files. These define the functions and data types used to handle network connection, and must be included in all network programs.

The `tcpserver.c` program first creates a socket using the `socket()` function, then binds the socket to TCP port 8000 on the local host using any local address. The `listen()` function is then used to listen for new connection attempts, allowing up to five connections to wait before refusing additional connections.

After the `listen()` function, the server program waits for a connection attempt at the `accept()` function. When a connection attempt occurs, the `accept()` function returns a new socket file descriptor, representing the new remote client connection. The original file descriptor can still be used to accept other client connections.

The new client connection is then used to send and receive data. The server first sends a welcome message to the client. Next, the server goes into a `while` loop, waiting for data from the client. If data is received, it is displayed on the console and then sent back to the client. Notice that when data is received, the buffer size returned by the `recv()` function is used to place a terminating NULL character in the buffer. This ensures that each string received is properly terminated.

When the remote client closes the connection, the `recv()` function returns with a value of zero. This is used to exit the while loop.

No special libraries are needed to compile the `tcpserver.c` program; just compile it as you would any other C program and run:

```
$ cc -o tcpserver tcpserver.c
$ ./tcpserver
```

The `tcpserver` program starts, then waits for a client to connect. To test the server, start another session on the Linux system (or another Linux system on the network), and Telnet to port 8000 on the server. If you are connecting from the same system, you can use the special `localhost` network address to reference the same server:

```
$ telnet localhost 8000
Trying 127.0.0.1...
Connected to localhost.localdomain.
Escape character is '^]'.
Welcome to my server
test
test
This is another test.
This is another test.
goodbye.
goodbye.
^]
telnet> quit
Connection closed.
$
```

The server accepts the connection, and sends its welcome message, which is displayed by the Telnet program. After that, the server echoes back any text you type. To end the session, press Ctrl-], then type `quit`. The client session terminates the TCP session, and the server program also terminates (due to the `recv()` function receiving a 0 value).

The Client Functions

In connection-oriented applications, the client must connect to a specific host address and port for the application. If you know the IP address of the remote client, you can use the `inet_addr()` function to convert it into the proper format:

```
remote_addr.sin_family = AF_INET;
remote_addr.sin_addr.s_addr = inet_addr("127.0.0.1");
remote_addr.sin_port = htons(8000);
```

In a client program, you must use the `socket()` function to establish a proper communications socket, but after the socket is created a `connect()` function is used instead of the `bind()` function. The `connect()` function attempts to establish a connection to a remote network device using a `sockaddr` address/port pair supplied:

```
int connect(int socket, sockaddr *addr, int addrlen);
```

The *socket* parameter again references the created `socket()` function value, while the *addr* parameter points to a created `sockaddr` structure containing the IP address and TCP port number of the remote network device you intend to communicate with.

If the `connect()` function fails, it returns a value of -1. If it succeeds, the client is connected to the server and can use the standard `send()` and `recv()` functions on the socket file descriptor to transmit data back and forth with the server.

The `tcpclient.c` program in Listing 5-2 demonstrates a simple client application.

Listing 5-2: A simple TCP client

```
/*
 *
 * Professional Linux Programming - Simple TCP client
 *
 */
#include <stdio.h>
#include <sys/types.h>
#include <sys/socket.h>
#include <netinet/in.h>
#include <arpa/inet.h>

int main(argc, argv)
{
        int s, len;
        struct sockaddr_in remote_addr;
        char buf[BUFSIZ];

        memset(&remote_addr, 0, sizeof(remote_addr));
        remote_addr.sin_family = AF_INET;
        remote_addr.sin_addr.s_addr = inet_addr("127.0.0.1");
        remote_addr.sin_port = htons(8000);

        if ((s = socket(AF_INET, SOCK_STREAM, 0)) < 0)
        {
                perror("socket");
                return 1;
        }

        if (connect(s, (struct sockaddr *)&remote_addr, sizeof(struct sockaddr)) < 0)
        {
```

```
                perror("connect");
                return 1;
        }

        printf("connected to server\n");
        len = recv(s, buf, BUFSIZ, 0);
        buf[len] = '\0';
        printf("%s", buf);
        while(1)
        {
                printf("Enter string to send: ");
                scanf("%s", buf);
                if (!strcmp(buf, "quit"))
                        break;
                len = send(s, buf, strlen(buf), 0);
                len = recv(s, buf, BUFSIZ, 0);
                buf[len] = '\0';
                printf("  received: %s\n", buf);
        }

        close(s);
        return 0;
}
```

The `tcpclient.c` program is designed to work with the `tcpserver.c` program presented earlier. It creates a socket and attempts a connection to TCP port 8000 on the local host. If the connection is successful, a message is displayed, and the `recv()` function is used to receive the welcome message that is sent by the server. When receiving string values from a network connection, you should append the terminating NULL character:

```
        len = recv(s, buf, BUFSIZ, 0);
        buf[len] = '\0';
        printf("%s", buf);
```

After receiving the welcome message, the client program goes into a `while()` loop, asking for a string to send, then using the `send()` function to send it to the server. The `scanf()` function is not necessarily a good choice for production programs, as it is susceptible to a buffer overflow exploit, but it will work just fine for this test.

Since the server echoes back what it receives, the client then uses the `recv()` function to receive the string echoed back. Again, the string is terminated with a NULL character before being used in the `printf()` function.

When the client program detects that the string "quit" has been entered, it closes the connection with the server, which forces the server program to terminate.

Closing the Connection

In both the `tcpserver.c` and `tcpclient.c` programs, you may have noticed that at the end of the program the created sockets were closed using the standard `close()` function call. While this is perfectly acceptable, sockets have another function that can be used to accomplish this feature with more precision.

The shutdown() function can be used with socket file descriptors to specify how the communication session should be terminated. The format of the shutdown() function is:

```
shutdown(int socket, int how)
```

The shutdown() function uses the *how* parameter to allow you to determine how gracefully the connection will close. The options available are:

- ❏ **0:** No more packets can be received.
- ❏ **1:** No more packets can be sent.
- ❏ **2:** No more packets can be sent or received.

By selecting values 0 or 1, you can disable the socket from receiving or sending more data, but allow the socket to either finish sending pending data, or finish receiving pending data. After the connection has a chance to flush out any pending data, the close() function can be called to terminate the connection without any data loss.

Using Connectionless Sockets

In the connection-oriented socket world, the connect() function is used by a client to establish a TCP connection with the server. Connectionless sockets do not create a dedicated connection between the network devices. Instead, messages are "thrown out onto the network" in the hope that they make it to the desired destination. The benefit of connectionless sockets is that there is much less overhead involved in moving data. Individual packets do not need to be meticulously tracked, greatly reducing the overhead required to handle packets. Because of this, connectionless sockets can have a better throughput than connection-oriented sockets.

Connectionless sockets are implemented using the SOCK_DGRAM socket Type. This commonly uses the User Datagram Protocol (UDP) to send data across the network between network devices. Since connectionless sockets do not need the overhead of establishing connections, both server and client programs look similar.

To send UDP messages, the socket does not need to be bound using the bind() function. The sendto() function is used to define the data and the destination where it is sent:

```
int sendto(int socket, void *msg, int msglen, int flags,
        struct sockaddr *to, int tolen)
```

The sendto() function specifies the local *socket* created using the socket() function, the message to send, the length of the message, any special flags, the destination address (using a sockaddr structure), and finally, the length of the address structure.

To receive UDP messages, the socket must be bound to a UDP port using the bind() function, just as with TCP connections. This specifies the UDP port to listen for incoming packets on. After the bind() function, packets can be received using the recvfrom() function:

```
int recvfrom(int socket, void *msg, int msglen, int flags,
        struct sockaddr *from, int fromlen)
```

Since the `recvfrom()` function is connectionless, it can accept data from any network device. The sending host's network address information is contained in the *from* structure, and the received message is in the *msg* buffer.

The `udpserver.c` program shown in Listing 5-3 demonstrates setting up a connectionless server program.

Listing 5-3: A simple UDP server

```c
/*
 *
 * Professional Linux Programming - Simple UDP server
 *
 */
#include <stdio.h>
#include <sys/types.h>
#include <sys/socket.h>
#include <netinet/in.h>
#include <arpa/inet.h>

int main(int argc, char *argv[])
{
        int s, fd, len;
        struct sockaddr_in my_addr;
        struct sockaddr_in remote_addr;
        int sin_size;
        char buf[BUFSIZ];

        memset(&my_addr, 0, sizeof(my_addr));
        my_addr.sin_family = AF_INET;
        my_addr.sin_addr.s_addr = INADDR_ANY;
        my_addr.sin_port = htons(8000);

        if ((s = socket(AF_INET, SOCK_DGRAM, 0)) < 0)
        {
                perror("socket");
                return 1;
        }

        if (bind(s,(struct sockaddr *)&my_addr,sizeof(struct sockaddr))<0)
        {
                perror("bind");
                return 1;
        }

        sin_size = sizeof(struct sockaddr_in);
        printf("waiting for a packet...\n");
        if ((len=recvfrom(s,buf,BUFSIZ,0,(struct sockaddr *)&remote_addr,
&sin_size)) < 0)
        {
                perror("recvfrom");
                return 1;
```

(continued)

Listing 5-3: *(continued)*

```
        }

        printf("received packet from %s:\n",
                inet_ntoa(remote_addr.sin_addr));
        buf[len] = '\0';
        printf(" contents: %s\n", buf);

        close(s);
        return 0;
}
```

The `udpserver.c` program creates a socket and binds it to UDP port 8000. Next, it waits for an incoming packet using the `recvfrom()` function. Note that at this point any device can send a packet to UDP port 8000. The socket is not connected to a specific endpoint. When a packet arrives, the sending device's network address is extracted, the packet data is displayed, and the socket is closed.

Listing 5-4 shows the companion program, `udpclient.c`, which demonstrates sending a UDP packet to a remote network device.

Listing 5-4: A simple UDP client

```
/*
 *
 * Professional Linux Programming - Simple UDP client
 *
 */
#include <stdio.h>
#include <sys/types.h>
#include <sys/socket.h>
#include <netinet/in.h>
#include <arpa/inet.h>

int main(int argc, char *argv[])
{
        int s, len;
        struct sockaddr_in remote_addr;
        char buf[BUFSIZ];

        memset(&remote_addr, 0, sizeof(remote_addr));
        remote_addr.sin_family = AF_INET;
        remote_addr.sin_addr.s_addr = inet_addr("127.0.0.1");
        remote_addr.sin_port = htons(8000);

        if ((s = socket(AF_INET, SOCK_DGRAM, 0)) < 0)
        {
                perror("socket");
                return 1;
        }

        strcpy(buf, "This is a test message");
```

```
        printf("sending: '%s'\n", buf);
        if ((len = sendto(s, buf, strlen(buf), 0, (struct sockaddr *)&remote_addr,
sizeof(struct sockaddr))) < 0)
        {
                perror("sendto");
                return 1;
        }

        close(s);
        return 0;
}
```

The udpclient.c program creates a UDP socket, and uses the sendto() function to send a message to a specific endpoint. To test these programs, start the udpserver program on the system; then, either from the same system or from another network system, run the udpclient program. You should see the message appear on the server display.

Moving Data

While knowing how to establish a socket connection to a remote device is helpful, it is not the end-all of network programming. Sending simple messages from one host to another in a controlled environment is impressive but not overly useful. Most likely, you will want to use network programming to move meaningful data across large networks (possibly even the Internet) between devices. This is where things get tricky. There are many things that can go wrong in network programming applications. This section shows one of the pitfalls of network programming and shows simple solutions for how to avoid them.

Datagrams vs. Streams

The core difference between TCP and UDP communications is the method data is sent across the network. The UDP protocol sends data in messages, called datagrams. Each time a datagram is sent using a sendto() function, it is sent as a single UDP packet through the network. The receiving program receives the UDP packet and processes it in a single recvfrom() function. UDP may not guarantee that the packet will get to the destination, but once it gets there it guarantees that the data sent in the sendto() function will be complete in the recvfrom() function call (assuming that the packet fits in the standard UDP packet size).

This is not true in TCP communications. TCP sockets use a streaming technology rather than datagram technology. Data sent in a send() function can be combined in a stream across the network to the receiving host. The receiving host can read parts of the stream using the recv() function. There is no control over what parts of the stream are read. You cannot guarantee that all of the data sent in a single send() function call will even be read in a single recv() function call.

The best way to demonstrate this principle is to create programs that exploit it. The badserver.c program shown in Listing 5-5 is one half of this demonstration.

Listing 5-5: Demonstration of a bad TCP server

```
/*
 *
 * Professional Linux Programming - A bad TCP server
 *
 */
#include <stdio.h>
#include <sys/types.h>
#include <sys/socket.h>
#include <netinet/in.h>
#include <arpa/inet.h>

int main(argc, argv)
{
    int i, s, fd, len;
    struct sockaddr_in my_addr;
    struct sockaddr_in remote_addr;
    int sin_size;
    char buf[BUFSIZ];

    memset(&my_addr, 0, sizeof(my_addr));
    my_addr.sin_family = AF_INET;
    my_addr.sin_addr.s_addr = INADDR_ANY;
    my_addr.sin_port = htons(8000);

    if ((s = socket(AF_INET, SOCK_STREAM, 0)) < 0)
    {
        perror("socket");
        return 1;
    }

    if (bind(s, (struct sockaddr *)&my_addr, sizeof(struct sockaddr)) < 0)
    {
        perror("bind");
        return 1;
    }

    listen(s, 5);
    sin_size = sizeof(struct sockaddr_in);
    if ((fd = accept(s, (struct sockaddr *)&remote_addr, &sin_size)) < 0)
    {
        perror("accept");
        return 1;
    }
    printf("accepted client %s\n", inet_ntoa(remote_addr.sin_addr));
    len = send(fd, "Welcome to my server\n", 21, 0);
    for (i = 0; i < 5; i++)
    {
        len = recv(fd, buf, BUFSIZ, 0);
        buf[len] = '\0';
        printf("%s\n", buf);
```

```
        }

        close(fd);
        close(s);
        return 0;
}
```

By now you should recognize most of the elements in the `badserver.c` program. It uses the standard functions to create a socket, bind to a local address, listen for connections, and accept a new connection. After the new connection is accepted, the server sends out a welcome message and then goes into a loop expecting to receive exactly five messages from the client. Each message is displayed individually as a line on the console output. After receiving the five messages the connection is closed.

Next, Listing 5-6 shows the `badclient.c` program is used for the other half of the demonstration.

Listing 5-6: Demonstration of a bad TCP client

```c
/*
 *
 * Professional Linux Programming - A bad TCP client
 *
 */
#include <stdio.h>
#include <sys/types.h>
#include <sys/socket.h>
#include <netinet/in.h>
#include <arpa/inet.h>

int main(argc, argv)
{
    int i, s, fd, len;
    struct sockaddr_in remote_addr;
    int sin_size;
    char buf[BUFSIZ];

    memset(&remote_addr, 0, sizeof(remote_addr));
    remote_addr.sin_family = AF_INET;
    remote_addr.sin_addr.s_addr = inet_addr("127.0.0.1");
    remote_addr.sin_port = htons(8000);

    if ((s = socket(AF_INET, SOCK_STREAM, 0)) < 0)
    {
        perror("socket");
        return 1;
    }

    if (connect(s, (struct sockaddr *)&remote_addr, sizeof(struct sockaddr)) < 0)
    {
        perror("connect");
        return 1;
```

(continued)

Listing 5-6: *(continued)*

```
        }

        printf("connected to server\n");
        len = recv(s, buf, BUFSIZ, 0);
        buf[len] = '\0';
        printf("%s", buf);
        len = send(s, "test message1", 13, 0);
        len = send(s, "test message2", 13, 0);
        len = send(s, "test message3", 13, 0);
        len = send(s, "test message4", 13, 0);
        len = send(s, "test message5", 13, 0);

        close(s);
        return 0;
}
```

The badclient.c program connects to the badserver.c program, receives the welcome message, then sends a series of five test messages to match the five messages the badserver is expecting.

Compile the programs, and if possible, run them on separate systems on your network (remember to change the s_addr value of the badclient.c program to match the IP address of the system the bad-server program is running on).

Try running the programs a few different times, and note the output on the badserver. Here is sample output from my system:

```
$ ./badserver
accepted client 10.0.1.37
test message1
test message2test message3test message4test message5


$
```

What happened? Obviously, not all of the messages made it in separate packets. The first message sent by the client was received by the server in the first recv() function just fine, but then the remaining four messages sent by the client were all received by the second recv() function as one message. The remaining three recv() functions exited with no data, as by then the remote client had closed the connection.

This example graphically demonstrates a basic principle of TCP that is often overlooked by novice network programmers. TCP does not respect message boundaries. As messages are sent using the send() function, and received using the recv() function, they are not necessarily sent and received using the same boundaries. This is due to internal buffering of TCP data.

On a Linux system, since TCP packets are subject to retransmissions, data sent by applications to a socket is buffered internally on the Linux system. This way if a packet retransmission is requested by the remote device, the system can just extract the packet data from the socket buffer and resend it without having to bother the application. The downside to this process is that often the socket buffer gets filled before all of the data goes out. This is illustrated in Figure 5-3.

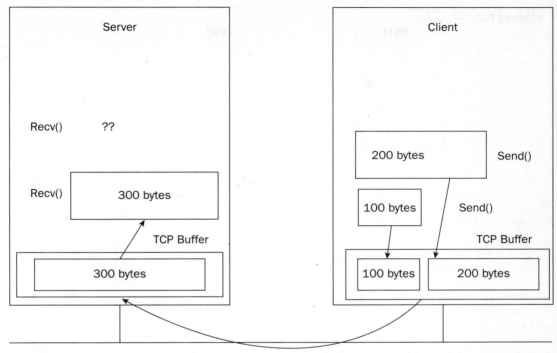

Figure 5-3

The two `send()` functions send data to the remote device, placing the data in its internal socket buffer for sending. When the data is sent to the remote device, it might be done in two packets, one packet, or a whole bunch of packets. We have no control over how the underlying socket process handles the buffered data. All TCP guarantees is that all of the data will appear at the remote device.

On the remote device side, the incoming packets are assembled in the socket buffer area. When a `recv()` function is called, whatever data is available in the buffer is sent to the application (depending on the size of the `recv()` function buffer). If the `recv()` function specifies a buffer large enough to accept all of the data in the socket buffer, all of the data is sent up to the application for processing. Thus, the data from the two `send()` function calls can be read by a single `recv()` function call.

Marking Message Boundaries

Since TCP does not provide a way of separating messages, you must do that yourself in your network program. There are two common methods used to delineate messages within a network stream:

❑   Use the message size

❑   Use an end-of-message marker

The following sections describe these methods.

Using Message Size

The first method uses the message size to identify message boundaries. If the receiving host knows the size of the message before it arrives, it knows how to handle the incoming data. There are two ways to use message size for data transmissions:

❏   Make every message the same size

❏   Mark every message with its message size

By making every message the same length, you know exactly how much data the recv() function should scoop up from the internal buffer by the size of the buffer supplied to the function call.

The betterserver.c program in Listing 5-7 fixes the badserver.c program by limiting the number of bytes of data scooped up by the recv() function.

Listing 5-7: Fixing the bad TCP server problem

```
/*
 *
 * Professional Linux Programming - A better TCP server
 *
 */
#include <stdio.h>
#include <sys/types.h>
#include <sys/socket.h>
#include <netinet/in.h>
#include <arpa/inet.h>

int main(argc, argv)
{
        int i, s, fd, len;
        struct sockaddr_in my_addr;
        struct sockaddr_in remote_addr;
        int sin_size;
        char buf[BUFSIZ];

        memset(&my_addr, 0, sizeof(my_addr));
        my_addr.sin_family = AF_INET;
        my_addr.sin_addr.s_addr = INADDR_ANY;
        my_addr.sin_port = htons(8000);

        if ((s = socket(AF_INET, SOCK_STREAM, 0)) < 0)
        {
                perror("socket");
                return 1;
        }

        if (bind(s, (struct sockaddr *)&my_addr, sizeof(struct sockaddr)) < 0)
        {
                perror("bind");
                return 1;
        }

        listen(s, 5);
```

```
        sin_size = sizeof(struct sockaddr_in);
        if ((fd = accept(s, (struct sockaddr *)&remote_addr, &sin_size)) < 0)
        {
                perror("accept");
                return 1;
        }
        printf("accepted client %s\n", inet_ntoa(remote_addr.sin_addr));
        len = send(fd, "Welcome to my server\n", 21, 0);
        for  (i = 0; i < 5; i++)
        {
                len = recv(fd, buf, 13, 0);
                buf[len] = '\0';
                printf("%s\n", buf);
        }

        close(fd);
        close(s);
        return 0;
}
```

Notice that the recv() function within the for loop now limits the number of bytes read by the recv() function:

```
len = recv(fd, buf, 13, 0)
```

Since each message sent by the client is 13 bytes long, this guarantees that no more than one message's worth of data will be processed by a single recv() function call. Compiling and running the betterserver.c program produces the following results when using the badclient program to send data:

```
$ ./betterserver
accepted client 10.0.1.37
test message1
test message2
test message3
test message4
test message5
$
```

No matter how many times I ran the programs, I got the same results. Now the server can cleanly separate messages from one another.

Sometimes it is not always efficient to send the same size messages in applications. Often messages are a mixture of sizes. Picking too large of a common message size can result in lots of padded data being sent across the network.

To solve this problem, programmers often use variable message sizes and send the message size to the remote device before the actual message. The receiving host must read the message size first and then loop until the complete message has been received. Once all of the bytes from the message have been received, the program can reset to accept another message size.

Using Message Markers

Instead of concentrating on message size, the second method of handling messages deals with message boundary markers. Boundary markers are a predetermined character (or set of characters) that delineate the end of a message. As the receiving program accepts data, it must scan the incoming data for the boundary marker. Once the boundary marker is found, the message is complete and passed on to the program for processing. Obviously, it is important to pick a message boundary marker that does not normally appear in the data sent in the message.

For many systems that use the ASCII character set, the standard message boundary marker is the carriage control–line feed combination. As each data packet is received by a host, it must examine each byte of data in the packet. As data is examined, if it is not the end-of-message marker, it is added to a temporary buffer. When the end-of-message marker is found, the data in the buffer is transferred to the permanent buffer for use. The temporary buffer can then be cleared and used to assemble the next message.

Using Network Programming Libraries

Writing raw socket code is the most robust way to develop networking applications, but it is not the only way. When you write your own client/server protocol, you are in control of how data is transferred from one network device to another. However, in today's network-savvy world, there are already many established network protocols that handle just about any type of data transfer. Instead of having to hand-code each network protocol your application uses from scratch, you can use one of the established network protocols to exchange data between systems. Once you find an established standard protocol to use, it is quite possible that there are free network programming libraries available that contain code for implementing that protocol.

These network programming libraries provide an application programming interface (API) to many common network protocols, such as FTP, HTTP, and Telnet. Sending data is as easy as calling a function with the destination address and your data. This makes your life much easier by allowing you to concentrate on the application code instead of the network programming features.

This section demonstrates how to use the libCurl network programming library. libCurl is one of the more popular packages for providing simple FTP, HTTP, and Telnet network programming functions.

The libCurl Library

The Curl package is an open source project that provides command line utilities for popular network protocols. Network communication with remote servers is as easy as executing a simple command line program. Any required parameters for the network connection (such as host names, user IDs, and passwords) are defined on the command line program. The command line utilities can be used in any shell script program, as well as within Perl and Python applications. Curl supports the FTP, Secure FTP (FTPS), TFTP, HTTP, HTTPS, Telnet, DICT, FILE, and LDAP network protocols from command line utilities.

libCurl is the sister project to Curl. libCurl is a standard library that provides C API functions to implement all the network protocols supported by Curl. This enables C and C++ programmers to easily incorporate network protocols in their applications.

This section describes how to download and install the libCurl library on a Linux system.

Downloading libCurl

The web page for Curl is located at curl.haxx.se. It contains documentation, tutorials, and of course, downloads for Curl and its sister project, libCurl. The Curl package can be downloaded as either a source code package, or a binary package. The binary package contains precompiled applications for specific operating system platforms. If you download a binary package for your platform, make sure that it includes the libCurl libraries (this feature is indicated on the download page).

If you prefer to build your own, you can download the current Curl source code package, and compile it yourself. The source code package includes the libCurl libraries, and automatically builds them during installation. At the time of this writing, the current source code package is curl-7.15-5 and can be downloaded in several compressed formats.

Installing libCurl

After downloading the source code package, you must extract the source code into a working directory. If you downloaded the .tar.gz file, this is done using the tar command:

```
$ tar -zxvf curl-7.15-5.tar.gz
```

This command automatically uncompresses the package and extracts the source code files into the curl-7.15.5 directory.

The Curl package utilizes the normal Linux toolset to build the executable and library files. The configure program is used to configure the desired options, and determine the build environment on your system. Go to the main directory (curl-7.15.5) and execute the configure command:

```
$ ./configure
```

After the configuration process completes, you can build the executable and library files using the standard make command. There are three steps to this process, making the files, testing the files, and installing the files. The first two steps can be performed as a normal user on the system. To install the files, you must have superuser privileges:

```
$ make
$ make test
$ su
Pasword:
$ make install
```

After the installation process completes, the libCurl library files are located in the /usr/local/lib directory. Not all Linux distributions include this directory in the default list of directories to locate library files. Check to ensure that this directory is included in the /etc/ld.so.conf file. If it is not, add it to the list of directories there.

Using the libCurl Library

The libCurl library is designed to be both versatile and easy. To meet these requirements, there are two formats for each of the C functions:

❑   Easy

❑   Multi

The easy format of the functions provides for simple functions that create synchronous connections to network devices. Since these are synchronous connections, only one connection can be active at a time. Alternatively, the multi format of the functions provides for more advanced functions that provide a higher level of control. The multi format functions also allow asynchronous connections to network devices. These functions allow you to perform multiple simultaneous connections within a single processing thread.

To compile a libCurl application, you must reference the libCurl header files in your application and link the program to the libCurl library. The libCurl header files are located in the /usr/local/include/curl directory. You can reference individual header files in the program relative to the curl directory:

```
#include <curl/curl.h>
```

When you compile the program, you must specify the /usr/local/include directory, as well as the curl library file:

```
$ cc -I /usr/local/include -o test test.c -lcurl
```

This command creates the executable program test from the test.c program.

The following sections demonstrate a few of the libCurl easy function formats and show how to use them in your application to connect to common network resources.

Connecting to Network Resources

The libCurl library provides many different functions for handling network connections. The main functions are handled by a CURL object handle. The CURL object is used to track the connection, handle the parameters used to establish the connection, and provide the data returned by the connection.

Before any functions can be performed, the Curl library must be initialized using the curl_easy_init() function:

```
CURL *curl;
curl = curl_easy_init();
if (!curl)
{
    perror("curl");
    return 1;
}
```

If the initialization is successful, the CURL object contains a new handle that can be used for connecting to a network resource. Parameters for the connection are defined using the curl_easy_setopt() function. The format for this function is:

```
curl_easy_setopt(curl, opt, value)
```

The *curl* parameter is an initialized CURL object. The *opt* parameter is the connection option to define, and the *value* parameter is the defined value for the option. There are tons of options that can be used to modify the network connection parameters. Some more common options that are available are shown in the following table.

Option	Description
CURLOPT_URL	Specify the URL to connect to.
CURLOPT_USERPWD	Specify the userid:password pair to use for the connection.
CURLOPT_PROXY	Specify a proxy server:port to use for the connection.
CURLOPT_VERBOSE	Specify if verbose mode should be on (1) or off (0).
CURLOPT_HEADER	Specify if the protocol header information should be displayed (1).
CURLOPT_WRITEFUNCTION	Specify a pointer to a function to handle received data. Otherwise, received data is displayed on the standard output.
CURLOPT_WRITEDATA	Data pointer to pass to the defined write function.
CURLOPT_READFUNCTION	Specify a pointer to a function to handle sending data.
CURLOPT_READDATA	Data pointer to pass to the defined read function.

After the connection parameters are defined, start the connection using the curl_easy_perform() function. This function uses the CURL object pointer as its only parameter, and returns a CURLcode object with the resulting data.

After you are done with the CURL object, it is wise to use the curl_easy_cleanup() function to remove it from memory.

The getweb.c program in Listing 5-8 demonstrates a basic libCurl application:

Listing 5-8: Using the libCurl library

```
/*
 *
 * Professional Linux Programming - A simple libCurl program
 *
 */
#include <stdio.h>
#include <curl/curl.h>

int main(int argc, char *argv[])
{
        CURL *curl;
        CURLcode res;

        curl = curl_easy_init();
        if(!curl)
```

(continued)

Listing 5-8: *(continued)*

```
        {
                perror("curl");
                return 1;
        }
        curl_easy_setopt(curl, CURLOPT_URL, argv[1]);
        curl_easy_setopt(curl, CURLOPT_PROXY, "webproxy:8080");
        res = curl_easy_perform(curl);

        curl_easy_cleanup(curl);
        return 0;
}
```

This program demonstrates how easy it is to do network programming using `libCurl`. In just a few lines of code, this program uses the `libCurl` library to connect to a remote website, and display the retrieved web page. If your network uses a proxy server for web connectivity, you will need to change the value of the `CURLOPT_PROXY` option to match your network settings. If your network does not use a proxy server, remove that option line.

Compile the `getweb.c` program using the command:

```
$ cc -I /usr/local/include -o getweb getweb.c -lcurl
```

After the compile completes, test the new program out on a few web pages. You can specify the full URL of the website (such as `http://curl.haxx.se`), or you can just specify the just website address (`curl.haxx.se`). The `libCurl` library attempts to determine the default protocol to use based on the URL name.

If the connection is successful, the HTML code for the web page will be displayed on your console:

```
$ ./getweb http://www.google.com
<html><head><meta http-equiv="content-type" content="text/html; charset=ISO-
8859-1"><title>Google</title><style><!--
body,td,a,p,.h{font-family:arial,sans-serif}
.h{font-size:20px}
.q{color:#00c}
--></style>
<script>
<!--
function sf(){document.f.q.focus();}
// -->
</script>
</head><body bgcolor=#ffffff text=#000000 link=#0000cc vlink=#551a8b alink=#ff0000
onLoad=sf() topmargin=3 marginheight=3><center><table border=0 cellspacing=0
cellpadding=0 width=100%><tr><td align=right nowrap><font size=-1><a href="/
url?sa=p&pref=ig&pval=3&q=http://www.google.com/ig%3Fhl%3Den&sig=__yvmOvIrk79QYmDkr
JAeuYO8jTmo=">Personalized Home</a>  | <a href="https://www.google.com/
accounts/Login?continue=http://www.google.com/&hl=en">Sign in</a></font></td></
tr><tr height=4><td><img alt="" width=1 height=1></td></tr></table><img src="/intl/
en/images/logo.gif" width=276 height=110 alt="Google"><br><br>
```

```
<form action=/search name=f><table border=0 cellspacing=0 cellpadding=4><tr><td
nowrap><font size=-1><b>Web</b>    <a class=q
href="/imghp?hl=en&ie=UTF-8&tab=wi">Images</a>    <a class=q
href="http://video.google.com/?hl=en&ie=UTF-8&tab=wv">Video<a          style="text-
decoration:none"><sup><font
color=red>New!</font></sup></a></a>    <a class=q
href="http://news.google.com/nwshp?hl=en&ie=UTF-
8&tab=wn">News</a>    <a class=q
href="/maps?hl=en&ie=UTF-8&tab=wl">Maps</a>    <b><a
href="/intl/en/options/" class=q onclick="this.blur();return
togDisp(event);">more &raquo;</a></b><script><!--
function togDisp(e){stopB(e);var elems=document.getElementsByName('more');for(var
i=0;i<elems.length;i++){var obj=elems[i];var
dp="";if(obj.style.display==""){dp="none";}obj.style.display=dp;}return false;}
function stopB(e){if(!e)e=window.event;e.cancelBubble=true;}
document.onclick=function(event){var
elems=document.getElementsByName('more');if(elems[0].style.display ==
""){togDisp(event);}}
//-->
</script><style><!--
.cb{margin:.5ex}
--></style>
<span name=more id=more
style="display:none;position:absolute;background:#fff;border:1px solid
#369;margin:-.5ex 1.5ex;padding:0 0 .5ex .8ex;width:16ex;line-height:1.9;z-
index:1000" onclick="stopB(event);"><a href=# onclick="return togDisp(event);"><img
border=0 src=/images/x2.gif width=12 height=12 alt="Close menu" align=right
class=cb></a><a class=q href="http://books.google.com/bkshp?hl=en&ie=UTF-
8&tab=wp">Books</a><br><a class=q
href="http://froogle.google.com/frghp?hl=en&ie=UTF-8&tab=wf">Froogle</a><br><a
class=q href="http://groups.google.com/grphp?hl=en&ie=UTF-
8&tab=wg">Groups</a><br><a href="/intl/en/options/" class=q><b>even more
&raquo;</b></a></span></font></td></tr></table><table cellspacing=0
cellpadding=0><tr><td width=25%> </td><td align=center><input type=hidden
name=hl value=en><input type=hidden name=ie value="ISO-8859-1"><input
maxlength=2048 size=55 name=q value="" title="Google Search"><br><input type=submit
value="Google Search" name=btnG><input type=submit value="I'm Feeling Lucky"
name=btnI></td><td valign=top nowrap width=25%><font size=-2>  <a
href=/advanced_search?hl=en>Advanced Search</a><br>  <a
href=/preferences?hl=en>Preferences</a><br>  <a
href=/language_tools?hl=en>Language
Tools</a></font></td></tr></table></form><br><br><font size=-1><a
href="/intl/en/ads/">Advertising Programs</a> - <a href=/services/>Business
Solutions</a> - <a href=/intl/en/about.html>About Google</a></font><p><font size=-
2>&copy;2006 Google</font></p>
$
```

The entire www.google.com web page HTML code is downloaded and displayed. Pretty good for just a few lines of code. Could you imagine how many lines of raw socket programming that would take in your application?

Storing Retrieved Data

The previous example showed that, by default, libCurl displays the retrieved data on the standard output. For many programs, this is most likely not what you want. Instead, you will want to process the retrieved data within the application and then present any pertinent information within your application to your customer. The libCurl library provides an option for you to do just that.

The CURLOPT_WRITEDATA option allows you to define a stream that the retrieved data is passed to instead of the standard output. You can perform whatever data-handling process you need to within the stream and control which data is displayed within your application.

If you want to process the data before sending it directly to the stream, you can use the CURLOPT_WRITEFUNCTION option. This allows you to define a callback routine that libCurl calls when data is received. Within the callback routine, you can process the data before sending it to the stream defined in the CURLOPT_WRITEDATA option.

In Listing 5-9 the getheaders.c program demonstrates defining a stream to a file to save the retrieved data from an HTTP connection. The retrieved data is separated into two files, one for the HTTP header data and one for the HTTP body data.

Listing 5-9: Using libCurl to store retrieved web data

```c
/*
 *
 * Professional Linux Progamming - Storing retrieved data
 *
 */
#include <stdio.h>
#include <curl/curl.h>

int main(int argc, char **argv)
{
    CURL *curl;
    CURLcode result;
    FILE *headerfile, *bodyfile;

    headerfile = fopen("header.txt", "w");
    bodyfile = fopen("body.txt", "w");
    curl = curl_easy_init();
    if (!curl)
    {
        perror("curl");
        return 1;
    }
    curl_easy_setopt(curl, CURLOPT_URL, argv[1]);
    curl_easy_setopt(curl, CURLOPT_WRITEHEADER, headerfile);
    curl_easy_setopt(curl, CURLOPT_WRITEDATA, bodyfile);

    curl_easy_setopt(curl, CURLOPT_VERBOSE, 1);

    result = curl_easy_perform(curl);
    curl_easy_cleanup(curl);

    fclose(headerfile);
```

```
        fclose(bodyfile);
        return 0;
    }
```

The getheaders.c program defines two file streams, headerfile and bodyfile. The special CURLOPT_
WRITEHEADER option is used to extract the HTTP header data and place it in the header.txt file. The
HTTP body data is placed in the body.txt file.

After compiling and running the program, the result from the program is seen in the header.txt file:

```
$ cat header.txt
HTTP/1.1 200 OK
Date: Sun, 08 Oct 2006 17:14:32 GMT
Server: Server
Set-Cookie: skin=noskin; path=/; domain=.amazon.com; expires=Sun, 08-Oct-2006
17:14:32 GMT
x-amz-id-1: 00Z0BGDZQZ7VKNKKTQ7E
x-amz-id-2: FPU2ju1jPdhsebipLULkH6d0uAXtsDBP
Set-cookie: session-id-time=11608956001; path=/; domain=.amazon.com; expires=Sun
Oct 15 07:00:00 2006 GMT
Set-cookie: session-id=002-7554544-2886459; path=/; domain=.amazon.com; expires=Sun
Oct 15 07:00:00 2006 GMT
Vary: Accept-Encoding,User-Agent
Content-Type: text/html; charset=ISO-8859-1
nnCoection: close
Transfer-Encoding: chunked

$
```

The HTTP header fields retrieved from the HTTP session to www.amazon.com are stored in the
header.txt file, while the body of the HTML page is stored in the body.txt file.

Summary

In today's networked world, a professional Linux programmer must know how to interface Linux applications with the network. This can be done using either socket programming or standard open source network libraries. Socket programming provides the most versatile way to interact with the network but
requires that you manually code all the features necessary to transport data across the network. You must
determine the proper protocol to interact with remote network devices, using either standard protocols or
your own protocol. There are different programming requirements for server and client applications.
Often, you must program different logic for each to ensure that they interact properly with each other.

Using network libraries makes network programming much simpler. There are many open source
libraries available that provide standard network protocols for C and C++ applications, as well as many
Linux scripting languages. The libCurl library is a popular open source library that provides an easy
interface to send and receive data with FTP, HTTP, Telnet, and other standard network protocols using
simple C function calls. Knowing how to interface with standard network libraries can save you from
having to hand-code each network protocol, making your life as a network programmer much easier.

6

Databases

As a Linux application runs, all of the data used in the program resides in system memory. Once the application stops running, the data contained in the memory area is lost. The next time you start the application, none of the data from the previous session is accessible. Most data-handling applications require that data be available between different sessions of the application (called data persistence). Persistent storage of information is crucial to any application that must handle historical data, such as employee records, inventory information, or class grades.

This chapter describes two methods used for implementing data persistence in Linux programs. First, a method that utilizes a built-in database engine is demonstrated. Incorporating a built-in database engine in your application provides simple persistent data features without the overhead and administration of a separate database server. Next, a method that utilizes a full-featured open source database server is demonstrated. By using a database server, customers can access your data from anywhere on the network, or even the Internet.

Persistent Data Storage

The key to persistent data storage is being able to quickly retrieve stored data. Modern database theory utilizes many techniques and methods to provide for quick retrieval of data. There are many schools of thought on exactly how databases should be designed, configured, and operated. Fortunately, Linux provides products that cover a wide range of solutions.

Data persistence is usually implemented in a Linux application using one of three different methods:

- ❏ Standard file reading and writing
- ❏ A built-in database engine
- ❏ An external database server

Each method has pros and cons that should be considered when creating a Linux application that must store data.

Using a Standard File

The most basic form of data persistence is saving data in a standard file on the system hard disk. In Linux you can write data elements to a file on the system, then access the same data elements when run again. You can use the Linux operating system to control access to the data files so that unauthorized users or applications cannot see the stored data.

In most Linux applications, using files is a multistep process. Figure 6-1 demonstrates the steps required to interact with files.

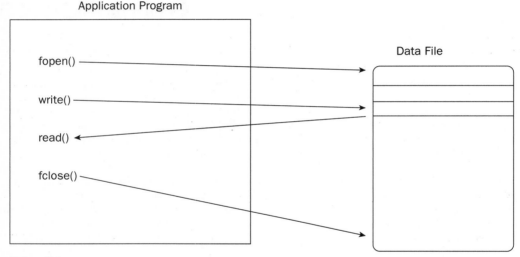

Figure 6-1

Most Linux programming languages provide the functions necessary for opening, writing data, reading data, and closing files. You must code the appropriate functions into your applications to store and retrieve data from the files.

The downside to using standard files for data persistence is performance. While it is easy to create a file and write data to it, trying to find the data within the file can become a challenge. Trying to find a single record in a 1000 record data file could mean having to read up to 1000 records before getting to the data you need. To solve this problem, you must use a database data persistence method.

Using a Database

Modern database theory provides many methods for increasing the performance of database data lookups. Instead of placing data records in a file in the order in which they are created, a database system can order data records based on values, called keys, and even create separate files with data keys and pointers to the complete record. Sorting data based on a unique data key helps databases retrieve stored information quickly, much faster than having to scan each record for the proper data.

The trick to implementing a database system is in the coding. Creating the proper logic to implement a database requires lots of lines of code. There are two schools of thought on how to implement the database logic in an application.

One school of thought is that simple database functions can be incorporated into applications using simple libraries that handle the database functions. This is demonstrated in Figure 6-2.

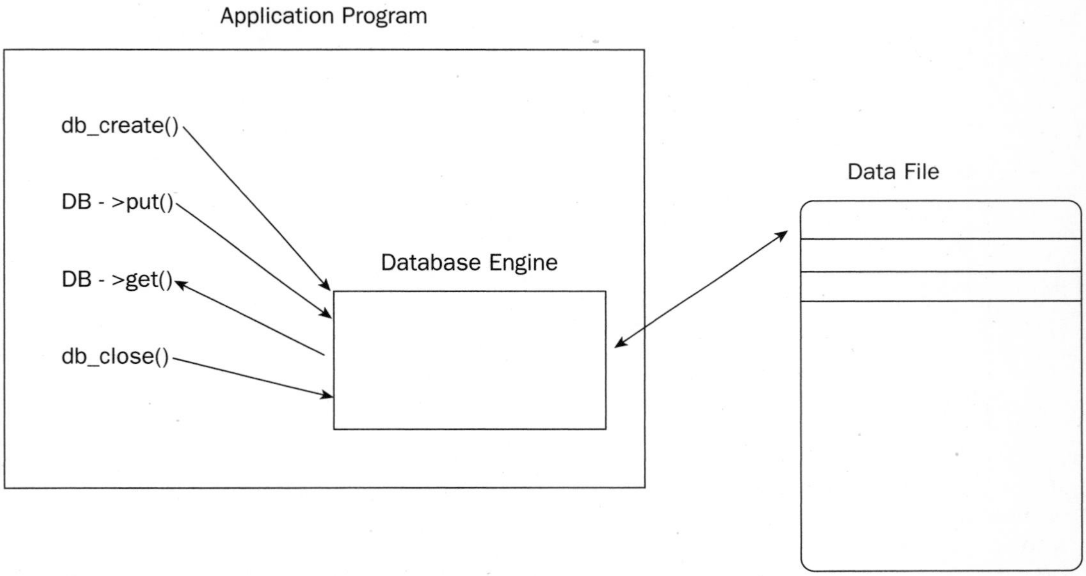

Figure 6-2

The database engine library provides functions for creating database files; inserting, modifying, and deleting data records in the database; and querying data elements within the database. By implementing the database functions within the application code, there is no need for a separate database server that must be managed. All of the database functions are contained in the application. Of course, this also means that it is up to the application to control the necessary data files and, of course, access to those files.

The downside to using a built-in database engine appears in multiuser environments. When using just a single application, there is no problem with accessing the file and updating it as necessary. If multiple users try accessing and updating the database file at the same time, all using a separate database engine, problems can occur with the integrity of the data. There needs to be a single entity controlling access to the data, and determining when updated data is available for the other users.

This is where the database server comes in. The database server provides all of the logic for handling the data in the database. Applications that must access data in the database must interact with the database server to access the data. The database server can control what data is presented to each user, and how data received from each user is placed into the database. A typical database server environment is shown in Figure 6-3.

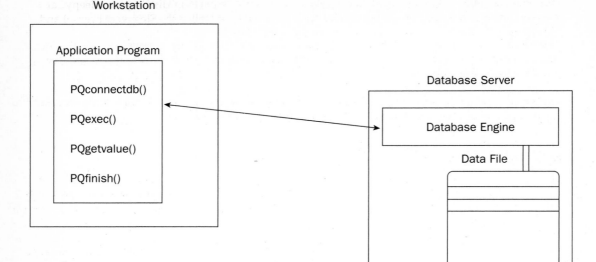

Figure 6-3

To interact with the database server, each application must again use a library of functions. The library includes functions to connect to the database server; insert, modify, and delete data within the database; and of course, query data contained within the database. Since many different clients must be able to connect and interact with the database server, many standards have been created to simplify the process. One of those standards is the Standard Query Language (SQL). This is a standard protocol used for sending commands to a database server, and retrieving results.

The following sections demonstrate two popular Linux database products. The Berkeley DB product demonstrates using a built-in database engine in your applications, while the PostgreSQL product demonstrates using a central database server.

The Berkeley DB Package

By far the most popular and useful built-in database engine package is the open source Berkeley DB package. It provides many advanced database features in a simple, easy-to-use library that can be linked to your C or C++ applications.

Unfortunately, the Berkeley DB product has had quite a checkered life cycle. As its name suggests, it started out as a simple database project at the University of California, Berkeley for the 4.4 version of the BSD operating system. It became so popular that in 1996 the Netscape Corporation asked the authors to release the product for general use. With that, a separate company, Sleepycat Software Incorporated, was created to continue working on Berkeley DB separate from the BSD UNIX distribution. SleepyCat Software released the software both under an open source license (called the Sleepycat license) and under a commercial license to support commercial installations.

Recently SleepyCat Software (and Berkeley DB) has been acquired by the Oracle corporation. Oracle, while a major commercial database vendor, maintains the open source status of Berkeley DB.

The following sections show how to download, compile, install, and use the Berkeley DB package in your Linux applications.

Downloading and Installing

Since it is such a popular package, many Linux distributions include the Berkeley DB package (and some even install it by default). You can choose to install the prebuilt package for your distribution (if it is not already installed), or if you prefer, you can download, compile, and install the latest version from the Oracle website.

If you choose to install a prebuilt package for your distribution, follow the standard software package installation directions for your Linux distribution. Make sure that you install both the library files and the development files. These are usually two separate packages that must be installed.

You can download the latest version of Berkeley DB from the Oracle website. The Berkeley DB area is currently at www.oracle.com/technology/products/berkeley-db/index.html. On this page, click the Download link at the top right of the web page.

At the time of this writing, the current version of Berkeley DB is 4.5.20. It is available in several different configurations and package formats. For installing in Linux, choose the .tar.gz package, either with AES encryption or without encryption.

Save the downloaded file in a working directory on your Linux system. Since the distribution package is the source code, it must be expanded and compiled. To expand the file, use the uncompression tool appropriate for the version you downloaded:

```
$ tar -zxvf db-4.5.20.tar.gz
```

This command creates the directory db-4.5.20 under the current directory and expands the source code files into the directory.

The Berkeley DB package compiles a little differently from some of the other open source products you may be used to. To compile the source code, you must go to the proper build_xxx directory under the main directory. For Linux systems, this is the build_unix directory. From there, you must run the configure program, which is located in the dist directory. The process looks like this:

```
[db-4.5.20]$ cd build_unix
[build_unix]$ ../dist/configure
```

The configure utility checks the system for features, and produces the necessary files to compile the application. When it completes, you can run the make command from the build_unix directory:

```
[build_unix]$ make
```

When the compiling is complete, you should install the library and development files onto your system using the make with the install option:

```
[build_unix]# make install
```

Remember that this step should be performed as the root account. Once the library and development files are installed, you are almost ready to start programming.

Building Programs

By default, the Berkeley DB library and development files are installed into directories under the /usr/local/BerkeleyDB.4.5 directory. This top-level directory contains the following directories:

- ❑ **bin:** Contains utilities for examining and fixing Berkeley DB database files
- ❑ **docs:** Contains HTML documentation for the C APIs and utilities
- ❑ **include:** Contains the C and C++ header files for compiling Berkeley DB applications
- ❑ **lib:** Contains the shared library files for compiling and running Berkeley DB applications

In order to run applications that use the Berkeley DB library, you must add the lib directory to the system's list of library directories. The /etc/ld.so.conf file contains the list of directories Linux will search for library files. As the root user, add the /usr/local/BerkeleyDB.4.5/lib directory to the list that is already present in the file (do not remove any of the existing entries, or bad things could happen on your system). Once you have updated the /etc/ld.so.conf file, you must run the ldconfig utility (as the root user) to update the system.

Now your system is ready to run Berkeley DB applications. To compile an application that uses the Berkeley DB functions, you must tell the compiler where the include directory is located, and also where the library files are located. You must also specify the db library to the linker. This is an example of compiling a Berkeley DB application:

```
$ cc -I/usr/local/BerkeleyDB.4.5/include -o test test.c -L/usr/local/BerkeleyDB.4.5
-ldb
```

The -I parameter is used to specify the location of the header files necessary to compile the application, and the -L parameter is used to specify the location of the library files necessary to link the application into an executable program.

Basic Data Handling

Now that you have the Berkeley DB libraries loaded and configured for your system, you are ready to start using them in your applications. This section describes the steps required to use the Berkeley DB functions to utilize databases in your applications.

Opening and Closing a Database

Before a Berkeley DB database file can be accessed, you must open a database file for access. When you are done working with the database file, you must close it, or risk corruption of the data. A DB handle is used to control access to a database file. The DB handle is created using the db_create() function:

```
int db_create(DB **dbp, DB_ENV *env, u_int32_t flags)
```

The dbp parameter specifies the DB handle used for access to the file. The env parameter specifies the environment the database file is open under. If the value is NULL, the database is considered a standalone database and all settings specified apply only to this file. Alternatively, you can specify a DB_ENV value to group this database with other databases into an environment. Any settings made to the environment (such as setting file locking) apply to all database files created in the environment. The flags parameter should be set to 0 for databases running on the Linux environment.

If the db_create() function succeeds, it returns a zero value. If it fails, the return value is nonzero.

Once a DB handle is created, the open() function is used to open a new or existing database file:

```
int DB->open(DB *db, DB_TXN *txnid, const char *file, const char *database,
             DBTYPE type, u_int32_t flags, int mode)
```

The open() function uses the DB handle db created using the db_create() function. The txnid parameter specifies an open transaction object if the command is part of a transaction. The file and database parameters specify a text name of the system file to use for the database, and the name of the database stored in the file. Berkeley DB allows you to store multiple databases within a single physical file. If only one database is used in the file, you can specify NULL for the database name. If multiple databases are used within a single file, you must open each one using a separate open() function call.

If you are creating a new database, you must specify the type of database used in the type parameter. The currently supported database types are:

❏ **DB_BTREE:** A sorted, balanced tree database structure, using the key values to sort data

❏ **DB_HASH:** An extended linear hash table, using a hashed value of the key to sort data

❏ **DB_QUEUE:** A queue of fixed-length records, using logical record numbers as keys

❏ **DB_RECNO:** A queue of fixed or variable length records using logical record numbers as keys

The DB_BTREE and DB_HASH types offer quick access to data by sorting data as it is entered into the database file. Of course, this also means that storing new data values takes a little longer, as the data must be placed in a specific place in the file. For extremely large databases, the DB_HASH method is known to perform better than DB_BTREE.

The DB_QUEUE and DB_RECNO types are often used for data that is sorted based on logical record number. The logical record number is used as the key value. Records can only be retrieved using the record number. However, inserting and retrieving records in these database types is extremely fast. If your application requires quick data storage and retrieval without sorting, these types will perform best.

If you are opening an existing database, you can also specify the DB_UNKNOWN value for the type parameter. If this value is used, Berkeley DB attempts to automatically determine the database type of the existing database. If it fails to recognize the database type, the open() function fails.

The flags parameter specifies how the database file should be opened. The valid values are shown in the following table.

Flag	Description
DB_AUTO_COMMIT	Use a transaction to open the database file. If the call succeeds, the open operation will be recoverable. If the call fails, no database file will be created.
DB_CREATE	Create the database if it does not already exist.
DB_DIRTY_READ	Read operations on the database may request the return of modified but not yet saved data.
DB_EXCL	Return an error if the database already exists.
DB_NOMMAP	Do not map the database file into memory.
DB_RDONLY	Open the database in read-only mode.
DB_THREAD	Cause the DB handle returned to be usable by multiple threads.
DB_TRUNCATE	Truncate any other databases that may have already existed in the database file

Flag values may be combined using the logical OR symbol (|). For example, you can specify the flag DB_CREATE | DB_EXCL, which will create a new database file but will fail if the database file already exists. By default, the DB_CREATE flag will open an existing database.

The mode parameter specifies the UNIX system filemode for the file. Entering a value of zero specifies that both the owner and group have read and write privileges, while everyone else has no privileges. This value can be specified using the normal octal UNIX filemode settings (such as 0664).

An example of creating a DB handle and opening a new database is shown here:

```
DB *dbp;
int ret;

ret = db_create(&dbp, NULL, 0);
if (ret != 0)
{
    perror("create");
    return 1;
}

ret = dbp->open(dbp, NULL, "test.db", NULL, DB_BTREE, DB_CREATE, 0);
if (ret != 0)
{
    perror("open");
    return 1;
}
```

In this short code snippet, the DB handle, dbp, is created using the db_create() function, then used to create (or open for use if it exists) the database file test.db using the B-Tree database format, and the default owner and group privileges.

Adding New Data

Now that you have a database file open, it is time to start putting some data into it. The function to do this is put(). The put() function format is:

```
int DB->put(DB *db, DB_TXN *txnid, DBT *key, DBT *data, u_int32_t flags)
```

The db and txnid parameters are the same as for the open() function, specifying the DB handle and the transaction to use for the function. The key and data parameters specify the database key and data pair used to store the data.

The DBT structure used for each defines a data element and a size element. Thus, the key.data element contains the record key value, and the data.data element contains the record data value.

The flags parameter specifies how the new data is placed in the database file. For DB_QUEUE and DB_RECNO databases, the DB_APPEND flag can be used to add the record to the end of the database file. For DB_BTREE and DB_HASH databases, the DB_NOUPDATA flag can be used to add the record to the database only if the key/data pair do not already exist. The DB_NOOVERWRITE flag is used to prevent new data from overwriting an existing key value.

The key/data pair combination can be misleading. Many people think this limits them to just a single data value in the record. The data value can be any data type required, including a structure. A C structure can be created containing as many data elements as required for the application. Each instance of the C structure is stored in the database file as a single data value.

This is demonstrated in the newemployee.c program shown in Listing 6-1.

Listing 6-1: Adding records to a Berkeley DB database

```c
/*
 *
 * Professional Linux Programming - Adding a new employee record
 *
 */
#include <stdio.h>
#include <db.h>

#define DATABASE "employees.db"

int main()
{
    DBT key, data;
    DB *dbp;
    int ret;
    struct data_struct {
        int empid;
        char lastname[50];
        char firstname[50];
```

(continued)

Listing 6-1: *(continued)*

```
      float salary;
  } emp;

  ret = db_create(&dbp, NULL, 0);
  if (ret != 0)
  {
     perror("create");
     return 1;
  }

  ret = dbp->open(dbp, NULL, DATABASE, NULL, DB_BTREE, DB_CREATE, 0);
  if (ret != 0)
  {
     perror("open: ");
     return 1;
  }

  while(1)
  {
     printf("Enter Employee ID: ");
     scanf("%d", &emp.empid);
     if (emp.empid == 0)
        break;
     printf("Enter Last name: ");
     scanf("%s", &emp.lastname);
     printf("Enter First name: ");
     scanf("%s", &emp.firstname);
     printf("Enter Salary: ");
     scanf("%f", &emp.salary);

     memset(&key, 0, sizeof(DBT));
     memset(&data, 0, sizeof(DBT));

     key.data = &(emp.empid);
     key.size = sizeof(emp.empid);
     data.data = &emp;
     data.size = sizeof(emp);

     ret = dbp->put(dbp, NULL, &key, &data, DB_NOOVERWRITE);
     if (ret != 0)
     {
        printf("Employee ID exists\n");
     }
  }

  dbp->close(dbp, 0);
  return 0;
}
```

The newemployee.c program creates a DB handle and opens the employees.db file as a single standalone database (note that using the .db file extension is not a requirement, but it is often used to identify Berkeley DB database files). Next, a while() loop is used to query the user for information on a new employee. The emp structure is used for the data element in the database. It contains an integer employee ID, character `lastname` and `firstname` strings, and a float salary value. As the values are obtained from the user, they are placed into an `emp` structure value.

Before using the `key` and `data` DBT objects, it is always a good idea to zero out the memory locations, using the `memset` function. This prevents stray bits from making their way into the data elements. Following that, the key value is set to the employee ID value, and the data value is set to the entire `emp` structure. Once everything is in place, the `put()` function is executed, using the `DB_NOOVERWRITE` flag to ensure that there will be an error if you attempt to use the same employee ID. Note, if you want to update an existing employee's record, just remove the `DB_NOOVERWRITE` flag.

The `while()` loop exits if the new employee ID entered is 0. When the loop exits, the `close()` function is used to properly close the database file.

Compile this application (remember to use the proper header and library files), then run it. You should be able to add employee records into the database. When you stop the program, you should see the new `employees.db` database file in the directory.

Retrieving Data

Once data is placed in the database file, at some point you will most likely want to retrieve it. The `get()` function is used for this:

```
int DB->get(DB *db, DB_TXN *txnid, DBT *key, DBT *data, u_int32_t flags)
```

Just as with the other functions, the `db` parameter specifies an opened database DB handle, and the `txnid` parameter specifies an existing transaction. The key and data parameters are both DBT objects which hold the key and data values. In the case of retrieving data, the key parameter holds the key value to retrieve, and the data parameter will be filled with the appropriate data when the function completes.

The flags parameter specifies the function to perform when retrieving the data. A value of zero only retrieves the data element with no actions. The following flags can also be used:

Flag	Description
DB_CONSUME	In a `DB_QUEUE` type database, the record data at the head of the queue is retrieved, and the record is deleted from the database.
DB_CONSUME_WAIT	Same as `DB_CONSUME`, except that if the queue is empty, wait for a record to appear.
DB_GET_BOTH	Return a key/data pair only if the specified key and data pair supplied match the database.
DB_SET_RECNO	Retrieve both the key and data values from the database, not just the data value. Can only be used in `DB_BTREE`-type databases.
DB_DIRTY_READ	Read modified but not yet committed data.
DB_MULTIPLE	Return multiple data elements. If the `data.size` value is not large enough, the data value is set to the size required to contain all of the data elements.
DB_RMW	Acquire a write lock instead of a read lock when performing the retrieval. Used in transactions.

In Listing 6-2, the `getemployee.c` program demonstrates how to retrieve data from a database file:

Listing 6-2: Retrieving records from a Berkeley DB database

```c
/*
 *
 * Professional Linux Programming - Retrieving an employee record
 *
 */
#include <stdio.h>
#include <db.h>

#define DATABASE "employees.db"

int main()
{
    DBT key, data;
    DB *dbp;
    int ret;
    struct data_struct {
        int empid;
        char lastname[50];
        char firstname[50];
        float salary;
    } emp;

    ret = db_create(&dbp, NULL, 0);
    if (ret != 0)
    {
        perror("create");
        return 1;
    }

    ret = dbp->open(dbp, NULL, DATABASE, NULL, DB_BTREE, DB_CREATE, 0);
    if (ret != 0)
    {
        perror("open: ");
        return 1;
    }

    while(1)
    {
        printf("Enter Employee ID: ");
        scanf("%d", &emp.empid);
        if (emp.empid == 0)
            break;

        memset(&key, 0, sizeof(DBT));
        memset(&data, 0, sizeof(DBT));
        key.data = &(emp.empid);
```

```
        key.size = sizeof(emp.empid);
        data.data = &emp;
        data.ulen = sizeof(emp);
        data.flags = DB_DBT_USERMEM;

        ret = dbp->get(dbp, NULL, &key, &data, 0);
        if (ret != 0)
        {
            printf("Employee ID does not exist\n");
        } else
        {
            printf("  Employee: %d - %s,%s\n", emp.empid, emp.lastname,
emp.firstname);
            printf("  Salary: $%.2lf\n", emp.salary);
        }
    }

    dbp->close(dbp, 0);
    return 0;
}
```

Listing 6-2 demonstrates the standard method used to create a DB handle and open the employees.db database file. The while() loop starts by querying the user to enter the employee ID value to search for. Again, the memset function is used to clear the key and data values, and the employee ID entered is placed in the key.data element. The data element is set to an empty instance of the data_struct structure.

The data element also contains flags that can be used to specify how the data is handled. The DB_DBT_USERMEM flag tells Berkeley DB that the program has set up its own memory area to handle the data once it is returned.

When the get() function is performed, the returned data is placed in the emp structure and displayed on the console. The while() loop continues until an employee ID of zero is entered.

Deleting Data

Another handy function is the ability to remove records from the database file. The del() function is used for that:

```
int DB->del(DB *dbp, DB_TXN *txnid, DBT *key, u_int32_t flags)
```

The deletion is based on the supplied key value in the function call. In the current version of Berkeley DB, the flags parameter is unused and should be set to zero.

The delemployee.c program shown in Listing 6-3 demonstrates using the del() function to delete a specified record in the employees.db database.

Listing 6-3: Removing a record from a Berkeley DB database

```c
/*
 *
 * Professional Linux Programming - removing an employee record
 *
 */
#include <stdio.h>
#include <db.h>

#define DATABASE "employees.db"

int main()
{
    DBT key;
    DB *dbp;
    int ret;
    struct data_struct {
        int empid;
        char lastname[50];
        char firstname[50];
        float salary;
    } emp;

    ret = db_create(&dbp, NULL, 0);
    if (ret != 0)
    {
        perror("create");
        return 1;
    }

    ret = dbp->open(dbp, NULL, DATABASE, NULL, DB_BTREE, DB_CREATE, 0);
    if (ret != 0)
    {
        perror("open: ");
        return 1;
    }

    while(1)
    {
        printf("Enter Employee ID: ");
        scanf("%d", &emp.empid);
        if (emp.empid == 0)
            break;

        memset(&key, 0, sizeof(DBT));
        key.data = &(emp.empid);
        key.size = sizeof(emp.empid);

        ret = dbp->del(dbp, NULL, &key, 0);
        if (ret != 0)
        {
            printf("Employee ID does not exist\n");
        } else
```

```
        {
            printf("  Employee %d deleted.\n", emp.empid);
        }
    }

    dbp->close(dbp, 0);
    return 0;
}
```

By now you should recognize most of the program. The user specifies the employee ID to delete, the value is stored in the key.data element, and the del() function is performed. If the deletion was successful, the function returns a zero value. If the key does not exist in the database, the del() function will return a DB_NOTFOUND value.

Using Cursors

The get() function can only retrieve data values if you already know a valid key value. Sometimes you may need to extract data from the database file without knowing what the key values are.

Berkeley DB uses a database concept called cursors to allow you to iterate over the records contained in the database. A cursor object is used to point to a record in the database. You can move the cursor either forward or backward in the database record by record to retrieve either the next or previous record. Once the cursor is at a record, you can retrieve the record data, delete the record it points to, or put a new record into the database in that location.

A DBC cursor object is created from the standard DB handle created for the database, using the cursor() function:

```
int DB->cursor(DB *db, DB_TXN *txnid, DBC **cursorp, u_int32_t flags);
```

The cursor() function creates a pointer to the cursor and assigns it to the DBC object pointer (cursorp). Once the cursor object is created, the c_get(), c_put() or c_del() functions can be used to get, put, or delete a record at the location the cursor points to in the database file.

Iterating through the database records comes in handy when you need to list every record contained in the database. The listemployees.c program, shown in Listing 6-4, demonstrates using a cursor in a database file to list all of the records contained in the database.

Listing 6-4: Retrieving multiple records from a Berkeley DB database

```
/*
 *
 * Professional Linux Programming - listing all employee records
 *
 */
#include <stdio.h>
#include <db.h>

#define DATABASE "employees.db"
```

(continued)

Listing 6-4: *(continued)*

```c
int main()
{
    DBT key, data;
    DBC *cursor;
    DB *dbp;
    int ret;
    struct data_struct {
        int empid;
        char lastname[50];
        char firstname[50];
        float salary;
    } emp;

    ret = db_create(&dbp, NULL, 0);
    if (ret != 0)
    {
        perror("create");
        return 1;
    }

    ret = dbp->open(dbp, NULL, DATABASE, NULL, DB_BTREE, DB_CREATE, 0);
    if (ret != 0)
    {
        perror("open: ");
        return 1;
    }

    ret = dbp->cursor(dbp, NULL, &cursor, 0);
    if (ret != 0)
    {
        perror("cursor: ");
        return 1;
    }

    memset(&key, 0, sizeof(DBT));
    memset(&data, 0, sizeof(DBT));
    data.data = &emp;
    data.size = sizeof(emp);
    data.flags = DB_DBT_USERMEM;

    while(ret = cursor->c_get(cursor, &key, &data, DB_NEXT) == 0)
    {
        printf("%d - %s,%s   $%.2lf\n", emp.empid, emp.lastname, emp.firstname,
emp.salary);
    }

    cursor->c_close(cursor);
    dbp->close(dbp, 0);
    return 0;
}
```

After creating the DB handle and opening the `employee.db` database file, a cursor object, `cursor`, is created to iterate through the database file. With each iteration, both the key and data DBT values are extracted from the database record using the `c_get()` function.

The `c_get()` function includes a flag that indicates where to move the cursor in the database. There are lots of options here, the most common being DB_NEXT, DB_PREV, DB_FIRST, DB_LAST, and DB_NEXT_DUP, used to find duplicate key/data pairs in the database.

When the key and data values are extracted from the record, a `data_struct` structure is used to extract the employee information stored in the data element. Since the program uses its own memory location, the DB_DBT_USERMEM flag must be used for the data element.

When the last record is reached in the database, the `c_get()` function returns a nonzero value, and the `while()` loop exits. Since the program is done with the cursor, it uses the `c_close()` function to close the cursor and release the memory it uses before closing the database file.

The PostgreSQL Database Server

The PostgreSQL database server is one of the most popular open source databases available. It supports many database features commonly found in commercial databases, such as stored procedures, views, triggers, functions, and hot backups.

Of course, the downside to using a database server is that it must be administered separately from the application programs. Often organizations hire database administrators whose only function is to ensure database servers are operating properly. An advantage to using a database server, though, is that you can place all of the data for every application supported in the company onto a single server, which is continually backed up.

Programming for a database server environment is not much different than when using the built-in database engine. Instead of opening a database file, you must establish a connection with the database server (either running on the local system, or remotely on the network). Once you have established a connection, you can send SQL commands to insert, delete, or update data in the database tables. You can also send SQL commands to query data within the tables. The database server returns the result of the query (called a result set) to your program, which can then iterate through the result set and extract the individual record data.

Downloading and Installing

Many Linux distributions include the PostgreSQL product as an installable package. If this is available for your Linux distribution, follow the appropriate instructions for installing software on your Linux platform to install PostgreSQL.

If you want to install the latest version of PostgreSQL, you can download either the source code package or the appropriate binary installation package for your Linux distribution. Go to the main PostgreSQL website (www.postgresql.org); then click the Download link at the top of the page.

The Downloads page contains a link to the FTP Browser page, which is where the various distribution packages are stored. The binary folder contains RPM distributions for Red Hat Linux installations. The source folder contains the source code distributions for various releases. At the time of this writing, version 8.1.5 is the latest version available.

If you are downloading the source code version, you must extract it into a working directory, using the `tar` command:

```
$ tar -zxvf postgresql-8.1.5.tar.gz
```

This creates the directory `postgresql-8.1.5`, which contains all of the source code to compile. Change to that directory, and run the configure and gmake utilities to build the executable files (PostgreSQL uses the GNU gmake utility instead of the standard make utility).

```
[postgresql-8.1.5]$ ./configure
...
[postgresql-8.1.5]$ gmake
...
All of PostgreSQL successfully made. Ready to install.
[postgresql-8.1.5]$ su
[postgresql-8.1.5]# gmake install
```

After building and installing the PostgreSQL database server software, you must create a special user account for the PostgreSQL server. To help prevent security problems, the PostgreSQL server will not run as the root user. It must be run as a normal user account. The standard is to create an account called `postgres` and give it access to the database directory:

```
# adduser postgres
# mkdir /usr/local/pgsql/data
# chown postgres /usr/local/pgsql/data
```

The PostgreSQL database directory can be located anywhere on the Linux system, this is just a recommendation by PostgreSQL. Make sure that wherever you place the data directory, the postgres user is the only one that has access to the directory.

Before starting the PostgreSQL server program, you must initialize the default PostgreSQL database. This is done using the initdb utility (as the postgres user):

```
$ su - postgres
$ /usr/local/pgsql/bin/initdb -D /usr/local/pgsql/data
```

The `initdb` program creates the necessary files for the default PostgreSQL database (called postgres). When the process completes, the `/usr/local/pgsql/data` directory contains the files for the database. You can now start the PostgreSQL server using the `pg_ctl` utility (again as the postgres user):

```
$ /usr/local/pgsql/bin/pg_ctl -D /usr/local/pgsql/data -l logfile start
```

The `pg_ctl` utility is used to stop, start, and reload the configuration of the PostgreSQL server. You must specify the location of the database directory using the `-D` parameter. You can also specify a location for the server logfile using the `-l` parameter. Make sure that the postgres user has write privileges to the logfile location. You can tell that the server is running by looking at the running processes. You should see a few different PostgreSQL processes running:

```
28949 pts/1    S      0:00 /usr/local/pgsql/bin/postmaster -D /usr/local/pgsql/d
28951 pts/1    S      0:00 postgres: writer process
28952 pts/1    S      0:00 postgres: stats buffer process
28953 pts/1    S      0:00 postgres: stats collector process
```

The postmaster process is the main controller for the server. It will spawn off other processes as necessary.

Building Programs

Just as with the Berkeley DB library, you must configure your Linux system for creating and running applications with the PostgreSQL library. The PostgreSQL C library is called libpq. The library files are located in the /usr/local/pgsql/lib directory. For PostgreSQL applications to work on your system, this directory must be added to the /etc/ld.so.conf file, and the ldconfig program run (as the root user).

To compile C programs that use the libpq library, you must include the header file location, as well as the libpq library file:

```
$ cc -I/usr/local/pgsql/include -o test test.c -L/usr/local/pgsql/lib -lpq
```

The -I parameter is used to specify the location of the header files necessary to compile the application, and the -L parameter is used to specify the location of the library files necessary to link the application into an executable program.

Creating an Application Database

Once the PostgreSQL software is installed and running on your system, you can begin creating databases, schemas, and tables for your applications.

The psql command line program provides a simple interface to the PostgreSQL server. You must specify a login ID (using the -U parameter) and password to connect to the database. By default, the administrator login ID is postgres, and the password is nothing:

```
$ /usr/local/pgsql/bin/psql -U postgres
Welcome to psql 8.1.5, the PostgreSQL interactive terminal.

Type:  \copyright for distribution terms
       \h for help with SQL commands
       \? for help with psql commands
       \g or terminate with semicolon to execute query
       \q to quit

postgres=#
```

You are now connected to the default database (called postgres) will full privileges!

The postgres database contains system tables that keep statistics. It is recommended that you create a separate database for your applications. You can create a new database using the SQL CREATE DATABASE command:

```
postgres=# create database test;
CREATE DATABASE
postgres=#
```

If the command is successful, you will see a terse message displayed. If it fails, you will see a longer error message explaining the problem.

To get ready for the programming examples, you should create a table in the newly created test database. First, you must use the \c metacommand to connect to the new database; then create the table within the database:

```
postgres=# \c test
You are now connected to database "test".
test=# create table employee (
test(# empid int4 primary key not null,
test(# lastname varchar,
test(# firstname varchar,
test(# salary float4);
NOTICE:  CREATE TABLE / PRIMARY KEY will create implicit index "employee_pkey" for
table "employee"
CREATE TABLE
test=#
```

The new table has been created. It is also a good idea to create a user so that your applications do not have to log in as the postgres user. The new user should be granted privileges to the newly created table:

```
test=# create role management with nologin;
CREATE ROLE
test=# create role earl in role management;
CREATE ROLE
test=# alter role earl login password 'bigshot' inherit;
ALTER ROLE
test=# grant all on employee to management;
GRANT
test=#
```

PostgreSQL provides both Group roles and Login roles. Login roles are used to allow individuals to log in to the database. Group roles contain Login roles and are granted privileges to database objects. This way you can move Login roles around to different Group roles as people change functions within an organization. This example creates a Group role called management that is granted all privileges on the employee table. A Login role called earl is created, and added to the management Group role. Now you can login as earl and access the employee table in the test database:

```
$ psql test -U earl -W
Password:
Welcome to psql, the PostgreSQL interactive terminal.

Type:  \copyright for distribution terms
```

```
        \h for help with SQL commands
        \? for help on internal slash commands
        \g or terminate with semicolon to execute query
        \q to quit

test=> select * from employee;
 empid | lastname | firstname | salary
-------+----------+-----------+--------
(0 rows)

test=>
```

To connect directly to the test database, you must specify it on the `psql` command line. Also, to log in as the `earl` Login role, you must specify the `-U` and `-W` parameters. After entering the password for earl (set to bigshot) you have access to the database. You are now ready to start programming.

Connecting to the Server

The libpq library provides five functions that are used for starting and stopping a connection to a PostgreSQL server:

Function	Description
`Pqconnectdb(const char *coninfo)`	Start a connection to a PostgreSQL server using parameters in `coninfo`, and wait for an answer
`PqconnectStart(const char * coninfo)`	Start a connection to a PostgreSQL server in non-blocking mode using parameters in `coninfo`.
`PqconnectPoll(PGconn *conn)`	Check on the status of a pending nonblocking connection attempt `conn`.
`Pqfinish(PGconn *conn)`	Close (end) an established PostgreSQL server session `conn`.
`Pqreset(PGconn *conn)`	Reset a PostgreSQL server session by closing a previous session `conn`, and starting a new session using the same parameters. This command will wait for an answer from the server.

The `PQconnectbd()` function is used to establish a new connection to a PostgreSQL server. The format of the `PQconnectdb()` function is:

```
PGconn *PQconnectdb(const char *conninfo)
```

The `PQconnectdb()` function returns a pointer to a `PGconn` data type. This value is used in all subsequent functions that send commands to the server using this connection.

The `conninfo` constant character pointer defines the values used to connect to the PostgreSQL server. These values are not much different from what you are already used to for connecting to a PostgreSQL server. As expected, there are several standard parameters that can be used to define the connection:

Connection Parameter	Description
host	The DNS host name or numeric IP address of the PostgreSQL server.
hostaddr	The numeric IP address of the PostgreSQL server.
port	The TCP port of the PostgreSQL server.
dbname	The database the session connects to.
user	The Login role to use to log into the server.
password	The password of the Login role.
connect_timeout	Maximum time (in seconds) to wait for the connection to establish. Use zero to wait indefinitely.
options	Command line options to send to the server.
sslmode	Sets SSL preference: disable for no SSL, allow to try SSL first, permit to negotiate with server, and require for only SSL.
service	Sets a service name to specify parameters in a pg_service.conf configuration file.

When listing multiple parameters in the character string, each parameter pair must be separated by one or more spaces. An example of creating a new connection is:

```
const char *conninfo;
Pconn *conn;
conninfo = "host = 127.0.0.1 dbname = test user = earl password = bigshot";
conn = PQconnectdb(conninfo);
```

This example connects to the PostgreSQL server running on the local system using the loopback address (127.0.0.1). It attempts to establish the session with the database test using the earl Login role.

The PQconnectdb() function is a blocking function. A blocking function stops (blocks) execution of the program until the function completes. If the PostgreSQL server specified in the connection string is unavailable, you will have to wait for connect_timeout seconds before control will return to your program. For applications which are event-driven, sometimes this can cause problems. While the program is blocking on a connection, it is not responding to events, such as mouse clicks or keyboard entries.

To solve this problem, you can use the nonblocking connection function. The PQconnectStart() function uses the same connection string information as PQconnectdb() and attempts the same type of connection to the specified PostgreSQL server. However, PQconnectStart() does not wait for the connection to either establish or fail.

Program execution continues immediately after the PQconnectStart() function is executed. In order to determine if the connection succeeded (or failed), you must call the PQconnectPoll() function. This function returns the status of the connection attempt. The PQconnectPoll() function can return one of several status values:

- ❑ **CONNECTION_STARTED:** Waiting for the connection to be established
- ❑ **CONNECTION_AWAITING_RESPONSE:** Waiting for a response from the PostgreSQL server
- ❑ **CONNECTION_SSL_STARTUP:** Negotiating SSL encryption scheme.
- ❑ **CONNECTION_AUTH_OK:** Authentication succeeded, waiting for server to finish the connection
- ❑ **CONNECTION_SETENV:** Negotiating session parameters
- ❑ **CONNECTION_MADE:** Connection established, waiting for commands

If the connection has not succeeded or failed, you must poll the connection again. This should continue until either the connection is established, or it has ultimately failed.

After you have established a connection to a PostgreSQL server, there are several functions you can use that allow you to check on the status of the connection, as well as the connection parameters used to establish the connection.

Function	Description
PQdb(PGconn *conn)	Returns the database name of the connection
PQuser(PGconn *conn)	Returns the Login role used for the connection
PQpass(PGconn *conn)	Returns the password of the Login role used for the connection
PQhost(PGconn *conn)	Returns the server host name of the connection
PQport(PGconn *conn)	Returns the TCP port of the connection
PQoptions(PGconn *conn)	Returns any command line options used to establish the connection
PQstatus(PGconn *conn)	Returns the status of the server connection
PQtransactionStatus(PGconn *conn)	Returns the transaction status of the server
PQparameterStatus(PGconn *conn, const char *param)	Returns the current setting of a parameter param on the server
PQprotocolVersion(PGconn *conn)	Returns the PostgreSQL back end protocol version
PQserverVersion(PGconn *conn)	Returns the server version as an integer value
PQerrorMessage(PGconn *conn)	Returns the most recently generated server error message
PQsocket(PGconn *conn)	Returns the server file descriptor of the socket connection
PQbackendPID(PGconn *conn)	Returns the server process ID (PID) of the PostgreSQL process
PQgetssl(PGconn *conn)	Returns NULL if SSL is not used, or an SSL structure if it is used for the connection

All of the status functions use the PGconn data value returned by the PQconnectdb() function to iden-tify the connection. Most of the status functions return a pointer to a string that contains the status infor-mation. An example of this is:

```
char *user;
user = PQuser(conn);
```

The user character pointer points to the Login role value used to establish the connection. The exception is the PQstatus() function. This function returns a ConnStatusType data type, which has two defined values:

❑   CONNECTION_OK for good connections

❑   CONNECTION_BAD for failed connections

In Listing 6-5 the version.c program demonstrates connecting to a database, checking the status of the connection, and extracting the PostgreSQL server version.

Listing 6-5: Connecting to a PostgreSQL database

```c
/*
 *
 * Professional Linux Programming - connecting to a database
 *
 */
#include <stdio.h>
#include <stdlib.h>
#include "libpq-fe.h"

int main(int argc, char **argv)
{
    const char *conninfo;
    const char *serverversion;
    PGconn *conn;
    const char *paramtext = "server_version";

    conninfo = "hostaddr = 127.0.0.1 dbname = test user = earl password = bigshot";

    conn = PQconnectdb(conninfo);
    if (PQstatus(conn) != CONNECTION_OK)
    {
        printf("Unable to establish connection: %s",
                PQerrorMessage(conn));
        return 1;
    } else
    {
        printf("Connection established!\n");
        serverversion = PQparameterStatus(conn, paramtext);
        printf("Server Version: %s\n", serverversion);
    }
    PQfinish(conn);
    return 0;
}
```

This small example demonstrates all the basics of connecting to and interacting with a PostgreSQL server in C. It connects to the `test` database on the localhost using the earl Login role created.

After attempting the connection, the `PQstatus()` function is used to test the status of the connection. If the connection is OK, the `PQparameterStatus()` function is used to obtain the value of the `server_version` parameter from the PostgreSQL server.

To compile the program, you must include the PostgreSQL libpq header (`libpq-fe.h`), and link with the libpq library files:

```
$ cc -I/usr/local/pgsql/include -o version version.c -L/usr/local/pgsql/lib -lpq
$ ./version
Connection established!
Server Version: 8.1.5
$
```

The program worked as expected. The next section moves on to show more advanced functions that can be executed on the server.

Executing SQL Commands

After establishing a connection with the PostgreSQL server, you will most likely want to execute SQL commands on the PostgreSQL server. There are quite a few command execution functions contained in the libpq library:

Function	Description
`PQexec(PGconn *conn, const char *command)`	Submit a string command to the server and wait for the result.
`PQexecParams(PGconn *conn, const char *command, int nParams, const Oid *paramTypes, const char *paramValues, const int *paramLengths, const int *paramFormats, int resultFormat)`	Submit a command that includes parameters to the server and wait for the result. The parameters are defined, along with lengths and formats, in the other parameters. This command also specifies the result format (0 for text or 1 for binary).
`PQprepare(PGconn *conn, const char *name, const char *query, int nParams, const Oid *paramTypes)`	Submit a command query to be prepared on the server using connection conn. The command may use parameters, defined in the `PQexecPrepared()` function. The prepared statement is referenced by name.

Table continued on following page

Function	Description
`PQexecPrepared(Pgconn *conn, const char *name, int nParms, const char *paramValues, const int paramLengths, const int paramFormats, int resultFormat)`	Submit a request to execute a previously prepared statement name. You may specify parameters, and the result format (0 for text or 1 for binary).
`PQresultStatus(Pgresult *result)`	Returns the result status of an executed command.
`PQresStatus(ExecStatuwsType status)`	Returns a string result status given a `PQresultStatus` value.
`PQresultErrorMessage(PGresult *result)`	Returns an error message string from an executed command or a `NULL` value if no error occurred.
`PQclear(PGresult *result)`	Clears (frees) the storage memory of result status result.

The `PQexec()` function is the basic function used for executing SQL commands on the PostgreSQL server. The libpq library uses a single function to execute both query and nonquery SQL commands. The result of the all commands is returned into the same `PGresult` data type object:

```
PGresult *PQexec(PGconn *conn, const char *command)
```

The `PQexec()` function requires two parameters. The first parameter is the `PGconn` object created when connecting to the server. The second parameter is a character string that contains the SQL command to execute on the server.

When the `PQexec()` function is executed in the program, the command is sent to the server, and the program waits for a response. The response is placed in an `PGresult` data object. Since there are many types of output associated with different SQL commands, this data object must be capable of handling lots of possibilities.

This data object must first be checked using the `PQresultStatus()` function to determine the status of the command, and the type of output available from the command. The result status can be:

❑ **PGRES_COMMAND_OK:** Command processed OK but with no result set returned.

❑ **PGRES_TUPLES_OK:** Command processed OK and returned a result set (even an empty result set).

❑ **PGRES_EMPTY_QUERY:** The command sent was empty.

❑ **PGRES_BAD_RESPONSE:** The response from the server could not be understood.

❑ **PGRES_NONFATAL_ERROR:** The server generated a notice or a warning.

❑ **PGRES_FATAL_ERROR:** The server generated a fatal error message.

These values are defined in the libpq library and can be directly checked in your code:

```
PGresult *result;
result = PQexec(conn, "SELECT lastname from employee");
if (PQresultStatus(result) != PGRES_TUPLES_OK)
{
    ...
```

If the result returned by the command is a result set, there are several "helper" functions that can be used to determine what the returned data looks like and how to handle it.

Function	Description
PQntuples(PGresult *res)	Returns the number of records (tuples) in a result set res.
PQnfields(PGresult *res)	Returns the number of columns (fields) in a result set res.
PQfname(PGresult *res, int column)	Returns a column name given a result set res and a column number column.
PQfnumber(PGresult *res, const char *colname)	Returns a column number given a result set res and a column name colname.
PQftable(PGresult *res, int column)	Returns the OID of the table that a given column column, was fetched from.
PQgetvalue(PGresult *res, int rec, int column)	Returns the value of column, column, of a single record rec in result set res.
PQgetisnull(PGresult *res, int rec, int column)	Tests if a value in column column of record rec in result set res is NULL. Returns 1 if the value is NULL and 0 if it is not.
PQgetlength(PGresult *res, int rec, int column)	Returns the length (bytes) of a value in column column in record rec in a result set res.

These functions are invaluable in sorting through the result set data returned within the PGresult object. The way your program handles the result set data depends on what type of data (if any) is returned. The following sections demonstrate how to handle different types of data returned from executing SQL commands in libpq.

Commands Returning No Data

SQL commands such as INSERT, UPDATE, and DELETE do not return data but return a status code indicating if the command succeeded or not. In these situations, you must check for the PGRES_COMMAND_OK status in the result, since there are no tuples (records) returned.

The update.c program in Listing 6-6 demonstrates this principle:

Listing 6-6: Inserting records in a PostgreSQL database

```c
/*
 *
 * Professional Linux Programming - insert a new record
 *
 */
#include <stdio.h>
#include <stdlib.h>
#include "libpq-fe.h"

int main(int argc, char **argv)
{
    const char *conninfo;
    PGconn *conn;
    PGresult *result;
    char *insertcomm;

    conninfo = "hostaddr = 127.0.0.1 dbname = test user = earl password = bigshot";
    conn = PQconnectdb(conninfo);
    if (PQstatus(conn) != CONNECTION_OK)
    {
        printf("Unable to establish connection: %s",
                   PQerrorMessage(conn));
        return 1;
    } else
    {
        insertcomm = "INSERT into employee values (100, 'Test', 'Ima', 35000)";
        result = PQexec(conn, insertcomm);
        if (PQresultStatus(result) != PGRES_COMMAND_OK)
        {
            printf("Problem with command: %s\n", PQerrorMessage(conn));
            PQclear(result);
            PQfinish(conn);
            return 1;
        }
        PQclear(result);
    }
    PQfinish(conn);
    return 0;
}
```

The update.c program establishes a connection to the test database on the PostgreSQL server running on the local system, using the earl Login Role. After the connection is established, a simple INSERT SQL command is executed on the server using the PQexec() function.

The status of the command is checked using the PQresultStatus() function and the PGRES_COM-MAND_OK value. If the status is not OK, the PQerrorMessage() function is used to display the error message generated by the server. Finally, the PQclear() function is used to clear the memory used by the PGresult object. It is always a good idea to clear this memory, especially if you reuse the PGresult object for another command.

After compiling the update.c program, execute it on your PostgreSQL system. If the INSERT command succeeds, nothing should be displayed (not too exciting). You can then look at the employee table and see the newly added record. If you run the program a second time, you should get an error message, indicating that the employee ID key value already exists:

```
$ ./update
ERROR:  duplicate key violates unique constraint "employee_pkey"
Problem with command: ERROR:  duplicate key violates unique constraint
"employee_pkey"

$
```

As expected, the record was not allowed to be added.

Commands Returning Data

For SQL commands that return data, you must use the PQgetvalue() function to retrieve the returned information. The PQgetvalue() function retrieves the data values as a character string data type, no matter what the actual data type of the table column data. For integer or floating point values you can convert the character string value into the appropriate data type using standard C functions, such as atoi() for integers, or atof() for floating point values.

The PQgetvalue() function allows you to retrieve data from the result set in any order. You are not limited in walking forward through each record in the result set. The format of the PQgetvalue() function is:

```
char *PQgetvalue(PGresult *result, int record, int column)
```

In the function you must specify the result set result, the desired record number record within the result set, and the column number column within the record to retrieve a value from. Records and column numbers both start at 0. For commands that produce only one record, that is always record 0.

The getvals.c program shown in Listing 6-7 demonstrates how to retrieve and convert data from a result set of an SQL function:

Listing 6-7: Querying records in a PostgreSQL database

```
/*
 *
 * Professional Linux Programming - retrieving values from queries
 *
 */
#include <stdio.h>
#include <stdlib.h>
```

(continued)

Listing 6-7: *(continued)*

```c
#include "libpq-fe.h"

int main(int argc, char **argv)
{
   const char *conninfo;
   PGconn *conn;
   PGresult *result;
   char *time, *pi;
   float fpi;

   conninfo = "hostaddr = 127.0.0.1 dbname = test user = earl password = bigshot";
   conn = PQconnectdb(conninfo);
   if (PQstatus(conn) != CONNECTION_OK)
   {
      printf("Unable to establish connection: %s",
                PQerrorMessage(conn));
      return 1;
   } else
   {
      result = PQexec(conn, "SELECT timeofday()");
      if (PQresultStatus(result) != PGRES_TUPLES_OK)
      {
         printf("Problem with command1: %s\n", PQerrorMessage(conn));
         PQclear(result);
         return 1;
      }
      time = PQgetvalue(result, 0, 0);
      printf("Time of day: %s\n", time);
      PQclear(result);

      result = PQexec(conn, "Select pi()");
      if (PQresultStatus(result) != PGRES_TUPLES_OK)
      {
         printf("Problem with command: %s\n", PQerrorMessage(conn));
         PQclear(result);
         return 1;
      }
      pi = PQgetvalue(result, 0, 0);
      fpi = atof(pi);
      printf("The value of pi is: %lf\n", fpi);
      PQclear(result);
   }

   PQfinish(conn);
   return 0;
}
```

After establishing the connection, the PQexec() function is used to send a standard SELECT SQL command to the server. Notice that to check the status of the result set, you must use the PGRES_TUPLES_OK value, since the query returns a result set. The PQgetvalue() function is used to retrieve the result set, using record 0 and column 0, since there is only one data value returned. In the first instance, the `timeofday()` PostgreSQL function returns a string value, which can be directly placed in a character string variable.

After using the `PQclear()` function to reset the `PGresult` value, another query is made with the `PQexec()` function. Again the `PQgetvalue()` function is used to retrieve the text result set from the query. This time, since the desired data type is a floating point value, the `atof()` C function is used to convert the string value to a floating point variable.

Running the program produces the following results:

```
$ ./getvals
Time of day: Wed Oct 18 19:27:54.270179 2006 EDT
The value of pi is: 3.141593
$
```

Handling Column Data

The `getvals.c` program was somewhat trivial in that we knew there was only one column of data in the result set. It was easy to extract the single record data from the result set. For more complicated result sets, you must determine the number records returned, and the order of the data columns in the result set. If there are multiple records in the result set, you must loop through the result set, reading all of the data records until you have read the last one.

To determine the number of records and columns in a result set, you can use the `PQntuples()` and `PQnfields()` functions, respectively:

```
int recs;
int cols;
result = PQexec(conn, "SELECT * from employee");
recs = PQntuples(result);
cols = PQnfields(result);
```

Once you know the number of records and columns in a result set, it is a snap to loop through the result set extracting individual data items:

```
for (i = 0; i < recs; i++)
{
    ...
```

There is one thing you must be careful about though when extracting the column data. Remember, the `PQexec()` function returns all data items in text format. This means that if you intend to use the table data within your application program as another data type, you must use standard C functions to convert the string to the appropriate data type:

❑   `atoi()` for converting to an integer value

❑   `atof()` for converting to a floating point value

The `getemployees.c` program in Listing 6-8 demonstrates how to extract individual column data elements from a result set.

179

Listing 6-8: Retrieving multiple records from a PostgreSQL database

```c
/*
 *
 * Professional Linux Programming - list all employees
 *
 */
#include <stdio.h>
#include <stdlib.h>
#include "libpq-fe.h"


int main(int argc, char **argv)
{
    const char *conninfo;
    PGconn *conn;
    PGresult *result;
    char *empid, *lastname, *firstname, *salary;
    float salaryval;
    int i;

    conninfo = "hostaddr = 127.0.0.1 dbname = test user = earl password = bigshot";

    conn = PQconnectdb(conninfo);
    if (PQstatus(conn) != CONNECTION_OK)
    {
        printf("Unable to establish connection: %s",
                    PQerrorMessage(conn));
        return 1;
    } else
    {
        result = PQexec(conn, "Select * from employee order by empid");
        if (PQresultStatus(result) != PGRES_TUPLES_OK)
        {
            printf("Problem with query: %s",
                        PQerrorMessage(conn));
            return 1;
        } else
        {
            printf("ID      Name            Salary\n");
            printf("---------------------------\n");
            for(i = 0; i < PQntuples(result); i++)
            {
                empid = PQgetvalue(result, i, 0);
                lastname = PQgetvalue(result, i, 1);
                firstname = PQgetvalue(result, i, 2);
                salary = PQgetvalue(result, i, 3);
                salaryval = atof(salary);
                printf("%s  %s,%s    $%.2lf\n", empid, lastname,
                        firstname, salaryval);
            }
            PQclear(result);
        }
    }
}
```

```
        PQfinish(conn);
        return 0;
}
```

The `getemployees.c` program starts off as usual, connecting to the sample database and using the `PQexec()` function to send a simple query. The number of records in the result set is obtained using the `PQntuples()` function, and a for loop is started to loop through the result set records.

Within the `for` loop, each iteration is a separate record in the result set. For each record, the individual column data values are extracted using the `PQgetvalue()` function. The function references the result set, the record number (controlled by the `for` loop value), and the individual column number for each data element.

Of course, this requires that you know what columns are produced by the query, and in what order. If you do not know this information, you can use the `PQfname()` function to find out which column number is which column name.

Each individual column data value is assigned to a character string variable, since `PQexec()` returns only string values. Since the `salary` column value is a floating point data type, the `atof()` C function is used to convert the string representation to a floating point value:

```
$ ./getemployees
ID      Name            Salary
---------------------------
100     Test,Ima        $35000.00
101     Test, Another   $75000.00
$
```

Using Parameters

In many cases, it is necessary to perform multiple queries using the same SQL command but different data elements. Instead of having to rewrite each `PQexec()` command, you can use the `PQexecParams()` function and a feature called parameters. Parameters allow you to use variables in the place of normal data values in the SQL command. Each variable is preceded by a dollar sign ($), and is numbered (1 for the first variable, 2 for the second, and so on). An example of using parameters is:

```
SELECT * from employee where lastname = $1 and firstname = $2
```

Variables can only be used for data values. You cannot use a variable for the table or column names. The format of the complete `PQexecParams()` function is:

```
PGresult *PQexecParams(Pgconn *conn, const char *command,
                       int nparams,
                       const Oid *paramTypes,
                       const char * const *paramValues,
                       const int *paramLengths,
                       const int *paramFormats,
                       int resultFormat)
```

As expected, you must declare the values used in the variables within the function. After specifying the connection to use, and the string command to send, you must define the variable values. The first value is `nparams`, which specifies the number of variables used. After that is the `paramTypes` value. This value is an array containing the OID of each variable type. You can also assign this value a NULL value. This value forces the PostgreSQL server to use the default data type for the column the data value is used for.

The next three values specify the variable values (paramValues), their lengths (paramLengths), and the format the variable is specified in (paramFormats). Each of these values is an array. The first element in the array references variable $1, the second, variable $2, and so on.

The format value of each variable can be either text mode (0), or binary mode (1). If the value is NULL, PostgreSQL assumes that all of the variables are in text mode. If the format of the variable is text mode, PostgreSQL assumes that the variable is specified as a text (or character) data type, and converts the variable value to the data type required for the SQL command specified.

Thus, you can specify an integer or floating point value as a text string and set the format value to 0; PostgreSQL automatically does the conversion for you. If you use text mode for variables, you can also set the length value to NULL, as PostgreSQL automatically determines the length of the text string variable.

Alternatively, if you set the value format type to binary mode (1), you must specify the variable values using the appropriate data type, and specify the length as the byte length of the value.

The result format value (resultFormat) is also interesting. It allows you to set the data type of the result value. It can be either text mode (0) or binary mode (1). In text mode, the result set is returned as text values, just as with the PQexec() function. The appropriate data type conversion must be performed for binary values. In binary mode, the result set data is returned in the appropriate binary format either integer or floating point. At this time, the result format value can only be one or the other; you cannot mix and match text and binary mode data elements.

Setting the PQexecParams() function can be confusing. For beginners, the easiest thing to do is set both the input and output formats as text mode. This cuts down on the amount of information you must collect and pass to the function.

In Listing 6-9 The empinfo.c program demonstrates using parameters with text mode for both input and output data values:

Listing 6-9: Using parameters in a PostgreSQL program

```
/*
 *
 * Professional Linux Programming - get employee info
 *
 */
#include <stdio.h>
#include <stdlib.h>
#include <sys/types.h>
#include "libpq-fe.h"

int main(int argc, char **argv)
{
    const char *conninfo;
    PGconn *conn;
    PGresult *result;
    char *paramValues[1];
```

```
const char *query;
char empid[4];
char *lastname, *firstname, *salary;
float salaryval;

conninfo = "hostaddr = 127.0.0.1 dbname = test user = earl password = bigshot";
conn = PQconnectdb(conninfo);
if (PQstatus(conn) != CONNECTION_OK)
{
   printf("Unable to establish connection: %s", PQerrorMessage(conn));
   return 1;
} else
{
   query = "SELECT * from employee where empid = $1";
   while(1)
   {
      printf("\nEnter employee id: ");
      scanf("%3s", &empid);
      if (!strcmp(empid,"0"))
         break;

      paramValues[0] = (char *)empid;
      result = PQexecParams(conn, query, 1, NULL,
                     (const char * const *)paramValues, NULL, NULL, 0);
      if (PQresultStatus(result) != PGRES_TUPLES_OK)
      {
         printf("Problem: %s", PQerrorMessage(conn));
         PQclear(result);
         PQfinish(conn);
         return 1;
      } else
      {
         if (PQntuples(result) > 0)
         {
            lastname = PQgetvalue(result, 0, 1);
            firstname = PQgetvalue(result, 0, 2);
            salary = PQgetvalue(result, 0, 3);
            salaryval = atof(salary);
            printf(" Employee ID: %s\n", empid);
            printf(" Name: %s,%s\n", lastname, firstname);
            printf(" Salary: $%.2lf\n", salaryval);
            PQclear(result);
         } else
            printf(" Employee ID not found\n");
      }
   }

}

PQfinish(conn);
return 0;
}
```

The paramValues pointer is declared as an array. Since there is only one parameter used in the SQL command, there only needs to be one value in the array. The string used for the query is declared, using a parameter variable $1 for the data element in the WHERE clause.

Next, an endless `while()` loop is used to continually loop through values until a stopping value is entered by the user. The C `scanf` function is used to allow the user to enter an employee value to look up in the database.

After the desired variable value is entered, it is assigned to the `paramValues` array, and the `PQexecParams()` function is declared. Since the input value is in text mode, the `paramLengths` and `paramFormats` values can be set to `NULL`. Also, the `resultFormat` value is set to 0, indicating that we want the output result set data in text mode as well.

After the `PQexecParams()` function is executed, the data in the result set is extracted using `PQgetvalue()`. Since the output data format is set to text, the `salary` value must be converted to floating point using the C `atof()` function.

After compiling the program, it can be run to see the employee information for a specific employee. A value of 0 should be entered to stop the program:

```
$ ./empinfo

Enter employee id: 100
 Employee ID: 100
 Name: Test,Ima
 Salary: $35000.00

Enter employee id: 103
 Employee ID not found

Enter employee id: 0
$
```

Summary

In today's environment, Linux applications must be able to store information for future retrieval. There are several methods available for programming data persistence in Linux applications. The most popular methods involve using a database to allow quick storage and retrieval of data. There are two popular methods for implementing database functions in Linux applications.

The Berkeley DB application allows you to code a database engine directly into your applications. Data can be inserted, deleted, and retrieved from simple data files using easy library functions. The Berkeley DB library supports B-Tree, hash, queue, and record number data storage.

The other method is to use an external database server to control access to database files. The PostgreSQL open source database provides many commercial features in a free database. PostgreSQL provides the libpq library, which can be used to interface C and C++ applications with the database server. All access is sent to the server, and the server controls what data can be accessed. The server incorporates all of the database engine functions. Applications send commands to the server and retrieve results returned by the server. Using a central database server, applications can easily share data among multiple users, even spread out across a network.

7

Kernel Development

Developing software for Linux systems occasionally requires a more intimate knowledge of the internal design of the operating system kernel itself. This is especially true if you need to write a Linux device driver, but there are other reasons that you may end up delving a little deeper. People who port the Linux kernel to new hardware platforms, fix bugs, add new functionality, work out performance bottlenecks, or improve scalability to huge (or tiny) systems are among those who have legitimate reasons to be hacking away at the core algorithms that make Linux (literally) tick.

Sometimes, it's not about changing the kernel in any way at all. The Linux kernel is a very unusual example of a program that follows few of the norms you may be used to in writing application code. When writing kernel code, you need to handle all memory allocations explicitly—nobody is going to free up memory on your behalf—and you need to worry about very real programming errors or dead/live locks that can bring the entire system crashing down around you. Consequently, many are simply morbidly curious to know more about how the kernel that they rely on is put together.

Whatever your interest in the internal design of the Linux kernel, this chapter will lay the groundwork. In this chapter, you'll learn how working with the kernel differs from writing regular user applications. You'll learn how to build the Linux kernel from the latest development releases, how to track the public mailing lists, and how to submit your first patches back into the community. The emphasis here is on a broad understanding, which will facilitate your progression into the chapters that follow.

Starting Out

Working with the Linux kernel is somewhat different from the other day-to-day activities of a professional Linux programmer. The Linux kernel isn't a regular user program that begins and ends in the usual way. It isn't easy to test out ideas without running the risk of crashing the entire machine, and it can be very difficult to debug when things do go wrong. But for all the potential pitfalls, many are motivated to get involved in the development process—and that obviously includes you. As you begin to develop with the Linux kernel, you'll discover that the process can be very rewarding indeed.

No matter what your personal interest in the Linux kernel, there are few things you need to get right from the start. You'll need to quickly become proficient at configuring and building the kernel, applying test patches, and packaging the end result. And that's before you actually begin writing any new code for yourself. There's simply no point in jumping in at the deep end and hoping it'll all work out, without at least having a grasp of the basics. Likewise, there are aspects of the development process that you'll need to understand. The Linux kernel development process is introduced to you later in this chapter.

Background Prerequisites

To begin working with the Linux kernel, you'll need to satisfy a few background prerequisites. For starters, you'll need to have a development machine available in order to test out your kernel code without interfering with the operation of your regular workstation. Virtual machines are okay for many purposes[1], but it's not really acceptable to try getting into kernel development on the same machine on which you are writing the code—you're going to make mistakes that crash the entire system; do you really want to reboot every 10 minutes? It's by far much more preferable to have an old test machine.

You should have a reasonably fast development machine with a good amount of RAM (kernel builds are memory intensive and will take longer as you reduce available memory) and as fast a CPU as you can reasonably justify (or afford!). Don't go crazy with the processor speed—it's far more important that the machine not spend every second thrashing the disks, so memory is the bottleneck here—but do try to ensure that you have sufficient resources available. If you're working in a commercial company, try justifying a new machine on the grounds of improved productivity—you won't be wrong.

Developing code for the Linux kernel is a disk-intensive operation. You'll need plenty of space available to store all of those test kernels and even more to track the daily development of the upstream kernel via the tools that will be introduced to you later in the chapter. As a guideline, a fully built 2.6 Linux kernel may require up to 2GB for storage of the source code and binary object files—more if you decide to enable every possible configuration option (don't do that—it'll massively increase build times), while a development tree tracking daily upstream development might need even more. Disk space is cheap though these days, so you'll want to ensure that you have plenty of it available for kernel work.

If you're half serious about kernel development and are working on a PC workstation, you'll want to have at least a 2GHz processor available, more than 1GB of RAM—after other system overhead—and a large dedicated area of storage for all those test kernel builds that might run into 50GB or much more with relative ease. Fortunately, none of these requirements is particularly strenuous on the pocket these days—which is why they form the basis for a recommendation here. Of course, it's possible to build Linux using an old 386 or even a Sun IPX[2]—if you have a week at a time to build the kernel and potentially unlimited amounts of patience. Failing that, get a reasonably fast build machine.

---

[1]In that sense, they don't count as being the same machine; however, a virtual machine with virtual hardware (however implemented) will never be quite the same as working with a real machine. For this reason, a 3–5-year-old machine that you can pick up for little money is worthy of investment.

[2]The author recalls many hours of his early teenage years building test kernels on an old 386. Those were days when building a kernel was something you started on an evening before sleeping. As to the Sun IPX—it took over three days to install Debian, so building a kernel was always going to be painful.

Kernel Sources

The overall Linux kernel source tree is composed of around 10,000 header files, 9000 C language source files, 800 architecture-specific assembly language files and many other miscellaneous linker, Makefile, and other support infrastructure needed to put the whole thing together. To understand the entirety of the Linux kernel source tree would be almost impossible at this point — and nobody does understand the whole thing — that's not important. What is important is that you understand how and where the source tree is laid out and where to go looking for those parts that matter right now.

The de facto "official" home of Linux kernel sources is at the kernel.org website. There you will find copies of every Linux kernel ever released (including signed checksums of the sources for anything other than ancient kernels solely available for their historical interest), alongside many thousands of patches from individual developers who have accounts on those machines. This really is the first place to look whenever you want something kernel related — you'll find many pointers to other information.

On the home page of the kernel.org website, you'll see a link to the latest official "stable" Linux kernel — in the form 2.6.x.y at the time of this writing (where "x" is the primary version differentiator and, optionally, "y" refers to special security (or other very urgent) errata that have been applied by the "-stable" kernel team). You'll also see a link to the latest "-mm" development kernel, and information about other older kernels, too. Don't try too hard to understand why there's no 2.7 kernel (yet) or when that development process for the stable 2.8 kernel will start. Nobody else knows any better anyway.

To get going with your own kernel development, you'll want to download the latest 2.6.x.y kernel, linked directly from the front page of the kernel.org website. Download the ~40MB `.tar.bz2`[3] kernel archive with the highest available release number (for example kernel 2.6.18) and unpack it into a new working directory, using the following commands:

```
$ tar xvfj linux-2.6.18.tar.bz2
linux-2.6.18
linux-2.6.18/COPYING
linux-2.6.18/CREDITS
linux-2.6.18/Documentation
linux-2.6.18/Documentation/00-INDEX
linux-2.6.18/Documentation/BUG-HUNTING
linux-2.6.18/Documentation/Changes
linux-2.6.18/Documentation/CodingStyle
...
```

The listing has been truncated for brevity — the full listing of files will run into many thousands of files.

Pay particular attention to those files under the `Documentation` directory. They're not all as up to date as the current kernel release — something really worth helping to improve if you have some time and are trying to figure the kernel out anyway (2.6 kernel maintainer Andrew Morton et al. will really thank you if you do that) — but certainly are a great place to look for a little extra information.

You will find a great guide to the kernel coding style in that CodingStyle document as well as guides to submitting bugs and overview documents on many of the most technical aspects of the internal implementation within the kernel. You can always write your own handy documentation, too.

---

[3].bz2 files were explained when you were introduced to tarballs back in Chapters 2–4, but you'll find a (legacy) description of their use in the Linux kernel on the kernel.org website.

A Tour of the Kernel Source

The Linux kernel source has a top-level directory structure that is always similar to the following:

```
arch/      crypto/          include/ kernel/       mm/             scripts/
block/     Documentation/   init/    lib/          net/            security/
COPYING    drivers/         ipc/     MAINTAINERS   README          sound/
CREDITS    fs/              Kbuild   Makefile      REPORTING-BUGS  usr/
```

The arrangement of these directories has grown organically over the past decade, with the vast bulk of the interesting core kernel functionality remaining in the arch, kernel, and mm directories. The majority of kernel drivers live in the drivers directory these days, while a few notable exceptions stand out like a sore thumb — for example, the sound and net directories remain at the top level, mostly for a variety of historical reasons. Table 7-1 shows a summary of what is contained within each of those top-level directories:

Table 7-1 Top-Level Directories

Directory name	Directory content
arch	Architecture-specific files, by architecture — arm, i386, powerpc, and so on. This is the location of low-level startup code as well as critical code necessary to support processor features, largely written in assembly. Look for the head.s assembly files for low-level kernel entry points.
block	Support for block devices such as hard disks. This directory contains the 2.6 Linux kernel implementation of struct bios and bio_vecs used to represent in-flight IO operations as well as the vast majority of the code necessary to support hard disks within the Linux kernel.
crypto	Cryptographic library functions. Prior to a change in United States law, it was not possible to host a kernel with strong cryptography within the United States for potential export overseas. This changed some time ago, and now strong cryptography is built into the kernel.
Documentation	Documentation supplied with the Linux kernel. Remember, there is no commercially funded documentation team working to keep this up to date, so it's not always in line with the current state of the art. As long as you bear this in mind, you should be fine in using it.
drivers	Device drivers for a huge variety of potential devices.
fs	Implementation of every filesystem supported by the Linux kernel.
include	Header files supplied with the Linux kernel, divided by architecture-specific arch and generic linux header files. Look for the include/linux/sched.h header file referenced later in this chapter.
init	Higher-level startup code responsible for getting the kernel going after the very low-level architecture-specific code has finished up. This is where the kernel calls lower-level functions to set up kernel virtual memory (paging) support, begins running processes (the first process — or task — will become init) and ultimately exec()s into the init process to begin the regular Linux startup scripts and the first user programs.

Directory name	Directory content
ipc	The location of the implementation of various Inter-Process Communication (IPC) primitives used in the Linux kernel.
kernel	The higher-level core kernel functions. Contains the Linux process — task — scheduler, as well as miscellaneous support code such as the printk() generic routine that allows kernel developers to send messages to the kernel log at runtime (which end up in /var/log, once klogd has received each message, depending upon its configuration).
lib	Library routines such as CRC32 checksum calculation and various other higher-level library code that is used elsewhere in the kernel.
mm	Memory management routines supporting the Linux implementation of virtual memory. Works in tandem with architecture-specific code.
net	Contains an implementation of each of the networking standards that are supported by the Linux kernel. Does not contain individual network device drivers — they live in drivers/net and similar locations.
scripts	Various miscellaneous scripts used to configure and build the Linux kernel.
security	Linux includes support for the SELinux (Security-Enhanced Linux) functionality originally produced by the NSA (National Security Agency) of the United States. This code has been well audited but is, naturally, an occasional source of media attention and hysteria.
sound	Contains an implementation of the ALSA (Advanced Linux Sound Architecture) sound subsystem as used in recent Linux kernels. An older sound system known as OSS is being phased out over time.
usr	Various support utilities for building initial ramdisks (used by almost all Linux vendors to bootstrap their distribution environment), and so on.

Kernel Versioning

The Linux kernel used to follow a simple numbering system. Back in the good old days, kernels were numbered a.b.c, where "a" referred to the major version number — there have only been two of these — "b" referred to the minor version number — where odd numbers were development kernels and even numbers were considered to be stable — and "c" referred to the release number of a particular kernel development series. For example, it used to be possible to determine that a 2.3.z kernel would be an unstable development release, while a 2.4.z kernel was allegedly stable (although a number of those early 2.4 kernels had virtual memory problems that needed working out). This is true no longer.

Following the release of the 2.4 Linux kernel, a large amount of work went into a development series known as the 2.5 series kernel. This development kernel series had a large amount of improvement made in the name of block IO and scalability[4] as well as a vast number of other more miscellaneous developments. After a considerable time, the 2.6 Linux kernel was eventually released and was quickly hailed as some kind of breakthrough in the history of Linux development (which is true; it really was). With the release of the 2.6 Linux kernel, Linus Torvalds changed the numbering.

---

[4]This being the first real release afforded significant development cooperation from big computer companies with huge machines suddenly needing to run a Linux kernel, due to customer demand.

The problem with previous Linux kernel development was the amount of time it took to get new features out into the stable kernel. It could take 6 to 12 months before a feature in a development kernel would make it into a stable kernel, and some never made it at all—the Linux 2.4 kernel series never had good support for many modern peripheral buses (for example) that the 2.5 kernel quickly gained new support for, but it took more than a year for the 2.6 kernel to be available with those features. Many vendors backported new features into older kernels, but the situation was certainly less than ideal.

It was, then, felt that in the 2.6 kernel timeframe the development process was working well enough that it was not necessary to open up a new development kernel. Developers were comfortable with one another, and the entire process was working well enough, so development continued in the mainline Linux kernel throughout the life of the 2.6 Linux kernel. And that's where things still are today. Until there is a 2.7 Linux kernel or 3.0 kernel development begins, you can expect the status quo to remain.

Vendor Kernels

The Linux kernel is widely used around the world by many different individuals and organizations. There are many with vested interests in the development and furthering of Linux (as well as a number of groups who would love to see the back of Linux altogether). Thus, many groups are working on their own versions of the Linux kernel. For example, you're almost certainly running a standard Linux distribution on your Linux workstation. That distribution probably comes with its own kernel—a "vendor kernel"—that will include whatever additional features and patches your vendor felt were necessary to improve your overall experience. Your vendor supports its official kernel.

While vendor kernels can be useful because of the additional development and testing that has gone into them to support specific systems and workloads, you should be wary of using a vendor kernel when you start out with your own kernel development. You'll want to throw that kernel away and use the upstream "official" Linux kernel sources as quickly as possible so that you can interact with the kernel development community and ask useful questions. Nobody is going to help you if you attempt to write your fancy device driver using a vendor kernel, and your inbox will quickly remind you of this fact.

There are exceptions of course. A number of vendors sell specific products that include Linux kernels intended for developers to work on specific types of systems—often for embedded devices that need a specific set of kernels and patches for optimum use in these environments. Of course, if you are writing a device driver for some fancy new device, you'll want to ultimately support various vendor kernels in the field. But always begin with a fresh set of upstream kernel sources if you ever expect to get help from the many other kernel developers who are ready and willing to talk to you (you do want this).

Configuring the Kernel

With a freshly unpacked set of Linux kernel sources, you'll have a top directory of files similar to those shown in the previous section on the kernel sources. You can't actually build the Linux kernel at this stage. Building the kernel can only be done once you have determined what features it will support. Linux has an extremely flexible set of configuration options that will enable to you enable and disable core functionality, as well as many optional device drivers that may not be needed on your system. You will want to spend a while looking through the kernel configuration in the beginning, paying attention to the "help screen"-style information provided alongside most of the available configuration options.

To configure the Linux kernel, enter into a directory of newly unpacked set of kernel sources and configure them using the text based `menuconfig` configuration utility, as follows:

```
$ make menuconfig
```

Linux kernel configuration has a set of reasonable defaults for a given architecture, so you'll probably be fine with little more than the base configuration presented. One thing you will want to do is ensure that any obscure hardware that needs to be supported on your test machine is currently enabled in the configuration presented — otherwise, the kernel may just fail to boot when you come to test it out. Don't be disheartened by the wide variety of configuration options. It will take a few tries before you figure out how this all goes together, and you'll just need to slog through it in order to come out on top.

Navigating around the configuration system takes a bit of getting used to, but you'll figure it out. If you get lost, use the help option to understand how the different parts of the menu system fit together. If graphical configuration tools are not for you, then it is possible to edit the kernel configuration by hand instead — it is after all just a flat text file filled with options that will result in C language constants and macros being defined during the build. The text representation of the kernel configuration is stored in a file called `.config` within the top level of the kernel directory. Rather than editing the file by hand, however, you are advised to look to the "make config" make target.

If you decide to edit the `.config` file by hand, you are strongly advised to run the "make oldconfig" Make target in order to import the changes cleanly — the same goes for importing a vendor-supplied configuration, which you can do if you want to start with the configuration that is currently running on your machine. Your vendor's configuration is often in their Linux kernel development package.

Here is an example of the interaction you typically have when using the make config target:

```
$ make config
scripts/kconfig/conf arch/powerpc/Kconfig
#
# using defaults found in .config
#
*
* Linux Kernel Configuration
*
64-bit kernel (PPC64) [N/y/?]
*
* Processor support
*
Processor Type
> 1. 6xx/7xx/74xx (CLASSIC32)
  2. Freescale 52xx (PPC_52xx)
  3. Freescale 82xx (PPC_82xx)
  4. Freescale 83xx (PPC_83xx)
  5. Freescale 85xx (PPC_85xx)
  6. AMCC 40x (40x)
  7. AMCC 44x (44x)
  8. Freescale 8xx (8xx)
  9. Freescale e200 (E200)
choice[1-9]:
AltiVec Support (ALTIVEC) [Y/n/?]
Symmetric multi-processing support (SMP) [N/y/?]
*
* Code maturity level options
*
Prompt for development and/or incomplete code/drivers (EXPERIMENTAL) [Y/n/?]
*
```

```
* General setup
*
Local version - append to kernel release (LOCALVERSION) []
...
```

The output has been truncated for brevity.

Note how every single option is presented one at a time — you simply answer yes and no questions one at a time to each of the many hundreds (or thousands) of possible configuration options, varying according to the architecture, platform, and any other options you may have already chosen. If this is your idea of fun, or if you really want to ensure that you've seen every single possible option, old school is the way to go every time. After a few years, you'll be glad for the alternatives that follow below.

For those who don't like curses (text-based) graphics, you might prefer to use the make xconfig make target within the kernel build system. This will compile up and present you with a graphical configuration tool written for the X Window system.[5] Alternatively, if you have purchased a commercial Linux kernel development product (for example, one that uses the Eclipse graphical development environment IDE), then you may have an even more sophisticated set of kernel configuration tools available for your use. Whatever you use, the result is the same — the flat .config file of options.

Once you have a kernel configuration, it is saved in the .config file within the kernel configuration directory. You'll want to back this up so that it's available each time you unpack a fresh kernel or clean out the kernel sources you're working on via the make mrproper target. Once you have a working kernel configuration, you can import this into a new set of kernel sources by copying it into the .config location and running make oldconfig to pull in the configuration file. Kernel developers usually prefer this mechanism when moving from one release to another, as it avoids reconfiguration.[6]

Here is a small except from a valid kernel configuration .config file:

```
#
# Automatically generated make config: don't edit
# Linux kernel version: 2.6.17
# Mon Jun 19 18:48:00 2006
#
# CONFIG_PPC64 is not set
CONFIG_PPC32=y
CONFIG_PPC_MERGE=y
CONFIG_MMU=y
CONFIG_GENERIC_HARDIRQS=y
CONFIG_RWSEM_XCHGADD_ALGORITHM=y
CONFIG_GENERIC_HWEIGHT=y
CONFIG_GENERIC_CALIBRATE_DELAY=y
CONFIG_PPC=y
CONFIG_EARLY_PRINTK=y
```

---

[5]Obviously, you need to have X running to use this. If you're on a remote machine, connected via SSH, and it has X installed, try using the "-X" flag to SSH in order to forward to the remote X display.

[6]Unless a new option has been added, in which case you'll see only those options that were added or changed. Watch out for changes to configuration options that suddenly remove your default enabled IDE/SATA (or even perhaps SCSI) disk support and prevent the system from booting.

Vendor Kernel Configurations

Depending upon your distribution, you may find that the default set of kernel configuration options is provided in /boot with a name such as config-2.x.y-a.b_FC6 (as is the case with Fedora kernels) and can be imported into a new set of kernel sources with very little work on your part. Most distributions provide a document that details their official kernel build process and will tell you where to find the configuration that was used to build their kernel — obviously, it may not have exactly the same features as the kernel you are building, but that's okay, make oldconfig will do its best to work around that.

On some recent Linux kernels, you'll find that the kernel configuration is available in /proc/config. gz. Although this costs some wasted kernel memory, it is a good idea during development to enable this in your kernel configuration — it's then extremely easy to see the configuration options that were used to build particular test kernels. A compressed kernel configuration in /proc can easily be installed in a fresh set of kernel sources by using the gunzip command and copying the uncompressed resultant file.

Configuring for Cross-Compilation

It is quite common for the Linux kernel to be built in a cross-compiled environment when it will be used on embedded devices of dramatically lower processing capability than the machine upon which it is being built. Cross-compilation not only saves time in such cases but also enables you to remain agnostic with respect to the build machine you use when compiling your kernels — you can use the fastest machine you have access to without caring about the architecture or platform used in builds.

To cross-compile the Linux kernel, set up the CROSS_COMPILE environment variable so that it contains the prefix for the gcc and binutils commands you will use during compilation. For example, if you have a GNU Toolchain built that supports the PowerPC family of processors through commands like powerpc-eabi-405-gcc, you might set CROSS_COMPILE equal to powerpc-eabi-405- before you carry out the configuration and build steps mentioned in this chapter. You'll also want to ensure that the environment variable ARCH is set to the appropriate build architecture, such as powerpc:

```
$ export CROSS_COMPILE="powerpc-eabi-405-"
$ ARCH=powerpc make menuconfig
$ ARCH=powerpc make
```

The Linux 2.6 Kbuild system has been optimized to support a variety of build targets. You'll see that it clearly displays whether individual files are being built with a cross-compiler or the host compiler. It is a far cry from just a few years ago, when building a Linux kernel with a cross-compiler was considered to be an unusual and experimental game played by a small group of embedded device enthusiasts.

Building the Kernel

Building the Linux kernel is actually quite straightforward. You simply use the GNU make command, and the kernel Kbuild system (that is layered upon make) will make the appropriate calls to those utilities that are needed to build the entire system. A successful build can take a long time (hours on a very slow machine and still many minutes on even the fastest workstations — from around 7 seconds on some of the largest and fastest machines with huge amounts of RAM). So, it's often the case that builds are made as regularly as resources permit at whatever state the kernel tree is in.

It is a good idea to build and test frequently. There are a number of regression test suites available, but even a simple compile, boot cycle is sufficient to let you know if you are really on the wrong track. Those lucky enough to have automated build and test systems benefit here. A perk of being a Linux vendor.

You will need to have a configured Linux kernel before instructing the build system to put the kernel together. Start the build process by using `make` as follows (first few lines of the build are shown only):

```
$ make
  CHK      include/linux/version.h
  UPD      include/linux/version.h
  SYMLINK  include/asm -> include/asm-powerpc
  SPLIT    include/linux/autoconf.h -> include/config/*
  CC       arch/powerpc/kernel/asm-offsets.s
  GEN      include/asm-powerpc/asm-offsets.h
  HOSTCC   scripts/genksyms/genksyms.o
  SHIPPED  scripts/genksyms/lex.c
...
```

The output has been truncated for brevity.

You will clearly see at each stage what type of action is being performed, thanks to the Kbuild system prepending the action type to each line of output. The output defaults to this new shortened form of display without the full compilation command being printed for each stage. For the more verbose version of this output, repeat the previous command, adding `V=1` to the `Make` command line.

Here is an identical run of the previous example, but this time with verbose mode enabled:

```
$ make V=1
rm -f .kernelrelease
echo 2.6.17-rc6 > .kernelrelease
set -e; echo ' CHK       include/linux/version.h'; mkdir -p include/linux/;       if [
`echo -n "2.6.17-rc6" | wc -c ` -gt 64 ]; then echo '"2.6.17-rc6" exceeds 64
characters' >&2; exit 1; fi; (echo \#define UTS_RELEASE \"2.6.17-rc6\"; echo
\#define LINUX_VERSION_CODE `expr 2 \\* 65536 + 6 \\* 256 + 17`; echo '#define
KERNEL_VERSION(a,b,c) (((a) << 16) + ((b) << 8) + (c))'; ) <
/data/work/linux_26/linus_26/Makefile > include/linux/version.h.tmp; if [ -r
include/linux/version.h ] && cmp -s include/linux/version.h
include/linux/version.h.tmp; then rm -f include/linux/version.h.tmp; else echo '
UPD       include/linux/version.h'; mv -f include/linux/version.h.tmp
include/linux/version.h; fi
  CHK       include/linux/version.h
if [ ! -d arch/powerpc/include ]; then mkdir -p arch/powerpc/include; fi
ln -fsn /data/work/linux_26/include/asm-ppc arch/powerpc/include/asm
make -f scripts/Makefile.build obj=scripts/basic
  SPLIT    include/linux/autoconf.h -> include/config/*
mkdir -p .tmp_versions
rm -f .tmp_versions/*
make -f scripts/Makefile.build obj=.
mkdir -p arch/powerpc/kernel/
  gcc -m32 -Wp,-MD,arch/powerpc/kernel/.asm-offsets.s.d  -nostdinc -isystem
/usr/lib/gcc/ppc64-redhat-linux/4.1.0/include -D__KERNEL__ -Iinclude  -include
include/linux/autoconf.h -Iarch/powerpc -Iarch/powerpc/include -Wall -Wundef -
Wstrict-prototypes -Wno-trigraphs -fno-strict-aliasing -fno-common -Os
-fomit-frame-pointer -g -msoft-float -pipe -Iarch/powerpc -ffixed-r2 -mmultiple -
mno-altivec -funit-at-a-time -mstring -mcpu=powerpc -Wa,-maltivec
-Wdeclaration-after-statement -Wno-pointer-sign    -D"KBUILD_STR(s)=#s" -
D"KBUILD_BASENAME=KBUILD_STR(asm_offsets)"
-D"KBUILD_MODNAME=KBUILD_STR(asm_offsets)" -fverbose-asm -S -o
arch/powerpc/kernel/asm-offsets.s arch/powerpc/kernel/asm-offsets.c
```

```
mkdir -p include/asm-powerpc/
        (set -e; echo "#ifndef __ASM_OFFSETS_H__"; echo "#define
__ASM_OFFSETS_H__"; echo "/*"; echo " * DO NOT MODIFY."; echo " *"; echo " * This
file was generated by /data/work/linux_26/linus_26/Kbuild"; echo " *"; echo " */";
echo ""; sed -ne "/^->/{s:^->\([^ ]*\) [\$#]*\([^ ]*\) \(.*\):#define \1 \2 /* \3
*/:; s:->::; p;}" arch/powerpc/kernel/asm-offsets.s; echo ""; echo "#endif" ) >
include/asm-powerpc/asm-offsets.h
make -f scripts/Makefile.build obj=scripts
make -f scripts/Makefile.build obj=scripts/genksyms
  gcc -Wp,-MD,scripts/genksyms/.genksyms.o.d -Wall -Wstrict-prototypes -O2 -fomit-
frame-pointer       -c -o scripts/genksyms/genksyms.o scripts/genksyms/genksyms.c
  gcc -Wp,-MD,scripts/genksyms/.lex.o.d -Wall -Wstrict-prototypes -O2 -fomit-frame-
pointer       -Iscripts/genksyms -c -o scripts/genksyms/lex.o scripts/genksyms/lex.c
...
```

As you can see from the level of detail given by the verbose output option to the Kbuild system, you will usually want to build without verbose mode enabled (otherwise, it can be hard to see the wood for the trees with all of that verbose and informative output). If all else fails, type `make help` for a series of `make` targets, optional flags, and a brief explanation of your available build options.

Here is a list of build options:

```
$ make help
Cleaning targets:
  clean          - remove most generated files but keep the config
  mrproper       - remove all generated files + config + various backup files

Configuration targets:
  config         - Update current config utilising a line-oriented program
  menuconfig     - Update current config utilising a menu based program
  xconfig        - Update current config utilising a QT based front-end
  gconfig        - Update current config utilising a GTK based front-end
  oldconfig      - Update current config utilising a provided .config as base
  randconfig     - New config with random answer to all options
  defconfig      - New config with default answer to all options
  allmodconfig   - New config selecting modules when possible
  allyesconfig   - New config where all options are accepted with yes
  allnoconfig    - New config where all options are answered with no

Other generic targets:
  all            - Build all targets marked with [*]
* vmlinux        - Build the bare kernel
* modules        - Build all modules
  modules_install - Install all modules to INSTALL_MOD_PATH (default: /)
  dir/           - Build all files in dir and below
  dir/file.[ois] - Build specified target only
  dir/file.ko    - Build module including final link
  rpm            - Build a kernel as an RPM package
  tags/TAGS      - Generate tags file for editors
  cscope         - Generate cscope index
  kernelrelease  - Output the release version string
  kernelversion  - Output the version stored in Makefile

Static analysers
```

```
     checkstack       - Generate a list of stack hogs
     namespacecheck   - Name space analysis on compiled kernel

  Kernel packaging:
    rpm-pkg            - Build the kernel as an RPM package
    binrpm-pkg         - Build an rpm package containing the compiled kernel
                         and modules
    deb-pkg            - Build the kernel as an deb package
    tar-pkg            - Build the kernel as an uncompressed tarball
    targz-pkg          - Build the kernel as a gzip compressed tarball
    tarbz2-pkg         - Build the kernel as a bzip2 compressed tarball

  Documentation targets:
    Linux kernel internal documentation in different formats:
    xmldocs (XML DocBook), psdocs (Postscript), pdfdocs (PDF)
    htmldocs (HTML), mandocs (man pages, use installmandocs to install)

  Architecture specific targets (powerpc):
  * zImage             - Compressed kernel image (arch/powerpc/boot/zImage.*)
    install            - Install kernel using
                         (your) ~/bin/installkernel or
                         (distribution) /sbin/installkernel or
                         install to $(INSTALL_PATH) and run lilo
    *_defconfig        - Select default config from arch/powerpc/configs

    cell_defconfig            - Build for cell
    g5_defconfig              - Build for g5
    iseries_defconfig         - Build for iseries
    maple_defconfig           - Build for maple
    mpc834x_sys_defconfig     - Build for mpc834x_sys
    mpc8540_ads_defconfig     - Build for mpc8540_ads
    pmac32_defconfig          - Build for pmac32
    ppc64_defconfig           - Build for ppc64
    pseries_defconfig         - Build for pseries

    make V=0|1 [targets] 0 => quiet build (default), 1 => verbose build
    make O=dir [targets] Locate all output files in "dir", including .config
    make C=1   [targets] Check all c source with $CHECK (sparse)
    make C=2   [targets] Force check of all c source with $CHECK (sparse)

  Execute "make" or "make all" to build all targets marked with [*]
  For further info see the ./README file
```

As you can see, the list of options is quite comprehensive and worthy of some study.

The Built Kernel

Once a kernel build has finished successfully, the output will be placed in an architecture- (and platform) specific location. On Intel IA32 (x86) computers, this default location is in the somewhat unusual `arch/i386/boot/bzImage` file. This is done for historical reasons, but you'll get used to it quickly. This file is suitable to replace (or better yet, sit alongside) the existing `/boot/vmlinuz-2.6.x.y` files that are likely already installed on your system. Later, you'll copy these files into place and update the system bootloader, which is typically lilo or grub on Intel machines, though numerous others exist.

Wherever the binary kernel output file is located on your system, you'll also need a few supporting files before you can test-boot the resulting kernel. The kernel build process will have created a file named System.map in the top-level kernel directory that you'll need to preserve and ultimately copy into place, also within the de facto /boot location. System.map contains a copy of each of the publicly exported symbols of the just-built kernel. These are used occasionally during debugging and by the top system utility if it needs to figure out one of the optional output display fields—the name of the function within the kernel which a given process is currently sleeping. This is the WCHAN display field in action.

You will want to keep a backup copy of the kernel binary itself and the System.map file that accompanies it. You will probably also want to keep a copy of the .config file containing the options you chose during configuration. You want to keep a copy of the last known-good kernel, too, for when the test-build kernel doesn't boot first time.

Don't blow away the kernel build directory just yet. It still contains all of those modules that need to live somewhere on your test system. More about that in the next section.

Testing the Kernel

On a typical Linux workstation, testing the kernel can be as simple as copying into place the binary kernel image (after renaming it appropriately with the vmlinuz-2.6.x.y syntax), System.map, and, optionally, the config file used during the build. You will then need to edit your Linux bootloader configuration to ensure that this new kernel is being booted by default. In the dim and distant past, it was necessary to rerun a bootloader configuration program every time a new kernel was written (because the bootloader would rely upon the hard-coded location of the kernel on disk—something that will change every time any file is written to, even if it's the same file that was written last time).

These days, most regular PC-based Linux systems use the GRUB bootloader, which has a configuration file in the /boot/grub/menu.lst file that you can use to override the default boot kernel. PowerPC-based workstations and servers will typically use /etc/yaboot.conf to reconfigure the yaboot bootloader, while specialist embedded devices typically boot Linux directly from the Das U-Boot universal boot loader (which supports directly booting Linux out of flash memory). Whatever the appropriate activity on your system, it's pretty easy to inform Linux about a new kernel before booting it for real—and it's pretty easy to keep an entry in your bootloader configuration for a few older kernels, so you have a fallback.

Most of the time that you are testing out Linux kernels, you'll be encouraged to set up a separate test rig. This test box should be running a distribution similar to that of your development box, if possible. The best plan of attack is for you to get an NFS server up and running somewhere (for example, on your development workstation) and serve out a shared filesystem between a normal development machine and the test box. It is then trivial to copy across new kernels to the test box without resorting to the pain of burning a CD, using a USB storage key, or even resorting to plain old-fashioned floppy disks.

You can find documentation on NFS server configuration online and (hopefully) in your distribution documentation. A variety of guides cover this topic, including in-kernel source documentation, so it is not covered in detail here. Booting using NFS really is one of the best ways to test kernels—unless you really, really need a local disk with a local filesystem at system boot time (not just afterward).

You can copy a new kernel and System.map into place on your test system as follows:

```
$ cp /mnt/nfs_on_dev_box/linux-2.6.x.y/arch/i386/boot/bzImage /boot/vmlinuz-2.6.x.y
$ cp /mnt/nfs_on_dev_box/linux-2.6.x.y/System.map /boot/System.map-2.6.x.y
```

With the kernel in place, you will need to install any kernel modules that are needed by the system (as well as any others that were just built anyway) using the make modules_install target. This make target will copy the newly built modules into the /lib/modules/2.6.x.y standard directory location and make them available for use (after you next run depmod—sometimes run during system startup anyway so that modules are available on a reboot of the machine, depending on the distribution's choices).

If you're using a network-mounted filesystem on your test box, are not installing any loadable kernel modules on the machine itself, and need to vary where the installation location will be, then pass the optional INSTALL_MOD_PATH environment variable to make, setting it to the appropriate path. This is important if you built the kernel on a different machine that shares (or exports) the root NFS filesystem of your test machine—you don't want to install it on the development machine in that case.

Here's an example of installing kernel modules onto your local system /lib/modules (using the sudo command to avoid having to be logged in as the root user):

```
$ sudo make modules_install
Password:
    INSTALL arch/powerpc/oprofile/oprofile.ko
    INSTALL crypto/aes.ko
    INSTALL crypto/anubis.ko
    INSTALL crypto/arc4.ko
    INSTALL crypto/blowfish.ko
    INSTALL crypto/cast5.ko
    INSTALL crypto/cast6.ko
    INSTALL crypto/crc32c.ko
    INSTALL crypto/crypto_null.ko
    INSTALL crypto/deflate.ko
...
```

The output from the example has been truncated after just a few modules. A completely configured set of modules might run into many hundreds of modules and over 150MB.

You can instruct depmod to make these loadable kernel modules available to your system's modprobe command—so that you don't need to use the more specific (and less flexible) insmod/rmmod commands on a specific .ko module file. modprobe takes care of dependency resolution, too.

Here's how to run depmod correctly for newly installed 2.6 Linux kernel modules:

```
$ depmod -a 2.6.x.y
```

where 2.6.x.y is substituted for the specific version of the kernel that you just built.

Initial Ramdisks: initrds

Many modern Linux distributions rely upon an initial ramdisk in order to boot up cleanly. The purpose of an initial ramdisk is to allow the kernel to be configured as modularly as possible and for necessary Linux kernel modules to be loaded by scripts located within the initial ramdisk image early on in the boot process, before they are needed by the kernel. The initial ramdisk, therefore, is nothing more than a specially created binary file containing a filesystem image for the ramdisk, along with various scripts and modules that must be loaded (often for disks, etc.) before the system can boot. Modern bootloaders support loading this file into memory on behalf of the Linux kernel and making it available for use.

Many distributions cannot easily boot without an initial ramdisk, due to the assumptions that are made about its presence. In the likely event that your system does need one of these, you'll see reference to a ramdisk in the configuration for your bootloader — for example in /boot/grub/menu.lst. Fortunately, it is quite easily to build an initrd for yourself, thanks to the scripts supplied by modern Linux distributions. On most distributions, there is a script known as `mkinitrd` that will do the right thing on your behalf. In any case, your Linux distribution will likely come with documentation, describing required actions.

To make an initrd, use the `initrd` command and supply the name of the initrd and the kernel version to build for, or as according to its UNIX manual page ("man initrd"). See the following example:

```
$ mkinitrd /boot/initrd-2.6.x.y.img 2.6.x.y
```

You will obviously need to be root when building an initrd (or run the command under the sudo utility). Not only does the `mkinitrd` process usually require write access to the `/boot` directory, but it must also do an ugly loopback mount on a dummy filesystem on a regular file in order to populate the ramdisk (depending upon the precise process and filesystem, this might not be necessary). Don't worry if you don't understand exactly what this is doing at this stage — it will take you a while to figure it out, as kernel developers have been working on the Linux kernel build process for many years by now.

Next step, packaging and installing.

Packaging and Installing Kernels

By this point, you should have a sufficient understanding of the kernel configuration and build process to begin building kernels for yourself, but how do you package up these kernels for general distribution? The answer is that you typically won't do this yourself — there's no reason to do this, as vendors take care of providing the latest kernels for their distributions and other third parties are unlikely to want to install a random kernel that you send to them without a really good reason for doing so.[7] Nevertheless, there are times when you might want to package up a kernel for your own use.

Most distributions provide an RPM spec file (in the case of Debian, a set of rules for building a Debian package that you can use for yourself) that encompasses the configuration and build process for that distribution. In the case of both the Fedora Linux and OpenSUSE Linux distributions, this process is actually very straightforward. You can simply install the kernel source RPM package, make a couple of line changes to the sources used in building the kernel, and rebuild the kernel RPM.

> *Installing a prepackaged kernel can make life easier on development and production machines, but it's not recommended for frequent testing — simply copying a test kernel in place is much faster.*

Kernel Concepts

Congratulations! By now, you've hopefully managed to configure and build your own test kernels. You have an overall view of the kernel configuration process and a high-level understanding (at the very least) of the kernel directory layout that is used by Linux. You also understand the importance of having a standalone test machine on which to test the kernels that you are happily building away on your development machine. Now, it's time for the fun to really begin as you delve into the code.

---

[7]There's a security nightmare somewhere in that idea. Never install a kernel from someone you would not give root access to — it's effectively the same thing, especially if the kernel is in a package with its own pre/postinstall scripts, which also run as the root user. Or just keep a test machine for this stuff.

The kernel is the core of any operating system. It occupies the unique role of a resource broker, designed to keep all those applications that run atop the kernel from interfering with one another. In order to make life easier for regular application programmers, who must write large amounts of code for Linux systems, the kernel is also responsible for providing a special multiprocessing abstraction. This abstraction gives each application the illusion of having the entire Linux machine to itself. As a consequence, applications don't usually need to worry one another unless they choose to interact.

Your application programs won't usually have to care about relinquishing the processor when their fair share of processor has been used, or about whether another application might be waiting for keyboard input at the same time that they are, or a million and one other things that would quickly get in the way of your sanity. Instead, the Linux kernel takes care of ensuring each application receives a fair amount of CPU time, appropriate access to peripheral resources, and any other resources to which it is entitled. The kernel provides many innovative solutions to hard computer science problems in achieving this.

In this section, you'll learn some of the concepts necessary to work on the Linux kernel.

A Word of Warning

A common mistake for those getting into kernel development for the first time is to assume that the Linux kernel is an all-knowing, all-seeing mystical program that has total control over the operation of a system and is constantly running in the background in some kind of supervisory role. Parts of this concept are true — the kernel certainly does take on a supervisory role within the system, and it does have ultimate control over the hardware within your computer. But the kernel is not a program. It is rather a collection of routines that occasionally get invoked to service user requests and other tasks.

Linux kernel code usually runs only in response to direct requests from user programs. Sure, there's a collection of routines that handle low-level hardware interrupts — asynchronous requests from your computer hardware devices, such as the system timer that helps Linux keep track of the passage of time — and some other special code that runs from time to time, but there's no magical kernel program that's always running. You should not view the kernel as a special program but more as a very privileged collection of library routines that just happen to be always available whenever they are needed.

With that warning out of the way, you'll need to learn about a few fundamental abstractions that are used by the Linux kernel. In the following pages, you'll discover how the task abstraction and virtual memory simplify the lives of kernel and application programmers. It's important that you understand these concepts before you attempt to write your own kernel code — too often, mailing list posts show basic misunderstanding of these concepts. All manner of problems can result when that happens.

The Task Abstraction

The Linux kernel is built on fundamental task abstraction. This allows each application program to run independently from other programs — unless of course interaction is deliberately introduced by you, as the developer of these application programs. A task encapsulates the entire state of a single running program within a Linux system, including all resources required by that task (open files, allocated memory, and so on), the state of the processor, and a few other miscellaneous details. Tasks are represented by `task_struct` structures, defined within `include/linux/sched.h` in the kernel sources.

Task structures are usually allocated as a result of an existing program `fork()`ing an existing process; however, they can also be created whenever a new thread is created within a program. Linux doesn't have an internal abstraction for a thread like other operating systems and instead treats both processes and threads in largely the same way. To the Linux kernel, a thread is a task structure sharing the same memory and other system resources as an existing task, while having its own processor state. Tasks can also be allocated for special threads known as *kernel threads* — more about those later in this chapter.

Once a task has been created, it will continue to exist until it either successfully terminates or is killed as a result of a signal or attempt to perform an illegal operation (such as attempting to access memory locations that have not been allocated to the task). Linux takes care of scheduling individual tasks so that they each have their fair share of processor time, according to the scheduling policy in use on the system. Special fields within the task struct are used to keep the processor state whenever a task is not running so that it can be restored whenever the task next receives some time on the processor.

Users generally don't use the term "task" when they talk about running programs on a Linux system. Instead, they refer to "processes" and "threads" running within a process. You'll learn later in this chapter about the internal distinction within the kernel between these different terms. Users visualize lists of running processes using utilities such as "top" and "ps". A typical Linux desktop system might have up to several hundred concurrently executing processes running at a single time: one for each user application, a few dozen for the GNOME desktop, and more for miscellaneous purposes.

> *Within kernel code, the* current *macro always points to the currently executing task on the current processor. You can use this whenever you just want to refer to "this task running now."*

The Scheduler

At the heart of any Linux system is the Linux scheduler. This piece of kernel code is responsible for keeping track of how often tasks should be granted time on a system CPU and how much time that should be — the timeslice or quanta for the current task. Scheduling is a massive trade-off between variously contrasting requirements for a system to be responsive to user interaction, provide the maximum possible processing throughput for user applications, and to fit in a variety of complex accounting simultaneously with all of this other miscellaneous system activity.

You can manually call the scheduler through the in-kernel schedule() function. It is occasionally useful to do this as a means to give over the CPU to another task inside long running code paths when servicing system calls (more about system calls in the next section and in Chapter 8). Depending on various factors, Linux may then choose to run another task and put the current task to sleep until some later time. That's a key point, some later time. You can't be sure just when the scheduler will wake up a blocked task again — unless you're blocking on a specific event, indirectly resulting in a schedule(). This is pretty complex stuff — it takes a while to figure it out.

> *Obviously, making a call to the* schedule() *function will likely cause the current task to block, or cease to run for the moment, so you should only explicitly call the scheduler when there is a current task to block. More importantly, many internal kernel functions will produce side-effect calls into the scheduler that result in a schedule you may not have intended — and sometimes this can lead to disastrous consequences. You'll learn more about why this is a potentially serious problem later in this chapter when the issue of differing kernel contexts and its impact on modules is discussed.*

When you write kernel code, you won't usually need to worry about the internal activities of the Linux scheduler — internal scheduler design is an issue for those who work on the scheduler itself and can't be discussed in the space of this book (books specifically on the design of the Linux kernel do cover this). Nevertheless, you do need to be aware that a Linux system must support many concurrently executing tasks in order to provide the illusion of multiprocessing that is offered to users of Linux systems. This can only be provided if the scheduler is called frequently enough to allow other tasks to have their fair share of time on one of the system processors (if there are more than one).

The Linux kernel is becoming more preemptive over time. Kernel preemption means that it's possible for a more important task to begin running as soon as it becomes runnable, rather than waiting for any existing activity that might be taking place in another task to finish executing. Preemption within the kernel is not always possible. For example, if code executing in the kernel holds a spinlock as part of a critical section, it is not possible to block that task, lest it later cause a system deadlock. Since it is not acceptable for you to introduce large delays to overall system throughput by preventing preemption for a long period of time, you will want to keep your critical sections down to the minimum size possible.

System Calls

The relationship between the kernel and tasks is similar to that of a software library being used within an application. User programs communicate with the kernel through a defined software interface, known as the system call. They make requests for specific operations to be carried out by the Linux kernel on their behalf by varying the system call number that is used. This results in an appropriate response (after the kernel performs appropriate sanity checking of the request, ensures that any appropriate security considerations are met, etc.) returned to the application on completion.

System calls are not usually made directly by application programs. Instead, when you write software, you will use the standard GNU C library that has been mentioned throughout this book. The C library presents a series of utility functions useful to your applications, which in turn rely upon system calls to carry out some of their operations. For example, writing text to an open file handle relies upon a call to the write() system call, wrapped up in a C library function of the same name. The C library code handles the process of setting up the system call and getting the return code back.

It is quite common that libraries such as the system C library will provide many additional functions that are not directly provided by the kernel through system calls. System calls are regarded as relatively expensive in terms of the time that is required for their operation—try using the time command on an application, and you'll see how much of its time is spent in the kernel via system calls—so it is desirable only to make a system call when it is necessary. For this reason, the GNU C library provides a set of functions (those beginning with "f" – fopen/fclose/fread/fwrite) that buffer common file operations in order to avoid calling the kernel to read or write every character. Similar optimizations are common.

You can track system call usage of a running program by using the strace utility on the command line. The strace command will show all system calls made, the return values from those syscalls, and any signals that are received by a specified program. It will also show any signals that are received from the Linux kernel as a result of other system process activity or whenever certain events take place.

Run a simple Linux command such as the ls command under strace by using the following commands from within a regular Linux terminal (output formatted for readability):

```
$ strace ls
execve("/bin/ls", ["ls"], [/* vars */]) = 0
brk(0)                                   = 0x1002b000
mmap(NULL, 4096, PROT_READ...)           = 0x30000000
open(".", O_RDONLY|O_DIRECTORY...)       = 3
fstat64(3, {st_mode=S_IFDIR|0755, ...})  = 0
fcntl64(3, F_SETFD, FD_CLOEXEC)          = 0
getdents64(3, /* 3 entries */, 4096)     = 80
```

```
getdents64(3, /* 0 entries */, 4096)    = 0
close(3)                                = 0
write(1, "foo.txt\n", foo.txt)          = 8
close(1)                                = 0
munmap(0x30001000, 4096)                = 0
exit_group(0)                           = ?
Process 3533 detached
```

The output shows how system calls are made to start a new process using execve() and then to extend the process's memory address space through calls to brk() and mmap() (more about address spaces later in this chapter). Finally, calls to open(), getdents64(), and other file operations are used to obtain information about individual files within the current directory.

Output from the strace command has been edited to remove additional system calls made to set up shared libraries and other program operations not relevant to this discussion.

Execution Contexts

Within a Linux system, tasks can execute in variously privileged contexts. A regular user program is unable to directly interact with the system hardware and is unable to interfere with the operation of other programs running on the system. It is said to be running in an unprivileged user context, where that user might be a regular system user or the system "root" superuser. Root doesn't have any special power over the hardware within the machine other than the trusted ability to request that the kernel perform special operations on its behalf (shutdown, killing tasks, and other superuser operations).

Regular user programs make frequent calls into the kernel via the system call mechanism in order to have various operations performed on their behalf. When entering the kernel, the system is executing code in a privileged context known as the *kernel context* and is said to be in kernel mode. In this elevated state, it's possible to directly interact with hardware devices and manipulate sensitive kernel data structures in order to satisfy whatever requests have been made of the kernel. All kernel code executes in this privileged state, which is usually implemented via special processor features.

Process vs. Interrupt Context

There is another set of execution contexts within standard Linux systems — that of the process and that of the interrupt. *Process context* is exactly what it sounds like. It means that the kernel is running some kernel code on behalf of a user process (usually as a result of a system call) and that it's possible to block, or put the current task to sleep and wait for some data to turn up from disk, for example. In that case, the system scheduler will pick another task to run in the interim. The sleeping task is woken up when the condition that caused it to block is no longer present and it can continue from its stored state.

The practical side of being able to block means that most of the time, you are able to perform a wide variety of operations from within kernel context. You can freely make a call to a kernel function that might put the current task to sleep, make a call to a memory allocation function that will require the system to swap out some data to disk, or a variety of other operations without concern for the impact upon the rest of the system. Large parts of the kernel code make assumptions that result in potential blocking of the current task being a possibility whenever you call certain routines.

Sometimes, it's not possible to block the current task because there is no current task to block. This is the case whenever an interrupt is running or another asynchronous event happens that causes code to run not on behalf of a user task, but for some more general system purpose. In this case, blocking is technically not possible (it results in kernel panic – a crash) but even if it somehow were, the system usually requires a very fast response when in interrupt context and can't wait for memory to be freed/data to be read in from disk or other operations that happen following a task blocking.

The practical side of not being able to block is that there are times when you have only a limited set of kernel functions available to you or can use only a limited subset of their functionality. For example, inside interrupt handlers that take care of hardware interrupts from specific hardware devices, it's a really bad idea to attempt to allocate memory using the kernel kmalloc() function without passing the GFP_ATOMIC flag to inform the function that it must not block at any cost — kmalloc will, in such cases, know to use a special pool of reserve memory if it is unable to satisfy the allocation or may instead return an error code, if there is simply not enough available memory without blocking.

Kernel Threads

Not all tasks execute on behalf of regular user programs. There are a number of specially privileged tasks in the average system. These special tasks are known as *kernel threads* and have the unique capability to run privileged kernel code inside of a process environment. Kernel threads are used whenever the kernel programmer desires an individually schedulable entity that can occasionally process some data and then go back to sleep before being woken up again.

Although there are many other ways to schedule deferred work in the Linux kernel, only kernel threads can perform the full range of operations of a regular user process. Kernel code is only allowed to block (call a function that might need to put the current task to sleep and wait for data, a memory allocation, etc.) from within a process context and the kernel thread provides that context. It's very common to use kernel threads as a means of providing some kind of heavyweight processing within the kernel. For example, the kernel swapper daemon (kswapd) runs as a kernel thread that occasionally prunes available memory and swaps out unused data to the system swap space.

You can identify kernel threads in your ps output by looking for processes listed in square brackets, which usually begin with the letter k. For example, on a typical system, you might see the following kernel threads listed in ps output (output edited to remove nonkernel threads):

```
$ ps fax
  PID TTY       STAT   TIME COMMAND
    2 ?         SN     0:00 [ksoftirqd/0]
    3 ?         S      0:00 [watchdog/0]
    4 ?         S<     0:02 [events/0]
    5 ?         S<     0:00 [khelper]
    6 ?         S<     0:00 [kthread]
   30 ?         S<     0:00  \_ [kblockd/0]
   34 ?         S<     0:00  \_ [khubd]
   36 ?         S<     0:00  \_ [kseriod]
   86 ?         S      0:00  \_ [pdflush]
   87 ?         S      0:00  \_ [pdflush]
   89 ?         S<     0:00  \_ [aio/0]
  271 ?         S<     0:00  \_ [kpsmoused]
  286 ?         S<     0:00  \_ [kjournald]
 1412 ?         S<     0:00  \_ [kmirrord]
 1437 ?         S<     0:00  \_ [kjournald]
 1446 ?         S<     0:00  \_ [kjournald]
 1448 ?         S<     0:00  \_ [kjournald]
 2768 ?         S<     0:00  \_ [kauditd]
   88 ?         S      0:02 [kswapd0]
```

```
1106 ?        S      0:00 [khpsbpkt]
1178 ?        S      0:00 [knodemgrd_0]
2175 ?        S<     0:00 [krfcommd]
```

As you can see, there are a number of kernel threads running on even an average desktop system. As the system becomes larger and more processors are added, an increasingly large number of kernel threads help to manage everything from process migration from one processor to another, to balancing IO.

Virtual Memory

Individual tasks managed by the Linux kernel each have their own memory environment, known as an address space. Each process address space is separated from that of any other process by means of a fundamental abstraction known as *virtual memory*. Virtual memory allows processes not to care about the memory use of other applications within the system and also forms a part of the barrier between user programs and the Linux kernel, thanks to a variety of circuitry in a system's MMU (Memory Management Unit). As you'll learn in this section, virtual memory is a very powerful abstraction indeed, but perhaps a little difficult to understand at first sight—hopefully, this section will help.

Virtual memory allows every program to be built and linked independently of any other. Each program can expect to have a wide range of memory locations from zero through to whatever upper limit exists for a particular system or individual process (administrator-defined per-user resource limits are often used to set a practical limit for a given process). On most 32-bit Linux systems, the upper limit for an individual process address space is at 3GB, allowing up to 3GB for each user program.[8] Subject to any system resource constraints in providing the necessary memory, each process is free to do with its own address space as it likes, although various de facto standards do affect what is done in practice. For example, there are de facto standardized locations for stacks, program code and data, and so on.

The Page Abstraction

Modern computer systems account memory usage in terms of units known as *pages*. A page is simply a set of sequential memory addresses and is usually quite small in size—4K pages are common on Linux systems, though the precise size will vary according to the architecture and platform in use. Pages form a key part of the implementation of the virtual memory concept. Physical memory within the system is divided into many thousands of individual pages (aligned in memory according to the size of page chosen—for example, aligned at 4K boundaries), which are tracked using a series of in-kernel lists—free page lists, allocated lists, and so on. The virtual memory hardware within the system MMU then handles the process of translating virtual memory addresses into physical addresses at the page level.

A given virtual address within a running process, such as 0x10001234, is translated by the virtual memory hardware in the system as necessary into a physical address by masking out the appropriate page frame from the virtual address and looking up the corresponding physical page before returning the data stored at that location—all transparently to the application (and in many respects to the kernel, too). Given the example address, with 4K page sizes, the virtual page frame number (PFN) in question of 0x10001 would map to a physical page somewhere in system memory, where the offset of 0x234 is applied before carrying out any memory read or write operation with that data.

The system virtual memory hardware doesn't just know what virtual addresses translate into what physical addresses using some magical process. The kernel maintains a series of hardware tables that are

---

[8]Just because 3GB of address space is available, this doesn't mean you can allocate 3GB of heap in application code. In fact, the average process address space is limited by a variety of factors, which helps to explain why 64-bit machines are more popular even for moderately sized memory hogs.

directly consulted as necessary by the MMU when it needs to perform a translation. Linux itself actually implements a variety of page-tracking mechanisms and lists, which are used to update the hardware tables as necessary. You won't need to worry about the precise mechanics of the page management process just to write regular kernel code, but you will need to be aware of the page abstraction and in particular of the struct page that is used to represent pages in the Linux kernel.

Memory Mappings

Whenever you load a program on your Linux machine, the Linux kernel ELF parser will pull out of the binary those addresses at which the program code, data, and other program sections should be loaded at within the process address space. In Chapter 2, you learned how to use the GNU Toolchain to determine various detail about a program from its binary, including where in memory it should be loaded. As part of the startup process for any application, the dynamic linker will take care of ensuring that any shared libraries are also dynamically mapped in to a process address space at the required addresses.

Running programs can alter their memory mappings by making use of the mmap() system call. This special system call can be used to map a specified file at a given memory range for reading, writing, and/or execution. mmap() is used to map in shared libraries and as a fast mechanism for working with data files directly, without making calls to file reading and writing routines in the C library. mmap() is also used to map anonymous memory — memory not backed by any real file on disk, that is, regular memory allocated via C library routines such as malloc() for a variety of general program uses.

You can look at the address space of any program executing on your Linux system by using the /proc/pid/maps interface. Use a utility such as cat to read the content of the "maps" file within one of the numbered directories under /proc, and you'll be viewing information about the address space for the process with that numeric ID. For example, to view information about a bash shell, open a terminal window and issue the following commands (bash will substitute $$ for its own process ID):

```
$ cat /proc/$$/maps
00100000-00103000 r-xp 00100000 00:00 0
0f494000-0f49f000 r-xp 00000000 03:0b 983069       /lib/libnss_files-2.4.so
0f49f000-0f4ae000 ---p 0000b000 03:0b 983069       /lib/libnss_files-2.4.so
0f4ae000-0f4af000 r--p 0000a000 03:0b 983069       /lib/libnss_files-2.4.so
0f4af000-0f4b0000 rw-p 0000b000 03:0b 983069       /lib/libnss_files-2.4.so
0f4c0000-0f4c3000 r-xp 00000000 03:0b 987547       /lib/libdl-2.4.so
0f4c3000-0f4d2000 ---p 00003000 03:0b 987547       /lib/libdl-2.4.so
0f4d2000-0f4d3000 r--p 00002000 03:0b 987547       /lib/libdl-2.4.so
0f4d3000-0f4d4000 rw-p 00003000 03:0b 987547       /lib/libdl-2.4.so
0f5c0000-0f71b000 r-xp 00000000 03:0b 987545       /lib/libc-2.4.so
0f71b000-0f72a000 ---p 0015b000 03:0b 987545       /lib/libc-2.4.so
0f72a000-0f72e000 r--p 0015a000 03:0b 987545       /lib/libc-2.4.so
0f72e000-0f72f000 rw-p 0015e000 03:0b 987545       /lib/libc-2.4.so
0f72f000-0f732000 rw-p 0f72f000 00:00 0
0fbc0000-0fbc5000 r-xp 00000000 03:0b 987568       /lib/libtermcap.so.2.0.8
0fbc5000-0fbd4000 ---p 00005000 03:0b 987568       /lib/libtermcap.so.2.0.8
0fbd4000-0fbd5000 rw-p 00004000 03:0b 987568       /lib/libtermcap.so.2.0.8
0ffc0000-0ffdd000 r-xp 00000000 03:0b 987544       /lib/ld-2.4.so
0ffed000-0ffee000 r--p 0001d000 03:0b 987544       /lib/ld-2.4.so
0ffee000-0ffef000 rw-p 0001e000 03:0b 987544       /lib/ld-2.4.so
10000000-100c6000 r-xp 00000000 03:0b 950282       /bin/bash
100d5000-100dc000 rw-p 000c5000 03:0b 950282       /bin/bash
100dc000-100e0000 rwxp 100dc000 00:00 0
```

```
100eb000-100f3000  rw-p  000cb000  03:0b  950282    /bin/bash
100f3000-10135000  rwxp  100f3000  00:00  0         [heap]
30000000-30001000  rw-p  30000000  00:00  0
30001000-30008000  r--s  00000000  03:0b  262661    /usr/lib/gconv/gconv-modules.cache
30008000-3000a000  rw-p  30008000  00:00  0
3001b000-3001c000  rw-p  3001b000  00:00  0
3001c000-3021c000  r--p  00000000  03:0b  199951    /usr/lib/locale/locale-archive
7fa8b000-7faa0000  rw-p  7fa8b000  00:00  0         [stack]
```

As you can see, the address space for even a simple application can appear complex. In the output, each line shows a range of memory address on the left, followed by the permissions associated with that address range, and finishing up with any file that might be backing that memory range on disk. In the output, you can see that each shared library is mapped into the bash process at low memory addresses, followed by the /bin/bash program code, and with the stack toward the upper limit of the address space (stacks grow down, so the stack will grow downward into the large unmapped range beneath it).

Kernel Memory Mapping

Programs don't have the entire range of possible memory locations available within their address space for their own use. Recall that 32-bit Linux systems typically impose an upper limit of 3GB on the range available to user programs (64-bit systems differ according to the conventions for a particular platform). This leaves 1GB of the possible memory for each process unavailable for the process's use. But that memory is not wasted—it's used by the Linux kernel. The kernel does this in order to provide a performance benefit over having its own memory address space each time a system call occurs.

When a system call happens on modern Linux systems, the processor switches to an elevated privilege level and is able to execute kernel code, which is located in that upper memory mapping within a user process. That kernel code executes with its own kernel stack and runs independently of the program for which it is providing some service, but it nevertheless retains full access to the entirety of the process address space and can freely manipulate the data within it—facilitating the easy transfer of buffers of data to and from the kernel during system calls as well as easy access to other program data as necessary.

Special hardware protection mechanisms prevent user application programs from attempting to access kernel data, although occasional bugs have existed in older Linux kernels that would allow a program to trick the kernel into gaining access to privileged kernel memory. Nevertheless, this optimization of the process address space is common enough on Linux and other operating systems that it remains the status quo. There are special patches to the kernel that give it its own kernel address space, and these have been picked up in some distribution kernels, but have around a 10% performance overhead.

Task Address Spaces

Within the kernel, memory exists in various forms and is accounted through a variety of elaborate lists, along with various other mechanisms too complex to do justice in the space of this chapter. Each task accounts for its own memory usage via an entry in its task_struct known as mm. The mm_struct in turn contains a range of pointers to other structures that account individual range mappings within the task—one for each of the ranges you saw in the /proc/pid/maps output previously. The overall address space for any one task can become very complex and that's before considering more advanced usage.

Whenever a task structure is created by the Linux kernel, its mm field is set to point to a freshly created mm_struct structure that stores information about the task's address space. This structure is consulted whenever it is necessary for the kernel to educate the MMU about valid memory ranges for a given task.

The `mm_struct` is consulted at these times in order to determine whether the kernel should tell the MMU to allow read, write and/or execute access to a given memory location. It's also used to determine whether a particular memory range needs to be swapped back in from disk before use.

One common situation in which a task's `mm_struct` is queried is during a page fault. You have already learned that Linux systems use pages to represent the basic unit of virtual memory and so it is that they are also the basic unit of memory access. Any attempt to read from, write to, or execute data at an address within a process that is not currently available — it's been swapped out to disk to free up space, is part of a file on disk that will not be loaded until it is actually needed, and so on — will result in a page fault. The system page fault handler will use the `mm` data structures within a task to determine whether a memory access was legitimate and populate the particular memory page if it was.

Not all tasks have their own `mm_struct` allocated for their unique use. As it turns out, threads within a process have their own `task_struct` but share the same memory address space (a special argument is passed to the `clone()` system call when the new task structure is created to preserve this pointer) and kernel threads don't even have an `mm_struct` of their own in the first place. You can find out more about the `mm_struct` by consulting the kernel sources — it's also defined in `include/linux/sched.h`.

Don't Panic!

This small section has introduced a lot of concepts very briefly and covered a lot of ground in a small amount of page[9] real estate. Remember, this is hard stuff and nobody would be expected to understand all of it instantly. The purpose of this brief overview is not to scare you off from pursuing your interest in kernel development by pointing out how much more there is to know but to help you have at least a 30,000 ft view of a few key ideas as you get started. The next few chapters will help you to get into a few more meaty examples, but even then, a single book can only cover so much in the space available.

You will learn far more than any book can teach you by cutting your teeth on some real-life problems and just jumping in — sure you'll make mistakes (that's the idea), but you'll also learn from them. With that in mind, the remainder of this chapter will introduce you to the kernel development process and provide you with a few pointers to online resources and groups you can consult for assistance.

Kernel Hacking

The Linux kernel is made up of a number of individual components, all of which must work together in order for the system as a whole to function. Linux is unlike many other operating system kernels. It is neither a microkernel (built from many modular components, fully isolated from one another, with a small trusted core) nor a pure monolithic kernel (everything built in, little flexibility at runtime). In fact, Linux draws upon experience gained over the past 30 years in developing UNIX kernels — and in that sense is a giant monolith — but also adds in a powerful module system for runtime expansion.

Inside the kernel, any code is able to interact with any other part of the system. There is no protection from yourself — as the saying goes, "Linux allows you to shoot yourself in both feet at once" — but this provides for a great deal of flexibility insomuch as you are able to do almost anything without undue hindrance. The kernel is written almost exclusively in the C programming language, with some small amount of assembly language to support specific low-level operations that must be in architecture (or platform) specific assembly code. The goal is to be as portable to other architectures as possible.

---

[9]Pun intended.

There is no provision in Linux for kernel code written in C++, nor is it possible to easily perform floating point arithmetic from within the kernel on all architectures — just don't do it. In fact, there are numerous other things that should never be done within the kernel. For example, you should never attempt to open a file and manipulate it from within the kernel — yes, it's possible, but it's also much easier to do this from userspace and supply the data to the kernel over an appropriate interface. You will quickly come to learn some of the obvious dos and don'ts as you begin developing for Linux.

Loadable Modules

One of the easiest ways of beginning Linux kernel development is to work on loadable Linux kernel modules (LKMs). These extend the core kernel functionality by providing new functions and features at runtime. It is not possible to extend every aspect of the kernel at runtime — you can't really touch core kernel functionality such as the scheduler or virtual memory subsystem very easily — but there's a lot that you can do with modules nonetheless. Modules have the added advantage of being individual self-contained entities that can be moved from one kernel to another with relative ease.

In this chapter, you'll look at a simple module example just to get into the process of building and working with Linux kernel modules. Over the course of the next few chapters, you'll learn how to develop your own powerful kernel modules from scratch — supporting new hardware peripherals and adding other useful functionality to an existing Linux system. But you can't run without learning to crawl first, so you'll want to go through the motions of building up a test module from source.

An Example Module

The following very simple example simply writes a greeting to the kernel ring buffer (kernel log) upon loading and unloading. It doesn't do anything particularly useful — that's not the point of its existence — but it does demonstrate how to build a kernel module and load it on your running system.

The `plp` example module is comprised from a single file, `plp.c`:

```
/*
 * plp.c - An example kernel module
 *
 * Copyright (C) 2006 Jon Masters <jcm@jonmasters.org>
 *
 * This program is free software; you can redistribute it and/or
 * modify it under the terms of the GNU General Public License as
 * published by the Free Software Foundation.
 *
 */

#include <linux/module.h>
#include <linux/init.h>

int __init hello_init(void)
{
        printk("plp: hello reader!\n");
        return 0;
}

void __exit hello_exit(void)
{
        printk("plp: thanks for all the fish!\n");
```

```
    }

    /* Module Metadata */

    MODULE_AUTHOR("Jon Masters <jcm@jonmasters.org>");
    MODULE_DESCRIPTION("PLP example");
    MODULE_LICENSE("GPL");

    module_init(hello_init);
    module_exit(hello_exit);
```

Notice a few things about this example module. First, there's no `main()` function. That's because this isn't a regular program. You can't build it using a regular call to the `gcc` front end and expect to be able to execute any resulting program binary. Instead, the module defines a couple of entry points that the kernel can use at specific times. All modules have `init` and `exit` functions, which are advertised to the kernel via the macro calls to `module_init()` and `module_exit()` — they simply munge the module ELF in order to provide this information in a special section that is consulted by the kernel at module load.

You'll see the that the module calls three macros that set up the author and licensing information. It's very important that you do this in your modules. There are many reasons why it's a good idea to understand the license under which the Linux kernel and its modules is distributed, but in addition to that, if you don't define a `MODULE_LICENSE`, your module will "taint" the kernel and result in a special flag being set so that developers will know your module source might not be available to aid debugging efforts. You don't want this, so always set an appropriate license — for example, the GNU GPL.

Building the example module is made easy, thanks to the 2.6 Linux kernel build system, Kbuild. The example sources contain a simple Kbuild file with the following single-line entry:

```
    obj-m           := plp.o
```

This file is read by the kernel build system when it is instructed to process the current directory and allows the kernel to locate the `plp.c` module source. In order to actually built the module, you'll need to have a freshly built kernel tree to hand — it's no good just having the kernel sources, you need to have a compiled kernel tree in order to build modules against it (vendors can be an exception to this — they provide a specially modified set of kernel headers for building such modules, but this is not normal). With a fresh tree to hand, use the following command within the module source:

```
    make -C /usr/src/linux-2.6.x.y modules M=$PWD
```

Where `/usr/src/linux-2.6.x.y` should be the sources for the kernel you'd like to build this module against.

Provided you got the command right and have the module source code correctly set up on your system, you'll see build output from the Kbuild system that is similar to the following:

```
$ make -C /usr/src/linux-2.6.x.y modules M=$PWD
make: Entering directory `/usr/src/linux-2.6.x.y'
  CC [M]  /home/jcm/PLP/src/kerneldev/plp.o
  Building modules, stage 2.
  MODPOST
  CC      /home/jcm/PLP/src/kerneldev/plp.mod.o
  LD [M]  /home/jcm/PLP/src/kerneldev/plp.ko
make: Leaving directory `/usr/src/linux-2.6.x.y'
```

The output from this build process is a loadable kernel module known as `plp.ko`. You can find out more about this module and the sources used to build it by using the standard Linux `modinfo` system utility:

```
$ /sbin/modinfo plp.ko
filename:       plp.ko
author:         Jon Masters <jcm@jonmasters.org>
description:    PLP example
license:        GPL
vermagic:       2.6.15 preempt gcc-4.1
depends:
srcversion:     C5CC60784CB4849F647731D
```

You can load and unload this module by using the `/sbin/insmod` and `/sbin/rmmod` commands and by passing those commands a full path to the kernel module itself. Note that you won't see the output from the module unless you're on a system console when you load and unload the module—use the `dmesg` command, consult your system logs, or ask your Linux vendor about their logging processes in the event that there's no kernel output available somewhere on your system when loading and unloading.

Here's an example of loading and unloading the example module from a system console:

```
$ /sbin/insmod plp.ko
plp: hello reader!
$ /sbin/rmmod plp
plp: thanks for all the fish!
```

Depending upon your system, you may also be able to install the `plp.ko` loadable kernel module into the standard system module directory (`/lib/modules`). To do this, use the "`modules_install`" Make target:

```
make -C /usr/src/linux-2.6.x.y modules M=$PWD modules_install
```

You can then load and unload the module using the `/sbin/modprobe` utility in the usual way:

```
$ /sbin/modprobe plp
$ /sbin/modprobe -r plp
```

`modprobe` takes care of figuring out where the module is and loading and unloading it. It will also satisfy any dependencies that the example module may have—loading other modules that it depends upon. You won't need to worry about multiple interdependent kernel modules unless you're working on some very large kernel projects—in which case, you'll probably know all of this material already.

Kernel Development Process

The upstream Linux kernel community development process is a little different from that used by other Free Software and open source development projects. For a start, Linux is a very large project compared to many others, and it has a wide range of contributors with an even wider range of interests. Linux development is very much an international affair, with many developers working all over the world and in all time zones. English is the semi-official language and is used in all mailing list posts, source code comments, and documentation, but you'll need to allow for non-native English speakers.

Kernel development happens in cycles of frantic patching activity, followed by stabilization, followed by a release, and then any necessary postrelease updates via the "-stable" kernel team. Development is driven by three key pieces of infrastructure—the git kernel SCM tool, the LKML mailing list, and a guy by the name of Andrew Morton. Each individual Linux kernel developer is able to keep track of Linus's upstream personal git tree via the kernel.org website, from which they can track those patches that will likely form a part of a future release as well as test out the current state of the art. Andrew Morton maintains his "-mm" kernel tree as a staging area for patches that are likely to be sent on to Linus.

Git: the "Stupid Content Tracker"

The Linux kernel development community makes use of an automated SCM (software configuration management) tool known as *git*. Git is covered as part of the SCM chapter (chapter 2) earlier in this book, but this section will provide a few kernel specific items of note. Git has rapidly been adopted as the de facto open source SCM tool for the kernel community—it was written over the course of a couple of weeks when a previous tool had to be withdrawn and is possibly one of the most ingenious and useful SCM tools that is widely available today. Git is fundamentally really a very fast "filesystem" and database rolled into a regular application program. It can keep track of many source code directories quickly.

You'll be able to pick up a copy of git via your Linux distribution. If it's not already installed, look for the prepackaged version to save you the hassle of building it up for yourself from source. The first task needed to begin using git is to clone an upstream Linux kernel tree for use as a reference. Most of the kernel development community use Linus Torvalds' git tree as a reference. You can clone Linus's tree by using the following commands from within a terminal:

```
$ git clone git://git.kernel.org/pub/scm/linux/kernel/git/torvalds/linux-2.6.git
linus_26
```

This will create a new copy of Linus's git source tree and call it `linus_26`. Once the clone is complete, you'll see what appears to be a regular kernel source tree within the `linus_26` directory. You can keep this tree up to date by issuing the `git pull` command from within the source tree. For example:

```
$ git pull
Unpacking 3 objects
 100% (3/3) done
* refs/heads/origin: fast forward to branch 'master' of
git://git.kernel.org/pub/scm/linux/kernel/git/torvalds/linux-2.6
  from ce221982e0bef039d7047b0f667bb414efece5af to
427abfa28afedffadfca9dd8b067eb6d36bac53f
Auto-following refs/tags/v2.6.17
Unpacking 1 objects
 100% (1/1) done
* refs/tags/v2.6.17: storing tag 'v2.6.17' of
git://git.kernel.org/pub/scm/linux/kernel/git/torvalds/linux-2.6
Updating from ce221982e0bef039d7047b0f667bb414efece5af to
427abfa28afedffadfca9dd8b067eb6d36bac53f
Fast forward
 Makefile |    2 +-
 1 files changed, 1 insertions(+), 1 deletions(-)
```

You can read more about using git in the earlier chapter on software configuration management (SCM) or by consulting the Linux kernel website, which contains a quick primer on kernel development with git. You can find out more at the git website: www.kernel.org/git.

gitk: the Graphical Git Tree Browser

Git is a very powerful SCM tool that is used by many of the Linux kernel developers around the world each day. Although git contains a wide array of commands for querying the current git tree for useful information, sometimes it's good to have a graphical tool that can help to visualize the tree. It's for this reason that gitk was written. Gitk presents the history for a particular tree using a graphical tool written in tcl that should run on most Linux systems. The gitk utility allows for easy browsing of changes to a git repository, such as the kernel repository in this example. Individual changesets, merges, and deletions are readily identified, alongside metadata associated with them - such as author name and email address. Look for a package to install on your particular system.

You can try out gitk for yourself by entering a git-managed kernel source directory and running `gitk`. A graphical display will appear (Figure 7-1).

The Linux Kernel Mailing List

Linux kernel development revolves around a core group of kernel hackers — little more than a couple of dozen — who hang out on the LKML (Linux Kernel Mailing List), another product of kernel.org. The LKML is a public mailing list where open discussion takes place concerning new features that may go into the kernel, patches are posted, new releases are announced and too many heated flame wars take place from time to time. There's never a dull moment to be had, although some wish there would be.

Figure 7-1

You'll want to subscribe to the LKML as soon as possible and start tracking posts that are made to the list—more information about your options is contained on the kernel.org website. Note that you don't necessarily need to subscribe to the email mailing list directly in order to track posts that are made. A good few archives are available. One such website is lkml.org, which also provides various statistics. For those who prefer to use Usenet feeds, gmane.org provides a free news gateway for LKML readers. Additionally, you can find many summaries of mailing list activity in certain Linux publications.

> *Don't post to the LKML until you've taken a look through the archives and gotten a feel for the list first. Many questions come up time and again and quickly annoy many regular LKML members.*[10]

Submitting Linux Kernel Patches

Linux kernel development relies heavily on the many individual patches that are sent to the Linux Kernel Mailing List on a daily basis. Although there are other ways to share code with other developers, the humble patch is the preferred mechanism because it provides a simple way to share code and keep an audit trail of who did what in the email archives at the same time—a good thing, especially when there are those who have occasionally made various claims about the origin of certain features.

Making a patch was covered earlier in this book. In the case of the Linux kernel, you'll want to submit patches between a fresh set of kernel sources and those containing whatever feature you are currently working on. For example, supposing that you have a new froozebar magical graphics card, which you have decided to write a driver for, you would work on this driver in your developmental kernel tree. Once the driver was ready for some public exposure, it would then be time to produce a patch using the unified diff format, between this development kernel and a fresh set of kernel sources:

```
diff -urN linux-2.6.x.y_orig linux-2.6.x.y_froozebar >froozebar.patch
```

The output from this command is a patch between the original kernel source and the newly modified kernel sources. Kernel patches are always made one directory above the top level of the kernel sources to avoid any ambiguity in later applying those patches to another kernel tree. Patches are submitted to the wider Linux kernel community for their consideration via the LKML in the first instance—unless there's a very obvious maintainer (check the MAINTAINERS file) who should be consulted first—and later discussed among specific groups that randomly form like flash mobs.

When you post a patch to the Linux Kernel Mailing List, you need to follow a standard etiquette in making that post. Begin with the word [PATCH] in the subject of the email, then a short introduction to the specific problem in the body, followed by a "Signed off by" line and then the patch. Here's an example of the ideal format to use when submitting your patches:

```
Subject: [PATCH] New froozebar driver for froozybaz-branded graphics cards

This driver adds new support for the exciting features in the froozebar chipset as
used in froozybaz-branded graphics cards. It's not perfect yet since at the moment
the image is displayed upside down, in reverse video, and the kernel crashes a few
minutes after loading this driver. But it's a start.

Signed off by: A developer <a.developer@froozybazfansunite.org>

diff -urN linux-2.6.x.y_orig/drivers/video/froozebar.c linux-
2.6.x.y_new/drivers/video/froozebar.c
--- linux-2.6.x.y_orig/drivers/video/froozebar.c        1970-01-01
01:00:00.000000000 +0100
```

[10]The author learned this the hard way, so it's a good idea not to repeat history yet again.

```
+++ linux-2.6.x.y_new/drivers/video/froozebar.c       2006-06-19 09:41:10.000000000
+0100
@@ -0,0 +1,4 @@
+/*
+ * froozebar.c - New support for froozybaz branded graphics cards
+ *
+ */
...
```

The Kernel Newbies Mailing List

If you're a newcomer to Linux kernel development, or even if you're not, you may be interested in participating in the kernelnewbies community. The kernelnewbies.org website hosts a very popular wiki-based website that anyone can edit and use to improve the state of the art in understanding of the kernel as well as general documentation on the kernel. In addition to the website, the group has a mailing list that is inhabited by a mixture of new comers and very experienced kernel folk.

> Next time you've got a question you're not quite sure is suitable for the LKML, but you don't think is suitable for a general-purpose audience such as your local LUG either, try asking it on the kernelnewbies mailing list. You may be pleasantly surprised at the number of other people with similar concerns. Just don't ask them about binary drivers or your favorite episode of Star Trek.

Kernel Janitors

Just like the kernelnewbies group, kernel janitors is all about helping people to find ways to contribute. Janitors aren't always newcomers to the Linux kernel community, however. The kernel janitors mailing list is a general clearing house for a variety of annoying (and some less annoying) "janitorial" problems that need to be resolved in the Linux kernel but that might not be getting attention from the regular kernel development community. You can help out — and learn in the process — by visiting the janitor.kernelnewbies.org subwebsite. You can also find out about the mailing list there.

The "mm" Development Tree

Andrew Morton forms a cornerstone in the Linux kernel development process, just like Linus and a few other developers who help to keep the show running. Andrew gets a special mention, however, because he maintains the "-mm" kernel tree and because he is the official maintainer of the 2.6 Linux kernel. If you want to get your kernel patches into the upstream Linux kernel, there's a good chance that they'll have to go through Andrew (akpm) at some point. In lieu of a development kernel tree, Andrew's "-mm" is proving to be as good a place as any to get developmental patches tested prior to going into the kernel.

You can track Andrew's "-mm" kernel via the Linux kernel website at kernel.org. Andrew doesn't use an SCM system like git often — instead electing to use regular patches and tarballs, but he does have his own system for quickly applying and testing patches, quilt.

You can find out more about Andrew's quilt patch-tracking utility at the GNU "Savanah" open source tracking website: `http://savannah.nongnu.org/projects/quilt`.

The Stable Kernel Team

The "-stable" team handle updating existing kernel releases when those occasional nasty security exploits come out, as well as when serious enough bugs warrant an update between regular kernel releases. The "-stable" team maintain the "y" in the 2.6.x.y kernel release number and was formed as a result of an effort to add a level of stabilization postrelease, following a new kernel release. Rather than waiting six weeks or more between releases, it's possible to deploy simple fixes via the "-stable" team. They've had their work cut out in recent times, especially following a number of reasonably ugly bugs being found by the various automated code coverage tools being run on the kernel.

The stable kernel team work closely with the security team and will always incorporate any of the latest security fixes when making new releases. You can help both the stable and security kernel teams out by keeping an eye out for any nasty bugs and security exploits and letting them know via their email alias (`security@kernel.org`). Never publicize a security exploit before giving these folks a heads up — this gives them time to prepare an appropriate response (and, hopefully, get some patches out the door).

LWN: Linux Weekly News

No chapter on Linux kernel development would be complete without mentioning *Linux Weekly News*. For many years now, Jonathan Corbet, Rebecca Sobol, and others at *Linux Weekly News* have worked tirelessly to bring you the latest news on the happenings in the Linux community. LWN run a weekly news bulletin that includes a summary of the week's kernel development and offers various unique insights into what might be coming up next. In addition, LWN offers a comprehensive listing of changes to the internal APIs within the Linux kernel as those APIs change between kernel releases.

Add LWN to your bookmarks `http://www.lwn.net` — you'll be very glad that you did.

Summary

This chapter has covered a wide range of topics in a relatively short time. The intention behind this approach is to introduce you to the kernel development process with as much of an overview as possible. Although you don't need to instantly understand every single aspect of the Linux kernel or its development process, it is important to have an overview of concepts such as tasks, virtual memory, and how the kernel fits into a system. You'll find it a lot easier to write kernel code for yourself with even as basic understanding of how it all fits together into a working system.

None of the information in this chapter would be useful without the ability to configure and build kernels for yourself. This chapter has equipped you with at least a basic understanding of the process behind building, installing, and testing kernels on real-life machines. Along the way, a number of supplemental notes on kernel cross-compiling, configuration management, and other topics, were thrown in, to aid your general understanding. Hopefully, this chapter has laid the groundwork for the following chapters, in which you'll apply some of the concepts to real-world examples.

The next chapter will take a look at interfacing with the kernel, before the final kernel chapter looks in further detail at building your own kernel modules.

## 8

Kernel Interfaces

In the last chapter, you learned about developing software to extend or otherwise modify the Linux kernel. You learned that the Linux kernel is, fundamentally, a mere collection of useful (and privileged) library routines that you can utilize through your program to carry out some operation on your behalf. You also learned how to write Linux kernel modules of your own. The brief examples of the previous chapter demonstrated some limited ways to interface between user programs (userland) and the kernel.

This chapter builds upon the knowledge you've already gained from previous chapters and explains what kinds of interfaces exist within the Linux kernel and also those interfaces that exist between the Linux kernel and other user-level application software. The term *interface* is a little ambiguous, but in the context of this chapter, it refers both to the range of interfaces between the kernel and user, and the internal API of the kernel itself. Both are discussed in this chapter, along with an explanation of key concepts — such as the lack of a stable kernel ABI against which to write Linux kernel modules.

After reading this chapter, you'll have a better understanding of how the kernel fits into a typical Linux system. Even if you're not writing your own kernel modules, the information in this chapter will aid your understanding of tools — such as the udev dynamic device filesystem daemon — and how messages are passed around the lower levels of the system. This will especially aid those who need to build their own Linux systems, and those who need to occasionally break formal interfaces in custom systems.

What Is an Interface?

The term interface can have many different meanings. In the context of this chapter, the term refers to software interfaces (APIs) that define the interaction between different parts of a Linux system. There are only so many ways that your application programs can legally interact with the Linux kernel — for example, by making a system call or by reading from/writing to a file or a socket. Defined interfaces exist to make life easier for everyone — and Linux is no different in that respect (making life easier).

There are a large number of different kinds of interfaces in the Linux kernel. This chapter will concentrate on two of these: the external interfaces between the Linux kernel and user application programs, and the internal interfaces that exist between individual parts of the Linux kernel itself. The latter involves an explanation of the lack of a standard kernel ABI and how this impacts the writing Linux kernel modules — especially those that must be portable to a wide range of target Linux systems.

The two different kinds of interfaces (external and internal) can be summarized as follows:

❑   External interfaces between the Linux kernel and userspace (user applications) are defined software barriers through which certain operations must pass. Interfaces such as system calls provide a defined mechanism for requests to be sent to the kernel, and replies returned. The netlink socket provides an interface into the kernel through which messages may be received, routing tables updated, and a variety of other possible operations performed. These interfaces cannot easily change, because a majority of user application programs rely upon them remaining consistent.[1]

❑   Internal interfaces are formed from the collection of exported kernel functions that are made available to loadable kernel modules (so called "publicly exported" kernel symbols, such as the printk() function). For example, the printk() function provides a message-logging capability to any loaded kernel module with such a requirement. Once a kernel has been compiled, it will contain a binary version of these functions against which all subsequent kernel modules must be built.

You will have encountered APIs before as part of programming toolkits, such as a graphical windowing system or standard system libraries. What's different with the Linux kernel is that externally accessible interfaces (such as system calls) cannot easily be changed without affecting the entire system for a very long time. When a regular software library is updated, an older version of that library can remain on the system for compatibility. This isn't possible with the Linux kernel, so externally visible changes must be carefully regulated. As a result, often it can take years to finally remove all obsolete interfaces.

Undefined Interfaces

Sometimes, in the real world, things aren't quite as straightforward as they may seem, and there are ways to break the rules. For example, it's possible to manually access physical system memory from within a user application on some platforms.[2] This process bypasses the normal kernel handling of whatever device is located at that specific memory address, so it can only be done with great care. For example, the X Window system has historically been very keen to poke directly at graphics hardware.

There are other ways to work around the system's standard interfaces, too. When you use Linux, you're not constrained to follow the rules — especially on custom-engineered systems that are entirely under your control. A large number of embedded devices ship with nonstandard hacks that are designed just to make life easier for the developers. The fact that this is possible should not necessarily serve as an encouragement for you to employ custom hacks, but it's always worth knowing what's possible.

You should never jump at the opportunity to bypass regular system interfaces. They're there to make life easier and for interoperability reasons — much like the posted speed limits on our highways.

---

[1]A great Linux kernel hacker T-shirt available online conveys this message with the words "The Linux kernel: breaking user space since 1991." The point being that breaking userspace is always unacceptable and must only happen after due notice has been given of an anticipated change.

[2]This might be a design "feature" of some limited hardware systems, or achieved through specific, controlled permissions on other systems. In either case, it is sometimes necessary to do this kind of thing for its relative performance gains — not going through regular kernel interfaces can save some overhead.

External Kernel Interfaces

External kernel interfaces are those through which regular user application software can talk to the Linux kernel. These include system calls, the UNIX file abstraction, and various other modern kernel event mechanisms that have been implemented over the past few years specifically for Linux. You totally rely upon the kernel both for your application programs to operate and to provide a stable environment through which your custom drivers can communicate with application software.

External interfaces, such as system calls, define very rigid APIs that cannot easily be changed. In fact, anything within the Linux kernel that is considered to be user facing equally cannot be changed without due notice and care in the process. For example, the kernel community voted to remove an older device filesystem (one that was responsible for creating files under /dev, much like udev now) several years ago, but it is only now that the community feels it is safe to finally remove this antiquated filesystem from the kernel without adversely impacting someone who is still relying on it.[3]

There are more external interfaces than you may think. Modern Linux systems have not only device filesystems but also the deprecated procfs (/proc), newer sysfs (/sys) and more. Each of these may be relied on by user software — for example, module-init-tools (which provides the module loading and management system utilities modprobe, insmod, rmmod, and modinfo, among others) relies upon specific files in /proc and will rely more upon the various files in /sysfs over time. It's only in recent times (well after sysfs was introduced) that users, developers, and vendors have truly come to appreciate the complexities introduced by adding yet more such mechanisms for interacting with the Linux kernel.

The bottom line: when you add new kernel interfaces, consider it to be for the long haul. You will get a very negative reaction from the Linux kernel community if you propose random new interfaces that seem to have been poorly thought out — they don't want that support burden five years from now.

System Calls

Perhaps the most used kernel interface is that of the system call. The average Linux workstation will make literally thousands of system calls every second under normal operation, even when apparently idle. All those system daemons, desktop applets, and graphical applications rely on the frequent use of kernel-provided functionality, such as access to the current time. Perhaps it never occurred to you, but even your desktop volume control is frequently querying the current audio mixer state.

System calls are used as an abstraction through which user programs can request some privileged operation be performed on their behalf. These are operations that cannot be safely delegated to user programs directly because they require direct access to hardware (and would break the underlying hardware abstractions of userspace) or would otherwise open up the system to abuse from a user. Typical examples of system calls include open()ing a file, mmap()ing some anonymous memory (used by standard memory allocation routines, such as malloc, as well as for more complex memory management) or other functionality you might think was purely provided by the GNU C library.

---

[3]Even then, this was only achieved because a compatible replacement was in place and had been for a sufficiently long period of time. Occasionally, vendors will add back such legacy interfaces after they've been removed from the "upstream" official Linux kernel in order to avoid forcing their customers' to update legacy software. Once again, this kind of fundamental system breakage is carefully controlled.

In fact, many system C library functions are simply wrappers around a system call that will actually carry out the requested task. The C library function is used to provide an easy means to perform the system call as well as to perform any lightweight processing that doesn't require kernel support. For example, when calling the GNU C library family of exec() functions to replace the current program code with a new program and begin execution of that new program, you are actually calling a single underlying system call that the C library wraps with some cosmetic logic to make life easier on you.

In some cases, functionality you might expect to be handled directly by the Linux kernel can be more efficiently performed from within the system C library without any overall detriment to the system. Whenever a system call is performed, a potentially expensive (in terms of computation, memory access, time, and other metrics) context switch from user mode into kernel mode must be performed[4] (as explained in the previous chapter). If this is avoided, throughput increases. For example, some systems don't need a system call to get a high-resolution time stamp from the CPU.

Tracing System Calls

You can take a look at the system calls being made on your system by using a tool such as strace, as you have seen previously in this book. Each system call made by an application run under strace (itself using the ptrace() system call to perform the trace — an extremely ugly code hack, not covered in this book, and best avoided in the interests of your sanity) will be displayed, along with any parameters passed to it. Take a look at the output from running the ls command under strace — you'll see output whenever ls makes a system call (including those in the C library functions that set up the program).

To run strace on any system command, wrap the program call with strace:

```
$ strace program_name
```

When the ls command opens the current directory in order to enumerate those files contained within it, the following open() system call becomes a good example of the system call process:

```
open(".", O_RDONLY|O_NONBLOCK|O_LARGEFILE|O_DIRECTORY) = 3
```

This open() call was made by the ls command when it called the C library opendir() function. opendir() needs to open the underlying file representing the directory contents and enumerate the file list. The open() call itself is implemented in a C library stub, which causes the appropriate system call to be made on behalf of the program. This allows the platform-specific intelligence of the system call API to be confined to a single per-platform part of the C library and avoids duplication for every system call. The section 2 manual page[5] for the open command states one possible prototype for open() is:

```
int open(const char *pathname, int flags);
```

---

[4]Internal CPU hardware known as TLBs (translation look-aside buffers) that cache userspace virtual memory mappings often need to be flushed at this point, and other similar activities will result in additional overhead once that user process runs again. Linux has low system call overhead compared with other operating systems but it can never be nonexistent. So, reducing system calls can aid throughput.

[5]As you may know, Linux manual pages are split into sections, according to type. Whenever someone refers to open(2) or something similar, you know that they mean the section 2 manual page for open. Refer to your system documentation for more information about manual sections, or see the "man" command help.

From the prototype of the open function, it is apparent that it expects to be given the pathname of an on-disk file or directory to open, along with some flags, too. In the example above, these flags specify that the current directory should be opened read-only, using nonblocking IO (in other words, subsequent IO operations will not block if they cannot be completed but will return with an error indicating that the IO should be retried later) and with the Linux-specifc O_DIRECTORY flag, specifying that the file should not be opened unless it represents an on-disk directory. The system call returns a new file descriptor (3).

Transferring Control to the Kernel: sys_open

Calls to the open function implemented within the system GLIBC library (/lib/libc.so.6 for example) ultimately result in a platform-specific process for transfer of control into the specific kernel function responsible for providing the real open() system call. For example, on the PowerPC platform, system calls are actually implemented using a special sc processor instruction. Intel IA32 (x86) platforms use a special processor *exception* number 0x80 (128) to achieve much the same thing.[6] Whatever the actual hardware-dependent process used, the result is a context switch into kernel sys_open() function:

```
asmlinkage long sys_open(const char __user *filename, int flags, int mode)
{
        long ret;

        if (force_o_largefile())
                flags |= O_LARGEFILE;

        ret = do_sys_open(AT_FDCWD, filename, flags, mode);
        /* avoid REGPARM breakage on x86: */
        prevent_tail_call(ret);
        return ret;
}
EXPORT_SYMBOL_GPL(sys_open);
```

The real workhorse of the open() system call is the much longer (and much more complex) do_sys _open() function provided by fs/open.c in the kernel sources. You can take a look if you want to see in more detail what happens in opening a file or directory for processing. Note that the sys_open() function specifies additional linkage information to the GNU C compiler via the prepended asmlinkage macro (saying that this function is directly called from lower-level trap- handling exception code) and that the EXPORT_SYMBOL_GPL(sys_open) makes this function available to external kernel modules.

Most system calls are implemented within the kernel by a function beginning sys_, as this has become the de facto way to recognize a system call. You will learn in the next section how the system call table provides the glue necessary to tie specific system call numbers into the corresponding function call.

---

[6]Newer Intel IA32 (x86) machines actually have a more modern approach, using cunning memory-mapped pages high in the userspace address space through which userspace functions in, for example, the GNU C library can call into the kernel much the same way they were calling just a regular function within the library itself. The stub code mapped into every userspace process uses a new SYSENTER processor instruction instead of sc.

The System Call Table

Each of the different Linux architectures has its own process for making system calls into the kernel. The usual process involves calling a special machine instruction (via inline assembly code). This causes the processor to enter into its privileged kernel mode and results in either hardware- or software-assisted lookup of the correct software routine to execute. This usually depends upon the system call number, which is usually passed in one of the processor registers when a system call is made. Again, this is an area where there's a lot of flexibility in the range of underlying hardware implementations.

On the IA32 (x86) architecture, system calls are defined in the system call table (`syscall_table.S`) in the `arch/i386/kernel` directory within the kernel sources. A similar process is used on other architectures (refer to the kernel sources for your particular architecture for details of the precise process[7]). The IA32 system call table defines system call number 5 to mean the open system call and, consequently, the fifth entry of the table contains a pointer to the `sys_open()` function. On a system call, the call number will be used as a direct offset into the system call table, and the corresponding function will be called.

Here's an extract of the system call table on Intel (x86) machines:

```
ENTRY(sys_call_table)
        .long sys_restart_syscall     /* 0 - old "setup()" system call,
                                              used for restarting */
        .long sys_exit
        .long sys_fork
        .long sys_read
        .long sys_write
        .long sys_open                /* 5 */
        .long sys_close
        .long sys_waitpid
        .long sys_creat
        .long sys_link
        .long sys_unlink              /* 10 */
```

A total of 317 system calls were defined at the time that this book was written, although the precise number will differ between different Linux architectures (and in theory even between platforms based on specific architectures — though that would be highly unusual) and generally will tend to increase with the passage of time. As you can see, newer calls such as those supporting the `kexec()` interface used in modern Linux kernel crash dump analysis are appended to the end of the table. System call numbers are never reused, merely replaced with dummy functions producing suitable warnings.

You can manually call any of the system calls defined in the in-kernel system call table from your user programs by using some simple macros provided by the C library. You don't normally need to worry about this, because the C library takes care of making system calls as part of its standard functions. But sometimes, a newer system call exists that the C library does not yet know about (especially, if you wrote that system call and added it to the system call table yourself). In that case, using the handy macros is the recommended process and alternative to rebuilding your C library from sources.

---

[7]Look in `arch/` for your particular architecture, from within the Linux kernel sources.

Here's an example of calling the time system call directly, using the C library headers to abstract the precise system call process in use on a particular platform:

```
/*
 * Manually call the sys_time system call.
 */

#include <errno.h>
#include <stdio.h>
#include <stdlib.h>
#include <syscall.h>
#include <unistd.h>
#include <linux/unistd.h>

#define __NR_time              13 /* normally defined in <asm/unistd.h> */
_syscall1(long,time,time_t *,tloc);

int main(int argc, char **argv)
{

        time_t current_time;
        long seconds;

        seconds = time(&current_time);

        printf("The current time is : %ld.\n",seconds);

        exit(0);

}
```

The system call number is first defined and assigned to the macro __NR_time. This macro is defined in the expected format subsequently used by the _syscall1 macro in the Linux unistd.h header file (take a look at the header file on your system for the specifics). The syscall1 macro is used to define a system call that takes one parameter and returns a result, though many, many more macros exist for different numbers of system call parameters. The macro will expand out into a stub function containing the necessary minimum amount of inline assembly code needed to make the actual system call.

In the example, the time() system call userspace stub is defined using the following macro:

```
_syscall1(long,time,time_t *,tloc);
```

Subsequent calls to the time() function from within your user program will result in the above system call being executed on behalf of your program and the result returned as a long.

Implementing Your Own Syscalls

You usually won't want to implement your own Linux system calls. There are far better mechanisms for interfacing with the kernel in your own loadable kernel modules and the like (read on for details). In fact, you should not write your own system calls without a very good reason—one that the kernel community are likely to accept—if you hope for your system call to be made available generally.

System calls have been covered for completeness — you'll need to understand them to make significant changes to the core Linux kernel — however, they should not be added without a compelling reason and certainly not without upstream community coordination to ensure uniqueness. Rather than writing a new system call, look at the next few sections on interfaces, such as the Linux sysfs, for alternatives.

Be aware that when you implement your own system calls you effectively change the binary ABI of your kernel in ways that may break future compatibility with other Linux kernels. This means that, if you were to add a new system call number 319 to the previous system call table, you would need to ensure that nobody else later used that number for another system call — changing your application code constantly to keep up with system call numbers is really not a fun activity to be involved with. Really.

The vsyscall Optimization

For completeness, you should be aware of the vsyscall optimization that has been added into modern Linux kernels. Whereas in the past it was always necessary to use a special processor instruction within the C library wrapper function making the system call, modern hardware offers a variety of alternatives that are less expensive in terms of overhead. The vsyscall capability in modern kernels allows all user applications on most platforms to rely upon the kernel to use the most appropriate entry mechanism.

Applications using vsyscall have an additional memory mapped page high in their address space that is directly shared with the Linux kernel. When the program is first started and a new process is created, the kernel populates this page with the correct (and, importantly, most optimal) set of instructions necessary to switch into the kernel and perform the system call. In many cases, this might simply involve special processor instructions, but on some platforms that have a more modern and efficient entry mechanism (such as the SYSENTER instruction on Intel IA32 [x86]), it's used instead.

You won't need to worry about vsyscall or the Intel SYSENTER instruction beyond vaguely being aware of its existence, since it is handled directly by the Linux kernel on your behalf. For more information about vsyscall and sysenter, refer to the kernel subdirectory for your particular Linux architecture of interest or look at the variety of articles written online around its introduction.

The Device File Abstraction

Linux and other UNIX-like systems rely upon the fundamental abstraction of the file as the primitive used to represent many different underlying operating system functions and devices. "Everything is a file," as they say. In fact, most devices in your Linux system are represented by files within the /dev directory of your Linux filesystem. On modern distributions, this directory usually serves as a mount-point for a RAM filesystem such as tmpfs. This allows device nodes (a type of special file used to represent an underlying physical hardware device) to be created freely at runtime.

You can take a look at the device files currently available on your Linux system using the ls utility:

```
$ ls -l /dev/
crw-rw----  1 root audio     14,   4 2006-06-13 19:41 audio
crw-rw----  1 root audio     14,  20 2006-06-13 19:41 audio1
lrwxrwxrwx  1 root root            3 2006-06-13 19:41 cdrom -> hdc
lrwxrwxrwx  1 root root            3 2006-06-13 19:41 cdrw -> hdc
```

```
crw-------  1 root root      5,   1 2006-06-13 19:41 console
lrwxrwxrwx  1 root root          11 2006-06-13 19:41 core -> /proc/kcore
drwxr-xr-x  3 root root          80 2006-06-13 19:41 cpu
brw-rw----  1 root cdrom    22,   0 2006-06-13 19:41 hdc
brw-rw----  1 root disk     33,   0 2006-06-13 19:41 hde
brw-rw----  1 root disk     33,   1 2006-06-13 19:41 hde1
brw-rw----  1 root disk     33,   2 2006-06-13 19:41 hde2
brw-rw----  1 root disk     33,   3 2006-06-13 19:41 hde3
```

The output shows just a few of the typical device files located within a Linux system.

Device files help to make representing underlying hardware much easier and much more uniform. There are only a few types of device files (or "nodes"), differentiated according to the overall characteristics of the type of hardware device being represented. By using files, it's possible to open devices and use regular IO functions to interact with underlying hardware devices. For example, you can open and read from a disk file, just as if the entire hard drive were a single giant file. There are very few exceptions to this rule.[8]

Historically, Linux systems have had many tens (or hundreds) of thousands of files in /dev to represent possible devices. These days, device filesystem daemons, such as udev, create these device nodes (files) on the fly when new devices are detected and suitable drivers are loaded to support them. This reduces the number of unnecessary device files (themselves needing a small amount of space). You can read more about udev later in this book in the Chapter 12, when you will also learn about D-BUS and Project Utopia and how they help to streamline the process of general system notification.

Character Files

Character devices are shown using a c in the first column of the ls output in the listing above. These include any devices that are always read from and written to sequentially (one character at a time). You may read or write an entire buffer of data from/to the device, but the underlying operations will take place sequentially. Typical character devices include keyboards and mice because they represent instantaneous state of hardware — you don't read from a random location in your mouse input.

In the device file listing shown, you can see several audio devices. These allow applications to play sounds via the system sound card, using one of the standard Linux sound APIs. Fundamentally, however, you can record a sound by reading from one of these devices and play it back by writing back to the device again. In reality, you need to set up the sound card so that the recording input is enabled, but the point is that your application only needs to worry about dealing with a couple of special files.

Creating a Character Device

The first Linux kernel module you write will probably involve a character device somewhere. It has certainly been the case traditionally that character devices are easy to implement and can also be a good way to learn about driver writing in general. In the 2.6 Linux kernel, character devices are more complex than they were in the past — for many very valid reasons — especially when it comes to the dynamic allocation of devices and handling the cdev structures that back every character device. In the twenty-first century, it is no longer possible to get away with many of the hacks that existed in older kernels.

---

[8]The obvious exception is Linux networking devices (netdevs), which are not represented as files.

Take a look at the following simple example code:

```c
/*
 * char.c - A simple example character device.
 *
 * Copyright (C) 2006 Jon Masters <jcm@jonmasters.org>
 *
 * This program is free software; you can redistribute it and/or
 * modify it under the terms of the GNU General Public License as
 * published by the Free Software Foundation.
 *
 */

#include <linux/init.h>
#include <linux/fs.h>
#include <linux/major.h>
#include <linux/blkdev.h>
#include <linux/module.h>
#include <linux/cdev.h>

#include <asm/uaccess.h>

/* function prototypes */

static int char_open(struct inode *inode, struct file *file);
static int char_release(struct inode *inode, struct file *file);
static ssize_t char_read(struct file *file, char __user *buf,
                         size_t count, loff_t *ppos);

/* global variables */

static struct class *plp_class;      /* pretend /sys/class */
static dev_t char_dev;               /* dynamically assigned at registration. */
static struct cdev *char_cdev;       /* dynamically allocated at runtime. */

/* file_operations */

static struct file_operations char_fops = {
        .read    = char_read,
        .open    = char_open,
        .release = char_release,
        .owner   = THIS_MODULE,
};

/*
 * char_open: open the phony char device
 * @inode: the inode of the /dev/char device
 * @file: the in-kernel representation of this opened device
 * Description: This function just logs that the device got
 *              opened. In a real device driver, it would also
 *              handle setting up the hardware for access.
 */

static int char_open(struct inode *inode, struct file *file)
{
        /* A debug messsage for your edutainment */
```

```
printk(KERN_INFO "char: device file opened.\n");
        return 0;
}

/*
 * char_release: close (release) the phony char device
 * @inode: the inode of the /dev/char device
 * @file: the in-kernel representation of this opened device
 * Description: This function just logs that the device got
 * closed. In a real device driver, it would also handle
 * freeing up any previously used hardware resources.
 */

static int char_release(struct inode *inode, struct file *file)
{
        /* A debug message for your edutainment */
printk(KERN_INFO "char: device file released.\n");
        return 0;
}

/*
 * char_read: read the phony char device
 * @file: the in-kernel representation of this opened device
 * @buf: the userspace buffer to write into
 * @count: how many bytes to write
 * @ppos: the current file position.
 * Description: This function always returns "hello world"
 * into a userspace buffer (buf). The file position is
 * non-meaningful in this example. In a real driver, you
 * would read from the device and write into the buffer.
 */

static ssize_t char_read(struct file *file, char __user *buf,
                    size_t count, loff_t *ppos)
{
        char payload[] = "hello, world!\n";

        ssize_t payload_size = strlen(payload);

        if (count < payload_size)
               return -EFAULT;

        if (copy_to_user((void __user *)buf, &payload, payload_size))
               return -EFAULT;

        *ppos += payload_size;
        return payload_size;

}

/*
 * char_init: initialize the phony device
 * Description: This function allocates a few resources (a cdev,
 * a device, a sysfs class...) in order to register a new device
```

```
 * and populate an entry in sysfs that udev can use to setup a
 * new /dev/char entry for reading from the fake device.
 */


static int __init char_init(void)
{
        if (alloc_chrdev_region(&char_dev, 0, 1, "char"))
                goto error;

        if (0 == (char_cdev = cdev_alloc()))
                goto error;

        kobject_set_name(&char_cdev->kobj,"char_cdev");
        char_cdev->ops = &char_fops; /* wire up file ops */
        if (cdev_add(char_cdev, char_dev, 1)) {
                kobject_put(&char_cdev->kobj);
                unregister_chrdev_region(char_dev, 1);
                goto error;
        }

        plp_class = class_create(THIS_MODULE, "plp");
        if (IS_ERR(plp_class)) {
                printk(KERN_ERR "Error creating PLP class.\n");
                cdev_del(char_cdev);
                unregister_chrdev_region(char_dev, 1);
                goto error;
        }
        class_device_create(plp_class, NULL, char_dev, NULL, "char");

        return 0;


error:
        printk(KERN_ERR "char: could not register device.\n");
        return 1;
}

/*
 * char_exit: uninitialize the phony device
 * Description: This function frees up any resource that got allocated
 * at init time and prepares for the driver to be unloaded.
 */


static void __exit char_exit(void)
{
        class_device_destroy(plp_class, char_dev);
        class_destroy(plp_class);
        cdev_del(char_cdev);
        unregister_chrdev_region(char_dev,1);
}

/* declare init/exit functions here */

module_init(char_init);
```

```
module_exit(char_exit);

/* define module meta data */

MODULE_AUTHOR("Jon Masters <jcm@jonmasters.org>");
MODULE_DESCRIPTION("A simple character device driver for a fake device");
MODULE_LICENSE("GPL");
```

The example driver `char.c` declares two public entry points via `module_init()` and `module_exit()`. These are used to handle driver loading and unloading and will be explained in more detail shortly. The driver also makes use of `MODULE_` macros to define the author and license and provide a very brief description of the driver's function. This information will show up in the output of the `modinfo` utility, if it is run against the module output from the build process, `char.ko`. Finally, notice that the module is fully documented in the kernel-doc style discussed previously — it's always a good idea to add verbose documentation.

Building the Driver

You can experiment with the example driver by building it with using the kernel kbuild system. The example was tested against Linux kernel release 2.6.15.6 (along with all other kernel examples in this book), but should work with any recent 2.6 Linux kernel that you may have installed (if not, try fixing it for the most recent kernel and mailing in a patch to the publisher!). As was explained in the previous chapter, `/lib/modules/2.6.15.6/build` should be a symlink to the actual kernel source directory, so you can always figure out the location of the source to your running kernel via a quick call to uname.[9]

Here, then, is the right way to build this Linux kernel module:

```
$ make -C /lib/modules/`uname -r`/build modules M=$PWD
make: Entering directory `/data/work/linux_26/linux-2.6.15.6'
  CC [M]   /home/jcm/PLP/src/interfaces/char/char.o
  Building modules, stage 2.
  MODPOST
  CC       /home/jcm/PLP/src/interfaces/char/char.mod.o
  LD [M]   /home/jcm/PLP/src/interfaces/char/char.ko
make: Leaving directory `/data/work/linux_26/linux-2.6.15.6'
```

After (hopefully) building successfully, the driver `char.ko` will be created. As in the previous chapter, you can find out more about this driver using the `modinfo` utility:

```
$ /sbin/modinfo char.ko
filename:       char.ko
author:         Jon Masters <jcm@jonmasters.org>
description:    A simple character device driver for a fake device
license:        GPL
vermagic:       2.6.15.6 preempt K7 gcc-4.0
depends:
srcversion:     B07816C66A436C379F5BE7E
```

---

[9]As you may already know, uname -r will return the version of the kernel in use. The modules for a running kernel should live in `/lib/modules/`uname -r``, with the build subdirectory being a link within that directory.

To load the driver into the currently running kernel, use the `insmod` utility:

```
$ sudo insmod char.ko
```

Since the driver `char.ko` is not present in the standard `/lib/modules` path, you cannot (yet) use the system-level modprobe utility to do the loading on your behalf. This means that you must use `insmod` with the specific location of the `.ko` kernel module file — something that your users are certainly not going to be accustomed to having to do on their own systems. Rather than using `insmod`, you should install the module into the standard system `/lib/modules` location so that it is generally available.

You could install the driver into `/lib/modules` by repeating the build step above, substituting the `make modules` target for `make modules_install`:

```
$ export INSTALL_MOD_DIR=misc
$ sudo make -C /lib/modules/`uname -r`/build modules_install M=$PWD
make: Entering directory `/data/work/linux_26/linux-2.6.15.6'
  INSTALL /home/jcm/PLP/src/interfaces/char/char.ko
make: Leaving directory `/data/work/linux_26/linux-2.6.15.6'
$ sudo depmod -a
```

Notice that `INSTALL_MOD_DIR` should be set to the location under your kernel's modules where you'd like the driver to be installed — misc is a good choice — for example, `/lib/modules/2.6.15.6/misc`. This isn't needed but helps to keep your module seperate from the standard system-supplied modules. Don't forget to run `depmod` — to update the `module.dep` database used by `modprobe`, as shown.

However you load the module (whether with `insmod` or with `modprobe`), you will want to confirm that it loaded correctly. To confirm that the driver really has been loaded, check out the kernel ring buffer output, where in this case, you can see that a lot of object registration has taken place (your system may be much quieter, depending upon whatever verbosity settings are in the kernel configuration of the running kernel). You can view the kernel ring buffer via the dmesg system utility:

```
$ dmesg|tail
[18023332.980000] kobject char: registering. parent: <NULL>, set: module
[18023332.980000] kobject_hotplug
[18023332.980000] fill_kobj_path: path = '/module/char'
[18023332.980000] kobject_hotplug: /sbin/udevsend module seq=1021 HOME=/
PATH=/sbin:/bin:/usr/sbin:/usr/bin ACTION=add DEVPATH=/module/char SUBSYSTEM=module
[18023332.996000] subsystem plp: registering
[18023332.996000] kobject plp: registering. parent: <NULL>, set: class
[18023332.996000] kobject char: registering. parent: plp, set: class_obj
[18023332.996000] kobject_hotplug
[18023332.996000] fill_kobj_path: path = '/class/plp/char'
[18023332.996000] kobject_hotplug: /sbin/udevsend plp seq=1022 HOME=/
PATH=/sbin:/bin:/usr/sbin:/usr/bin ACTION=add DEVPATH=/class/plp/char SUBSYSTEM=plp
```

To top it off, the driver actually works! Try using the cat command on the newly created `/dev/char` device file (as root, the device file's default permissions are unlikely to include your regular user account):

```
$ sudo cat /dev/char
hello, world!
```

```
hello, world!
hello, world!
...
```

You'll see a never ending stream of "hello,world!" coming from the device file. In addition, after reading from the device, you can see that the kernel ring buffer also contains a log of the activity:

```
$ dmesg|tail
[18023447.656000] char: device file opened.
[18023449.544000] char: device file released.
```

Those messages were written by the driver using the printk() logging function whenever the device file in /dev was itself opened and closed, hence the output in the kernel log buffer — a useful minimal form of debugging technique, but something that a real driver probably wouldn't want to shout in the logs.

One you're done playing around, don't forget to unload the driver:

```
$ rmmod char
```

Or, using modprobe to unload:

```
$ modprobe -r char
```

You should see the example Linux Kernel Module log appropriate output to the kernel ring buffer.

A Note on Dynamic Devices

Although you will learn more about udev and dynamic device management later on in this chapter and in this book — and specifically just how this driver is able to automatically register its own dynamic device entry in /dev — you might want to check out the newly created sysfs class for the simple character driver via its /sys directory (obviously, only visible while the driver is loaded — it's a pseudo-filesystem representation of data structures within the driver) while you have the driver built and actually loaded:

```
$ ls /sys/class/plp/char/
dev  uevent
$ cat /sys/class/plp/char/dev
254:0
```

When the driver was loaded, /sys/class/plp was created (by the driver) and populated with an entry for the char device being offered by this driver. When those directory entries were created, a message was sent to the system's udev dynamic device daemon, which read the dev file and ascertained that a new device called /dev/char with major 254 and minor 0 should be created — that's how /dev/char came into being and that's how it's supposed to be done with more Linux kernels. No more hard-coded devices.

You should never hard-code the device number on newly created device nodes for your own modules.

Driver Initialization

The example driver is loaded by ether modprobe or insmod, and the kernel then takes charge of running the initialization function — char_init() — that was declared to be the module initialization function for this example Linux kernel module through use of the `module_init()` macro. The driver first attempts to allocate a new device number — a major device used to represent a class of devices supported by the driver. The major device number will be present in the `/dev/char` device file later. The magic is handled by `alloc_chrdev_region()`, which in this case is told to allocate just one device number.

Once a device number for the filesystem device node has been allocated, a corresponding `cdev` structure provides the kernel with an in-memory representation of the character device and its properties. The `cdev` contains a `kobject` used to reference count the number of different parts of the kernel and tasks have a reference (are in some way using) to the `cdev`. The name `char_cdev` is associated with the embedded `kobject` inside the `cdev` for improved readability and debugging later on. In older kernels, it would also show up within the `/sys/cdev` directory — before superfluous cruft was removed from `sysfs`.

The `char_cdev` cdev also stores a pointer to the file operations, `char_fops`, which will be associated with various different kinds of IO against the device file. In this driver, only a handful of file operations are implemented — opening, releasing, and reading from the device file. Other unimplemented file operations attempted (for example, an ioctl or a write) will return an error instead. The allocated `cdev` is then associated with the device major number using `cdev_add`, gluing device and operations together.

Finally, the example driver makes a call to the `class_create()` function and creates a new "plp" sysfs class under `/sys/class/plp` to house any attributes of the driver that are exported via `sysfs` (forming part of the interface between kernel and userspace). One of these attributes is the `dev` file entry that is created following a call to `class_device_create()` — that's what kicks off the frenzy of activity that results in the user space `udev` daemon creating the `/dev/char` device node. Don't worry too much about how this happens — it is complex stuff that very few mainstream kernel drivers really get right anyway!

Notice that errors are handled using gotos. Despite what Edsger Dijkstra may have once said about goto being now considered harmful, it's still heavily used in kernel code — but only in error paths. The fact is that it's clearer when you need to unwind memory allocations or free up partly allocated resources if you reuse error-handling code as much as possible within a function, hence the error label and goto.

Driver Uninitialization

All good things must come to an end, and so it is with the example module. Once a call has been made to either of the `modprobe` or `rmmod` utilities in order to remove the driver from the kernel, `char_exit()` takes care of freeing up those `sysfs` classes, the previously allocated `cdev` structure and unregistering the major device node from the system before the module is pulled and removed from memory. Notice that `cdev_del()` has to deal with the likely situation that someone is still trying to use the device — it'll just wait until the `cdev ref`. count is zero before actually freeing up the underlying structure from memory.

Driver payload

The purpose of the example module is to provide a simple character device from which a never-ending stream of test data can be read. This is implemented via a custom `char_read()` function that populates a userspace-supplied data buffer and returns the amount of data written. The `char_read()` function is actually hooked up via the `file_operations` (fops) structure pointed to by the ops member of the character device driver's `cdev`. The actual data writing to a user buffer must be done via a dedicated function, `copy_to_user`, in order to ensure that the user buffer is in memory at the time it is written. [10]

---

[10]Since userspace can be freely swapped in and out, there is no guarantee that any user buffer is loaded in memory at the time that the kernel wants to write to it. Furthermore, there is no guarantee that the kernel can even directly write into a userspace buffer — so you really want to use the `copy_to_user` function.

You are encouraged to experiment with the example code and to extend it in new ways. Why not allocate a large memory buffer when the device is opened (in char_open()) and use that to store data that is read from or written to the device? You can find some useful examples of the use of character devices in the kernel sources under the subdirectory drivers/char/.

Block Devices

Block devices are shown in the earlier /dev example file listing using a "b" in the first column of the output. These include any devices that are completely randomly addressable, such as disk drives. It doesn't matter what data you want to read from a regular disk, you are always able to specify where you'd like that data to be read from. Disk drives are represented using files such as /dev/hda or /dev/sda. Individual partitions within partitionable block devices are represented using files such as /dev/hda1.

When you write block device drivers, you don't deal directly with user IO in the way that you saw with character devices. Instead, you implement a series of functions that allow the kernel to perform block-orientated IO in an efficient manner (that's the top priority for a block device), and the kernel takes care of presenting the device to users when they choose to mount a filesystem on it or perform some other kind of block-device-related activity—such as partitioning the device and making a filesystem.

Creating your own block device drivers is tough and requires a lot more understanding about the Linux block layer than can be reasonably conveyed to you in the space of this chapter. If you're interested in writing a block device driver then you'll want to take a look at your existing Linux kernel sources for examples of other disk/block device drivers—why not see how your disk controller's driver implements the abstraction that is the block device containing your filesystem? You'll also want to check out some of the third-party resources that mentioned previously—especially the *Linux Device Drivers* book.

Everything Is a File?

Linux tries as hard as it can to always maintain the file abstraction, where it makes sense to do so. But in the real world, it's neither always practical nor always possible to use a file abstraction to represent every underlying device within a Linux system. There are exceptions to every rule, especially when it comes to more unusual devices or software stacks with unique performance requirements—such as is the case with the Linux networking and packet-filtering stacks being used on every Linux system.

The only widely adopted devices that aren't represented via some form of file abstraction in Linux (but are in other UNIX-like operating systems, as well as more radical alternatives, such as Plan 9) are network devices. The Linux networking stack instead uses special interfaces (such as netlink) and special system calls to set up and tear down networking configurations. This means that it's not trivially possible to read raw network packets using a command like cat, but there are tools that do this instead.[11]

Mechanism vs. Policy

Implementing mechanism, not policy, is the fundamental goal of the Linux kernel programmers. For example, the kernel doesn't need to know that only Bob should be able to read or write to the system sound card between the hours of 9 to 5. All that's necessary is a mechanism to add file permissions to the /dev/audio and /dev/dsp sound card interfaces and other system utilities (such as the PAM library) can handle setting the appropriate permissions. That way, it's trivial to change the policy later on.

---

[11]The *libpcap* library provides a generic enough way to do this on most Linux systems.

Sometimes, file abstractions are used, but desired functionality cannot be represented through file operations. The ioctl() system call (or, more recently, special sysfs files) is used for special control of devices. This is designed to compensate for the occasional inadequacies of using regular file IO operations to control devices. For example, telling a tape drive to rewind isn't a typical kind of file operation (there's no standard tape_rewind() system call or C library function), so it's implemented within the kernel via the ioctl() system call. ioctl()s are performed directly on the device file itself.

You can see an example of an ioctl in practice every time you change the volume of your soundcard mixer — a special ioctl() is used to instruct the sound card driver that you wish to modify the mixer and another special ioctl is used in order to determine what the current sound level is set at. To learn more, refer to the many examples of ioctl()s in existing Linux kernel drivers or on the Internet.

Procfs

Traditionally, the procfs pseudo-filesystem has been the main command and control interface into the Linux kernel outside of system calls. Using /proc, it's possible for a wide range of user applications and utilities to ascertain the current system state or modify system tunables, all through reading and writing simple files. What started out as a simple mechanism for querying the state of running processes (hence the name procfs) was quickly overloaded as it became clear just how easily procfs could be extended.

Take a look at the typical entries in the procfs filesystem on your Linux system by looking at /proc:

```
$ ls /proc
1       2115    27205   31915   4773    5703    7337    9271        kmsg
1063    22311   27207   31918   4918    5727    7339    9521        loadavg
115     23732   27209   31921   4994    5730    7341    9804        locks
116     24831   27210   31926   5       5732    7344    acpi        mdstat
13266   2493    27456   31929   5003    5745    7352    asound      meminfo
13278   24933   27457   32020   5012    5747    7360    buddyinfo   misc
13286   25065   28597   32024   5019    5749    7379    bus         modules
13289   25483   2870    32183   5026    5764    7381    cmdline     mounts
13330   26136   28711   32186   5045    5781    7383    config.gz   mtrr
13331   26410   28749   32189   5116    5784    7385    cpuinfo     net
14193   26557   2982    32193   5149    5814    7390    crypto      partitions
1727    2677    3       32195   5154    5816    7395    devices     pci
1738    26861   30191   32199   5162    5826    7397    diskstats   schedstat
1744    26952   30230   32221   5170    5884    7399    dma         scsi
1831    26962   30234   32226   5190    5906    7400    dri         self
19074   26965   30237   32236   5197    5915    7403    driver      slabinfo
19077   26966   30240   32280   5216    5918    7417    execdomains stat
19078   26969   30270   32287   5256    5921    7429    fb          swaps
19162   26984   30273   32288   5263    5924    7601    filesystems sys
19176   26997   3045    32416   5266    5927    7605    fs          sysrq-trigger
1929    27007   31079   32420   5267    6       8       ide         sysvipc
1935    27030   31118   3792    5269    6589    889     interrupts  tty
19411   27082   31415   3837    5290    704     9       iomem       uptime
19607   27166   31446   3848    5376    7253    9000    ioports     version
2       27174   31490   3849    5382    731     9016    irq         vmnet
20113   27180   31494   4       5388    7329    9023    kallsyms    vmstat
20270   27185   31624   4121    5397    7330    9024    kcore       zoneinfo
20278   27187   31799   4131    5401    7332    9025    keys
20670   27193   31912   4260    5531    7335    9029    key-users
```

You can query information about a particular system, such as the processor model:

```
$ cat /proc/cpuinfo
processor        : 0
vendor_id        : AuthenticAMD
cpu family       : 6
model            : 4
model name       : AMD Athlon(tm) processor
stepping         : 4
cpu MHz          : 1402.028
cache size       : 256 KB
fdiv_bug         : no
hlt_bug          : no
f00f_bug         : no
coma_bug         : no
fpu              : yes
fpu_exception    : yes
cpuid level      : 1
wp               : yes
flags            : fpu vme de pse tsc msr pae mce cx8 sep mtrr pge mca cmov pat
pse36 mmx fxsr syscall mmxext 3dnowext 3dnow
bogomips         : 2806.44
```

You can also set various system tunables, such as enabling IP forwarding (as root):

```
$ echo 1 >/proc/sys/net/ipv4/ip_forward
```

The ease with which these operations can be performed has made `procfs` very enticing to kernel developers who just want a simple interface into the kernel. For example, `/proc/meminfo` and `/proc/slabinfo` are used by numerous hackers in order to ascertain the current performance of the multitude of memory allocation and management functions within the kernel. Of course, `procfs` originally was designed to provide information about processes, so it can do that too.

Take a look at the information available for the init process (process 1):

```
$ sudo ls /proc/1
attr      cwd       fd         mem       oom_score  seccomp  statm    wchan
auxv      environ   loginuid   mounts    root       smaps    status
cmdline   exe       maps       oom_adj   schedstat  stat     task
```

You can see a series of directories containing links to the current file (`fd`) descriptors in use by the process, the command line used to invoke it (`cmdline`) and the memory mappings of the process (`maps`). Many additional pieces of information within `/proc` are extracted by the numerous tools and utilities installed on a typical Linux workstation or other system. Various operations require the user to posses appropriate security capability to carry them out properly, normally including the root user account (unless one of the other Linux security systems is in place and limiting even the activities of "root").

Creating procfs Entries

`procfs` has traditionally tried to have a sufficiently low barrier to entry that anyone can create a `proc` file. In fact, functions like `create_proc_read_entry`() make this process even easier and even less painful than before. You can find the full family of `procfs` functions in `include/linux/proc_fs.h` along with brief comments about what each of the functions does. Do bear in mind, however, that `procfs` is no longer considered as sexy as it once was — but it's still very easy to use indeed, for small sets of data.

The following example code creates a single readable entry in `/proc` called `plp`, which when read returns the message "hello, world!":

```
/*
 * procfs.c - Demonstrate making a file in procfs.
 *
 * Copyright (C) 2006 Jon Masters <jcm@jonmasters.org>
 *
 * This program is free software; you can redistribute it and/or
 * modify it under the terms of the GNU General Public License as
 * published by the Free Software Foundation.
 *
 */

#include <linux/init.h>
#include <linux/module.h>
#include <linux/proc_fs.h>

/* function prototypes */

static int procfs_read_proc(char *page, char **start, off_t off,
                      int count, int *eof, void *data);
/* global variables */

static struct proc_dir_entry *procfs_file;

/*
 * procfs_read_proc: populate a single page buffer with example data.
 * @page: A single 4K page (on most Linux systems) used as a buffer.
 * @start: beginning of the returned data
 * @off: current offset into proc file
 * @count: amount of data to read
 * @eof: eof marker
 * @data: data passed that was registered earlier
 */

static int procfs_read_proc(char *page, char **start, off_t off,
                            int count, int *eof, void *data)
{

        char payload[] = "hello, world!\n";
        int len = strlen(payload);

        if (count < len)
                return -EFAULT;

        strncpy(page,payload,len);

        return len;
```

```
}


/*
 * procfs_init: initialize the phony device
 * Description: This function allocates a new procfs entry.
 */


static int __init procfs_init(void)
{

        procfs_file = create_proc_read_entry("plp", 0, NULL,
                                             procfs_read_proc, NULL);

        if (!procfs_file)
                return -ENOMEM;
        return 0;
}

/*
 * procfs_exit: uninitialize the phony device
 * Description: This function frees up the procfs entry.
 */


static void __exit procfs_exit(void)
{

        remove_proc_entry("plp", NULL);
}

/* declare init/exit functions here */

module_init(procfs_init);
module_exit(procfs_exit);

/* define module meta data */

MODULE_AUTHOR("Jon Masters <jcm@jonmasters.org>");
MODULE_DESCRIPTION("A simple driver populating a procfs file");
MODULE_LICENSE("GPL");
```

The guts of the example above are similar enough to the previous example Linux kernel module that they need not be dissected in any great detail. One thing that should be pointed out, however, is that procfs works in terms of pages. This means that when you write out data, you have at most around a 4K (arch and platform-dependent) buffer to play around with at any one time. Trying to present a lot of data via procfs is definitely not fun—and not what it was designed to do. Notice that most of the existing files in /proc are very tiny text files, for a good reason. Besides, 4K ought to be enough for anyone.

Building the Driver

The build process is extremely similar to the previous example involving character devices. First, you need to enter into the module source directory and call the kernel `kbuild` system to build the driver:

```
$ make -C /lib/modules/`uname -r`/build modules M=$PWD
make: Entering directory `/data/work/linux_26/linux-2.6.15.6'
  CC [M]  /home/jcm/PLP/src/interfaces/procfs/procfs.o
  Building modules, stage 2.
  MODPOST
  CC       /home/jcm/PLP/src/interfaces/procfs/procfs.mod.o
  LD [M]  /home/jcm/PLP/src/interfaces/procfs/procfs.ko
make: Leaving directory `/data/work/linux_26/linux-2.6.15.6'
```

You can then load and test the driver:

```
$ sudo insmod procfs.ko
$ cat /proc/plp
hello, world!
```

Sysfs

Modern Linux systems include a new user-visible kernel interface, known as `sysfs`. `sysfs` was created originally as a mechanism to represent the state of the Linux kernel power management subsystem. By representing physical devices within a device tree under `/sys`, it's possible for the system to track not only the current power state (on, off, hibernate, etc.) of a device but also how it relates to other devices within the system. Initially, this was done in order for Linux to ascertain the ordering of various operations.

For example, suppose that you have a USB device B, attached to a USB bus A. In an ideal world, the kernel would not attempt to power down the USB bus A before any devices (B), which may be attached to it. Without knowing something about the topological structure of the physical buses within the system, Linux might attempt to turn off a bus before any device drivers running devices attached to that bus have had time to put those devices into quiescent states. This lead could lead not only to data loss but also to kernel corruption, if the device drivers for attached devices were not adequately prepared.

`sysfs` has done a very good job of representing the associations between different system devices, but has itself suffered from feature creep. Since its underlying implementation is tied to an in-kernel data structure known as a `kobject` — used for reference counting and numerous other functions within the Linux kernel — and again due to the ease with which `sysfs` entries can be created, it is being used for an array of additional functions now that are no longer directly related to its original purpose.

Kernel Events

A variety of mechanisms exist for sending messages between the kernel and userspace. One of the more interesting of these is the kernel events layer that was added around the time of kernel 2.6.10. Events exist in the form of messages referring to a specific `sysfs` path — a specific `sysfs` `kobject` — that are passed to userspace. It is expected that userspace will handle the message according to whatever rules are in place — usually, that's the job of a daemon such as the `udev` dynamic device daemon.

The implementation of kernel events has changed somewhat since the original proposal was made. Originally, arbitrary events could be defined on the fly, but now `kobject_uevent.h` defines a list of standard events that may be called — for example `KOBJ_ADD` is used to tell userspace that some new hardware (or driver) just came along and might need some additional processing.

You will learn more about standard system events when you read about the FreeDesktop.org project later in this book. For now, it's worth checking out your kernel source for more examples. You will want to look for use of the netlink socket type if you want to understand the implementation.

Ignoring Kernel Protections

Sometimes, it's desirable to override the various protections offered by the Linux kernel and its abstractions in order to improve efficiency or just to get something done that would not otherwise be possible. This is typically the case with custom-engineered systems in which there are no regular users to worry about and no system integrity to compromise but that already being provided by your needed modifications. Many Embedded Linux systems utilize such hacks, where appropriate.

It is possible to communicate directly with physical hardware devices without having to use a kernel device driver or the underlying device file abstractions that other applications programs need to be concerned about. There are some limitations to what is possible in mmap()ing hardware directly:

❑   Not all hardware can be memory mapped in this fashion on all platforms. Common uses of mmap()ed hardware occur in 32-bit Embedded Linux environments with block mappings.

❑   It is not possible to handle interrupts or have them delivered (routed) to a userspace program, without patching your kernel with experimental userspace interrupt signal routing patches. Hardware that relies upon interrupt driven IO will certainly need kernel assistance.

❑   You cannot guarantee the timeliness of hardware interactions that occur within userspace. Even if you are using the latest low latency ("real-time") patches with the highest priority possible, your program will still be subject to the interference of internal kernel activity.

If you are able to work within these constraints, the following example demonstrates how you can open and memory map ranges of physical memory via the /dev/mem device node:

```c
/*
 * peekpoke.c
 * Jon Masters <jcm@jonmasters.org>
 */

#include <linux/stddef.h>

#include <stdio.h>
#include <stdlib.h>
#include <unistd.h>
#include <string.h>
#include <sys/mman.h>
#include <sys/types.h>
#include <sys/stat.h>
#include <fcntl.h>

#define MMAP_FILE "/dev/mem"    /* physical direct. */
#define MMAP_SIZE 4096          /* 4K. */

/* #define DEBUG 1 */

int use_hex = 0;

void display_help(void);
```

```
int valid_flag(char *flag_str);
void peek(char *address_str);
void poke(char *address_str, char *value_str);
unsigned long *map_memory(unsigned long address);

void display_help() {

  printf("Usage information: \n"
  "\n"
  "     peekpoke [FLAG] ADDRESS [DATA]\n"
  "\n"
  "Valid Flags: \n"
  "\n"
  "     -x      Use Hexadecimal.\n");
  exit(0);
}

int valid_flag(char *flag_str) {

  if (strncmp(flag_str,"-x",2) == 0) {
     use_hex = 1;
#ifdef DEBUG
     printf("DEBUG: using hexadecimal.\n");
#endif
     return 1;
  }

#ifdef DEBUG
  printf("DEBUG: no valid flags found.\n");
#endif
  return 0;

}

void peek(char *address_str) {

  unsigned long address = 0;

  unsigned long offset = 0;
  unsigned long *mem = 0;

#ifdef DEBUG
  printf("DEBUG: peek(%s).\n",address_str);
#endif

  if (use_hex) {
     sscanf(address_str,"0x%lx",&address);
     /* printf("hexadecimal support is missing.\n"); */
  } else {
     address = atoi(address_str);
  }

#ifdef DEBUG
  printf("DEBUG: address is 0x%x.\n",address);
#endif

  offset = address - (address & ~4095);
```

```
    address = (address & ~4095);

#ifdef DEBUG
  printf("DEBUG: address is 0x%x.\n",address);
  printf("DEBUG: offset is 0x%x.\n",offset);
#endif

  mem = map_memory(address);

  printf("0x%lx\n",mem[offset]);

}

void poke(char *address_str, char *value_str) {

  unsigned long address = 0;
  unsigned long value = 0;

  unsigned long offset = 0;
  unsigned long *mem = 0;

#ifdef DEBUG
  printf("DEBUG: poke(%s,%s).\n",address_str,value_str);
#endif

  if (use_hex) {
    sscanf(address_str,"0x%lx",&address);
    sscanf(value_str,"0x%lx",&value);
    /* printf("hexadecimal support is missing.\n"); */
  } else {
    address = atoi(address_str);
    value = atoi(value_str);
  }

#ifdef DEBUG
  printf("DEBUG: address is 0x%x.\n",address);
  printf("DEBUG: value is 0x%x.\n",value);
#endif

  offset = address - (address & ~4095);
  address = (address & ~4095);

#ifdef DEBUG
  printf("DEBUG: address is 0x%x.\n",address);
  printf("DEBUG: offset is 0x%x.\n",offset);
#endif

  mem = map_memory(address);

  mem[offset] = value;

}

unsigned long *map_memory(unsigned long address) {

  int fd = 0;
```

```c
    unsigned long *mem = 0;

#ifdef DEBUG
  printf("DEBUG: opening device.\n");
#endif

  if ((fd = open(MMAP_FILE,O_RDWR|O_SYNC)) < 0) {
    printf("Cannot open device file.\n");
    exit(1);
  }

  if (MAP_FAILED == (mem = mmap(NULL, MMAP_SIZE, PROT_READ|PROT_WRITE, MAP_SHARED,
fd, address))) {
    printf("Cannot map device file.\n");
    exit(1);
  }

  return mem;

} /* map_memory */

int main(int argc, char **argv) {

  /* test we got a sensible invocation. */

  switch(argc) {

  case 0:
    printf("Impossibility Reached.\n");
    exit(1);
  case 1:
    display_help();
    break;
  case 2:
    peek(argv[1]);
    break;
  case 3:
    if (valid_flag(argv[1])) {
      peek(argv[2]);
    } else {
      poke(argv[1],argv[2]);
    }
    break;
  case 4:
    if (valid_flag(argv[1])) {
      poke(argv[2],argv[3]);
    } else {
      printf("Sorry that feature is not supported.\n");
      display_help();
    }
    break;
  default:
    printf("Sorry that option is not supported.\n");
    display_help();
    break;
```

```
    }

    exit(0);

} /* main */
```

If you have access to an embedded reference board, you might try using the example to flash an LED residing in a GPIO region (for example, by writing to a fictitious control register at 0xe1000000):

```
$ ./peekpoke -x 0xe1000000 1
```

Assuming that by writing one to that control register, the LED is on and by writing zero it is off, you could script a one-second flash using some simple shell commands:

```
$ while true; do
        ./peekpoke -x 0xe1000000 1
        sleep 1
        ./peekpoke -x 0xe1000000 0
done
```

The key part of example program is in the map_memory() function. This function takes a given physical memory address and attempts to map it into the virtual address space of the program via a call to mmap(). The special device file /dev/mem is first opened with the special MMAP_FILE flag before a subsequent call to mmap() sets up a desired mapping on the newly opened file descriptor, which is returned as the function return value. The peek() and poke() functions are simply wrappers that will additionally read from or write to the mapped range. The program supports a few command flags.

Internal Kernel Interfaces

You should now have an overview understanding of the variety of ways that user application programs interface with the Linux kernel. But there's another side to the Linux kernel and that's in the internal interactions of those functions that make up the API made available to third-party drivers, such as those that you may write. There are literally thousands of functions within the Linux kernel, but only a subset of these are exported — this section aims to give you a quick overview of the APIs available to you.

Note that there is only so much that can ever be covered in any book, especially one that is not specifically about kernel programming. For more detailed coverage of available kernel functions, you will want to check out one of the many online references, mailing lists or books like *Understanding the Linux Kernel and Linux Device Drivers*. Ultimately, however, there's no better place to look than in the kernel sources themselves — they tend to be more up to date than any book could ever hope to be.

The Kernel API

The Linux kernel contains many thousands of individual functions spread across many hundreds of individual source files. The public API used by loadable modules comes about thanks to the use of EXPORT_SYMBOL and EXPORT_SYMBOL_GPL macros spread throughout the kernel source. The former function makes a symbol available for use by third-party modules, while the latter places the additional restriction that the function is not available to modules that profess not to be GPLed. Without getting into legal arguments, suffice it to say there's compelling reason to always GPL kernel modules.

Although there is no officially published standardized Linux kernel API and even though there are no guarantees about not breaking things, the community doesn't like the fallout from major API changes any more than anyone else — so they're avoided when possible. A variety of tools, such as LXR — the Linux source Cross Reference — parse the Linux kernel sources and build a web-browsable list of functions, structures, and other data types to aid in figuring out where functions are defined and how they work together. Coywolf maintains an upstream LXR at `http://www.sosdg.org/~coywolf/lxr`.

The set of publicly exported functions (along with their location) within any given Linux kernel are listed in the `Module.symvers` file within the compiled kernel sources. It is this file that is consulted when building out of tree modules with versioning enabled and in combination with the standard `System.map` file can be used to locate any symbol of interest in the running kernel.

The folks at *Linux Weekly News* (LWN) maintain an up-to-the-minute listing of API changes to the Linux kernel. You can find that listing by visiting the kernel page at `http://www.lwn.net`.

The kernel ABI

Once a Linux kernel has been compiled, the binary version of the collection of publicly exported symbols (exported to loadable kernel modules) is known as the kernel ABI — Application Binary Interface — or kABI. There is no official Linux API or ABI in the upstream kernel. This means that terms like kABI can refer only to the specific set of interfaces provided by a particular compilation of the Linux kernel. Upgrade to a new version of the kernel and the kABI may be very different indeed.

Although you may not realize it, whenever you build a module against a Linux kernel, various kABI-dependent information is added to the module. This is especially true in the case that you use module versioning (modversions) in your Linux kernel — in this case, the module will also contain checksum information about the kernel interfaces used to build it. Any kernel with a compatible kABI can then be used with the driver in question. Although there are no guarantees about compatibility, this mechanism often allows a module to be used with a kernel version close to that of the kernel for which it was built.

Linux doesn't want a stable kABI upstream. The idea has been posited many times — Microsoft has a stable set of ABIs in its Windows Driver Model, so wouldn't it be a good idea to have a similar thing with Linux? In theory, this would be a good idea. But the downside of a stable kABI is that it's tough to make changes in the name of efficiency or simply to rewrite old hackish code. Microsoft (and others) is forced to work around rewrites by providing compatibility layers — and that gets complex very quickly. They might need such a mechanism, but it doesn't really fit with the official Linux kernel.

While upstream kernel developers are not interested in a stable kABI, vendors often are. Although the goal for most parties is that Linux kernel drivers end up in the official upstream kernel, it's a fact of life that there are numerous examples of "out-of-tree" drivers that aren't going to be in the upstream kernel anytime soon. As a result, vendors often like to preserve kernel ABI compatibility in order to ensure that out-of-tree drivers can be built and used with as wide as possible variety of installed systems.

Kernel Module Packages

Two of the larger Linux vendors — Novell (OpenSuSE) and Red Hat (Fedora Core) have begun working on packaging mechanisms to take advantage of kABI tracking at the package level. Typically, these systems work by extracting the same information used in module versioning and making that available as a package dependency. For example, on a Fedora Core system, the kernel package might contain the following additional kABI dependencies (shorted for brevity):

```
kernel(kernel) = 329af1d5c0ddc4ac20696d3043b4f3e1cbd6a661
kernel(drivers_media_video_bt8xx) = 727583b2ef41a0c0f87914c9ef2e465b445d1cde
kernel(crypto) = d5a2dff1c7bb7a101810ce36149f4b9f510780c4
kernel(drivers_cpufreq) = 4bd57712e2f886b4962a159bcd28fcef34f88f86
kernel(sound_i2c_other) = c2e9f7ce21f9465661ec7cbff8ed0b18545b3579
kernel(net_802) = 887bebd345ad585ecff84f3beb9b446e82934785
kernel(fs_configfs) = 844ef6e77e9da3e17f8cfe038d454265cabc17e6
```

Collections of related kABI dependencies are grouped together (in order to avoid 8000 dependencies) into checksums that can be required by third-party supplied modules at a later stage. If the checksums match, then the third-party driver can be made available to the kernel in a standardized location. It is possible for various system scripts to keep the available compatible modules updated.

Both Fedora and OpenSuSE publish instructions for building drivers with these dependencies added — you might like to check it out next time you have to package up a driver for use on these distributions. For further information about packaging modules in such a fashion, consult the community website (maintained by the author of this book) at http://www.kerneldrivers.org.

Summary

In this chapter, you learned about interfacing with the Linux kernel. You learned that there are a multitude of standardized interfaces that user programs must rely upon in communicating with the kernel. These interfaces must remain consistent for long periods of time, as it can take many years following a modification to the external kernel interfaces before all applications have caught up.

This chapter was intended to serves as glue, explaining a number of important concepts from the point of view of the internal and external interfaces presented by the Linux kernel. In the next chapter, you'll take a few of the things that you've learned over the last couple of chapters and help to debug drivers using the standard tools available to Linux kernel programmers.

## 9

Linux Kernel Modules

In the previous two chapters, you learned how the Linux kernel development process works. You learned about the upstream kernel community and how the kernel is a constantly evolving project. The last chapter was written in order to explain to you just how much of a moving target Linux really is (this is complex stuff, don't worry — there's no class test at the end of this book), while this chapter sets the stage for you to begin writing your very own Linux kernel modules. These are often referred to as Linux kernel drivers because a majority of modules support specific devices.

You already wrote a simple Linux kernel module called plp back in Chapter 7. That simple loadable Linux kernel module simply printed a greeting into the kernel ring buffer (displayed using the dmesg command) and demonstrated the fundamental concept of writing a module, without delving deeper. This chapter builds upon the examples from the previous chapter by introducing many more of the concepts that you need to work with when writing real Linux kernel modules for real-world uses.

Not all kernel development takes place in the form of third-party modules. There are many parts of the kernel that cannot be modified through loadable kernel modules alone, requiring core code changes instead of a simple module load. Although you will experience your first taste of kernel development in the form of loadable modules, you won't be modifying core kernel algorithms by the end of this chapter. To do that, you will need to allocate a serious amount of time to the necessary further study and community involvement. Remember, this is complex stuff — it can't be learned in a week.

How Modules Work

The Linux kernel is capable of dynamic runtime extension, through the use of loadable kernel modules. Dynamically loaded Linux kernel modules (or LKMs) are similar to the drivers that you can obtain for Microsoft Windows, some proprietary UNIX (for example Sun Solaris), Mac OS X, and others besides. LKMs are built against a particular set of Linux kernel sources and partially linked into a module object file with the extension .ko. These are then loaded into a running Linux kernel using special system calls.

When a module is loaded into the kernel, the kernel will allocate sufficient memory for the module and extract information from the "modinfo" ELF section,[1] added to the module during its build, in order to satisfy any other requirements that the module may have. At load time, the module is finally linked to the running kernel's versions of any exported kernel functions that it depends on, and its publicly exported symbols become a part of the running kernel. The module is part of the kernel.

You are probably relying on loadable kernel modules right now. Your Linux system will almost certainly be built to support loadable kernel modules if it is running a standard Linux distribution. The system will have several modules loaded to support a variety of hardware detected at boot time within your computer and loaded by automatic device managers such as udev (which maintains the /dev filesystem as well as loading modules for newly detected devices).

You can see a list of loaded modules with the lsmod command:

```
$ /sbin/lsmod
Module               Size  Used by
procfs               1732  0
char                 2572  0
raw                  7328  0
tun                  9600  0
snd_rtctimer         2636  0
vmnet               35172  13
vmmon              111244  0
capability           3336  0
commoncap            5504  1 capability
thermal             11272  0
fan                  3588  0
button               5200  0
processor           19712  1 thermal
ac                   3652  0
battery              7876  0
8250_pnp             8640  0
8250                25492  3 8250_pnp
serial_core         18944  1 8250
floppy              59972  0
pcspkr               1860  0
rtc                 10868  1 snd_rtctimer
usbnet              14024  0
sd_mod              16704  2
eth1394             18376  0
ohci1394            33268  0
ieee1394           292568  2 eth1394,ohci1394
emu10k1_gp           3072  0
ehci_hcd            32008  0
usb_storage         64128  1
scsi_mod            94760  2 sd_mod,usb_storage
ohci_hcd            19652  0
via686a             16712  0
```

---

[1]As explained back in Chapter 2, Linux uses ELF binaries extensively as the de facto binary format for all modern user programs (replacing the older, deprecated a.out format). ELF simply defines a standard container format for binary data—including programs—split into many different sections.

```
i2c_isa                 3968   1 via686a
uhci_hcd               31504   0
usbcore               120452   6 usbnet,ehci_hcd,usb_storage,ohci_hcd,uhci_hcd
parport_pc             38276   0
parport                33608   1 parport_pc
shpchp                 44512   0
pci_hotplug            11780   1 shpchp
tsdev                   6336   0
md_mod                 64916   0
dm_mod                 54552   0
psmouse                36420   0
ide_cd                 38212   0
cdrom                  37152   1 ide_cd
snd_cmipci             32288   1
gameport               12808   3 emu10k1_gp,snd_cmipci
snd_opl3_lib            9472   1 snd_cmipci
snd_mpu401_uart         6720   1 snd_cmipci
snd_emu10k1_synth       7040   0
snd_emux_synth         36160   1 snd_emu10k1_synth
snd_seq_virmidi         6464   1 snd_emux_synth
snd_seq_midi_emul       6784   1 snd_emux_synth
snd_seq_oss            32960   0
snd_seq_midi            7328   0
snd_seq_midi_event      6400   3 snd_seq_virmidi,snd_seq_oss,snd_seq_midi
snd_seq                50512   8
snd_emux_synth,snd_seq_virmidi,snd_seq_midi_emul,snd_seq_oss,snd_seq_midi,snd_seq_m
idi_event
snd_emu10k1           119652   5 snd_emu10k1_synth
snd_rawmidi            21600   4
snd_mpu401_uart,snd_seq_virmidi,snd_seq_midi,snd_emu10k1
snd_seq_device          7628   8
snd_opl3_lib,snd_emu10k1_synth,snd_emux_synth,snd_seq_oss,snd_seq_midi,snd_seq,snd_
emu10k1,snd_rawmidi
snd_ac97_codec         94304   1 snd_emu10k1
snd_pcm_oss            50784   1
snd_mixer_oss          17728   3 snd_pcm_oss
snd_pcm                83460   4 snd_cmipci,snd_emu10k1,snd_ac97_codec,snd_pcm_oss
snd_timer              22404   5
snd_rtctimer,snd_opl3_lib,snd_seq,snd_emu10k1,snd_pcm
snd_ac97_bus            2176   1 snd_ac97_codec
snd_page_alloc          8904   2 snd_emu10k1,snd_pcm
snd_util_mem            3776   2 snd_emux_synth,snd_emu10k1
snd_hwdep               7840   3 snd_opl3_lib,snd_emux_synth,snd_emu10k1
snd                    47844  20
snd_cmipci,snd_opl3_lib,snd_mpu401_uart,snd_emux_synth,snd_seq_virmidi,snd_seq_oss,
snd_seq,snd_emu10k1,snd_rawmidi,snd_seq_device,snd_ac97_codec,snd_pcm_oss,snd_mixer
_oss,snd_pcm,snd_timer,snd_hwdep
soundcore               8224   4 snd
r128                   46912   1
drm                    68308   2 r128
agpgart                29592   1 drm
8139too                23424   0
mii                     5120   1 8139too
```

That's a lot of output, just for one single regular desktop computer.

The lsmod output shows that a total of 77 modules are loaded on this one Linux system alone. Some of these modules have no other modules using symbols that they export into the kernel namespace (a zero in the third column), whereas others form complex hierarchies of module stacks — for example, in the case of the ALSA sound drivers providing support for the two installed sound cards (Creative Labs emu10k chipset and C-Media cmpci chipset) and in the case of the various installed USB modules.

Extending the Kernel Namespace

Loadable Linux kernel modules often export new functions for use by other parts of the Linux kernel (you'll discover how this works later in this chapter). These new symbols will show up within procfs though /proc/kallsyms (if you have support for this built into your kernel), along with the address of those new symbols that have been added within the kernel image. Here's an extract from a running kernel displaying /proc/kallsyms. First, the top of the symbol table:

```
$ cat /proc/kallsyms | head
c0100220 T _stext
c0100220 t rest_init
c0100220 T stext
c0100270 t do_pre_smp_initcalls
c0100280 t run_init_process
c01002b0 t init
c0100430 t try_name
c0100620 T name_to_dev_t
c01008e0 t calibrate_delay_direct
c0100a60 T calibrate_delay
```

And now the bottom of the kernel symbol table. Since new module symbol additions are added to the end of the table, you can see several module symbols in this output (the module name is listed in square brackets — in this case for the MII Ethernet device management and control standard module):

```
$ cat /proc/kallsyms | tail
e0815670 T mii_check_media        [mii]
e08154f0 T mii_check_gmii_support        [mii]
c023d900 U capable        [mii]
e0815600 T mii_check_link        [mii]
c011e480 U printk        [mii]
e08155a0 T mii_nway_restart        [mii]
c032c9b0 U netif_carrier_off        [mii]
e0815870 T generic_mii_ioctl        [mii]
c032c970 U netif_carrier_on        [mii]
e0815000 T mii_ethtool_gset        [mii]
```

Loadable modules show up towards the end of the kernel symbol table and have the corresponding module name inside square brackets, as in [mii] above. You can also easily note the loaded kernel modules by the address in the first column of the output in the symbol listing. Since the Linux kernel is usually linked to run from 3GB in virtual memory, built-in symbols appear at small offsets over 3GB (0xc0000000); however, loaded modules exist in kernel-allocated memory, in this case over 0xe0000000. This is because module memory is allocated by the kernel at runtime.

The example Linux system has been deliberately tainted to make a point to you. It has a non-GPL-licensed module loaded into the running kernel to support a popular commercial virtual machine product. This is also often the case with modern graphics chipsets. Such modules are widely disliked by the

Linux kernel community and, in general, you will want to remove any such kernel modules from your own test machines — you won't get any support from the kernel community otherwise.

No Guaranteed Module Compatibility

Unlike other operating systems, Linux (intentionally) has no standardized driver model against which you can build your drivers in order to guarantee compatibility between one Linux system and the next. This means that Linux is optimized for the case that module source code is available (which should normally be the case — many people consider non-GPL-licensed drivers to infringe upon the rights of kernel developers, so it's a really good idea not to try the binary driver game when writing modules).

In general, you should not assume that modules built for your desktop Linux kernel will run in prebuilt binary form on another Linux machine. Instead, those modules will usually need to be recompiled from the sources for each different Linux machine upon which they run. There are notable exceptions to this — vendor kernels are often compatible with one another — but don't count on it.

Finding Good Documentation

One of the biggest problems faced by new Linux developers — especially those working on the kernel — is that of finding good API documentation for each of the many hundreds and thousands of functions that they must work with in order to make good use of the facilities offered by the Linux kernel. Unless you're working on the Linux kernel on a daily basis, it's unlikely that you will immediately have such an in-depth knowledge at this moment so good documentation will be an essential part of your work.

The problem, as you may have guessed, is that there is not such a wealth of good documentation. In fact, the Linux kernel is constantly evolving, so even good documentation might be out of date by the time you read it. In this book, you'll notice that the authors have not attempted to write documentation on the Linux kernel. Rather, this book explains the nature of the kernel and offers examples that will demonstrate concepts, which you can apply for yourself. The ultimate source of documentation on writing new kernel modules comes in the form of existing modules already in the upstream kernel.[2]

Linux Kernel Man Pages

Fortunately, one good source of API documentation that does exist is the Linux kernel man pages. This collection of documentation does attempt to be as up to date as possible with respect to new releases of the Linux kernel and is available from the kernel.org master website, along with a lot of other resources: `http://www.kernel.org/pub/linux/docs/manpages`. You can also build these kernel manual pages for yourself from your Linux kernel sources by using the `mandocs` make target to the make command:

```
$ make mandocs
   MAN      Documentation/DocBook/usb.9
Writing struct_usb_ctrlrequest.9 for refentry
Writing struct_usb_host_endpoint.9 for refentry
Writing struct_usb_interface.9 for refentry
etc.
```

---

[2]That is, the Linux kernel available from the http://www.kernel.org website.

Install them with the `installmandocs` make target so that they're available to the man command.

Your Linux distribution may have packaged prebuilt versions of these Linux kernel manual pages alongside their regular Linux distribution man pages so that you don't even need to do the build step for yourself. As an example of this, look for "linux-manual" in Debian, Ubuntu, and derivatives.

Here, then, is how you can view the man page for the `vmalloc()` kernel memory allocation function:

```
$ man vmalloc

VMALLOC(9)                    LINUX                    VMALLOC(9)

NAME
       vmalloc - allocate virtually contiguous memory

SYNOPSIS
       void * vmalloc  (unsigned long size);

ARGUMENTS
       size    allocation size

DESCRIPTION
       Allocate  enough  pages to cover size from the page level allocator and
       map them into contiguous kernel virtual space.

       For tight cotrol over page level allocator  and  protection  flags  use
       __vmalloc instead.

DESCRIPTION
       Allocate  enough  pages to cover size from the page level allocator and
       map them into contiguous kernel virtual space.

       For tight control over page level allocator  and  protection  flags  use
       __vmalloc instead.

Kernel Hackers Manual            July 2006                    VMALLOC(9)
```

You will probably find these manual pages very useful as you start working with the kernel. Don't forget to help document those parts of the kernel whose lack of documentation causes frustration. If everyone helps to document those parts that are lacking, then things will be less painful for others.

Writing Linux Kernel Modules

Back in Chapter 7, you began developing for the Linux kernel with a very simple example. The example demonstrated how kernel modules are built and loaded into a (binary compatible) running kernel. Using the kernel's `printk()` function, the module could log as it was loaded and unloaded from the kernel. You should now be aware of the basic process of building a kernel and of compiling modules for that kernel. If you missed or skipped over Chapter 7, take a look back now and make sure that you're comfortable.

This section aims to cover a few of the basics of writing useful kernel modules, while equipping you to educate yourself by using available resources. It's not possible to explain all of the intricacies of writing kernel code in the space of one chapter (or actually even in the space of a book — it takes real practice) but you should be able to use what you read here in combination with a study of existing code, and the documentation mentioned above to write some pretty complex Linux kernel modules of your own.

Finally, it's not all about loadable modules kept away from the upstream, mainline Linux kernel. Linux is so much more than just a kernel for which you will write drivers — it's a whole community out there. The goal should always be to get new code into the mainline kernel as soon as possible. Likewise, you will discover that some of the things you may want to do cannot be implemented using modules and instead require changes to the "core kernel" code itself. This book doesn't cover that specifically, since making changes to the core kernel involves many issues best left to larger tomes on the subject.

Before You Begin

You learned about appropriate development and testing environments back in Chapter 7. Remember that even the most experienced of Linux engineers make mistakes, have accidental typos, and do other silly things that result in a destabilization of their test environment. Once you have lost track of pointers and other resources within the kernel, then they are lost forever. Likewise, when writing to memory you are able to freely and happily trash the entire contents of system RAM with nothing in your way.

The bottom line is that if you test kernel code on the machine on which you are writing that code, there is a good chance that you'll end up with a number of nasty crashes and constant rebooting. So, just don't do it. Get a really old throwaway machine to test out your code on when you start out — and if you later need specific hardware devices for development, add those to a suitable test machine rig. You are *strongly* advised to use network shares on your development machine to make kernels and modules available to your test machine — for details on how to do this, refer to the many online references.

This is an important point that bears repeating: never expect test machines to be stable. Period.

Essential Module Requirements

Every Linux kernel module needs a defined entry and exit point. The entry and exit points denote functions that will be called at module load and unload. In addition, each module should define an author, version number and provide a description of the services it makes available so that users, administrators and developers can easily obtain information about compiled driver modules using standard module-init-tools utilities, such as `modinfo` (as was demonstrated in Chapters 7 and 8).

Here's an example of the bare minimum loadable module that you can build on:

```
/*
 * plp_min.c - Minimal example kernel module.
 */

#include <linux/kernel.h>
#include <linux/init.h>
#include <linux/module.h>

/* function prototypes */

static int __init plp_min_init(void);
```

```
static void __exit plp_min_exit(void);

/*
 * plp_min_init: Load the kernel module into memory
 */

static int __init plp_min_init(void)
{
        printk("plp_min: loaded");
        return 0;
}

/*
 * plp_min_exit: Unload the kernel module from memory
 */


static void __exit plp_min_exit(void)
{
        printk("plp_min: unloading");
}

/* declare init/exit functions here */

module_init(plp_min_init);
module_exit(plp_min_exit);

/* define module meta data */

MODULE_AUTHOR("Jon Masters <jcm@jonmasters.org>");
MODULE_DESCRIPTION("A minimal module stub");

MODULE_ALIAS("minimal_module");
MODULE_LICENSE("GPL");
MODULE_VERSION("0:1.0");
```

Compile this module in the usual fashion:

```
$ make -C `uname -r`/build modules M=$PWD
```

Take a look at the output from running modinfo against the built module:

```
$ /sbin/modinfo plp_min.ko
filename:      plp_min.ko
author:        Jon Masters <jcm@jonmasters.org>
description:   A minimal module stub
alias:         minimal_module
license:       GPL
version:       0:1.0
vermagic:      2.6.15.6 preempt K7 gcc-4.0
depends:
srcversion:    295F0EFEC45D00AB631A26C
```

Notice that the module version is displayed along with a generated checksum to match against the version generated. Get into the habit of always adding a version to your modules, so that those who must later package them are able to use tools like modinfo to retrieve this information automatically.

module.h

All Linux kernel modules must include <linux/module.h>, along with the other headers that they make use of. Module.h defines a number of macros that are used by the kernel build system to add necessary metadata to compiled module files. You can see how these macros are used during build by looking out for generated C source files ending in .mod.c during the build. They have been heavily annotated with compiler directives that tell the GNU toolchain how to link the resulting module together into a special ELF file that can be linked into a kernel. You can also see a special module struct defined therein.

The following table shows some of the special header macros and functions that are available. Those shown in the table should be used in every module, where appropriate. These should all be treated as functions (even though some are in fact macros) and are usually inserted toward the end of the module source.

Macro/Function Name	Description
MODULE_ALIAS(_alias)	Provide an alias for userspace. Allow tools that load and unload modules to recognize an alias. The intel-agp module, like many PCI drivers, specifies a series of PCI device IDs supported by the driver that can be used by userspace tools to find the driver automatically: MODULE_ALIAS("pci:v00001106d00000314sv*sd*bc06sc00i00*")
MODULE_LICENSE(_license)	The license used by this module. Note that some kernel functions are only available to LKMs licensed under an accepted Free license. For example, to define a module as licensed under the GPL: MODULE_LICENSE("GPL")
MODULE_AUTHOR	Specify the module author in the form of a name and email address. For example: MODULE_AUTHOR("Jon Masters jcm@jonmasters.org")
MODULE_AUTHOR	Specify (briefly) the purpose and functionality of the LKM. For example, in the case of the toshiba_acpi module: MODULE_DESCRIPTION("Toshiba Laptop ACPI Extras Driver")

Table continued on following page

Macro/Function Name	Description

`module_param`, `MODULE_PARM_DESC`	module_param defines a load-time parameter for the module (which can be specified on the insmod/modprobe line, or /etc/modules.conf. Parameters include the name, type and permissions for the sysfs-file representation. For example, the ndb (network block device) driver defines a parameter and accompanying description in a similar fashion to the following:
	
	 `module_param(nbds_max, int, 0444);`
	
	 `MODULE_PARM_DESC(nbds_max, "Number of nbds to init.")`

`MODULE_VERSION`	Specify the version of the module in the form `[<epoch>:]<version>[-extra-version]`. The epoch and extra version may be omitted or used as needed. For example, the iscsi_tcp module defines the following version: `MODULE_VERSION("0:4.409")` You should always specify a module version in every module that you produce, since it will aid those using automatic packaging tools.

init.h

Linux kernel modules (LKMs) should also include `<linux/init.h>`. This header file contains numerous definitions that are used to support booting the kernel and also to support inserting and removing modules through the `module_init` and `module_exit` macros. These two macros should always be used to define an entry and exit point for your module, since they will take care of building the entry and exit functions into the kernel statically in the event that the kernel is built without loadable module support.

You will notice from the example modules in this book that entry and exit functions are defined thus:

```
static int __init kmem_init(void);
static void __exit kmem_exit(void);
```

Notice the use of the __init and __exit attributes. These are also defined in `init.h` and are used to tag functions that are only used at module load and unload so that, if the kernel is statically built then it automatically frees the memory used by those functions once normally booted. In the event that the module is actually loaded and unloaded at runtime in the "normal" fashion, then these don't have any effect other than to serve as a useful form of documentary annotation to your source code.

Logging

The Linux kernel provides a logging mechanism, via `/proc/kmsg`, that can be read from userland by tools such as klogd. Take a look at your Linux system and you'll see that you have a klogd process running silently in the background. klogd opens `/proc/kmsg` and passes all received kernel messages on to the standard `syslog` daemon for logging into the system log files defined by your distribution. The exact location of the kernel messages will vary by distribution and the treatment by the associated priority of the message — higher-priority messages may be displayed on a system console directly.

Within the kernel, messages are sent to the kernel log using the `printk()` function:

```
printk("my_module: This message is logged.");
```

This function can optionally be called with a priority (otherwise the default preset level is used):

```
printk(KERN_INFO "This is a regular message.");
printk(KERN_EMERG "The printer is on fire!");
```

The priority is simply another string that determines how the message will be processed. These are defined within `<linux/kernel.h>`, alongside the actual `printk` function itself. For example, on a 2.6.15.6 kernel, the following priorities were defined:

```
#define KERN_EMERG    "<0>"  /* system is unusable                 */
#define KERN_ALERT    "<1>"  /* action must be taken immediately   */
#define KERN_CRIT     "<2>"  /* critical conditions                */
#define KERN_ERR      "<3>"  /* error conditions                   */
#define KERN_WARNING  "<4>"  /* warning conditions                 */
#define KERN_NOTICE   "<5>"  /* normal but significant condition   */
#define KERN_INFO     "<6>"  /* informational                      */
#define KERN_DEBUG    "<7>"  /* debug-level messages               */
```

Internally, `printk()` is a magical function. It's magical because it is guaranteed to always work, no matter where it is called, in what context and with whatever locks being held. It works so well because it writes into a (reasonably large) circular buffer that is flushed periodically before it fills up completely. This is intended to allow logging in even the most unpleasant of error situations but does mean that it is indeed possible to loose logged messages, if a very large number are sent before they can be read by klogd.

> *There's even an early version of printk on some architectures, that's designed to allow logging to a serial console even from within very low-level code — if that's your thing, check it out.*

Exported Symbols

The Linux kernel is filled with many thousands of individual functions and global data structures. Take a look at the `System.map-kernelversion` file that's likely in your /boot directory, or the file generated during a kernel build, and you'll see just how many symbols you are dealing with here. Once upon a time, these symbols were all globally visible from within every piece of kernel code; however, over time efforts have been made to reduce the level of namespace pollution of unnecessarily exported symbols.

You can see the symbols that are visible to loadable kernel modules via the `Module.symvers` file that is also generated during a kernel build. It's in the root of the kernel build directory (for example in the `/lib/modules/`uname -r`/build` symlink directory) after a successful build and is used by the kernel build system when building kernel modules in order to automatically resolve any symbol dependencies that need to be expressed in the module object file for use by the runtime module loading mechanism.

On a typical system, there might be more than 4000 symbols being defined in `Module.symvers`:

```
$ cat /lib/modules/`uname -r`/build/Module.symvers | wc -l
4555
```

These are symbols and data structures that have been explicitly made available for use by other parts of the kernel, through the use of macros like `EXPORT_SYMBOL`. The kernel defines several variants.

EXPORT_SYMBOL

`EXPORT_SYMBOL` is a macro that allows a single kernel symbol to be made available outside of the module within which it is being defined. You will frequently see this used in subsystem and driver code that forms part of larger driver stacks, since each individual module requires particular functions to be made available to it. There is a continual effort to reduce the number of symbols being exported, as even more at being added to the kernel over time through the addition of new functionality.

EXPORT_SYMBOL_GPL

A significant percentage of the Linux kernel development community feels that, since the Linux kernel is licensed under the GNU General Public License, this extends to kernel modules, too. It is felt that all kernel modules should necessarily be under the GPL, since they are extensions of the Linux kernel. Whatever the legal reality of the situation, there is an ongoing effort to increase the use of this macro.

`EXPORT_SYMBOL_GPL` makes a symbol available to loadable modules, but only on the condition that the module is licensed under a compatible license. Those that are not licensed under a compatible license never actually see symbols that have been exported in this way — though there is a token kind of guarantee that the community won't go unexporting certain widely used symbols that have always been available in the past. If you write GPL-licensed code, you don't need to worry about this.

Don't Fight the System

Having read this section, you're probably puzzled. Since the kernel can access any memory it feels like touching (Linux isn't a multilayered microkernel), surely it is possible for your module or other kernel code to do whatever it wants within the confines of the kernel. If your module wants to access a nonexported symbol, it has only to jump through a few extra hoops — calculating the offset or some other suitable magic should be enough to get at whatever memory location you need to get to, right?

Please don't do that. Ever. It is a real issue with some kernel code and will only result in trouble.

The kernel is free to touch whatever memory it wants, so it's possible to always access any data or functions from anywhere inside the kernel. However, if a function or data structure is not being exported, then you should not use it. Too often, new kernel programmers decide to employ hacks to get at data structures that should not be used from within modules (the system call table is an example). You don't want to touch these symbols because they are not protected with suitable locks or other mechanisms.

Take the system call table as an example. People complained when, during the 2.5-2.6 kernel development cycle, the system call table was unexported and it became "impossible" for kernel modules to add in their own system calls at runtime. In the past, books and other references had recommended modification as a way of adding or modifying system calls — especially modules designed to allow interception — or those runtime patching a system call security vulnerability.

Unfortunately, patching up the system call table causes nasty side effects both during the patchup and when the module is later removed and must decide what to revert the table entry to. If sys_open is to be overridden at runtime, you cannot know for sure that it needs to go back to sys_open once the module that does the patching is removed. It might have been changed twice. Or the system call might be called at just the moment it is being removed — causing an invalid pointer to be deferenced inside the kernel.

The system call table and other structures were unexported and removed from the global kernel names- pace for very valid reasons, and you don't want to use them from within loadable modules. If a symbol that you need is not being exported, consider why this is the case before petitioning on the public mail- ing lists for it to be re-exported. It'll end in bad things happening if you don't.

Allocating Memory

The Linux kernel is not like any userspace program and cannot make use of standard library functions such as malloc. Besides, malloc actually relies upon the kernel for its low-level memory allocations and makes frequent calls into the kernel to get more backing memory for its internal bucket memory alloca- tion structures as necessary. The majority of the time, you've probably never had to consider where your application memory is coming from; it was just there when you asked for some. Once you start working with the Linux kernel, you'll find things aren't quite as comfortable.

Internal memory is managed in a variety of different ways within the Linux kernel, according to the type of the memory that is being requested, when it is asked for, and a variety of other criteria. You'll usually use one of two allocation functions as a matter of course: kmalloc or vmalloc. In this section, you'll dis- cover what the differences are between these two and how you can make sensible use of (precious) ker- nel memory. You'll also learn more about more advanced allocation mechanisms.

kmalloc

The most primitive memory allocation function that you will normally use in your own modules is kmalloc. This is a low-level physical page-level allocator that guarantees all of its allocations are con- tiguous in physical memory. kmalloc takes a size and a set of flags and returns a pointer to the allocated memory, as might be expected (as might be expected, the kernel NULL returns NULL whenever an alloca- tion cannot be performed due to various errors):

```
pointer = kmalloc(SIZE_IN_BYTES, ALLOCATION_FLAGS)
```

The size of an allocation is very limited and should not exceed a few kilobytes because you are relying on various activities since boot having not deprived the system of sufficient contiguous physical mem- ory. Once you are done using the memory, you must return it to the kernel by calling kfree():

```
kfree(pointer)
```

If you do not return memory to the kernel, then it is lost forever. There is no garbage collector running, there is no automatic cleanup when your module is removed from the kernel — the memory is simply lost and cannot be used again until the system is rebooted. You will want to be very sure that you are correctly tracking all of your memory use in your driver or the system will slowly starve of memory.

You should specify one of the following flags to the allocation (defined by including it in <linux/mm.h>):

GTP_ATOMIC

The allocation should be performed immediately without sleeping. This is typically invoked in those situations where it is not possible to sleep — for example, in kernel interrupt handlers. Memory is either allocated immediately, from a special reserve if needed, or the allocation will fail without blocking.

GFP_KERNEL

Normal kernel memory allocations should be performed using this flag. It is formed by combining __GFP_WAIT, __GFP_IO, and __GFP_FS. This set of flags allows the kernel to block and wait for some more memory to become available. It allows that memory to come as a result of synchronously flushing filesystem buffers, or from other IO activity. A variant of this, GFP_NOFS is used in various filesystem code when it is not possible to reenter the kernel to flush a filesystem buffer.

GFP_USER

You should use this flag whenever you allocate memory that will be returned to userland. It results in the memory being pre-zeroed but otherwise is very similar to GFP_KERNEL above.

A variety of other allocation flags are available. Consult <linux/mm.h> (and its included <linux/gfp.h> for the specific set of available flags — although you almost certainly won't need to use them).

vmalloc

Many times, you won't need a large contiguous block of physical system RAM, but you will need a large enough buffer for some internal use within the kernel. The vmalloc function exists to service this requirement of kernel code and allows for much larger allocations, with the caveat that they are noncontiguous in physical memory. This means that many devices, which want to deal with contiguous memory (for example in regular DMA operations not involving complex scatter-gather lists of many individual buffers in memory) won't be able to handle vmalloc()'d memory properly.

You can allocate memory using vmalloc() as follows:

```
pointer = vmalloc(SIZE_IN_BYTES)
```

And free the memory with vfree():

```
vfree(pointer)
```

You don't have the same level of control over allocations as you do with kmalloc (so there are situations where you should not use vmalloc). Typical uses include large internal buffers allocated at module startup or smaller buffers allocated whenever a device is opened for some new operation. The kernel takes care of allocating physical memory to back the contiguous virtual memory.

plp_kmem: a Kernel Memory Buffer

You can test the various memory allocation functions by writing a simple kernel module that allows the user to read from and write to a memory buffer. The module will need to allocate a large buffer for backing storage and should use the vmalloc function to do this, since the memory does not need to be contiguous within physical RAM but will be larger than a limited allocation available from kmalloc.

The following example code provides a new device in /dev called plp_kmem that represents a (by default) 1MB memory buffer, to and from which you can read and write data. The module uses the kernel vmalloc function to allocate a large buffer of PLP_KMEM_BUFSIZE (1MB) byres:

```
if (NULL == (plp_kmem_buffer = vmalloc(PLP_KMEM_BUFSIZE))) {
                printk(KERN_ERR "plp_kmem: cannot allocate memory!\n");
                goto error;
        }
```

Note the use of error handling, since all memory allocations within the kernel might fail. The allocation in plp_kmem_init sits alongside many other function calls that can result in memory being allocated as a side effect of their operation. For example, a function called class_create is called (to create the entry /sys/class/plp_kmem for use with the dynamic device registration mechanisms explained in the previous chapter) that internally may need to perform small memory allocations using kmalloc:

```
plp_kmem_class = class_create(THIS_MODULE, "plp_kmem");
        if (IS_ERR(plp_kmem_class)) {
                printk(KERN_ERR "plp_kmem: Error creating class.\n");
                cdev_del(plp_kmem_cdev);
                unregister_chrdev_region(plp_kmem_dev, 1);
                goto error;
        }
```

Since the internal operation of class_create might fail when the system is under heavy memory pressure there is a more substantive amount of error handling put in place. Remember that the kernel is not like a regular program, where memory leaks won't normally bring down the system. Within the kernel, all of the allocations and registrations of data structures with other parts of the kernel must be undone as part of the error path handling. Gotos are frequently used in the kernel for the purpose of simplifying error handling, as functions can drop through to common blocks of error-handling code when necessary.

Once the kernel module has done its work and you request that it be unloaded from your running kernel, it is necessary that any allocated memory is again returned to the kernel. The example module does this by making calls to vfree():

```
vfree(plp_kmem_buffer);
```

In the example, you'll see a few constructs that won't be introduced until later in the book — but don't worry about that, since the device creation, deletion, and sysfs bits will be fully explained.

```
/*
 * plp_kmem.c - Kernel memory allocation examples.
 */

#include <linux/kernel.h>
#include <linux/init.h>
#include <linux/module.h>
#include <linux/vmalloc.h>

#include <linux/fs.h>
#include <linux/major.h>
#include <linux/blkdev.h>
```

```
#include <linux/cdev.h>

#include <asm/uaccess.h>

#define PLP_KMEM_BUFSIZE (1024*1024) /* 1MB internal buffer */

/* global variables */

static char *plp_kmem_buffer;

static struct class *plp_kmem_class;    /* pretend /sys/class */
static dev_t plp_kmem_dev;              /* dynamically assigned char device */
static struct cdev *plp_kmem_cdev;      /* dynamically allocated at runtime. */

/* function prototypes */

static int __init plp_kmem_init(void);
static void __exit plp_kmem_exit(void);

static int plp_kmem_open(struct inode *inode, struct file *file);
static int plp_kmem_release(struct inode *inode, struct file *file);
static ssize_t plp_kmem_read(struct file *file, char __user *buf,
                        size_t count, loff_t *ppos);
static ssize_t plp_kmem_write(struct file *file, const char __user *buf,
                        size_t count, loff_t *ppos);

/* file_operations */

static struct file_operations plp_kmem_fops = {
 .read          = plp_kmem_read,
 .write         = plp_kmem_write,
 .open          = plp_kmem_open,
 .release       = plp_kmem_release,
 .owner         = THIS_MODULE,
};

/*
 * plp_kmem_open: Open the kmem device
 */

static int plp_kmem_open(struct inode *inode, struct file *file)
{

#ifdef PLP_DEBUG
 printk(KERN_DEBUG "plp_kmem: opened device.\n");
#endif

 return 0;
}

/*
 * plp_kmem_release: Close the kmem device.
 */

static int plp_kmem_release(struct inode *inode, struct file *file)
```

```
{

#ifdef PLP_DEBUG
 printk(KERN_DEBUG "plp_kmem: device closed.\n");
#endif

 return 0;
}

/*
 * plp_kmem_read: Read from the device.
 */

static ssize_t plp_kmem_read(struct file *file, char __user *buf,
                        size_t count, loff_t *ppos)
{
 size_t bytes = count;
 loff_t fpos = *ppos;
 char *data;

 if (fpos >= PLP_KMEM_BUFSIZE)
         return 0;

 if (fpos+bytes >= PLP_KMEM_BUFSIZE)
         bytes = PLP_KMEM_BUFSIZE-fpos;

 if (0 == (data = kmalloc(bytes, GFP_KERNEL)))
         return -ENOMEM;

#ifdef PLP_DEBUG
 printk(KERN_DEBUG "plp_kmem: read %d bytes from device, offset %d.\n",
         bytes,(int)fpos);
#endif

 memcpy(data,plp_kmem_buffer+fpos,bytes);

 if (copy_to_user((void __user *)buf, data, bytes)) {
         printk(KERN_ERR "plp_kmem: cannot write data.\n");
         kfree(data);
         return -EFAULT;
 }

 *ppos = fpos+bytes;

 kfree(data);
 return bytes;
}

/*
 * plp_kmem_write: Write to the device.
 */

static ssize_t plp_kmem_write(struct file *file, const char __user *buf,
                        size_t count, loff_t *ppos)
```

```
{
 size_t bytes = count;
 loff_t fpos = *ppos;
 char *data;

 if (fpos >= PLP_KMEM_BUFSIZE)
         return -ENOSPC;

 if (fpos+bytes >= PLP_KMEM_BUFSIZE)
         bytes = PLP_KMEM_BUFSIZE-fpos;

 if (0 == (data = kmalloc(bytes, GFP_KERNEL)))
         return -ENOMEM;

 if (copy_from_user((void *)data, (const void __user *)buf, bytes)) {
         printk(KERN_ERR "plp_kmem: cannot read data.\n");
         kfree(data);
         return -EFAULT;
 }

#ifdef PLP_DEBUG
 printk(KERN_DEBUG "plp_kmem: write %d bytes to device, offset %d.\n",
         bytes,(int)fpos);
#endif

 memcpy(plp_kmem_buffer+fpos,data,bytes);

 *ppos = fpos+bytes;

 kfree(data);
 return bytes;
}

/*
 * plp_kmem_init: Load the kernel module into memory
 */

static int __init plp_kmem_init(void)
{
 printk(KERN_INFO "plp_kmem: Allocating %d bytes of internal buffer.\n",
             PLP_KMEM_BUFSIZE);

 if (NULL == (plp_kmem_buffer = vmalloc(PLP_KMEM_BUFSIZE))) {
         printk(KERN_ERR "plp_kmem: cannot allocate memory!\n");
         goto error;
 }

 memset((void *)plp_kmem_buffer, 0, PLP_KMEM_BUFSIZE);

 if (alloc_chrdev_region(&plp_kmem_dev, 0, 1, "plp_kmem"))
         goto error;

 if (0 == (plp_kmem_cdev = cdev_alloc()))
         goto error;

 kobject_set_name(&plp_kmem_cdev->kobj,"plp_kmem_cdev");
```

```
        plp_kmem_cdev->ops = &plp_kmem_fops; /* file up fops */
        if (cdev_add(plp_kmem_cdev, plp_kmem_dev, 1)) {
                kobject_put(&plp_kmem_cdev->kobj);
                unregister_chrdev_region(plp_kmem_dev, 1);
                goto error;
        }

        plp_kmem_class = class_create(THIS_MODULE, "plp_kmem");
        if (IS_ERR(plp_kmem_class)) {
                printk(KERN_ERR "plp_kmem: Error creating class.\n");
                cdev_del(plp_kmem_cdev);
                unregister_chrdev_region(plp_kmem_dev, 1);
                goto error;
        }
        class_device_create(plp_kmem_class, NULL, plp_kmem_dev, NULL, "plp_kmem");

        printk(KERN_INFO "plp_kmem: loaded.\n");

        return 0;

error:
        printk(KERN_ERR "plp_kmem: cannot register device.\n");
        return 1;
}

/*
 * plp_kmem_exit: Unload the kernel module from memory
 */


static void __exit plp_kmem_exit(void)
{

        class_device_destroy(plp_kmem_class, plp_kmem_dev);
        class_destroy(plp_kmem_class);
        cdev_del(plp_kmem_cdev);
        unregister_chrdev_region(plp_kmem_dev,1);

        vfree(plp_kmem_buffer);

        printk(KERN_INFO "plp_kmem: unloading.\n");
}

/* declare init/exit functions here */

module_init(plp_kmem_init);
module_exit(plp_kmem_exit);

/* define module meta data */

MODULE_AUTHOR("Jon Masters <jcm@jonmasters.org>");
MODULE_DESCRIPTION("Demonstrate kernel memory allocation");

MODULE_ALIAS("memory_allocation");
MODULE_LICENSE("GPL");
MODULE_VERSION("0:1.0");
```

Build and Test the Example

You can compile the example module as follows:

```
$ make -C /lib/modules/`uname -r`/build modules M=$PWD
make: Entering directory `/usr/src/kernels/2.6.17-1.2517.fc6-ppc'
  CC [M]  /home/jcm/modules/plp_kmem/plp_kmem.o
  Building modules, stage 2.
  MODPOST
  CC      /home/jcm/modules/plp_kmem/plp_kmem.mod.o
  LD [M]  /home/jcm/modules/plp_kmem/plp_kmem.ko
make: Leaving directory `/usr/src/kernels/2.6.17-1.2517.fc6-ppc'
```

Load the resulting kernel module into your running system kernel as follows:

```
$ /sbin/insmod ./plp_kmem.ko
```

You will see some activity in the kernel log:

```
$ dmesg|tail
plp_kmem: Allocating 1048576 bytes of internal buffer.
plp_kmem: loaded.
```

The module has also registered and created a device in /dev/plp_kmem to and from which you can read and write:

```
$ echo "This is a test" >/dev/plp_kmem
$ cat /dev/plp_kmem
This is a test
```

Attempting to write too much data to the device results in the expected error:

```
$ cat /dev/zero >/dev/plp_kmem
cat: write error: No space left on device
```

The device can be unloaded once you are finished using it:

```
$ /sbin/rmmod plp_kmem
```

The module logs the unload to the kernel log:

```
$ dmesg|tail
plp_kmem: unloading.
```

A Note on udev

In the next chapter, you will learn how the dynamic device node in /dev/plp_kmem is created when you load the module and is destroyed when you unload the module. A side effect of the dynamic device filesystem is that it will use default permissions for device nodes that it does not recognize — and nobody told udev about plp_kmem! The result of this is that it has some very restrictive default permissions. On a Debian system, these default permissions might be:

```
$ ls -l /dev/plp_kmem
crw-rw---- 1 root root 253, 0 2006-08-14 13:04 /dev/plp_kmem
```

Whereas a Fedora system might be even more restrictive:

```
$ ls -l /dev/plp_kmem
crw------- 1 root root 253, 0 2006-08-14 13:04 /dev/plp_kmem
```

You can work around this by explicitly telling udev about the new module. To do this, add the following to a new file called /etc/udev/rules.d/99-plp.rules:

```
# Add a rule for plp device
KERNEL=="plp_*", OWNER="root" GROUP="root", MODE="0666"
```

Locking considerations

The Linux kernel provides the usual wealth of locking primitives that one would expect to see in any programming environment. Chief among these are the two major workhorses of mutual exclusion — spinlocks and semaphores (also known as mutexes when in a binary two state mode of operation). Each of these addresses a different problem and typical modules make use of both these (and other more complex locking primitives) whenever there is a need to protect data against multiple access.

Semaphores

The semaphore is used to control concurrent use of a given resource. Also known as a sleeping lock, a semaphore allows you to ensure that only one (or a specified number) user is accessing a given resource at a particular moment. Whenever you need to enter into a critical section of code, you can call down() on a given semaphore, perform the necessary operation on some data, and then call up() to release the semaphore and cause the next task waiting for that semaphore to become available to wake up again.

Obviously, semaphores are only available where it is appropriate to sleep within the kernel. This makes them ideal in functions that service user system calls, because the kernel can simply put the user task to sleep if it is unable to acquire the desired resource when it is requested. Once another user (usually another task) has finished performing some operation on the protected data and released the semaphore, the waiting, sleeping, task can be woken up and can take control of the semaphore for itself.

Semaphores are defined in <asm/semaphore.h> and can be declared as follows:

```
struct semaphore my_sem;
```

You will often use a special form of semaphore called a mutex. Mutexes can only be held by one task at a time, whereas full semaphores can actually be initialized to handle a greater number if so desired. You can declare and initialize a mutex using the following macro (which will then be available for use):

```
DECLARE_MUTEX(my_lock);
```

The semaphore must be taken with a call to down():

```
down(&my_sem);
```

Or (preferably) via a call to `down_interruptible()`:

```
down_interruptible(&my_sem);
```

You will often want to use `down_interruptible()`, since it allows you to avoid blocking signals to the current task whenever you make a call to `down()`. It will return a positive value if the call was interrupted by a signal that was delivered to the task trying to acquire the semaphore while it was waiting. You will usually want this because you otherwise could end up blocking tasks indefinitely if hardware problems with the physical device your module is helping to drive mean the task is never woken up again. Since it won't respond to signals, the task then becomes completely unkillable.

Semaphores are released with call to `up()`:

```
up(&my_sem);
```

Here is an example declaration and use of a semaphore:

```
static DECLARE_MUTEX(my_lock);
down(&my_lock);
/* perform some data manipulation */
up(&my_lock);
```

Spinlocks

The Linux kernel also provides another kind of locking primitive, known as the spinlock. Spinlocks are similar to semaphores in that they guard against simultaneous access to a given resource, but spinlocks are not sleeping locks — they are used mainly to protect critical sections of code from interference from code running on another processor rather than to restrict user access to shared resources. Whenever a function attempts to acquire a spinlock and is unable to do so, it will sit and literally spin (do nothing very quickly via a processor NOP operation) while whatever task on another processor holds the lock.

Spinlocks should not be held for very long periods of time. They are a great way to protect a single item of data or a structure against concurrent access while a member is being manipulated, but they will also happily cause other processors in the system to sit in a tight loop and wait if they attempt to acquire the same lock while it is being held by some other function. Spinlocks have also been evolving over time, since there is ongoing work to address their impact upon performance in real-time applications. Spinlocks are defined in `<linux/spinlock.h>` and can be declared as follows:

```
struct spinlock my_lock;
spin_lock_init(&my_lock);
```

A spinlock is taken using the `spin_lock()` function:

```
spin_lock(&my_lock);
```

And it is released using the `spin_unlock()` function:

```
spin_unlock(&my_lock);
```

Depending upon whether you also want to protect against interrupts running on other processors, you might want to call a special variant of the spinlock functions that also disables interrupts:

```
unsigned long flags;
spin_lock_irqsave(&my_lock, flags);
spin_unlock_irqrestore(&my_lock, flags);
```

The flags variable must be declared locally to the function and must not be passed to any other function. You don't need to worry about the content of the flags variable because it is used internally by the spin-lock implementation to track local interrupt status and determine whether to really enable or disable the hard interrupts on the machine (they might already be disabled by another call to a spinlock function for a different lock, so it's necessary to verify that isn't the case before turning interrupts back on again).

plp_klock: Adding User Tracking to plp_kmem

The previous example demonstrated some very useful memory allocation mechanisms, but it had one major flaw. This is exposed whenever multiple users are attempting to read from or write to the device at the same time. Try it out for yourself using the reader.sh and writer.sh example scripts included in the online version of the module source code. You'll quickly see how trivial it is for many different users to trash the content of a shared resource, such as the large buffer from the previous example.

It would be ideal if access to the module buffer device could be restricted to just one real user at a time. After all, two users attempting to read and write to a shared buffer will quickly result in corruption of the shared data without some kind of mutual exclusion being put in place. This isn't a typical "locking" problem per se, it's a shared resource problem introduced whenever individual independent users are sharing a device. To solve it, you will need to use a few of the new locking primitives, however. In this section, you will learn how to build a plp_klock example that's based upon the previous plp_kmem.

First, you need to keep track of which system user has opened the device and is using it. You will learn more about filesystem activity later in the book, but it suffices to know for now that the open function within the module is passed a struct file from which you can extract the current user ID. The file->f_uid will contain the UID of the system user, where 0 is always the root user and most regular system UIDs are allocated beginning at 500. The current user of the device will be stored in a global variable.

The global variable plp_klock_owner will contain the UID of the current system user who has the device open, while plp_klock_count will be used to count the number of times the device is opened. It is assumed that it is safe for the same system user to have the device opened more than once — that can be changed with a simple adjustment to the semantics in the plp_klock_open function. There is one problem with the introduction of the new global variables however — they are not protected.

Locking Considerations for plp_klock

Shared global data that will be used in different code paths simultaneously must be protected using some form of locking. In this case, a semaphore is chosen to protect critical sections of code that will manipulate plp_klock_owner and plp_klock_count from affecting one another. The semaphore will be taken on entry to plp_klock_open when the device is opened before a test is made against the current user ID of the user attempting to open the device (debugging removed for readability):

```
down(&plp_klock_sem);

if ((plp_klock_owner != file->f_uid) &&
    (plp_klock_count != 0)) {
        up(&plp_klock_sem);
        return -EBUSY;
```

```
        }

        plp_klock_count++;
        plp_klock_owner=file->f_uid;

        up(&plp_klock_sem);
```

Notice that error paths must necessarily release any locks that have been acquired. Just because an error has occurred, does not mean that the kernel should not continue operating normally and recover from that error gracefully. If the device is in use by another user then any attempt to open it will result in the error -EBUSY being returned. Applications know that this is a temporary error caused because the device is busy performing another operation and cannot be made available at that moment in time.

```
/*
 * plp_klock.c - Add locking to the previous kmem example.
 */

#include <linux/kernel.h>
#include <linux/init.h>
#include <linux/module.h>
#include <linux/vmalloc.h>

#include <linux/fs.h>
#include <linux/major.h>
#include <linux/blkdev.h>
#include <linux/cdev.h>

#include <asm/uaccess.h>

#define PLP_KMEM_BUFSIZE (1024*1024) /* 1MB internal buffer */

/* global variables */

static char *plp_klock_buffer;

static struct class *plp_klock_class;   /* pretend /sys/class */
static dev_t plp_klock_dev;             /* dynamically assigned char device */
static struct cdev *plp_klock_cdev;     /* dynamically allocated at runtime. */

static unsigned int plp_klock_owner;    /* dynamically changing UID. */
static unsigned int plp_klock_count;    /* number of current users. */

/* Locking */

static DECLARE_MUTEX(plp_klock_sem);    /* protect device read/write action. */

/* function prototypes */

static int __init plp_klock_init(void);
static void __exit plp_klock_exit(void);

static int plp_klock_open(struct inode *inode, struct file *file);
static int plp_klock_release(struct inode *inode, struct file *file);
static ssize_t plp_klock_read(struct file *file, char __user *buf,
                        size_t count, loff_t *ppos);
```

```
static ssize_t plp_klock_write(struct file *file, const char __user *buf,
                    size_t count, loff_t *ppos);

/* file_operations */

static struct file_operations plp_klock_fops = {
 .read          = plp_klock_read,
 .write         = plp_klock_write,
 .open          = plp_klock_open,
 .release       = plp_klock_release,
 .owner         = THIS_MODULE,
};

/*
 * plp_klock_open: Open the ksem device
 */

static int plp_klock_open(struct inode *inode, struct file *file)
{

 down(&plp_klock_sem);

 if ((plp_klock_owner != file->f_uid) &&
     (plp_klock_count != 0)) {

#ifdef PLP_DEBUG
        printk(KERN_DEBUG "plp_klock: device is in use.\n");
#endif
        up(&plp_klock_sem);
        return -EBUSY;
 }

 plp_klock_count++;
 plp_klock_owner=file->f_uid;

#ifdef PLP_DEBUG
 printk(KERN_DEBUG "plp_klock: opened device.\n");
#endif

 up(&plp_klock_sem);
 return 0;
}

/*
 * plp_klock_release: Close the ksem device.
 */

static int plp_klock_release(struct inode *inode, struct file *file)
{

 down(&plp_klock_sem);
 plp_klock_count--;
 up(&plp_klock_sem);

#ifdef PLP_DEBUG
```

```
      printk(KERN_DEBUG "plp_klock: device closed.\n");
#endif

 return 0;
}

/*
 * plp_klock_read: Read from the device.
 */

static ssize_t plp_klock_read(struct file *file, char __user *buf,
                        size_t count, loff_t *ppos)
{
 size_t bytes = count;
 loff_t fpos = *ppos;
 char *data;

 down(&plp_klock_sem);

 if (fpos >= PLP_KMEM_BUFSIZE) {
        up(&plp_klock_sem);
        return 0;
 }

 if (fpos+bytes >= PLP_KMEM_BUFSIZE)
        bytes = PLP_KMEM_BUFSIZE-fpos;

 if (0 == (data = kmalloc(bytes, GFP_KERNEL))) {
        up(&plp_klock_sem);
        return -ENOMEM;
 }

#ifdef PLP_DEBUG
 printk(KERN_DEBUG "plp_klock: read %d bytes from device, offset %d.\n",
        bytes,(int)fpos);
#endif

 memcpy(data,plp_klock_buffer+fpos,bytes);

 if (copy_to_user((void __user *)buf, data, bytes)) {
        printk(KERN_ERR "plp_klock: cannot write data.\n");
        kfree(data);
        up(&plp_klock_sem);
        return -EFAULT;
 }

 *ppos = fpos+bytes;

 kfree(data);
 up(&plp_klock_sem);
 return bytes;
}

/*
 * plp_klock_write: Write to the device.
```

```
     */

static ssize_t plp_klock_write(struct file *file, const char __user *buf,
        size_t count, loff_t *ppos)
{

 size_t bytes = count;
 loff_t fpos = *ppos;
 char *data;

 down(&plp_klock_sem);

 if (fpos >= PLP_KMEM_BUFSIZE) {
        up(&plp_klock_sem);
        return -ENOSPC;
 }

 if (fpos+bytes >= PLP_KMEM_BUFSIZE)
        bytes = PLP_KMEM_BUFSIZE-fpos;

 if (0 == (data = kmalloc(bytes, GFP_KERNEL))) {
        up (&plp_klock_sem);
        return -ENOMEM;
 }

 if (copy_from_user((void *)data, (const void __user *)buf, bytes)) {
        printk(KERN_ERR "plp_klock: cannot read data.\n");
        kfree(data);
        up (&plp_klock_sem);
        return -EFAULT;
 }

#ifdef PLP_DEBUG
 printk(KERN_DEBUG "plp_klock: write %d bytes to device, offset %d.\n",
        bytes,(int)fpos);
#endif

 memcpy(plp_klock_buffer+fpos,data,bytes);

 *ppos = fpos+bytes;

 kfree(data);
 up(&plp_klock_sem);
 return bytes;
}

/*
 * plp_klock_init: Load the kernel module into memory.
 */

static int __init plp_klock_init(void)
{
 printk(KERN_INFO "plp_klock: Allocating %d bytes of internal buffer.\n",
                PLP_KMEM_BUFSIZE);

 if (NULL == (plp_klock_buffer = vmalloc(PLP_KMEM_BUFSIZE))) {
```

```
                printk(KERN_ERR "plp_klock: cannot allocate memory!\n");
                goto error;
        }

        memset((void *)plp_klock_buffer, 0, PLP_KMEM_BUFSIZE);

        if (alloc_chrdev_region(&plp_klock_dev, 0, 1, "plp_klock"))
                goto error;

        if (0 == (plp_klock_cdev = cdev_alloc()))
                goto error;

        kobject_set_name(&plp_klock_cdev->kobj,"plp_klock_cdev");
        plp_klock_cdev->ops = &plp_klock_fops; /* file up fops */
        if (cdev_add(plp_klock_cdev, plp_klock_dev, 1)) {
                kobject_put(&plp_klock_cdev->kobj);
                unregister_chrdev_region(plp_klock_dev, 1);
                goto error;
        }

        plp_klock_class = class_create(THIS_MODULE, "plp_klock");
        if (IS_ERR(plp_klock_class)) {
                printk(KERN_ERR "plp_klock: Error creating class.\n");
                cdev_del(plp_klock_cdev);
                unregister_chrdev_region(plp_klock_dev, 1);
                goto error;
        }
        class_device_create(plp_klock_class, NULL, plp_klock_dev, NULL, "plp_klock");

        printk(KERN_INFO "plp_klock: loaded.\n");

        return 0;

error:
 printk(KERN_ERR "plp_klock: cannot register device.\n");
 return 1;
}

/*
 * plp_klock_exit: Unload the kernel module from memory.
 */


static void __exit plp_klock_exit(void)
{

 class_device_destroy(plp_klock_class, plp_klock_dev);
 class_destroy(plp_klock_class);
 cdev_del(plp_klock_cdev);
 unregister_chrdev_region(plp_klock_dev,1);

 vfree(plp_klock_buffer);

 printk(KERN_INFO "plp_klock: unloading.\n");
```

```
    }

    /* declare init/exit functions here */

    module_init(plp_klock_init);
    module_exit(plp_klock_exit);

    /* define module meta data */

    MODULE_AUTHOR("Jon Masters <jcm@jonmasters.org>");
    MODULE_DESCRIPTION("Demonstrate kernel memory allocation");

    MODULE_ALIAS("locking_example");
    MODULE_LICENSE("GPL");
    MODULE_VERSION("0:1.0");
```

Deferring work

There are times when kernel code wishes to delay or defer some action until a later time, when it can more easily be handled. This can occur for many different reasons, but it is especially useful to be able to schedule some function to execute when the system is less busy and able to devote some spare time to housekeeping operations. Interrupt handlers are a good example of deferred work, since they often temporarily stop the system from performing other tasks. To avoid a needlessly large amount of overhead, interrupt handler to arrange for some of their work to happen at a later time.

Broadly speaking, there are two kinds of delayed or deferred work functions available in the Linux kernel. The first are those that run the work in an interrupt-like context, completely separated from any user process and in quite a constrained environment. These are fast (so useful if you need to perform a lot of work very frequently or with very low overhead), but ultimately many people are now favoring (slightly more heavyweight) functions to perform delayed work in process context.

Remember, when you run your work in process context, you can call functions that might cause a reschedule without worrying about a system lockup happening if that actually occurs. For example, you can grab a semaphore, or make a call to kmalloc with flags other than GFP_ATOMIC (which obviously works even when in the most resource-constrained situations — that's the whole point) or do many other things that weren't possible in the past. Try to make life easier for yourself if possible.

Work Queues

One of the simplest ways to schedule deferred work is to use the Work Queue interface of Linux 2.6. Work Queues are essentially a mechanism for running a single function at a later time. They are defined in the <linux/workqueue.h> header file along with many other support functions — a few of which are documented here. In order to use a Work Queue, you must first write a function that will be executed whenever the work queue is being run. It has this prototype:

```
    void my_work(void *data);
```

Then, you need to call the DECLARE_WORK macro to create a schedulable work entity:

```
    DECLARE_WORK(my_work_wq, my_work, data);
```

The macro arranges for a new structure of type `workqueue_struct` called `my_work_wq` to be defined and sets it up to run the function `my_work` whenever it is called. The third argument, `data`, is an optional void pointer argument that can point to some data in the case that you want to make particular data available to the function that processes the work each time that it does so. The work is actually run whenever a call is made to one of the `schedule_work` functions:

```
int schedule_work(my_work_wq);
```

The `my_work` function will then be executed as soon as the system is less busy. Should you wish to place a constraint upon how long you would like the kernel to wait before considering running your work function, you can use the `schedule_delayed_work` function to add a delay:

```
int schedule_delayed_work(my_work_wq, delay)
```

Delay should be specified in jiffies. For example, to delay 10 seconds, you can use the HZ macro to automatically derive the number of jiffies for delay as 10*HZ.

Kernel Threads

Work Queues are great, but they usually run within the context of a single kernel thread that is used by a number of other items of work as a schedulable entity for that work. You can go one better by defining your own kernel thread that will always be available to run whatever you want, and nothing else. This way, you can have your own kernel thread that will wake up from time to time, perform some data process, and then go back to sleep until it is needed again. To set up a kernel thread, you can use the `kthread` API functions in `<linux/kthread.h>`, which were created to make kernel threads easier to handle.

kthread_create

Kernel threads can be easily created by a helper function. These take as an argument the name of a regular function that will be run by the newly created thread. Here is an example of a newly created kernel thread that will be used to run the `plp_kwork_thread` function, which has a NULL argument and shall be called "plp_work_kthread." The function returns a new `task_struct`:

```
(struct task_struct *)plp_kwork_ts = kthread_create(plp_kwork_thread, NULL,
"plp_work_kthread");
```

You can also call the `kthread_run` variant, which will create the kernel thread and also start it:

```
(struct task_struct *)plp_kwork_ts = kthread_run(plp_kwork_thread, NULL,
"plp_work_kthread");
```

To signal that a kernel thread should stop running, call `kthread_stop` and pass the task:

```
kthread_stop(plp_kwork_ts);
```

This will block until the kernel thread has completed. To facilitate *that*, the thread function should, from time to time, check the value returned by the `kthread_should_stop()` function. Here is an example of a simple kernel thread function, which will wake up every 10 seconds, process data, and then go back to sleep for another 10 seconds — unless it's woken up by a signal, such as that which is sent as a result of `kthread_stop()` being called by another part of the module:

```
static int plp_kwork_kthread(void *data)
{

        printk(KERN_INFO "plp_kwork: kthread starting.\n");

        for(;;) {

                schedule_timeout_interruptible(10*HZ);

                if (!kthread_should_stop()) {

                        /* If nobody has the device open, reset it after
                         * a period of time.
                         */

                        down(&plp_kwork_sem);
                        if (!plp_kwork_count) {
                                plp_kwork_owner = 0;
                                memset((void *)plp_kwork_buffer, 0,
                                        PLP_KMEM_BUFSIZE);
                        }
                        up(&plp_kwork_sem);

                } else {
                        printk(KERN_INFO "plp_kwork: kthread stopping.\n");
                        return 0;
                }
        }
}
```

The example function checks to see if nobody is currently using the memory buffer defined by the kmem example previously. If the virtual device is not in use, then the memory is reset by memset.

Kernel Thread Example

Here is the previous kmem and klock example, modified to support a kernel thread that keeps an eye on the device, resetting the memory buffer if the device is not being used:

```
/*
 * plp_kwork.c - Example of scheduling deferred work via kernel threads.
 */

#include <linux/kernel.h>
#include <linux/init.h>
#include <linux/module.h>
#include <linux/vmalloc.h>

#include <linux/fs.h>
#include <linux/major.h>
#include <linux/blkdev.h>
#include <linux/cdev.h>

#include <linux/kthread.h>

#include <asm/uaccess.h>
```

```
#define PLP_KMEM_BUFSIZE (1024*1024) /* 1MB internal buffer */

/* global variables */

static char *plp_kwork_buffer;

static struct class *plp_kwork_class;   /* pretend /sys/class */
static dev_t plp_kwork_dev;             /* dynamically assigned char device */
static struct cdev *plp_kwork_cdev;     /* dynamically allocated at runtime. */

static unsigned int plp_kwork_owner;    /* dynamically changing UID. */
static unsigned int plp_kwork_count;    /* number of current users. */

static struct task_struct *plp_kwork_ts; /* task struct for kthread. */

/* Locking */

static DECLARE_MUTEX(plp_kwork_sem); /* protect device read/write action. */

/* function prototypes */

static int __init plp_kwork_init(void);
static void __exit plp_kwork_exit(void);

static int plp_kwork_open(struct inode *inode, struct file *file);
static int plp_kwork_release(struct inode *inode, struct file *file);
static ssize_t plp_kwork_read(struct file *file, char __user *buf,
                        size_t count, loff_t *ppos);
static ssize_t plp_kwork_write(struct file *file, const char __user *buf,
                        size_t count, loff_t *ppos);

static int plp_kwork_kthread(void *data);

/* file_operations */

static struct file_operations plp_kwork_fops = {
 .read          = plp_kwork_read,
 .write         = plp_kwork_write,
 .open          = plp_kwork_open,
 .release       = plp_kwork_release,
 .owner         = THIS_MODULE,
};

/*
 * plp_kwork_open: Open the ksem device
 */

static int plp_kwork_open(struct inode *inode, struct file *file)
{

 down(&plp_kwork_sem);

 if ((plp_kwork_owner != file->f_uid) &&
     (plp_kwork_count != 0)) {

#ifdef PLP_DEBUG
```

```
                printk(KERN_DEBUG "plp_kwork: device is in use.\n");
#endif

        up(&plp_kwork_sem);
        return -EBUSY;
 }

 plp_kwork_count++;
 plp_kwork_owner=file->f_uid;

#ifdef PLP_DEBUG
 printk(KERN_DEBUG "plp_kwork: opened device.\n");
#endif

 up(&plp_kwork_sem);
 return 0;
}

/*
 * plp_kwork_release: Close the ksem device.
 */

static int plp_kwork_release(struct inode *inode, struct file *file)
{

 down(&plp_kwork_sem);
 plp_kwork_count--;
 up(&plp_kwork_sem);

#ifdef PLP_DEBUG
 printk(KERN_DEBUG "plp_kwork: device closed.\n");
#endif

 return 0;
}

/*
 * plp_kwork_read: Read from the device.
 */

static ssize_t plp_kwork_read(struct file *file, char __user *buf,
                        size_t count, loff_t *ppos)
{
 size_t bytes = count;
 loff_t fpos = *ppos;
 char *data;

 down(&plp_kwork_sem);

 if (fpos >= PLP_KMEM_BUFSIZE) {
        up(&plp_kwork_sem);
        return 0;
 }

 if (fpos+bytes >= PLP_KMEM_BUFSIZE)
```

```
                bytes = PLP_KMEM_BUFSIZE-fpos;

   if (0 == (data = kmalloc(bytes, GFP_KERNEL))) {
           up(&plp_kwork_sem);
           return -ENOMEM;
   }

#ifdef PLP_DEBUG
   printk(KERN_DEBUG "plp_kwork: read %d bytes from device, offset %d.\n",
           bytes,(int)fpos);
#endif

   memcpy(data,plp_kwork_buffer+fpos,bytes);

   if (copy_to_user((void __user *)buf, data, bytes)) {
           printk(KERN_ERR "plp_kwork: cannot write data.\n");
           kfree(data);
           up(&plp_kwork_sem);
           return -EFAULT;
   }

   *ppos = fpos+bytes;

   kfree(data);
   up(&plp_kwork_sem);
   return bytes;
}

/*
 * plp_kwork_write: Write to the device.
 */

static ssize_t plp_kwork_write(struct file *file, const char __user *buf,
                        size_t count, loff_t *ppos)
{

   size_t bytes = count;
   loff_t fpos = *ppos;
   char *data;

   down(&plp_kwork_sem);

   if (fpos >= PLP_KMEM_BUFSIZE) {
           up(&plp_kwork_sem);
           return -ENOSPC;
   }

   if (fpos+bytes >= PLP_KMEM_BUFSIZE)
           bytes = PLP_KMEM_BUFSIZE-fpos;

   if (0 == (data = kmalloc(bytes, GFP_KERNEL))) {
           up (&plp_kwork_sem);
           return -ENOMEM;
   }

   if (copy_from_user((void *)data, (const void __user *)buf, bytes)) {
```

```
                printk(KERN_ERR "plp_kwork: cannot read data.\n");
                kfree(data);
                up (&plp_kwork_sem);
                return -EFAULT;
    }

#ifdef PLP_DEBUG
 printk(KERN_DEBUG "plp_kwork: write %d bytes to device, offset %d.\n",
        bytes,(int)fpos);
#endif

 memcpy(plp_kwork_buffer+fpos,data,bytes);

 *ppos = fpos+bytes;

 kfree(data);
 up(&plp_kwork_sem);
 return bytes;
}

/*
 * plp_kwork_init: Load the kernel module into memory
 */

static int __init plp_kwork_init(void)
{
 printk(KERN_INFO "plp_kwork: Allocating %d bytes of internal buffer.\n",
                PLP_KMEM_BUFSIZE);

 if (NULL == (plp_kwork_buffer = vmalloc(PLP_KMEM_BUFSIZE))) {
        printk(KERN_ERR "plp_kwork: cannot allocate memory!\n");
        goto error;
 }

 memset((void *)plp_kwork_buffer, 0, PLP_KMEM_BUFSIZE);

 if (alloc_chrdev_region(&plp_kwork_dev, 0, 1, "plp_kwork"))
        goto error;

 if (0 == (plp_kwork_cdev = cdev_alloc()))
        goto error;

 kobject_set_name(&plp_kwork_cdev->kobj,"plp_kwork_cdev");
 plp_kwork_cdev->ops = &plp_kwork_fops; /* file up fops */
 if (cdev_add(plp_kwork_cdev, plp_kwork_dev, 1)) {
        kobject_put(&plp_kwork_cdev->kobj);
        unregister_chrdev_region(plp_kwork_dev, 1);
        goto error;
 }

 plp_kwork_class = class_create(THIS_MODULE, "plp_kwork");
 if (IS_ERR(plp_kwork_class)) {
        printk(KERN_ERR "plp_kwork: Error creating class.\n");
        cdev_del(plp_kwork_cdev);
        unregister_chrdev_region(plp_kwork_dev, 1);
```

```
                goto error;
        }
        class_device_create(plp_kwork_class, NULL, plp_kwork_dev, NULL, "plp_kwork");

        plp_kwork_ts = kthread_run(plp_kwork_kthread, NULL, "plp_work_kthread");
        if (IS_ERR(plp_kwork_ts)) {
                printk(KERN_ERR "plp_kwork: can't start kthread.\n");
                cdev_del(plp_kwork_cdev);
                unregister_chrdev_region(plp_kwork_dev, 1);
                goto error;
        }

        printk(KERN_INFO "plp_kwork: loaded.\n");

        return 0;

error:
        printk(KERN_ERR "plp_kwork: cannot register device.\n");
        return 1;
}

/*
 * plp_kwork_exit: Unload the kernel module from memory
 */


static void __exit plp_kwork_exit(void)
{

        kthread_stop(plp_kwork_ts);

        class_device_destroy(plp_kwork_class, plp_kwork_dev);
        class_destroy(plp_kwork_class);
        cdev_del(plp_kwork_cdev);
        unregister_chrdev_region(plp_kwork_dev,1);

        vfree(plp_kwork_buffer);

        printk(KERN_INFO "plp_kwork: unloading.\n");
}

static int plp_kwork_kthread(void *data)
{

        printk(KERN_INFO "plp_kwork: kthread starting.\n");

        for(;;) {

                schedule_timeout_interruptible(10*HZ);

                if (!kthread_should_stop()) {

                        /* If nobody has the device open, reset it after
                         * a period of time.
```

```
                         */

                 down(&plp_kwork_sem);
                 if (!plp_kwork_count) {
                         plp_kwork_owner = 0;
                         memset((void *)plp_kwork_buffer, 0,
                                 PLP_KMEM_BUFSIZE);
                 }
                 up(&plp_kwork_sem);

         } else {
                 printk(KERN_INFO "plp_kwork: kthread stopping.\n");
                 return 0;
         }
 }

 return 0;
}

/* declare init/exit functions here */

module_init(plp_kwork_init);
module_exit(plp_kwork_exit);

/* define module meta data */

MODULE_AUTHOR("Jon Masters <jcm@jonmasters.org>");
MODULE_DESCRIPTION("Demonstrate kernel memory allocation");

MODULE_ALIAS("kthread_example");
MODULE_LICENSE("GPL");
MODULE_VERSION("0:1.0");
```

Further Reading

The previous section has given you a brief introduction to several different APIs that exist within the Linux kernel. You've seen how certain parts of the kernel provide support for memory allocations, locking primitives, and handling deferred work. There's a lot more to the Linux kernel than just what you've seen in this chapter, but it is hoped that this has given you a feel for the operation of the kernel. You should feel inspired to learn more, by referring to other texts on the subject and online resources.

One of the issues not covered in this chapter is that of working with specific hardware devices. This is because it is difficult to determine what hardware you might have available as you read this book and there is not room to cover all of the alternatives in the space of a single chapter. You can locate specific hardware examples in a book such as *Linux Device Drivers*, which is made available online from the *Linux Weekly News* website at www.lwn.net. Take a look at their kernel commentary, too.

In addition, a number of online tutorials make use of virtual machine technology, such as that offered by qemu and UML to synthesize artificial devices against which you can write your own drivers. You can find some examples on the website accompanying this book. No matter what you do, however, the best source for high-quality driver examples remains the Linux kernel itself. Take a look at the "drivers" subdirectory of the Linux kernel sources, and you will find plenty of simple example modules.

Distributing Linux Kernel Modules

There are a number of different ways of making your own modules available to third parties. The first and most obvious is to simply post patches to the Linux kernel mailing list. That might not always be practical, however, so this section discusses several alternatives for shipping your drivers independently of the Linux kernel — at least until the kernel has your module built right in.

Going Upstream

The ultimate goal for anyone writing a Linux kernel module should be to get that module into the upstream Linux kernel. This means that the module becomes a part of the mainstream Linux kernel and is maintained by you, in conjunction with anyone else wanting to provide fixes, updates, or suggestions for ways to improve the module. Modules that remain out-of-tree will have to be constantly updated to reflect the changing pace of Linux kernel development over recent years. The module will have to handle API changes when they occur upstream, and you will have to live with upstream decisions.

Over time, fewer interfaces are being exported to loadable modules. Kernel developers have little concern about removing entirely an API that is relied upon only by known out-of-tree modules. For example, the LSM (Linux Security Modules) framework is, at the time of writing this book, under constant debate for removal from the kernel since it has only one in-kernel user (and a bunch of known out-of-tree users who have not sent their code upstream after many requests). The bottom line is that it's much safer to get your code upstream if at all possible — even if you're the only user of that code!

Getting your module into the upstream kernel is hardly trivial. You must first pass the "Christoph" test. This means that you must first post patches for your code to the Linux Kernel Mailing List (LKML) and await the comments of other kernel developers. Certain developers are well known to be opinionated on various topics and will likely post criticisms of your code, but you should swallow your pride and listen to their comments as they often turn out to be right. Don't take it personally — these guys are trying to ensure that the Linux kernel is of the utmost quality, so they are going to be pretty pedantic about it.

Shipping Sources

Another good solution for those who don't yet have their module in the Linux kernel is to provide a set of sources via a website and allow third parties to build the driver for themselves using instructions and processes similar to those discussed over the last couple of chapters. Bear in mind that you will need to keep your module up to date with respect to those kernels that are being used by your users. And that means that you'll need to verify your module against some of the more unusual vendor kernels, too.

Many more experienced users are comfortable following these instructions, but for those who are not, you might be interested in looking at the DKMS project. DKMS supports automated building of drivers in the target environment and came out of a lot of interesting work being done by a major computer manufacturer. To find out more about the DKMS, see `http://linux.dell.com/dkms`.

Shipping Prebuilt Modules

A growing number of Linux distributions provide infrastructure for prepackaged drivers. They may not officially support out-of-tree drivers, but if you can't get your kernel module into the upstream kernel (yet), then you might decide to follow the packaging guidelines for your distribution. Several of the big-name Linux companies have banded together and even worked on tools that support verifying module symbol versioning at the package level — allowing you to use one module with several compatible kernels at the same time. That should help prepackaged drivers to need fewer constant updates.

For more information about packaging up prebuilt kernel modules, contact your vendor.

Summary

In this chapter, you learned about Linux kernel modules (LKMs). You learned how they are constructed from numerous functions and macros. You learned how LKMs are compiled with the GNU Toolchain and linked into objects that can extend a running Linux kernel. You also learned about a few of the standard Linux kernel APIs that are available to most loadable kernel modules and saw a few examples of these APIs in action through a virtual-memory-based buffer device.

Although this chapter cannot possibly convey all of the complexities and intricacies of writing modules, you should now feel more comfortable with the concepts involved and empowered to learn more about both the Linux kernel and module development in particular. In the next chapter, you will learn about interfacing with the Linux kernel, how tools such as udev and D-BUS are able to receive messages, indicating various events are happening within the system and how the kernel fits into the picture.

10

Debugging

Throughout this book, you have learned about a wide range of technologies that are available for Linux systems. You have studied a variety of examples and (hopefully) have tested some of these examples out for yourself. But it is also quite likely that you have experienced at least one or two bugs in the course of working with Linux — an inevitable consequence of working with any computer software. Linux may be openly developed by skillful people all around the world, but no software is bug free.

In this chapter, you will learn about some of the debugging techniques available to you as you write code for Linux systems. The chapter is divided into three logical sections. First, you'll learn about the gdb command line GNU debugger utility and how to use some of its powerful command set. Then, you will learn about higher level graphical debugging built upon gdb, using tools such as ddd and Eclipse. Finally, you will delve into kernel debugging using a UML (User Mode Linux) kernel as an example.

By the end of this chapter, you should have a good understanding of the range of debugging tools available to Linux programmers. You should feel comfortable in the basic use of these tools and be empowered to learn more through your own experimentation. Bear in mind that debugging is, by its very nature, a complex and difficult task that can take many years to fully master. Don't expect that you'll be an expert after reading this chapter alone — you need to put these techniques into practice.

Debugging Overview

You will almost certainly have some experience and involvement with debugging applications. This might be as a programmer but perhaps also as a user who has experienced frustration whenever an application failed to behave in the manner anticipated. Software bugs occur for a wide variety of reasons (there are, in fact, whole academic disciplines involved in their study) but whatever the cause, the outcome is often a negative experience for the user[1] and in any case necessitates some kind of software fix. The hard part (usually) is finding exactly what caused the bug in the first place.

There are a variety of common types of bugs, such as the trivial (and annoying) "off by one error" that will occur whatever the operating system you're working with and lead to certain types of tell-tale application misbehavior. But there are also more Linux- and UNIX-specific issues with which you may be less familiar. These will be briefly discussed here, but for a really comprehensive coverage, you will want to purchase a good academic text on the subject. In any case, keep in mind as you write code for Linux this famous quote from UNIX co-creator Brian W. Kernighan:

> *"Debugging is twice as hard as writing the code in the first place. Therefore, it you write the code as cleverly as possible, you are, by definition, not smart enough to debug it."*

A Word about Memory Management

One of the most common (and most annoying) areas in which bugs occur on Linux and UNIX-like systems is in individual application memory handling. Incorrectly allocating, not freeing, using freed memory, and many other typical kinds of bugs occur frequently and can take a considerable amount of time to isolate on any platform. Fortunately, erroneous memory handling in a regular application won't bring down the entire system thanks to the Linux kernel's handling of the virtual memory environment.

Two typical memory-related errors you will encounter when writing software for Linux are:

❑ **Segmentation Faults:** This ugly error occurs whenever your program attempts to access memory outside of its official data storage areas. The Linux kernel is able to detect these accesses due to its virtual memory subsystem handling the underlying (bad) page faults[2] that occur on such accesses. The application is forcibly terminated, optionally with a core file being created containing the state of the program, depending on the system's configuration.

❑ **Memory leaks:** These are universal in any programming environment. However, because the kernel provides a virtual memory environment for applications, a memory leak in a regular program will unlikely bring the entire system down. Once the application crashes or is terminated, the leaked memory is available once again to other applications. Often, system administrators impose resource limits, restricting memory available to any one program.

The former is perhaps the most annoying error you will receive, but is a good alternative to having erroneous memory use outside of that which is provided to your application. Most memory-related problems that lead to a crash also leave sufficient clues that a little time spent in gdb is all that is required; however, there are times when subtle misuse of memory can go undetected. This is where tools such as Valgrind (discussed later) can come in helpful, monitoring runtime program execution.

---

[1] Examples of ATMs giving away free money due to software glitches notwithstanding.

[2] Literally, the kernel tried to make data available that wasn't there (and wasn't in the swap space at the time). There are other reasons for and complexity to this not covered here—but then, there always are in life.

Essential Debugging Tools

Linux programmers have come to rely upon a small collection of essential debugging tools, on which many of the more complex alternatives now available have been built. The GNU Debugger (gdb) is by far the most popular debugging tool for tracing and debugging applications, but it is not the only option available to you if you wish to do more than insert a few breakpoints and monitor your application as it runs through some test data. In recent times, a number of whole-system analysis tools (such as system-tap and frysk) have aided in performance enhancement of applications, for example.

The GNU Debugger

GDB is one of the most well-known and renowned pieces of Free and open source software available today. It is used by a large number of GNU software projects as well as numerous third parties with no connection, other than a desire for a high-quality debugger. In fact, many third-party tools incorporate gdb as the basis for their debugging capability, even if they build levels of graphical abstraction on top. Indeed, it's highly likely that you've already encountered GDB — perhaps even without realizing it.

GDB is built on the fundamental concept that there are two parts to any debugger. First, there's the low-level handling required to start and stop individual processes and threads, to trace execution, and to insert and remove breakpoints from running code. GDB supports a vast number of different platforms and mechanisms for achieving these (seemingly simple) operations on a wide range of architectures. The precise functionality available will occasionally vary, subject to underlying hardware features.

> *GDB even supports connecting to hardware debugging equipment, such as the Abatron BDI2000, a specialist CPU-level debugger that can be used to debug the Linux kernel running on another system remotely, by stopping and starting the CPU itself. GDB is favored over reinventing the wheel with some other inferior debugger design. You may encounter this if you are an Embedded developer.*

Built upon the low-level functionality necessary for debugging applications is the need for a higher level interface that can be used by the programmer in an efficient fashion. GDB provides one interface with one set of commands that is standard, no matter what hardware it is running on. This is perhaps one of the reasons it has become so popular — you need only learn the core commands once.

Compiling Code for Use with GDB

The GNU Debugger comes in the form of a deceptively simple-looking command line utility known as gdb. It expects to take a program name as one of its arguments, or otherwise expects to be asked to load a program before proceeding. It will then fire up the debugger environment and await commands. The program will not begin until you actually instruct gdb to begin program execution under the debugger.

As an example, create a simple "Hello World" program to use with gdb:

```
/*
 * hello.c - test program.
 */

#include <stdio.h>

void print_hello()
```

```
{

 printf("Hello, World!\n");

}

int main(int argc, char **argv)
{

        print_hello;

        return 0;

}
```

The example code uses a subroutine to display the greeting, since this will result in at least one function call being made by the main program. When it comes to using the debugger, you will notice that a new stack frame is created and be able to see the effects of the function call more than if the program had simply been a standard test program — the point is, there's a good reason for the subroutine call in the example, because you're going to take advantage of that later on when you test out GDB features.

You can compile the example program, using GCC:

```
$ gcc -o hello -g hello.c
```

Notice the –g flag specified on the GCC command line. This informs GCC that it must add additional debugging symbols and source-level information to the resulting executable, so that GDB can provide more verbose information than it could from a regular binary. GDB really needs this additional information — which is usually stripped from Linux binaries to save space — in order to be able to provide source file line numbers and other related information. Try the following examples without building in debugging information and you'll quickly see the difference in the level of the output.

In addition to the –g flag, you might wish to supply additional GCC command flags on some platforms, especially those that optimize machine code instruction scheduling for performance reasons. This is often the case on modern non-x86 processors with simplified instruction sets, since the tendency is toward having optimization in the compiler rather than complexity in the machine instruction set. This means, in practice, that turning off instruction rescheduling will lead to sensible GDB output. Please refer to the earlier Chapter 2 for a description of suitable GCC command line flags.

Starting GDB

Once your application is appropriately built with the correct command flags passed to GDB, you can load the hello example into GDB by calling the gdb command, as follows:

```
$ gdb ./hello
GNU gdb Red Hat Linux (6.3.0.0-1.122rh)
Copyright 2004 Free Software Foundation, Inc.
GDB is free software, covered by the GNU General Public License, and you are
welcome to change it and/or distribute copies of it under certain conditions.
Type "show copying" to see the conditions.
There is absolutely no warranty for GDB.  Type "show warranty" for details.
```

```
This GDB was configured as "ppc-redhat-linux-gnu"...Using host libthread_db library
"/lib/libthread_db.so.1".

(gdb)
```

GDB loads the `hello` ELF binary into memory and sets up an environment for the program to run in. At this point, it'll look for useful symbols in both the program binary as well as any libraries that are linked into the program itself. The `run` command can be used to run the program normally:

```
(gdb) run
Starting program: /home/jcm/PLP/src/debugging/hello
Reading symbols from shared object read from target memory...done.
Loaded system supplied DSO at 0x100000
Hello, World!

Program exited normally.
```

This is all very well, but it's not particularly useful merely to run a program from beginning to end. This is where GDB's powerful selection of commands comes in very useful. A few of these commands are individually discussed below, but you can find a complete listing of commands as well as a summary of their use through the help system built right into GDB, as well as existing system documentation (and whole books devoted to GDB). The GDB help is split into classes:

```
(gdb) help
List of classes of commands:

aliases -- Aliases of other commands
breakpoints -- Making program stop at certain points
data -- Examining data
files -- Specifying and examining files
internals -- Maintenance commands
obscure -- Obscure features
running -- Running the program
stack -- Examining the stack
status -- Status inquiries
support -- Support facilities
tracepoints -- Tracing of program execution without stopping the program
user-defined -- User-defined commands

Type "help" followed by a class name for a list of commands in that class.
Type "help" followed by command name for full documentation.
Command name abbreviations are allowed if unambiguous.
```

For example, to obtain a list of commands controlling program execution, type "help running" at the prompt. Spend a few minutes looking through the lists of commands available in GDB; it'll come in very helpful later on not to have to constantly look up the names of commands.

Setting Breakpoints

Using GDB to run programs isn't particularly exciting unless it is possible to also control the execution of the program at runtime. This is where the `break` command becomes very useful. By inserting breakpoints into an application at runtime, you can have GDB stop program execution when a particular point in the program instructions is reached. It is common (even traditional) to insert such a breakpoint at the very beginning of a program by breaking on entry into the main function:

```
(gdb) break main
Breakpoint 1 at 0x1000047c: file hello.c, line 17.
Now that a breakpoint has been inserted, program execution will cease immediately
upon entry into the main function. You can test this by re-issuing the run command
to GDB:
```

You can also use the shorted form of break, simply:

```
(gdb) b main
```

will achieve the same thing.

Run the program using the run command:

```
(gdb) run
Starting program: /home/jcm/PLP/src/debugging/hello
Reading symbols from shared object read from target memory...done.
Loaded system supplied DSO at 0x100000

Breakpoint 1, main (argc=1, argv=0x7fed6874) at hello.c:17
10              printf("Hello, World!\n");
```

Notice how GDB has temporarily halted program execution at the breakpoint specified, while you decide whether to proceed or to carry out another operation. You can move forward through the program by using the step and next commands. The command step will continue the program until it reaches a new line in the program source code, while stepi will move forward one machine instruction only (one line of source may represent many individual machine code instructions to the processor).

The next and nexti variants behave similarly, except that they proceed through subroutine calls — a good way to debug your code without worrying about library calls. This is especially useful because it's likely that your C library will not have been built with the same level of debugging information as applications you are currently debugging. Therefore, it may not make sense to trace through calls to standardized C library functions, even if you're interested to know more about their implementation.

> Note that inserting a breakpoint on entry to the main function does not technically halt execution at the absolute very beginning of the program, since all C-based programs running on Linux systems make use of the GNU C library runtime to help get set up. Thus, by the time the breakpoint is reached, many incidental library functions have already performed a great deal of setup work.

Visualizing Data

You can use GDB to query data stored by an individual program, using the print command. For example, you can visualize optional arguments passed to the example program via the run command. Arguments passed to the run command are passed to the called program as its regular argv argument list. Here is the output produced by GDB when the simple program is called with added arguments:

```
(gdb) break main
Breakpoint 1 at 0x1000047c: file hello.c, line 17.
(gdb) run foo baz
Starting program: /home/jcm/PLP/src/debugging/hello foo baz
Reading symbols from shared object read from target memory...done.
Loaded system supplied DSO at 0x100000

Breakpoint 1, main (argc=3, argv=0x7f8ab864) at hello.c:17
10              printf("Hello, World!\n");
(gdb) print argv[0]
$1 = 0x7f8ab9d8 "/home/jcm/PLP/src/debugging/hello"
(gdb) print argv[1]
$2 = 0x7f8ab9fa "foo"
(gdb) print argv[2]
$3 = 0x7f8ab9fe "baz"
(gdb) print argv[3]
$4 = 0x0
```

You can see here the list of program arguments, followed by a NULL character in the argv list. It doesn't matter whether the example program uses the argument list—it's still supplied and return following a quick call to the GDB print command, as shown in the output.

Backtrace

GDB provides many useful stack frame management commands and includes several commands designed solely to see how the program got to the point that it is at. One of the most useful commands, backtrace, has a simplified mnemonic, bt, which can be used to see all stack frames leading up to the current one. Here is an example of the kind of information provided by the backtrace command:

```
(gdb) break main
Breakpoint 1 at 0x100004b4: file hello.c, line 17.
(gdb) run
Starting program: /home/jcm/PLP/src/debugging/hello
Reading symbols from shared object read from target memory...done.
Loaded system supplied DSO at 0x100000

Breakpoint 1, main (argc=1, argv=0x7ff96874) at hello.c:17
17              print_hello();
(gdb) step
print_hello () at hello.c:10
10              printf("Hello, World!\n");
(gdb) bt
#0  print_hello () at hello.c:10
#1  0x100004b8 in main (argc=1, argv=0x7ff96874) at hello.c:17
```

In the above GDB session, you can clearly see how stepping through the print_hello subroutine results in two stack frames being listed by the bt (backtrace) command. The first and innermost is the current stack frame, covering the function call into print_hello, while the outer stack frame is used by the global main function in order to store its local variables ahead of calling print_hello.

A Buggy Example

Thus far, you have seen some examples of commands available within the GDB environment. You have not, however, tried debugging a real program containing an actual bug! The following examples will show you how you can begin to use GDB to perform routine debugging tasks — locating a bad pointer reference, backtrace following a program crash, and other related actions.

You can use the following simple example program to beginning debugging with GDB. The code in the source file buggy.c defines a linked_list struct and allocates 10 elements using a head-first list insertion algorithm. Unfortunately, the data elements in the list are assigned to unallocated memory (using a call to strncpy without preallocated memory). To make matters worse, the program doesn't free allocated memory — but there's more about detecting memory leaks later in this section.

Here's a simple buggy program:

```
/*
 * buggy.c - A buggy program.
 */

#include <stdio.h>
#include <stdlib.h>
#include <string.h>

struct linked_list {

        struct linked_list *next;
        char *data;

};

int main(int argc, char **argv)
{

        struct linked_list *head = NULL;
        struct linked_list *tmp = NULL;
        char *test_string = "some data";
        int i = 0;

        for (i=0;i<10;i++) {
                tmp = malloc(sizeof(*tmp));
                strncpy(tmp->data,test_string,strlen(test_string));
                tmp->next = head;
                head = tmp;
        }

        return 0;

}
```

You can compile and run this program using GCC as follows:

```
$ gcc -o buggy -g buggy.c
$ ./buggy
Segmentation fault
```

As you can see, the program has unfortunately crashed due to a segmentation fault, meaning that it tried to access memory outside its allocated data storage. Typically, this happens when a pointer is deferenced that points to trash instead of a legitimate memory location (there's often no easy way to know whether a number stored in a memory location is in fact a genuine pointer until it's too late). In this case, it's because code is attempting to write into a string for which memory has not been allocated.

You can load this buggy program into GDB and run it once again:

```
$ gdb ./buggy
GNU gdb Red Hat Linux (6.3.0.0-1.122rh)
Copyright 2004 Free Software Foundation, Inc.
GDB is free software, covered by the GNU General Public License, and you are
welcome to change it and/or distribute copies of it under certain conditions.
Type "show copying" to see the conditions.
There is absolutely no warranty for GDB.  Type "show warranty" for details.
This GDB was configured as "ppc-redhat-linux-gnu"...Using host libthread_db library
"/lib/libthread_db.so.1".

(gdb) run
Starting program: /home/jcm/PLP/src/debugging/buggy
Reading symbols from shared object read from target memory...done.
Loaded system supplied DSO at 0x100000

Program received signal SIGSEGV, Segmentation fault.
0x0f65a09c in strncpy () from /lib/libc.so.6
```

This time, the program crash was detected by GDB, which is ready to help in debugging. You can now use the bt (backtrace) command to find out what the program was doing when it received the fatal signal as a result of an errant memory deference. Use the bt mnemonic to make life easier:

```
(gdb) bt
#0  0x0f65a09c in strncpy () from /lib/libc.so.6
#1  0x10000534 in main (argc=1, argv=0x7f9c5874) at buggy.c:26
```

According to the backtrace above, something on line 26 of the buggy program caused a call to be made to the C library strncpy subroutine, at which point the program crashed. At this point, it should be quite obvious enough from looking at the program source just what the problem is:

```
strncpy(tmp->data,test_string,strlen(test_string));
```

This line of code copies test_string into the data member of the tmp linked list element, but data is not initialized first, so random memory locations are used to store the string. Such memory misuse quickly results in an expected and somewhat inevitable application crash. A simple call to malloc prior to the strncpy is all that is required (or a malloc calling string alternative). In this case, however, you can avoid any string copy by simply setting the data elements to point to the static string test_string.

To work around the bug, replace the particular call to strncpy in the example source with this:

```
tmp->data = test_string;
```

The program should now compile and run normally:

```
$ gcc -o buggy -g buggy.c
$ ./buggy
```

Debugging a Core File

Traditionally, UNIX and UNIX-like systems have dumped core or provided a binary output of their state upon crashing. These days, a number of Linux distributions disable core file creation for regular users to save on space (having core files cluttering up the disk that the average user may know nothing about is both wasteful and disconcerting for the user). Normally, a particular Linux distribution will use `ulimits` (user limits) to control the creation of core files.

You can view your current user limits by using the `ulimit` command:

```
$ ulimit -a
core file size          (blocks, -c) 0
data seg size           (kbytes, -d) unlimited
max nice                        (-e) 0
file size               (blocks, -f) unlimited
pending signals                 (-i) 4096
max locked memory       (kbytes, -l) 32
max memory size         (kbytes, -m) unlimited
open files                      (-n) 1024
pipe size            (512 bytes, -p) 8
POSIX message queues     (bytes, -q) 819200
max rt priority                 (-r) 0
stack size              (kbytes, -s) 10240
cpu time               (seconds, -t) unlimited
max user processes              (-u) 4096
virtual memory          (kbytes, -v) unlimited
file locks                      (-x) unlimited
```

As you can see, the limit on core file size is set to zero (disabled). You can reset this value by passing a new value to the `ulimit` command `-c` command line optional flag. The value should be the maximum core file size as measured in disk blocks. Here is an example of resetting the core file size in order to cause a core file to be created for the example program (output shortened for brevity):

```
$ ulimit -c 1024
$ ulimit -a
core file size          (blocks, -c) 1024
```

Note that this may not be necessary on your Linux distribution, depending upon its configuration.

With suitable limits in place on core file creation size, rerunning the example program should cause a real core dump to occur:

```
$ ./buggy
Segmentation fault (core dumped)
```

You can see a new core file in the current directory:

```
$ ls
buggy  buggy.c  core.21090  hello  hello.c
```

Note that, in the case of this particular Linux distribution, core files include the number of the process that was running the original program. This is an optional feature, which may not have been enabled in the kernel configuration supplied by your particular Linux distribution.

GDB includes the option to read in a core file and begin a debugging session based upon that. Since the core file results from a program that is no longer running, not all commands are available — for example, it makes no sense to try stepping through a program that is no longer running. Core files are useful, however, because you can debug them in an offline fashion, so your users can mail you[3] a core file alongside information about their local machine environment to facilitate your remote debugging.

You can run GDB against the example core file:

```
$ gdb ./buggy core.21090
GNU gdb Red Hat Linux (6.3.0.0-1.122rh)
Copyright 2004 Free Software Foundation, Inc.
GDB is free software, covered by the GNU General Public License, and you are
welcome to change it and/or distribute copies of it under certain conditions.
Type "show copying" to see the conditions.
There is absolutely no warranty for GDB.  Type "show warranty" for details.
This GDB was configured as "ppc-redhat-linux-gnu"...Using host libthread_db library
"/lib/libthread_db.so.1".

Failed to read a valid object file image from memory.
Core was generated by `./buggy'.
Program terminated with signal 11, Segmentation fault.

warning: svr4_current_sos: Can't read pathname for load map: Input/output error

Reading symbols from /lib/libc.so.6...done.
Loaded symbols for /lib/libc.so.6
Reading symbols from /lib/ld.so.1...done.
Loaded symbols for /lib/ld.so.1
#0  0x0f65a09c in strncpy () from /lib/libc.so.6
```

Then continue your debugging session in the same way that was covered before. Just remember that program flow control commands won't be available to you — the program is long since dead.

---

[3] Or, perhaps — and somewhat more likely to succeed in returning useful bug reports that can be worked on — you could write a tool to do this on their behalf. That's just what tools like GNOME bug buddy will do.

Valgrind

Valgrind is a runtime diagnostic tool that can monitor the activities of a given program and notify you of a wide variety of memory management problems that may be present in your code. It is similar to the older Electric Fence utility (which replaces standard memory allocation routines with its own for the purpose of improved diagnostics) but is regarded as easier to use and is generally more feature-rich in several respects — it's also supplied by most major Linux distributions at this point, so using it won't take you much time beyond installing a simple package onto your particular Linux distribution.

A typical Valgrind run might look like this:

```
$ valgrind ./buggy
==2090== Memcheck, a memory error detector.
==2090== Copyright (C) 2002-2006, and GNU GPL'd, by Julian Seward et al.
==2090== Using LibVEX rev 1658, a library for dynamic binary translation.
==2090== Copyright (C) 2004-2006, and GNU GPL'd, by OpenWorks LLP.
==2090== Using valgrind-3.2.1, a dynamic binary instrumentation framework.
==2090== Copyright (C) 2000-2006, and GNU GPL'd, by Julian Seward et al.
==2090== For more details, rerun with: -v
==2090==
==2090==
==2090== ERROR SUMMARY: 0 errors from 0 contexts (suppressed: 2 from 1)
==2090== malloc/free: in use at exit: 80 bytes in 10 blocks.
==2090== malloc/free: 10 allocs, 0 frees, 80 bytes allocated.
==2090== For counts of detected errors, rerun with: -v
==2090== searching for pointers to 10 not-freed blocks.
==2090== checked 47,492 bytes.
==2090==
==2090== LEAK SUMMARY:
==2090==    definitely lost: 80 bytes in 10 blocks.
==2090==      possibly lost: 0 bytes in 0 blocks.
==2090==    still reachable: 0 bytes in 0 blocks.
==2090==         suppressed: 0 bytes in 0 blocks.
==2090== Use --leak-check=full to see details of leaked memory.
```

The output shows that 80 bytes worth of memory were lost by the program by the time it ended. By specifying the leak-check option, it's possible to find just where this leaked memory came from:

```
==2101== 80 (8 direct, 72 indirect) bytes in 1 blocks are definitely lost in loss
record 2 of 2
==2101==    at 0xFF7BBE0: malloc (vg_replace_malloc.c:149)
==2101==    by 0x100004B0: main (buggy.c:25)
```

You should get into a habit of using tools such as Valgrind, where available, to automate the process of finding and fixing memory leaks and other programming errors. Take a look at the extensive online documentation for a more comprehensive coverage of the capabilities of Valgrind, as this just scratches the surface. Indeed, a growing number of open source projects are relying on Valgrind as a part of their regression tests — an important part of any reasonably sized software project.

Automated Code Analysis

There are a growing number of third-party tools that can be used to perform automated code analysis, searching for various typical kinds of defects in software. Such code coverage tools typically offer static, dynamic, or a hybrid form of code analysis. What this means is that the tool may simply examine the source code in order to determine potential defects, or it may attempt to hook into some other process in order to obtain data necessary to determine where defects in the software may lie.

The commercial Coverity code analysis tool, based on the Stanford University Checker, is often used on Linux systems. It hooks into the compilation process and extracts a large quantity of useful information, which can be used to isolate numerous potential problems. In fact, Coverity are offering free code analysis to a growing number of open source projects. They have even found a reasonably large number of previously undetected bugs in the Linux kernel. These are addressed, once raised.

One of the more interesting uses for static code analysis is looking for GPL violations in source code. Blackduck software offers just such a tool, which can help you to scan your large software projects to look for source code borrowed from open source projects and determine how to respond to it. This is useful for compliance testing, as well as a number of other activities your legal team might advise you on.

Graphical Debugging Tools

Although you can use GDB for most (if not all) of your Linux debugging experience, many people find that they are much more comfortable using a graphical tool, such as DDD or Eclipse, as opposed to sitting in front of the GDB command line for protracted periods. At the end of the day, most of the somewhat more fancy graphical debugging tools are simply an abstraction built upon GDB anyway, so it's really a matter of personal choice which you choose to use for yourself.

This section mentions two such tools available, though many others (including the GNU insight front end to GDB) do exist and are in use by various groups of developers.

DDD

The Data Display Debugger, or DDD, was first written as part of a college engineering project but quickly became extremely popular in the community for its friendly, easy-to-use interface and its powerful data visualization tools. DDD is simply a direct driver of GDB, which runs in the lower window, while source code and data displays are shown in windows above that. DDD should come preinstalled as part of your Linux distribution. You can build it up from sources if it's not prepackaged.

You can start DDD by typing ddd at the command line or by clicking on the appropriate menu option. Once loaded, you need to tell DDD which program it is going to open. Go to the File menu, select Open Program, and load the buggy example program into the debugger. If you have built the example code correctly, informing GCC to leave debugging information in the binary itself, then the program source (if available) will also show up in the source code window along with disassembly and status.

The main DDD graphical interface window is shown in Figure 10-1.

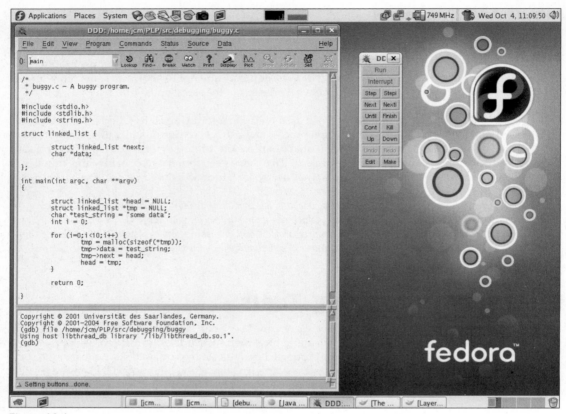

Figure 10-1

You can insert and remove breakpoints in your program with ease, simply by right-clicking with the mouse over part of the program text. The contextual menu that is displayed will include the option to add or remove any predefined breakpoints, as well as to continue program execution up to the point of the mouse cursor (an alternative to setting an explicit breakpoint). Refer to Figure 10-2, where a break-point is being set within the main function of the buggy program.

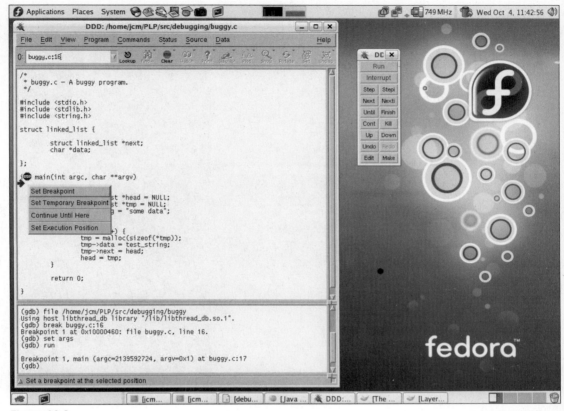

Figure 10-2

Since DDD is the Data Display Debugger, it stands to good reason that its data presentation capabilities are reasonably good. In fact, by clicking View and then Data Window, you can turn on another area in which different kinds of data visualizations are possible, as shown in Figure 10-3. Within the data window, you simply insert predefined expressions defining the data you would like to view, for example `tmp->head` to display the char string value contained within the temporarily linked list item, `tmp`.

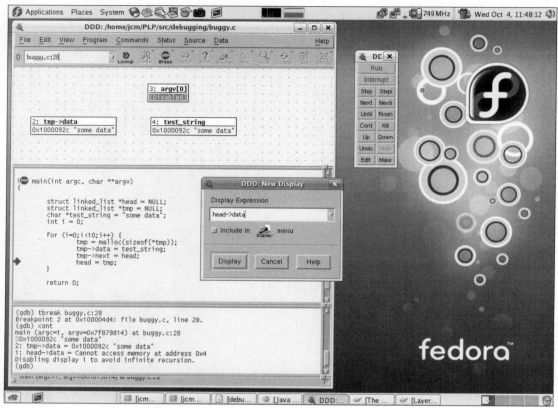

Figure 10-3

Eclipse

These days, everyone is interested in using integrated tools such as eclipse as effectively as possible. Eclipse actually includes yet another graphical front-end to the GNU debugger (GDB) that you can use directly from within the eclipse environment. First, load up eclipse by typing eclipse into a command line or by clicking on the option on your desktop menu. You will want to follow through the New Project wizard and create a project called buggy. Next, create a new C source file by clicking File, then New, and finally Source File. Name this file buggy.c and populate it with the contents of the example, as shown in Figure 10-4.

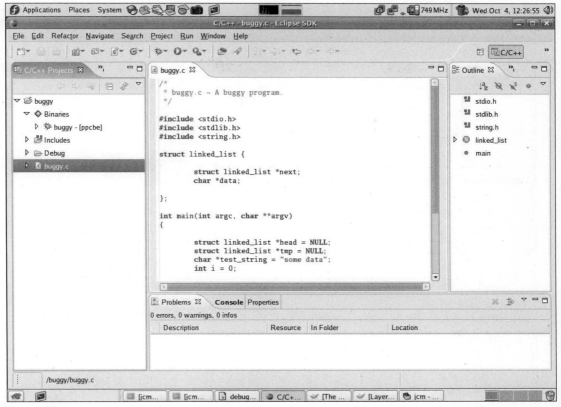

Figure 10-4

Eclipse will automatically build the source file when it is saved, but you can also use the options under the Project menu to achieve the same effect (for example, if you have disabled automatic workspace building in your Eclipse preferences). You can see the binary output file listed in the left-hand pane under the `Binaries` heading. It's of type `ppcbe` because it was built on a Big Endian PowerPC laptop (an Apple Macintosh running Linux), but your output will vary according you your choice of platform.

To begin debugging the buggy program, you need to switch to the Debug Perspective, shown in Figure 10-5. You will find the option to switch perspectives via an icon in the top-right corner of the Eclipse main window. You should see a Debug Perspective offered in the list, alongside any others that your vendor or third-party Eclipse packager has made available to you (and they may have offered you a lot of "value add").

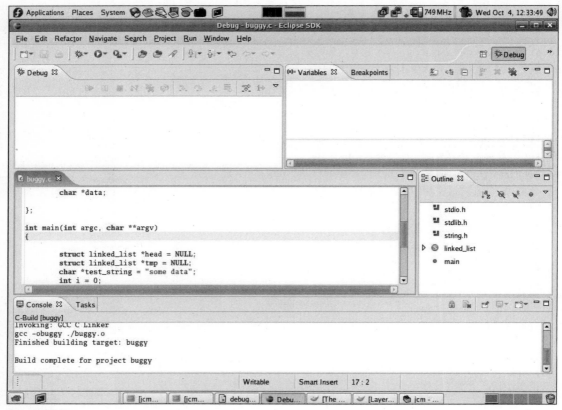

Figure 10-5

To begin debugging the program, choose Debug from the Run menu. You will be presented with a list of options, depending upon whether you wish to debug the program on the local machine, on a remote target or if you wish to use the output of a core file to figure out where things went wrong previously. In this case, you simply want to debug the current program on the local machine, so you want to choose C/C++ Local Application and define a new debug configuration in the wizard dialog presented to you.

Once a valid debug configuration has been created, the Debug button on the wizard dialog is activated and you can continue onto actually debugging your application. Clicking the button will result in the program entering into debug mode, the program will be started (with whatever options were specified via the wizard) and an automatic breakpoint will be inserted on entry into the main function.

You should see a screen similar to that shown in Figure 10-6.

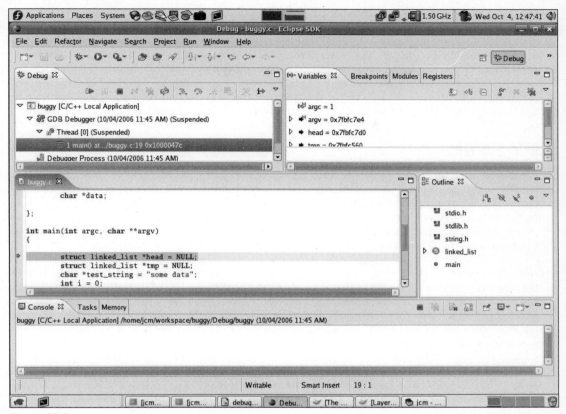

Figure 10-6

You can now continue to debug your application as you did before in GDB and within DDD. For further information about Eclipse debugging and its various options, check out the online Eclipse IDE documentation, where you will learn about some of the more advanced features, including support for remote target debugging of Embedded Linux devices — controlling the entire machine from Eclipse.

Kernel Debugging

In the last few sections, you learned about debugging regular Linux application programs running under the control of the Linux kernel. In such situations where you are debugging normal programs, you are able to directly benefit from numerous supporting infrastructure facilities offered by the Linux kernel. The Linux kernel provides a trace system call to handle tracing regular programs; it watches out for erroneous memory handling and prevents an application from running awry through its many other scheduling and process management abstractions that you are ordinarily able to take for granted.

The Linux kernel is, however, fundamentally just a complex piece of software, and like all other complex software, it is prone to occasionally unpleasant bugs. And when the kernel experiences a bug, the chances are that you'll quickly hear about it — glitches in the kernel tend to do very bad things for overall system stability. Fortunately, the Linux kernel is a well written and expertly maintained software project with many thousands of people constantly working to remove any such bugs.

This section will briefly introduce kernel debugging, but due to its complex nature, you may wish to consult additional online reference materials before embarking on a kernel debugging marathon.

Don't Panic!

Depending upon the nature of the kernel bug and where precisely it occurs (whether in the core kernel, in a device driver, and in what context) the system may be able to continue, or it may not. Often, the system will be able to proceed with some loss in functionality (and normally with a very ugly message in the system logs to that effect) following what is known as an oops.[4] An oops results in the current task (process) being killed, and any resources it was using being left in an often inconsistent state. At the very minimum, you should reboot a system that has experienced an oops as soon as possible.

In the case that the system is unable to safely continue, the kernel will call an immediate halt to its normal operation and force the system to die a sudden and horrible death. In such situations, the kernel is said to panic, after the function names used historically (and even today) within UNIX and UNIX-like kernels to effect the forced system crash. Although some data loss is likely following a panic (anything not previously committed to disk, including stale disk buffers), the system has safely prevented further (and substantially more serious) data corruption. It's a safety trade-off.

Note that your system may support kernel crash dumps using the kexec and kdump mechanisms recently introduced into 2.6 Linux kernels (older systems use a variety of alternatives). You should consult your distribution documentation to find out whether you can take advantage of this in order to preserve crash output on a kernel panic — it's a great alternative to manually writing down or having to digitally photograph (yes, really) the quantity of kernel debugging information that may otherwise adorn your screen on a crash. Sometimes, it's the only way to get at the important diagnostic data.[5]

> You can take a look at the wide variety of panic screens available on Linux and other UNIX and UNIX-like systems (and fool your friends and coworkers into thinking your system is constantly crashing) by activating the panic xscreensaver, if it is installed on your system.

---

[4] Certain Enterprise Linux vendors customize their kernel to panic whenever an oops happens. Effectively, this means that even a minor kernel hiccup will cause the system to crash immediately — the benefit being an absence of kernel data corruption, destroyed filesystems, and other much greater hidden damage later.

[5] This is especially true when you use the X Window system. Since X configures your graphics card for graphical output, it's often not possible for the kernel to write meaningful data to the display. The situation is compounded for those without displays, while those using genuine framebuffer devices (typically on non-Intel x86 platforms) will often see the kernel output superimposed over their graphical display.

Making Sense of an oops

Whenever the Linux kernel experiences a nonfatal (but still very serious) error, an oops occurs. In this case, a kernel stack backtrace alongside register contents and other pertinent information is printed to the system console and also recorded to the system logs. Note that your X Window system display is not the system console. You may never see real-time oops output as it happens on the console if you're using the graphical system but you should still have the oops output itself recorded in system logs.

Here is an example oops, from a recent mail to the LKML (Linux Kernel Mailing List):

```
Unable to handle kernel NULL pointer dereference at virtual address 0000025c
 printing eip:
d118143f
*pde = 00000000
Oops: 0000 [#1]
PREEMPT
Modules linked in: saa7134 i2c_prosavage i2c_viapro ehci_hcd uhci_hcd
usbcore 8250_pci 8250 serial_core video_buf compat_ioctl32 v4l2_common
v4l1_compat ir_kbd_i2c ir_common videodev via_agp agpgart snd_via82xx
snd_ac97_codec snd_ac97_bus snd_mpu401_uart snd_rawmidi snd_seq_device
snd_rtctimer snd_pcm_oss snd_pcm snd_timer snd_page_alloc
snd_mixer_oss snd soundcore it87 hwmon_vid hwmon i2c_isa video fan
button thermal processor via_rhine uinput fuse md5 ipv6 loop rtc
pcspkr ide_cd cdrom dm_mod
CPU:    0
EIP:    0060:[<d118143f>]    Not tainted VLI
EFLAGS: 00010246    (2.6.16-rc4 #1)
EIP is at saa7134_hwinit2+0x8c/0xe2 [saa7134]
eax: 00000000   ebx: cc253000   ecx: 00000000   edx: 0000003f
esi: cc253000   edi: cdc36400   ebp: cc2530d8   esp: c05d3e44
ds: 007b   es: 007b   ss: 0068
Process modprobe (pid: 7451, threadinfo=c05d2000 task=cb24fa70)
Stack: <0>cc253000 cc253000 00000000 d1181ae7 cc253000 d1180fdc
24000000 cc2530d8
       cc253000 00000003 d118b1cd fffffffed cdc36400 d1199920 d119994c c02188ad
       cdc36400 d1198ef4 d1198ef4 d1199920 cdc36400 d119994c c02188ea d1199920
Call Trace:
 [<d1181ae7>] saa7134_initdev+0x332/0x799 [saa7134]
 [<d1180fdc>] saa7134_irq+0x0/0x2d6 [saa7134]
 [<c02188ad>] __pci_device_probe+0x5f/0x6d
 [<c02188ea>] pci_device_probe+0x2f/0x59
 [<c026b26a>] driver_probe_device+0x93/0xe5
 [<c026b325>] __driver_attach+0x0/0x69
 [<c026b38c>] __driver_attach+0x67/0x69
 [<c026a747>] bus_for_each_dev+0x58/0x78
 [<c026b3b4>] driver_attach+0x26/0x2a
 [<c026b325>] __driver_attach+0x0/0x69
 [<c026acba>] bus_add_driver+0x83/0xd1
 [<c026b883>] driver_register+0x61/0x8f
 [<c026b80e>] klist_devices_get+0x0/0xa
 [<c026b818>] klist_devices_put+0x0/0xa
 [<c0218b33>] __pci_register_driver+0x54/0x7c
 [<c011be9a>] printk+0x17/0x1b
```

```
[<d1182229>] saa7134_init+0x4f/0x53 [saa7134]
[<c0137d75>] sys_init_module+0x138/0x1f7
[<c0102f65>] syscall_call+0x7/0xb
Code: 24 04 e8 68 aa f9 ee 89 1c 24 e8 d8 81 00 00 89 1c 24 e8 74 3e
00 00 83 bb d0 00 00 00 01 ba 3f 00 00 00 75 a9 8b 8b d4 00 00 00 <8b>
81 5c 02 00 00 a9 00 00 01 00 75 0e a9 00 00 04 00 74 2e ba
```

At first sight, this oops appears rather daunting in nature, but it is relatively easily broken down. First, notice the message: Unable to handle kernel NULL pointer dereference at virtual address 0000025c. This is, effectively, the equivalent of a Segmentation Fault in kernel space, but this time there's nothing to save the kernel from trying to manipulate unallocated memory or follow a NULL pointer someplace. In this case, the EIP (instruction pointer) is at 0xd118143f, which the kernel later handily translates to:

```
EIP is at saa7134_hwinit2+0x8c/0xe2
```

This means that the kernel was executing code 0x8c bytes into the function saa7134_hwinit2, which is 0xe2 bytes long in its compiled form. To locate the precise line in the source code, you can use the objdump utility to dump a dissassembly of that function from the kernel vmlinux file, as was covered earlier in Chapter 2. Often, simply knowing which function was being executed alongside a stacktrace and current register context from the oops report is enough to work on the problem.

The oops output confirms that this is the first oops which has occurred since boot (see below) and that the kernel was built with PREEMPTive kernel support (see "Low-Level Linux" for further details). The kernel also furnishes a complete list of modules that were loaded into the kernel at the time of the oops. There will be many of these on a typical Linux system, since the trend these days is toward increasing modularization of drivers and other nonessential core kernel infrastructure that can be modularized.

Next comes output describing the type and nature of CPU(s) installed on the system and what their register contents was at the time of the oops. From the output of this Intel IA32 (x86) processor, you can see that register EAX (eax) contained the NULL value that the kernel attempted to use as a pointer value, leading to the oops that occurred. The kernel tells us that the current task was modprobe, so we can reasonably deduce that this oops occured in the saa7134 driver immediately upon load.

Oops reports end with a (possibly lengthy) stack backtrace showing what caused the kernel to reach the point it is at. From the trace given, it is apparent that saa7134_init registered a new PCI device driver that immediately resulted in a call to the module's PCI probe function and that somewhere in the saa7134_initdev function a NULL pointer dereference occurred that caused the oops. Don't worry if this isn't obvious at this point – it will take you while of reading through oopses to get good at it.

Don't Trust Subsequent oopses

Bear in mind that oopses occur after "something bad happened"™ within the Linux kernel. This means that you really don't want to continue to expect your system to be stable or for any subsequent oops output to make any sense whatsoever (it might be influenced by the unstable system environment that follows the first oops). Sometimes, it's not easy to capture useful output before the system locks hard or otherwise panics. In such cases, it is very worthwhile investing in a null modem cable and setting up your system to log console output remotely. You can find examples in various online resources.

Reporting Bugs to Upstream

In the case that you can't figure out what caused an oops and would like to go ahead and file a kernel bug report with the upstream maintainers, you'll want to check out the REPORTING-BUGS file in the top level of your Linux kernel sources. It describes the correct process that you should follow and the format of the mail that you should send. Note that you are unlikely to receive support from the kernel community if you use an old kernel (contact your vendor instead) or choose to use proprietary drivers.

Note that the kernel community can tell when you're using proprietary non-GPL drivers. Often, people will file upstream bugs with lists of binary modules removed from the bug report but the kernel community has gotten wise to this. They are they able to figure this out (and refrain from offering support in the future if they choose). Several distributions now even modify the output formatting of oops reports in order to make it much harder to conceal this information from the kernel developers.

Using UML for Debugging

Debugging real hardware can be a difficult task, especially given the plethora of platforms and architectures that are available today. Providing an example that could realistically hope to address even a fraction of these was never likely to be easy – at least until tools such as UM Linux, qemu and other kernel virtualization technologies became available. Now, it's possible to trivially debug certain kinds of kernel problem safely and without the risk of a system crash, by using an emulator.

There are various types of emulation technology available that can be used to run the Linux kernel in all manner of simulated environments. One of the most straightforward to use is the User Mode (UM) kernel since it's now built right into the mainstream Linux kernel and available as a compile time option when building a new Linux kernel. User Mode Linux (UML) runs the Linux kernel as a regular application process. It simulates hardware such as clocks and interrupts using signals and does not talk directly to real hardware. Nonetheless, it is still a Linux kernel and is useful for testing certain features.

Note that you should not expect to be able to test out your own Linux kernel hardware device drivers using UML – that's not what it's designed for – but you can trace through kernel execution and test out pure software features. For example, you could test out your latest pure software filesystem.

Building a UML Kernel

The UM Linux kernel is a type of artificial Linux architecture that must be specified during kernel compilation. To proceed, you will need a fresh copy of Linux kernel sources from the kernel.org website and some free disk space to build and test out the UM kernel, using the GNU Toolchain.

Begin by calling tar to unpack the Linux kernel source tree in a fresh directory:

```
$ tar xvfj linux-2.6.18.tar.bz2
```

Next, configure the new kernel sources, specifying the UM architecture in place of whatever your regular system architecture (normally automatically detected) would be:

```
$ make ARCH=um menuconfig
```

Notice that the Linux kernel target architecture is specified using the ARCH environment variable.

Select the compilation options you would like to have in your UM kernel and then compile:

```
$ make ARCH=um
```

The output from the build process is a regular Linux ELF executable called linux. You can run this special Linux kernel just like any other regular application program:

```
$ ./linux
Checking that ptrace can change system call numbers...OK
Checking syscall emulation patch for ptrace...missing
Checking for tmpfs mount on /dev/shm...OK
Checking PROT_EXEC mmap in /dev/shm/...OK
Checking for the skas3 patch in the host:
  - /proc/mm...not found
  - PTRACE_FAULTINFO...not found
  - PTRACE_LDT...not found
UML running in SKAS0 mode
Checking that ptrace can change system call numbers...OK
Checking syscall emulation patch for ptrace...missing
Linux version 2.6.18 (jcm@panic) (gcc version 3.3.5 (Debian 1:3.3.5-13)) #1 Wed Oct
4 16:00:55 BST 2006
Built 1 zonelists.  Total pages: 8192
Kernel command line: root=98:0
PID hash table entries: 256 (order: 8, 1024 bytes)
Dentry cache hash table entries: 4096 (order: 2, 16384 bytes)
Inode-cache hash table entries: 2048 (order: 1, 8192 bytes)
Memory: 30116k available
Mount-cache hash table entries: 512
Checking for host processor cmov support...Yes
Checking for host processor xmm support...No
Checking that host ptys support output SIGIO...Yes
Checking that host ptys support SIGIO on close...No, enabling workaround
Using 2.6 host AIO
NET: Registered protocol family 16
NET: Registered protocol family 2
IP route cache hash table entries: 256 (order: -2, 1024 bytes)
TCP established hash table entries: 1024 (order: 0, 4096 bytes)
TCP bind hash table entries: 512 (order: -1, 2048 bytes)
TCP: Hash tables configured (established 1024 bind 512)
TCP reno registered
Checking host MADV_REMOVE support...MADV_REMOVE failed, err = -22
Can't release memory to the host - memory hotplug won't be supported
mconsole (version 2) initialized on /home/jcm/.uml/INfrHO/mconsole
Host TLS support detected
Detected host type: i386
VFS: Disk quotas dquot_6.5.1
Dquot-cache hash table entries: 1024 (order 0, 4096 bytes)
io scheduler noop registered
io scheduler anticipatory registered (default)
io scheduler deadline registered
io scheduler cfq registered
TCP bic registered
NET: Registered protocol family 1
NET: Registered protocol family 17
```

```
Initialized stdio console driver
Console initialized on /dev/tty0
Initializing software serial port version 1
Failed to open 'root_fs', errno = 2
VFS: Cannot open root device "98:0" or unknown-block(98,0)
Please append a correct "root=" boot option
Kernel panic - not syncing: VFS: Unable to mount root fs on unknown-block(98,0)

EIP: 0073:[<40043b41>] CPU: 0 Not tainted ESP: 007b:40152fbc EFLAGS: 00000246
    Not tainted
EAX: 00000000 EBX: 00001594 ECX: 00000013 EDX: 00001594
ESI: 00001591 EDI: 00000000 EBP: 40152fc8 DS: 007b ES: 007b
08897b10:  [<0806cdd8>]  show_regs+0xb4/0xb6
08897b3c:  [<0805aa84>]  panic_exit+0x25/0x3f
08897b4c:  [<0807e41a>]  notifier_call_chain+0x1f/0x3e
08897b6c:  [<0807e4af>]  atomic_notifier_call_chain+0x11/0x16
08897b80:  [<08071a8a>]  panic+0x4b/0xd8
08897b98:  [<08049973>]  mount_block_root+0xff/0x113
08897bec:  [<080499d8>]  mount_root+0x51/0x56
08897c00:  [<08049aab>]  prepare_namespace+0xce/0xfa
08897c10:  [<0805644d>]  init+0x73/0x12a
08897c24:  [<08066be8>]  run_kernel_thread+0x45/0x4f
08897ce0:  [<0805aee0>]  new_thread_handler+0xc3/0xf5
08897d20:  [<ffffe420>]  _etext+0xf7e72405/0x0

 <3>Trying to free already-free IRQ 2
Trying to free already-free IRQ 3
```

As you can see, the kernel crashed because it was not given a root filesystem. You can download copies of fake Linux filesystems that you can use with UML but for straightforward experimentation with the Linux kernel, this is not necessary (and hence is not covered here). The fact that the kernel did panic and produce the output above shows that it is as true to real life as is possible for UML (in that the Linux kernel will panic whenever it cannot mount its root filesystem and has no fallback to go to).

UM Linux can be run under GDB, when called with the debug option. First, start GDB:

```
$ gdb ./linux
GNU gdb 6.3-debian
Copyright 2004 Free Software Foundation, Inc.
GDB is free software, covered by the GNU General Public License, and you are
welcome to change it and/or distribute copies of it under certain conditions.
Type "show copying" to see the conditions.
There is absolutely no warranty for GDB.  Type "show warranty" for details.
This GDB was configured as "i386-linux"...Using host libthread_db library
"/lib/tls/libthread_db.so.1".
```

Then start UM Linux, passing the debug parameter (it will otherwise be difficult to debug due to the way that UM Linux uses signal handlers for internal interrupts – this option changes the default behavior of UM Linux so that it uses an alternative mechanism for communicating with itself):

```
(gdb) run debug
Starting program: /home/jcm/linux-2.6.18/linux debug
'debug' is not necessary to gdb UML in skas mode - run
```

```
'gdb linux' and disable CONFIG_CMDLINE_ON_HOST if gdb
doesn't work as expected
Checking that ptrace can change system call numbers...OK
Checking syscall emulation patch for ptrace...missing
Checking for tmpfs mount on /dev/shm...OK
Checking PROT_EXEC mmap in /dev/shm/...OK
Checking for the skas3 patch in the host:
  - /proc/mm...not found
  - PTRACE_FAULTINFO...not found
  - PTRACE_LDT...not found
UML running in SKAS0 mode

Program received signal SIGUSR1, User defined signal 1.
0x40043b41 in kill () from /lib/tls/libc.so.6
```

Try inserting a breakpoint at the beginning of the higher level C startup code present in all Linux kernels. To do this, set a breakpoint at the start_kernel function.

You can trace through kernel startup, following start_kernel:

```
(gdb) break start_kernel
Breakpoint 1 at 0x80493fd: file init/main.c, line 461.
(gdb) continue
Continuing.

Breakpoint 1, start_kernel () at init/main.c:461
461             smp_setup_processor_id();
```

You can, of course, do a great many more powerful things than simply trace kernel startup. By running the kernel under a debugger, you're able to insert breakpoints and exploit the full power of GDB and all without the need for expensive hardware debuggers running on real machines. You are encouraged to spend some time with UM Linux as you experiment more with extending and enhancing the kernel.

An Anecdotal Word

An interesting anecdotal point to this chapter was that this book helped to find a bug in the kernel. The book manuscript was written using the Open Office text editor, but some post-processing work was done using special Microsoft Word templates running within Microsoft Word on a CrossOver office installation (CrossOver is a commercial version of wine, the Free windows emulator, which allows various Windows applications to run within a graphical Linux environment without modification).

It turns out that Microsoft Office likes to open the sound device (for whatever reason) when it is loaded. Wine happily obliges by emulating the Windows API calls and passing through the results to the Word application, at least, that's what should happen. What actually happened was that the sound card driver would attempt to initialize its non-existent MIDI interface and get very unhappy when it learned that it didn't actually have one installed. This lead to a hard lockup every time Microsoft Word was loaded.

Hard lockups are one of the worst kind of kernel problem. They happen spontaneously, there's little you can do about them (except reboot, or perhaps try out some of the newer Linux kernel deadlock detect patchsets) and you probably won't have a lot of useful logs afterward. Still, with a little careful thought and a few well placed printk statements, it is possible to figure out what the kernel was doing right before it crashed. Once the problem was isolated, fixing the sound card driver didn't take long.

Now, it's possible load Microsoft Windows applications without having system crashes.

A Note about In-Kernel Debuggers

"I don't think kernel development should be 'easy'. I do not condone single-stepping through code to find the bug. I do not think that extra visibility into the system is necessarily a good thing".

When Linus Torvalds (the creator of the Linux kernel) wrote the above a few years ago, he was repeating a point he has made many times before – that he considers kernel debuggers to be more harmful than they are good, in many situations. His view appears to be that kernel developers should know the code inside out and should not need a debugger – they should be able to feel with their gut instinct where a bug might be with only a few helpful hints (such as an oops report) to guide them.

More importantly, kernel debuggers usually alter the environment in which the kernel is operating. Because they make changes to the way the kernel works, there is a valid argument that the debugger could introduce problems where none exist, or could cause an error to go otherwise undetected due to the unique set of circumstances in which it would otherwise occur. The apparent unlikeliness of this occurring aside, there are cases where using a debugger can adversely alter that which is debugged.

Of course, not everybody agrees with the philosophy that there should be no kernel debuggers. While it is commendable that someone such as Linus could be smart enough to figure out these problems with minimal assistance, many other people feel that a debugger would be of considerable use to them. For this reason, a variety of third party patches and projects exist to modify the kernel such that it can be debugged remotely using, for example, GDB over the network, a null modem cable or even FireWire.

> *Note that in-kernel debuggers for Linux are non-standard, so they are not covered in this Linux book. You can, however, find a great deal of information available on the Internet about projects such as KGDB. These projects, written by third parties, generally provide the necessary functionality.*

Summary

In this chapter, you learned about debugging applications on Linux systems. You learned about GDB and its graphical front-ends in the form of DDD, Eclipse, and other projects besides. You also learned about certain types of typical bug that can occur on Linux systems and saw a simple debugging session in progress. Finally, you learned a little about kernel debugging, deciphering and filing oopses, and the reasons for the lack of a full Linux kernel debugger being built right into the Linux kernel itself.

You should now feel equipped to learn more about tools such as GDB in your own time.

11

The GNOME Developer Platform

You are probably familiar or at least acquainted with the popular GNOME desktop environment. Often seen as a competitor to the similarly popular K Desktop Environment (KDE), GNOME is one of the flagship open source projects and one of the best ways to make GNU/Linux systems usable by the average person.

The desktop environment is based upon a stack of libraries known as the *GNOME Developer Platform*; the applications such as the panel, session manager, and web browser, which form the user's experience of GNOME are known as the *GNOME Desktop*. Both Platform and Desktop are released simultaneously on a strict every-six-month schedule, so the development philosophy is generally one of incremental improvement instead of radical change and rewriting. Some libraries usually considered as part of the Platform are not released on this schedule — Glib and GTK+ are developed on their own schedule, as they are not a part of the GNOME Project even though they share many core developers.

This chapter explores the GNOME Developer Platform by building a simple music player application using only libraries found within the Platform. By the end of the chapter, you should have a good starting point for further exploration of the libraries and the development of new GNOME applications. To assist you, a number of possible improvements to the music player will be presented, which will require some research to discover the appropriate solutions for. It is assumed that you have a basic understanding of object-oriented programming.

Before beginning to code, it is worthwhile to take a look at some of the most important libraries in the GNOME Developer Platform.

GNOME Libraries

There are lots of libraries available for the GNOME system. The trick to successful GNOME program-ming is using just the libraries you need to support your application. The GNOME libraries interact in a layered manner — lower-level core libraries provide an interface to the GNOME Desktop, and a founda-tion for the higher-level graphical libraries to build on.

This section shows the GNOME libraries used to create the music player application. The libraries pre-sented here each build upon some or all of those mentioned before it. A developer working with the GNOME Platform can use only those libraries considered necessary, although for full integration with the GNOME Desktop, a more significant number may be required.

Glib

The core of the GNOME Platform is Glib. Essentially a "booster" to the C standard library, Glib provides a selection of portable data types useful in many programs, such as Unicode strings and linked lists. It also offers basic algorithms, and portable methods for tasks such as the construction of filesystem paths, parsing command line options and determining the user's home directory.

Glib was originally part of GTK+ but was split into a separate library to allow it to be used in programs that don't require a GUI.

GObject

GObject builds on Glib to provide a capable single-inheritance object-orientation system in C. While the implementation of the library is complex, and the creation of new classes is not comparable in ease even to C++, the use of GObject-based libraries is generally consistent and straightforward. GObject is built in its own library, but is distributed in the same package as Glib.

Some of the complexity of GObject is due to one of its design principles: it should be easy to create bind-ings for GObject-based libraries in any language. As a result, most of the GNOME platform libraries have bindings for a large number of languages, including C++, C# (and the rest of the .NET languages), Perl, Python, Ruby, and Haskell. These bindings are able to take full advantage of the language's native object orientation and memory management features.

Cairo

A graphics library with an API modeled after PostScript's drawing model, Cairo offers a relatively easy way to draw high-quality, resolution-independent graphics on any output device. It has multiple output back ends, allowing straightforward drawing to the screen using Xlib or the Windows graphics model, or generation of PostScript or PDF for printing. Cairo applications are, therefore, largely independent of platform with regard to their drawing code.

An interesting work in progress is the Glitz back end for Cairo on Linux, which implements all drawing operations using hardware-accelerated Open GL commands. This offers the potential to greatly speed up complex graphics across the GNOME desktop on the many modern desktop systems with 3-D graph-ics hardware available.

GDK

GDK (The GIMP Drawing Kit) is the graphics library used by GTK+ to draw its widgets. It is packaged as part of GTK+ itself, and so is not suitable for standalone use. Since GTK+ 2.8, GDK has been implemented on top of Cairo, and Cairo drawing commands are now preferred where applications need to draw their own graphics.

Pango

Pango is a sophisticated text-rendering system for laying out text in a multitude of international languages. It is used by GTK+ to render all text within the user interface, and also supports various screen display enhancements such as antialiasing and subpixel rendering. Pango relies on other libraries such as Freetype and Fontconfig to provide the actual glyph generation and font selection; its own code is primarily concerned with text layout.

GTK+

The original GTK library was developed for the GIMP (GNU Image Manipulation Program) image editor project, which needed a toolkit with a free license to replace the commercial Motif toolkit that the project initially used and which was deemed unsuitable. GTK+, which stands for *GIMP Tool Kit*, was the eventual product of this effort and was so successful on its own that it became a separate project and was chosen as the basis of the GNOME Desktop. Since then it has been extensively developed, most significantly with the development of GTK+ 2.0. Since 2.0, all releases of GTK+ have been API and ABI-compatible, allowing library upgrades without breaking existing applications — although many newer applications require features only added in more recent versions of GTK+. This policy will not change until at least the development of GTK+ 3.0, a milestone which is not currently on the developers' roadmap. The current GTK+ API is largely successful, so compatible API additions are expected to be sufficient for some time to come.

Major features of GTK+ include its mostly straightforward GObject-based API, a comprehensive selection of available widgets, full Unicode support, and a high level of portability. It has been designed to be easily bound by other languages, and there are mature and successful GTK+ bindings for many languages, including gtkmm for C++, GTK# for C# and .NET/Mono, ruby-gtk for Ruby, and even a GTK+ binding for PHP.

Although there are GNOME-specific UI libraries such as `libgnomeui`, GTK+ provides the bulk of the widgets used in any GNOME application, and this proportion is increasing as the developers attempt to move all generally applicable widgets into GTK+ in order to simplify the platform stack.

As an aid to consistency of the user interface and to internationalization, GTK+ provides a wide selection of stock items: icons, text, and suitable accelerator keys that can be used to construct common entries on menus and toolbars that automatically follow the current theme and language settings. While the rest of the application still need to be translated, stock items handle a lot of common cases easily and help to ensure consistency of the user interfaces of GNOME applications.

libglade

libglade is a library to assist in the construction of user interfaces. It reads XML files produced by the Glade interface design application and uses them to build the application user interface at runtime, avoiding the necessity of writing large amounts of code to build the interfaces for complex applications. It also makes it easier to alter the interface during development, as adjustments to layout can be easily made within Glade with no change to the application code, except where widgets directly manipulated by code are changed.

Due to its extreme utility and popularity, libglade is expected to be incorporated into the forthcoming 2.10 release of GTK+. The beginnings of this work can already be seen in the GtkUIManager class introduced in GTK+ 2.6, which allows the construction of menu systems based on XML descriptions.

GConf

GConf is GNOME's centralized configuration system. Somewhat akin to the Windows Registry, it stores a database of configuration keys which applications may use to save their settings and other information. The default presentation of this information is as a tree of XML files on disk, with system-wide defaults located typically in /usr/share on a GNU/Linux system, and each user's settings in his or her own home directory. These files are not intended to be user-editable, although if necessary they can be modified with a text editor.

The primary means of accessing GConf is through the library's API as used by applications, although there is also a Configuration Editor application provided with the GNOME Desktop. GConf should only be used for storing small pieces of information — if your application requires the storage of large data, use your own datafiles instead.

GConf also provides facilities for administrators to lock down certain application preferences, a useful feature in large multiuser deployments such as within a business. Applications using the GConf-based configuration can support these facilities without the necessity of writing large amounts of code.

GStreamer

A streaming multimedia framework, GStreamer is the basis for GNOME's sound and video handling. GStreamer handles each sound clip or video frame as an individual element. GStreamer is based around the idea of assembling the provided elements into pipelines for processing. Each pipeline provides the necessary processing steps to play the sound clip or display the video frame.

GStreamer allows programmers to easily build video or audio playback into their applications, with a wide range of codecs and output devices supported. Media encoding, transcoding and other tasks are also possible. Elements are also available for detecting filetypes, reading metadata, and introducing effects.

At the time of writing, the latest stable GStreamer version is the 0.10 series, used in this chapter and in the GNOME 2.14 release. GStreamer is not yet API-stable, so the code shown here may need modification as GStreamer moves towards an eventual 1.0 release and a stable API.

Building a Music Player

Our example application for this chapter is a simple music player. While only capable of opening and playing one file at a time, the completed program features filetype detection, artist and title metadata reading, and the ability to seek within tracks. It demonstrates basic GTK+ programming ideas, and the use of the standard FileChooser and About dialogs. At the end of the chapter are several suggestions for improvements to the music player, which may prove a useful starting point for those wishing to learn more about GTK+ programming.

Requirements

To begin, we need GTK+ and GStreamer installed, along with their dependencies. Most Linux distributions provide packages, and the source code is readily available with a standard GNU autotools build procedure. The code in this chapter requires GTK+ 2.8.0 or greater, as it uses some features introduced for the 2.8 series; and GStreamer 0.10.0 or later API-compatible version, and some appropriate GStreamer plugins for media playback—exactly which plugins will vary depending on the format of available media files, and the system's sound drives, but the `gst-plugins-good` package should provide everything necessary for playback of Ogg Vorbis files on most systems.

Changes may be made to the GStreamer API for version 0.11 and later, but it is unlikely that the core concepts will change, so consultation of updated GStreamer documentation should allow the code here to be adapted.

Users of distributions with binary packages will need to ensure that they have any necessary GTK+ and GStreamer development packages installed. On many distributions installing the packages `gtk+-devel` and `gstreamer-devel` should suffice.

Getting Started: The Main Window

The best way to explain the basic principles behind GTK+ programming is with sample code. Create a directory for the music player project to live in, and edit a new file called `main.h`, which should contain the following:

```
#ifndef MAIN_H
#define MAIN_H

#include <gtk/gtk.h>

#endif
```

This does very little other than including the global GTK+ header file, which imports declarations for all classes and functions in the GTK+ toolkit. An alternate approach would be to include only those parts of the toolkit required at any time; large projects with many source files may take that approach, as it can reduce compilation times if not much of the toolkit is being used.

Now create `main.c`. The code below is enough to create and display an empty window:

```c
#include "main.h"

static GtkWidget *main_window;

static void
destroy(GtkWidget *widget, gpointer data)
{
  gtk_main_quit();
}

int main(int argc, char *argv[]) {
  /* Initialise GTK+ */
  gtk_init(&argc, &argv);

  /* Create a window */
  main_window = gtk_window_new(GTK_WINDOW_TOPLEVEL);

  /* Set main window title */
  gtk_window_set_title(GTK_WINDOW(main_window), "Music Player");

  /* Connect the main window's destroy handler */
  g_signal_connect(G_OBJECT(main_window), "destroy",
    G_CALLBACK(destroy), NULL);

  /* Make everything visible */
  gtk_widget_show_all(GTK_WIDGET(main_window));

  /* Start the main loop */
  gtk_main();

  return 0;
}
```

This is almost the minimal code for a GTK+ application. A few concepts specific to the toolkit are introduced here. `gtk_init()` sets up the library and processes command line arguments which GTK+ knows about, modifying the `argc` and `argv` variables so that the application programmer does not have to worry about arguments that have already been handled.

The window itself is created with `gtk_window_new()`. This is an object constructor, which returns a pointer to a new `GtkWindow` object. The naming convention is important, as it is followed by all object constructors and methods in GTK+ - the first part of the name is the class name, here `GtkWindow` (written for a function as `gtk_window` to distinguish it from the class data type itself), followed by the method name. `gtk_window_new()` takes a single parameter, which is a constant specifying the type of window to create. `GTK_WINDOW_TOPLEVEL` is a normal application window that can be closed, minimized, and resized by the window manager.

`gtk_window_set_title()`, a method of `GtkWindow`, sets the window's title as you might expect. With all nonconstructor methods, the first parameter must be an object of an appropriate type — either an instance of the class that the method is part of or an instance of a class that inherits from the method's class. `main_window` is a `GtkWindow` object, so it may be passed directly to `gtk_window_set_title()`. The macro `GTK_WINDOW()` ensures that what the function sees really is a `GtkWindow` object, and raises an error if it cannot perform the appropriate conversion. In this case, the macro is not necessary, but it would be if we wished to use this method to set the title of a `GtkDialog`.

All classes have such conversion macros, and they are used extensively in all GTK+ code.

`g_signal_connect()` sets up a signal handler. A fundamental concept in the design of the GTK+ toolkit is that of signals and callbacks — callbacks being functions which are called when the signal to which they are connected is emitted. Signals exist for such events as buttons being clicked, the mouse being moved, keyboard focus changing, and many other things. Here, the signal in question is the "destroy" signal of `GtkWindow`, which is emitted when X indicates that the window should close — such as when the user presses the close button in the title bar. Connecting it to the `destroy()` function ensures that closing this window will cause the program to quit, as `destroy` simply calls `gtk_main_quit()`, which does what you might expect.

`gtk_main()` begins the GTK+ main loop. This blocks until the main loop finishes, and any further interaction between the user and the application code happens through the calling of signal handlers.

Compilation

To compile the code, create a `Makefile` that uses the program `pkg-config` to get the correct compiler and linker flags for GTK+ and GStreamer:

```
CFLAGS=`pkg-config --cflags gtk+-2.0 gstreamer-0.10`
LIBS=`pkg-config --libs gtk+-2.0 gstreamer-0.10`

all: player

player: main.o
    gcc -o player main.o $(LIBS)

%.o: %.c
    gcc -g -c $< $(CFLAGS)
```

Compile the program and run the resulting executable "player." Closing the window should cause the program to terminate in accordance with the "destroy" signal handler.

Building the GUI

Now you have a window, but it is of little use without some other widgets to provide a useful user interface. Windows in GTK+ are a subclass of `GtkBin`, which is a container object that may contain one child widget. This may not sound very useful, but GTK+ provides a variety of other subclasses of `GtkBin`, which can contain multiple widgets. A window layout in GTK+ is, therefore, always constructed by one multiple-widget container being added to a `GtkWindow`. The most useful of these containers are `GtkVBox`, `GtkHBox`, and `GtkTable`. `GtkVBox` allows an arbitrary number of widgets to be stacked vertically. `GtkHBox` is the same, but provides horizontal alignment. `GtkTable` is a combination of the two, allowing widgets to be laid out on a flexible grid.

These three layout widgets provide almost all layout functionality necessary. It is important to note that GTK+ rarely deals with absolute positions or sizes of objects — containers and the widgets within them will be resized to fit the available space. The user may, however, alter the constraints on such sizing to gain the desired effect, and `GtkFixed` is available as a last resort if precise pixel layouts are required.

The flexible box model layout is preferred, as it copes more readily with different screen sizes and the variety of themes which users may be using.

The final result of the GUI construction will look something like Figure 11-1

Figure 11-1

Figure 11-1 shows the music player's window before a file has been loaded for playback. From the top down, observe a menu bar, labels for title and artist metadata, a label showing the current state of the player next to a label showing the elapsed time, then a slider for seeking through the current file, and finally three buttons for controlling playback. This screenshot represents the ClearLooks GTK+ theme, which is the default in GNOME 2.14. Customizations by GNOME packagers and end users may cause the window to look different on other systems, but the basic layout will not change.

The Top-Level Container

The top-level container of the window layout will be a GtkVBox, as the window may be seen as a series of widgets stacked atop each other. You will need to add some new global variables for widgets that will be created and referred later.

```
static GtkWidget *play_button;
static GtkWidget *pause_button;
static GtkWidget *stop_button;
static GtkWidget *status_label;
static GtkWidget *time_label;
static GtkWidget *seek_scale;
static GtkWidget *title_label;
static GtkWidget *artist_label;
```

Add a function above main() that will construct the GUI:

```
GtkWidget *build_gui() {
  GtkWidget *main_vbox;
  GtkWidget *status_hbox;
  GtkWidget *controls_hbox;

  /* Create the main GtkVBox. Everything else will go inside here */
  main_vbox = gtk_vbox_new(0, 6);
```

Here a GtkVBox is created. The parameters affect how widgets are packed into the box. The first indicates if widgets within the box must all be the same height, a false value indicating that the widgets may have different heights depending on their requirements. The second parameter is the spacing in pixels between the widgets. Six pixels is the spacing recommended in the *GNOME Human Interface Guidelines*.

Text Labels

You should now add the labels which will display the title and artist names from the song metadata:

```
title_label = gtk_label_new("Title");
gtk_misc_set_alignment(GTK_MISC(title_label), 0.0, 0.5);
gtk_box_pack_start(GTK_BOX(main_vbox), title_label, FALSE, FALSE, 0);
```

GtkMisc is one of GtkLabel's parent classes, and contains the mechanism by which you can control the alignment of the text within the GtkLabel. The alignment parameters range from 0 to 1, and in this case mean full left (0.0), and vertically centered (0.5). The default is for horizontal and vertical centering (0.5, 0.5), which does not look good in this window layout.

gtk_box_pack_start() instructs the main GtkVBox to pack the title_label in from the start (i.e., the top) of the box, although it is packed after any widgets that were previously packed using pack_start. gtk_box_pack_end(), which is not used in this chapter, packs from the opposite direction, and is of use if you wish to pack widgets in such a way that the widgets separate somewhere in the middle of the container when the enclosing container is expanded.

The final three parameters of gtk_box_pack_start() — and indeed gtk_box_pack_end() — indicate the way the packed widget should be allocated space. The first of these three parameters is called *expand* and affects the widget spacing: if extra space should be allocated to the box in which the widget is contained, expand says whether or not this widget's segment of the containing box should be given some of that space or not. Extra space is divided evenly between all segments with expand set to TRUE. The second value is called *fill*, and in situations were extra space has been allocated to the widget's segment, indicates if the widget should grow to fill that space, or whether the space should be used for padding. The third parameter gives the number of pixels of padding that should be maintained between this widget's segment and its neighbor.

The artist label is created in a similar manner:

```
artist_label = gtk_label_new("Artist");
gtk_misc_set_alignment(GTK_MISC(artist_label), 0.0, 0.5);
gtk_box_pack_start(GTK_BOX(main_vbox), artist_label, FALSE, FALSE, 0);
```

There are two more labels: one to show the status of the player and one to show the elapsed time of the current track. Because these are both short, place them side by side in a GtkHBox:

```
status_hbox = gtk_hbox_new(TRUE, 0);
```

Note that for this box the widgets should be equally sized, so you pass TRUE to the constructor. Extra spacing is not required in this case.

```
gtk_box_pack_start(GTK_BOX(main_vbox), status_hbox(FALSE, FALSE, 0);

status_label = gtk_label_new("<b>Stopped</b>");
gtk_label_set_use_markup(GTK_LABEL(status_label), TRUE);
gtk_misc_set_alignment(GTK_MISC(status_label), 0.0, 0.5);
gtk_box_pack_start(GTK_BOX(status_hbox), status_label, TRUE, TRUE, 0);
```

By now, you should see the attraction of using `libglade` for the GUI instead of hand-coding. For a project this size it is acceptable, but it quickly becomes difficult for larger applications. Note that in this code the label's text contains HTML-style markup. After calling `gtk_label_set_use_markup()`, this allows bold text to be displayed in a label very easily.

An alternative method to achieve the bold text would be to modify the label's font style, but when you only wish to change one attribute this seems unnecessarily complex. It would, though, free you of the need to include the bold markup every time you set the label's text, and is definitely to be recommended when multiple font attributes need to be changed but will remain constant during the lifetime of the program. Markup excels where the formatting requirements will change often compared to the updates of the label's text, and also allows the label to display multiple font styles for different parts of its contents.

```
time_label = gtk_label_new("--:--.--");
gtk_misc_set_alignment(GTK_MISC(time_label), 1.0, 0.5);
gtk_box_pack_start(GTK_BOX(status_hbox), time_label, TRUE, TRUE, 0);
```

The only new thing in this code is to note that the alignment of `time_label` has been set to right-justify the text, rather than left justification as we have done so far. This is because the label will need to appear to sit flush with the right-hand side of the window.

The Slider Control

The next widget to add to the GUI is the slider used for seeking and showing progress through the track. This is provided by a `GtkHScale` widget (as you might expect, `GtkVScale` is also available). These widgets are subclasses of `GtkScale`, where most of the scale-specific methods can be found, and that in turn is a subclass of `GtkRange`, which contains other useful functionality relating to maintaining a range with minimum and maximum extents and a current position.

```
seek_scale = gtk_hscale_new_with_range(0, 100, 1);
gtk_scale_set_draw_value(GTK_SCALE(seek_scale), FALSE);
gtk_range_set_update_policy(GTK_RANGE(seek_scale),
  GTK_UPDATE_DISCONTINUOUS);
gtk_box_pack_start(GTK_BOX(main_vbox), seek_scale, FALSE, FALSE, 0);
```

The `HScale` and its sibling the `VScale` have a number of different constructors. The one chosen here builds the widget with the given range; another constructor uses the default range, and a third is available that associates the widget with an existing `GtkRange` object. Here, a range from 0 to 100 is used, which will allow progress through the current track to be expressed as a percentage, removing the need to change the range parameters when a track of a different length is opened. The third parameter indicates the granularity of the range — here one unit is quite suitable.

`gtk_scale_set_draw_value()` is used to ask the scale widget not to draw a numeric representation of its current position next to the drag handle. The final setting modified is the widget's update policy, which indicates when a scale will emit a signal indicating that the value has changed after the user has altered it by dragging the slider or otherwise manipulating it. `GTK_UPDATE_DISCONTINUOUS` indicates that a signal will only be emitted once the user has finished dragging. Other options include one that emits signals while the user is dragging, which would be far more suitable for the sliders in a color picker.

The Control Buttons

The final part of the GUI for now is the HBox with the playback control buttons in it.

```
controls_hbox = gtk_hbox_new(TRUE, 6);
gtk_box_pack_start_defaults(GTK_BOX(main_vbox), controls_hbox);
```

gtk_box_pack_start_defaults() simply frees the programmer from the necessity of providing the three sizing and spacing parameters if he or she is happy with the default values, and in this case the default values serve perfectly.

```
play_button = gtk_button_new_from_stock(GTK_STOCK_MEDIA_PLAY);
gtk_widget_set_sensitive(play_button, FALSE);
gtk_box_pack_start_defaults(GTK_BOX(controls_hbox), play_button);
```

Here, you have created your first button. Because GTK+ 2.8 introduced stock items for common media playback functions such as play, pause, and stop, they can be used to build buttons with the correct icons, captions, and tooltips automatically. Even better, stock items will automatically adopt the user's language settings, assuming that the relevant translation files are installed, meaning that you only need to translate any nonstock functions in your application, if you wish to make it localizable. For any large application, this could still be a significant amount of translation, but by using stock items you can ensure that common functionality is at least translated consistently. Stock items also adapt to the user's icon theme preferences, allowing your application to blend in more easily with the surrounding desktop environment.

Here, the button's "sensitive" property is set to FALSE. This causes it to appear "grayed out" and to be unresponsive to clicks or keyboard events. This is a good state for the button to be when the program starts up, as there will be no file available for the user to play until he or she has selected one.

The rest of the buttons are made in a similar manner, although since the pause button is a GtkToggleButton to allow it to stay in a depressed state when paused, GTK+ makes the programmer jump through an extra hoop. In GTK+ 2.8, there is no gtk_toggle_button_new_from_stock() constructor, so instead the button must be constructed with its label being the desired stock ID, and then gtk_button_set_use_stock() (inherited from GtkButton) must be used to set up the button as a stock button. This is the procedure used by the new_from_stock() constructor of GtkButton, which is really just a convenience wrapper.

```
pause_button =
  gtk_toggle_button_new_with_label(GTK_STOCK_MEDIA_PAUSE);
gtk_button_set_use_stock(GTK_BUTTON(pause_button), TRUE);
gtk_widget_set_sensitive(pause_button, FALSE);
gtk_box_pack_start_defaults(GTK_BOX(controls_hbox), pause_button);

stop_button = gtk_button_new_from_stock(GTK_STOCK_MEDIA_STOP);
gtk_widget_set_sensitive(stop_button, FALSE);
g_signal_connect(G_OBJECT(stop_button),
  "clicked",
  G_CALLBACK(stop_clicked),
  NULL);
gtk_box_pack_start_defaults(GTK_BOX(controls_hbox), stop_button);
```

The function is finished off by returning the GtkVBox. GTK+ widgets, like all GObjects, are reference-counted, and since pointers are used to access them, the objects themselves will not be destroyed until the reference count reaches zero. Most of the time, the exact decrement of reference counting is of less importance, as most widgets are destroyed when the application closes anyway. Attention does need to be paid if widgets are being created and destroyed during runtime, as incorrect reference counting can cause memory leaks and segmentation faults.

```
    return main_vbox;
}
```

Add a line to main(), just before the call to gtk_widget_show_all():

```
    gtk_container_add(GTK_CONTAINER(main_window), build_gui());
```

This places the VBox containing the window layout into the window itself. The existing call to gtk_widget_show_all() will make it visible, so compile and run the program, and you should have most of a user interface.

Menus

There's still something missing: a menu bar. Conventional UI design would suggest that a menu bar is useless in a small program such as this, but it is important to demonstrate GTK+'s method for constructing menus.

There are several methods for building menus, but with recent versions of GTK+ the action-based menu and toolbar construction using GtkUIManager objects has become preferred. Somewhat resembling libglade, although on a more limited scope, GtkUIManager generates menu structures from XML provided by the programmer. Each menu item is associated with a GtkAction object, which describes its caption, icon, tooltip, and what to do when it is clicked on. GtkAction objects may also be used to generate toolbar buttons, and this offers considerable convenience when enabled/disabled states of menu and toolbar items must be kept consistent, as altering the enabled state of the GtkAction object automatically updates the state of the corresponding menu and toolbar items.

Then first task then is to describe the actions that we will create menu items for. Just before the build_gui() function definition, add an array of GtkActionEntry structures:

```
static GtkActionEntry mainwindow_action_entries[] = {
  { "FileMenu, "NULL", "_File" },
  {
    "OpenFile",
    GTK_STOCK_OPEN,
    "_Open",
    "<control>O",
    "Open a file for playback",
    G_CALLBACK(file_open)
  },
  {
    "QuitPlayer",
    GTK_STOCK_QUIT,
```

```
      "_Quit",
      "<control>Q",
      "Quit the music player",
      G_CALLBACK(file_quit)
    },
    { "HelpMenu", "NULL", "_Help" },
    {
      "HelpAbout",
      GTK_STOCK_ABOUT,
      "_About",
      "",
      "About the music player",
      G_CALLBACK(help_about)
    }
};
```

Two different kinds of `ActionEntry` are defined here. The first kind represents a menu rather than a menu item — `"FileMenu"` and `"HelpMenu"` in this case. These simply provide captions for the menus. The other items are more detailed, and represent menu items with, respectively, action names, icons, labels, keyboard accelerators, tooltips, and callback functions. In the labels, an underscore before a letter indicates that letter will be underlined when the label is displayed, and it will therefore be the letter used to active the menu item when navigating the menus by keyboard.

Keyboard Shortcuts

The keyboard accelerator is specified using GTK+'s accelerator syntax. In this case, all the accelerators are a simple letter pressed while holding the Control key. Tooltips are simple strings, and the callbacks are no different from the callbacks you have seen already.

Note that these callback specifiers refer to functions that do not exist yet. It will be time to add them soon, but first add two variables to the `build_gui()` function:

```
GtkActionGroup *actiongroup;
GtkUIManager *ui_manager;
```

A `GtkActionGroup` is an object that maintains a set of `GtkActions` used by a `UIManager`. The code to construct the `ActionGroup` and the `UIManager` goes before the code for constructing any other widgets in `build_gui()`, as the menu bar will be placed at the top of the window, and it is helpful for code maintainability to construct widgets and related objects in roughly the order in which they will appear in the window.

```
actiongroup = gtk_action_group_new("MainwindowActiongroup");
gtk_action_group_add_actions(actiongroup,
  mainwindow_action_entries,
  G_N_ELEMENTS(mainwindow_action_entries),
  NULL);

ui_manager = gtk_ui_manager_new();
gtk_ui_manager_insert_action_group(ui_manager, actiongroup, 0);
gtk_ui_manager_add_ui_from_string(ui_manager,
    "<ui>"
    "  <menubar name='MainMenu'>"
```

```
"        <menu action='FileMenu'>"
"          <menuitem action='OpenFile'/>"
"          <separator name='fsep1'/>"
"          <menuitem action='QuitPlayer'/>"
"        </menu>"
"        <menu action='HelpMenu'>"
"          <menuitem action='HelpAbout'/>"
"        </menu>"
"    </menubar>"
"</ui>",
 -1,
 NULL);
```

This should be fairly straightforward, although it looks quite different from the widget construction code that you have seen so far. The GtkActionGroup is initialized with the array created earlier, and then associated with the UI Manager. G_N_ELEMENTS() is a Glib macro that determines the number of elements in an array. The XML description of the user interface is merely a specification of the structure, and what sort of item each action corresponds to. GtkUIManager also provides functions that allow the loading of such structures directly from files.

After the construction of main_vbox, add the menu bar to it:

```
gtk_box_pack_start(
    GTK_BOX(main_vbox),
    gtk_ui_manager_get_widget(ui_manager, "/ui/MainMenu"),
    FALSE, FALSE, 0);
```

GTK+ treats menu bars like any other widget, so you simply pack them into the VBox at the top. The menu bar is retrieved by asking the UI Manager for the widget at a particular path, which is determined from the names given to the items in the XML provided. Using similar paths, any widget built by the UI manager can be requested. This is convenient should you wish to obtain a pointer to one of the menu items in order to modify it manually.

At this point, you may have noticed the similarity between defining menu structure in XML as seen here and the description of libglade at the start of the chapter. GtkUIManager can be thought of as representing a starting point for the integration of libglade's functionality into GTK+, something currently intended for GTK+ 2.10.

Callbacks

Obviously, without connecting the UI widgets to some callback functions, the program isn't going to do very much. At this stage full functionality cannot be produced, as there is no sound playback code yet, but the skeletons of the required callbacks can be added and connected up. There is enough present to produce the full implementation of the Help ⇨ About menu item, which is provided below.

The callbacks required by the actions in the menu structure have the return type void, and take one GtkAction pointer as a parameter. When the callback is called, this will be the action that invoked the callback. Using this parameter, a programmer could associate the same callback with multiple actions and have it behave differently depending on which action triggered it.

```
static void file_open(GtkAction *action) {
  /* We will write this function later */
}

static void file_quit(GtkAction *action) {
  gtk_main_quit();
}

static void help_about(GtkAction *action) {
  GtkWidget *about_dialog = gtk_about_dialog_new();

  gtk_about_dialog_set_name(GTK_ABOUT_DIALOG(about_dialog), "Music Player");
  gtk_about_dialog_set_version(GTK_ABOUT_DIALOG(about_dialog), "0.1");
  gtk_about_dialog_set_copyright(GTK_ABOUT_DIALOG(about_dialog), "Copyright 2006,
The Author");

  gtk_dialog_run(GTK_DIALOG(about_dialog));
}
```

In `help_about`, you meet your first `GtkDialog`. `GtkAboutDialog` is a simple object that provides a complete dialog box ideal for "about this application" functions. The application's name, version, and copyright are all set with simple method calls, and then `gtk_dialog_run()` displays it. You will encounter `gtk_dialog_run()` later, when implementing the `file_open()` callback.

```
static void play_clicked(GtkWidget *widget, gpointer data) {
}

static void pause_clicked(GtkWidget *widget, gpointer data) {
}

static void stop_clicked(GtkWidget *widget, gpointer data) {
}
```

These three callbacks provide the functionality for the play, pause, and stop buttons, so go back to `build_gui()` and connect them to the "`clicked`" signals of the buttons.

```
g_signal_connect(G_OBJECT(play_button), "clicked",
  G_CALLBACK(play_clicked), NULL);
g_signal_connect(G_OBJECT(pause_button), "clicked",
  G_CALLBACK(pause_clicked), NULL);
g_signal_connect(G_OBJECT(stop_button), "clicked",
  G_CALLBACK(stop_clicked), NULL);
```

The program should now compile, and if run, the Help ⇨ About menu item should be functional, as should File ⇨ Quit.

Introducing GStreamer

Now that most of the GUI is in place, it is possible to add the ability to actually play music. This functionality will be provided by the GStreamer multimedia framework.

GStreamer operates by requiring application developers to create pipelines. Each pipeline is composed of a number of elements, each of which performs a particular function. Typically, a pipeline will begin with some kind of source element. This could be the element called `filesrc`, which reads files from disk and makes their contents available, or an element that brings buffered data in over a network connection, or even one which retrieves data from a video capture device. There will then typically be a number of other elements, which are likely to be decoders (used to convert sound files into a standard format for processing), demuxers (used to separate multiple sound channels from a sound file), or other such processors. The pipeline finishes with an output element, which could be anything from a file writer to an Advanced Linux Sound Architecture (ALSA) sound output element to an Open GL–based video playback element. These output elements are referred to as "sinks."

Thus a typical pipeline designed for playing Ogg Vorbis audio files from disk using ALSA might contain a `filesrc` element, then a `vorbisdecoder` element, and then an `alsasink`.

Elements are connected together by linking them using "pads." Each pad advertises a set of capabilities, which indicate what the pad is for. Some pads provide data of a particular type — for example, raw data from a file, or decoded audio from a decoder element. Others accept data of a particular type or types, while still others will provide metadata or synchronization information.

To simplify the code that we have to write, we will take advantage of a convenience element provided by GStreamer 0.10 called `playbin`. This is a sophisticated element that is actually a prebuilt pipeline. Using GStreamer's filetype detection, it can read from any given URI and will determine the appropriate decoders and output sinks to play it back correctly. In our case, this means that it should identify and correctly decode any audio file that the GStreamer installation has plugins for (you can get a list of all your GStreamer 0.10 plugins by running gst-inspect-0.10 in a terminal).

You will put all the GStreamer code in another file. Create `playback.h` as follows:

```
#ifndef PLAYBACK_H
#define PLAYBACK_H

#include <gst/gst.h>

gboolean load_file(const gchar *uri);
gboolean play_file();
void stop_playback(void);
void seek_to(gdouble percentage);

#endif
```

This header file provides an interface for `main.c` to call those functions that it needs. Modify `main.c` to include `playback.h`; then create `playback.c`, which should include `playback.h` and `main.h`. Also update the `Makefile` to link `playback.o` into the executable. Then lay out the basis for `playback.c`.

```
#include "main.h"
#include "playback.h"

static GstElement *play = NULL;
static guint timeout_source = 0;

gboolean load_file(const gchar *uri) {
  if (build_gstreamer_pipeline(uri)) return TRUE;
  return FALSE;
}
```

The function `build_gstreamer_pipeline()` takes a URI and constructs a `playbin` element, a pointer to which will be stored in the variable play for later use.

```c
static gboolean build_gstreamer_pipeline(const gchar *uri) {
  /* If there is already a pipeline, destroy it */
  if (play) {
    gst_element_set_state(play, GST_STATE_NULL);
    gst_object_unref(GST_OBJECT(play));
    play = NULL;
  }

  /* Create a playbin element */
  play = gst_element_factory_make("playbin", "play");
  if (!play) return FALSE;
  g_object_set(G_OBJECT(play), "uri", uri, NULL);

  /* Connect the message bus callback */
  gst_bus_add_watch(gst_pipeline_get_bus(GST_PIPELINE(play)), bus_callback, NULL);

  return TRUE;
}
```

Note that this code will not compile, due to the lack of a `bus_callback()` function. This will be attended to momentarily.

`build_gstreamer_pipeline()` is a fairly simple function. It checks if the play variable is not `NULL`, indicating that a `playbin` is already present. If a `playbin` is present, `gst_object_unref()` is used to decrease the `playbin`'s reference count. Since only one reference is held on the `playbin` in this code, decreasing the reference count causes the `playbin` to be destroyed. The pointer is then set to `NULL` to indicate that no `playbin` is currently available.

The construction of the `playbin` element happens with a call to `gst_element_factory_make()`, which is a general-purpose construction function capable of constructing any GStreamer element. Its first parameter is the name of the element to construct. GStreamer uses string names to identify element types to facilitate the addition of new elements — a program may, if required, accept element names from a configuration file or from the user and make use of new elements without need of recompilation to include header files for them. Provided that the specified elements have the correct capabilities (and this may be checked in code at runtime), they will operate perfectly with no code changes being required. In this case, you construct a `playbin` element, and give it a name, `play`, which is the second parameter to `gst_element_factory_make()`. The name is not used in the rest of the program, but it does have a use in identifying elements in complicated pipelines.

The code then checks that the pointer received from `gst_element_factory_make()` is valid, indicating that the element was correctly constructed. If it is, `g_object_set()` allows the standard `GObject` property `uri` of the `playbin` element to be set to the supplied URI of the file to play. Properties are used extensively by Gstreamer elements to configure their behavior, and the set of available properties will vary among elements.

Finally, `gst_bus_add_watch()` connects a callback function that watches the pipeline's message bus. GStreamer uses a message bus for pipelines to communicate with their applications. By providing this, pipelines that run in a different thread — such as playbin — may communicate information to the application without the application author needing to worry about cross-thread data synchronization issues. A similar encapsulation allows messages and commands to flow the other way.

This callback function does, of course, need to be defined to be of any use. When called, GStreamer provides it with the GstBus object for which the callback has been triggered, a GstMessage object containing the message being sent, and a user-supplied pointer, which in this case is not used.

```
static gboolean bus_callback (GstBus *bus,
  GstMessage *message, gpointer data)
{
  switch (GST_MESSAGE_TYPE (message)) {
    case GST_MESSAGE_ERROR: {
      GError *err;
      gchar *debug;

      gst_message_parse_error(message, &err, &debug);
      g_print("Error: %s\n", err->message);
      g_error_free(err);
      g_free(debug);

      gtk_main_quit();
      break;
    }
```

The error-handling routine is straightforward: it simply prints the error message and terminates the program. In a more sophisticated application, a more intelligent error-handling technique would be used based on the exact nature of the error encountered. The error message itself is an example of a GError object, a generic error description object provided by Glib.

```
    case GST_MESSAGE_EOS:
      stop_playback();
      break;
```

EOS is the message that indicates that the pipeline has reached the end of the current stream. In this case, it calls the stop_playback() function, which is defined below.

```
    case GST_MESSAGE_TAG: {
      /* The stream discovered new tags. */
      break;
    }
```

The TAG message indicates that GStreamer has encountered metadata in the stream, such as title or artist information. This case will also be implemented later, although it is of little importance to the task of actually playing a file.

```
    default:
      /* Another message occurred which we are not interested in
       * handling. */
      break;
  }
```

The default case simply ignores any message that is not handled explicitly. GStreamer generates numerous messages, only a few of which are useful in a simple audio playback such as this.

```
    return TRUE;
}
```

Finally the function returns TRUE, which indicates that it has handled the message and no further action need be taken.

To complete this function, you need to define stop_playback(), which will set the state of the GStreamer pipeline and clean up appropriately. To understand it, you will first need to define the function play_file(), which does more or less what you would expect:

```
gboolean play_file() {

  if (play) {
    gst_element_set_state(play, GST_STATE_PLAYING);
```

The element state GST_STATE_PLAYING indicates a pipeline which is playing. Changing the state to this starts the pipeline playing, and is a no-op if playback was already in progress. States control whether a pipeline is actually processing a stream or not, and so you will also encounter states such as GST_STATE_PAUSED, the functionality of which should be self-explanatory.

```
      timeout_source = g_timeout_add(200,
        (GSourceFunc)update_time_callback, play);
```

g_timeout_add() is a Glib function that adds a timeout handler in the Glib main loop. The callback function update_time_callback will be called every 200 milliseconds, with the pointer play as a parameter. This function is used to retrieve the progress of the playback and update the GUI appropriately. g_timeout_add() returns a numeric ID for the timeout function, which can be used to remove or modify it later.

```
    return TRUE;
  }

  return FALSE;
}
```

The function returns TRUE to show that the playback started or FALSE if the playback did not start.

Barring the lack of definition of update_time_callback(), stop_playback() may now be defined, giving the program the ability to start and stop the playback of files — although as yet the GUI is not capable of providing a file URI to the playback code.

```
void stop_playback() {
  if (timeout_source) g_source_remove(timeout_source);
  timeout_source = 0;
```

This uses the saved timeout ID to remove the timeout from the main loop, as it is not desirable to have the update function called five times per second when no playback is taking place, and there is, thus, no need for it.

```
if (play) {
    gst_element_set_state(play, GST_STATE_NULL);
    gst_object_unref(GST_OBJECT(play));
    play = NULL;
  }
}
```

The pipeline is deactivated and destroyed. GST_STATE_NULL causes the pipeline to stop playing and reset itself, freeing any resources it might be holding, such as playback buffers or file handles on the sound devices.

The callback function for updating the GUI's idea of time uses gst_element_query_position() and gst_element_query_duration(). These two methods allow an element's position and the stream's duration to be retrieved in a specified format. Here, the standard GStreamer time format is used. This is a high-resolution integer showing the precise position in the stream.

The two methods return if they are successful, and place the values in the addresses provided. To format the time into a string for display to the user, g_snprintf() is used. This is the Glib version of snprintf(), provided to ensure portability across systems which may not have snprintf(). GST_TIME_ARGS() is a macro that converts a position into suitable arguments for use with printf()-style functions.

```
static gboolean update_time_callback(GstElement *pipeline) {
  GstFormat fmt = GST_FORMAT_TIME;
  gint64 position;
  gint64 length;
  gchar time_buffer[25];

  if (gst_element_query_position(pipeline, &fmt, &position)
      && gst_element_query_duration(pipeline, &fmt, &length))
  {
    g_snprintf(time_buffer, 24,
      "%u:%02u.%02u", GST_TIME_ARGS(position));
    gui_update_time(time_buffer, position, length);
  }

  return TRUE;
}
```

This function also calls a new function, gui_update_time(). Add this to the GUI code in main.c, with a suitable declaration in main.h to allow the code in playback.c to call it. It simply takes the formatted time string and the position and length, and updates the widgets in the GUI appropriately.

```
void gui_update_time(const gchar *time,
  const gint64 position, const gint64 length)
{
  gtk_label_set_text(GTK_LABEL(time_label), time);
```

```
    if (length > 0) {
      gtk_range_set_value(GTK_RANGE(seek_scale),
        ((gdouble)position / (gdouble)length) * 100.0);
    }
  }
```

Needless to say, there are some other things that should be updated in the GUI when events in the playback engine occur. To ensure that all this code stays close together, write the function gui_status_update():

```
void gui_status_update(PlayerState state) {
  switch (state) {
    case STATE_STOP:
      gtk_widget_set_sensitive(GTK_WIDGET(stop_button), FALSE);
      gtk_widget_set_sensitive(GTK_WIDGET(pause_button), FALSE);
      gtk_label_set_markup(GTK_LABEL(status_label), "<b>Stopped</b>");
      gtk_range_set_value(GTK_RANGE(seek_scale), 0.0);
      gtk_label_set_text(GTK_LABEL(time_label), "--:--.--");
      break;
    case STATE_PLAY:
      gtk_widget_set_sensitive(GTK_WIDGET(stop_button), TRUE);
      gtk_widget_set_sensitive(GTK_WIDGET(pause_button), TRUE);
      gtk_label_set_markup(GTK_LABEL(status_label), "<b>Playing</b>");
      break;
    case STATE_PAUSE:
      gtk_label_set_markup(GTK_LABEL(status_label), "<b>Paused</b>");
      break;
    default:
      break;
  }
}
```

Responding to each of the three states STOP, PAUSE, and PLAY, this function simply sets the state of various parts of the GUI appropriately. The only new method used is gtk_label_set_markup(), which changes a label's text and ensures that the use_markup property of the label is switched on. Add a declaration for gui_status_update() to main.h, and place calls to it in the appropriate places in playback.c where playback starts and stops.

Opening Files

The code is now almost read to begin playback; all that remains is to give the user the ability to choose which file he or she wishes to play. For this, the obvious choice is the GtkFileChooserDialog widget, a complete dialog box that allows the opening and saving of files. It also has a mode for opening directories; in the example, you only need to open files.

```
static void file_open(GtkAction *action) {
  GtkWidget *file_chooser = gtk_file_chooser_dialog_new(
      "Open File", GTK_WINDOW(main_window),
      GTK_FILE_CHOOSER_ACTION_OPEN,
      GTK_STOCK_CANCEL, GTK_RESPONSE_CANCEL,
      GTK_STOCK_OPEN, GTK_RESPONSE_ACCEPT,
      NULL);
```

This constructor deserves some explanation. The first parameter is the title to use for the window that will be shown to the user. The second parameter is the window that the dialog will specify as its parent, which helps the window manager to layout and link windows correctly. In this case, the obvious parent window is main_window—the only other window in the application and also the window from which the command to display the FileChooserDialog is invoked. GTK_FILE_CHOOSER_ACTION_OPEN indicates that the FileChooser should allow the user to choose a file to open. Specifying a different action here could have dramatically altered the appearance and functionality of the dialog, as GNOME save dialogs (GTK_FILE_CHOOSER_ACTION_SAVE) differ quite substantially to their counterparts for opening files.

The next four parameters are the buttons to use in the dialog, and their *response IDs*, ordered from left to right as they appear on a system running with a left-to-right language such as English (GTK+ automatically inverts some window layouts in right-to-left locales). This ordering is consistent with the *GNOME Human Interface Guidelines* as the code first specifies a stock "cancel" button, then a stock "open" button. The final parameter indicates that there are no more buttons to follow.

Response IDs are important, as these are the values that are returned when the buttons are pressed. Because the dialog will be called with gtk_dialog_run(), the program blocks until the dialog returns— that is, until the user closes it by choosing one of the buttons or pressing a keyboard accelerator, which performs the equivalent function.

Nonmodal dialogs may also be implemented by remembering that GtkDialog is a subclass of the familiar GtkWindow, and by handling some events—the button clicks in particular—manually. The returned value from gtk_dialog_run() is the response ID of the activated button (GTK_RESPONSE_ACCEPT is considered by GTK+ to be the response ID of the default button, and so the button with that response ID becomes the button that is triggered by the user pressing Enter). Therefore, the code for opening a file need only be run if the dialog returns GTK_RESPONSE_ACCEPT:

```
if (gtk_dialog_run(GTK_DIALOG(file_chooser)) == GTK_RESPONSE_ACCEPT)
{
  char *filename;
  filename = gtk_file_chooser_get_uri(GTK_FILE_CHOOSER(file_chooser));
```

Because it is known that the user selected a file, the URI of that file can be retrieved from the FileChooser widget contained in the FileChooserDialog. We could retrieve only its UNIX file path, but since playbin expects a URI, it is far easier to stick to the same format throughout. Note that this URI might not be a file://—with GNOME present on the system, GTK+'s FileChooser will use GNOME libraries to enhance its capabilities, including gnome-vfs, the virtual filesystem layer. Therefore, GtkFileChooser may in some circumstances be capable of providing URIs to documents hosted on network shares or inside other files. A truly gnome-vfs-aware application would be able to handle such URIs without problems—and in fact the use of playbin in this application means that some network URIs may work, depending on your system's configuration.

```
g_signal_emit_by_name(G_OBJECT(stop_button), "clicked");
```

Because a new file is being opened, the code needs to ensure that any existing file is no longer being played. The simplest way to do this is to pretend that the user clicked the stop button, so the code causes the stop button to emit its clicked signal.

The local copy of the current URI is then updated, and `load_file()` called to prepare the file for playback:

```
    if (current_filename) g_free(current_filename);
    current_filename = filename;
    if (load_file(filename))
      gtk_widget_set_sensitive(GTK_WIDGET(play_button), TRUE);
  }

  gtk_widget_destroy(file_chooser);
}
```

Finally, the `FileChooser` is destroyed using `gtk_widget_destroy()`.

The program should now compile, run, and allow the playback of a music file. But there are two things missing: metadata and seeking.

Metadata

Metadata is simple. First, you should provide an interface method allowing the playback code to change the metadata labels in the GUI. This should have a declaration in `main.h` and a definition in `main.c` as follows:

```
void gui_update_metadata(const gchar *title, const gchar *artist) {
  gtk_label_set_text(GTK_LABEL(title_label), title);
  gtk_label_set_text(GTK_LABEL(artist_label), artist);
}
```

The code itself is straightforward. As you may have already realized, this function needs to be called from within the player's message handler in the case where the message type is `GST_MESSAGE_TAG`. In this case, the `GstMessage` object contains a tag message, which has several methods you can use to extract the information that the user is interested in. The code looks like this:

```
case GST_MESSAGE_TAG: {
  GstTagList *tags;
  gchar *title  = "";
  gchar *artist = "";
  gst_message_parse_tag(message, &tags);
  if (gst_tag_list_get_string(tags, GST_TAG_TITLE, &title)
  && gst_tag_list_get_string(tags, GST_TAG_ARTIST, &artist))
  gui_update_metadata(title, artist);
  gst_tag_list_free(tags);
  break;
}
```

Tags arrive in a `GstMessage` enclosed in a `GstTagList` object, which can be extracted with `gst_message_parse_tag()`. This generates a new copy of the `GstTagList`, so it is important to remember to free it with `gst_tag_list_free()` when it is no longer required. Failing to do so could cause a substantial memory leak.

Once the tag list has been extracted from the message, it is a straightforward matter to use `gst_tag_list_get_string()` to extract the title and artist tags. GStreamer provides predefined constants to extract standard metadata fields, although arbitrary strings can also be provided to extract other fields that the media may contain. `gst_tag_list_get_string()` returns `true` if it succeeds in finding a value for the requested tag and `false` otherwise. If both calls succeed, the function updates the GUI with the new values.

Seeking

To allow seeking within the file, the ideal scenario is to allow the user to click on the `seek_scale`'s position handle and drag it to the new location, with the stream immediately changing position accordingly. Fortunately, this is exactly the functionality GStreamer allows you to implement. When the user changes the value of a `GtkScale` widget, it emits the signal `value-changed`. Connect a callback to this signal:

```
g_signal_connect(G_OBJECT(seek_scale),
  "value-changed", G_CALLBACK(seek_value_changed), NULL);
```

You should then define the callback function in `main.c`:

```
static void seek_value_changed(GtkRange *range, gpointer data) {
  gdouble val = gtk_range_get_value(range);

  seek_to(val);
}
```

`seek_to()` takes a percentage figure, which represents how far through the stream the user wishes to seek. It is declared in `playback.h` and defined in `playback.c` as follows:

```
void seek_to(gdouble percentage) {
  GstFormat fmt = GST_FORMAT_TIME;
  gint64 length;

  if (play && gst_element_query_duration(play, &fmt, &length)) {
```

The function first checks that there is a valid pipeline. If there is, and if the duration of the current stream can be successfully retrieved, it uses that duration and the percentage supplied by the user to calculate the GStreamer time value of the place the user wishes to seek to.

```
    gint64 target = ((gdouble)length * (percentage / 100.0));
```

The actual seek is attempted by calling `gst_element_seek()`.

```
if (!gst_element_seek(play, 1.0, GST_FORMAT_TIME,
      GST_SEEK_FLAG_FLUSH, GST_SEEK_TYPE_SET,
      target, GST_SEEK_TYPE_NONE, GST_CLOCK_TIME_NONE))
    g_warning("Failed to seek to desired position\n");
  }
}
```

The `gst_element_seek()` function uses several parameters that define seek. Fortunately, for the default behavior, most of the parameters can be set using predefined library constants. These set the format and type of the element, as well as the seek ending time and type. The only parameters we need to worry about providing are the element to send the event to (the play variable), and the time value for the seek (the target variable).

Because gst_element_seek() returns true if it succeeds, the function checks for a false value and prints a message if the seek failed. This is of little real use to the user, but you can easily imagine providing a more helpful message, especially if you were to query the pipeline to check its actual status.

With seeking added, the stated functionality of the music player is nearly complete. The pause function is left as an exercise for the reader, along with some other suggestions in the "Improvements" section below.

Unfortunately, there is a major flaw in seeking as it currently stands: if the seek_scale's position is updated by the playback engine while the user is dragging it, its position jumps about. To stop this, you need to prevent the playback code from updating the slider during a drag. Because the playback code calls gui_update_time() to accomplish this, this restriction can be kept entirely within the GUI code. At the top of main.c, add a new flag variable:

```
gboolean can_update_seek_scale = TRUE;
```

Modify the gui_update_time() function so that it only updates seek_scale's position if can_update_seek_scale is true. You should leave the update of the time label, as this will not cause any problems, and some indication of continued playback is useful while the user is dragging to seek within the track.

To ensure that this variable is always correct, it needs to be updated when the user starts and stops dragging the slider. This can be accomplished through the use of events provided by the GtkWidget class, an ancestor of GtkHScale, the class of the seek_scale widget. button-press-event is triggered when the user presses a mouse button when the cursor is over the widget. button-release-event is triggered when the button pressed in the button-press-event is released — even if the user has moved the mouse pointer away from the widget. This ensures that no release events are missed. The clicked signal that you have already encountered is a combination of these two events, and is triggered after the widget observes the pressing and releasing of the primary mouse button.

Write some signal handlers for the button press and release events of seek_scale. These are nice and straightforward:

```
gboolean seek_scale_button_pressed(
  GtkWidget *widget, GdkEventButton *event, gpointer user_data) {
  can_update_seek_scale = FALSE;
  return FALSE;
}

gboolean seek_scale_button_released(
  GtkWidget *widget, GdkEventButton *event, gpointer user_data) {
  can_update_seek_scale = TRUE;
  return FALSE;
}
```

Each function updates the flag variable appropriately, then returns FALSE. Signals that have callback prototypes returning gboolean usually use the return value to indicate whether or not they have completely handled the signal. Returning TRUE tells GTK+ that the signal has been completely handled, and no further signal handlers should be executed for this signal. Returning FALSE allows the signal to propagate to other signal handlers.

In this case, returning FALSE allows the default signal handler for the widget to also handle the signal, and thus the behavior of the widget is preserved. Returning TRUE would prevent the user from adjusting the position of the slider.

Signals that behave in this way are usually events such as those relating to mouse buttons and movement, rather than signals like clicked, which is a signal emitted after mouse events have been received and interpreted by the widget.

Summary

The program as specified in this chapter falls short in a few areas, but with the information presented here and the documentation for GTK+ and GStreamer, the interested reader should be able to implement the following:

❑   The FileChooserDialog is destroyed after each use, thus forgetting where the user navigated to. Modify the program to use one FileChooserDialog, which is built and reused each time the user opens another file.

❑   Pause functionality has deliberately been left as an exercise for the reader. Implement it, with the appropriate GUI state changes, using the GStreamer pipeline state GST_STATE_PAUSED.

❑   File metadata is not read until the pipeline begins playing, as GStreamer cannot read it without beginning to play the file. Modify load_file to build another pipeline from lower-level elements that can retrieve this metadata but that will not cause any sound to be output. Its message-handling function should stop the pipeline after the metadata message has been received with the appropriate information in it. You should investigate the filesrc, decodebin, and fakesink GStreamer elements to achieve this.

By now, you should be familiar with the basic concepts of programming GNOME applications in C. This chapter, by necessity, does not touch on all the areas needed to make full-blown applications for GNOME, but with an understanding of GObject and GTK+, you should not have a great deal of trouble beginning to use other libraries such as Gconf. GNOME offers a great deal to application developers, and although the situation is beginning to change in favor of languages like C#, C is still the language of choice for core desktop applications.

## 12

The FreeDesktop Project

While GTK+ provides a great toolkit for building applications, and GNOME itself provides a great set of applications, there are many important features related to the desktop that do not belong in either a widget toolkit library or an individual application set for various reasons. Certain features may be a little lower level than application builders should deal with, and/or ought to be done with desktop neutrality in mind (so that things still work when using a different desktop environment, such as KDE). Fortunately for programmers there is a middle ground. The FreeDesktop project provides several projects that work in any Linux desktop environment. It provides a common application programming interface (API) for many commonly used desktop features.

The Desktop Bus, the Hardware Abstraction Layer, and the Network Manager are three popular FreeDesktop projects that provide useful interfaces to common desktop problems. This chapter demonstrates how to write code that utilizes these FreeDesktop project applications to interact with any Linux desktop environment that implements FreeDesktop. Finally, you will be introduced to a few more FreeDesktop projects that may come in handy in your Linux programming.

D-BUS: The Desktop Bus

D-Bus is an Inter-Process Communication (IPC) mechanism that is part of the FreeDesktop.org project. It was designed to replace Common Object Request Broker Architecture (CORBA) and Desktop Communication Protocol (DCOP), the IPC mechanisms previously used by GNOME and KDE, respectively, D-Bus is tailored specifically for the Linux Desktop. Because of this, it is much simpler to use in many instances. The key to the power of D-Bus lies within its name: the bus daemons. Instead of using a binary bytestream, as is common in other IPC mechanisms, D-Bus uses a concept of binary messages, which are composed of headers and corresponding data.

This section discusses how D-Bus works, then demonstrates how to write an application that uses the D-Bus to pass messages in a client/server environment.

What Is D-Bus?

It is important to note that while D-Bus is an IPC mechanism, it is not a general-purpose IPC mechanism. It was designed for the desktop and is likely not suited for other applications. Specifically, it was designed with two goals in mind. It should facilitate multiple applications in the same desktop session to communicate with each other. It should also facilitate desktop applications to communicate with the operating system. That includes the kernel, and system daemons and processes.

With those in mind, it seems natural that D-Bus employs both a system and a session bus. The first bus instance on the system is the *system bus*, which is a machinewide privileged daemon, similar to `inetd` or `httpd`. There are heavy restrictions on what types of messages the system bus can accept. Additionally, D-Bus has integration for SELinux contexts, which further improves its security. When a user logs in to the desktop, another bus is created using that person's user context. This is the session bus and will allow the user's applications to communicate with each other. When applications employ both buses, they can do powerful things like get notification of system events such as loss of network, and perform tasks based on network status. Later in this chapter, you will learn how the powerful NetworkManager application takes full advantage of both the system and session bus.

Under D-Hood of D-Bus

The D-Bus API is not tied to a specific language or framework. For example, there are D-Bus bindings for Glib (which is written in C), Qt (written in C++), Python, and C#. Since you just learned a little about GNOME, which is written in C and uses Glib, in the previous chapter, this chapter focuses on the C and Glib bindings to D-Bus. All the general principles apply to the other bindings, however.

To use D-Bus in an application, first include the headers.

```
#include <dbus/dbus.h>
#include <dbus/dbus-glib.h>
```

Each application must then connect to the message bus daemon. Remembering that there are two message bus daemons we can connect, it is time to decide which to connect to. To connect to the session bus, use the following bit of code:

```
DBusError error;
DBusConnection *conn;

dbus_error_init (&error);
conn = dbus_bus_get (DBUS_BUS_SESSION, &error);

if (!conn) {
    fprintf (stderr, "%s: %s\n", error.name, error.message);
    /* Other error Handling */;
}
```

To connect to the session bus, simply replace DBUS_BUS_SESSION with DBUS_BUS_SYSTEM. Connecting to the system bus can be a little trickier because of restrictions on who can connect to it. You may be required to provide a `.service` file with details about who can and cannot connect to a given service. This chapter focuses on connecting to the session bus, but the principles are the same for connecting to the system bus.

When an application connects to either the system or session bus, D-Bus assigns a unique connection name to the application. This name begins with a colon (:) character, for example :80-218 and is the only type of name that can start with a colon. These are unique per daemon instance and are never reused during the lifetime of the bus. However, applications can request that connections be referenced by a more common name. For example, org.foo.bar.

D-Bus communicates to objects within an application instead of the application itself (although using the application's top-level object exclusively would have the same effect as talking directly to the application). In your Glib applications, this means GObjects and its derivatives. In your application, these are passed around as memory addresses in your application's address space, so it would not make sense to pass these around to other applications. Instead, D-Bus passes object paths. These look similar to filesystem paths; for example, /org/foo/bar could denote the top-level object path for a Foo Bar application. While it is not required to namespace object paths, it is highly recommended to avoid clashes.

There are four different types of messages that D-Bus can send to an object:

❑ *Signal messages* notify an object that a given signal has been emitted or an event has occurred,

❑ *Method call messages* request a method to be invoked on a particular object.

❑ *Method return messages* return the result of invoking a method on an object.

❑ *Error messages* return any exceptions raised by invoking a method on an object.

The following bit of code can be used to emit a signal:

```c
#include <dbus/dbus.h>
#include <stdlib.h>
#include <stdio.h>

int main (int argc, char *argv[])
{
    DBusError dberr;
    DBusConnection *dbconn;
    DBusMessage *dbmsg;
    char *text;

    dbus_error_init (&dberr);
    dbconn = dbus_bus_get (DBUS_BUS_SESSION, &dberr);
    if (dbus_error_is_set (&dberr)) {
        fprintf (stderr, "getting session bus failed: %s\n", dberr.message);
        dbus_error_free (&dberr);
        return EXIT_FAILURE;
    }

    dbmsg = dbus_message_new_signal ("/com/wiley/test",
                                     "com.wiley.test",
                                     "TestSignal");
    if (dbmsg == NULL) {
        fprintf (stderr, "Could not create a new signal\n");
        return EXIT_FAILURE;
    }

    text = "Hello World";
```

```
        dbus_message_append_args (dbmsg, DBUS_TYPE_STRING, &text, DBUS_TYPE_INVALID);

        dbus_connection_send (dbconn, dbmsg, NULL);
        printf ("Sending signal to D-Bus\n");

        dbus_message_unref (dbmsg);

        dbus_connection_close (dbconn);
        dbus_connection_unref (dbconn);

        return EXIT_SUCCESS;
}
```

Of course, sending out signals is nice, but in order for them to be useful, one has to know how to process D-Bus signals. This is slightly more complicated, but not too much. It starts off very similarly to emitting a signal:

```
int main (int argc, char *argv[])
{
    DBusError dberr;
    DBusConnection *dbconn;

    dbus_error_init (&dberr)
    dbconn = dbus_bus_get (DBUS_BUS_SESSION, &dberr);
    if (dbus_error_is_set (&dberr)) {
        fprintf (stderr, "getting session bus failed: %s\n", dberr.message);
        dbus_error_free (&dberr);
        return EXIT_FAILURE;
    }
```

Next, to properly receive signals, we need to make sure we "own" the com.wiley.test namespace. This matters more when dealing with the system bus, but it is a common mistake to make.

```
    dbus_bus_request_name (dbconn, "com.wiley.test",
                        DBUS_NAME_FLAG_REPLACE_EXISTING, &dberr);
    if (dbus_error_is_set (&dberr)) {
        fprintf (stderr, "requesting name failed: %s\n", dberr.message);
        dbus_error_free (&dberr);
        return EXIT_FAILURE;
    }
```

Adding a filter function is a good way to receive signals as well as filter out the signals you wish to process and how you want to process them. For now, we will simply register one but won't define it until later.

```
    if (!dbus_connection_add_filter (dbconn,
                                filter_func, NULL, NULL))
        return EXIT_FAILURE;
```

Also, as we are expecting to receive a signal, we need to make sure that we don't ignore it. By default, signals are ignored to prevent "spam," as there are many signals sent across the bus that not all applications want to hear, even if they are on the same interface.

```
dbus_bus_add_match (dbconn,
                    "type='signal',interface='com.wiley.test'",
                    &dberr);

if (dbus_error_is_set (&dberr)) {
    fprintf (stderr, "Could not match: %s", dberr.message);
    dbus_error_free (&dberr);
    return EXIT_FAILURE;
}
```

Last, it is important to make sure that the program doesn't exit right away; there must be some kind of continuous polling for signals. D-Bus provides a low-level API function that will take care of this for us.

```
while (dbus_connection_read_write_dispatch (dbconn, -1))
    ; /* empty loop body */


return EXIT_SUCCESS;
}
```

With the basic control of the program squared away, it is now possible to implement the filter function.

```
static DBusHandlerResult
filter_func (DBusConnection *connection,
             DBusMessage *message,
             void *user_data)
{
    dbus_bool_t handled = FALSE;
    char *signal_text = NULL;

    if (dbus_message_is_signal (message, "com.wiley.test", "TestSignal")) {
        DBusError dberr;

        dbus_error_init (&dberr);
        dbus_message_get_args (message, &dberr, DBUS_TYPE_STRING, &signal_text,
DBUS_TYPE_INVALID);
        if (dbus_error_is_set (&dberr)) {
            fprintf (stderr, "Error getting message args: %s", dberr.message);
            dbus_error_free (&dberr);
        } else {
            DBusConnection *dbconn = (DBusConnection*) user_data;

            printf ("Received TestSignal with value of: '%s'\n", signal_text);

            handled = TRUE;
        }
    }

    return (handled ? DBUS_HANDLER_RESULT_HANDLED :
DBUS_HANDLER_RESULT_NOT_YET_HANDLED);
}
```

It is fairly straightforward. It checks to make sure the signal is a `TestSignal` using the `com.wiley.test` interface. Then, it gets the arguments expected (which are known from the emitted signal) and simply prints them to the console. Running `dbus-get-hello` and then `dbus-say-hello` in different consoles will print out:

```
% ./dbus-get-hello
Received TestSignal with value of: 'Hello World'

% ./dbus-send-hello
Sending signal to D-Bus
```

Congratulations! You now have a working D-Bus client and server!

D-Bus Methods

Sometimes, sending signals back and forth do not suit a program's needs. For example, one might wish to "ask a question" or invoke some function and get a result back. The NetworkManager applet might want to tell its system daemon to connect to a specific network and then return the properties of the network. As mentioned previously, D-Bus allows for method call and reply messages as well.

D-Bus signal messages were created with `dbus_message_new_signal()`. To call a D-Bus method, simply create a message using `dbus_message_new_method_call()`. Let's call a method that adds three integers and returns the integer sum. We simply grab the integers from the current hours, minutes, and seconds.

First, include the needed files and prepare D-Bus. These steps are very similar to what was needed for emitting signals.

```
#include <dbus/dbus.h>
#include <stdlib.h>
#include <stdio.h>
#include <time.h>

int main (int argc, char *argv[])
{
    DBusError dberr;
    DBusConnection *dbconn;
    DBusMessage *dbmsg, *dbreply;
    DBusMessageIter dbiter;
    int arg1, arg2, arg3, result;
    struct tm *cur_time;
    time_t cur_time_t;

    dbus_error_init (&dberr);
    dbconn = dbus_bus_get (DBUS_BUS_SESSION, &dberr);
    if (dbus_error_is_set (&dberr)) {
        fprintf (stderr, "getting session bus failed: %s\n", dberr.message);
        dbus_error_free (&dberr);
        return EXIT_FAILURE;
    }
```

Instead of emitting a signal, we want to call a method, so prepare the method call:

```
dbmsg = dbus_message_new_method_call ("com.aillon.test",
                                      "/com/aillon/test",
                                      "com.aillon.test",
                                      "add_three_ints");
if (dbmsg == NULL) {
    fprintf (stderr, "Couldn't create a DBusMessage");
    return EXIT_FAILURE;
}
```

Now, the method call is ready. It simply needs to know what arguments to call the method with. Let's get the current time and supply it with some integers.

```
cur_time_t = time (NULL);
cur_time = localtime (&cur_time_t);
arg1 = cur_time->tm_hour;
arg2 = cur_time->tm_min;
arg3 = cur_time->tm_sec;

dbus_message_iter_init_append (dbmsg, &dbiter);
dbus_message_iter_append_basic (&dbiter, DBUS_TYPE_INT32, &arg1);
dbus_message_iter_append_basic (&dbiter, DBUS_TYPE_INT32, &arg2);
dbus_message_iter_append_basic (&dbiter, DBUS_TYPE_INT32, &arg3);
```

You'll note that the preceding code uses a DBusMessageIter to append arguments. Previously, arguments were appended with dbus_message_append_args(). Both are equally correct; they are simply two different ways of performing the same task.

Next, it is time to call the method:

```
printf ("Calling add_three_ints method\n");
dbus_error_init (&dberr);
dbreply = dbus_connection_send_with_reply_and_block (dbconn, dbmsg, 5000,
&dberr);
if (dbus_error_is_set (&dberr)) {
    fprintf (stderr, "Error getting a reply: %s!", dberr.message);
    dbus_message_unref (dbmsg);
    dbus_error_free (&dberr);
    return EXIT_FAILURE;
}

/* Don't need this anymore */
dbus_message_unref (dbmsg);
```

Finally, extract the results from the reply, print out the results to the console, and clean up:

```
dbus_error_init (&dberr);
dbus_message_get_args (dbreply, &dberr, DBUS_TYPE_INT32, &result);
if (dbus_error_is_set (&dberr)) {
    fprintf (stderr, "Error getting the result: %s!", dberr.message);
    dbus_message_unref (dbmsg);
    dbus_error_free (&dberr);
    return EXIT_FAILURE;
```

```
    }

        printf ("Result of : add_three_ints (%d, %d, %d) is %d\n", arg1, arg2, arg3,
    result);

        dbus_message_unref (dbreply);

        dbus_connection_close (dbconn);
        dbus_connection_unref (dbconn);

        return EXIT_SUCCESS;
    }
```

Of course, the method needs to be implemented now. Start off by getting the session bus:

```
int main (int argc, char *argv[])
{
        DBusError dberr;
        DBusConnection *dbconn;

        dbus_error_init (&dberr);
        dbconn = dbus_bus_get (DBUS_BUS_SESSION, &dberr);

        if (dbus_error_is_set (&dberr)) {
            fprintf (stderr, "getting session bus failed: %s\n", dberr.message);
            dbus_error_free (&dberr);
            return EXIT_FAILURE;
        }
```

Next, request ownership of the name so that D-Bus knows we own the namespace and it should forward method calls to us. There is no need to explicitly add a match for method calls; D-Bus will automatically forward those, but let's also add a filter function, as we did before, and then start our loop to poll for D-Bus messages.

```
        dbus_bus_request_name (dbconn, "com.aillon.test",
                               DBUS_NAME_FLAG_REPLACE_EXISTING, &dberr);
         if (dbus_error_is_set (&dberr)) {
            fprintf (stderr, "requesting name failed: %s\n", dberr.message);
            dbus_error_free (&dberr);
            return EXIT_FAILURE;
        }

        if (!dbus_connection_add_filter (dbconn, filter_func, dbconn, NULL))
            return EXIT_FAILURE;

        while (dbus_connection_read_write_dispatch (dbconn, -1))
            ; /* empty loop body */


        return EXIT_SUCCESS;
    }
```

The filtering function simply needs to check to make sure that the method call we are receiving is the correct one, and then forward the call:

```
static DBusHandlerResult
filter_func (DBusConnection *connection,
             DBusMessage *message,
             void *user_data)
{
    dbus_bool_t handled = FALSE;

    if (dbus_message_is_method_call (message, "com.aillon.test",
"add_three_ints")) {
        printf ("Handling method call\n");
        add_three_ints (message, connection);
        handled = TRUE;
    }

    return (handled ? DBUS_HANDLER_RESULT_HANDLED :
DBUS_HANDLER_RESULT_NOT_YET_HANDLED);
}
```

The meat of the entire thing is the actual function call. In this case, add_three_ints(). Start off by extracting the expected arguments from the DBusMessage passed in.

```
static void
add_three_ints (DBusMessage *message, DBusConnection *connection)
{
    DBusError dberr;
    DBusMessage *reply;
    dbus_uint32_t arg1, arg2, arg3, result;

    dbus_error_init (&dberr);
    dbus_message_get_args (message, &dberr, DBUS_TYPE_INT32, &arg1,
DBUS_TYPE_INT32, &arg2, DBUS_TYPE_INT32, &arg3, DBUS_TYPE_INVALID);
```

If the arguments are not what was expected, create an error reply message back to send back to the caller. Otherwise, create a method return message and append the arguments.

```
    if (dbus_error_is_set (&dberr)) {
        reply = dbus_message_new_error_printf (message, "WrongArguments", "%s",
dberr.message);
        dbus_error_free (&dberr);
        if (reply == NULL) {
            fprintf (stderr, "Could not create reply for message!");
            exit (1);
        }
    } else {
        result = arg1 + arg2 + arg3;

        reply = dbus_message_new_method_return (message);
        if (reply == NULL) {
            fprintf (stderr, "Could not create reply for message!");
            exit (1);
        }

        dbus_message_append_args (reply, DBUS_TYPE_INT32, &result,
DBUS_TYPE_INVALID);
    }
```

Finally, send the message and clean up:

```
dbus_connection_send (connection, reply, NULL);

dbus_message_unref (reply);
}
```

A few invocations should yield output similar to:

```
% ./dbus-call-method
Calling add_three_ints method
Result of : add_three_ints (16, 19, 7) is 42
% ./dbus-call-method
Calling add_three_ints method
Result of : add_three_ints (16, 19, 8) is 43
% ./dbus-call-method
Calling add_three_ints method
Result of : add_three_ints (16, 19, 9) is 44
```

Perfect, the intended method was successfully called and the result returned. Using these two basic concepts, you can create your own applications that utilize the features of D-Bus.

Hardware Abstraction Layer

You learned in the previous section how powerful D-Bus is and how to utilize it. But naturally, applications need to standardize on signals and messages to send. This section shows you what the Hardware Extraction Layer (HAL) is, how it relates to D-Bus, and how to use HAL from your applications.

Making Hardware Just Work

Long-time users of Linux remember times when acquiring a new piece of hardware was somewhat troublesome. One would spend time trying to figure out what kernel module needed to be present for the device to work. If the device was hot swappable, a USB device for example, one might not want a module loaded at times when the device was not in use. When switching between many devices, it was easy to become confused as to which module to load.

Of course, even when things did work smoothly, the process was rather tedious, and casual computer users might get frustrated when their camera was not working as they expected upon plugging it into the computer, or they couldn't immediately access their USB hard disk, or perhaps a printer. Applications couldn't care what the specifics of the hardware were, lest authors be required to update their software for each new piece of hardware they wanted to support.

Eventually, Havoc Pennington of Red Hat, Inc. wrote a paper entitled "Making Hardware Just Work" (http://ometer.com/hardware.html), which outlined the set of problems as he deemed them, and proposed his ideas for resolving the issues using a Hardware Abstraction Layer (HAL). A few months later, the first chunk of code was committed to a CVS repository. Today, HAL is able to discover storage devices, network devices, printers, media players such as an iPod, digital cameras, and more.

HAL is a system daemon that monitors the hardware currently on the system. It listens to hot-plug events as hardware devices are added and removed from the system by installing a script in /etc/dev.d, which gets run as udev modifies entries in /dev. HAL also requests a list of all devices on the system from udev when it starts up. In addition to information on devices, HAL also can perform certain tasks such as locking a hardware device for applications to gain exclusive access to devices.

The HAL API is entirely in D-Bus, but as it is a rather large API, and many programs are written in C, there exists a C helper library called libhal. Using HAL is fairly straightforward. Let's start by creating an application that will simply listen for the next device to be added to or removed from the system, print out a short message, and then exit.

```
#include <libhal.h>
#include <dbus/dbus.h>
#include <dbus/dbus-glib.h>
#include <glib.h>
#include <stdlib.h>
#include <stdio.h>
```

Let's get the meat of the app done first and worry about our callbacks later on. To wait around for events, let's use a GMainLoop, which Glib provides. We have to open a D-Bus connection to the system bus.

```
int main (int argc, char *argv[])
{
        GMainLoop *mainloop;

        DBusConnection *dbconn;
        DBusError dberr;

        LibHalContext *hal_ctx;

        mainloop = g_main_loop_new (NULL, FALSE);
        if (mainloop == NULL) {
            fprintf (stderr, "Can't get a mainloop");
            return EXIT_FAILURE;
        }

        dbus_error_init (&dberr);
        dbconn = dbus_bus_get (DBUS_BUS_SYSTEM, &dberr);
        if (dbus_error_is_set (&dberr)) {
            fprintf (stderr, "Can't get D-Bus system bus!");
            return EXIT_FAILURE;
        }

        dbus_connection_setup_with_g_main (dbconn, NULL);
```

With that out of the way, it's now possible to create a LibHalContext and tell it what events the callback should handle. Note that the order of doing things here is important. First, a LibHalContext must be created with libhal_ctx_new() and then, prior to calling libhal_ctx_init(), all the callbacks, D-Bus connection, and so on must be registered.

```
        hal_ctx = libhal_ctx_new ();
        if (hal_ctx == NULL) {
```

```
            fprintf (stderr, "Can't create a LibHalContext!");
            return EXIT_FAILURE;
    }

    /* Associate HAL with the D-Bus connection we established */
    libhal_ctx_set_dbus_connection (hal_ctx, dbconn);
    /* Register callbacks */
    libhal_ctx_set_device_added (hal_ctx, my_device_added_callback);
    libhal_ctx_set_device_removed (hal_ctx, my_device_removed_callback);
    /* We will be breaking out of the mainloop in a callback */
    libhal_ctx_set_user_data (hal_ctx, mainloop);

    dbus_error_init (&dberr);
    libhal_device_property_watch_all (hal_ctx, &dberr);
    if (dbus_error_is_set (&dberr)) {
            fprintf (stderr, "libhal_device_property_watch_all() failed: '%s'",
    dberr.message);
            dbus_error_free (&dberr);
            libhal_ctx_free (hal_ctx);
            return EXIT_FAILURE;
    }

    dbus_error_init (&dberr);
    libhal_ctx_init (hal_ctx, &dberr);
    if (dbus_error_is_set (&dberr)) {
            fprintf (stderr, "libhal_ctx_init() failed: '%s'. Is hald running?",
                             dberr.message);
            dbus_error_free (&dberr);
            libhal_ctx_free (hal_ctx);
            return EXIT_FAILURE;
    }
```

HAL is finally ready to go. To receive events, though, the main loop must be started:

```
    g_main_loop_run (mainloop);

    return EXIT_SUCCESS;
    }
```

And now, all that is needed is to implement the callback functions that HAL is expecting to call when a device is added or removed. This test application just cares about whether a device was added or removed, and will exit (after of course cleaning up and shutting down the connection to HAL).

```
static void all_done (LibHalContext *hal_ctx)
{
    DBusError dberr;
    GMainLoop *mainloop;

    mainloop = (GMainLoop*) libhal_ctx_get_user_data (hal_ctx);

    dbus_error_init (&dberr);
    libhal_ctx_shutdown (hal_ctx, &dberr);
    if (dbus_error_is_set (&dberr)) {
            fprintf (stderr, "libhal shutdown failed: '%s'", dberr.message);
            dbus_error_free (&dberr);
```

```
        }
        libhal_ctx_free (hal_ctx);

        g_main_loop_quit (mainloop);
}

static void my_device_added_callback (LibHalContext *hal_ctx, const char *udi)
{
        printf ("Device added: '%s'\n", udi);

        all_done (hal_ctx);
}

static void my_device_removed_callback (LibHalContext *hal_ctx, const char *udi)
{
        printf ("Device removed: '%s'\n", udi);

        all_done (hal_ctx);
}
```

After compiling, start the program and then insert a device, such as a USB mouse or camera. The output should look similar to:

```
% ./halloworld
Device added: '/org/freedesktop/Hal/devices/usb_device_46d_c016_noserial'
% ./halloworld
Device removed:
'/org/freedesktop/Hal/devices/usb_device_46d_c016_noserial_if0_logicaldev_input'
```

Hal Device Objects

The previous section showed you the basics of connecting to HAL and having it notify you when devices are added and removed. Now, it is time to explore the details of HAL device objects.

A HAL device object is composed of a few things. Each HAL device has a Unique Device Identifier (UDI), which no two devices share at the same time. The UDI is computed using information on the bus and is meant to be static across device insertions. However, this may not be entirely possible for devices that do not provide a serial number. HAL will use product and vendor information and sometimes a device's physical location (e.g., PCI slot 2 on bus 42) in these instances to generate the UDI, so it is possible to have UDIs across device insertions that vary slightly.

HAL device objects also have key/value properties associated with them. The key is an ASCII string. The values can be one of several types:

- ❑　`bool`, `int` (32-bit signed)
- ❑　`uint64`, `string` (UTF-8 string)
- ❑　`strlist` (sorted list of UTF-8 strings)
- ❑　`double`

Property keys use namespaces delimited by a "`.`" (period) character, for example: `info.linux.driver` and `net.80211.mac_address`.

353

HAL property keys can be thought of as belonging to four categories:

❑ *Metadata properties* are set by HAL to describe the relationship of how devices are interconnected and the type of device.

❑ *Physical properties* are determined by HAL from the device itself or device information files and contain information such as product and vendor IDs.

❑ *Functional properties* are properties that give out information about a device's current state. Examples are network link status, filesystem mount location, laptop battery charge, and so on.

❑ *Policy properties* define how devices may be used by users and are typically set by a system administrator in a device information file.

HAL also provides information about device capabilities. These are given in the `info.capabilities` property, which provide information about what a device can do. For example, a portable music player, such as an iPod, can also be used as a storage device. In this case, `info.capabilities` would be a `strlist` containing `portable_music_player` and `storage.disk`. The `info.category` key denotes the primary type and would be set to `portable_music_player`.

Finally, it also is important to note that HAL device objects do not necessarily map one to one with physical devices. For example, a multifunction printer could have three HAL device objects, for printing, scanning, and storage. Other devices that serve multiple purposes may only have one HAL device interface. The main device would have a single listing with all of the capabilities listed, and there would be three devices under it in HAL's tree, one to correspond to each capability.

Now that you have a basic understanding of how HAL device objects work, let's write a program that finds the optical drives on the system and prints a few details about them. Optical drives have the `storage.cdrom` capability, so that should be what is requested of HAL. To determine whether the drive also supports reading DVDs, ask HAL for the value of the `storage.cdrom.dvd` property. It would be somewhat useful to find the max read speed of the drive, as well. That is determined by the `storage.cdrom.read_speed` property.

HAL needs to be initialized similarly to the previous program. Note that because, this time, all that is required is to get the list of current devices, there is no need for event listening or a `mainloop`, the Glib requirement is gone.

```
#include <libhal.h>
#include <stdlib.h>
#include <stdio.h>

int main (int argc, char *argv[])
{
    DBusConnection *dbconn;
    DBusError dberr;

    LibHalContext *hal_ctx;
    LibHalPropertyType property_type;
    char *property_key;
    dbus_bool_t bool_value;
    int int_value;
    char **udis;
    int num_udis;
```

```
    int i;

    dbus_error_init (&dberr);
    dbconn = dbus_bus_get (DBUS_BUS_SYSTEM, &dberr);
    if (dbus_error_is_set (&dberr)) {
        fprintf (stderr, "Can't get D-Bus system bus!");
        return EXIT_FAILURE;
    }

    hal_ctx = libhal_ctx_new ();
    if (hal_ctx == NULL) {
        fprintf (stderr, "Can't create a LibHalContext!");
        return EXIT_FAILURE;
    }

    /* Associate HAL with the D-Bus connection we established */
    libhal_ctx_set_dbus_connection (hal_ctx, dbconn);

    dbus_error_init (&dberr);
    libhal_ctx_init (hal_ctx, &dberr);
    if (dbus_error_is_set (&dberr)) {
        fprintf (stderr, "libhal_ctx_init() failed: '%s'. Is hald running?",
                        dberr.message);
        dbus_error_free (&dberr);
        libhal_ctx_free (hal_ctx);
        return EXIT_FAILURE;
    }
```

With HAL initialized, it's time to look for devices that have the `storage.cdrom` capability.

```
    /* Looking for optical drives: storage.cdrom is the capability */
    udis = libhal_find_device_by_capability (hal_ctx, "storage.cdrom", &num_udis,
&dberr);
    if (dbus_error_is_set (&dberr)) {
        fprintf (stderr, "libhal_find_device_by_capability error: '%s'\n",
dberr.message);
        dbus_error_free (&dberr);
        libhal_ctx_free (hal_ctx);
        return EXIT_FAILURE;
    }
```

The `udis` variable now contains an array of `udis` that HAL found matching the `storage.cdrom` capability. Iterating through them is the next step, so properties on each individual device can be obtained. We will first use `libhal_device_get_property_type` to make sure that the properties are each of the type we're expecting.

```
    printf ("Found %d Optical Device(s)\n", num_udis);
    for (i = 0; i < num_udis; i++) {
        /* Ensure our properties are the expected type */
        property_type = libhal_device_get_property_type (hal_ctx,
                                            udis[i],
                                            "storage.cdrom.dvd",
                                            &dberr);
        if (dbus_error_is_set (&dberr) ||
            property_type != LIBHAL_PROPERTY_TYPE_BOOLEAN)
```

```
                {
                        fprintf (stderr, "error checking storage.cdrom.dvd type");
                        dbus_error_free (&dberr);
                        libhal_ctx_free (hal_ctx);
                        return EXIT_FAILURE;
                }

                property_type = libhal_device_get_property_type (hal_ctx,
                                                                 udis[i],

        "storage.cdrom.read_speed",
                                                                        &dberr);
                if (dbus_error_is_set (&dberr) || property_type !=
        LIBHAL_PROPERTY_TYPE_INT32) {
                        fprintf (stderr, "error checking storage.cdrom.read_speed type");
                        dbus_error_free (&dberr);
                        libhal_ctx_free (hal_ctx);
                        return EXIT_FAILURE;
                }
```

Now that we know that the property value types are indeed correct, it is safe to get the values and print them out to stdout. Because the properties are of type bool and int, we need to use libhal_device_get_property_bool and libhal_device_get_property_int. There are other methods that correspond to their respective types. They are pretty straightforward, but see libhal.h for more details on these methods.

```
                /* Okay, now simply get property values */
                bool_value = libhal_device_get_property_bool (hal_ctx, udis[i],
                                                              "storage.cdrom.dvd",
                                                              &dberr);
                if (dbus_error_is_set (&dberr)) {
                    fprintf (stderr, "error getting storage.cdrom.dvd");
                    dbus_error_free (&dberr);
                    libhal_ctx_free (hal_ctx);
                     return EXIT_FAILURE;
                }
                int_value = libhal_device_get_property_int (hal_ctx, udis[i],
                                                            "storage.cdrom.read_speed",
                                                            &dberr);
                if (dbus_error_is_set (&dberr)) {
                        fprintf (stderr, "error getting storage.cdrom.dvd");
                        dbus_error_free (&dberr);
                        libhal_ctx_free (hal_ctx);
                        return EXIT_FAILURE;
                }

                /* Display the info we just got */
                printf ("Device %s has a maximum read spead of %d kb/s and %s read
        DVDs.\n",
                        udis[i], int_value, bool_value ? "can" : "cannot");
        }

        return EXIT_SUCCESS;
}
```

Compile the program and execute it. The output should look similar to:

```
% ./hal-optical-test
Found 2 Optical Device(s)
Device /org/freedesktop/Hal/devices/storage_model_HL_DT_STDVD_ROM_GDR8162B has a
maximum read spead of 8467 kb/s and can read DVDs.
Device /org/freedesktop/Hal/devices/storage_model_HL_DT_ST_GCE_8483B has a maximum
read speed of 8467 kb/s and cannot read DVDs.
```

For a better listing of properties of which HAL is aware, check the output of the program lshal. It outputs all of the devices HAL knows about and all properties on the devices that it knows about. The output listing will look similar to:

```
% lshal
Dumping 99 device(s) from the Global Device List:
...
udi = '/org/freedesktop/Hal/devices/storage_model_HL_DT_STDVD_ROM_GDR8162B'
  info.addons = {'hald-addon-storage'} (string list)
  block.storage_device =
'/org/freedesktop/Hal/devices/storage_model_HL_DT_STDVD_ROM_GDR8162B'  (string)
  info.udi = '/org/freedesktop/Hal/devices/storage_model_HL_DT_STDVD_ROM_GDR8162B'
(string)
    storage.cdrom.write_speed = 0  (0x0)  (int)
    storage.cdrom.read_speed = 8467  (0x2113)  (int)
    storage.cdrom.support_media_changed = true  (bool)
    storage.cdrom.hddvdrw = false  (bool)
    storage.cdrom.hddvdr = false  (bool)
    storage.cdrom.hddvd = false  (bool)
    storage.cdrom.bdre = false  (bool)
    storage.cdrom.bdr = false  (bool)
    storage.cdrom.bd = false  (bool)
    storage.cdrom.dvdplusrdl = false  (bool)
    storage.cdrom.dvdplusrw = false  (bool)
    storage.cdrom.dvdplusr = false  (bool)
    storage.cdrom.dvdram = false  (bool)
    storage.cdrom.dvdrw = false  (bool)
    storage.cdrom.dvdr = false  (bool)
    storage.cdrom.dvd = true  (bool)
    storage.cdrom.cdrw = false  (bool)
    storage.cdrom.cdr = false  (bool)
    storage.requires_eject = true  (bool)
    storage.hotpluggable = false  (bool)
    info.capabilities = {'storage', 'block', 'storage.cdrom'} (string list)
    info.category = 'storage'  (string)
    info.product = 'HL-DT-STDVD-ROM GDR8162B'  (string)
    storage.removable = true  (bool)
    storage.physical_device = '/org/freedesktop/Hal/devices/pci_8086_24db_ide_1_0'
(string)
    storage.firmware_version = '0015'  (string)
    storage.vendor = ''  (string)
    storage.model = 'HL-DT-STDVD-ROM GDR8162B'  (string)
    storage.drive_type = 'cdrom'  (string)
    storage.automount_enabled_hint = true  (bool)
    storage.media_check_enabled = true  (bool)
    storage.no_partitions_hint = true  (bool)
```

```
        storage.bus = 'ide'  (string)
        block.is_volume = false  (bool)
        block.minor = 0  (0x0)  (int)
        block.major = 22  (0x16)  (int)
        block.device = '/dev/hdc'  (string)
        linux.hotplug_type = 3  (0x3)  (int)
        info.parent = '/org/freedesktop/Hal/devices/pci_8086_24db_ide_1_0'  (string)
        linux.sysfs_path_device = '/sys/block/hdc'  (string)
        linux.sysfs_path = '/sys/block/hdc'  (string)
    ...
    Dumped 99 device(s) from the Global Device List.
    -------------------------------------------------
```

Just like the standard `ls` command does for files, `lshal` produces a listing of every device on the system recognized by HAL. This is a handy quick-and-dirty method you can use for determining what hardware devices the Linux system recognized and how they were configured.

That shows you the basics of using HAL and how to extract hardware information from it. The next section dives into the networking world with the FreeDesktop Network Manager.

The Network Manager

NetworkManager was introduced as part of Red Hat's Stateless Linux Project. The general premise is that networking in Linux should just work. It aims to make sure that a user never has to manually configure a wireless network card by typing in various `iwconfig` commands and then obtaining an IP address.

As you've learned, it harnesses the power of HAL and D-Bus in order to give the user a seamless wireless experience when connecting. But to get a true stateless experience, other applications need to be network aware. For example, a web browser might want to know whether the machine is connected to the network to decide whether to attempt to load web pages over the network or to attempt to read them out of its disk cache. A music player may wish to display possible Internet radio stations when the user is connected to a network; the Internet radio stations might be disabled otherwise. Mail applications may have similar requirements.

Desktop applications can listen over the same D-Bus interfaces that NetworkManager does to determine network state. NetworkManager also exposes an interface for applications using Glib to gain a quick way of determining network state, without having to figure out its D-Bus signals. The interface, called `libnm` (for NetworkManager), is easy to use.

First, include the header file and initialize `libnm-glib`:

```
#include <libnm_glib/libnm_glib.h>

int main(int argc, char* argv[])
{
    GMainLoop      *loop;
    libnm_glib_ctx *ctx;
    guint id;

    ctx = libnm_glib_init ();
```

```
            if (ctx == NULL)
            {
                  fprintf (stderr, "Could not initialize libnm.\n");
                  exit (1);
            }
```

Then, register the callback (the callback function will be defined later on):

```
            id = libnm_glib_register_callback (ctx, status_printer, ctx, NULL);
```

Finally, make sure that Glib's main loop is running:

```
            loop = g_main_loop_new (NULL, FALSE);
            g_main_loop_run (loop);

            exit (0);
      }
```

Of course, the callback function still needs to be defined. Because this is simply a test application, printing the status should suffice:

```
      static void status_printer (libnm_glib_ctx *ctx, gpointer user_data)
      {
            libnm_glib_state      state;

            g_return_if_fail (ctx != NULL);

            state = libnm_glib_get_network_state (ctx);
            switch (state)
            {
                  case LIBNM_NO_DBUS:
                        fprintf (stderr, "Status: No DBUS\n");
                        break;
                  case LIBNM_NO_NETWORKMANAGER:
                        fprintf (stderr, "Status: No NetworkManager\n");
                        break;
                  case LIBNM_NO_NETWORK_CONNECTION:
                        fprintf (stderr, "Status: No Connection\n");
                        break;
                  case LIBNM_ACTIVE_NETWORK_CONNECTION:
                        fprintf (stderr, "Status: Active Connection\n");
                        break;
                  case LIBNM_INVALID_CONTEXT:
                        fprintf (stderr, "Status: Error\n");
                        break;
                  default:
                        fprintf (stderr, "Status: unknown\n");
                        break;
            }
      }
```

With Network Manager, it is easy to check the status of the network connection. Instead of having to search for hardware network cards and query features, with just a few lines of code we were able to interact with the underlying network configuration on the Linux system and retrieve the status.

Other Freedesktop Projects

The FreeDesktop project has a few other important pieces of software. While this book won't discuss any of them in detail, it's important to have a basic knowledge of a few of them.

One of the pros of using an open source operating system such as Linux is that there is no shortage of applications. There are plenty of text editors, image viewers, web browsers, and media players that users can install. However, it becomes hard to keep track of which application can open which types of files and whether they are installed on the system. Additionally, there are so many file types these days that it simply is unreasonable to expect users to know what types of files they have. Sure, the user could simply run the `file` command on the file, but the typical user should not have to do that. Attempting to open it from a file viewer such as Nautilus should launch a viewer for it. Additionally, a user should be able to configure his or her own preference for which application should launch.

FreeDesktop.org to the rescue: the `shared-mime-info` project (`http://freedesktop.org/wiki/Standards/shared-mime-info-spec`) effectively compiles a static database indicating how files should map to MIME types. The database provides rules that allow applications to determine that certain filenames (such as `*.txt` files) should be treated as certain types (such as text/plain). With this information, the OS can make better choices as to which applications to launch when the user requests a file to be opened.

To make these decisions, the system needs to know which applications can handle which types. The desktop file specification (`http://freedesktop.org/wiki/Standards/desktop-entry-spec`) provides this information along with other details about the application that can be used by menuing systems and application launchers. The desktop file is a key/value text file that provides the name for the application to display in UI, icons that can be used to denote the application, what executable to launch, and of course which MIME types the application can handle. On a Red Hat/Fedora system, desktop files can be found in `/usr/share/applications/`. They are straightforward enough that looking at a few desktop files will go a long way toward helping you understand how to write them.

You must make sure the desktop file is properly installed. Use the latest `desktop-file-utils` package available at `http://www.freedesktop.org/software/desktop-file-utils`. The `desktop-file-install` program will make sure that all caches are properly updated.

As you can see, there is a wide range of applications that the FreeDesktop project provides for Linux programmers. The ones demonstrated here are just the tip of the iceberg. There are many more applications for you to play with and use in your programs available at the FreeDesktop.org website. Feel free to peruse that website and program to your heart's content.

Summary

In this chapter, you've learned that D-Bus is the IPC mechanism used by the Linux Desktop. You've learned that there is both a system and a session bus. You've learned there are four different types of messages that D-Bus can send and how to send and receive them. You've implemented a D-Bus client and server. You've learned what the HAL project is and how it utilizes D-Bus. You've learned how to listen for HAL events. You've learned what a HAL device object is and how to get information about it. You've also learned about NetworkManager and how to listen for network status events. You've learned a little bit about the desktop file specification and the `shared-mime-info` project. Most importantly, you've learned how all these pieces fit in to enhance the Linux Desktop experience.

13

Graphics and Audio

Many facets of professional programming require advanced graphics and audio support. Everything from creating mathematical models to writing the latest action game requires the ability to draw (and often animate) complex geometric objects. Likewise, with today's multimedia craze, many applications are required to handle audio files, both as digital files and directly from audio music CDs. Unfortunately, the standard programming tools included with most Linux systems do not provide methods for developing these advanced graphics and audio programs. This chapter describes two tools that can be added to your programming toolbox that help you create programs that add advanced graphics and audio to your Linux applications.

Linux and Graphics

Most Linux distributions today are graphics based. When you boot the system, you are greeted by a graphical login screen that often contains a fancy background image and a graphical list of users and options. Once you log in to the Linux system, your are presented with a graphical desktop environment that contains various icons for programs and devices, as well as a menu icon for selecting applications. Launching programs is as easy as clicking a desktop icon or selecting the appropriate option from a menu.

To get to this point though, the Linux system has to do a lot of things behind the scenes. There is a lot of program code used to display graphics on a Linux system. Graphics programming is one of the most complicated programming environments in Linux. Manipulating graphics objects requires knowledge of how the video card and monitor interact to produce screen images.

Fortunately, there are a few tools to help Linux graphics programmers out. This section describes four of the tools used to get graphics working on a Linux system: X Windows, OpenGL, GLUT, and SDL.

X Windows

The most common form of graphics provided by operating systems today is the windows system. Besides the famous Microsoft operating system called by that name, there are several other windows-based operating systems that provide a graphical window environment for programmers. Linux has joined the graphical revolution by supporting multiple types of graphical window environments.

In all operating systems there are two basic elements that control the video environment: the video card installed in the system and the monitor used to display the images. Both of these elements must be detected and controlled to properly display graphics in a program. The trick is gaining easy access to these elements.

Linux distributions use the X Windows standard for managing graphics. The X Windows standard defines protocols that act as an interface between graphical applications and the system's video card and monitor combination.

Since it acts as a middleman, the X Windows standard provides a common interface for a multitude of video cards and monitors. Applications written to interact with the X Windows standard can run on any system using any combination of video cards and monitors, as long as the video card and monitor provide an X Windows interface. This is shown in Figure 13-1.

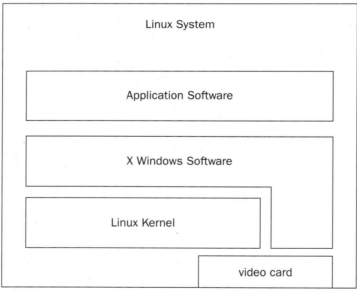

Figure 13-1

The X Windows standard itself is only a specification, not a product. Individual operating systems use different implementations of X Windows software to implement the X Windows standard. In the Linux world, there are currently two software packages that implement X Windows:

❑   XFree86

❑   X.org

The XFree86 software package is the oldest implementation of the X Windows standard. For a long time it was the only X Windows package available for Linux. As its name implies, it is a free, open source implementation of the X Windows software that was designed to run on Intel x86 systems.

Recently, a new package, called X.org, has come onto the Linux scene. The X.org software started as a development fork of the XFree86 software and quickly gained popularity among various Linux distributions by adding more advanced features than were available in Xfree86. Many Linux distributions are now using the X.org software instead of the older XFree86 system.

Both packages work the same way, controlling how Linux interacts with the video card to display graphical content on a monitor. To do that, the X Windows software has to be configured for the specific hardware system it is running on. In the old days of Linux, you had to pour through a huge configuration file to manually configure the XFree86 software for the specific type of video card and monitor used. Using the wrong configuration could mean burning out an expensive monitor. Now, most Linux distributions automatically detect video card and monitor features when the Linux system is installed, and create the appropriate configuration file without any intervention from the user.

At installation time, Linux detects the video card and monitor by probing for information, then creates the appropriate X Windows configuration file that contains the information found. When you are installing a Linux distribution, you may notice a time when it scans the monitor for supported video modes. Sometimes, this causes the monitor to go blank for a few seconds. Since there are lots of different types of video cards and monitors out there, this process can take a little while to complete.

Unfortunately, sometimes the installation can not autodetect what video settings to use, especially with some of the newer, more advanced video cards. To add insult to injury, some Linux distributions will fail to install if they can't find a specific video card's settings. Other distributions will fail the autodetect part, then resort to asking a few questions during installation to gather the required information. Still others just default to the lowest common denominator if the autodetect fails, and produce a screen image that is not customized for a specific video environment.

Many PC users have fancy video cards, such as 3-D accelerator cards, so they can play high-resolution games. 3-D accelerator cards provide hardware and software that increases the speed of drawing three-dimensional objects on the screen. In the past, the special video hardware caused lots of problems when you tried to install Linux. But lately, video card companies are helping to solve this problem by providing Linux drivers with their products. And many of the customized Linux distributions now even include drivers for specialty video cards.

Once the X Windows interface is available, application programs can use it to interact with the video environment installed on the Linux system. The popular KDE and GNOME desktops run on top of the X Windows environment, using X Windows application programming interface (API) calls to perform all of the drawing functions.

While the X Windows system is great for creating programs in a windows environment, there are limitations to what the X Window system can do. Since it is an older standard, there are lots of things X Windows can not provide for the programmer looking to write advanced graphics applications, especially when working with three-dimensional objects. For this type of programming, you must turn to other packages.

Open Graphics Library

The Open Graphics Library (OpenGL) was created to provide a common API to access advanced graphics features contained in advanced 3-D video accelerator cards. While the X Windows standard focuses on providing a windowed environment for programmers, the OpenGL project focuses on providing APIs specifically for drawing advanced two-dimensional (2-D) and three-dimensional (3-D) objects.

Much like X Windows, the OpenGL project is not a specific software library of functions. Instead, it is a generic specification of what functions would be required to perform tasks to draw objects on a graphical workstation. Individual vendors of video cards license the OpenGL specifications to produce APIs for their specific video cards. Programmers can then use the same APIs to interact with different OpenGL-licensed video cards.

Instead of using a specific OpenGL library for a specific video card, you can use a generic OpenGL library that is implemented entirely in software. The software library converts all of the 2-D and 3-D objects into standard X Windows function calls, which can be handled by standard video cards. This is demonstrated in Figure 13-2.

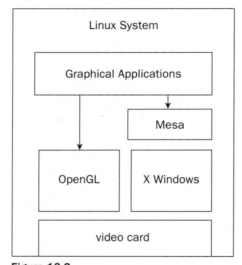

Figure 13-2

The Mesa program is a popular package that provides a software implementation of the OpenGL library of functions. The Mesa software is often installed by default in Linux systems that do not have fancy 3-D video cards installed, but need to implement advanced 3-D graphics. The Mesa software also includes developer libraries so you can utilize it to create your own 2-D and 3-D applications without having to purchase a fancy 3-D accelerator video card. Any software program written to run in Mesa will also work using OpenGL on an advanced video card.

OpenGL Utilities Toolkit

The OpenGL library provides functions for advanced 2-D and 3-D graphics, but unfortunately it does not provide functions for standard windows programming. To help compensate for the window short-comings of OpenGL, Mark Kilgard developed the OpenGL Utility Toolkit (GLUT). GLUT takes the OpenGL specifications and incorporates them with generic window functions to create a complete library of functions to build windows, interact with the user, and draw 2-D and 3-D objects.

The GLUT library becomes a middleman between OpenGL and the X Windows system. As with OpenGL, many video card manufacturers provide a specific GLUT library for their video cards. Also, the Mesa software provides a GLUT implementation completely in software for less advanced video systems. If you are using OpenGL for creating graphical objects, most likely you will want to include the GLUT library to help make your life easier.

Simple Directmedia Layer

The OpenGL and GLUT libraries are great if you need to draw polygons and spin them around on an axis, but in some graphical environments, you need to do more. Many programs (especially game programs) also need to quickly display full images on the screen besides drawing objects. Also, most game programs need access to the audio system to play sound effects and music, as well as access the keyboard, mouse, and joystick to interact with the game user. Doing these things using GLUT is not an easy task.

This is where higher-level game libraries come in handy. The most popular full-featured graphics and audio library available for Linux is the Simple Directmedia Layer (SDL) library. The SDL library provides many advanced functions for manipulating image files on the screen, creating animation from image files, accessing audio, and handling keyboard, mouse, and even joystick events.

The SDL library is a cross-platform library. There are implementations of SDL for most operating systems. You can develop an application using SDL on your Linux system and easily port it to a Microsoft Windows or Apple Macintosh environment. This feature has made the SDL library become a popular tool for professional game programmers. Many commercial game developers are switching to SDL to port Windows games to the Linux environment.

Writing OpenGL Applications

To create OpenGL applications, you must have both the OpenGL runtime library and development library installed on your Linux system. This requirement can be tricky.

The OpenGL library is not Open Source software. It is a licensed specification controlled by Silicon Graphics Incorporated (SGI). You must have a licensed copy of the software to run it on your Linux system. Many commercial video card vendors provide licensed OpenGL libraries for their specific video cards. However, if you do not have a video card that has specific OpenGL drivers, and still want to do OpenGL programming, you can use an OpenGL software implementation.

By far the most popular OpenGL software implementation is the Mesa project. *Mesa* is an open source project that was created by Brian Paul as a simple implementation of the OpenGL library. However, Mark does not claim that Mesa is a compatible replacement for OpenGL, and thus does not possess an OpenGL license for Mesa.

Instead, Mesa provides an environment that is similar to the OpenGL command syntax and has been authorized by SGI to be distributed as open source. Using Mesa does not violate any licensing restrictions. You can develop OpenGL applications using the Mesa programming environment that will work on any OpenGL implementation, and you can run the Mesa runtime libraries on your Linux system without requiring licensing from SGI.

As mentioned earlier in the "OpenGL Utilities Toolkit" section, the OpenGL library does not provide the necessary windows functions to write useful code. Fortunately, the Mesa project also provides the GLUT libraries as well, allowing you to write full-featured graphical window applications with one development environment.

This chapter uses the Mesa libraries to demonstrate how to develop OpenGL applications. The following sections describe how to download and install the Mesa libraries and how to use them to create OpenGL applications that can run on any OpenGL implementation.

Downloading and Installing

Many Linux distributions include installation packages for Mesa. Most Linux distributions install the Mesa runtime libraries by default. This allows you to run OpenGL applications, even if you do not have an advanced 3-D video card.

To develop OpenGL applications most likely you will have to install the Mesa development header and library files yourself. These are often bundled in installation packages with names such as `mesa-devel`. If you cannot find the Mesa development installation package for your particular Linux distribution, or if you prefer to work from the latest version of the package, you can download that from the Mesa web page.

The Mesa project web page is located at `www.mesa3d.org`. From the main web page, click the Downloading/Unpacking link to find the Download web page. From there you can download the latest Mesa libraries.

There are three software package bundles that can be downloaded:

❏ **MesaLib-*x.y.z*:** The main Mesa OpenGL library files

❏ **MesaDemos-*x.y.z*:** A set of OpenGL example programs to demonstrate OpenGL programming

❏ **MesaGLUT-*x.y.z*:** An implementation of the OpenGL Utility Toolkit for Mesa

The `x.y.z` nomenclature identifies the version of the Mesa library package, where x is the major version number, y is the minor version number, and z is a patch number. Mesa follows a release rule whereby all even numbered minor release numbers are stable releases, and all odd numbered minor release numbers are development releases. At the time of this writing, the latest stable release is version 6.4.2, and the latest development release is 6.5.1.

To create OpenGL applications on your Linux system, you should download at least the `MesasLib` and `MesaGLUT` packages. This provides a complete OpenGL and GLUT development environment for you to create your OpenGL applications.

You can download the files in either `.tar.gz` or `.zip` format, whichever is easiest for your particular Linux distribution. Download the distribution packages to a working directory, and use the `tar` or `unzip` commands to extract the files. All three packages extract to the same directory of Mesa-*x.y.z*.

After downloading and extracting the packages, you can build the libraries (and example programs if the Demo package was also downloaded). The Mesa software does not use the `configure` program to determine the compiler environment. Instead, it uses multiple make targets, one for each type of supported environment.

To see all of the available targets, type `make` from the command line by itself. A listing of all the available make targets is displayed. For Linux systems, you can use the generic `linux` target or a target specific to your environment, such as `linux-x86`. Just type the appropriate target name after the make command:

```
$ make linux-x86
```

After compiling the library files on your system, you can choose to install them into the standard library and header file locations on your system. By default the `make install` target installs the header files in the `/usr/local/include/GL` directory, and the library files in the `/usr/local/lib` directory.

One of the neat things with OpenGL is that you can have multiple versions of the OpenGL library files installed in separate locations (such as one version specific to your video card, plus the Mesa software libraries). When you run an application, you can choose which library is used to implement the OpenGL functions, and compare performance between the different libraries.

Programming Environment

With the Mesa OpenGL and GLUT header files libraries installed, you are ready to start writing programs. You must include the OpenGL and GLUT header locations in your applications using the standard `#include` statements:

```
#include <GL/gl.h>
#include <GL/glut.h>
```

When you compile your OpenGL application, you must include the locations for the Mesa OpenGL and GLUT header files, and the Mesa OpenGL and GLUT libraries for the linker using the `-l` parameter:

```
$ cc -I/usr/local/include -o test test.c -L/usr/local/lib -lGL -lglut
```

Notice that the Mesa OpenGL library (GL) is specified in uppercase but the GLUT library is in lowercase. You should also include the `/usr/local/lib` directory in the `/etc/ld.so.conf` library file so that Linux can find the OpenGL and GLUT dynamic library files. Remember to run `ldconfig` after you modify the file. You are now ready to start creating some OpenGL applications.

Using the GLUT Library

As would be expected, the GLUT library contains many functions for creating windows, drawing objects, and handling user input. This section demonstrates a few of the basic principles behind using the GLUT library to create simple graphical applications:

❑   Creating a window

❑   Drawing objects within a window

❑   Processing user input

❑   Animating your drawings

Before you can draw anything, you must have a workspace. The workspace used in GLUT is the window. The first topic shows how to use the GLUT library to create a window in a standard X Windows environment. After creating a window, you can use basic GLUT library commands to draw objects such as lines, triangles, polygons, and other complex mathematical models.

When working in a windows environment, capturing user input is crucial. Your application must be able to detect keyboard entries as well as any mouse movement. Finally, just about every game program requires animation. The GLUT library provides simple animation commands that can bring your objects to life.

Creating a Window

The most basic element of any graphics program is to create the window where the graphical elements are placed. There are five functions that are normally used to initialize the GLUT environment and establish a window:

```
void glutInit(int argc, char **argv);
void glutInitDisplayMode(unsigned int mode);
void glutInitWindowSize(int width, int height);
void glutInitWindowPosition(int x, int y);
int glutCreateWindow(char *name);
```

This series of function calls are present in just about every OpenGL program. The `glutInit()` function initializes the GLUT library and uses command line parameters passed to the program as function parameters to define how GLUT interacts with the X Window system. The command line parameters are:

❑   **display:** Specifies the X server to connect to

❑   **geometry:** Specifies the location to place the window on the X server

❑   **iconic:** Requests all top-level windows to be created in an iconic state

❑   **indirect:** Forces using indirect OpenGL rendering contexts

❑   **direct:** Forces the use of direct OpenGL rendering contexts

❑ **gldebug:** Calls `glGetError` after every OpenGL function call

❑ **sync:** Enables synchronous X Window protocol transactions

The `glutInitDisplayMode()` function specifies the display mode used for the OpenGL environment. The display mode is defined by ORing a series of flag values:

Flag	Description
GLUT_SINGLE	Provide a single buffered window.
GLUT_DOUBLE	Provide two buffered windows that can be swapped.
GLUT_RGBA	Control window colors based on red-green-blue (RGB) values.
GLUT_INDEX	Control window colors based on a color index.
GLUT_ACCUM	Provide a accumulation buffer for the window.
GLUT_ALPHA	Provide an alpha shading component for the window color.
GLUT_DEPTH	Provide a window with a color depth buffer.
GLUT_STENCIL	Provide a window with a stencil buffer.
GLUT_MULTISAMPLE	Provide a window with multisampling support.
GLUT_STEREO	Provide a stereo window buffer.
GLUT_LUMINANCE	Provide a luminance component for the window color.

The `glutInitWindowSize()` and `glutInitWindowPosition()` functions do what they say; they allow you to set the initial window size (in pixels) and position (based on the window coordinate system). The window coordinate system bases point (0,0) in the lower-left corner of the window display. The x-axis goes along the bottom of the display, while the y-axis is located along the left side of the display.

The `glutCreateWindow()` function creates the actual window in the display. The parameter used specifies the name of the window, which is displayed in the title bar at the top of the window.

After the window is created, the real fun can start. GLUT is similar to all other windows-based programming languages in that it uses event-driven programming. Instead of linearly stepping through the application code executing commands, GLUT waits for events to happen within the created window. When an event occurs, it executes a function tied to the event (called a callback function), then waits for the next event.

All of the work in a windows program happens in the callback functions. You must provide the code for events that happen without your application (such as when the user clicks on a mouse button or presses a key on the keyboard). GLUT provides several function calls that enable you to register your own callback functions to be called by GLUT when a specific event occurs:

Function	Description
`GlutDisplayFunc(void (*func)(void))`	Specifies a function to call when the contents of the window need to be redrawn
`GlutReshapeFunc(void (*func)(int width, int height))`	Specifies a function to call when the window is resized or moved
`GlutKeyboardFunc(void (*func)(unsigned int key, int x, int y))`	Specifies a function to call when an ASCII keyboard key has been pressed
`GlutSpecialFunc(void (*func)(int key, int x, int y))`	Specifies a function to call when a special keyboard key, such as F1–F12, or an arrow key, has been pressed
`GlutMouseFunc(void (*func)(int button, int state, int x, int y))`	Specifies a function to call when a mouse button is pressed or released
`GlutMotionFunc(void (*func)(int x, int y))`	Specifies a function to call when the mouse pointer is moved within the window
`GlutTimerFunc(int msec, void (*func)(int value), value)`	Specifies a function to call at *msec* milliseconds time, passing *value*
`GlutPostRedisplay(void)`	Marks the current window as needing to be redrawn

If you do not register a function with an event, GLUT does not attempt to pass those types of events occurrences to your program, and ignores the events. After registering your functions with the events, you must use the `glutMainLoop()` function to start GLUT waiting for events.

The `testwin.c` program, shown in Listing 13-1, demonstrates creating a window in the GLUT environment, and drawing a simple object within the window.

Listing 13-1: A sample OpenGL window program

```
/*
 *
 * Professional Linux Progamming - OpenGL window test
 *
 */
#include <GL/gl.h>
#include <GL/glut.h>

void display(void)
{
    glClearColor(0, 0, 0, 0);
    glClear(GL_COLOR_BUFFER_BIT);
    glColor3f(1.0, 1.0, 1.0);
    glRotatef(30, 1.0, 0.0, 0.0);
    glRotatef(30, 0.0, 1.0, 0.0);
```

```
        glutWireTetrahedron();
        glFlush();
}

int main(int argc, char **argv)
{
        glutInit(&argc, argv);
        glutInitDisplayMode(GLUT_SINGLE | GLUT_RGBA);
        glutInitWindowSize(250, 250);
        glutInitWindowPosition(0, 0);
        glutCreateWindow("Test Window");

        glutDisplayFunc(display);
        glutMainLoop();
        return 0;
}
```

The main() section of the testwin.c program uses the standard GUT initialization functions to create the window that displays the OpenGL drawing. A callback function is registered to handle the window display; then the GLUT main event loop is started.

The callback function, display, is used to control what is placed in the window. This is where the action happens. Before placing anything in the window, it is always a good idea to clear what may already be there. The glClear() function is used to clear the window. You can set the background color used to clear the window, using the glClearColor() function.

The glClearColor() function uses four parameters:

```
glClearColor(float red, float green, float blue, float alpha)
```

The *red*, *green*, and *blue* parameters specify the amount of red, green, and blue color added to the background color, with the value 0.0 being none at all, and the value 1.0 being all of that color. If you are like me and do not know how to create colors using the red, green, and blue combination, here is a table showing some of the basic color combinations:

Red	Green	Blue	Color
0.0	0.0	0.0	Black
1.0	0.0	0.0	Red
0.0	1.0	0.0	Green
1.0	1.0	0.0	Yellow
0.0	0.0	1.0	Blue
1.0	0.0	1.0	Magenta
0.0	1.0	1.0	Cyan
1.0	1.0	1.0	White

Remember, these are floating point values, so there are lots of color shades in between 0.0 and 1.0, but this should give you an idea of how to create some basic colors. The *alpha* parameter controls the amount of shading applied to the color. A value of 0.0 indicates that no shading is used, and a value of 1.0 applies full shading.

After setting the background color and clearing the background, you can start your drawing. The color of the drawn object is set using the `glColor3f()` function. This function defines colors by using the three RGB values (red, green, and blue), with floating point values from 0.0 to 1.0. The same color combinations shown for the `glClearColor()` function work just fine with this function.

After setting a color, it is time to draw an object. For this simple example, a built-in geometric object from the GLUT library is used. There are several types of built-in shapes to use, ranging from simple objects such as cubes, spheres, and cones to more advanced objects, such as octahedrons, tetrahedrons, and dodecahedrons. The `glutWireTetrahedron()` function used creates the outline of a tetrahedron. By default the object is displayed centered on the axis origin point. To help spice things up a bit, I used the `glRotatef()` function to rotate the view of the image. The `glRotate()` function uses four parameters:

```
glRotatef(float angle, float x, float y, float z)
```

The first parameter, *angle*, specifies the amount to rotate the object in degrees (I chose a 30 degree rotation). The next three parameters specify a coordinate point direction from the origin to rotate the object toward. The two `glRotatef()` function calls rotate the object 30 degrees on the x-axis, and then 30 degrees on the y-axis. This allows you to get more the 3-D feel of the object. The `glFlush()` function is used to ensure the drawing gets sent to the display at the end of the callback function call.

Once you have the `testwin.c` code typed in, you must compile it for your system:

```
$ cc -I/usr/local/include -o testwin testwin.c -L/usr/local/lib -lGL -lglut
```

To run the program, you must have an X Windows session open on your system. If you are using a desktop management system, such as KDE or GNOME, you can open a command prompt window to start the `testwin` program. The program window should appear on your desktop, along with the object, as shown in Figure 13-3.

Figure 13-3

Since this test program did not register a callback function to handle mouse or keyboard events, nothing you type or click will affect the program window. You can stop the program by closing the window. One thing you might notice is the way the window repaints the image. The display callback function is called every time the window needs to be repainted, for example if the window is moved or resized. Each time this happens, the glRotatef() functions add another 30 degrees to the image rotation. By resizing the window, you can watch the image rotate around the axis. In a couple of sections, you will learn how to make images move automatically.

Drawing Objects

Now that you have seen how to create a window and draw something in the window, it is time to learn what you can draw. Besides the built-in 3-D objects, GLUT uses the OpenGL library for drawing 2-D and 3-D objects.

In OpenGL, all objects are defined by one or more points. A point is created by the glVertex() function. The glVertex() function can be defined in several formats:

```
void glVertex{234}{sidf}[v](TYPEcoords)
```

As you can see, there are several versions of the function name that can be used. The function name used defines how the glVertex() object is defined:

❑   How many coordinates are used (2, 3, or 4)

❑   The data type of the coordinates specified (single, integer, double, or floating point)

❑   Whether the coordinate is a set of points or a vector

By default, OpenGL specifies all points as a 3-D object (x,y,z). If you are only drawing a 2-D object, you can use the two-coordinate option, with the z-axis value assumed to be 0. For example, to define a 2-D point using two integer coordinates, you would use:

```
glVertex2i(3, 6);
```

or to define a point in 3-D using floating point coordinates, you would use:

```
glVertex3f(1.0, 0.0, 3.4);
```

You can also define the point as a vector:

```
Gldouble vec[3] = {1.0, 0.0, 3.4};
glVertex3fv(vec);
```

A set of glVertex() points define an object. The set is defined using a glBegin() and glEnd() pair:

```
glBegin(mode);
glVertex2i(0,0);
glVertex2i(1,0);
glVertex2I(0,1);
glEnd();
```

The *mode* parameter defines how the points are related. There are several primitive modes that can be used:

Primitive Mode	Description
GL_POINTS	Individual, unconnected points
GL_LINES	Two points interpreted as a line segment
GL_LINE_STRIP	A series of two or more connected line segments
GL_LINE_LOOP	A series of two or more connected line segments, with the first and last segment also connected
GL_TRIANGLES	Three points interpreted as a solid triangle.
GL_TRIANGLE_STRIP	A series of two or more connected solid triangles
GL_TRIANGLE_FAN	A series of two or more connected solid triangles with the first and last triangle also connected
GL_QUADS	Four points interpreted as a four-sided solid polygon
GL_QUAD_STRIP	A series of two or more connected solid polygons
GL_POLYGON	Five or more points interpreted as the boundary of a simple, convex solid polygon

Note that the GL_LINE_ STRIP and GL_LINE_LOOP modes just create outlines of an object, while the other modes create a solid object. The inside of the solid objects is colored to match the color selected for the individual points.

Also notice that the same set of points can be interpreted in several different ways, depending on the primitive mode defined. Three points can be interpreted as three individual points, as two line segments, as a line loop with three segments, or as a solid triangle object.

When creating solid objects, be careful about the order you define for the glVertex() points. The object will be drawn in the order the points are specified. Crossing lines while drawing the object will result in a mismatched object.

The glVertex() function uses a coordinate system to define the location of the points. The tricky part to this is knowing what coordinate system is being used when you are drawing your objects. This is a somewhat complicated topic, especially when working with windows.

The coordinates used in the window change each time the window is resized. To make life simpler, OpenGL allows you to set a viewport within your window. The viewport allows you to map a generic coordinate system into the available space allocated within the physical window.

To set the viewport every time the window is resized, you must create a callback function for the glutReshapeFunc() function. Remember, the glutReshapeFunc() callback function is called every time the window size changes. The code contained in the callback function looks like this:

```
void resize(int width, int height)
{
    glViewport(0, 0, (GLsizei)width, (GLsizei)height);
    glMatrixMode(GL_PROJECTION);
    glLoadIdentity();
    gluOrtho2D(0.0, (GLdouble) width, 0.0, (GLdouble)height);
}
```

The `glViewport()` function adjusts the coordinate system to the new size of the window (the width and height values are passed by the `glReshapeFunc()` function. The `glMatrixMode()` function is used to define how 3-D objects are displayed on the 2-D monitor. The `GL_PROJECTION` matrix mode projects the 3-D image onto the 2-D screen, much as a camera projects a 3-D image onto a 2-D picture. You can also try to `GL_MODELVIEW` matrix mode for a slightly different effect. The `glLoadIdentity()` function is used to establish the matrix mode used in the window. The `gluOrtho2D()` function is used to set the location of the origin point (0,0) on the viewport. This format sets the origin in the lower-left corner of the window. The `gluOrtho2D()` function is not used in all drawing applications, as it conflicts with the GLUT coordinate system. If you must process mouse events using GLUT, do not remap the OpenGL coordinates using `gluOrtho2D()`, or you will easily get confused.

Now that you have seen the pieces required to draw an object, it is time to look at an example. The `testdraw.c` program shown in Listing 13-2 demonstrates how to draw a simple 2-D object using OpenGL.

Listing 13-2: Drawing objects using OpenGL

```
/*
 *
 * Professional Linux Programming - OpenGL drawing test
 *
 */
#include <GL/gl.h>
#include <GL/glut.h>

void display(void)
{
    glClearColor(0, 0, 0, 0);
    glClear(GL_COLOR_BUFFER_BIT);

    glBegin(GL_LINE_LOOP);
    glColor3f(1.0, 1.0, 1.0);
    glVertex2i(20,30);
    glVertex2i(60,30);
    glVertex2i(20,60);
    glEnd();

    glBegin(GL_TRIANGLES);
    glColor3f(1.0, 0.0, 0.0);
    glVertex2i(180, 30);
    glVertex2i(220, 30);
```

(continued)

Listing 13-2: *(continued)*

```
        glVertex2i(180, 60);

        glEnd();

        glBegin(GL_QUADS);
        glColor3f(1.0, 1.0, 0.0);
        glVertex2i(20, 130);
        glVertex2i(20, 160);
        glVertex2i(60, 160);
        glVertex2i(60, 130);
        glEnd();

        glBegin(GL_LINE_LOOP);
        glColor3f(0.0, 0.0, 1.0);
        glVertex2i(180, 130);
        glVertex2i(180, 160);
        glVertex2i(220, 160);
        glVertex2i(220, 130);
        glEnd();

        glFlush();
}

void resize(int width, int height)
{
        glViewport(0, 0, (GLsizei)width, (GLsizei)height);
        glMatrixMode(GL_PROJECTION);
        glLoadIdentity();
        gluOrtho2D(0.0, (GLdouble)width, 0.0, (GLdouble)height);
}

int main(int argc, char **argv)
{
        glutInit(&argc, argv);
        glutInitDisplayMode(GLUT_SINGLE | GLUT_RGBA);
        glutInitWindowSize(250, 250);
        glutInitWindowPosition(0, 0);
        glutCreateWindow("Test Drawing");

        glutDisplayFunc(display);
        glutReshapeFunc(resize);
        glutMainLoop();

        return 0;
}
```

The first thing to notice about the testdraw.c program is that the main() section is just about exactly the same as the testwin.c program. The only change is the addition of the glutReshapeFunc() function. Since all of the real work is being done in the display() callback function, you can often use a standard template for the main() section of all your OpenGL programs.

Also notice that the resize() callback function is the same one that was demonstrated earlier in this section. Again, often the callback function used to resize the viewport stays the same between OpenGL programs.

The display() callback function clears the window, then defines four different types of objects to draw within the window. At the end of the object definitions, the glFlush() function is used to ensure that the new objects are displayed in the window.

After compiling the program, try running it on your system. You should get an output window similar to the one shown in Figure 13-4.

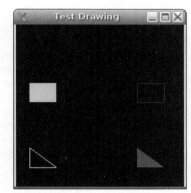

Figure 13-4

Try experimenting with the glVertex() function points defined, along with the glBegin() function modes to create your own shapes and objects. More complex objects can be created by overlapping several basic shapes.

Processing User Input

The next step in the process is to handle user input. As mentioned earlier in the "Creating a Window" section, you must provide a callback function for GLUT to call when a keyboard or mouse event is detected.

The glutKeyboardFunc() and glutSpecialFunc() functions define callback functions that are called when a keyboard event is processed. The glutKeyboardFunc() function listens for standard ASCII keyboard keys to be pressed or released, while the glutSpecialFunc() function only listens for special keys, such as the F1 through F12 function keys, the Escape key (ESC), or any of the up, down, left, or right arrow, Home, End, PgDn, or PgUp keys. The format for the glutKeyboardFunc() function is:

```
glutKeyboardFunc(void (*func)(unsigned char key, int x, int y))
```

The callback function is defined as *func*. The glutKeyboardFunc() function passes the *key* pressed, as well as the mouse pointer x- and y-coordinates in the window at the time the key was pressed.

If a multikey combination using the Shift, Ctrl, or Alt keys is selected, the ASCII key or special key value is used to trigger the callback function. The glutGetModifiers() function can then be used within the callback function to determine what modifying keys were pressed along with the ASCII or special key. The glutGetModifiers() function returns an integer value that can be compared to the values GLUT_ACTIVE_SHIFT, GLUT_ACTIVE_CTRL, or GLUT_ACTIVE_ALT to determine which modifier key was selected.

Similarly, the mouse buttons and movement can be tracked within the window using the glutMouseFunc() and glutMotionFunc() functions. The glutMouseFunc() function format is:

```
glutMouseFunc(void (*func)(int button, int state, int x, int y))
```

The function sends an integer value to your callback function *func* identifying the mouse *button* selected (GLUT_LEFT_BUTTON, GLUT_MIDDLE_BUTTON, or GLUT_RIGHT_BUTTON), an integer value showing the state (GLUT_UP or GLUT_DOWN), along with the *x* and *y* point location that the mouse pointer was at when the button was pressed. The mouse point location uses a coordinate system with the origin at the upper-left corner of the screen. This can often become confusing, so be careful if you must handle mouse locations.

The testkey.c program, shown in Listing 13-3, demonstrates capturing keyboard keys to control the movement of a drawn object.

Listing 13-3: Handling keyboard events in OpenGL

```
/*
 *
 * Professional Linux Programming - OpenGL keyboard test
 *
 */
#include <GL/gl.h>
#include <GL/glut.h>

int xangle = 0;
int yangle = 0;

void display(void)
{
    glClearColor(0, 0, 0, 0);
    glClear(GL_COLOR_BUFFER_BIT);
    glColor3f(1.0, 1.0, 1.0);
    glRotatef(xangle, 1.0, 0.0, 0.0);
    glRotatef(yangle, 0.0, 1.0, 0.0);
    glutWireCube(1);
    glFlush();
}

void keyboard(unsigned char key, int x, int y)
{
    if (key == 'q' || key == 'Q')
        exit(0);
}

void special(int key, int x, int y)
```

```
{
    switch(key)
    {
        case(GLUT_KEY_UP):
            xangle += 15;
            break;
        case(GLUT_KEY_DOWN):
            xangle -= 15;
            break;
        case(GLUT_KEY_RIGHT):
            yangle += 15;
            break;
        case(GLUT_KEY_LEFT):
            yangle -= 15;
            break;
    }
    glutPostRedisplay();
}

void resize(int width, int height)
{
    glViewport(0, 0, (GLsizei)width, (GLsizei)height);
    glMatrixMode(GL_MODELVIEW);
    glLoadIdentity();
}

int main(int argc, char **argv)
{
    glutInit(&argc, argv);
    glutInitDisplayMode(GLUT_SINGLE | GLUT_RGBA);
    glutInitWindowSize(500, 500);
    glutInitWindowPosition(0, 0);
    glutCreateWindow("Test Keyboard");

    glutDisplayFunc(display);
    glutReshapeFunc(resize);
    glutKeyboardFunc(keyboard);
    glutSpecialFunc(special);
    glutMainLoop();

    return 0;
}
```

The testkey.c program controls the viewing angle of the drawn object using two global variables, xangle and yangle. The initial values are set to 0. The display() callback function controls drawing the object (a cube created using the glutWireCube() function) in the window. The resize() callback function is almost the same as was used in the other examples. In this case, the gluOrtho2D() function is removed to keep the axis origin in the middle of the screen so that the rotation works properly.

The keyboard() and special() callback functions are used to control what happens when a key is pressed. The keyboard() callback function only checks to see if the key was either a q or a Q. All other keys are ignored. If the pressed key was a q or a Q, the program is stopped.

The `special()` callback function uses predefined GLUT values to check if one of the arrow keys had been pressed. For each arrow key, the rotation angle for the specific axis is changed using the appropriate global variable. (Note that this is not a correct mathematical model for altering rotation, as the previous rotation values are not cleared.)

After the rotation angle is changed, the `glutPostRedisplay()` function is called. This function forces OpenGL to redraw the contents of the window, again using the `display()` callback function. Since the rotation angle has been changed, the image view will rotate when the object is redrawn.

After compiling the program, run it and watch the window. A cube should appear, and you should be able to control the viewing angle of the cube by pressing the arrow keys. Pressing the `q` key closes the window and stops the program cleanly.

Animation

So far, you have seen how to alter a drawn image based on if the window size changes, or if the user hits a keyboard key or mouse button. However, for many applications (such as games) you need to move objects even when nothing else is happening. The OpenGL library provides the tool you need to automatically animate your drawn objects.

The `glutTimerFunc()` function allows you to specify a callback function, along with the time in milliseconds to call the callback function. The program waits the specified amount of time, then triggers the callback function. This allows you to perform specific functions at predetermined intervals within the program.

The contents of the timer callback function usually include a `glutPostRedisplay()` function to force the window to be redrawn with the new images. The timer `glutTimerFunc()` function can be added to the `display()` callback function to trigger another timer to update the display again later.

The `testtimer.c` program, shown in Listing 13-4, demonstrates using the `glutTimerFunc()` feature to animate an object drawn in the window.

Listing 13-4: Animating objects in OpenGL

```
/*
 *
 * Professional Linux Programming - OpenGL timer test
 *
 */
#include <GL/gl.h>
#include <GL/glut.h>

int millisec = 100;

void timer(int value)
{
    glutPostRedisplay();
}

void display(void)
{
```

```
        glutTimerFunc(millisec, timer, 1);
        glClearColor(0, 0, 0, 0);
        glClear(GL_COLOR_BUFFER_BIT);
        glColor3f(1.0, 1.0, 1.0);
        glRotatef(1, 0.0, 1.0, 1.0);
        glutWireCube(1);
        glutSwapBuffers();
}

void resize(int width, int height)
{
        glViewport(0, 0, (GLsizei)width, (GLsizei)height);
        glMatrixMode(GL_PROJECTION);
        glLoadIdentity();
}

void keyboard(unsigned char key, int x, int y)
{
        if (key == 'q' || 'Q')
            exit(0);
}

void special(int key, int x, int y)
{
        switch(key)
        {
            case(GLUT_KEY_UP):
                if (millisec >= 10)
                    millisec -= 10;
                break;
            case(GLUT_KEY_DOWN):
                millisec += 10;
                break;
            case(GLUT_KEY_HOME):
                millisec = 100;
        }
}

int main(int argc, char **argv)
{
        glutInit(&argc, argv);
        glutInitDisplayMode(GLUT_DOUBLE | GLUT_RGBA);
        glutInitWindowSize(500, 500);
        glutInitWindowPosition(0, 0);
        glutCreateWindow("Test Window");

        glutDisplayFunc(display);
        glutReshapeFunc(resize);
        glutKeyboardFunc(keyboard);
        glutSpecialFunc(special);
        glutMainLoop();

        return 0;
}
```

You should recognize most of the features in the `testtimer.c` program. The `display()` callback function displays a simple cube object using the `glutWireCube()` function and rotates it by one degree on the x-axis using the `glRotatef()` function. Notice that, instead of using the standard `glFlush()` function to push the image onto the window, a different function is used.

The `glutSwapBuffer()` function is a handy function provided by GLUT that allows you to manipulate two display buffers. When the `glutInitDisplayMode()` function is called in the `main()` program, it specifies the `GLUT_DOUBLE` parameter, which creates two display buffers. One buffer is always the active buffer. Its contents are displayed on the window. The other buffer is used when new objects are drawn. Any OpenGL drawing function performed is done on the inactive buffer. The `glutSwapBuffer()` immediately swaps the active buffer with the second buffer. This helps make animation appear smoother on the screen, as opposed to trying to update an active screen buffer.

Also, notice that the first statement in the `display()` callback function is a call to the `glutTimerFunc()` function. This starts a timer for a preset interval (100 milliseconds) and calls the `timer()` callback function when the timer expires. The `timer()` callback function's only job is to trigger the `glutPostRedisplay()` function, which forces the `display()` callback function to execute again, which in turn starts another `glutTimerFunc()`. This cycle is what continually redraws the window image every 100 milliseconds.

The `special()` callback function is used to handle the up and down arrow keys. If the up arrow key is pressed, the value of the `timer()` delay is decreased to speed up the animation refresh rate. If the down arrow key is pressed, the value of the `timer()` delay is increased, slowing down the animation refresh rate. If the Home key is pressed, the value is set back to 100 milliseconds.

Compile the program, and run it on your system. You should see a window appear, with a rotating cube drawn inside. Notice how smoothly the cube is drawn in the animation. Pressing the up arrow key increases the rotation rate, until there is no delay, creating quite a blur. Often, determining the optimal refresh rate for applications is a tricky thing. Most commercial-quality animations attempt a rate of 24 frames per second.

Writing SDL Applications

The OpenGL and GLUT libraries are excellent for drawing 2-D and 3-D objects, but they have their limitations. For more advanced graphical programming, and for incorporating audio into your applications, the SDL library provides functions that make life much easier.

This section describes how to download and install the SDL library on your Linux system and demonstrates some of the capabilities of the SDL library.

Downloading and Installing

The SDL library can be downloaded from the SDL website (`www.libsdl.org`). The main page contains a link to the download page for the latest version of SDL (currently SDL-1.2.11). On the download page, you can download a binary distribution of SDL or the complete source code package to compile. The complete source code can be downloaded as either a gzipped tar file, or a zip file.

If you choose to build the SDL library yourself from the source code, download the source code distribution file to a working directory, and extract the files using the appropriate method:

```
$ tar -zxvf SDL-1.2.11.tar.gz
```

This creates a directory called SDL-1.2.11 under the working directory. The SDL distribution uses the standard configure program to detect the platform-dependent compile configurations. Use the standard ./configure command, then the make command to build the libraries:

```
$ ./configure
$ make
$ su
Password:
# make install
#
```

The SDL header files are installed in the /usr/local/include/SDL directory, while the library files are installed in the /usr/local/lib directory.

Programming Environment

To create programs using the SDL library, you must include the path to the header and library files, as well as link with the SDL library:

```
$ cc -I/usr/local/include -o test test.c -L/usr/local/lib -lSDL
```

Also, in your application, you must reference the SDL/SDL.h header file, using the #include statement.

Make sure that your library environment uses the /usr/local/lib directory to reference dynamic libraries. This can be found in the /etc/ld.so.conf file.

Using the SDL Library

The SDL library contains functions to control video, audio, the keyboard, the mouse, the joystick, and the CD-ROM drive if one is present. Before you can use these functions, you must initialize the SDL library from your application. Also, at the end of your application you must close the SDL library.

The SDL_Init() function is used to initialize the library, while the SDL_Quit() function is used to close it. When you initialize the SDL library, you must specify which parts of the library you will use:

- ❏ **SDL_INIT_VIDEO:** Initializes the video functions

- ❏ **SDL_INIT_AUDIO:** Initializes the audio functions

- ❏ **SDL_INIT_CDROM:** Initializes the CD-ROM functions

- ❏ **SDL_INIT_TIMER:** Initializes the timer functions

You can initialize more than one portion by using the OR operation, like this:

```
#include "SDL.h"

int main(int argc, char**argv)
{
    if(SDL_Init(SDL_INIT_AUDIO | SDL_INIT_VIDEO) < 0
    {
        perror("SDLInit");
        exit(1);
    }
    ...
    SDL_Quit();
    Return 0;
}
```

This code initializes the video and audio SDL libraries. The following sections demonstrate some of the activities that are possible using the SDL library.

Displaying an Image

Although drawing images by hand on the window is nice, it can become cumbersome for large images. Often it would be nice to load and manipulate a premade image directly into the window. The SDL library allows you to do just that.

SDL displays images on an SDL_Surface object. The SDL_Surface object is then displayed on the viewing screen, which can be either in a window or the full screen. Individual images are loaded into an SDL_Surface object, with multiple images loaded into multiple SDL_Surface objects. The SDL_Surface objects can then be quickly swapped in and out of the viewing screen.

Before you can display images, you must set the video mode used for the images. The SDL_SetVideoMode() function is used for this. The format of this function is:

```
SDL_Surface *SDL_SetVideoMode(int width, int height, int bpp, Uint32 flags)
```

The SDL_Surface pointer returned by the SDL_SetVideoMode() function becomes the active viewing surface. Objects must be loaded into this surface to be seen on the display. The function call requests a specific video width, height, and bits per pixel (*bpp*). The *flags* parameter defines additional video mode features requested. The flags can be one or more of the following items:

Flag	Description
SDL_SWSURFACE	Create the video surface in system memory.
SDL_HWSURFACE	Create the video surface in the video card's memory.
SDL_ASYNCBLIT	Enables asynchronous blitting, used for multiprocessor machines.
SDL_ANYFORMAT	If the bpp requested is not available, SDL uses the available video bpp.
SDL_HWPALETTE	Give SDL exclusive access to the video card color palette.
SDL_DOUBLEBUF	Enable double buffering. Available only with SDL_HWSURFACE.

Flag	Description
SDL_FULLSCREEN	Attempt to use fullscreen video mode.
SDL_OPENGL	Create an OpenGL rendering context.
SDL_OPENGLBLIT	Create an OpenGL rendering context, but allow image blitting.
SDL_RESIZABLE	Create a resizable window. By default the window is not resizable.
SDL_NOFRAME	If possible, SDL will create a window with no title bar or frame.

The video mode defined in the function call is not necessarily what is allowed by the video system. The phrase "request what you like, and work with what you get" is often used in graphical programming. The SDL_Surface object returned by the SDL_SetVideoMode() function can be checked to determine what was actually allowed by the video system.

After creating an SDL_Surface to work with, you can load an image into an inactive SDL_Surface object, then move that object into the active SDL_Surface object. This process is called *blitting*. The first step, loading an image into an SDL_Surface object, is done with the SDL_LoadBMP() function:

```
SDL_Surface *SDL_LoadBMP(const char *file)
```

The image, obviously, must be in .bmp format, and specified by the *file* parameter. If there was an error loading the image into the surface, a NULL value is returned.

Once the new image is loaded into an SDL_Surface object, you can blit that image onto the active SDL_Surface object, using the SDL_BlitSurface() function:

```
int SDL_BlitSurface(SDL_Surface *src, SDL_Rect *srcrect, SDL_Surface *dst, SDL_Rect *dstrect)
```

As expected, the *src* and *dst* parameters represent the source SDL_Surface object to load, and the destination (active) SDL_Surface object. The two SDL_Rect parameters define a rectangular area of pixels, defining the regions to blit. The SDL_Rect object is a structure, with the following definition:

```
typedef struct {
      Sint16 x, y;
      Uint16 w, h;
} SDL_Rect;
```

The w and h fields define the width and height of the object, while the x and y parameters define the position of the upper-left corner of the rectangle.

If you are loading only a portion of the new image onto the screen, you can define the rectangular area using the SDL_Rect definition. If you are loading the entire image onto the screen, you can specify a NULL value for the *srcrect* parameter. The *dstrect* parameter is a little bit trickier. This specifies where on the screen the new image will be loaded. Usually the width (w) and height (h) values are set to the width and height of the image. The x and y values depend on where you want to place the image on the screen.

This can all start to seem confusing, but it is not all that bad. To create a screen, load an image, then center it on the screen, you can use the following code:

```
SDL_Surface *screen, *image;
SDL_Rect location;
screen = SDL_SetVideoMode(800, 600, 0, 0);
image = SDL_LoadBMP("test.bmp");
location.x = (screen->w - image->w) / 2;
location.y = (screen.h - image.h) / 2;
location.w = image->w;
location.h = image->h;
SDL_BlitSurface(image, NULL, screen, &location);
SDL_UpdateRects(screen, 1, &location);
```

The location object defines how the new image is blitted onto the active screen. The x and y values of location are set to center the new image on the screen. Notice that after the SDL_BlitSurface() function is called, the SDL_UpdateRects() function is used to perform the actual update of the active SDL_Surface object. As mentioned, you do not need to update the entire screen image if it is not necessary.

The imagetest.c program, shown in Listing 13-5, demonstrates loading images onto a screen using SDL.

Listing 13-5: Displaying image files, using SDL

```
/*
 *
 * Professional Linux Programming - SDL image test
 *
 */
#include <stdio.h>
#include <SDL/SDL.h>

int main(int argc, char **argv)
{
    SDL_Surface *screen, *image1, *image2;
    SDL_Rect location1, location2;
    int delay = 4;

    if (SDL_Init(SDL_INIT_VIDEO) < 0)
    {
        perror("SDLInit");
        return 1;
    }
    printf("SDL initialized.\n");

    screen = SDL_SetVideoMode(800, 600, 0, 0);
    if (screen == NULL)
    {
        printf("Problem: %s\n", SDL_GetError());
        return 1;
    }
```

```
        printf("Video mode set.\n");

        SDL_WM_SetCaption("SDL test image", "testing");
        image1 = SDL_LoadBMP("image1.bmp");
        if (image1 == NULL)
        {
          printf("Problem: %s\n", SDL_GetError());
            return 1;
        }
        printf("image1 loaded.\n");

        image2 = SDL_LoadBMP("image2.bmp");
        if (image2 == NULL)
        {
         printf("Problem: %s\n", SDL_GetError());
         return 1;
        }
        printf("image2 loaded.\n");


        location1.x = (screen->w - image1->w) / 2;
        location1.y = (screen->h - image1->h) / 2;
        location1.w = image1->w;
        location1.h = image1->h;

        location2.x = (screen->w - image2->w) / 2;
        location2.y = (screen->h - image2->h) / 2;
        location2.w = image2->w;
        location2.h = image2->h;

        if (SDL_BlitSurface(image1, NULL, screen, &location1) < 0)
        {
            printf("Problem: %s\n", SDL_GetError());
            return 1;
        }
        SDL_UpdateRects(screen, 1, &location1);
        SDL_Delay(delay * 1000);

        if (SDL_BlitSurface(image2, NULL, screen, &location2) < 0)
        {
         printf("Problem: %s\n", SDL_GetError());
         return 1;
        }
        SDL_UpdateRects(screen, 1, &location2);
        SDL_Delay(delay * 1000);
        SDL_Quit();
        return 0;
    }
```

The `imagetest.c` program uses `SDL_SetVideoMode()` function to request an 800x600-sized screen area, using the system default bpp and screen image. For most systems, the default will produce a window within the currently running X Window system. If you would like to try the program in fullscreen mode, add the `SDL_FULLSCREEN` flag in place of the last 0.

The the `SDL_LoadBMP()` function to load two images (`image1.bmp` and `image2.bmp`) into two `SDL_Surface` objects. You will need to have two images handy (named `image1.bmp` and `image2.bmp`) for this to work. After each image is loaded, the `SDL_Rect` location of the image is calculated to place the image in the middle of the viewing screen. Then, the `SDL_BlitSurface()` and `SDL_UpdateRects()` functions are used to load each image. The `SDL_Delay()` function provides an easy timer to use. The program uses it to pause four seconds between each image being displayed.

Compile the application and run it with a couple of test images. Notice that the switch between the two images is very quick and clean (especially if you are using an advanced video card). It is not hard to imagine what quickly blitting a few images on the screen can accomplish.

Playing an Audio File

Every successful game requires good sound effects. Being able to send audio files to the audio system can sometimes be a tricky thing in Linux. The SDL library provides an excellent interface for easily playing audio files on any operating system that supports audio.

SDL handles audio files using an `SDL_AudioSpec` structure. The format of this structure is:

```
typedef struct {
        int freq;
        Uint16 format;
        Uint8 channels;
        Uint8 silence;
        Uint16 samples;
        Uint32 size;
        void (*callback)(void *userdata, Uint8 *stream, int len);
        void *userdata;
} SDL_AudioSpec;
```

The `SDL_AudioSpec` structure contains all of the information needed to handle an audio file. The structure fields are:

Field	Description
freq	Audio frequency in samples per second
format	Audio data format
channels	Number of channels (1 for mono, 2 for stereo)
silence	Audio buffer silence value
samples	Audio buffer size in samples
size	Audio buffer size in bytes
callback	Callback function used for filling audio buffer
userdata	Pointer to audio data passed to the callback function

Most of the SDL_AudioSpec values are automatically filled in when the audio file is loaded. The SDL_LoadWAV() function is used to load a .wav audio file into an SDL_AudioSpec structure:

```
SDL_AudioSpec *SDL_LoadWAV(const char *file, SDL_AudioSpec *spec,
                    Uint8 **audio_buf, Uint8 *audio_len)
```

The SDL_LoadWAV() function loads the audio file *file* into the SDL_AudioSpec object *spec*. It also sets the *audio_buf* pointer to the buffer where the audio data is loaded, and the *audio_len* parameter to the length of the audio data.

The audio data length and pointer are important items that need to be tracked along with the SDL_AudioSpec information. The most common way to handle this information is with another structure:

```
struct {
        SDL_AudioSpec spec;
        Uint8 *sound;
        Uint32 soundlen;
        int soundpos;
} wave;
SDL_LoadWAV("test.wav", &wave.spec, &wave.sound, &wave.soundlen);
```

This structure provides all of the information needed to handle the audio file in one easy location. The audio data buffer location is pointed to using the sound pointer, and the length of the audio data buffer is kept in the soundlen variable. The soundpos variable will be used when we start playing the file. Once the audio file is loaded into memory, you can get ready to play it.

Unfortunately, this is where things get a little complicated. Remember, the SDL_AudioSpec object specifies a callback function to use for actually playing the audio data. The callback function is where things get complex.

SDL handles audio data as a stream. The audio stream might be stopped and restarted several times during the duration of playing the audio data. Each time the stream is restarted, the callback function is called. It must know where it left off in the audio data file, or it will just keep playing the file from the beginning each time.

To handle this, the callback function must be able to keep a pointer to the location in the stream where the audio file was stopped, and use the pointer to pick up where it left off. This is where the soundpos variable comes in handy. Here is a short callback function that uses the SDL_MixAudio() function to play an audio file stream:

```
void SDLCALL playit(void *unused, Uint8 *stream, int len)
{
    Uint32 amount = wave.soundlen - wave.soundpos;
    if (amount > len)
        amount = len;
    SDL_MixAudio(stream, &wave.sound[wave.soundpos], amount, SDL_MIX_MAXVOLUME);
    wave.soundpos += amount;
}
```

When the SDL_AudioSpec object is created, it passes the audio stream and its length to the callback function playit. The local variable amount is used to determine how much of the audio file is left to play, based on the current value of the soundpos variable. The SDL_MixAudio() function is used to send the audio stream to the audio system. The format of the SDL_MixAudio() function is:

```
void SDL_MixAudio(Uint8 *dst, Uint8 *src, Uint32 length, int volume)
```

The call to SDL_MixAudio() adds the current location of the audio file to the audio stream, attempting to play the entire left over amount. The last parameter, volume, specifies the relative volume to play the audio at. This value ranges from 0 to SDL_MIX_MAXVOLUME. Each time a portion of the audio file is played, the soundpos variable is updated to the next unplayed location in the audio file.

As soon as the SDL_MixAudio() function is called, it attempts to send the audio file data to the audio system. The SDL_PauseAudio() function controls if the audio should play or not. Using a parameter of 1 pauses the audio playing, while using a parameter of 0 starts the playing. By default, the parameter is set to 1, pausing playing until the next SDL_PauseAudio() function call.

The audiotest.c program, shown in Listing 13-6, demonstrates playing a .wav file using the SDL library.

Listing 13-6: Playing audio files using SDL

```c
/*
 *
 * Professional Linux Programming - SDL audio test
 *
 */
#include <stdio.h>
#include <SDL/SDL.h>
#include <SDL/SDL_audio.h>

struct {
        SDL_AudioSpec spec;
        Uint8 *sound;
        Uint32 soundlen;
        int soundpos;
} wave;

void SDLCALL playit(void *unused, Uint8 *stream, int len)
{
   Uint32 amount = wave.soundlen - wave.soundpos;
   if (amount > len)
      amount = len;
   SDL_MixAudio(stream, &wave.sound[wave.soundpos], amount, SDL_MIX_MAXVOLUME);
   wave.soundpos += amount;
}

int main(int argc, char **argv)
{
   char name[32];

   if (SDL_Init(SDL_INIT_AUDIO) < 0)
   {
      perror("Initializing");
```

```
        return 1;
    }
    if (SDL_LoadWAV(argv[1], &wave.spec, &wave.sound, &wave.soundlen) == NULL)
    {
        printf("Problem: %s\n", SDL_GetError());
        return 1;
    }
    wave.spec.callback = playit;
    if (SDL_OpenAudio(&wave.spec, NULL) < 0)
    {
        printf("Problem: %s\n", SDL_GetError());
        SDL_FreeWAV(wave.sound);
        return 1;
    }
    SDL_PauseAudio(0);
    printf("Using audio driver: %s\n", SDL_AudioDriverName(name, 32));
    SDL_Delay(1000);
    SDL_CloseAudio();
    SDL_FreeWAV(wave.sound);
    SDL_Quit();
    return 0;
}
```

The `audiotest.c` program uses the command line parameter to pass along the name of the audio file to load. The `SDL_OpenAudio()` function is used to open an audio device using the `SDL_AudioSpec` parameters required for the loaded `.wav` file. If there is not an audio device on the system that can play the file, the `SDL_OpenAudio()` function returns a -1 value. After opening the audio device, the `SDL_PauseAudio()` function is used with a 0 parameter value, starting the playback of the audio file.

The audio will only play while the program is active. Because of this, an `SDL_Delay()` function is added to wait a second for the audio clip to complete. For longer audio clips, you will have to alter the delay value. After the audio file plays, the `SDL_CloseAudio()` function is used to release the audio device, and the `SDL_FreeWAV()` function is used to free the buffer space allocated for the audio file.

Accessing the CD-ROM

In today's multimedia world, many Linux systems contain CD-ROM drives. The SDL library allows you the ability to use the CD-ROM drive to play music CD's in your application.

The `SDL_CDOpen()` function is used to initialize a CD-ROM device and examine the CD loaded in the drive. The `SDL_CDOpen()` function takes a single parameter, the CD-ROM drive number to access (CD-ROM drives are numbered starting at 0 for the first detected drive).

The `SDL_CDOpen()` function returns an `SDL_CD` object. This object is a structure that contains information about the CD:

```
typedef struct {
    int id;
    CDstatus status;
    int numtracks;
    int cur_track;
    int cur_frame;
    SDL_CDTrack track[SDL_MAX_TRACKS+1];
} SDL_CD;
```

The CDstatus field returns the current status of the CD-ROM drive:

- ❏ CD_TRAYEMPTY
- ❏ CD_STOPPED
- ❏ CD_PLAYING
- ❏ CD_PAUSED
- ❏ CD_ERROR

The numtracks and cur_track fields are somewhat obvious, showing the number of tracks in the CD if one is loaded in the CD-ROM drive and the currently selected track number. The track field contains the descriptions of each of the tracks of the CD. The cur_frame field is not so obvious. It contains the frame location within the current track. The frame is a base unit of measurement on a CD track. It is equal to 1 second of audio. You can use the FRAMES_TO_MSF() function to convert the frame value to minutes, seconds, and frames.

Once you know that a CD is loaded in the CD-ROM drive, playing tracks from it is as easy as using the SDL_CDPlayTracks() function:

```
int SDL_CDPlayTracks(SDL_CD *cdrom, int start_track, int start_frame,
                     int ntracks, int nframes)
```

where *cdrom* is an SDL_CDROM object opened from the SDL_CDOpen() function, *start_track* is the track to start playing from, *start_frame* is frame offset to start playing, *ntracks* is the number of tracks from the start to play, and *nframes* is the number of frames from the beginning of the last track to stop playing.

Opening a CD in the default CD-ROM drive and playing the first track looks like this:

```
SDL_CD *cdrom
cdrom = SDL_CDOpen(0);
SDL_CDPlaytrack(cdrom, 0, 0, 1, 0);
```

And that is all you need! Playing music from a CD could not be simpler. There are a few other functions that SDL incorporates to help glean information about the CD.

The cdtest.c program, shown in Listing 13-7, demonstrates using a few of the SDL CD functions to play a music selection from a CD.

Listing 13-7: Playing music CDs, using SDL

```
/*
 *
 * Professional Linux Programming - SDL CD test
 *
 */
#include <stdio.h>
#include <SDL/SDL.h>

int main()
{
    SDL_CD *cdrom;
```

```c
    int track, i, m, s, f;

    if (SDL_Init(SDL_INIT_CDROM) < 0)
    {
        perror("cdrom");
        return 1;
    }

    cdrom = SDL_CDOpen(0);
    if (cdrom == NULL)
    {
        perror("open");
        return 1;
    }

    if (CD_INDRIVE(SDL_CDStatus(cdrom)))
    {
        printf("CD tracks: %d\n", cdrom->numtracks);
        for( i = 0; i < cdrom->numtracks; i++)
        {
            FRAMES_TO_MSF(cdrom->track[i].length, &m, &s, &f);
            if (f > 0)
                s++;
            printf("\tTrack %d: %d:%2.2d\n", cdrom->track[i].id, m, s);
        }
    } else
    {
        printf("Sorry, no CD detected in default drive\n");
        return 1;
    }

    while(1)
    {
        printf("Please select track to play: ");
        scanf("%d", &track);
        if(track = -1)
            break;
        printf("Playing track %d\n", track);
        track--;

        if (SDL_CDPlayTracks(cdrom, track, 0, 1, 0) < 0)
        {
            printf("Problem: %s\n", SDL_GetError());
            return 1;
        }
        SDL_Delay((m * 60 + s) * 1000);
    }

    SDL_CDClose(cdrom);
    SDL_Quit();
    return 0;
}
```

The `cdtest.c` program starts out as expected, using the `SDL_CDOpen()` function to open the default CD-ROM drive for use. The `CD_INDRIVE()` function is used to determine if a CD is available, incorporating the results of the SDL_CDStatus() function. This provides an easy interface for interpreting the SDL_CDStatus() results.

If a CD is present, a loop is started to loop through each track on the CD, using the information in the SDL_CD object to obtain the tracks, track ID, and frames in each track. The FRAMES_TO_MSF() function is used to convert the frames to the standard minute:second format.

After the information is displayed, the user is asked which track to play. Selecting a track value of -1 stops the program. Since SDL numbers the tracks starting at 0, you have to be careful when working with track numbers. The SDL_CDPlayTracks() function is used to play the selected track.

The SDL_CDPlayTracks() function is nonblocking. That is, it will not stop execution of the program while the track plays. Instead, the program will start the CD playing, then go on its merry way. To halt the program and wait for the CD track to play, the cdtest.c program uses the SDL_Delay() function to pause for the duration of the CD track selected.

Compile the program, place a music CD in your CD-ROM tray, and test it:

```
$ ./cdtest
CD tracks: 11
        Track 1: 3:56
        Track 2: 3:33
        Track 3: 4:28
        Track 4: 3:12
        Track 5: 4:23
        Track 6: 5:16
        Track 7: 3:30
        Track 8: 4:07
        Track 9: 4:08
        Track 10: 3:32
        Track 11: 4:08
Please select track to play:
```

The program successfully read my music CD information, and played the track I selected.

Summary

In today's multimedia world, it is crucial to be able to create programs that contain graphics and audio. There are several methods for incorporating graphics and audio into your programs. The OpenGL library is used to provide advanced 2-D and 3-D graphical programming features for applications. The OpenGL Utility Toolkit (GLUT) can be used along with OpenGL to provide a window-based graphical programming environment. Many 3-D video cards provide an OpenGL library interface so that advanced 3-D objects can be drawn using the onboard hardware in the video card. For less advanced video cards, you can use software emulation to produce 3-D objects. The Mesa software library is an open source project that provides OpenGL-compatible capabilities for standard video cards by using software emulation.

Another popular graphical and audio library is the Simple Directmedia Layer (SDL) library. The SDL library is a cross-platform library that allows you to create programs using advanced graphics and audio features that will run on any operating system platform. The SDL library includes functions to handle playing music CDs, as well as standard .wav formatted files.

14

LAMP

In today's world where practically everything revolves around the Internet, making your Linux applications network-accessible is almost a necessity. Fortunately, there is plenty of help available in the open source community. The Linux-Apache-MySQL-PHP (LAMP) combination of software provides the elements for a complete web application environment. While not a single package per se, this combination of open source packages is easy to assemble and gets you going in the Web world.

This chapter aims to provide an existing programmer with a kick-start in web application development using the open source LAMP platform. It covers the basics of the LAMP environment, showing how to incorporate an Apache web server, MySQL database server, and PHP programming language together on a Linux server. After that, a complete web application is shown, demonstrating the ease of using the LAMP environment to implement web applications.

What Is LAMP?

Unknown to many, some of the largest brand-name websites run on open source software. Sites such as Google, BBC, Yahoo!, Slashdot, and Wikipedia are all built on components that anyone can obtain for free and modify for their own use. According to the regular Netcraft survey (`http://news .netcraft.com/archives/web_server_survey.html`) around 70% of all web domains are hosted on LAMP platforms.

LAMP is an all-encompassing label for web applications built around open source technologies (and sometimes proprietary ones). A LAMP application is traditionally viewed as one made up of the following open source components:

- ❏ Linux
- ❏ Apache
- ❏ MySQL
- ❏ PHP (or Perl)

However, all the above are open source projects developed by different groups of developers each with their own itch to scratch. Because of this, there are no strong dependencies among components, and it is quite normal for one or more of these components to be replaced by a substitute: PostgreSQL instead of MySQL, Perl instead of PHP, IIS instead of Apache, Microsoft Windows instead of Linux, Java/Tomcat instead of Apache and PHP, and so on).

Because of this flexibility, it is not easy to provide a hard-and-fast definition of LAMP, but perhaps a close fit is:

> **An open web application platform, where there is choice and flexibility as to which component is selected.**

Readers with experience of other web applications should be able to compare this with platforms or languages such as Microsoft's .NET, ColdFusion or WebLogic, where the commercial product provides the entire stack from web server to programming language and data access layer. The closed nature of these platforms restricts the choice developers have in selecting the components for their application. However, it is arguable that this provides for greater integration of components, which reduces complexity and may result in more efficient development.

As this book is about *Linux* Programming, other operating system options will not be discussed — other than to mention that many of the components discussed have versions for at least Microsoft Windows and other UNIX variants (Solaris, FreeBSD, NetBSD, OSX, etc.).

Apache

Apache was born as a fork of an existing NSCA `httpd` web server in February 1995. Its name reflects the early development, when sets of patches were exchanged through a mailing list — hence "A Patchy" web server. Netcraft surveys have shown Apache in a position of dominance in the server market since 1996. Its popularity has been due to its open source nature, excellent security, scalability, and flexibility — making it rare to find a deployment of a LAMP application without it. A number of alternative application servers (such as Tomcat [Java] or Zope [Python]) can be used as alternative web servers — although they tend to use Apache as a front end for security and configuration issues. There are two major versions of Apache available — 1.3 (the final release in the V1 branch) and version 2. The latter offers improved performance, so it should be used where possible, although you may need to use the earlier version in order to utilize some third-party modules such as mod_jk, or older versions of PHP.

MySQL

MySQL is the de facto database option for LAMP applications. This is partly due to superior support for it in early versions of PHP, but other factors include the speed of the MyISAM table type for simple applications, good graphical development tools, windows support and good marketing on the part of MySQL's commercial arm — MySQL AB. There are many alternatives, one of the most common being PostgreSQL. Amusingly, the choice of database is one that inspires many emotional debates among developers and administrators. MySQL is available under dual licenses — GPL or commercial — depending on the application, allowing redistribution as part of closed source applications without inheriting the restrictions of the GPL.

PHP

PHP is the most widely used language for web application development—according to the February 2006 Netcraft survey just under 1/3 of domains report that they run on PHP. PHP is a flexible web-oriented scripting language that provides extensive support for a wide range of database storage engines and tools such as zip, PDF, Flash, and image rendering to name but a few.

Development of PHP as was started by Rasmus Lerdorf in 1995 in response to the lack of tools for building simple websites. It began life as a collect of Perl scripts. As use of these tools increased, more developers began to work on them, and they were reimplemented in C with additional functionality. By 1997, the project's original name— "Personal Home Page Tools"—was changed to the recursive acronym "PHP Hypertext Preprocesso,r" and a complete rewrite formed version 3. The year 2000 saw the release of version 4—with support for limited object-oriented (OO) functionality—and the formation of the commercial company Zend, one of the driving forces behind PHP. The release of version 5 in 2005 was seen by many as a huge leap forward, with full object orientation functionality (including exceptions).

There are many alternatives (of which, coincidently, several also begin with P): Python, an object-oriented scripting language; Perl, which has a long history (often given the epithet "the duct tape of the Internet"); Java (with J2EE); and relative newcomers like Ruby. Each language has its own selection of frameworks which may make building applications easier (e.g., J2EE, Tapestry, Hibernate, Ruby on Rails, PHPNuke, Drupal, Zope, and Plone).

The Rebel Platform

Some industry analysts class LAMP as a "rebel platform" (as opposed to "industry-standard" platforms like .NET, or J2EE). The label comes from the perception of LAMP (and PHP in particular) as subversive in an industry historically (in the short history of the industry) dominated by single-vendor-driven platforms such as ColdFusion or .NET. The significantly reduced financial costs of setting up the application environment lowers the bar of entry into the industry, fueling the growth of many smaller and one-man-band development companies—and changing the face of the web development industry.

In this case, the term "industry standard" is somewhat misleading, as LAMP has become a de facto industry standard due to its market share. Nevertheless, the lack of significant backing from any large IT supplier (such IBM, Microsoft, Sun) means that it does not have the resources (or the centralized organization) to play the same sort of marketing games as the big names and can cause it lose out in larger projects (often those with a corporate decision-making structure behind them, where brand can be everything). On the other hand, the absence of a single large corporate backer has its advantages—resulting in less formality, and transparent and open development (e.g., public bug tracking and discussion).

Evaluating the LAMP Platform

There are various issues to consider when deciding whether to go with a LAMP-based application. Many of these are not technical but will depend on the decision-making culture of the organization(s) that you are working with or within.

- ❑ Cost and licensing
- ❑ Certification
- ❑ Support and services

- ❑ Vendor/developer community relationship
- ❑ Integration with and support for other technologies

Cost and Licensing

A common misconception about open source projects is that they must be free — financially speaking. Many licenses allow one to charge for products, and although the majority of the components in the LAMP stack are actually free to download and use in most circumstances, there are exceptions, such as MySQL (for commercial applications) or third-party modules or plugins. The general assumption that can be made about the costs of building a LAMP application is that they will be mostly developer and administrator time rather than from software licenses. With other platforms, license costs can be a significant portion of the overall project costs — especially when charges for some licenses will be applied to each "unit" of software sold.

The open licensing of the components of the LAMP platform — and of many of the applications built with it — provide excellent opportunities for software reuse, which can further reduce development costs. If you have the skills, you are free to adapt or extend the components to fit your needs

Certification

Certification has traditionally been an important element in the software industry, with all the big players providing a certification scheme for the users of their products. This is something that has always been popular with employers and people who commission software — anything that provides a benchmark for evaluating the skills of potential employees or development companies will save them valuable time. As a result, developers and administrators have always been keen to gain such certification.

Certification for the components of the LAMP platform is a relatively new development. The lack of corporate backing for these products has meant that there has been no recognized source of validation for such certification. However, with the growth of commercial companies supporting various components, industry-recognized certifications such as the Zend Certified PHP developer, MySQL certification from MySQL AB and the LPI, RedHat and Suse Linux Administration certifications have appeared and quickly gained popularity. Such certification theoretically helps people looking to hire developers to ensure that potential employees meet particular standards.

Support and Services

For many years, the "accepted" way to acquire software (including programming languages and development platforms) was to purchase a package from a vendor that included a certain amount of support. It was (any in some sectors is still) expected that both the software and the services would come from the same place.

Where open source software is concerned, this causes a problem. When they do not purchase software from a vendor, companies that wish to purchase support for it are often unsure as to where to go. There are several solutions to this problem. The first is following the traditional route. Sometimes the application is developed by a company and released as open source to take advantage of the developer community (or companies form around the product purely to support it). In these cases, there is a single entity to approach for support. Alternatively, there is an increasingly large industry growing up around the support of open source applications — often this takes the form of individual contractors or small companies who provide support, knowledge, and expertise in a particular niche. Third, large-scale users of products might find it more cost-effective to employ or train in-house support.

Vendor/Developer Community Relationship

Open source, by its nature, tends to result in a more transparent and reactive development process where bugs are resolved and new features reach users more quickly. Many open source projects provide mailing lists that allow interested parties to participate in and follow the discussion around feature development, and potentially influence the future direction of the project. Immediate access to source code, coupled with the ability to build the application, results in a never-ending stream of "beta" releases—although care should be taken not to use untested software in a live or hostile environment.

Some open source projects allow interested parties to fund development of a particular feature—this may be through donation of code or development time, or a financial donation—known as a bounty. Bounties are generally not centrally managed but are offered as an open proposition, which developers can choose to work on. Offering a bounty is no guarantee that a feature will be implemented.

In a commercial setting, the relationship between developers and the community tends to be more formal and less flexible. While license and support agreements ensure a certain level of responsibility of the provider toward the customer, there are rarely agreements in place to give the customer a chance to influence the direction of the product's development.

For vital new features, users of open source products often have the option of offering to employ key developers to implement what they require. This is something that would be somewhat more difficult with developers of a closed system. Less drastically, if you are having problems with a particular product, if it is open source, you are much more likely to have access to developers (or others in the community) through a variety of means such as mailing lists, instant relay chat (IRC), and online forums.

Integration with and Support for Other Technologies

Open source products, in general, have good integration with other open source products. Integration with closed source components can be more problematic; however, it is easier than trying to integrate two closed source applications. As an example, PHP has support for Oracle, Sybase, Microsoft SQL Server, and Java. Imagine seeing Microsoft supporting PHP from within ASP.

Now that you have an overview of what LAMP is, it is time to dive into the individual components of LAMP and see how to install them and use them. The next sections each cover a different LAMP component, showing how to get them installed and running on your Linux system.

Apache

This section illustrates some of the useful Apache-specific elements relevant to an example LAMP application. We will cover setting up an example virtual host for Apache, integrating Apache with PHP, and implementing HTTP authentication. Finally, we will show how SSL encryption can be used.

Nearly all Linux distributions come with Apache preinstalled. Our examples below use a version of Apache 2.x that can be found on any Debian-derived Linux system.

If you do not have Apache installed on your Debian system, running the following command should suffice:

```
apt-get install apache2
```

For other Linux distributions, consult your specific installation software instructions for how to load the Apache packages. For Red Hat–derived systems, this usually requires installing a .rpm file or two.

Virtual Hosting

Most installations of Apache create a generic configuration file to start the Apache server. To do any real-world work, you will have to customize the configuration files for your environment. One feature commonly used in real-world web servers is virtual hosting.

Virtual hosting is a means of having multiple websites listen on the same IP address. This is very useful, as it allows for an infinite number of websites, while we have only a finite number of IPv4 addresses available.

As you may recall from the earlier section on HTTP, upon making a connection to a server over TCP port 80, the client sends a "Host:" message which is used by the server to match the name of the site the client is visiting with that of the virtual host.

To define a virtual host, we need to create a file similar to the following in /etc/apache2/sites-available as "root":

```
<VirtualHost *>
    ServerName test.example.com
    ServerAlias test www.test.example.com
    ErrorLog /var/log/apache2/test-error_log
    CustomLog /var/log/apache2/test-access_log common
    DocumentRoot /www/test.example.com
    DirectoryIndex index.php
    <Directory "/www/test.example.com/">
        Options Indexes MultiViews FollowSymLinks
        AllowOverride All
        Order allow,deny
        Allow from all
    </Directory>
</VirtualHost>
```

The ServerName directive, specifies what the site advertises itself as, while ServerAlias allows the same site to match multiple other URLs (for instance, on an internal network you may skip the domain name). The ErrorLog and CustomLog directives specify where Apache will log messages relevant for this site to (requests to view content, etc.). The DocumentRoot directive specifies where on the filesystem, files for the site can be found. The DirectoryIndex specifies what page will be used if only a directory name is supplied in the URL.

<Directory> allows anyone to view the contents of the directory (hence Allow from all).

Now, to tell Apache to load your configuration you need to do the following:

```
a2ensite the_file_name
/etc/init.d/apache2 reload
```

As long as you have appropriate entries in DNS or your local /etc/hosts file, you will now be able to access the site through a web browser.

Installation and Configuration of PHP 5

While this sounds like we are jumping ahead, installing the PHP5 software is actually a part of the Apache installation. The Apache distribution includes the PHP5 installation software as a module. A module in Apache is a self-contained feature that can be added to the Apache server.

Just as with the basic Apache server installation, installation and configuration of the PHP5 Apache module will vary according to the distribution of Linux that you are using. All of the major distributions will have packaged versions of PHP that you can install in the normal way. Look for an installation file labeled `php-mod`, or something along those lines.

After you get the PHP5 module installed on your Apache server, you will want to check that it is working. To test your setup, create an HTML file in your website document root that contains the following:

```php
<?php
phpinfo();
?>
```

Accessing this file through a web browser should show a page containing information about PHP. if it does, you have successfully installed the PHP5 module. If not, you may have to consult your specific Linux installation software instructions to determine which modules you must load.

PHP Configuration

Typically, there is no need to change the default PHP configuration; however, for your reference the following information may be of use.

There are a number of settings which can be changed within PHP, by changing the `php.ini` file. There are normally different configuration files for the CLI version (PHP from the command line) and the Apache module.

Installation of PHP Modules

PHP itself contains several features that can be individually installed on the Linux system. PHP is generally distributed for Linux in a number of packages, allowing you some choice over what is installed on your server. Default packages often have no database-specific extensions installed, so they would not be able to immediately communicate with a PostgreSQL or MySQL database. You must install the PHP MySQL module to enable your PHP installation to communicate with a MySQL database (another component in the LAMP environment).

For Debian-derived systems, you can install the php-mysql module to include the linking components in PHP to communicate with a MySQL database. After installing additional packages, you can once again test your setup with a `phpinfo()` page. Now, it should show that it is capable of connecting and communicating with a MySQL database.

> Note: It is generally considered to be good practice to not leave `phpinfo()` style pages accessible on a live website, as it potentially provides malicious individuals access to move information than is necessary about your site and configuration.

Apache Basic Authentication

If you want to restrict your website (or even just parts of it) to specific customers, you should implement basic authentication. Apache can provide simple authentication of resources, on a per-directory (or sometimes per-file) basis. This can be specified in the site's global Apache configuration file (in this case, within the VirtualHost container specified earlier), or it can be placed within a .htaccess file, which is placed in the directory to be protected.

The authentication mechanism provided by Apache should not be regarded as being secure (i.e., passwords are transmitted in effectively plain text). If security is an issue, see the section on Authentication with SSL as well.

An Apache configuration that requires a login for a resource (in this case /admin) might look like the following, which should be placed within the VirtualHost container, as shown previously.

```
<VirtualHost *>
......
    <Location "/admin">
        AuthType Basic
        AuthName "Administration Site"
        AuthUserFile /etc/apache2/htpasswd
        AuthGroupFile /etc/apache2/htgroup
        Require group dvd-admin
    </Location>
.......
</VirtualHost>
```

It is necessary for you to create the files /etc/apache2/htpasswd and /etc/apache2/htgroup (these are arbitrary — specified in the configuration file above — but sensible names) as follows, where you create two users and a group file referencing them:

```
$> htpasswd2 -c -m /etc/apache2/htpasswd my_user_name
$> htpasswd2 -m /etc/apache2/htpasswd an_other_user
$> echo "dvd-admin: my_user_name an_other_user" > /etc/apache2/htgroup
```

Note that, the −c flag should not be used on an existing file; otherwise, you'll lose its contents!

Now, if you attempt to access the /admin part of your website, you will be presented with a pop-up authentication window.

Apache and SSL

Besides basic authentication, you may want to implement encryption on your website. For websites that deal with personal information, this should be a requirement. SSL is used to encrypt the transport layer below HTTP. Therefore, from a developer's or user's point of view, there is no difference between sites that do or don't use HTTP + SSL (HTTPS), aside from the fact that use of SSL ensures that the content was transmitted securely. Mechanisms for setting up SSL will depend on your distribution. In Debian-based systems, you would use the following command:

```
$> apache2-ssl-certificate
```

If you have an existing SSL certificate, you will need to provide the `-force` *option to this script. If you wish the certificate to last for a set period, use the* `-days` *parameter.*

This will guide you through a series of questions, asking for information about the site you wish to protect with the SSL certificate. After this successfully runs, you will need to reconfigure your web server to contain something similar to the following:

```
NameVirtualHost *:443
<VirtualHost *:443>
        SSLEngine On
        SSLCertificateFile /etc/apache2/ssl/apache.pem
        ServerName mysecureserver.example.com
        ServerAlias mysecureserver
        ........other directives as before.....
</VirtualHost>
```

Note how the `VirtualHost` definition has changed slightly — this is to bind it to the correct port for SSL (443).

Integrating SSL with HTTP Authentication

There is no reason why you can't just make everyone use the HTTPS-style links. However, this may be a slight inconvenience for your users because they must update their bookmarks and the like, and ideally it's best if it "just happens." Also, if you do not have a registered certificate, you are asking your users to take your SSL certificate on trust. Thankfully, in the case of the bookmarking issue, we can use Apache's `mod_rewrite` module to allow us to redirect people accessing <http://myserver/admin to https://myserver/admin> to a location where they will be prompted to log in using the `htpasswd`-style authentication as discussed above.

In your original non-SSL site, add the following to the `VirtualHost` container:

```
RewriteEngine on

RewriteCond %{REQUEST_URI} ^/admin(.*)
RewriteRule ^/(.*) https://securesite/$1
```

Now, should any user access the URL <http://mysite/admin/anything>, the following will occur:

1. The URL will match the rule in Apache for `^/admin` in the `RewriteCond` statement.

2. Apache will redirect the user to <https://securesite/admin/anything>.

3. The user will be prompted to accept the SSL certificate for `https://securesite` (if it is not trusted via, for example, Thwate).

4. The SSL session will start, and the browser will request the user for authentication details.

5. The user enters authentication details, which are encrypted via SSL.

6. The server returns the content requested by the user, again via SSL.

Now, you have a running Apache web server that supports PHP5 programs, which in turn can access a MySQL database. The next step, of course, is to install a MySQL database to store your web data.

MySQL

Following the LAMP model, the next component you need is a MySQL database. This section discusses how to install the MySQL database and configure it for your environment. Once you have your MySQL server running, you will need to configure a few tables for your database. This section wraps up by showing you some basic database programming commands so that you can build your database.

Installing MySQL

Similarly to installing Apache and PHP5, installing MySQL on most Linux distributions is just a matter of finding the proper installation file and using your installation software to install it. MySQL is so popular in the Linux world that now some Linux distributions install it by default. You can check your specific distribution's installed software list to see if MySQL is already installed (or you can type `mysql` in the command line and see if anything happens).

If MySQL is not installed on your system, for Debian-derived systems you can use the `apt-get` program to install the basic package:

```
apt-get install mysql
```

Some Linux distributions separate the MySQL server and client programs into separate installation packages. If your distribution does that, you will want to install the client package as well. This provides applications for interacting with the MySQL server from a command prompt. This makes creating and managing databases much easier.

In most Linux distributions, the installation package installs the MySQL database software but either provides a basic configuration or does not configure it for you at all. The next step is to configure and start your MySQL database.

Configuring and Starting the Database

Before you can start the MySQL server, you must create the system databases that MySQL uses to track tables, users, and other database information. You do this by running a premade script provided by MySQL, `mysql_install_db`, as the root user.

When you run this script, you should see messages showing the progress of the script. The script will build several tables:

```
Creating db table
Creating host table
Creating user table
Creating func table
Creating tables_priv table
Creating columns_priv table
```

When the script completes, you are ready to start the MySQL server. Again, this is somewhat distribution specific. Some distributions place the MySQL database startup script in the autostart area, automatically starting the server when the Linux system is booted. If your distribution does not do this, you must start the MySQL server manually:

```
/usr/local/bin/safe_mysqld --user=mysql &
```

The `safe_mysqld` script starts the MySQL database using the supplied user account (it is a considered a security risk to start the server as the root user). Most all distributions use the `mysql` user account for this purpose. The ampersand (&) at the end of the command forces the server to run in background mode.

Changing the Default Password

The MySQL server maintains its own list of users, separate from the Linux system. The administrator account for the server is root. By default, the root user account does not have a password. This can be a bad thing for a database exposed to the Internet.

The `mysqladmin` program allows you to perform administrative functions on the server, such as stopping the server, displaying the status of a running server, and of course, changing users' passwords. The format to change the root user password is:

```
/usr/local/bin/mysqladmin -u root -p password 'newpassword'
```

Of course, to use the `mysqladmin` program you must be the root user, so the first thing it will do is ask you for the root user password. Since the default password is null, just press the Enter key. The password will then be changed to whatever you place in the command line.

The MySQL Client Interface

After you have a complete MySQL server running you can try to log in with an interactive prompt. The `mysql` command starts a command line program that allows you to connect to a database and execute SQL commands. To connect to the default MySQL database using the root user account, you type:

```
mysql -u root -p
```

After entering the password, you should see the MySQL prompt:

```
$ mysql -u root -p
Enter password:
Welcome to the MySQL monitor. Commands end with ; or \g.
Your MySQL connection id is 250 to server version: 3.23.36

Type 'help;' or '\h' for help. Type '\c' to clear the buffer

mysql>
```

Now, you are ready to start entering SQL commands to build your database.

Relational Databases

In many fields of programming today, *relational databases (RDB)* are used as a matter of course. Traditional UNIX flat file databases have been discussed in earlier chapters. However, these traditional data formats leave many of the regular tasks necessary to build a good data model for an application to the programmer, ensuring that they are reimplemented each time a new application is developed. There are often physical constraints on data that is taken from the real world, and these constraints need to be reflected somewhere in the application. Many people chose to put them in their application logic code, but these more properly belong in the data layer itself (especially in applications where you can have more than one front end to your data). Relational databases and their associated software—*relational database management systems (RDBMS)* can reflect these constraints in the data definition and enforce them any time data is entered or modified, ensuring that developers cannot accidentally not implement a constraint that might already exist in another user interface—creating inconsistent data.

SQL

Data in your RDB is defined, created, accessed and modified using *Structured Query Language (SQL)*. This is the element of RDBs that most developers are familiar with, as even a basic understanding of this (often code cut and pasted from other resources) is enough to get you started with an application that basically works. This section is being included before the explanation of the relational model (even though it's kind of the wrong way round) because many developers already have a familiarity with SQL, even if they have not come across the relational model, and this can be exploited to help explain the mathematical model. If you have such familiarity, you can skip ahead; otherwise, the concepts here will help the comparisons in the next section to make sense.

This section is not intended in any way to be an exhaustive reference but rather a simple "getting started" guide. It explains some of the most basic statements and provides information that will help you if you have no previous experience with SQL.

Data of a particular type is stored in a table (so a person's data would all be collected into a table called Person, and so on), and the attributes of that data are the fields in the table. Records (or rows) are individual occurrences of that type, so "Jane Smith" and all her associated data would be stored in a record in the Person table.

All of the SQL statements in this section are standard statements. This means that they conform to the SQL92 standard that most relational database management systems implement. These statements will work with a wide range of RDBMSs, which will allow you to create vendor-independent applications.

Some of the data types in these examples are PostgreSQL-specific. If your RDBMS of choice does not accept these data types, you should be able to make a simple substitution in your table definitions according to the types defined in the DBMS's documentation.

Some notes about SQL statements:

❑ SQL statements are terminated using a semicolon (;), although most programming interfaces to relational databases automatically append them to single statements.

❑ All SQL statements have a basic syntax, which can be supplemented with optional parameters that will make the statement more specific.

❑ By convention, all SQL keywords are typed in capitals—this makes differentiating between keywords and data or functions quite simple.

Creating Tables

The basic syntax to create a *table* (relation) is:

```
CREATE TABLE tablename(fieldname type, fieldname type, ... fieldname type);
```

From our example:

```
CREATE TABLE dvd(title character varying(150), director character varying(150),
release_date int4);
```

would create a table called dvd, with three fields — two size-limited text fields for title and director, and one integer field for the release year.

Inserting a Record

Once you have defined a table, you will want to insert some data into it. There are two basic forms of the syntax for this:

```
INSERT INTO tablename VALUES (value, value, ... value)
INSERT INTO dvd VALUES ('How to Lose a Guy in 10 Days', '2003', 'Donald Petrie',
'12', 'Comedy');
```

This takes each of the values in turn and attempts to store them in the fields in the order in which they were defined when the table was created.

However, it is often required that only a select number of fields be inserted and/or that they need to be inserted in a different order to the one they were defined in. In that case, the following syntax can be used to name the appropriate fields and the order in which the corresponding values are going to be passed.

```
INSERT INTO tablename (fieldname, fieldname, ... fieldname) VALUES (value, value,
... value)
```

To insert values into the DVD table, per the previous statement, without knowing the director, the following statement can be used:

```
INSERT INTO dvd (title, release_year, rating, genre) VALUES ('How to Lose a Guy in
10 Days', '2002', '12', 'Comedy');
```

Searching for Records

Locating records according to various criteria is probably the most common database operation for most systems. The syntax for this is simple, but there are a few options. The simplest version is:

```
SELECT * FROM tablename WHERE field = value;
```

This will return all of the records for the table where the field matches the given value exactly. The two main parts of a query to carry out a search are the SELECT statement and the WHERE clause.

The SELECT Clause

The SELECT part involves defining which fields you want to display from your query, narrowing down your output. Multiple fields are provided in the form of a comma-separated list:

```
SELECT title FROM dvd;
SELECT title, director FROM dvd;
```

would list the titles of all of the records in the DVD table.

The WHERE Clause

Having no WHERE clause gives every record in the table. The WHERE clause restricts the number of records that are returned, according to the criteria given. The WHERE clause is also used in other SQL statements.

To find all DVDs that were released before 2000, we could use the following statement:

```
SELECT * FROM dvd WHERE release_year < 2000;
```

To narrow that down further an AND (or OR) could be added to the WHERE to find all DVDs directed by Terry Gilliam:

```
SELECT * FROM dvd WHERE release_date < 2000 AND director = 'Terry Gilliam';
```

In a WHERE clause, the = operator matches equality exactly and is case sensitive. In addition, there are many other comparison operators to use, for example:

- ❏ > (greater than)
- ❏ < (less than)
- ❏ AND / OR / NOT
- ❏ != (or <>)
- ❏ >= or <= (greater or equal to, less than or equal to)
- ❏ IS NULL / IS NOT NULL

Editing a Record

Once a database table contains some data, it is quite likely that it will need to be updated. The UPDATE statement is used to achieve this:

```
UPDATE tablename SET fieldname = value, fieldname = value, ... fieldname = value
WHERE fieldname = value;
```

The WHERE clause here is used to identify the record to update. If a WHERE clause matches multiple records, it will update them all, so you need to ensure that the criteria only selects the records you want to update. Its often a good idea to test the WHERE clause on a SELECT statement before using it in an UPDATE (or DELETE).

To update a single field in the DVD table — for example, if the release date for cinemas rather than for the DVD version had been entered, the following statement can be used:

```
UPDATE dvd SET release_year = 2003 WHERE title = 'How to Lose a Guy in 10 Days';
```

Deleting Records

Deleting records is much like updating them, except that because the whole record must be deleted, there is no need to specify which parts of the record are needed. The syntax is:

```
DELETE FROM tablename WHERE field = value;
```

For example:

```
DELETE FROM tablename WHERE title = 'How to Lose a Guy in 10 Days';
```

would only delete "How to Lose a Guy in 10 Days" as no other records would match the title.

The Relational Model

Many casual (and some not so casual!) users of relational databases are unfamiliar with the mathematical principles that define and constrain how a RDBMS behaves. To really understand how to structure and search your data, it is highly advisable to get a good understanding of the theory behind it all. This section is not intended to provide that level of understanding but aims to provide an overview of some of the terminology and principles. It is highly simplified and will need to be followed up.

If you have an interest in building well-defined, robust RDB applications, you should follow up your reading with one of the many excellent books on database theory, such as C. J. Date's Database in Depth: Relational Theory for Practitioners.

Relations, Tuples, and Attributes

The building blocks of the relational model is the *relation*. Roughly equivalent to the concept of a table in SQL, it is the main unit of data in an RDB. The relation represents the set of data of a particular type. In the PHP sample application, which will bring the LAMP chapter to an end, a very simple DVD library is implemented. In that case, the basic relations are as dvd, library_user, and genre. Our *tuples* are broadly the same as our rows, so the set of values that includes Serenity, 2005, Joss Whedon, 15, and Sci Fi are a tuple. An *attribute* equates generally to the concept of a column, so Director would be an attribute of the relation dvd.

Keys and Relationships

To be able to perform actions such as searching on the data, each tuple needs to have a way of being *uniquely identifiable*. The attribute or combination of attributes that can be used to uniquely identify a tuple are known as *keys*. Keys can be of various types. *Candidate* keys are any key that could potentially identify the record as unique. However, a relation may have several potentially unique combinations of attributes, so a *primary* key is the one selected to be maintained as unique — this is more of an implementation issue with an RDBMS though, as operations based on the relational model will be performed on any of the candidate keys. In practice, keys are used to identify precisely how relations are related, so a primary key for one table that appears in another — to link the two together — is a *foreign key* in the table for which is not a candidate key.

Relations, tuples, and attributes alone cannot reflect the real structure of your data. Each relation taken individually might accurately reflect that small subset of data, but it is the *relationships* between the items of data — and the limits and restrictions on those relationships — that helps you to gain a much more accurate representation of it. Our relationships in the sample application are not the best example, as they represent a categorization of the data in the dvd relation into genres — something that is imposed on the data. A better example here might be a representation of a school structure, where students and classes have a defined relationship. Relationships are defined in terms of the number of participants on each side of the relationship. Values can be 0, 1, or many, and you can have a minimum and maximum value for each relationship. An example of this will be explained when data modeling is covered.

Relational Operators

Once you have a set of data, you will want to be able to manipulate it — and to do this, you need some operators. The *relational assignment* operator is used to assign values to a relation (in SQL terms, INSERT, UPDATE, or DELETE). In addition to this, you also have relational operators, classified into *Restrict, Project, Product, Intersect, Union, Difference, Join,* and *Divide.* Covering all of these operators would be far too much detail, but suffice it to say that many of them relate to different types of *join* (e.g., union is a special case of join). Understanding these concepts and how they affect a data set will help you to select the right — and most efficient — SQL for your task.

Data Integrity

Your real-world data set — such as your DVDs sitting on your shelf at home, or your children going to school — have actual constraints that the world (be it the government, their parents, or the rules of physics) places upon them. Often, you can define a few constraints that are absolute within the bounds of your system and should never be broken. You can have constraints at various levels — from the size of an attribute (a UK National Insurance number is always nine characters) to the contents of a tuple (a tuple from a dvd relation must have a title that is not blank) to the relationships between relations.

Data Modeling and Normalization

Deciding what the bounds of your system are, and what its constraints should be, is perhaps the most vital part of the design of any system. Ensuring that your data storage system accurately models the data being represented will increase the chances of the application as a whole meeting the user's actual requirements, but this is a very difficult thing to do. When a system is modeled, you should ensure that you understand the data and its relationships thoroughly, or at the least painstakingly gather the information from whoever has the best understanding of it (unfortunately, often such a person may not exist, or you may not have access to them) and resolve any queries carefully.

When modeling the data of a system, you need to start by gathering as much information about the system and the way it works as possible. The following types of information can help with this:

❑ Requirements specifications

❑ Existing records (from a previous electronic system or paper-based records)

❑ Descriptions of how users carry out their tasks (either produced by the user or from interview)

❑ Observation of people working

Once you have a set of documents, you can begin to examine them and pick out pertinent information. From this you can identify rules about the system — known as *integrity rules* — they can be sentences picked straight out of a document, or they might be conclusions drawn from various sources of information. These rules may or may not be directly relevant to the data, but picking them out will assist in making that decision. In a school system, some of the integrity rules might look like this (from an imagined requirements specification for a school records system):

```
...
Each teacher teaches only one "form group"
Each pupil can belong to only one form group at a time, and every pupil must belong
to a form group
```

```
    Information must be retained about pupil's addresses and parental contact details
    in case of an emergency
    Form groups are made up of pupils who are all in the same school year
    Teachers must record a value (present or absent) for each pupil at each
    registration session
    Absent values within a registration record should, wherever possible, be
    accompanied by an approved reason.
    ...
    ...
```

Initially these integrity rules can be used to identify *entities* (concrete or abstract concepts such as people, books, schools, etc.) and *attributes* (things that describe entities). In this example, several possible entities can be identified, including "teacher," "pupil," and "form_group." Possible attributes for pupils could be "address" and "parental contact details," although it is fairly obvious that these would need further definition. These entities and attributes are roughly equivalent to the starting set of relations and attributes in the database design.

Once there are a set of entities and attributes that make up the system, the data and the relationships can be examined to produce an effective and efficient design. This is accomplished through a process called *normalization*. Normalization takes a set of data — initially roughly grouped into relations — and organizes it in such a way that the relational model can be effectively and efficiently applied to that data — for example, by removing repeated information. There are various stages or levels in normalization, each one more "strict" than the previous one — those commonly applied to database designs are: *first normal form* (1NF), *second normal form* (2NF), *third normal Form* (3NF), and *Boyce-Codd normal form* (BCNF). Fourth and fifth normal forms deal with some quite rare situations involving data and are not often applied.

Many developers will find that if they have been using a relational database for some time — even without knowledge of the normal forms — they will already be applying some of the steps performed in normalization, as they become apparent through design and use of a database. Going through a normalization example in this context would be getting into too much detail, but there are many excellent reference books that will go through this process step by step on sample data. Applying the principles to some real-world data — perhaps from a real application — will help the process to make sense that much more quickly and easily.

PHP

PHP is a programming language specifically aimed at development of dynamic web applications. Unlike languages such as Perl and Python, PHP was originally conceived of as set of tools to aid dynamic web page creation, and has evolved (and gone through several rewrites) with that purpose obviously kept firmly in mind.

The PHP Language

The final piece of the LAMP environment is the PHP programming language. PHP is a simple scripting language that allows you to perform complex functions within an HTML web page. This section assumes that you already have some experience programming in PHP. It focuses on version 5 of the PHP language, because of its enhanced object-oriented implementation (interfaces, abstract classes, etc.).

This section covers some of the basic principles of PHP, and highlights major differences PHP has from other mainstream languages. It then moves on to cover a few basic optimization techniques specific to PHP. With that under your belt, it will show you how to create a simple web form with appropriate script for processing of results and then build this into a more realistic example with multiple pages and a database back end. By the end of the section, you will have experience of using the Smarty templating language, the PEAR Log for logging events, xdebug for profiling and debugging, some object-oriented examples, error and exception handling, and the PEAR database libraries.

This chapter is not going to spend time explaining the language constructs and the like of PHP, partly because it is assumed that the reader already has some experience of programming. It does attempt to point out some of the quirks of the language, which make it stand out, and may catch the unwary.

If you wish to find out more about a particular PHP function, the online PHP API is an excellent resource with plenty of user contributed notes and examples. For any particular function, go to www.php.net *followed by the function name, for example* www.php.net/microtime.

The syntax, and constructs for PHP are similar to many other languages (Perl, C, Java), and anyone familiar with at least one of these languages should find PHP easy to pick up.

Language Basics

A block of PHP code is conventionally stored in a file with a .php suffix. The code may be intermingled with HTML, and begins with <?php and ends with ?>. In some environments, <% ... %> or <? ... ?> can be used as well.

The language supports all common conditional statements (for, while, do/while, if). A variable always begins with a $ (as with Perl). PHP does not require the definition of types, and magically casts types from one to another, depending on the context.

For example, a file containing the following:

```
<?php
$variable1 = "Bob";
$variable2 = Array("This", "Is", "an", "Array");
echo "Variable 1 is : $variable1\n";
echo "The second item in the array is : " . $variable2[1] . "\n";
?>
```

when executed would produce output like:

```
Variable 1 is : Bob
The second item in the array is : Is
```

When writing PHP code, the programmer has a choice of including the variables within a double-quotation-marked string (as with the variables in Variable 1 is : Bob above) or appending the variable onto the end of a string, using "." notation. Either way is valid, although in most circumstances including the variable within the string looks neater—but it does come with a performance impact—as discussed in the optimization section later.

The example below shows how PHP and regular HTML can be mixed on one page. When reading the web page, the PHP parser understands the opening tag (<?, <?php, or <%, depending on configuration) and executes the appropriate code:

```
<html>
<head><title>My first PHP page</title></head>
<body>
<?php
$count = 0;
while($count<50) {
    echo "<br/>Hello World\n";
    $count++;
}
?>
</body>
</html>
```

Which writes out "Hello World" 50 times on a web page.

PHP can be written as a standalone script and executed with the /usr/bin/php command.

For example:

```
#!/path/to/php
<?php
for($i=0; $i<50; $i++) {
    print "Hello world\n";
}
?>
```

Requiring/Including Files

In an effort to reduce code duplication, PHP can import code from external text files, through use of the require or include functions. An example is shown below. Such practice is encouraged, as it allows you to define certain global constants in, for example, config.php or to group together related functions in other files.

config.php contains:

```
<?php
$debug=true;
?>
```

and index.php contains:

```
<?php
require("config.php");

if($debug) {
    echo "We are set to debug";
}
?>
```

There is very little difference between the use of require and include (if require fails, there is a fatal error, while include only causes a warning). Often in larger projects, it can become hard to track which files are imported where, and importing a file twice can cause problems (for example errors about a function being already defined). To solve this problem, there are sister functions called `require_once` and `include_once` which do exactly as their names suggest.

Magic Type Casting

PHP, by default, dynamically converts from one data type to another, depending on the context — so for instance:

```php
<?php
// string + int = int
echo "5" + 5; // 10
// string + string = number
echo "5" + "5"; // 10
// string . int = string
echo "5" . 5 ; // 55
// string * string = int
echo "5" * "5abcdef" ; // 25
// string / string = .666...
echo "2a" / "3b"; //    division by zero error ( 0 / 0 )
// hex + int = int
echo 0x05 + 10; // 15
?>
```

An empty string is evaluated to zero, as is an undefined variable. Because of this, the === and !== operators exist, which check the type and contents of the variable.

```php
<?php
$tmp1="";
$tmp2=False;

if ($tmp1 == $tmp2)
    echo "Equal with ==\n";
else
    echo "Not equal with ==\n";

if ($tmp1 === $tmp2)
    echo "Equal with ===\n";
else
    echo "Not equal with ===\n";
?>
```

Produces:

```
Equal with ==
Not equal with ===
```

Undefined variables can be detected with the `isset` function or by using an `if` statement, as shown below:

```php
<?php
if(!$tmp) { echo 'tmp not defined'; };
?>
```

```
or :
<?php
if(!isset($tmp)) { echo 'tmp is not set'; }
?>
```

Note, however, that if $tmp contained "0" or "" it would pass the isset test but fail the if(!$tmp) test. For this reason, it is best to use isset instead of a simple if check.

Arrays/Lists/Dictionaries

PHP does not differentiate between a hash (or associative list) and an array. For example:

```
<?php
$array = Array(5,4,3,2,1);
echo var_dump($array);
?>
```

Produces an output similar to:

```
array(5) {
  [0]=>
  int(5)
  [1]=>
  int(4)
  [2]=>
  int(3)
  [3]=>
  int(2)
  [4]=>
  int(1)
}
```

Note how PHP has automatically assigned the variables to the appropriate array index based on the order in which they were inserted.

```
<?php
$foo = Array(55 => "Bob", 4 => 9, "Roger" => "Rover");
echo var_dump($foo);
?>
```

Gives:

```
array(2) {
  [55]=>
  string(3) "Bob"
  [4]=>
  int(9)
  ["Roger"]=>
  "Rover"
}
```

You can use the `array_push` and `array_pop` functions to utilize an array like a stack/queue, or alternatively the `$array[]` syntax can be used to append to the end of an array. As shown here:

```php
<?php
$foo = Array();
array_push($foo, "Bar");
$foo[] = "Foo"; // Array("Bar", "Foo")
$last = array_pop($foo); // returns "Foo", Array("Bar")
?>
```

From a computer science perspective, it is interesting to note that the order of items within an array is retained, even though it may be used strictly as a hash. This is one of the powerful aspects of PHP and makes building complex, dynamic data structures very easy.

Functions

The following is an example of a function within PHP:

```php
<?php
function increment($arg1) {
    return $arg1 + 1;
}
echo "10 increments to : " . increment(10);
?>
```

Functions allow you to write blocks of code that can be reused. Please be sure to read the next section on scope before using them.

Scope

Within PHP the scope of a variable is generally global, which spans files that may be imported through `include` or `require`. However, user-defined functions have their own local scope, and if you wish to access a variable assigned outside the function, it is necessary to use the `global` keyword (or the `$GLOBALS` array), as illustrated in the example below.

```php
<?zphp
$foo = "Something";
function do_something() {
    $tmp = $GLOBALS['foo'];
    echo "We should do " . $tmp . "\n";
}
function do_something_else() {
    global $foo;
    echo "We should do " . $foo . " else\n";
}
function destructive_call() {
    global $foo;
    $foo = "nothing";
}

do_something();
do_something_else();
destructive_call();
echo "Finally \$foo is : $foo\n";
?>
```

gives output of:

```
We should do Something
We should do Something else
Finally $foo is nothing
```

If you wish for a variable to remain after a function has been called, the `static` keyword can be used.

Loops and Iterators

If you wish to iterate through an array, there are several ways of accomplishing this:

```
foreach($array as $value) {
      echo "value is $value";
}
foreach($array as $key => $value){
      echo "key is $key and value is $value";
}
```

If you wish to iterate over a random object, it needs only to define a `next()` method, for instance:

```
<?php
class Shelf {
      $objects = Array("a", "b", "c");
      function next() {
              // delegate the next call to the array
              return next($objects);
      }
}
$a = new Shelf();
foreach($a as $string) {
      echo "Shelf Entry : $string\n";
}
?>
```

Objects

When calling an object's method in PHP, the following syntax is used: `object->method(parameters,...)`. If you wish to access a public variable from an object you can use: `object->`.

PHP4's object orientation implementation was not particularly sophisticated. However, with PHP5 it was totally rewritten and the language now supports multiple levels of inheritance, abstraction, exceptions, and interfaces.

Much of the syntax used is similar to other object-oriented languages; however, there are differences, which this example illustrates:

```
<?php
class Foo {
    protected $name;
    function __construct($name) {
        $this->name = $name;
    }
    public function getName() {
```

```
            return $this->name;
        }
    }
    class Bar extends Foo {
        protected $password;
        function __construct($name, $password) {
            $this->password = $password;
            parent::__construct($name);
        }
        public function getPassword() {
            return $this->password;
        }
    }
    $foo = new Foo("Joe");
    $bar = new Bar("Joe", "secret");
    echo "Name: " . $bar->getName() . "\n";
    echo "Password: " . $bar->getPassword() . "\n";
    ?>
```

Note, how the $this keyword is used to reference class variables. Otherwise, it is assumed that you are returning a variable that only exists in the function's scope.

As with other languages, PHP supports constructors and polymorphism. It is not, however, possible to overload a method with multiple definitions (different parameters). If you wish to do this, you need to use optional arguments, as illustrated here:

```
<?php
class Foo {
    function do_something($arg1, $arg2, $arg3 = FALSE) {
        if($arg3 === FALSE) {
            // do one thing
        }
        else {
            // do something else...
        }
    }
}
$foo = new Foo();
$foo->do_something("a", "b");
$foo->do_something("a", "b", Array(1,2,3,"four"));
?>
```

The arguments allow us to fake out PHP to create the different definitions. If the third argument is not present, it is assumed to be a value from the constructor.

Pass by Reference/Pass by Value?

Traditionally PHP has been a pass-by-value language, where a copy-on-write approach was taken. So for example, if a large array was passed into a function that iterated over the array and changed one item near the end of the array, the original array would be iterated through, and only when the array was written to would an additional copy be made.

If you wish to force a pass-by-reference approach, then a variable needs to have an ampersand (&) next to it, as shown below.

The general rule is that everything is passed by value, unless you're using objects, in which case:

```php
<?php
class MyObject {
        public $foo = 0;
}

function do_it($foo) {
        $foo++;
}
function doItObj($object) {
        $object->foo++;
}

$bar = 0;
$myobject = new MyObject();

do_it($bar);
echo "Bar is $bar\n";
do_it(&$bar);
echo "Bar is $bar\n";

do_it($myobject->foo);
echo "Object has {$myobject->foo}\n";

doItObj($myobject);
echo "Object has {$myobject->foo}\n";
?>
```

prints out:

```
Bar is 0
Bar is 1
Object has 0
Object has 1
```

When using PHP, in a procedural context, all variables are passed by value, not reference. If you wish to pass something by reference, use the &$variable notation or &= for assignment.

(As a side note, it is generally frowned upon to use call time pass by reference, as was done in the above example, because it complicates the code somewhat (and the function may not be safe for pass by reference anyway). Normally, a better practice is to do the following:

```php
function do_it(&$foo) {
    $foo++;
}
$bar=0;
do_it($bar)
echo "Bar is now : $bar\n";
```

With this approach, it is obvious that everywhere the function is called, it operates in a pass-by-reference manner.

Error Handling

In this section, we will cover some methods of detecting and handling errors during the execution of a PHP script.

PHP's traditional approach to error handling is for the programmer to check the return value after executing a function; so, for example, it's not unusual to see something like:

```php
<?php
$db_conn = mysql_connect(......);
if(!$db_conn) {
    // handle error condition here. Call mysql_error() to get error message.
}
?>
```

Unfortunately, this relies on the programmer remembering to check the return values from various functions. It also tends to make the code more verbose than it needs to—as there are a lot of additional if statements to check return values. One approach around this is to use the trigger_error function (available since PHP version 4.0.1) as follows:

```php
<?php
$foo = bar("54");
function bar($arg1) {
    if($arg1 > 50) {
        trigger_error("argument to function bar cannot be greater than 50",
E_USER_ERROR);
    }
}
```

For more information on error handling, see http://uk2.php.net/manual/en/function.error-reporting.php.

Warnings like this will normally be displayed inline within the HTML document. This is generally not desirable and doesn't make your application appear very professional. If you deem that the error isn't that significant, you can squish it out using the error_reporting function—or alternatively ini_set(), as shown below.

```php
<?php
// display all warnings and notices - ideal for use during development.
error_reporting(E_STRICT | E_ALL);
// alternatively :
// ini_set("error_reporting", E_ALL);
ini_set("display_errors", true);
// Note: won't be of any use for fatal startup errors.
// Useful for debugging only.
ini_set("log_errors", true);
ini_set("error_log" , "/tmp/php.error.log");
?>
```

Sometimes it is necessary to suppress an error message, this can be done by prepending a function name with an @ sign, as follows:

```php
<?php
$file = @file("http://www.example.com");
if(!$file) {
    // handle error condition.
}
?>
```

In most cases however, it is best to define a global error handling function, as follows:

```php
<?php
function my_error_handler($errno, $errstr, $errfile, $errline){
    // generate pretty html page
}
set_error_handler("my_error_handler");
.... code that may generate errors ....
?>
```

This error-handling function can handle any error passed, and display the appropriate error message in a generic format. You can now use this error-handling function anywhere in the PHP program to display error events if they occur.

Error-Handling Exceptions

Since PHP 5, PHP has supported a full OO model with exceptions and multiple levels of inheritance. PHP's exception-handling code looks very similar to that of Java's. For example:

```php
<?php
try {
    // something that can cause problems here
}
catch(DbException $ex) {
    echo "Database error : " . $ex->getMessage();
}
catch(Exception $ex) {
    echo "Unknown Error : " . $ex->getMessage();
}
?>
```

The language offers a global exception handler, which can be used to provide the end user with "friendly" error messages, for example:

```php
<?php
class DbException extends Exception {
}
class ValidationException extends Exception {
}

function my_exception_handler($exception) {
    if($exception instanceof DbException) {
```

```
            echo "Database error occurred. Please contact support\n";
            // don't print db exceptions to users; they're meaningless.
        }
        if($exception instanceof ValidationException) {
            echo "The page was unable to validate the data you supplied to it. Please
try again\n";
            echo "Error: " . $exception->getMessage();
        }
        // etc.
    }
    set_exception_handler('my_exception_handler');

    // randomly throw one or the other.
    $rand = rand(0,1);
    if($rand == 0) {
        throw new DbException('sql error at line 44');
    }
    else {
        throw new ValidationException("invalid input, can't contain '-'");
    }
?>
```

Running this code produces a user-friendly error rather than an ugly PHP error message:

```
$ php php-04.php
The page was unable to validate the data you supplied to it. Please try again
Error: invalid input, can't contain '-'
$ php php-04.php
Database error occurred. Please contact support
```

As mentioned earlier, PHP generally works on a pass-by-value approach when using objects or functions, unless you specify `&$foo` as a parameter or `&=` in an assignment or pass an object into a function, in which case it uses pass by reference.

Optimization Techniques

This section illustrates some of the simple ways of optimizing PHP code, which can be universally applied. It also introduces the xdebug PHP module, which can be used for code profiling.

As with nearly all other languages, it is best to develop in a relatively unoptimizing manner. Significant optimization often requires the expenditure of significant time on the part of the programmer, and without proper investigation may have minimal impact on the performance of the application. While in general, some simple techniques can be applied (for example, those shown below), they may have a negligible impact on implementation speed or code clarity, so optimization should be left until the end of development. In most circumstances, the time the programmer spends on optimization during development may have a greater cost than benefit.

Strings

If you are using a large amount of looping, PHP is required to scan all double-quotation-marked strings for `$variables`, as the following example shows:

```php
<?php
$number = 500000;

echo "It is now : " . microtime(true) . "\n";
$start = microtime(true);
for($i=0;$i<$number;$i++){
        $temp = "This is a plain double quoted string";
}
$end = microtime(true);
echo "$number double quotes (variable-less) took : " . ($end - $start) . "\n";

$start = microtime(true);
for($i=0;$i<$number;$i++){
        $temp = 'This is a plain single quoted string';
}
$end = microtime(true);
echo "$number single quotes (variable-less) took : " . ($end - $start) . "\n";

$start = microtime(true);
for($i=0;$i<$number;$i++) {
        $temp = "This is a string $i";
}
$end=microtime(true);
echo "$number double quotes took : " . ($end - $start) . "\n";

$start = microtime(true);
for($i=0;$i<$number;$i++) {
        $temp = 'This is a string' . $i;
}
$end = microtime(true);
echo "$number single quotes took : " . ($end - $start) . "\n";
?>
```

The output is:

```
It is now : 1141551380.13
500000 double quotes (variable-less) took : 1.12232685089
500000 single quotes (variable-less) took : 1.11122107506
500000 double quotes took : 3.25105404854
500000 single quotes took : 1.71430587769
```

Notice the various time differences between the four examples. Obviously, adding the $variables to the string significantly decreased the performance of the loop.

Arrays

Using the for each notation when iterating through an array, is very convenient and offers better performance than using alternative methods, as shown below:

```php
<?php
$number=50000;

$array1 = Array();
```

```
for($i=0;$i<$number;$i++) {
        $array1[] = $i;
}

$start = microtime(true);
reset($array1);
foreach($array1 as $key => $value) {
        $foo = $value;
}
echo "It took : " . (microtime(true) - $start) . " using a foreach over $number
\n";

$start = microtime(true);
$array_len = sizeof($array1);
for($i=0;$i<$array_len;$i++) {
        $foo = $array1[i];
}
echo "It took : " . (microtime(true) - $start) . " using a for loop.\n";

$start = microtime(true);
reset($array1);
while(list($key, $value) = each($array1)) {
        $foo = $value;
}
echo "It took : " . (microtime(true) - $start) . " using each/list etc.\n";
?>
```

The output is:

```
It took : 0.161890029907 using a foreach over 50000
It took : 0.309633970261 using a for loop.
It took : 2.0244410038 using each/list etc.
```

The for each loop almost halved the performance time of the for loop, and was a dramatic increase over the while loop. This is an important feature to remember when creating looping code.

xdebug: Profiling and/or Debugging PHP Code

xdebug is an open source third-party module that can be installed into your PHP environment. It provides a number of useful features for development, notably: code profiling, script execution analysis, and debugging support. This section focuses on using xdebug version 2.0.

xdebug can be downloaded from www.xdebug.org, *which also contains installation instructions.*

Once xdebug is installed, and PHP configured to load it, you will immediately benefit from a pretty stack trace produced when error messages are generated. However, it can do even more.

Due to its nature, xdebug needs to be loaded and configured during PHP's own initialization. It is, therefore, not possible to change the xdebug settings using the ini_set PHP functionality. You will recall that earlier we briefly touched on the php.ini file — here we get to make a meaningful change:

```
zend_extension=xdebug.so
xdebug.profiler_enable=1
```

```
xdebug.profiler_output_dir = "/tmp"
xdebug.auto_profile = 1
```

The settings above, instruct it to automatically profile code, saving the output to a file in /tmp (with a name like /tmp/cachegrind.out.$number).

Therefore, if we execute the following PHP file, xdebug "magically" generates a cachegrind.out file for us, which we can view in an application like kcachegrind.

```php
<?php
if(!extension_loaded('xdebug')) {
        die("<a href='http://xdebug.org'>Xdebug needed</a>");
}
function foo($string) {
        $val = preg_replace("/foo/", "bar", $string);
        $tmp = explode(" ", $val);
        $val = implode(" ", $tmp);
        echo "Val: $val\n";
}
function bar($string) {
        return $string . "BAR";
}


for($i=0;$i<100;$i++) {
        foo("kettle of fish near a foo bar");
}
?>
```

When the output from the above is loaded into kcachegrind, you see something similar to Figure 14-1.

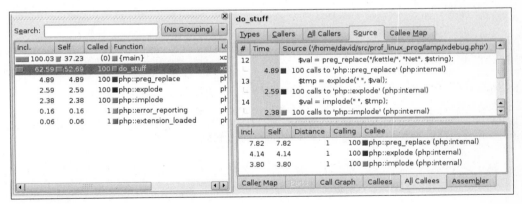

Figure 14-1

Although the page used is relatively simple, it does provide suitable timing (and additionally, not shown, memory usage). This should allow you to optimize functions that run regularly, and undertake a before and after approach to testing.

kcachegrind gives a complete graphical output showing function names (including whether they are internal to PHP or from an included file), memory and CPU usage, percentages, and counts (number of times a function was called), and if the source code is present (i.e., not a built-in function) it can be viewed.

It should be noted that use of xdebug may result in excessive memory or disk activity — but it can be invaluable in diagnosing performance issues with a script.

xdebug can also be configured to connect to a remote debugger in the event of an error occurring, and it integrates nicely with ActiveState's Komodo IDE — a screenshot of which is shown in Figure 14-2.

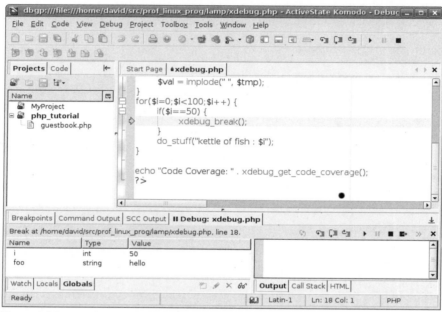

Figure 14-2

Komodo allows the user to set breakpoints, change variable values, and do all the other things a debugger will allow you to do.

To configure xdebug and komodo, it's necessary to make the following changes to the appropriate `php.ini` file:

```
xdebug.remote_host=IP_Address_of_Host_Running_Komodo
xdebug.remote_mode=req
xdebug.remote_autostart=On
xdebug.remote_enable=On
xdebug.remote_port = 56973
```

The `remote_port` setting used matches that shown by Komodo in its Debug ➪ Listener Status. It appears to pick a random port each time it is started.

> *ActriveState's Komodo can be downloaded from* www.activestate.com/Products/Komodo *and has a free 90-day trial period.*

Installing Additional PHP Software

The PEAR project (`http://pear.php.net`) contains a vast selection of useful add-on packages for PHP. This should be installed by default this should be installed; if not you may find it necessary to use `apt-get install pear`.

Once `pear` is installed, there are a number of useful classes that can be seen in the `/usr/share/php` directory. Full documentation for all classes can be found on the PEAR project website. If you wish to install additional software, you may be able to use the `apt-get` command to install it, or alternatively you can use the inbuilt pear command shown here:

```
pear list-all | grep -i xml
pear install XML_Util
```

This command demonstrates how to install the `XML_Util` PHP package.

The `pear` command also allows you to update the installed packages, with newer (and hopefully, better) versions from online. Depending upon the package, this may require that you have a compiler or other tools installed on your system.

```
$> pear list-upgrades
Available Upgrades (stable):
==============================
Package                Local          Remote         Size
Archive_Tar            1.1 (stable)   1.3.1 (stable) 14.8kB
Date                   1.4.5 (stable) 1.4.6 (stable) 53kB
HTML_Template_IT       1.1 (stable)   1.1.3 (stable) 18.9kB
HTTP_Request           1.2.4 (stable) 1.3.0 (stable) 13.6kB
Log                    1.9.0 (stable) 1.9.3 (stable) 34kB
Net_UserAgent_Detect   2.0.1 (stable) 2.1.0 (stable) 9.5kB
PEAR                   1.3.6 (stable) 1.4.7 (stable) 274kB
XML_RPC                1.4.0 (stable) 1.4.5 (stable) 29kB
$> pear upgrade-all
```

Be careful that `pear` does not upgrade an existing package that is managed by your distributions package management, as you may encounter problems in the future should both mechanisms attempt to update the same files with different versions.

Logging

Logging errors, information, and general debug messages is a necessary part of any project — whether large or small. In some circumstances, it is acceptable to just use `echo` and show the debug messages inline with, or example, HTML. However, this is not an ideal approach and when possible writing to an external log file is always preferred. As well as being an essential aspect of development, logging is just as critical for deployed applications. However, care should be taken not to log excessively, as this may hinder performance or result in gigantic log files that consume all the disk space on an active site! Post-deployment logging offers advantages for support and maintenance — for instance detecting security probes, tracking the application's usage, and looking back to see what went wrong two days ago when a customer encountered an error.

For the examples, we've concentrated on showing the PEAR::Log package

The command `pear install Log` *can be used to install the necessary files, if they are not installed already.*

The Log package is relatively straightforward to use. However, for the sake of keeping you sane, it is best if its configuration and setup is done in one place, allowing you to turn it on or off (or tweak it) easily. In the example application this is done in the config.php file, which is included within each page.

An example of log usage is:

```
require_once 'Log.php';

$logger = Log::factory('file', '/path/to/log.file', 'ANameForThisLogger');
$mask = Log::UPTO(PEAR_LOG_DEBUG);
$logger->setMask($mask);

$logger->debug("this is a debug message");
$logger->error("this is an error message");
```

For further information see the Log projects home pages at `http://pear.php.net/package/Log` *and* `www.indelible.org/pear/Log`.

By having different logging methods (debug, error, info, emerg[ency]), it is possible for messages to be classified and optionally squelched (for instance, debug messages may be too verbose and resource consuming to log on an active application site) — this can be done using the setMask functionality.

The log messages can be easily directed to a console, email message, or file (as shown above).

Parameter Handling

When accepting values from a user's request — either GET or POST, it is advisable to undertake some sort of validation. This can be something as simple as a length check or a more complex regular expression. Unfortunately, adding such checks to user-supplied input is tedious and relatively repetitive. Some frameworks (for example: Symfony, `www.symfony-project.com`, can assist in this).

An example of checking user supplied input from a HTML form is given below:

```
<html>
<head></head><body>
<form action='$PHPSELF' method='post'>
Name <input type='text' name='the_name' value=''>
<input type='submit'>
</form>

<?php
if(isset($_POST['the_name'])) {
    $name = $_POST['the_name'];
    if(preg_match("/[^A-Za-z0-9 ]/, $name) {
        // name contains a character that isn't ABCDE....Z, abc...z,
        // 0123456789 or a space.
```

```
            // Display error message, or send user back to entry form
            // for resubmission.
        }
        // Do something with $name.
        echo "<p>You entered : $name</p>";
    }
    ?>
</body></html>
```

Furthermore, care needs to be taken when either displaying a user-supplied variable on a web page, or when storing user-supplied variables within a database. With respect to databases, the use of prepared statements is one of the best approaches, as the parameters will be correctly sanitized by the library used. Care must be taken to ensure that users are not able to embed HTML < or > brackets in fields, which are then redisplayed unaltered to them — this could allow users to embed JavaScript or other Cross-Site-Scripting (XSS) attacks. When developing an application for an internal network, you may decide that such checks are not necessary.

To counter XSS attacks, PHP contains the `htmlentities` function. This converts, for example, < to a `&lt;`, which will be rendered by the browser as a "<" and not as part of the structure of the page.

General parameter handling takes the form of (as shown above in the last example) accessing parameters in a `$_` array (`$_POST`, `$_GET`, `$_SESSION`, or `$_COOKIE`). PHP itself handles the population of this array, and as programmers all we need to do is to check the contents of the value supplied and use it in an appropriate fashion.

It is quite common to find a PHP page that undertakes two tasks — one, the default, will be to display data, while the second will be to update the data. Upon executing the page, a check will be made to see if a particular `POST`/`GET`/`COOKIE`/`SESSION` parameter is set, and if so the data will be updated.

Register Globals

`register_globals` *is a* php.ini *setting; see the section on PHP configuration for more information.*

Previous versions of PHP included functionality where variables submitted from a form (or contained with a cookie) were automatically made available within the scope of the script as their name (i.e., form element name `my_name` becomes `$my_name`). Unfortunately, this has resulted in a number of vulnerabilities within PHP applications, as it allows malicious users to potentially alter the normal execution of code by setting what would otherwise be unset variables. To counter this, all recent versions of PHP have had this functionality turned off by default, and nearly all PHP applications have been rewritten not to use it — however, some do. If you are installing an application that requires `register_globals` to be turned on, be wary.

Session Handling

PHP handles some of the session features behind the scenes — for instance sending of cookie headers to the client. PHP can be set to automatically start sessions if the appropriate `php.ini` setting (`session.auto_start`) is enabled. Under most circumstances, this is not recommended; you may encounter problems if you are storing objects with a session and starting the session before the definition of the object is loaded.

For more information on `php.ini` *settings, see the section on PHP installation and configuration for more information.*

By default you will need to use the `session_start()` function to use HTTP sessions. When you use `session_start()`, it needs to take place before any text is outputted to the user, as this will cause the HTTP headers to be sent to the client and prevent the sending of a cookie for session tracking.

```php
<?php
session_start();
$_SESSION['key'] = "Something";
$_SESSION['key'] = Array("some", $values);
?>
```

There are historical functions called `session_register` and `session_unregister`; however, these are really superfluous and tend to be confusing. Accessing the `$_SESSION` array directly is easier (and requires less typing).

Unit Testing

The practice of *unit testing* — long accepted in, for example, the Java community — has more recently gained popularity within the PHP world, and for good reason. The ability to modify code in a scripting language can introduce errors. While the script still executes perfectly well 99% of the time, this is something that has surely bitten all script developers at one time or another. Most developers find testing to be dull and repetitive — and it is. Using a testing framework requires quite a lot of work to implement the initial tests, which are still fairly boring and repetitive. However, this framework makes repeating the tests easy and automatic, and also reduces the chance of user error in the running of the tests.

There are a number of unit testing frameworks for PHP, all of which generally seem to be based on the `junit` approach.

For further information on junit, see http://junit.sf.net.

PHPUnit2 is a PEAR project that provides a complete unit testing framework and also integrates nicely with `xdebug` to provide a code-test coverage indication. Unfortunately, it causes problems with the passing of globals to functions — for this reason, we have used `SimpleTest` in our examples.

SimpleTest is another PHP testing framework, which is very similar to `PHPUnit`, and the code used to produce tests for either is nearly identical (which does at least make changing test framework very easy).

`SimpleTest` *can be found at www.lastcraft.com/simple_test.php.*

As with all `junit`-derived test harnesses, the `setUp` and `tearDown` routines are defined to create and clear the testing environment. These are run before each test to ensure data is initialized to a known state before running a test.

A test is defined by having a method name starting with the word "test." The test harness uses reflection/introspection to examine the class and call all methods starting with this prefix.

A very simple example is shown here:

```php
<?php
require_once 'simpletest/unit_tester.php';
require_once 'simpletest/reporter.php';

class VerySimpleTest extends UnitTestCase {

    public function setUp() {
        $this->foo = "Bar";
    }
    public function tearDown() {
        unset($this->foo);
    }
    public function testSimple1() {
        $this->assertTrue(isset($this->foo), "this->foo not defined!");
    }
    public function testSimple2() {
        $this->assertTrue($this->foo === "Bar", "Bar != Bar ??");
    }
}
$test = new VerySimpleTest();
$test->run(new TextReporter());
?>
```

Readers wishing to see a more complex example should look at the `dvd-lib-smarty-test` *code (specifically the* `DBTest.php` *and* `LogTest.php` *source files) on the CD-ROM.*

The test harness itself provides the assertion methods (`assertTrue`, `assertFalse`, and `assertEqual`). Providing a message in case of failure is normally a good idea to aid debugging.

When running the above tests, the following is seen:

```
VerySimpleTest
OK
Test cases run: 1/1, Passes: 2, Failures: 0, Exceptions: 0
```

`SimpleTest` can be configured to "fake" submission of form values to a certain file, allowing for the automated testing of forms and associated logic. Such functionality should be the bare minimum expected from any test suite you use. In more complex scenarios, it is possible to run a multitude of tests together in one larger batch.

If you are working in a team project, it is a good idea to schedule an hourly job on a central server, where the source code is checked out from subversion, tests are run, and any errors are reported to the entire team. Such an automatic approach helps to ensure that the quality of code within subversion (i.e., it all works) and should save you from having to wait for someone to come into work to fix what ever they inadvertently broke last night at 9 pm. Eventually after a few bouts of embarrassment, most developers will run the tests themselves on the code they have just edited *before* checking their changes into subversion (or other versioning system). Such a routine does require that tests be kept up to date, added to, and maintained; however, the benefits from such an approach are huge.

After all, anything is better than spending hours manually testing an application, only to discover and fix a bug and then have to repeat all the tests manually again!

Databases and PHP

Out of the box, PHP may support either MySQL or PostgreSQL or both. Vendors normally ship a php-(mysql | pgsql) package, which should be installed (usually as an Apache module as discussed earlier in the Apache section).

The inbuilt database functions are all unique, and they all have individual function names (e.g., `mysql_connect`, `pgsql_query` etc.). The result of this naming is that it is difficult to create cross-database applications — historically, applications have tended to support MySQL, and support for other databases has been either nonexistent or lagged behind the main development branch. Some projects implement their own database independence layer, but this really places an unneeded burden on the development of the application.

To solve the above, the PEAR (PHP Extension and Application Repository (`http://pear.php.net`) project has a DB transparency module, which will work with a range of database back ends without the need to change more than the connection string. Care does still need to be taken to stick to using standard SQL, however, as it is easy to pop in something that is specific to your RDBMS or that the RDBMS you might need to migrate to in the future has not chosen to implement. Code examples of `PearDB` in use can be seen in the DVD Library example at the end of the chapter.

PHP Frameworks

When you start to write that magic application that pushes everything to "the next level," it's often desirable to build upon work done by others. This has advantages of code reuse, reduced maintenance requirements, and, hopefully, improved performance/security and faster time to market/development.

There are numerous PHP frameworks available. At the lower end, there are projects like the PEAR libraries, which aim to provide some of the best practices building blocks for PHP applications — for instance nondatabase-specific database methods, logging methods, and the like.

At a higher level, there are CMS applications like Drupal or Joomla (or Mambo). These provide nearly all the infrastructure required (login, user tracking, search facilities, shopping baskets, etc.) and can be modified and customized to a huge extent, to provide the basis for almost any sort of web application.

One of the problems with PHP application development is that it is all too easy to develop a working page where the thee main concerns (Model, View, and Controller) are intermingled. This is partly due to the fact that PHP is a powerful language in its own right that can also be used for simple templating purposes.

Smarty is one of a number of PHP projects, which provides a simple yet quite powerful templating framework for PHP. It features useful constructs to aid the generation of forms. If necessary it is also possible to embed PHP within a Smarty template.

Smarty templates have the file ending of `.tpl` (by convention). An example of using Smarty is shown in the DVD library example later in this chapter.

Smarty also provides some helpful (although not particularly elegant) routines that help handle the input of dates and other awkward data (e.g., times).

The DVD Library

The DVD library set of examples brings together much of what has been covered in this chapter in a coherent group. Rather than provide just one, best practice example, a progression of versions of this application have been provided to show how code can be improved in terms of readability and maintainability.

The DVD library is the start of a simple DVD rental application, which is intended to allow users to find and rent DVDs. This example covers a subset of this behavior — a basic search and viewing interface for "public" users, and a management interface — allowing users to maintain information about DVDs in the library (add, edit, and delete).

The look and feel does not change throughout the examples, as all versions after v1 use the same head and foot files. The functionality remains the same throughout — except where, for reasons of convenience, a particular version has been implemented using a subset of the features.

Version 1: The Developer's Nightmare

Anybody who's ever been called upon to work on existing code will tell you that their worst nightmare is to find something that looks a bit like the first example. Taking a couple of the features of the DVD library, and showing them in the worst possible way, this set of examples shows an application that is hard to read, is hard to maintain, and a provides a real soul-destroying experience if you have to work on it. It becomes an even greater nightmare when the application gets bigger, and you don't have the remit to rebuild it from scratch (or at least refactor it into a state where it is no longer recognizable!) This example has been implemented for just a couple of the features, to show how easy it is to let your code become a complete mess. In this example, the HTML (which is often, unfortunately, also included in the same file as everything else (and repeated in all the others) has not been shown. This code is taken from `list-all.php` in the version 1 directory.

```php
<?php
echo "<h2>All DVDs in the catalogue</h2>";
$db_host = 'localhost';
$db_user = 'prof';
$db_password = 'linuxprog';
$db_name = 'dvd';

$connection = mysql_connect($db_host, $db_user, $db_password);
if(!$connection) {
    print "Failed to connect:\n" . mysql_error() . "\n";
    die;
}

$sel = mysql_select_db($db_name, $connection);

if(!$sel) {
```

```
        print "Failed to connect to database $db_name.\n" . mysql_error();
        die;
}

$sql = "SELECT title from dvd";

$res = mysql_query($sql, $connection);

if(!$res) {
    trigger_error("Error executing query :" . mysql_error());
    die;
}

$all_dvds = array();
while($row = mysql_fetch_row($res)){
    array_push($all_dvds, $row);
}
if(!$all_dvds) {
    trigger_error("Error retrieving all_dvds :" . mysql_error());
    die;
}

mysql_close($connection);

if (sizeof($all_dvds)>0){
    echo "<ul>\n";
    foreach($all_dvds as $dvd){
        echo "<li><a
href='view_dvd.php?part_title={$dvd[0]}'>{$dvd[0]}</a></li>\n";
    }
    echo "</ul>\n";
}
?>
```

Of course, this is only a few lines of code and looks fairly readable in this example. However, look at it in context, with the HTML around it; then look at the second feature implemented in view_dvd.php. This is a bit bigger and a bit messier. Note that both examples are for very simple features.

Then you decide that you want to change the look of your site. It's a fairly common horror for people who are not using any templating mechanism, and it would be a brave (and fairly silly) developer who would go through the code for even a small system and change the HTML in each file. However, what if you wanted to switch databases? What about the customer who always uses PostgreSQL for everything and wants your product to use it too? They're going to pay you to port it, so you'll do it, but with your current structure this would be ridiculously difficult and error prone. A good refactoring is in order.

Version 2: Basic Application with DB-Specific Data Layer

Taking the application a step forward from the monolithic, duplication ridden system in version 1, there are several basic steps to making your application more maintainable. The first, and probably most important, is to separate your basic presentation from your logic (as this is where most duplication will occur, and even when you have a stable application in terms of features, where you will want to make most of the changes). In practice, it is difficult to separate them entirely, but a good start is to separate them out into simple header and footer files, containing the basic HTML and any PHP, such as menu-generation or authentication-checking code. Example headers and footers, as used in all of the subsequent examples, can be found in the common directory of the examples.

The next step is to factor out the database related code into a separate file. You will notice that the two files in the first example have a lot of repeated code to connect to and disconnect from the database, and to do simple fetching of results. This repeated code can be made into generic functions that can be reused elsewhere. Taking these two elements out of the code turns the above lines into the following:

```php
<?php

session_start();
require_once("dvd-db.php");
require_once("dvd-util.php");
include "../dvd-lib-common/head.php";

echo "<h2>All DVDs in the catalogue</h2>";

$all_dvds = get_dvd_titles("dvd");
if (sizeof($all_dvds)>0){
    echo "<ul>\n";
    foreach($all_dvds as $title){
        echo "<li><a
href='view_dvd.php?part_title=$title'>$title</a></li>\n";
    }
    echo "</ul>\n";
}

include "../dvd-lib-common/foot.html"; ?>
```

While it relies on code from other files, including the snippets from the database file (in this case dvd-db_mysql.php although the Postgres version can be substituted by changing this to dvd-db.php), the code is already smaller, cleaner, and far easier to read. The file sticks to performing only the actions needed display the required information (other examples would also include code required to process form input data).

The database file contains simple, generic connect, disconnect, execute_query (for queries with data results), and execute_update (for insert, update, and delete statements with no results) functions that can be used by any of the specific functions.

```php
<?php

function connect(){
    $db_host = 'localhost';
    $db_user = 'prof';
    $db_password = 'linuxprog';
    $db_name = 'dvd';

    $connection = pg_connect("host=$db_host user=$db_user password=$db_password
dbname=$db_name");
    if(!$connection) {
        print "Failed to connect:\n" . pg_last_error($connection) . "\n";
```

```php
        die;
    }
    return $connection;
}

function disconnect($db){
    pg_close($db);
}


function execute_query($sql) {
    $db = connect();
    $res = pg_query($db, $sql);
    if(!$res) {
        trigger_error("Error executing query :" . pg_last_error($db));
        die;
    }

    $results = array();
    while($row = pg_fetch_row($res)){
        array_push($results, $row);
    }
    disconnect($db);
    return $results;
}

function execute_update($sql) {
    $db = connect();
    $res = pg_query($db, $sql);
    if(!$res) {
        trigger_error("Error executing update :" . pg_last_error($res));
        die;
    }
    disconnect($db);
}
?>
```

Completing the picture is a the small function, `get_dvd_titles()`, used to fetch the DVD titles from the database and bring everything together:

```php
<?php
/**
 * Retrieve all titles for a DVD
 * @return an array containing the titles
 */
function get_dvd_titles(){
    $querystring = "SELECT title from dvd";
    $results = execute_query($querystring);
    $names = array();
    foreach($results as $row) {
        array_push($names, $row[0]);
    }
    return $names;
}
?>
```

Having the code separated into functions, in appropriate files, makes each section easier to read and understand without having to trawl though pages of code to find the appropriate section. Of course, if your main php file (the one presented to the user, which is where you will often start viewing) has many different files included, and you are not familiar with the structure of the application, you may have to look through a few files (or use your favorite search tool) to find the right place, but overall, this is an improvement in maintainability.

You might also note that there are two versions of the database files — one for PostgreSQL and one for MySQL. While these are very similar syntactically, they use different function names and, therefore, cannot be made generic. The only real way to do this is to create two versions with the same function definitions and behavior. Thankfully, however, because all of the database code is removed from the individual files, this only requires making a substitution in one file, which can then be included where needed. As there is an interface that gives us a level of abstraction between the display code and the database, we can include appropriate code according to the differences in the particular MySQL- or PostgreSQL-specific functions — and the same approach would work for other databases with PHP access functions.

While making these changes, it will become apparent that there more things causing problems than the readability of your code. If you made these types of changes to an application, you would soon find yourself needing to debug code. It then becomes painfully obvious that the application is in dire need of some logging facilities to record information for debugging (and other) purposes. Without these, you can either use a dedicated debugger (see the earlier xdebug section) or fall back on the old — and very error-prone — method of including print (or echo) statements within your code. These often requires painstaking work to add (and remove when you're done), and can change the behavior of your application.

The last thing to note with this version of the code is the error handling (or in many cases, lack of it). Where there is checking, it takes the traditional form of checking the return value of a function, as in the case of this extract from the edit_dvd.php script:

```
$success = edit_dvd($data);
if($success) {
    echo "\nDVD updated!\n";
}
else {
    echo "Problems were encountered while trying to update the DVD";
}
```

While this is not too messy at this level, it can involve checking return values through a whole stack of function calls, which can add a lot of fairly boilerplate code to your application — especially in a larger application with several layers of abstraction.

Version 3: Rewriting the Data Layer, Adding Logging and Exceptions

The next version of the application addresses many of the problems demonstrated in the code from the previous version.

Adding Database Abstraction

Using the database-specific mysql_ and pg_ functions means that you actually have to write two versions of the code. Using a database abstraction layer, however, as explained earlier in the section

"Databases and PHP," can allow you to produce "write once, run anywhere" style code. In this case, we have used the PEAR DB module to provide an interface to our databases. Now, to change databases, in theory, the only modification that would need to be made would be to the connection string. (However, in this case, due to the MySQL's not having an ILIKE operator — it uses LIKE instead on plain-text character strings in a case-insensitive manner — the search function would, unfortunately, have to be changed).

So, we now have a new set of generic functions for use by the other functions. (Note that we have now moved the connection string out into a configuration file):

```php
<?php
require_once 'config.php';
require_once 'DB.php';

class DbException extends Exception{
    function DbException($msg){
        $this->message = "Error in DB Communications: " . $msg;
    }
}

function connect(){
    global $connection_string;
    global $logger;
    $db = DB::connect($connection_string/*, $options*/);
    if (DB::isError($db)) {
        $err = "Failed to Connect: " . $db->getMessage();
        $logger->err($err);
        throw new DbException($err);
    }
    $logger->debug("Connected to DB successfully!");
    return $db;
}

function disconnect($db){
    $db->disconnect();
}

function execute_query($sql, $values = false) {
    global $logger;
    $db = connect();
    $prep = $db->prepare($sql);
    if($values === false) {
        $values = Array();
    }
    $res = $db->execute($prep, $values);
    if(DB::isError($res)){
        $err = "Could not execute $sql in query: " . $res->getMessage();
        $logger->err($err);
        throw new DbException($err);
    }
    while($row =& $res->fetchRow()) {
        $results[] = $row;
    }
    return $results;
```

```
}
/**
 * Retrieve all titles for a DVD
 * @return an array containing the titles
 */
function get_dvd_titles(){
    global $logger;
    $querystring = "SELECT title from dvd";
    $results = execute_query($querystring, Array());
    $names = Array();
    foreach($results as $row) {
        array_push($names, $row['title']);
    }
    $logger->debug("Found : " . sizeof($names) . " dvd titles");
    return $names;
}
```

Exceptions

The code above also illustrates the addition of exceptions quite nicely. The PEAR DB code itself does not throw convenient exceptions for us to pass back up to the user. Where there are errors, instead of returning an error code, or a blank or empty object or array, it returns a DB_Error object, which contains (normally) useful information about the error that occurred. We can detect if an error has occurred by checking the returned value, and then we can throw our custom exception, containing a bit of information about where the error happened and the message from the DB_Error object.

Note that the get_dvd_titles function does not do any error checking. Neither did the previous one, but that exactly the sort of omission that happens when checking is required at every level. In that case, if a fatal error happens at a lower level, the user will see an unpleasant error screen, and if a nonfatal error occurs, it may just be silently ignored — which is not ideal behavior!). In this case, that is what we want, as the exception is then passed up until it reaches a catch block, or is not caught at all (in which case it will be displayed to the user like any other error). By catching the exception, we can specify where we want to deal with the exception and what we want to happen when one is caught — so we can extract the information from the caught exception, and use it as we wish. The final edit page is a nice example of how using exceptions can keep your code clean. It makes it as very easy to separate your "successful" code — things that happen sequentially when everything works as expected — from your "failed" code. In this example, all of the normal operations for the page are at the top (after the necessary checks and the opening of the try block), and the error handling is all cleanly tucked away at the bottom.

```
<?php
session_start();
require_once "dvd-db.php";
require_once "dvd-util.php";
ensure_authenticated();

if(array_key_exists('title', $_POST)){
    try{
        edit_dvd($_POST);
        add_message("\nDVD updated!\n");
        $_SESSION['last_edit'] = $title;
        header("Location: index.php");
    }catch(DbException $dbe){
        echo "<h3 class='error'>An error occurred while trying to update the DVD:
{$dbe->getMessage()}</h3>";
```

```
        }
    }
    else {
        echo "<h3 class='error'>No DVD was selected for editing. Please <a
    href='edit-select.php'>Try Again</a></h3>";
    }
    ?>
```

Logging

To make debugging this application simpler, and to improve the maintainability of the system, we have also added a system for logging various sorts of messages, using the PEAR logging package, as explained earlier. This is easily set up with a few lines in the configuration file (config.php), which can then be included wherever logging is needed:

```
require_once 'Log.php';

$logger = Log::factory('file', '/tmp/php.log', 'AdvancedDVDLibrary');
$mask = Log::UPTO(PEAR_LOG_DEBUG);
$logger->setMask($mask);
```

Here is another function from the database-handling file (dvd-db.php) that includes various levels of logging:

```
function check_password($username, $password){
    global $logger;

    $querystring = "SELECT password from library_user WHERE username = ?";
    $results = execute_query($querystring, Array($username));
    $numRows = sizeof($results);

    if($numRows > 1){
        $err = "Error fetching password for $username for checking: 1 row expected,
$numRows found";
        $logger->err($err);
        throw new DbException($err);
    }
    elseif($numRows == 0){
        $logger->info("No record matching $username" );
        return FALSE;
    }
    $row = $results[0];
    $enc_password = md5($password);
    if($enc_password == $row['password']){
        $logger->info("Password authenticated for $username");
        return TRUE;
    }
    else return FALSE;
}
```

In this example, you can see the logger being used to provide info and error messages: info to record when someone successfully logs in, or tries to log in, with a user name that doesn't exist (very useful if someone is using a script which is trying to log in repeatedly using random user names to see what works) and the error to record when something out of the ordinary happens (in this case, if more than one record is returned that matches a field that should be unique—which should never happen). Note that the logger is not given any sensitive information such as the password, because if your system is compromised, log files can often be easily accessed and in some systems can be the source of some very interesting information!

Output written to the log files in this instance looks something like this:

```
Mar 06 20:58:16 AdvancedDVDLibrary [info] Password authenticated for david
Mar 06 20:58:16 AdvancedDVDLibrary [debug] Connected to DB successfully!
Mar 06 20:58:16 AdvancedDVDLibrary [debug] Found : 11 dvd titles
Mar 06 20:58:16 AdvancedDVDLibrary [debug] Connected to DB successfully!
```

If you don't wish the debug messages to be recorded once, for example, your application has gone live, you can simply change the logging level set in the configuration file.

Version 4: Applying a Templating Framework

At this point, we have a fairly clean and tidy application, but there is more that can be done to separate the displaying of the pages from the logic code. To keep code volume down, the Smarty templates have only been applied to the display sections of the page. The Smarty templating system, introduced earlier, offers a clean and simple mechanism for doing this. As previously explained, Smarty integrates with PHP through defined templates that can then be populated and displayed. The listing of the DVDs in the database from the initial nightmare code version of the example is now generated and displayed using a normal PHP file and a template. The PHP file contains the normal logic, along with:

```php
<?php

session_start();
require_once("config.php");

$smarty = new Smarty;
$smarty->compile_check=true;

require_once("dvd-db.php");
require_once("dvd-util.php");

try {
    $all_dvds = get_all("dvd");
    $dvd_list = array();
    foreach($all_dvds as $dvd){
        array_push($dvd_list, $dvd['title']);
    }

    $smarty->assign("dvd_list", $dvd_list);
    $smarty->assign("header", "All DVDs in the Library");
}catch(DbException $dbe){

    display_error_page($smarty, "An error ocurred while feching the list of DVDs:
{$dbe->getMessage()}");
}
$smarty->display("list_dvds.tpl");
```

Also note the `display_error_page` function, which looks like the following (from `dvd-util.php`). This is used to display a simple error message:

```
function display_error_page($smarty, $error){
    $smarty->assign("message", $error);
    $smarty->display("error.tpl");
    return;
}
```

Its associated template is very simple:

```
{include file="header.tpl"}
<h2>An Error has ocurred</h2>
<ul>
    <p class='error'>{$message}</p>
</ul>
{include file="footer.tpl"}
```

The template file simply displays the variables that have been assigned to the Smarty object. The special case is the list, which is used in a special Smarty tag that loops over the list provided. The `name` attribute is then used to determine the position in the loop (and therefore the array).

```
{include file="header.tpl"}
<h2>{$heading}</h2>
<ul>
{section name=dvd loop=$dvd_list}
    <li><a
href='view_dvd.php?part_title={$dvd_list[dvd]}'>{$dvd_list[dvd]}</a></li>
{/section}
</ul>
{include file="footer.tpl"}
```

Although with these two files, there is probably more code overall, I suspect (especially using templates without loops) that it would be far less error prone to hand a Smarty template over to a nonprogramming web designer to implement, than some PHP code.

Summary

This chapter discussed the popular Linux-Apache-MySQL-PHP (LAMP) web programming environment. These components can be combined to produce a complete open source web server, database and web page programming solution. While each of the components is an individual open source project, they are easily incorporated into a single server environment.

The Apache and PHP software programs are usually loaded together, using installation software packages designed for specific Linux distributions. The MySQL software is a separate installation package that is also available in Linux distributions. Installing the three packages on a Linux server is as easy as running the native software installation program for your distribution.

Finally, the chapter demonstrated how to use PHP programs to access database data from standard HTML code. This technique is used in commercial web applications all around the world. Now you have the same capability as some of the large commercial websites.

Index

Index

GNU General Public License

Version 2, June 1991

Copyright © 1989, 1991 Free Software Foundation, Inc.

59 Temple Place - Suite 330, Boston, MA 02111-1307, USA

Preamble

The licenses for most software are designed to take away your freedom to share and change it. By contrast, the GNU General Public License is intended to guarantee your freedom to share and change free software—to make sure the software is free for all its users. This General Public License applies to most of the Free Software Foundation's software and to any other program whose authors commit to using it. (Some other Free Software Foundation software is covered by the GNU Library General Public License instead. You can apply it to your programs, too.)

When we speak of free software, we are referring to freedom, not price. Our General Public Licenses are designed to make sure that you have the freedom to distribute copies of free software (and charge for this service if you wish), that you receive source code or can get it if you want it, that you can change the software or use pieces of it in new free programs; and that you know you can do these things.

To protect your rights, we need to make restrictions that forbid anyone to deny you these rights or to ask you to surrender the rights. These restrictions translate to certain responsibilities for you if you distribute copies of the software, or if you modify it.

For example, if you distribute copies of such a program, whether gratis or for a fee, you must give the recipients all the rights that you have. You must make sure that they, too, receive or can get the source code. And you must show them these terms so they know their rights.

We protect your rights with two steps: (1) copyright the software, and (2) offer you this license which gives you legal permission to copy, distribute and/or modify the software.

Also, for each author's protection and ours, we want to make certain that everyone understands that there is no warranty for this free software. If the software is modified by someone else and passed on, we want its recipients to know that what they have is not the original, so that any problems introduced by others will not reflect on the original authors' reputations.

Finally, any free program is threatened constantly by software patents. We wish to avoid the danger that redistributors of a free program will individually obtain patent licenses, in effect making the program proprietary. To prevent this, we have made it clear that any patent must be licensed for everyone's free use or not licensed at all.

The precise terms and conditions for copying, distribution and modification follow.

Terms and Conditions for Copying, Distribution and Modification

0. This License applies to any program or other work which contains a notice placed by the copyright holder saying it may be distributed under the terms of this General Public License. The "Program", below, refers to any such program or work, and a "work based on the Program" means either the Program or any derivative work under copyright law: that is to say, a work containing the Program or a portion of it, either verbatim or with modifications and/or translated into another language. (Hereinafter, translation is included without limitation in the term "modification".) Each licensee is addressed as "you".

    Activities other than copying, distribution and modification are not covered by this License; they are outside its scope. The act of running the Program is not restricted, and the output from the Program is covered only if its contents constitute a work based on the Program (independent of having been made by running the Program). Whether that is true depends on what the Program does.

1. You may copy and distribute verbatim copies of the Program's source code as you receive it, in any medium, provided that you conspicuously and appropriately publish on each copy an appropriate copyright notice and disclaimer of warranty; keep intact all the notices that refer to this License and to the absence of any warranty; and give any other recipients of the Program a copy of this License along with the Program.

    You may charge a fee for the physical act of transferring a copy, and you may at your option offer warranty protection in exchange for a fee.

2. You may modify your copy or copies of the Program or any portion of it, thus forming a work based on the Program, and copy and distribute such modifications or work under the terms of Section 1 above, provided that you also meet all of these conditions:

    a) You must cause the modified files to carry prominent notices stating that you changed the files and the date of any change.

    b) You must cause any work that you distribute or publish, that in whole or in part contains or is derived from the Program or any part thereof, to be licensed as a whole at no charge to all third parties under the terms of this License.

    c) If the modified program normally reads commands interactively when run, you must cause it, when started running for such interactive use in the most ordinary way, to print or display an announcement including an appropriate copyright notice and a notice that there is no warranty (or else, saying that you provide a warranty) and that users may redistribute the program under these conditions, and telling the user how to view a copy of this License. (Exception: if the Program itself is interactive but does not normally print such an announcement, your work based on the Program is not required to print an announcement.)

    These requirements apply to the modified work as a whole. If identifiable sections of that work are not derived from the Program, and can be reasonably considered independent and separate works in themselves, then this License, and its terms, do not apply to those sections when you distribute them as separate works. But when you distribute the same sections as part of a whole which is a work based on the Program, the distribution of the whole must be on the terms of this License, whose permissions for other licensees extend to the entire whole, and thus to each and every part regardless of who wrote it.

Thus, it is not the intent of this section to claim rights or contest your rights to work written entirely by you; rather, the intent is to exercise the right to control the distribution of derivative or collective works based on the Program.

In addition, mere aggregation of another work not based on the Program with the Program (or with a work based on the Program) on a volume of a storage or distribution medium does not bring the other work under the scope of this License.

3.   You may copy and distribute the Program (or a work based on it, under Section 2) in object code or executable form under the terms of Sections 1 and 2 above provided that you also do one of the following:

    a)   Accompany it with the complete corresponding machine-readable source code, which must be distributed under the terms of Sections 1 and 2 above on a medium customarily used for software interchange; or,

    b)   Accompany it with a written offer, valid for at least three years, to give any third party, for a charge no more than your cost of physically performing source distribution, a complete machine-readable copy of the corresponding source code, to be distributed under the terms of Sections 1 and 2 above on a medium customarily used for software interchange; or,

    c)   Accompany it with the information you received as to the offer to distribute corresponding source code. (This alternative is allowed only for noncommercial distribution and only if you received the program in object code or executable form with such an offer, in accord with Subsection b above.)

The source code for a work means the preferred form of the work for making modifications to it. For an executable work, complete source code means all the source code for all modules it contains, plus any associated interface definition files, plus the scripts used to control compilation and installation of the executable. However, as a special exception, the source code distributed need not include anything that is normally distributed (in either source or binary form) with the major components (compiler, kernel, and so on) of the operating system on which the executable runs, unless that component itself accompanies the executable.

If distribution of executable or object code is made by offering access to copy from a designated place, then offering equivalent access to copy the source code from the same place counts as distribution of the source code, even though third parties are not compelled to copy the source along with the object code.

4.   You may not copy, modify, sublicense, or distribute the Program except as expressly provided under this License. Any attempt otherwise to copy, modify, sublicense or distribute the Program is void, and will automatically terminate your rights under this License. However, parties who have received copies, or rights, from you under this License will not have their licenses terminated so long as such parties remain in full compliance.

5.   You are not required to accept this License, since you have not signed it. However, nothing else grants you permission to modify or distribute the Program or its derivative works. These actions are prohibited by law if you do not accept this License. Therefore, by modifying or distributing the Program (or any work based on the Program), you indicate your acceptance of this License to do so, and all its terms and conditions for copying, distributing or modifying the Program or works based on it.

6. Each time you redistribute the Program (or any work based on the Program), the recipient automatically receives a license from the original licensor to copy, distribute or modify the Program subject to these terms and conditions. You may not impose any further restrictions on the recipients' exercise of the rights granted herein. You are not responsible for enforcing compliance by third parties to this License.

7. If, as a consequence of a court judgment or allegation of patent infringement or for any other reason (not limited to patent issues), conditions are imposed on you (whether by court order, agreement or otherwise) that contradict the conditions of this License, they do not excuse you from the conditions of this License. If you cannot distribute so as to satisfy simultaneously your obligations under this License and any other pertinent obligations, then as a consequence you may not distribute the Program at all. For example, if a patent license would not permit royalty-free redistribution of the Program by all those who receive copies directly or indirectly through you, then the only way you could satisfy both it and this License would be to refrain entirely from distribution of the Program.

   If any portion of this section is held invalid or unenforceable under any particular circumstance, the balance of the section is intended to apply and the section as a whole is intended to apply in other circumstances.

   It is not the purpose of this section to induce you to infringe any patents or other property right claims or to contest validity of any such claims; this section has the sole purpose of protecting the integrity of the free software distribution system, which is implemented by public license practices. Many people have made generous contributions to the wide range of software distributed through that system in reliance on consistent application of that system; it is up to the author/donor to decide if he or she is willing to distribute software through any other system and a licensee cannot impose that choice.

   This section is intended to make thoroughly clear what is believed to be a consequence of the rest of this License.

8. If the distribution and/or use of the Program is restricted in certain countries either by patents or by copyrighted interfaces, the original copyright holder who places the Program under this License may add an explicit geographical distribution limitation excluding those countries, so that distribution is permitted only in or among countries not thus excluded. In such case, this License incorporates the limitation as if written in the body of this License.

9. The Free Software Foundation may publish revised and/or new versions of the General Public License from time to time. Such new versions will be similar in spirit to the present version, but may differ in detail to address new problems or concerns.

   Each version is given a distinguishing version number. If the Program specifies a version number of this License which applies to it and "any later version", you have the option of following the terms and conditions either of that version or of any later version published by the Free Software Foundation. If the Program does not specify a version number of this License, you may choose any version ever published by the Free Software Foundation.

10. If you wish to incorporate parts of the Program into other free programs whose distribution conditions are different, write to the author to ask for permission. For software which is copyrighted by the Free Software Foundation, write to the Free Software Foundation; we sometimes make exceptions for this. Our decision will be guided by the two goals of preserving the free status of all derivatives of our free software and of promoting the sharing and reuse of software generally.

NO WARRANTY

11. BECAUSE THE PROGRAM IS LICENSED FREE OF CHARGE, THERE IS NO WARRANTY FOR THE PROGRAM, TO THE EXTENT PERMITTED BY APPLICABLE LAW. EXCEPT WHEN OTHERWISE STATED IN WRITING THE COPYRIGHT HOLDERS AND/OR OTHER PARTIES PROVIDE THE PROGRAM "AS IS" WITHOUT WARRANTY OF ANY KIND, EITHER EXPRESSED OR IMPLIED, INCLUDING, BUT NOT LIMITED TO, THE IMPLIED WARRANTIES OF MERCHANTABILITY AND FITNESS FOR A PARTICULAR PURPOSE. THE ENTIRE RISK AS TO THE QUALITY AND PERFORMANCE OF THE PROGRAM IS WITH YOU. SHOULD THE PROGRAM PROVE DEFECTIVE, YOU ASSUME THE COST OF ALL NECESSARY SERVICING, REPAIR OR CORRECTION.

12. IN NO EVENT UNLESS REQUIRED BY APPLICABLE LAW OR AGREED TO IN WRITING WILL ANY COPYRIGHT HOLDER, OR ANY OTHER PARTY WHO MAY MODIFY AND/OR REDISTRIBUTE THE PROGRAM AS PERMITTED ABOVE, BE LIABLE TO YOU FOR DAMAGES, INCLUDING ANY GENERAL, SPECIAL, INCIDENTAL OR CONSEQUENTIAL DAMAGES ARISING OUT OF THE USE OR INABILITY TO USE THE PROGRAM (INCLUDING BUT NOT LIMITED TO LOSS OF DATA OR DATA BEING RENDERED INACCURATE OR LOSSES SUSTAINED BY YOU OR THIRD PARTIES OR A FAILURE OF THE PROGRAM TO OPERATE WITH ANY OTHER PROGRAMS), EVEN IF SUCH HOLDER OR OTHER PARTY HAS BEEN ADVISED OF THE POSSIBILITY OF SUCH DAMAGES.

END OF TERMS AND CONDITIONS